D1078032

Graded exercises in
Advanced level mathematics

# Graded exercises
# in pure mathematics

Edited by Barrie Hunt

COLEG MEIRION - DWYFOR
PENRALLT
PWLLHELI
GWYNEDD
LL53 5UB

CAMBRIDGE
UNIVERSITY PRESS

PUBLISHED BY THE PRESS SYNDICATE OF THE UNIVERSITY OF CAMBRIDGE
The Pitt Building, Trumpington Street, Cambridge, United Kingdom

CAMBRIDGE UNIVERSITY PRESS
The Edinburgh Building, Cambridge CB2 2RU, UK
40 West 20th Street, New York, NY 10011-4211, USA
10 Stamford Road, Oakleigh, VIC 3166, Australia
Ruiz de Alarcón 13, 28014 Madrid, Spain
Dock House, The Waterfront, Cape Town 8001, South Africa

http://www.cambridge.org

© Cambridge University Press 2001

This book is in copyright. Subject to statutory exception and to the provisions of relevant collective licensing agreements, no reproduction of any part may take place without the written permission of Cambridge University Press.

First published 2001

Printed in the United Kingdom at the University Press, Cambridge

Typeface *Times*          System *3B2*

*A catalogue record for this book is available from the British Library*

ISBN 0 521 63753 8 paperback

ACKNOWLEDGEMENTS

The authors gratefully acknowledge the following for permission to use questions from past papers:

| | |
|---|---|
| AQA | Assessment and Qualifications Alliance |
| Edexcel | |
| OCR | Oxford, Cambridge and RSA Examinations |
| | |
| AEB | Associated Examining Board |
| Cambridge | The University of Cambridge Local Examinations Syndicate |
| London | The University of London Examinations and Assessment Council |
| MEI | The Oxford and Cambridge Schools Examination Board |
| NEAB | Northern Examination and Assessment Board |
| O&C | The Oxford and Cambridge Schools Examination Board |
| SMP | The Oxford and Cambridge Schools Examination Board |
| WJEC | Welsh Joint Education Committee |
| | |
| Authors | Robin Bevan |
| | Bob Carter |
| | Andy Hall |
| | Barrie Hunt |
| | Lorna Lyons |
| | Lucy Norman |
| | Sarah Payne |
| | Caroline Petryszak |
| | Rachel Williams |
| | |
| Edited by | Barrie Hunt |

# Contents

# How to use this book

This is *not* a textbook. It has been designed to supplement your A level studies by providing further examples for practice. In this book you should find questions on all the topics in your A level syllabus, at four levels. You should select topics for practice where you need it and at the right level to match your degree of understanding at the time.

**Chapter 0** covers the background knowledge needed for the study of A level mathematics. This will not be explicitly tested in your A level examination, but you will be expected to be able to use the techniques on the way to solving A level problems.

**Basic** questions are questions which have no frills – they are designed to provide you with routine practice in standard techniques. The minimum knowledge of other topics is required and numbers have normally been chosen to ensure that solutions can be found readily. They will provide a good introduction to AS level questions.

**Intermediate** questions are designed to be more challenging. Solutions may involve more than one or two stages and will often require you to adopt a strategy for solving the problem. They may also involve using more than one area of mathematics. You should find that they provide a good introduction to the type of questions that you will get in the A2 papers at A level. Alternatively, you may like to use them early in your course if you feel that you understand a topic and need more challenging questions.

**Advanced** questions are even more challenging. They include more demanding A level style questions and a small number of 'S' level standard. Those labelled STEP are taken from the Sixth Term Examination Papers for the University of Cambridge. If you are aiming for the highest grades at A level, then these will make you think! If you are also studying Further Mathematics you may well find that these questions can be used to make you think more deeply about topics with which you are already familiar.

**Revision** questions are generally quite straightforward and are intended to provide a set of questions which you can use to revise a particular topic thoroughly in order to gain confidence. They should be used in conjunction with past papers from your own syllabus.

**Answers** are given to all questions (except those which involve proving a given result). A small number of questions are marked with an asterisk (*). These have **full worked solutions** and are intended to help you understand key topics.

# 0 Background knowledge

## 0.1 Basic arithmetic – highest common factor; lowest common multiple; fractions

$$\frac{a}{b} + \frac{c}{d} = \frac{ad + bc}{bd} \qquad \frac{a}{b} \times \frac{c}{d} = \frac{ac}{bd}$$

**1** Express as a product of prime factors:

(a) 30      (b) 49      (c) 53      (d) 84
(e) 108      (f) 693      (g) 1144      (h) 14 553

**2** Find the highest common factor (HCF) of:

(a) 6, 10      (b) 7, 14      (c) 30, 42
(d) 24, 40, 64      (e) 42, 70, 182      (f) 169, 234, 299
(g) 252, 378, 567      (h) 51, 527, 1343

**3** Find the lowest common multiple (LCM) of:

(a) 6, 10      (b) 7, 14      (c) 30, 42      (d) 2, 3, 4
(e) 5, 25      (f) 5, 7, 11      (g) 4, 21, 22      (h) 14, 18, 21

**4** Express each fraction in its lowest terms, without using a calculator:

(a) $\frac{7}{35}$      (b) $\frac{15}{125}$      (c) $\frac{26}{39}$      (d) $\frac{16}{80}$

(e) $\frac{81}{108}$      (f) $\frac{3a}{12a}$      (g) $\frac{42a^2}{56a}$      (h) $\frac{22ab^2}{121b}$

**5** Complete:

(a) $\frac{3}{4} = \frac{}{24}$      (b) $\frac{4}{5} = \frac{}{20}$      (c) $\frac{4}{7} = \frac{}{21}$      (d) $\frac{7}{8} = \frac{}{64}$

(e) $\frac{7}{4} = \frac{}{20}$      (f) $\frac{2a}{3} = \frac{}{9}$      (g) $\frac{a}{b} = \frac{}{bx}$      (h) $\frac{2}{a} = \frac{}{a^2}$

**6** Simplify, without using a calculator:

(a) $\frac{3}{4} + \frac{2}{3}$      (b) $\frac{2}{7} - \frac{1}{5}$      (c) $\frac{4}{13} + \frac{2}{7}$      (d) $\frac{5}{12} - \frac{3}{8}$

(e) $1\frac{3}{4}+2\frac{7}{8}$  (f) $5\frac{2}{3}-3\frac{1}{9}$  (g) $2\frac{1}{7}+\frac{3}{4}$  (h) $3\frac{2}{5}+2\frac{2}{3}$

**7** Express as a single fraction:

(a) $\frac{3a}{4}+\frac{2a}{3}$  (b) $\frac{2a}{7}-\frac{a}{5}$  (c) $\frac{3}{a}+\frac{2}{a}$  (d) $\frac{3}{a}+\frac{2}{b}$

(e) $\frac{1}{u}+\frac{1}{v}$  (f) $\frac{5}{a}-\frac{2}{a^2}$  (g) $p-\frac{2}{q}$  (h) $\frac{3}{ab}-\frac{5}{ac}$

**8** Without using a calculator, simplify and express each fraction in its lowest terms:

(a) $6\times\frac{2}{3}$  (b) $\frac{1}{2}\times\frac{3}{4}$  (c) $\frac{3}{5}\times\frac{4}{7}$  (d) $\frac{3}{5}\times\frac{4}{9}$

(e) $\frac{3a}{7}\times\frac{2}{5a}$  (f) $\frac{4a^2}{11}\times\frac{3}{2ab}$  (g) $x\times\frac{1}{x}$  (h) $x^2\left(\frac{3}{x}+\frac{2}{x^2}\right)$

**9** Without using a calculator, simplify and express each fraction in its lowest terms:

(a) $6\div\frac{2}{3}$  (b) $\frac{1}{2}\div\frac{3}{4}$  (c) $\frac{3}{5}\div\frac{6}{25}$  (d) $\frac{3}{5}\div\frac{4}{9}$

(e) $\frac{3a}{7}\div\frac{2a}{5}$  (f) $\frac{4}{11a^2}\div\frac{2}{3ab}$  (g) $x\div\frac{1}{x}$  (h) $\frac{1}{x^2}\div\frac{1}{x}$

**10** Which is larger, $\frac{77}{78}$ or $\frac{78}{79}$?

**11** (a) The fraction $\frac{20}{91}$ is written as $\frac{1}{7}+\frac{1}{a}$. Find $a$.

(b) Calculate:   (i) $(1-\frac{1}{2})(1-\frac{1}{3})(1-\frac{1}{4})$

(ii) $(1-\frac{1}{2})(1-\frac{1}{3})(1-\frac{1}{4})\ldots(1-\frac{1}{n})$

**12** Find the greatest number which, when divided into 1407 and 2140, leaves remainders of 15 and 23 respectively.

## 0.2    Laws of indices

$$a^m\times a^n=a^{m+n}\qquad\frac{a^m}{a^n}=a^{m-n}\qquad(a^m)^n=a^{mn}$$

**1** Simplify:

(a) $a^3\times a^4$    (b) $a^7\times a^6$    (c) $a\times a^3$
(d) $2a^3\times 3a^2$    (e) $5a^2\times a^7$    (f) $\frac{1}{3}a^3\times 6a^4$

**2** Simplify:

(a) $\frac{x^9}{x^2}$  (b) $\frac{p^4}{p^3}$  (c) $\frac{x^{12}}{x}$  (d) $\frac{12a^7}{4a^2}$  (e) $\frac{12a^5}{8a^3}$  (f) $\frac{2a^2b}{6ab^2}$

**3** Simplify:

(a) $(a^5)^3$     (b) $(2a)^4$     (c) $(5a^3)^2$     (d) $5(a^3)^2$

(e) $(-2a^2)^4$     (f) $(3a^2b^3)^3$

**4** Simplify:

(a) $\sqrt{x^2}$     (b) $\sqrt{x^6}$     (c) $\sqrt{a^2b^2}$     (d) $\sqrt{4a^2}$

(e) $\sqrt[3]{-x^6}$     (f) $\sqrt{9a^{10}b^4}$

**5** Expand:

(a) $(1+x^2)^2$     (b) $(3-a^3)^2$     (c) $\left(x^2-\dfrac{1}{x^2}\right)^2$

**6** Simplify:

(a) $\dfrac{x^2+x^5}{x}$     (b) $\dfrac{3x^8+2x^4}{x^4}$

(c) $3x^2+(5x)^2-\dfrac{3x^3}{x}$     (d) $\dfrac{10x^2y+6xy^2-8x^2y^2}{2xy}$

## 0.3    Similar figures

**1** Find the sides marked $x$ and/or $y$ in each of the following pairs of similar triangles.

(a)

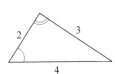 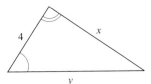

(b)

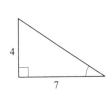 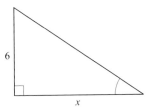

(c)

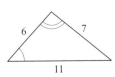 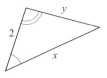

(d)

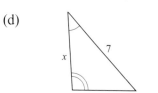 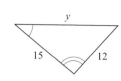

(e)

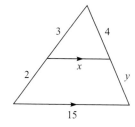

(f)

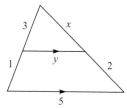

(g)

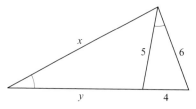

**2**  $OAB$ is the cross-section of a
cone, radius $r$, height $h$.
Express $y$ in terms of $r$, $h$ and $x$.

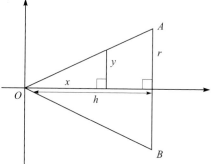

**3**  The coordinates of $Q$ are (4, 0).
What are the coordinates of P?

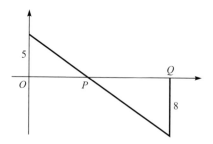

**4**  A sphere has radius 8 cm and a second sphere has radius 12 cm.
What is the ratio of their (a) areas, (b) volumes?

**5** A solid metal cylinder of radius 6 cm and height 12 cm weighs 6 kg. A second cylinder is made from the same material and has radius 8 cm and height 16 cm. How much does this cylinder weigh?

**6** A liquid is poured into a hollow cone, which is placed with its vertex down. When $400 \text{ cm}^3$ has been poured in, the depth of water is 100 cm. What is the depth of water after (a) $1000 \text{ cm}^3$, (b) $x \text{ cm}^3$ has been poured in? Plot the graph to show how depth varies with volume.

## 0.4 Basic algebra – multiplying brackets, factorising quadratics, solution of simultaneous equations

$$(a + b)(c + d) = ac + ad + bc + bd$$

**1** Expand:

    (a) $3(4 + a)$      (b) $6(2 - 3a)$      (c) $a(a + 3)$

    (d) $a(2a + 3b)$      (e) $3a(5a - 2b)$      (f) $x\left(2 + \dfrac{3}{x}\right)$

**2** Multiply out the brackets:

    (a) $(x + 2)(x + 5)$      (b) $(x - 3)(x + 4)$      (c) $(2x + 1)(3x + 5)$

    (d) $(5x - 2)(5x + 2)$      (e) $(3a + 2)^2$      (f) $(p + 3q)(2p - 5q)$

    (g) $\left(x + \dfrac{2}{x}\right)^2$      (h) $(2x^2 + 1)(x + 3)$

**3** Factorise:

    (a) $4x + 8y$      (b) $x^2 - 3x$      (c) $5x^2 + 2xy$

    (d) $2\pi r^2 + 2\pi rh$      (e) $ut + \frac{1}{2}at^2$      (f) $2x^3 + 3x^4$

**4** Factorise:

    (a) $x^2 + 4x + 3$      (b) $x^2 + 2x - 3$      (c) $a^2 - 6a + 9$

    (d) $x^2 + 7x + 10$      (e) $p^2 + p - 30$      (f) $2a^2 + 7a + 3$

    (g) $6y^2 - 7y - 5$      (h) $p^2 - 4q^2$      (i) $p^2 + 4pq - 12q^2$

    (j) $15p^2 - 34pq - 16q^2$      (k) $9x^2 + 30xy + 25y^2$      (l) $10a^2 + 31a - 14$

**5** Simplify:

    (a) $\dfrac{3x + 6}{3}$      (b) $\dfrac{x^2 + 2x}{x}$      (c) $\dfrac{x^2 + 3x + 2}{x + 1}$      (d) $\dfrac{16 - x^2}{x + 4}$

**6** Solve the simultaneous equations:

    (a) $x + y = 4$      (b) $x + 2y = 8$      (c) $2x + 3y = 2$

        $x - y = -6$        $x + 5y = 17$        $x - 2y = 8$

(d)  $3x - 2y = 1$        (e)  $2x + 5y = -14$        (f)  $5x - 3y = 23$
     $-5x + 4y = 3$               $3x + 2y = 1$                 $7x + 4y = -17$
(g)  $4x - 3y = 0$        (h)  $2x + 3y + 4 = 0$
     $6x + 15y = 13$                 $5x - y - 7 = 0$

**7**   Multiply out the brackets:

(a)  $(x - 1)(x^2 + x + 1)$        (b)  $(a + b)^3$        (c)  $(a + b)^4$
(d)  $(x + \sqrt{2})(x - \sqrt{2})$

**8**   Simplify:

(a)  $(a + b)^2 - (a - b)^2$        (b)  $\dfrac{x^3 + 2x^2 + x}{x^2 + x}$        (c)  $\dfrac{x^4 - 13x^2 + 36}{(x - 2)(x^2 - 9)}$

**9**   Solve the pairs of simultaneous equations below, explaining your results graphically.

(a)  $2x + 3y = 8$        (b)  $2x + 3y = 8$
     $6x + 9y = 12$                $6x + 9y = 24$

## 0.5     Solving equations; changing the subject of a formula

**1**   Solve the following equations.

(a)  $2x + 1 = 7$                           (b)  $2 - 3x = 8$
(c)  $5x + 2 = 3x - 5$              (d)  $6x + 3 = 8 - 2x$
(e)  $3(x + 2) = 9x$                (f)  $4(2x - 7) = 3(5x + 1)$
(g)  $x^2 = 81$                          (h)  $x^2 - 25 = 0$
(i)  $x = \dfrac{16}{x}$                        (j)  $x^3 + 27 = 0$
(k)  $x^2 = 7x$                         (l)  $x - \dfrac{4}{x} = 0$
(m)  $x(x - 4) = 0$               (n)  $(x + 3)(x - 7) = 0$
(o)  $(2x - 3)(x + 4)(3x + 2) = 0$

**2**   Rearrange to make the given variable the subject of the formula:

(a)  $Q = CV$  $(C)$                   (b)  $C = 2\pi r$  $(r)$
(c)  $F = \frac{9}{5}C + 32$  $(C)$         (d)  $y = mx + c$  $(m)$
(e)  $P = 2(\ell + w)$  $(\ell)$          (f)  $S = \frac{1}{2}n(a + \ell)$  $(a)$
(g)  $v^2 = u^2 + 2as$  $(a)$          (h)  $s = ut + \frac{1}{2}at^2$  $(a)$
(i)  $u = a + (n - 1)d$  $(d)$       (j)  $s = \frac{n}{2}\{2a + (n - 1)d\}$  $(d)$

**3** Rearrange to make the given variable the subject of the formula:

(a)    $E = mc^2$    (c)

(b)    $V = \frac{4}{3}\pi r^3$    (r)

(c)    $V = \frac{1}{3}\pi r^2 h$    (r)

(d)    $y = \frac{4}{x^2}$    (x)

(e)    $I = \frac{1}{2}m(v^2 - u^2)$    (v)

(f)    $y = 2\sqrt{x} + 3$    (x)

(g)    $T = 2\pi\sqrt{\frac{\ell}{g}}$    (ℓ)

(h)    $A = \pi(r^2 - r_1^2)$    (r)

(i)    $y = \frac{1}{x - a}$    (x)

(j)    $c = \sqrt{a^2 + b^2}$    (a)

**4** In each case, show clearly how the second formula may be obtained from the first.

(a) $I = \frac{iR}{R + r}$,    $r = \frac{(i - I)R}{I}$

(b) $\frac{x^2}{a^2} + \frac{y^2}{b^2} = 1$,    $y = \frac{b}{a}\sqrt{(a^2 - x^2)}$

(c) $y = \frac{x - 2}{x}$,    $x = \frac{2}{1 - y}$

(d) $y = \frac{3x + 2}{5 - x}$,    $x = \frac{5y - 2}{y + 3}$

(e) $I = \frac{Er}{R + r}$,    $r = \frac{IR}{E - I}$

(f) $\frac{1}{R} = \frac{1}{u} + \frac{1}{v}$,    $v = \frac{Ru}{u - R}$

**5** The surface area, $S$, of a cylinder is given by $S = 2\pi r^2 + 2\pi rh$.
Its volume, $V$, is given by $V = \pi r^2 h$. Express $V$ in terms of $S$ and $r$ only.

## 0.6    The straight line $y = mx + c$; gradient and intercept

> The line $y = mx + c$ has gradient $m$, intercept $c$

**1** Plot the graph of $y = 4x + 2$ for $-3 \leq x \leq 3$. Calculate the gradient of the line.
Write down where it crosses the $y$-axis (the $y$-intercept).

**2** Complete the table.

| | Equation | Gradient | Intercept |
|---|---|---|---|
| (a) | $y = 5x - 2$ | | |
| (b) | $y = 1 - 3x$ | | |
| (c) | $y = \frac{1}{2}x$ | | |
| (d) | $y = -4 - 3x$ | | |
| (e) | | 2 | 5 |
| (f) | | 6 | $-2$ |
| (g) | | 7 | $\frac{1}{2}$ |
| (h) | | 1 | 0 |
| (i) | $2y = 4x + 1$ | | |
| (j) | $5y = 2x$ | | |

**3** Sketch the following lines.

(a) $y = 2x + 5$     (b) $y = \frac{1}{2}x + 2$     (c) $y = -x$     (d) $y = -x + 1$

**4** Write down the equation of each of the lines shown.

(a)

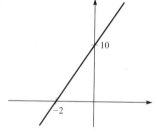

(b)

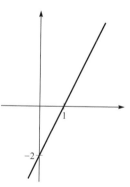

(c)

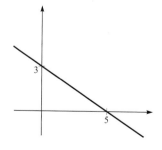

(d)

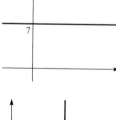

(e)

**5**   Find the equation of the line perpendicular to $y = 2x - 1$ which passes through $(0, 3)$.

**6**   State the coordinates of the point where the line $\dfrac{y}{4} + \dfrac{x}{6} = 1$ crosses
(a) the $x$-axis, (b) the $y$-axis.

## 0.7   The distance between two points

**1**   (a)   $P$ and $Q$ are two points with coordinates $(2, 3)$ and $(5, 7)$ respectively. By applying Pythagoras' theorem to triangle $PQR$, find the distance $PQ$.

    (b)   By drawing a suitable diagram, find a formula for the distance $PQ$ where $P$ and $Q$ have coordinates $(x_1, y_1)$, $(x_2, y_2)$ respectively.

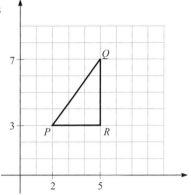

**2**   Find the distance between the following pairs of points.

    (a)   $(1, 2)$, $(6, 14)$     (b)   $(3, 2)$, $(6, 3)$     (c)   $(-1, 4)$, $(2, 7)$
    (d)   $(4, 2)$, $(1, -3)$

**3**   Show that the triangle with vertices at $(1, 0)$, $(3, 0)$, $(2, \sqrt{3})$ is equilateral.

**4**   Which of the points $(6, 4)$, $(-3, 6)$, $(2, -4)$ is nearest to $(1, 2)$?

**5**   Find the distance of the point $P(x, y)$ from (i) $O(0, 0)$ (ii) $R(4, 3)$. If $P$ is equidistant from $O$ and $R$, find the equation of the locus of $P$.

## 0.8   Trigonometry – right-angled triangles; sine and cosine rules

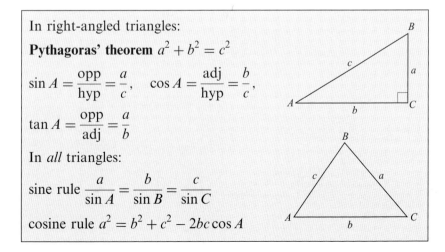

In right-angled triangles:

**Pythagoras' theorem** $a^2 + b^2 = c^2$

$$\sin A = \frac{\text{opp}}{\text{hyp}} = \frac{a}{c}, \quad \cos A = \frac{\text{adj}}{\text{hyp}} = \frac{b}{c},$$

$$\tan A = \frac{\text{opp}}{\text{adj}} = \frac{a}{b}$$

In *all* triangles:

$$\text{sine rule} \quad \frac{a}{\sin A} = \frac{b}{\sin B} = \frac{c}{\sin C}$$

$$\text{cosine rule } a^2 = b^2 + c^2 - 2bc \cos A$$

**1**  Find the angles marked $x$.

(a)
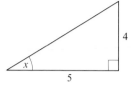

(b)
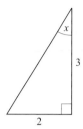

(c)
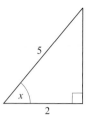

(d)
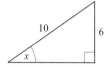

**2**  Find the sides marked $x$.

(a)
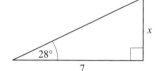

(b)
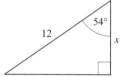

(c)
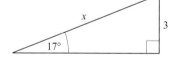

(d)
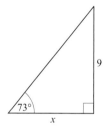

(e)
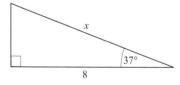

(f)
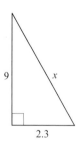

(g)
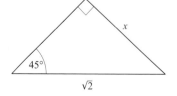

(h)
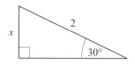

**3** (a) Find the lengths of (i) *BC*, (ii) AB giving your
   answer in the form $\sqrt{a}$.
   (b) Write down exact values for
   (i) $\sin 45°$, (ii) $\cos 45°$, (iii) $\tan 45°$.

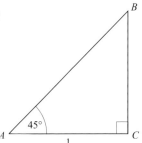

**4** Use the sine rule to find the value of *x*.

(a)

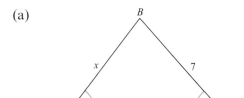

(b)

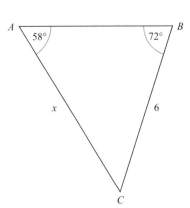

(c)

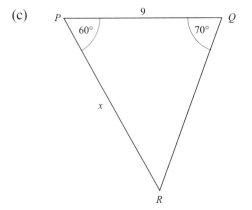

(d)

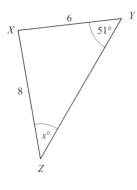

(e)

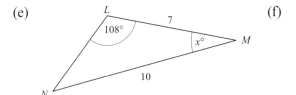

(f)

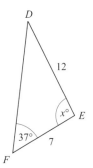

**5**  Use the cosine rule to find the value of *x*.

(a)
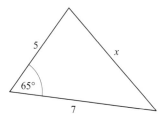

(b)
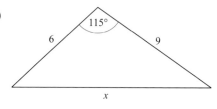

(c)
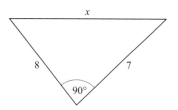

(d)
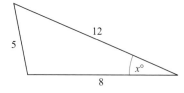

(e)
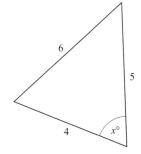

(f)
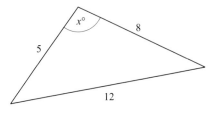

**6**  Use appropriate methods to find all sides and angles for:

(a)
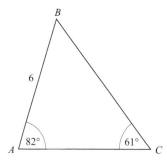

(b)
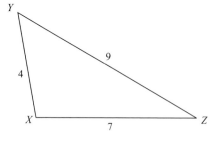

## 0.9    The cone and sphere

Volume of cone = $\frac{1}{3}\pi r^2 h$,    Volume of sphere = $\frac{4}{3}\pi r^3$

Surface area of cone = $\pi r \ell$,    Surface area of sphere = $4\pi r^2$

1 Find the volumes of the following solid objects, giving your answers as multiples of $\pi$.

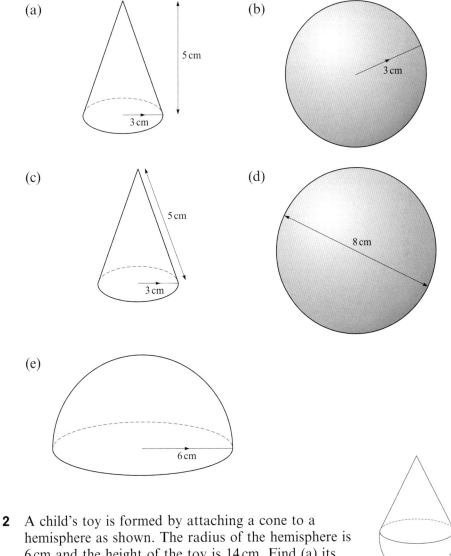

(a)

5 cm

3 cm

(b)

3 cm

(c)

5 cm

3 cm

(d)

8 cm

(e)

6 cm

2 A child's toy is formed by attaching a cone to a hemisphere as shown. The radius of the hemisphere is 6 cm and the height of the toy is 14 cm. Find (a) its volume, (b) its surface area.

3 The earth may be treated as a sphere of radius 6370 km. Find (a) its surface area, (b) its volume.

4 Twelve balls, each of radius 3 cm, are immersed in a cylinder of water, radius 10 cm, so that they are each fully submerged. What is the rise in the water level?

**5**  A solid metal cube of side 4 cm is melted down and recast as a sphere. Show that its radius is $\sqrt[3]{48/\pi}$.

**6**  A gas balloon, in the shape of a sphere, is made from $1000\,\text{m}^2$ of material. Estimate the volume of gas in the balloon. What assumptions have you made?

**7**  A hollow sphere has internal diameter 10 cm and external diameter 12 cm. What is the volume of the material used to make the sphere?

**8**  A bucket is in the shape of the frustrum of a cone. The radius of the base is 15 cm and the radius of the top is 20 cm. Find the volume of the bucket, given that its height is 30 cm.

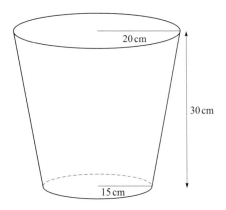

## 0.10     Properties of a circle

**Angle facts:**

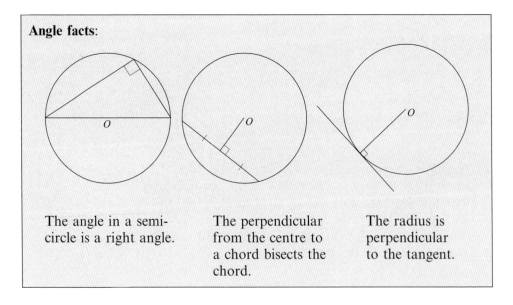

The angle in a semi-circle is a right angle.

The perpendicular from the centre to a chord bisects the chord.

The radius is perpendicular to the tangent.

**1** Find the value of $x$ in each of the following.

(a)

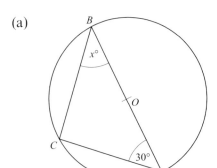

(b)

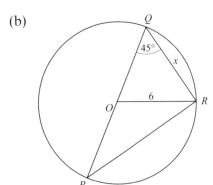

(c)

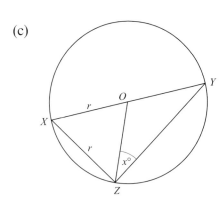

**2** (a) $AB$ is a chord of a circle, radius 5 cm, at a distance of 3 cm from the centre $O$. Find (i) the length $AB$, (ii) the angle $\theta$.

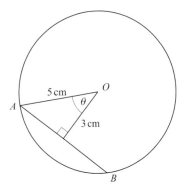

(b) Find the angle $\theta$ subtended by the chord $AB$ in the diagram.

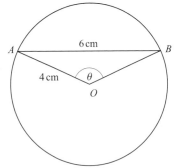

(c) Find the area of triangle $AOB$ and hence find the area of the minor segment cut off by $AB$.

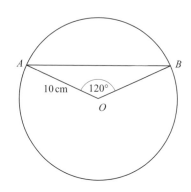

**3** (a) $AP$ and $BP$ are tangents to the circle with centre $O$ and radius 5 cm. $OP = 13$ cm. Find (i) $AP$, (ii) $\theta$.

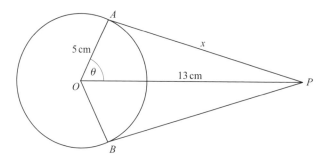

(b) $OP_1P_2$ is a tangent to two circles with centres $O_1$, $O_2$. $OP_1 = 12$ cm. The radius of the circle with centre $O_1$ is 5 cm. Find the radius of the circle with centre $O_2$.

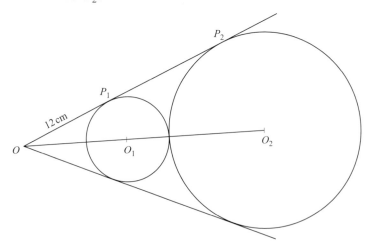

(c) In the diagram, $OA$ is parallel to $PQ$. Find the angle $QPR$ in terms of $\theta$.

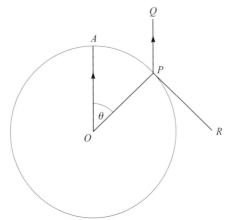

**4** Two circles, radii 3 cm and 5 cm, have centres $P$, $Q$ respectively, $PQ = 7$ cm. If the circles intersect at $A$ and $B$, find the length $AB$.

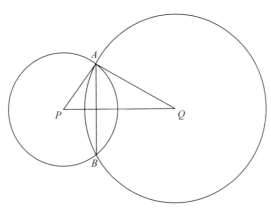

**5** The distance from the Earth to the sun is $1.50 \times 10^8$ km. The diameter of the sun is $1.39 \times 10^6$ km.
Find the angle subtended by the sun from a point on the Earth.
What assumptions have you made?

# 1

## Algebra

### 1.1 Surds; laws of indices

$$\sqrt{ab} = \sqrt{a}\sqrt{b} \qquad \sqrt{\frac{a}{b}} = \frac{\sqrt{a}}{\sqrt{b}}$$

$$a^m a^n = a^{m+n} \qquad a^m / a^n = a^{m-n} \qquad (a^m)^n = a^{mn} \qquad a^0 = 1$$

$$a^{-n} = \frac{1}{a^n} \qquad a^{1/q} = \sqrt[q]{a} \qquad a^{p/q} = \sqrt[q]{(a^p)}$$

**Basic**

1  Evaluate without using a calculator:

(a) $2^0$     (b) $9^{\frac{1}{2}}$     (c) $3^{-3}$

2  Simplify:

(a) $2x^2 y \times 3xy$     (b) $6xy^2 \div 2y$     (c) $\dfrac{x^2}{\sqrt{x}}$

3  Find the value of $x$ which satisfies each equation:

(a) $3^x = 27$     (b) $2^x = \frac{1}{8}$     (c) $3^{x+1} = \frac{1}{3}$

4  Simplify:

(a) $9^{\frac{3}{2}} - 27^{\frac{2}{3}}$     (b) $3^{2x} \div 9$     *(c) $\dfrac{12^x}{6^x}$

5  Simplify:

(a) $\dfrac{x^{\frac{2}{3}} x^{\frac{1}{2}}}{x^{\frac{1}{6}}}$     (b) $\dfrac{x^{\frac{1}{2}} + x^{-\frac{1}{2}}}{x^{\frac{1}{2}}}$     (c) $\dfrac{(x+1)^{\frac{3}{2}} - (x+1)^{-\frac{1}{2}}}{(x+1)^{-\frac{1}{2}}}$

6  Express $\dfrac{1}{(\sqrt[3]{x})^{\frac{6}{5}}}$ in the form $x^n$.

7  Express in terms of the simplest possible surds:

(a) $\sqrt{45}$     (b) $\sqrt{12} - \sqrt{3} + \sqrt{27}$     (c) $\sqrt{8} - 2\sqrt{2}$

8  Express as single square roots:

(a) $2\sqrt{3}$     (b) $4\sqrt{5}$     (c) $a^2\sqrt{b}$

**9** Rationalise the denominators:

(a) $\dfrac{1}{\sqrt{2}}$    (b) $\dfrac{3}{2\sqrt{3}}$    (c) $\dfrac{\sqrt{5}-1}{\sqrt{5}}$

**10** Write in the form $a + b\sqrt{c}$:

(a) $(3 - \sqrt{5})(1 + \sqrt{5})$    (b) $(\sqrt{3} + 2)(2\sqrt{3} - 1)$    *(c) $\dfrac{\sqrt{2}+1}{\sqrt{2}-3}$

(d) $\dfrac{1}{8 + \sqrt{5}}$

**11** Given that $\alpha$ is acute and that $\tan\alpha = \frac{1}{7}$, find the value of $\sin\alpha$ and $\cos\alpha$, leaving your answers in surd form, with rational denominators.

**12** Solve, leaving your answers in surd form:

(a) $x^2 + 2x - 7 = 0$    (b) $2x^2 - 6x - 1 = 0$

### Intermediate

**1** Evaluate without using a calculator:

(a) $\left(\frac{4}{9}\right)^{\frac{1}{2}}$    (b) $\left(3\frac{3}{8}\right)^{-\frac{1}{3}}$    (c) $64^{\frac{2}{3}}$

**2** For each of the following, find the value of $a$.

(a) $3^{n+1} + 3^{n+2} = a \times 3^n$
(b) $4(2^{n+2}) + 2^{n+1} = a \times 2^n$
(c) $9^n - 3^{2n} = a \times 3^n$

**3** Express as a power of $x$:

(a) $\sqrt{x^{\frac{1}{2}} x^{\frac{7}{2}}}$    (b) $\dfrac{\sqrt{x^3}}{\sqrt[3]{x^2}}$    (c) $\sqrt[n]{\dfrac{x^{\frac{n}{2}} x^{\frac{3n}{2}}}{x^{4n}}}$

**4** Find integers $a$ and $b$ such that $3^a \times 5^b = 45^6$.

**5** Simplify $\left(a^{\frac{1}{4}} - b^{\frac{1}{4}}\right)\left(a^{\frac{3}{4}} + a^{\frac{1}{2}} b^{\frac{1}{4}} + a^{\frac{1}{4}} b^{\frac{1}{2}} + b^{\frac{3}{4}}\right)$.

**\*6** Simplify:

(a) $(x + 3)^2 + 2(x + 3)^3$    (b) $32^{\frac{1}{2}} - 18^{\frac{1}{2}}$    (c) $2x\sqrt{\dfrac{1}{x^2} - \dfrac{1}{4}}$

**7** Without using a calculator, write the following in order of size, smallest first.

$$2\sqrt{6},\ 2\sqrt{5},\ 5,\ 2\sqrt{7},\ 3\sqrt{2}$$

**8** Simplify:

(a) $\sqrt{800} \div \sqrt{50}$

(b) $(\sqrt{3}+2)(\sqrt{3}-2)$

(c) $\sqrt{18}+\sqrt{20}-\sqrt{80}+\sqrt{2}$

**9** (a) Show that, if $y=2^x$, the equation $2^{2x}-3(2^x)-4=0$ reduces to $y^2-3y-4=0$. Hence solve $2^{2x}-3(2^x)-4=0$.

(b) Solve:

(i) $3^{2x}-28(3^x)+27=0$

(ii) $16^x-5(2^{2x})+4=0$

(iii) $3^{2x}-10(3^{x+1})+3^4=0$

**10** Solve the simultaneous equations: $2^{x+1}+3^y=5$

$$2^x+2(3^y)=7$$

**11** Given that $\beta$ is acute and that $\sin\beta=\frac{1}{7}$, write, in simplified surd form, the values of $\cos\beta$ and $\tan\beta$.

**12** (a) Rationalise the denominators of the following.

(i) $\dfrac{2}{\sqrt{3}-1}$

(ii) $\dfrac{2+\sqrt{3}}{2-\sqrt{3}}$

(iii) $\dfrac{3\sqrt{5}+2}{3\sqrt{5}+1}$

(b) Find the reciprocals of the following in the form $a+b\sqrt{c}$.

(i) $\sqrt{2}+1$

(ii) $3\sqrt{2}-2$

(iii) $\dfrac{\sqrt{3}-2}{1+\sqrt{3}}$

**13** Find the square roots of the following in the form $a+b\sqrt{c}$.

*(a) $9+4\sqrt{5}$

(b) $19-6\sqrt{2}$

(c) $13-4\sqrt{3}$

**14** Solve the following, leaving your answers in surd form.

(a) $\dfrac{x+1}{x-2}=3x$

(b) $(x-3)(2-x)=x-7$

(c) $\dfrac{a}{a\sqrt{3}+2}=\dfrac{\sqrt{3}-1}{2}$

**15** Given that $(a+\sqrt{3})(b-\sqrt{3})=7+3\sqrt{3}$ and that $a$ and $b$ are positive integers, find the values of $a$ and $b$.

**16** Simplify the following, giving your answers in the form $a+b\sqrt{c}$.

(a) $\dfrac{1}{\sqrt{2}}+\dfrac{2+\sqrt{2}}{3}$

(b) $\dfrac{\sqrt{3}-2}{2}+\dfrac{\sqrt{3}+1}{4}$

(c) $\dfrac{1+2\sqrt{3}}{1-\sqrt{3}} + \dfrac{1-\sqrt{3}}{2}$

(d) $\dfrac{1+\sqrt{2}}{2\sqrt{2}-1} - \dfrac{1+\sqrt{2}}{1-\sqrt{2}}$

## Advanced

1  If $y = a^x + b$, and $y = 5$ when $x = 1$ and $y = \frac{7}{3}$ when $x = -1$, find the value of $y$ when $x = 2$.

2  By writing $z = x^{\frac{1}{3}}$, solve the equation $x^{\frac{1}{3}} - 2x^{-\frac{1}{3}} = 1$.

3  Write down the square of $\sqrt{p} + q\sqrt{s}$ in the form $a + b\sqrt{c}$.
   Hence show that $\sqrt{8} + 4\sqrt{3} < 10$.

4  Solve the equation $x^2 - (6\sqrt{3})x + 24 = 0$, giving your answers in terms of surds, simplified as far as possible.
   Hence:

   (i)  solve the inequality $x^2 - (6\sqrt{3})x + 24 < 0$,
   (ii) find all four solutions of the equation $x^4 - (6\sqrt{3})x^2 + 24 = 0$, giving your answers correct to two decimal places.

   [OCR (Cambridge), 1995]

5  (a) Express $\dfrac{\sqrt{a} + \sqrt{b}}{\sqrt{a} - \sqrt{b}}$ as a fraction with a rational denominator.
   (b) Explain why, if $x$ is positive, $\sqrt{x(x+1)}$ lies between $x$ and $x+1$.
   (c) If $y$ is an integer, find two consecutive integers between which the

   value of $\dfrac{\sqrt{y+1} + \sqrt{y}}{\sqrt{y+1} - \sqrt{y}}$ lies.

6  Simplify:

   (a) $\dfrac{x^{\frac{3}{2}} - x^{-\frac{1}{2}}}{x^{\frac{1}{2}} - x^{-\frac{1}{2}}}$

   (b) $\dfrac{(\sqrt{p+1} - \sqrt{p})(p + \frac{1}{2} + \sqrt{p^2 + p})}{\sqrt{p+1} + \sqrt{p}}$

7  (a) Write $\sin 30°$, $\cos 30°$, $\sin 45°$, $\cos 45°$, $\sin 60°$ and $\cos 60°$ exactly, using surds where appropriate.

(b)  Use the formulae

$$\sin(A \pm B) = \sin A \cos B \pm \cos A \sin B$$
$$\cos(A \pm B) = \cos A \cos B \mp \sin A \sin B$$

to find the values of (i) $\sin 15°$, (ii) $\cos 75°$, (iii) $\sin 105°$, leaving your answers in surd form.

**8**  Use the formulae in question 7(b) to show that $\tan 105° = -2 - \sqrt{3}$.

**9**  Let $p = a + b\sqrt{2}$, where $a$ and $b$ are integers such that $a^2 - 2b^2 = 1$, and let $q = c + d\sqrt{2}$, where $c$ and $d$ are integers such that $c^2 - 2d^2 = 1$.

(a)  Express $\dfrac{1}{p}$ in the form $A + B\sqrt{2}$ and show that $A^2 - 2B^2 = 1$.

(b)  Express $pq$ in the form $C + D\sqrt{2}$ and show that $C^2 - 2D^2 = 1$.

**10**  Given that $2y = a^x + a^{-x}$, where $a > 1$, $x > 0$, prove that $a^x = y + \sqrt{(y^2 - 1)}$.

If, further, $2z = a^{-3x} + a^{3x}$, prove that $z = 4y^3 - 3y$.

[OCR (Cambridge), 1973]

## Revision

**1**  Evaluate without using a calculator:

(a)  $4^{-\frac{1}{2}}$     (b)  $(2\frac{1}{4})^{\frac{1}{2}}$     (c)  $64^{\frac{2}{3}}$

**2**  Simplify:

(a)  $\dfrac{x^2 \times x}{\sqrt{x}}$     (b)  $(\sqrt{x})^5$     (c)  $(x^4)^{\frac{1}{2}}$

**3**  Find the value of $x$ which satisfies each of the following equations.

(a)  $2^{\frac{x}{2}} = \frac{1}{8}$     (b)  $(2\frac{1}{4})^x = \frac{2}{3}$     (c)  $2^{2x+1} - 9(2^x) + 4 = 0$

**4**  Simplify:

(a)  $4 \times 2^{x-2}$     (b)  $(x - 1)^{-\frac{1}{2}} + (x - 1)^{\frac{1}{2}}$     (c)  $x\sqrt{1 - \dfrac{8}{x} + \dfrac{16}{x^2}}$

**5**  Without using a calculator, state which is the greater in each of the following pairs.

(a)  $3\sqrt{3}$ or $4\sqrt{2}$     (b)  $8\sqrt{3}$ or $9\sqrt{2}$     (c)  $10\sqrt{10}$ or $12\sqrt{7}$

**6**  Simplify:

(a)  $2\sqrt{5} + \sqrt{20}$     (b)  $3\sqrt{2} \times 5\sqrt{6}$     (c)  $(2\sqrt{5} - 1)(2\sqrt{5} + 1)$

**7** Rationalise the denominators:

(a) $\dfrac{2}{\sqrt{5}}$     (b) $\dfrac{\sqrt{3}+2}{\sqrt{3}}$     (c) $\dfrac{2+\sqrt{7}}{\sqrt{7}-1}$

**8** Write the following in the form $a+b\sqrt{c}$.

(a) $(7-5\sqrt{5})^2$     (b) $(2+\sqrt{3})(3-2\sqrt{3})$

**9** Find integer values of $a$ and $b$ such that $(a+b\sqrt{3})^2 = 31+12\sqrt{3}$.

**10** Giving your answers in the form $a+b\sqrt{c}$, find:

(a) the reciprocal of $2-\sqrt{3}$     (b) the square root of $49+12\sqrt{5}$

**11** Solve the following, leaving your answers in surd form.

(a) $x^2-3x-2=0$     (b) $\dfrac{5}{3x-2}=x-1$     (c) $2^{2x}-3(2^x)+2=0$

**12** Simplify the following, leaving your answers in rationalised surd form.

(a) $\dfrac{\sqrt{3}}{1-\sqrt{3}}-\dfrac{1}{\sqrt{3}}$     (b) $\dfrac{1}{\sqrt{5}+1}\div\dfrac{2}{\sqrt{5}-1}$

## 1.2    Arithmetic of polynomials; factor theorem; remainder theorem; graphs of $y=kx^n$ ($n=\frac{1}{2}$ or an integer)

> **Factor theorem**: if $f(a)=0$, then $x-a$ is a factor of $f(x)$.
> **Remainder theorem**: $f(a)$ is the remainder when $f(x)$ is divided by $x-a$.

### Basic

**1** Factorise:

(a) $f(x)=x^2-5x$
(b) $f(x)=4x^2-49$
(c) $f(x)=x^2-13x-48$

**2** For each of the following polynomials, write down (i) the degree of the polynomial, (ii) the coefficient of $x^2$.

(a) $3x^4-x^3-2x^2+1$
(b) $2x^5+x^4-3x+7$
*(c) $(1-x)(1+2x^2)$

**3** If $f(x)=4x^3+2x^2-x+1$ and $g(x)=2x^3-7x^2+8$, what is the degree of:

(a) $f(x)+g(x)$     (b) $f(x)-2g(x)$     (c) $f(x)\cdot g(x)$

**4**   Simplify:

(a) $(x^2 - 1)(x + 2) - (x^2 + 1)(x - 3)$
*(b) $(x + 5)(x^2 + x - 1) - (x + 3)^2$
(c) $(x + 2)^2 + (x - 4)^2 - 3(x + 1)(x - 2)$

**5**   Multiply:

(a) $(x^3 - 2x^2 + x + 1)$ by $(x - 3)$
(b) $(x^2 - x + 1)$ by $(x^2 + 2x - 1)$
(c) $(x - 5)^2$ by $(x + 1)^2$

**\*6**   Show that $(x - 2)$ is a factor of $y = x^4 + x^3 - 7x^2 + 5x - 6$.

**7**   Find the remainder when the following polynomials are divided by the given linear factor.

*(a) $3x^4 - 2x^3 + x^2 - 3x + 1$,   $x - 2$
(b) $x^3 - 3x^2 + 4x - 6$,   $x + 1$
(c) $3x^3 - 8x^2 - 4x + 4$,   $x - 3$

**8**   Given that $f(x) = x^3 + 2x^2 - 5x - 6$:

(a) find the remainder when $f(x)$ is divided by $(x + 2)$,
(b) find the remainder when $f(x)$ is divided by $(x - 2)$,
(c) factorise $f(x)$ completely.

**9**   Factorise:

(a) $x^3 - 7x + 6$
(b) $x^3 + 5x^2 - 4x - 20$
(c) $x^3 + 13x^2 + 51x + 63$

**10** Match graphs (a)–(f) below with equations (i)–(vi).

(a)

(b)

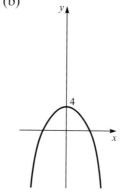

(c)

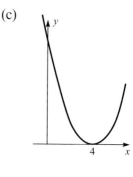

(d)

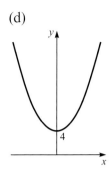

(e)

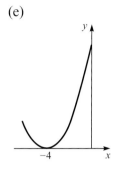

(f)

(i)  $y = x^2$

(ii)  $y = 4x^2$

(iii)  $y = x^2 + 4$

(iv)  $y = (x - 4)^2$

(v)  $y = (x + 4)^2$

(vi)  $y = 4 - x^2$

**11** Match graphs (a)–(f) below with equations (i)–(vi).

(a)

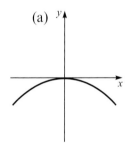

(b)

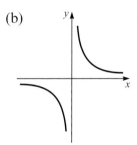

(c)

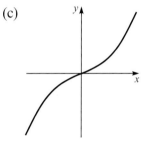

(d)

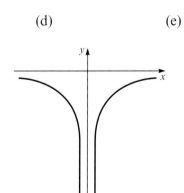

(e)

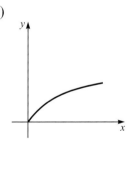

(f)

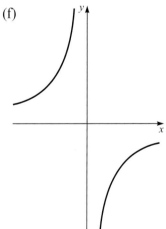

(i)  $y = \dfrac{1}{x}$

(ii)  $y = -\dfrac{2}{x}$

(iii)  $y = -\dfrac{1}{x^2}$

(iv)  $y = \sqrt{x}$

(v)  $y = -x^4$

(vi)  $y = x^5$

**12** Match graphs (a)–(f) below with equations (i)–(vi).

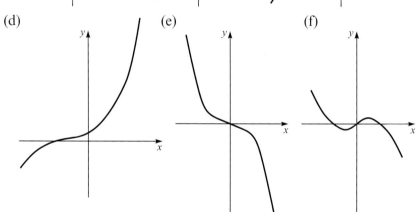

(i)  $y = x^3$                           (ii)  $y = -2x^3$
(iii)  $y = x(x - 1)(x + 1)$             (iv)  $y = x(x + 1)(1 - x)$
(v)  $y = (x + 1)(x^2 + x + 1)$          (vi)  $y = x(x + 1)^2$

### Intermediate

**1** Sketch a cubic function with the following properties:

(a)  three real roots and two turning points,
(b)  two real roots and two turning points,
(c)  one real root and two turning points,
(d)  one real root and no turning points,
(e)  one real root and one stationary point.

**2** Factorise $f(x) = 3 + 4x - 5x^2 - 2x^3$ and hence sketch the graph of $y = f(x)$. For what values of $x$ is $f(x) > 0$?

**3** Factorise $f(x) = x^4 - a^4$. Hence find the number of real roots for the equation $x^4 - a^4 = 0$.

**4** If $f(x) = 2x^3 + 3x^2 - x + 1$ and $g(x) = 4x^2 + 3x - 5$, find:

(a) $f(x) \cdot g(x)$
(b) $g(x + 1)$
(c) $f(2x)$

**5** The diagram opposite shows the graph of
$y = (x - p)^2(q - x)$.
Write down the values of $p$, $q$ and $r$.

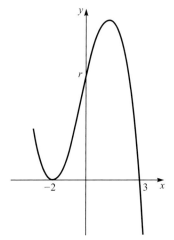

**6** Suggest a possible equation for each of the
graphs (a)–(f) below.

*(a)

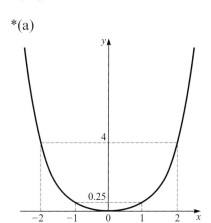

(b)

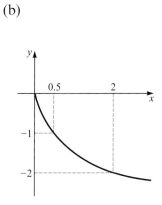

(c)

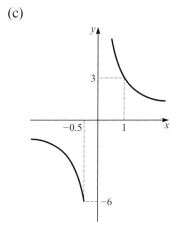

(d)

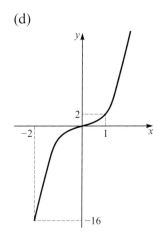

(e)                              (f)

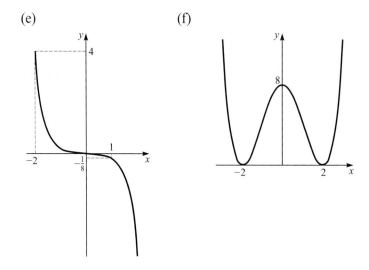

**7** (a) Find the roots of $f(x) = 24 + 26x - 7x^2 - 11x^3 - 2x^4$ and hence sketch the graph of $y = f(x)$.
   (b) For what values of $x$ is $f(x) > 0$?

**8** Find the number of real roots of the equation $x^3 - 3x^2 - x - 12 = 0$.

**9** The polynomial $ax^3 + x^2 + bx - 24$ is divisible by $x^2 - x - 6$. Find the values of $a$ and $b$.

**10** Factorise $f(x) = x^4 - 10x^2 + 9$ and hence sketch the graph of $f(x)$. (Hint: write $y = x^2$.)

**11** Suggest a possible equation for each of the graphs below. There is no need to simplify your answers.

(a)                    *(b)                    (c)

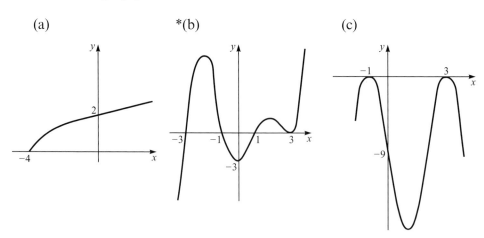

**12** Sketch the graph of $f(x) = x^3 - 12x^2 + 36x$. What is the maximum value of $f(x)$? Hence find the possible values of $k$ so that the equation $x^3 - 12x^2 + 36x = k$ has three distinct solutions.

**13** The polynomial $f(x) = 2x^3 + ax^2 + bx - 12$ has a remainder of 42 when divided by $x - 2$ and a remainder of 6 when divided by $x + 2$.
Find $a$ and $b$ and hence factorise $f(x)$ completely. State the values of $x$ for which $f(x) \leq 0$.

**14** (a)  Factorise $f(x) = 2x^3 - 7x^2 + 9$.
 (b)  Show that $f(x)$ has turning points at $(0, 9)$ and $(\frac{7}{3}, -3.7)$ and hence sketch the graph of $y = 2x^3 - 7x^2 + 9$.
 (c)  Use your graph to find the number of solutions to each of these equations:
   (i)   $2x^3 - 7x^2 + 8 = 0$
   (ii)  $2x^3 - 7x^2 + 13 = 0$
   (iii) $2x^3 - 7x^2 - x + 9 = 0$
   (iv)  $2x^3 - 7x^2 + 2x + 6 = 0$
   (v)   $2x^3 - 9x^2 + x + 15 = 0$

**15** (a)  Find where the graph of $f(x) = 28 - 23x + 12x^2 - 2x^3$ crosses the $x$-axis. Sketch the curve.
 (b)  Find the equation of the normal to the curve at the point $x = 2$.
 (c)  Find the coordinates of the other two points where this normal crosses the curve.

**16** (a)  Find the turning points and roots of $y = x^3 - 3x^2 - 9x - 5$
 (b)  Find the values of $k$ for which the line $y = k - 9x$

   (i)   is a tangent to the curve,
   (ii)  meets the curve three times,
   (iii) cuts the curve once.

### Advanced

**1**  The polynomial $p^3 + ap^2 + bp + 13$ has three integer roots. Find the values of $a$ and $b$.

**2**  $x - 1$ is a factor of the polynomial $f(x) = x^3 + px^2 + qx - 4$.

 (a)  Show that $p + q = 3$.
 (b)  Find the range of values of $p$ for which $f(x)$ has three real roots.

**3**  (a)  Given that $-1$ is a root of the equation $2x^3 - 5x^2 - 4x + 3 = 0$, find the two positive roots.
 (b)  Hence, by substituting $x = \cos t$, solve the equation
    $2\cos^3 t - 5\cos^2 t - 4\cos t + 3 = 0$, for $0 \leq t < 2\pi$, giving your answer in radians in terms of $\pi$.

(c) Solve the equation $2e^{3u} - 5e^{2u} - 4e^{u} + 3 = 0$, giving your answers to three decimal places.

[Edexcel (London), 1996]

4   When the spherical container shown is filled with liquid to a depth of $d$ cm, the volume of liquid is given by $V = \pi(ad^2 - d^3/3)$. Find the value of $d$ when the container is $\frac{5}{32}$ full.

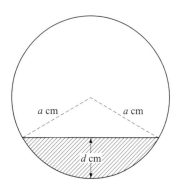

5   If $f(x) = x^4 + x^3 + x + 1 \equiv (x^2 - 1)(x^2 + px + q) + rx + s$, find the values of $p$, $q$, $r$ and $s$. Hence find the remainder when $10\,001\,000\,000\,010\,001$ is divided by $99\,999\,999$.

6   If $f(x) \equiv x^6 - 5x^4 - 10x^2 + k$, find the value of $k$ for which $x - 1$ is a factor of $f(x)$. When $k$ has this value, find another factor of $f(x)$, of the form $x + a$, where $a$ is a constant.

[OCR (Cambridge), 1973]

7   Let $f(x) = x^4 + 2x^3 + 6x^2 + 5x - 7$. Calculate $f(-2)$, $f(-1)$, $f(0)$ and $f(1)$ and deduce that the equation $f(x) = 0$ has at least one root for $-2 < x < -1$, and also at least one root for $0 < x < 1$. Sketch the graph of $f'(x)$, and use it to deduce that $f(x) = 0$ has precisely two roots.

[OCR (SMP), 1978]

8   (a) When divided by $(x^2 + x + 1)$, a cubic polynomial $F(x)$ leaves remainder $(2x + 3)$. When $F(x)$ is divided by $x(x + 3)$, the remainder is $5(x + 1)$. Find $F(x)$.

   (b) $f(x)$, $g(x)$ and $G(x)$ are cubic polynomials in $x$. The polynomials $h(x)$ and $H(x)$ are respectively the remainders left when $f(x)$ is divided by $g(x)$ and by $G(x)$. Prove that, if $ax^3$ and $Ax^3$ are respectively the terms of highest degree in $g(x)$ and $G(x)$, then

$$[aG(x) - Ag(x)]f(x) = aG(x)h(x) = Ag(x)H(x).$$

[OCR (Cambridge), 1964]

9   The positive or zero integer $r$ is the remainder when the positive integer $n$ is divided by the positive integer $p$. Show that $p$ is an exact divisor of $(n^p - n) - (r^p - r)$. Factorise $r^p - r$ in each of the special cases $p = 3$, $p = 5$ and $p = 7$, and deduce that in these cases $p$ is an exact divisor of $n^p - n$. Determine whether this result holds when $p = 4$.

[OCR (Cambridge), 1968]

**10** Let $p(x) = x^3 - 6x^2 + 9x - 1$. Sketch the graph of $p(x)$ for $x > 0$, and show that the zeros of p are all real, distinct and positive. Suppose that these zeros are $\alpha$, $\beta$, $\gamma$ (where $\alpha > \beta > \gamma > 0$) and that for $r \geq 0$ the expression $\alpha^r + \beta^r + \gamma^r$ is denoted by $s_r$ (with the convention that $s_0 = 3$). Use the result $p(x) = (x - \alpha)(x - \beta)(x - \gamma)$ to find the value of $s_1$.
Show, by considering the expression $(\alpha + \beta + \gamma)^2 - 2(\alpha\beta + \beta\gamma + \gamma\alpha)$, or otherwise, that $s_2 = 18$.
By considering the sum $\alpha^n p(\alpha) + \beta^n p(\beta) + \gamma^n p(\gamma)$, or otherwise, prove that $s_{n+3} = 6s_{n+2} - 9s_{n+1} + s_n$ for $n \geq 0$. Hence find the values for $s_3$ and $s_4$.
Evaluate $s_n^{1/n}$ for $n = 1, 2, 3, 4$ and explain why these values appear to be approaching a limit.
[OCR (SMP), 1980]

### Revision

**1** (a) Factorise:
  (i) $x^4 - 9x^2$   (ii) $x^3 - 7x^2 + 7x + 15$
 (b) Given that $x + 3$ is a factor of $x^3 + ax^2 - 9$, find $a$.

**2** $f(x) = 2x^3 + x^2 - 13x + 6$

 (a) Show that $2x - 1$ is a factor of $f(x)$.
 (b) Factorise $f(x)$ completely.
 (c) Solve the equation $f(x) = 0$.

**3** Factorise $f(x) = x^4 - x^3 - 4x^2 - 5x - 3$.
Hence state the number of real roots of $f(x) = 0$.

**4** Given that $x + 3$ and $x - 4$ are factors of $f(x) = x^3 + ax^2 + bx - 12$ find the values of $a$ and $b$. Hence factorise $f(x)$ completely.

**5** Find the values of $x$ for which $4x^3 - 3x^2 + 4 > 16x^2 - 11x$.

**6** Find the values of $x$ for which $f(x) = x^4 + 2x^3 - 3x^2 - 4x + 4$ is zero.
Find the coordinates of the turning points of $f(x)$, distinguishing between the maximum and minimum. Sketch the graph of $f(x)$.

**7** The polynomial $f(x) = 3x^3 + ax^2 + bx + 16$ has a double root at $x = 2$.
Find the values of $a$ and $b$.

**8** Find the equation of the tangent to the curve $y = x^3 - 3x^2 + 2x + 7$ at the point when $x = 2$. Find the coordinates of the point where this tangent crosses the curve.

**9** (a) Sketch the graph of $y = x^3 - 6x$.
 (b) (i) Find the equation of the tangent to the curve at the point $x = -1$.

(ii) Find the coordinates of the point where the tangent crosses the curve.

(c) Solve the inequality $x^3 - 6x > 8x^2 - 17x - 20$.

**10** The polynomial $f(x) = x^3 + 3x^2 - 24x + k$ has a repeated root. Show that this repeated root must be either $-4$ or $2$. In each case, find the value of $k$ and the other root.

**11** The quadratic $x^2 + 4x + 7$ gives the same remainder when divided by $x + a$ and $x - 2a\,(a \neq 0)$. Find the value of $a$.

**12** The polynomial $f(x) = px^3 + qx^2 + 20x - 12$ gives a remainder of 36 when divided by $x - 1$ and $-14$ when divided by $x + 1$.

(a) Find the values of $p$ and $q$ and hence factorise $f(x)$ completely.

(b) State the values of $x$ for which $f(x) \geq 0$.

## 1.3      Modulus sign; linear and quadratic equations and inequalities (including graphical methods); sum and product of roots of quadratic equations; simultaneous equations – one linear and one quadratic

For the quadratic equation $ax^2 + bx + c = 0$, the solution is

$$x = \frac{-b \pm \sqrt{b^2 - 4ac}}{2a}$$

If $\alpha$ and $\beta$ are roots of the equation, $\alpha + \beta = -\dfrac{b}{a}$; $\alpha\beta = \dfrac{c}{a}$.

### Basic

**1** Draw sketch graphs of the following functions.

(a) $y = |x| + 4$      (b) $y = 2|x| - 3$      (c) $y = 3(|x| + 2)$

**2** Use the appropriate sketch graphs from question 1 to solve the following equations.

(a) $|x| + 4 = 7$      (b) $2|x| - 3 = 1$      (c) $3(|x| + 2) = 9$

**3** Draw sketch graphs of the following functions.

(a) $|x - 5|$      (b) $|3x + 4|$      (c) $2|x + 3|$

**4**  Using your graphs from question 3, solve the following equations.

(a)  $|x - 5| = 3$     (b)  $2|x + 3| = 8$     (c)  $|3x + 4| = 10$

**5**  Solve the following equations.

(a)  $3(x + 3) - 4(2 - 3x) = 5x - 9$     (b)  $\dfrac{2x - 3}{5} - \dfrac{x + 3}{2} = \dfrac{2 - 3x}{4}$

**6**  Find the ranges of values of $x$ for which:

(a)  $3x - 5 \leq 7$     (b)  $4 + 5x < 8 - 11x$

*(c)  $3(4x - 1) - 2(1 + 2x) > 4(x + 3) + 5$

**7**  Find the solution sets of the following inequalities.

(a)  $|x| \leq 2$     (b)  $|5x + 3| > 18$     *(c)  $|2x - 5| < |x - 7|$

**8**  Solve the following equations, using the method given, giving your answers to two decimal places where appropriate.

(a)  $3x^2 + 13x - 10 = 0$   (factorisation)

(b)  $5x = \dfrac{12x + 9}{x}$   (factorisation)

(c)  $\dfrac{16}{x} = x$   (inspection)

(d)  $x^2 - 8x - 3 = 0$   (completing the square)
(e)  $10x^2 - 5x - 2 = 0$   (completing the square)
(f)  $2x^2 + 5x - 4 = 0$   (formula)

**9**  Find the ranges of values of $x$ which satisfy the following inequalities.

(a)  $x^2 - x - 12 \leq 0$     (b)  $2 - 5x - 12x^2 \geq 0$

(c)  $4x^2 + 23x + 15 < 0$

**10** (a)  Express $x^2 + 2x + 3$ in the form $(x + a)^2 + b$. Hence show that $x^2 + 2x + 3 > 0$ for all values of $x$.
(b)  Show that $-x^2 + 6x - 10 < 0$ for all values of $x$.

**11** Illustrate graphically the inequalities $x \geq 0$, $y \geq 0$, $3x + 2y \leq 24$, $2x + y \geq 8$.

**12** Solve the simultaneous equations:

(a)  $y = 3x$          *(b)  $x - y = 4$
     $y = x^2 - 4$           $3x^2 + 4xy + y^2 = 0$

**13** Find the sum and product of the roots, $\alpha$, $\beta$, of each of the equations:

(a)  $x^2 - 3x + 2 = 0$     (b)  $2x^2 - 5x - 4 = 0$
(c)  $5x^2 + 3x - 7 = 0$     (d)  $3x^2 + x + 8 = 0$

**14** Find, in the form, $ax^2 + bx + c = 0$, where $a$, $b$, $c$ are integers, the equations whose roots are:

(a) $-1, 4$     (b) $\frac{1}{3}, -\frac{1}{6}$     (c) $-\frac{2}{5}, -2$

## Intermediate

**1** (a) Sketch the graph of $f(x) = 8 - 2x - x^2$. Hence sketch the graph of $y = |f(x)|$.
(b) Sketch the graph of $y = \left|4 - \dfrac{16}{x}\right|$.

**2** Use your answers to question 1 to solve the following equations, giving your answers to two decimal places.

(a) $|8 - 2x - x^2| = 4$     (b) $\left|4 - \dfrac{16}{x}\right| = |x|$

**3** For what ranges of values of $x$ are each of the following inequalities true?

(a) $\dfrac{x-3}{x+4} > 0$     (b) $\dfrac{x+1}{(x-3)(x-2)} > 0$     (c) $\dfrac{x^2 - x - 2}{x+7} < 0$

**4** (a) Show that the inequality $\dfrac{x-2}{x+3} \geq 2$ is equivalent to $\dfrac{x+8}{x+3} \leq 0$.

Hence find the range of values of $x$ that satisfy the inequality.
(b) Solve the inequality:

$$\frac{x+4}{x-3} \leq \frac{x+2}{x-1}$$

**5** (a) Solve the equations:
*(i) $3x(x+5) = 9x - 2$     (ii) $x - \dfrac{3}{x} = 2 - x$.
(b) Solve the inequalities:
(i) $(x+2)(x-3) > 14$     (ii) $4x^2 + 4x - 1 \geq 0$

**6** Solve the inequality $2x^3 - 9x^2 + x + 12 \geq 0$.

**7** Solve the simultaneous equations:
(a) $y = x - 3$           (b) $y = 3x - 2$              (c) $xy = 12$
   $3x^2 - 2xy - y^2 = 3$       $2x^2 - xy + y^2 = 2$           $x^2 + y^2 = 40$

**8** Find the value of $c$ for which the line $y = 3x + c$ is a tangent to the curve $y^2 = 5x$.

**9** A straight line has gradient 3 and passes through the point $(-1, 4)$. A circle has centre $(2, 4)$ and radius 5. Find the equations of the line and the circle and hence find the coordinates of the points where the line intersects the circle.

**10** (a)  Solve the equation $x^2 - 3\sqrt{5}x + 10 = 0$, giving your answers in terms of surds.

(b)  Solve the inequality $x^2 - 3\sqrt{5}x + 10 < 0$.

(c)  Solve $x^4 - 3\sqrt{5}x^2 + 10 = 0$, giving your answers correct to two decimal places.

**11**  Find the range of values of $x$ for which:

(a)  $\left|\dfrac{x}{x-5}\right| > 6$     (b)  $\dfrac{3}{|x+1|} \le \dfrac{2}{|x-3|}$

**12**  Verify that $x^3 - y^3 = (x - y)(x^2 + xy + y^2)$. Hence solve the equations:

$$x - y = 5$$
$$x^3 - y^3 = 35$$

**13**  If $\alpha$, $\beta$ are the roots of the equation $3x^2 + 5x + 4 = 0$, find the values of:

(a)  $\alpha^2 + \beta^2$     (b)  $\alpha^3 + \beta^3$     (c)  $\dfrac{\alpha}{\beta} + \dfrac{\beta}{\alpha}$

**14**  If $\alpha$ and $\beta$ are the roots of the equation $3x^2 + 6x - 2 = 0$, find the quadratic equation whose roots are:

(a)  $2\alpha, 2\beta$     *(b)  $\alpha^2, \beta^2$     (c)  $\alpha + 5\beta, 5\alpha + \beta$

**15**  If the roots of the equation $px^2 + qx + r = 0$ differ by 4, show that

$$q^2 = 4p(4p + r)$$

**16**  If one root of the equation $x^2 - 2x + 3r = 0$ is the square of the other, find the possible values of $r$.

## Advanced

**1**  Solve the simultaneous equations:

$$4x + 3y = 3$$
$$20x^2 + 9y^2 = 6$$

**2**  If $a, b$ are positive numbers and $b > a$, show that

$$(a + 2b)\left(\dfrac{1}{a} + \dfrac{1}{2b}\right) > 4$$

**3**  (a)  Find the values of $k$ for which the equation $x^2 + (k - 4)x - 4k = 0$ has real roots.

(b)  If $x$ is real, find the set of possible values of the function $\dfrac{3 - 2x}{x^2 + 2x - 5}$.

**4** Find the range of values of $p$ for which the quadratic equation in $x$,

$$px^2 + (p+3)x + p = 0 \quad (p \neq 0)$$

has real roots. Find the value of $p$ if $x = -2$ is a root, and find the other root in this case. Give, in each case, a sketch of the graph of the function $y = px^2 + (p+3)x + p$ when $p = 2$ and when $p = -2$.
[OCR (Cambridge), 1971]

**5** If $\alpha$ and $\beta$ are the roots of the equation $ax^2 + bx + c = 0$ and $\alpha + 1/\beta = 1$, show that $(a+c)(a+b+c) + ac = 0$.

**6** (a) Find $x$, $y$, $z$ in terms of $a$, $b$, $c$ if

$$y + z = 2a, \quad z + x = 2b, \quad x + y = 2c$$

Deduce the solution of the equations

$$\frac{1}{y} + \frac{1}{z} = \frac{2}{a}, \quad \frac{1}{z} + \frac{1}{x} = \frac{2}{b}, \quad \frac{1}{x} + \frac{1}{y} = \frac{2}{c}$$

(b) Solve the simultaneous equations:

$$\frac{x^2}{3y^2} - \frac{x}{y} = \frac{9}{4}$$

$$2x - 3y = 12$$

[OCR (Cambridge), 1963]

**7** Show that, if the coordinates $(x, y)$ of a point $P$ satisfy the relation

$$|(1 - 2|x|)| + |(1 - |y|)| \leq 1$$

then so do the coordinates $(-x, y)$, $(-x, -y)$, $(x, -y)$ of the three images of $P$ under reflection in the coordinate axes. Hence show on a diagram of the Cartesian plane the region defined by the points whose coordinates satisfy the above relation.
[OCR (Cambridge), 1976]

**8** Find the maximum values of the function $x^2 + y^2$ consistent with the inequalities

$$y \geq 1, \quad x + 4 \geq 2y, \quad 9 \geq 3y + 2x$$

[OCR (Cambridge), 1962]

**9** Find the range of values of $c$ such that the simultaneous equations

$$\cos\theta + \sin\phi = 1$$

$$\sec\theta + \operatorname{cosec}\phi = c$$

are satisfied by real values of $\theta$ and $\phi$.
Obtain the general solutions of these equations when $c = 6\frac{1}{4}$.
[OCR (Cambridge), 1967]

**10** If $x$, $y$ and $z$ are any three real numbers, prove that

$$k(x^2 + y^2 + z^2) - 2(yz + zx + xy)$$

can never be negative if $k \geq 2$. Find conditions for the expression to vanish, distinguishing between the cases $k > 2$ and $k = 2$. A closed rectangular box has total surface area $A$, and the sum of the lengths of its twelve edges is $p$. The diagonal (i.e. the straight line joining the intersection of three faces to the intersection of the remaining three faces) is of length $d$. Prove that $48d^2 > p^2 > 24A$, unless the box is cubical.
[OCR (Cambridge), 1967]

### Revision

**1** Using the same axes and scales, sketch the graphs of $y = |x + 2|$ and $y = |x^2 + 2x - 3|$. Hence state the number of solutions to the equation $|x^2 + 2x - 3| = |x + 2|$.

**2** Find the ranges of values of $x$ which satisfy the following inequalities.

(a) $-7 \leq 5x + 3 \leq 8$       (b) $|3x + 5| \geq 11$

**3** Find the ranges of values of $x$ for which:

(a) $\dfrac{3x + 2}{x - 5} < 2$       (b) $3|x - 1| > |x + 2|$       (c) $\dfrac{(x + 2)(x - 3)}{x - 1} \leq 2$

**4** Show that the minimum value of $(p + 2)x^2 - 2px + 1$ is given by

$$\frac{-p^2 + p + 2}{(p + 2)^2}$$

Hence find the set of values of $p$ for which $(p + 2)x^2 - 2px + 1$ is positive for all real values of $x$.

**5** Solve the equations:

(a) $x^4 - 13x^2 + 36 = 0$       (b) $\sqrt{4 + x} - \dfrac{3}{\sqrt{4 + x}} = 2$

**6** Solve the simultaneous equations:

$$x + 2y = 5$$
$$2x^2 + 7y + y^2 = 32$$

**7** Find the value of $p$ if the line $px + y = 3$ is a tangent to the curve $y^2 = 4x$.

**8** Find the range of values of $c$ such that the line $x + cy = 5$ intersects the circle whose equation is $x^2 + y^2 = 9$.

**9** Find the range of values of $q$ which makes the function $q - 3qx - 2x^2$ negative for all values of $x$.

**10** The diagram shows a sketch of

$$f(x) = \frac{p}{x - q}, \text{ where } p \text{ and } q \text{ are}$$

constants. The curve intersects the $y$-axis at the point $P(0, -3)$. The $x$-axis and the line $x = 2$ are asymptotes to the curve.

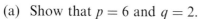

(a) Show that $p = 6$ and $q = 2$.
(b) Sketch the graph of $y = |f(x)|$.

(c) Solve $\left| \dfrac{6}{x - 2} \right| = 3$.

(d) Find the set of values of $x$ for which $\left| \dfrac{6}{x - 2} \right| < 3$.

**11** Solve the inequality $\left| \dfrac{x - 5}{x} \right| \le |x + 3|$.

**12** If $\alpha$ and $\beta$ are the roots of the equation $px^2 + qx + r = 0$, find the equations whose roots are

(a) $\dfrac{1}{\alpha}, \dfrac{1}{\beta}$     (b) $\alpha^2, \beta^2$     (c) $3\alpha, 3\beta$

## 1.4     Partial fractions

### Basic

**1** Evaluate:

(a) $\dfrac{3}{4} + \dfrac{4}{5}$     (b) $\dfrac{a}{7} - \dfrac{b}{9}$     (c) $\dfrac{2}{x} + \dfrac{3}{y}$

**2** Without the use of a calculator, solve the following equations to find $k$.

(a) $\dfrac{3}{10} = \dfrac{4}{5} + \dfrac{k}{4}$     (b) $\dfrac{4}{15} = \dfrac{4}{5} - \dfrac{k}{3}$     (c) $\dfrac{7}{24} = \dfrac{1}{2} + \dfrac{k}{3} - \dfrac{k}{4}$

**3** Multiply both sides of each equation to remove all fractions, leaving all the coefficients as integers, with no common factors.

(a) $\dfrac{4}{6} = \dfrac{a}{5} + \dfrac{b}{4}$     (b) $\dfrac{13}{3} = \dfrac{a}{51} - \dfrac{b}{17}$     *(c) $\dfrac{7}{x} = \dfrac{3}{x + 1} + \dfrac{1}{4}$

**4**   In each case, obtain an equation with integer coefficients and use this to find, by inspection, possible integer values for the unknown constants.

(a) $\dfrac{a}{11} + \dfrac{b}{7} = \dfrac{25}{77}$     (b) $\dfrac{4}{39} = \dfrac{a}{3} - \dfrac{b}{13}$     (c) $\dfrac{13}{15} = \dfrac{a}{5} - \dfrac{b}{15} + \dfrac{c}{3}$

**5**   Express as a single fraction:

(a) $\dfrac{2}{x+1} + \dfrac{3}{x+2}$     (b) $\dfrac{4}{x-3} - \dfrac{2}{x+5}$     (c) $\dfrac{2}{2x+1} - \dfrac{3}{3x+2}$

**6**   Verify that the following identities are valid for all values of $x$ for which the expressions are defined.

(a) $\dfrac{6}{2x+1} - \dfrac{3}{x+1} \equiv \dfrac{3}{(2x+1)(x+1)}$     (b) $\dfrac{2}{x+1} + \dfrac{3}{x-1} \equiv \dfrac{5x+1}{x^2-1}$

**7**   Consider the expression $\dfrac{10x+2}{(x+3)(2x-1)}$ and the equivalent partial

fractions, $\dfrac{A}{x+3} + \dfrac{B}{2x-1}$

(a) Explain why $(10x+2) \equiv A(2x-1) + B(x+3)$.
(b) Explain how the values $x = \frac{1}{2}$ and $x = -3$ can be used to determine values for $A$ and $B$.
(c) Find the required values for $A$ and $B$.

**8**   Find the values of the constants $A$ and $B$:

*(a) $\dfrac{A}{2x+1} + \dfrac{B}{x+2} \equiv \dfrac{x+8}{(2x+1)(x+2)}$

(b) $\dfrac{A}{x-7} + \dfrac{B}{4x+1} \equiv \dfrac{29}{7(x-7)(4x+1)}$

**9**   Express each algebraic fraction as the sum of two partial fractions.

(a) $\dfrac{x-9}{(2x+3)(x-2)}$     (b) $\dfrac{1}{(x+1)(x-1)}$

(c) $\dfrac{x}{(x+1)(x-1)}$     (d) $\dfrac{3x+4}{(2x+1)(5x+4)}$

**10**  Verify that the following identities are valid for all values of $x$ for which the expressions are defined.

(a) $\dfrac{2}{2x+1} - \dfrac{2}{3x-2} \equiv \dfrac{2x-6}{6x^2-x-2}$

(b) $\dfrac{5}{x-7} + \dfrac{3}{2x+5} \equiv \dfrac{13x-20}{2x^2-9x-35}$

**11** Prove algebraically, or disprove with a counter-example, each identity.

(a) $\dfrac{1}{3x+1} - \dfrac{1}{3x-2} \equiv \dfrac{-3}{9x^2+3x-2}$

(b) $\dfrac{2}{x-1} - \dfrac{3}{5x-4} \equiv \dfrac{7x-11}{5x^2-9x+4}$

(c) $\dfrac{5}{1-5x} - \dfrac{2}{x+3} \equiv \dfrac{15x+13}{3-14x-5x^2}$

**12** In each case factorise the denominator, and then determine the two related partial fractions with linear denominators.

(a) $\dfrac{x-21}{x^2-2x-15}$

(b) $\dfrac{9x}{2x^2-3x-9}$

(c) $\dfrac{x}{4x^2-1}$

## Intermediate

**1** Express as partial fractions:

*(a) $\dfrac{4x-1}{(2x+1)(x+2)}$

(b) $\dfrac{5x}{(6x+8)(3x-1)}$

(c) $\dfrac{9x-5}{10x^2+28x-6}$

**2** Express $\dfrac{14x+18}{(x+1)(x+2)(x-3)}$ in partial fractions.

**3** By expanding both expressions into partial fractions, show that

$$\frac{2x+12}{x^2+10x+21} + \frac{x+16}{2x^2+10x-28} \equiv \frac{3}{2(x+3)} + \frac{1}{x-2}$$

Hence, verify that

$$\frac{2x+12}{x^2+10x+21} + \frac{x+16}{2x^2+10x-28} \equiv \frac{5x}{2x^2+2x-12}$$

**4** (a) Show that $\dfrac{2x}{x^2-1}$ may be expressed in the form $\dfrac{A}{x-1} + \dfrac{B}{x+1}$, finding the values of the constants $A$ and $B$.

(b) Sketch on the same axes the two graphs $\mathrm{f}(x) = \dfrac{A}{x-1}$ and $\mathrm{g}(x) = \dfrac{B}{x+1}$.

(c) Use these sketches to superimpose the principal features of the curve
$$\mathrm{h}(x) = \frac{2x}{x^2-1}.$$

**5** Apply the method of partial fractions to sketch the graph of
$$y = \frac{x+3}{2x^2-3x-2}.$$

**6**  Consider the cubic mapping defined by $p(x) = 2x^3 + 5x^2 + 5x + 3$.

(a)  Show that $-\frac{3}{2}$ is a root of the equation $p(x) = 0$.

(b)  Hence express $p(x)$ in the form $(Ax + B)(Cx^2 + Dx + E)$.

(c)  By considering the quadratic expression $Cx^2 + Dx + E$, explain why it is **not** possible to decompose $\dfrac{1}{p(x)}$ into three partial fractions with linear denominators.

**\*7**  (a)  If $(Ax + B)(x - 2) + C(x^2 + 1) \equiv 7x + 1$, find $A$, $B$ and $C$.

(b)  Find values of $A$, $B$, and $C$ that satisfy the following identity:

$$\frac{5x + 4}{(2x + 3)(x^2 + x + 1)} \equiv \frac{Ax + B}{x^2 + x + 1} + \frac{C}{2x + 3}$$

**8**  (a)  Prove that

$$\frac{Ax + B}{(x + k)^2} \equiv \frac{A}{x + k} + \frac{B - kA}{(x + k)^2} \quad (x \neq -k)$$

(b)  Hence, obtain directly partial fractions for:

(i)  $\dfrac{x + 7}{(x + 3)^2}$    (ii)  $\dfrac{5x - 3}{x^2 - 8x + 16}$

**\*9**  Given that the cubic expression $x^3 + 3x^2 - 9x + 5$ has a repeated root at $x = 1$, factorise the polynomial completely. Hence express

$$\frac{14x - 2}{x^3 + 3x^2 - 9x + 5}$$

as the sum of three partial fractions.

**10** (a)  Find the values of $A$, $B$ and $C$, such that $\dfrac{(x^2 + 25)}{(x + 7)^3}$ may be expressed as the sum of three partial fractions

$$\frac{A}{x + 7} + \frac{B}{(x + 7)^2} + \frac{C}{(x + 7)^3}$$

(b)  By attempting to express $\dfrac{2x}{(2x + 3)^3}$ as the sum of three partial fractions, show that one of the numerators is zero, and hence that it is only necessary to use two partial fractions.

**11** (a)  Verify that $\dfrac{x^2 + 6x + 13}{x^2 + 5x + 6}$ may be expressed as $1 + \dfrac{x + 7}{x^2 + 5x + 6}$.

(b)  Hence obtain $\dfrac{x^2 + 6x + 13}{x^2 + 5x + 6}$ as the sum of a constant and two fractions with linear denominators.

(c)  Express $\dfrac{4x^2 + 16x - 30}{x^2 + 2x - 8}$ in the form $a + \dfrac{b}{x - 2} + \dfrac{c}{x + 4}$.

**12 (a)** Using polynomial division, or otherwise, show that it is possible to express $\dfrac{2x^3 + 7x^2 + 5x + 6}{2x^2 + x + 1}$ in the form $x + 3 + \dfrac{Ax + B}{2x^2 + x + 1}$.

**(b)** Find the values of the constants $A$ and $B$.

**(c)** Explain why it is not possible to decompose the original expression any further into partial fractions.

**13 (a)** Find both the quotient and the remainder when the cubic $3x^3 - 27x^2 + 65x + 25$ is divided by $x(x - 5)^2$.

**(b)** Use this result to express $\dfrac{3x^3 - 27x^2 + 65x + 25}{x(x - 5)^2}$ as the sum of a constant and three partial fractions.

**14** Given the two cubic approximations $\dfrac{1}{1 + x} \approx 1 - x + x^2 - x^3$ and $\dfrac{1}{1 - x} \approx 1 + x + x^2 + x^3$, which are valid for small $x$, show, by using partial fractions, that $\dfrac{2x}{1 - x^2} \approx 2x + 2x^3$.

**15 (a)** **(i)** Show that

$$\frac{-4x}{(1 + x)^2} \equiv \frac{-4}{1 + x} + \left(\frac{2}{1 + x}\right)^2$$

**(ii)** By substituting the quadratic approximations $\dfrac{1}{1 + x} \approx 1 - x + x^2$ and $\dfrac{1}{1 - x} \approx 1 + x + x^2$ into the result from (i), show that

$$\frac{-4x}{(1 + x)^2} \approx -4x + 8x^2.$$

**(b)** Confirm that the same result is obtained by writing $\dfrac{-4x}{(1 + x)^2}$ as $-4x\left(\dfrac{1}{1 + x}\right)^2$ and then applying the quadratic approximation.

**16** Show that $f(x) = \dfrac{26 - 6x^2}{(1 - 2x)(x + 3)^2} \equiv \dfrac{2}{1 - 2x} + \dfrac{4}{x + 3} - \dfrac{5}{(x + 3)^2}$

Hence show that

**(a)** $f'(0) = \frac{106}{27}$,

**(b)** $\displaystyle\int f(x)\,dx = \ln\dfrac{(x + 3)^4}{1 - 2x} + \dfrac{5}{x + 3} + c$,

**(c)** the series expansion of $f(x)$ as far as the term in $x^2$ is $\frac{1}{27}(75 + 106x + 215x^2)$.

**Advanced**

1   Express as partial fractions:

(a) $\dfrac{2bx}{x^2 - a^2}$     (b) $\dfrac{bx - a^2}{x^2 - a^2}$

2   It is required to find the value of the sum $\displaystyle\sum_{n=2}^{100} \dfrac{1}{n^2 - 1}$ without performing all of the constituent calculations.

(a) Express $\dfrac{1}{n^2 - 1}$ as partial fractions.

(b) Using these partial fractions, write down the terms in the sum

$$\sum_{n=2}^{5} \dfrac{1}{n^2 - 1}.$$

(c) Confirm that $\displaystyle\sum_{n=2}^{100} \dfrac{1}{n^2 - 1} = \dfrac{1}{2} + \dfrac{1}{4} - \dfrac{1}{200} - \dfrac{1}{202} = \dfrac{14\,949}{20\,200}.$

3   Simplify $(x^2 + \sqrt{2}x + 1)(x^2 - \sqrt{2}x + 1)$.

Hence express $\dfrac{1}{x^4 + 1}$ as the sum of two partial fractions with quadratic denominators.

4   Show that, if $f(x) = \dfrac{1}{ax + b}$, $f^{(n)}(x) = (-1)^n \dfrac{a^n n!}{(ax + b)^{n+1}}$.

Hence find the $n$th derivative of $\dfrac{15x}{(x + 1)(3x - 2)}$.

5   (a) Express $\dfrac{12n + 12}{n^4 + 4n^3 + 4n^2}$ as partial fractions.

(b) Hence show that the sum $\displaystyle\sum_{n=1}^{20} \dfrac{12n + 12}{n^4 + 4n^3 + 4n^2}$ has the value

$3 + \frac{3}{4} - \frac{3}{441} - \frac{3}{484}.$

6   By expressing $f(x) = \dfrac{7x + 7}{(x + 3)(x - 4)}$ in partial fractions, prove that $f'(x) < 0$ for all values of $x$. Sketch the graph of $f(x)$.

7   $S_n$ and $T_n$ are defined as the sum to $n$ terms of the two series

$\dfrac{1}{1.2.3} + \dfrac{1}{2.3.4} + \dfrac{1}{3.4.5} + \cdots$ and $\dfrac{1}{1.3} + \dfrac{1}{2.4} + \dfrac{1}{3.5} + \cdots$ respectively

(a) Prove that $T_n - S_n = \dfrac{n}{2(n + 2)}$.

(b) If $S$ is the sum to infinity of the first series, find $S$.

(c) How large must $n$ be to ensure that $|S - S_n| < 10^{-3}$?

**8** A quadratic function $f(x)$ takes values 4, $-1$ and 2 when $x = 1$, $x = 2$ and $x = 3$ respectively. Put into partial fractions the function defined by

$$g(x) = \frac{f(x)}{(x-1)(x-2)(x-3)}, \text{ and hence or otherwise find } f(x).$$

Sketch the graph of $g(x)$ and determine where it crosses the axis of $x$.
[OCR (Cambridge), 1968]

**9** Express $\dfrac{x}{1-x^2}$ in partial fractions.

Prove that it is not possible to find constants $a$, $b$ such that, for all values of $x$, where $x^2 \neq 1$,

$$\frac{x}{\sqrt{(1-x^2)}} = \frac{a}{\sqrt{(1-x)}} + \frac{b}{\sqrt{(1+x)}}.$$

Prove also that $\sin^2 \alpha - \sin^2 x = \sin(\alpha - x)\sin(\alpha + x)$ and determine whether it is possible to express $\dfrac{\sin x}{\sin^2 \alpha - \sin^2 x}$ for all values of $x$, where $\sin^2 x \neq \sin^2 \alpha$, in the form $\dfrac{A}{\sin(\alpha - x)} + \dfrac{B}{\sin(\alpha + x)}$ where $A$, $B$ are constants, possibly involving $\alpha$ but independent of $x$, and give the values for $A$ and $B$ if they exist.
[OCR (Cambridge), 1982]

**10** A sequence $f_1(x), f_2(x), f_3(x), \ldots$, is defined for all real values of $x$ other than $\pm 1$, by

$$\frac{d^n}{dx^n}\left(\frac{1}{1-x^2}\right) = \frac{f_n(x)}{(1-x^2)^{n+1}}.$$

By expressing $1/(1-x^2)$ in partial fractions, or otherwise, prove that $f_n(x)$ is a polynomial of degree $n$, and find the coefficient of $x^n$ in this polynomial.
[OCR (Cambridge), 1975]

## Revision

**1** Verify that the identities are valid for all values of $x$ for which the expressions are defined:

(a) $\dfrac{6}{5x-2} - \dfrac{3}{2x+1} \equiv \dfrac{12-3x}{(2x+1)(5x-2)}$

(b) $\dfrac{1}{x+7} + \dfrac{3}{7x-1} \equiv \dfrac{10x+20}{7x^2+48x-7}$

**2**  Find the values of the constants $A$ and $B$:

(a) $\dfrac{A}{2x-1} + \dfrac{B}{x+3} \equiv \dfrac{x-32}{(2x-1)(x+3)}$

(b) $\dfrac{A}{2x-7} + \dfrac{B}{x+5} \equiv \dfrac{85}{(2x-7)(x+5)}$

**3**  Decompose each algebraic fraction into the sum of two partial fractions:

(a) $\dfrac{x-4}{2x^2-x-1}$     (b) $\dfrac{7x+1}{9x^2-1}$

**4**  $f(x) = \dfrac{2}{x^2-2x}$

(a)  Express $f(x)$ in partial fractions.
(b)  Show that $f'(1) = 0$.
(c)  Show that $\int_3^4 f(x)\,dx = \ln\frac{3}{2}$

**5**  Find values of $A$, $B$ and $C$ that satisfy:

(a) $\dfrac{3x(2x-1)+4}{(x+2)(2x^2-x+7)} \equiv \dfrac{Ax+B}{2x^2-x+7} + \dfrac{C}{x+2}$

**6**  Given that $x = -5$ is a root of the equation $x^3 + 4x^2 - 3x + 10 = 0$,

(a)  factorise $x^3 + 4x^2 - 3x + 10$,

(b)  express $\dfrac{x(9x+2)+9}{x^3+4x^2-3x+10}$ in partial fractions.

**7**  Obtain partial fractions for:

(a) $\dfrac{5x}{(x-2)^2}$     (b) $\dfrac{2x-2}{4x^2-12x+9}$

**8**  Express $\dfrac{2x^2}{(x+1)^3}$ in the form $\dfrac{A}{x+1} + \dfrac{B}{(x+1)^2} + \dfrac{C}{(x+1)^3}$, where $A$, $B$ and $C$ are constants.

**9**  If $\dfrac{(4x^2-27x+41)}{(3x^2-18x-21)} \equiv A + \dfrac{B}{(x-7)} + \dfrac{C}{(x+1)}$, find the values of $A$, $B$ and $C$.

**10** (a)  Show that $\dfrac{6x-4}{3x+2} \equiv 2 - \dfrac{8}{3x+2}$;

(b)  Express $\dfrac{5-2x}{3x+1}$ in the form $A + \dfrac{B}{3x+1}$, where $A$ and $B$ are to be stated.

(c)  Find $\displaystyle\int \dfrac{5-2x}{3x+1}\,dx.$

**11** Given that $\dfrac{1}{1+2x} \approx 1 - 2x + 4x^2$ and $\dfrac{1}{1-3x} \approx 1 + 3x + 9x^2$ for small $x$,

show, using partial fractions, that, near the origin, the graph

$y = \dfrac{35x - 5}{1 - x - 6x^2}$ is approximately linear with gradient 30 and $y$-intercept $-5$.

**12** Express as partial fractions:

(a) $\dfrac{x^2 + 2}{x^2(x - 2)}$    (b) $\dfrac{1}{x(x^2 + 1)}$    (c) $\dfrac{x + 2}{(x + 1)^2}$    (d) $\dfrac{4x + 5}{2x + 1}$

## 1.5     Complex numbers

---

If $z = a + bi$, where $i^2 = -1$, the **complex conjugate** $z^* = a - bi$.

$$(z_1 + z_2)^* = z_1^* + z_2^* \qquad (z_1 z_2)^* = z_1^* z_2^* \qquad \left(\dfrac{z_1}{z_2}\right)^* = \dfrac{z_1^*}{z_2^*}$$

The **modulus** of $z$, $|z|$ or $r = \sqrt{(a^2 + b^2)}$; the **argument**, $\theta$, of $z$ is such that $\tan\theta = \dfrac{b}{a}$.

The **polar** (or **modulus-argument**) form of $z$ is written $[r, \theta] = r(\cos\theta + i\sin\theta)$.
In polar form:
$$[r, \theta] \times [s, \phi] = [rs, \theta + \phi]$$
$$[r, \theta] \div [s, \phi] = \left[\dfrac{r}{s}, \theta - \phi\right]$$
$$[r, \theta]^n = [r^n, n\theta], \text{ where } n \in \mathbb{Z}^+.$$

---

### Basic

**1** State the two square roots of each of the following real numbers.

(a) 1    (b) 4    (c) $-1$    (d) $-9$    (e) $-\frac{1}{4}$    (f) $-1.44$

**2** Write down the results of the following calculations.

(a) $(-i)^2$    (b) $i^3$    (c) $i^5$    *(d) $(-i)^{100}$

**3** Evaluate:

(a) $(3 + i) + (-3 + i)$    (b) $5(-2 - i) - (2 + 3i)$
(c) $(a + bi) + (a - bi)$    (d) $(a + bi) - (a - bi)$

**4**  Determine the value of each of the following products.

(a) $(2 + i) \times i$    (b) $(1 - 2i) \times (-3i)$    (c) $(1 + 2i) \times (3 + 4i)$
(d) $(-2 + \frac{1}{3}i) \times (1 - 6i)$    (e) $(a + bi)^2$    (f) $(a + bi) \times (a - bi)$

**5**  Verify, for the equation stated, that the value given is a possible solution.

(a) $z^2 + 9 = 0$          when $z = -3i$
*(b) $z^2 + 3 = 4i$        when $z = 1 + 2i$
(c) $3z^2 - 12z + 15 = 0$  when $z = 2 + i$
(d) $z^3 - 9z^2 + 1 = 99i$ when $z = 2 - 3i$

**6**  Find the value of (i) $z^*$, (ii) $z + z^*$, (iii) $z - z^*$, (iv) $zz^*$, (v) $\dfrac{1}{(zz^*)}$, when:

(a) $z = 1 + i$    (b) $z = 1$        (c) $z = i$
(d) $z = 2 - 3i$   (e) $z = a + bi$

Use your results for (e) to explain why $zz^*$ is always a positive real number (unless $z = 0$).

**7**  Evaluate, and then express the results of these calculations in the form $\alpha + \beta i$.

(a) $\dfrac{1}{1 + i} \times \dfrac{5 - i}{1 - i}$    (b) $\dfrac{-3i}{-2 - i} \times \dfrac{2i}{-2 + i}$    (c) $\dfrac{2 + 3i}{6i} \times \dfrac{1}{-6i}$

**8**  Multiply each expression by $\dfrac{z^*}{z^*}$ where $z$ is the value of the denominator and $z^*$ is the complex conjugate; and hence express each fraction in the form $\alpha + \beta i$.

(a) $\dfrac{1}{2 - i}$    *(b) $\dfrac{2i}{5 + 7i}$    (c) $\dfrac{5 + i}{1 - i}$    (d) $\dfrac{1}{a + bi}$

**9**  Plot carefully an Argand diagram which illustrates the complex numbers given by:

(a) $3 + 4i$    (b) $-5i$    (c) $-3 + 4i$    (d) $-\dfrac{5}{\sqrt{2}} - \dfrac{5}{\sqrt{2}}i$

By drawing an appropriate circle, verify that these complex numbers have the same magnitude. What is the radius of the circle?

**10** State the modulus and argument $(-\pi < \theta \le \pi)$ of:

(a) $3i$    (b) $1 + 2i$    (c) $3 + i$    (d) $-2i$    (e) $-2 - 2i$

**11** Express each of the complex numbers on the diagram in the form $\alpha + \beta i$, giving your answer to two decimal places where necessary.

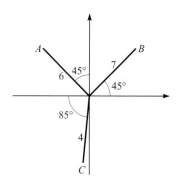

**12** In this question $a$ and $b$ are both positive and the complex conjugate of $z = a + bi$ is given by $z^* = a - bi$.

(a) Draw a diagram showing the origin and the points $A$ at $2z$, $B$ at $z + z^*$, and $C$ at $z - z^*$.

(b) What type of quadrilateral is $OBAC$?

(c) What is the area of $OBAC$?

## Intermediate

**1** Simplify:

(a) $i(3i^2 + 5i)(i + 1)$     (b) $(3 - 4i)(1 - 2i)/i$     (c) $(1 + i + i^2)^3$

**2** Evaluate $\sum\limits_{n=0}^{100} i^n$.

**3** Solve the following quadratic equations, by completing the square.

*(a) $z^2 + 2z + 5 = 0$     (b) $z^2 - 3z + 3 = 0$     (c) $2z^2 - 6z + 5 = 0$

**4** Find the complex solutions of the following quadratic equations, using the quadratic formula.

(a) $4z^2 - 4z + 5 = 0$     (b) $9z^2 - 6z + 5 = 0$     (c) $7z^2 - 2z + 8 = 0$

**5** Given that both of the following expressions are satisfied by $z = -2$ as a root, fully factorise the cubic polynomials incorporating complex numbers.

*(a) $z^3 + 2z^2 + z + 2$     (b) $z^3 - 2z^2 - 3z + 10$

**6** *(a) Apply the quadratic formula to solve $4iz^2 + 5z - i = 0$.
(b) Verify that $z = 1 + \frac{1}{2}i$ is a solution of the complex cubic $24iz^3 - 8iz^2 + 25 = 0$.

**7** Obtain the values of $a$ and $b$, where $a$ and $b$ are real constants, in each of the following equations.

(a) $(a - 2) + \frac{b}{5}i = 2 + 3i$          *(b) $(a + 2b) - \frac{b}{3}i = 1 + \frac{1}{2}i$

(c) $(4a + b) + 10i = 25 - (b - a)i$

**8** It is known that, when $z$ takes the value 3i, the expression $A(z^3 - z^2) + B(1 - z)$ takes the value $-2 + 6i$. Use this information to show that $9A + B + 2 = 0$.

**9** The three cube roots of 1 may be found by solving the equation $z^3 = 1$.

(a) Rewrite the equation as $z^3 - 1 = 0$, and explain why $(z - 1)$ must be a factor.
(b) Find the other quadratic factor, and hence the other two cube roots.
(c) Illustrate the three cube roots on an Argand diagram, stating the modulus and argument.

**10** Describe fully the transformation that occurs on the Argand diagram when $a + bi$ is subject to the specified changes:

(a) $a + bi$ is multiplied by i,
(b) $a + bi$ is multiplied by 2,
(c) $a + bi$ is mapped to the complex conjugate $a - bi$.

**11** In this question $[r, \theta]$ refers to the complex number with modulus $r$ and argument $\theta$. Evaluate, giving your answer in $[r, \theta]$ form:

(a) $[2, \pi] \times \left[3, -\dfrac{\pi}{2}\right]$  (b) $[1, 0] \times \left[-1, \dfrac{\pi}{7}\right]$  (c) $\left[\sqrt{5}, \dfrac{\pi}{4}\right] \times \left[\sqrt{5}, \dfrac{\pi}{4}\right]$

(d) $[1, \theta_1] \times [1, \theta_2]$  (e) $\left[\sqrt{r}, \dfrac{\theta}{2}\right]^2$  (f) $\left[3, \dfrac{3\pi}{4}\right] \times \left[5, \dfrac{3\pi}{4}\right]$

**12** (a) Explain why $[r, \theta]^n = [r^n, n\theta]$.

(b) Verify that $[2, 0]$, $\left[2, \dfrac{2\pi}{3}\right]$, $\left[2, -\dfrac{2\pi}{3}\right]$ are the three cube roots of 8.

Sketch the three cube roots on an Argand diagram.

(c) Deduce, using a similar method, that the fifth roots of 32 include $\left[2, \dfrac{2\pi}{5}\right]$. Find the four other values in $[r, \theta]$ form.

**13** (a) Show that $\dfrac{1 + \sqrt{3}i}{1 - i} = \tfrac{1}{2}((1 - \sqrt{3}) + i(1 + \sqrt{3}))$.

(b) Show that $\dfrac{1 + \sqrt{3}i}{1 - i} = [\sqrt{2}, \theta]$, where $\tan\theta = \dfrac{1 + \sqrt{3}}{1 - \sqrt{3}}$.

(c) Express in the form $[r, \theta]$, (i) $1 + \sqrt{3}i$, (ii) $1 - i$.

(d) Use the result $[r_1, \theta_1] \div [r_2, \theta_2] = \left[\dfrac{r_1}{r_2}, \theta_1 - \theta_2\right]$ to express $\dfrac{1 + \sqrt{3}i}{1 - i}$ in

the form $[r, \theta]$ and hence show that $\tan\dfrac{5\pi}{12} = \dfrac{1 + \sqrt{3}}{\sqrt{3} - 1}$.

**14** It is required to find the square roots of $(3 - 4i)$ in the form $A + Bi$.

   (a) Given that $A + Bi = \sqrt{3 - 4i}$, explain why $A^2 - B^2 = 3$ and $AB = -2$.

   (b) Find the possible values for $A$ and $B$ and confirm in both cases that $(A + Bi)^2 = 3 - 4i$.

**15** (a) Use an Argand diagram to verify that one of the possible square roots of $[r, \theta]$ is given by $\left[\sqrt{r}, \dfrac{\theta}{2}\right]$.

   (b) Find a general expression for the other square root.

   (c) Apply this method to find the square roots of $\dfrac{9\sqrt{2}}{2}(1 + i)$ in the form $[r, \theta]$.

**16** (a) Confirm, with a diagram, that $[1, \alpha] \equiv \cos \alpha + i \sin \alpha$.

   (b) Given that $[1, \theta]^2 \equiv [1, 2\theta]$, use the expression in (a) to establish that:

      (i) $\cos^2 \theta - \sin^2 \theta \equiv \cos 2\theta$     (ii) $2 \cos \theta \sin \theta \equiv \sin 2\theta$.

## Advanced

**1** (a) The quadratic equation $z^2 + 6z + 34 = 0$ has complex roots $\alpha$ and $\beta$.

      (i) Find the roots, in the form $a + bi$.

      (ii) Find the modulus and argument of each root, and illustrate the two roots on an Argand diagram.

      (iii) Find $|\alpha - \beta|$.

   (b) You are given the complex number $w = 1 - i$.

      (i) Express $w^2$, $w^3$ and $w^4$ in the form $a + bi$.

      (ii) Given that $w^4 + 3w^3 + pw^2 + qw + 8 = 0$, where $p$ and $q$ are real numbers, find the values of $p$ and $q$.

      (iii) Write down two roots of the equation
$z^4 + 3z^3 + pz^2 + qz + 8 = 0$, where $p$ and $q$ are the real numbers found in (ii).

[OCR (MEI), 1998]

**2** If $a$, $b$ are real numbers, define the conjugate of $a + ib$. Write $(a + ib)^2$ in the form $\alpha + i\beta$ and show that $(a - ib)^2$ is the conjugate of $(a + ib)^2$. Solve $(a + ib)^2 = 3 + 4i$ for $a$ and $b$. Write down the solutions of $z^2 = 3 - 4i$.
Solve $z^4 - 6z^2 + 25 = 0$. Draw a sketch showing the position of your solutions in the complex plane. Using the above information, or otherwise, express $z^4 - 6z^2 + 25$ as a product of two quadratic factors, each with *real* coefficients.
[OCR (SMP), 1984]

**3**  The complex numbers $\alpha$ and $\beta$ are given by $(\alpha + 4)/\alpha = 2 - i$ and $\beta = -\sqrt{6} + \sqrt{2}i$.

(a)  Show that $\alpha = 2 + 2i$.
(b)  Show that $|\alpha| = |\beta|$. Find arg $\alpha$ and arg $\beta$.
(c)  Find the modulus and argument of $\alpha\beta$. Illustrate the complex numbers $\alpha$, $\beta$ and $\alpha\beta$ on an Argand diagram.
(d)  Describe the locus of points in the Argand diagram representing complex numbers $z$ for which $|z - \alpha| = |z - \beta|$. Draw this locus on your diagram.
(e)  Show that $z = \alpha + \beta$ satisfies $|z - \alpha| = |z - \beta|$. Mark the point representing $\alpha + \beta$ on your diagram and find the exact value of $\arg(\alpha + \beta)$.
[OCR (MEI), 1998]

**4**  Five complex numbers $a, b, c, d, e$ are connected by the equations

$$b = ia$$
$$c - 1 = i(b - 1)$$
$$d = ic$$
$$e - 1 = i(d - 1)$$

where $i^2 = -1$. Find expressions (as simple as possible) for $c$ and $d$ in terms of $a$, and prove that $e = a$.
Draw an Argand diagram on graph paper, to a scale of 2 cm to 1 unit. Mark the origin $O$ and the point $I$ representing $1 + 0i$. Taking $a = 1 + 2i$, mark on your diagram the points $A, B, C, D, E$, representing the complex numbers $a, b, c, d, e$ respectively.
Starting from $A$, the points $B, C, D, E$ can be obtained in succession by rotations through a certain angle about either $O$ or $I$. Describe each of these rotations precisely.
[OCR (SMP), 1987]

**5**  The complex number $z$ satisfies the equation $|z| = |z + 2|$. Show that the real part of $z$ is $-1$.
The complex number $z$ also satisfies the equation $|z| = 2$. By sketching two loci in an Argand diagram, find the two possible values of the imaginary part of $z$ and state the two corresponding values of arg $z$.
The two possible values of $z$ are denoted by $z_1$ and $z_2$, where $\operatorname{Im} z_1 > \operatorname{Im} z_2$.

(a)  Find a quadratic equation whose roots are $z_1$ and $z_2$, giving your answer in the form $az^2 + bz + c = 0$ where the coefficients $a$, $b$ and $c$ are real.

(b) Determine the square roots of $z_1$, giving your answers in the form $x + iy$.

[OCR (Cambridge)]

6  (a) Sketch in the Argand diagram the curve $z = \dfrac{1}{1 + is}$ as $s$ varies from $-\infty$ to $+\infty$.

(b) Given that $3 - 4i$ is a root of the equation $z^4 + 2z^3 + 2z^2 + 50z + c = 0$, where $c$ is a real constant, find the value of $c$. Find also the other roots of the equation.

7  The **impedance**, $Z$, of an electrical circuit is a complex number that satisfies $\left( Z - \dfrac{1}{i\omega C} \right)\left( \dfrac{1}{z} + \dfrac{1}{i\omega L} \right) = 1$, where $L$, $C$ and $\omega$ are positive real numbers.

(a) Solve the equation for $Z$.

(b) Show that $Z$ is purely imaginary if $\omega \le \omega_0$, where $\omega_0^2 = \dfrac{1}{4LC}$.

(c) If $\alpha = 1 - \dfrac{1}{i\omega CZ}$, prove that $|\alpha| = 1$ if $\omega \ge \omega_0$ and that $\alpha$ is real if $\omega \le \omega_0$.

8  For any complex number $z$ prove that $|z|^2 = z\bar{z}$. For any two complex numbers $z_1$ and $z_2$ show that

$$(1 + \bar{z}_1 z_2)(1 + z_1 \bar{z}_2) - (z_1 + z_2)(\bar{z}_1 + \bar{z}_2) = (1 - z_1 \bar{z}_1)(1 - z_2 \bar{z}_2)$$

and deduce that if $|z_1| \le 1$, $|z_2| \le 1$ then

$$|z_1 + z_2| \le |1 - \bar{z}_1 z_2|.$$

By putting $z_1 = \cos\theta + i\sin\theta$ and $z_2 = \cos\varphi + i\sin\varphi$, or otherwise, show that if $|z_1| = |z_2| = 1$ then $|1 + \bar{z}_1 z_2| \le 2$, with equality if, and only if, $z_1 = z_2$.

[OCR (Cambridge), 1976]

9  For a complex number $z$, give an expression for $|z|^2$ in terms of $z$ and its complex conjugate $z^*$. Show that, for any complex numbers $z$ and $w$, $|z + w|^2 + |z - w|^2 = 2|z|^2 + 2|w|^2$. Let $s$ be a complex number with $|s| \le 1$. Use the above identity (with $z = 1 + s$ and $w = s(1 - s)$) to show that

$$|1 + 2s - s^2|^2 \le 2|1 + s|^2 + 2|1 - s|^2$$

By applying the identity a second time (for suitable values of $z$ and $w$), deduce that

$$|1 + 2s - s^2| \le \sqrt{8}.$$

Find the values of $s$, if any, for which $|1 + 2s - s^2| = \sqrt{8}$, $|s| \le 1$.

[OCR (SMP), 1977]

**10** A **Gaussian integer** is a complex number whose real and imaginary parts are both integers. Given any complex number $z$, show that there is a Gaussian integer $w$ such that $|z - w|^2 \leq \dfrac{1}{\sqrt{2}}$. Suppose that $s$, $t$ are Gaussian integers with $t \neq 0$. By considering the complex number $\dfrac{s}{t}$, show that there are Gaussian integers $q, r$ such that $s = qt + r$, $|r| < |t|$. Find $q$ and $r$ in the case where $s = 5 + 4i$ and $t = 1 + 2i$.
(The Gaussian integers $q$ and $r$ are not unique; you are only asked to find *one* possible pair of values that satisfy the above conditions.)
[OCR (SMP), 1976]

### Revision

**1** Simplify the following expressions, when $a = 5 - 3i$, $b = 2 + 7i$, $c = -3 - i$.

    (a) $a + b + c$    (b) $(a^* + b^* + c^*)^*$    (c) $(b - c^*)$    (d) $(b^* - c)^*$

**2** Verify that $|(2 + 3i)(1 - 4i)| > |(2 + 4i)(1 - 3i)| > |(2 + i)(3 - 4i)|$.

**3** Simplify each of the following and verify that they are equal.

    (a) $\dfrac{1 + 5i}{3 + 2i}$    (b) $\dfrac{-4 - 2i}{-3 + i}$    (c) $\dfrac{i\sqrt{8}}{\sqrt{2}(1 + i)}$

**4** Consider the cubic equations $2z^3 - 21z^2 + 302z - 146 = 0$.

    (a) Show that $(2z - 1)$ is a factor of the left-hand side.
    (b) Find the three roots of the equation.

**5** The complex number $z$ is given by $z = (1 + 3i)^2 + \dfrac{1 + 2i}{2 - i}$.

    (a) Express $z$ in the form $x + iy$.
    (b) Find the modulus and argument of $z$.

**6** Find, in surd form, the complex roots of the following quadratics.

    (a) $z^2 + 5z + 17 = 0$    (b) $3z^2 - z + 9 = 0$    (c) $z^2 + iz + 6 = 0$

**7** Express, in polynomial form, a cubic equation which has i, 2i, and 3i as roots.

**8** If $\sqrt{-16 + 30i} = a + ib$, where $a$ and $b$ are real, find $a$ and $b$.

**9** (a) Find the area enclosed on the Argand diagram by the polygon $OABCD$, where $O$ is the origin and $A$, $B$, $C$ and $D$ are respectively the points $[\sqrt{2}, 0]$, $[2, \frac{1}{4}\pi]$, $[2, \frac{1}{2}\pi]$, and $[2, \frac{3}{4}\pi]$.
    (b) What is the new area when each of the points is transformed by multiplying by $1 + i$?

**10** Sketch on separate Argand diagrams the positions of:

(a) the square roots of 1,     (b) the cube roots of 1,

(c) the cube roots of i.

Explain why $[1, \frac{1}{6}\pi]$ is one of the points on the third diagram.

**11** Sketch the locus of points on the Argand diagram that satisfy each of these conditions:

(a) $|z| = 5$     (b) $|z - 4| = 2$     (c) $\arg z = \dfrac{3\pi}{4}$

In each case obtain the Cartesian equation of the line or curve.

**12** (a) When $z = i\theta$, evaluate $z^2$, $z^3$, $z^4$ and $z^5$.

(b) Using the series expansion for $e^z$, show that

$$e^{i\theta} = \left(1 - \frac{1}{2!}z^2 + \frac{1}{4!}z^4 - \frac{1}{6!}z^6 + \cdots\right) + i\left(z - \frac{1}{3!}z^3 + \frac{1}{5!}z^5 - \frac{1}{7!}z^7 + \cdots\right).$$

(c) Deduce that $e^{i\theta} = \cos\theta + i\sin\theta$.

# 2

# Coordinate geometry

## 2.1 Equation of a straight line in the forms $y - y_1 = m(x - x_1)$ and $ax + by + c = 0$; finding the equation of a linear graph; parallel and perpendicular lines; distance between two points in two and three dimensions; mid-point of two points; equation of a circle

The equation of a straight line of gradient $m$, $y$-intercept $c$, is $y = mx + c$.

The equation of a straight line of gradient $m$ through $(x_1, y_1)$ is $y - y_1 = m(x - x_1)$.

Two lines of gradients $m$, $m_1$ are perpendicular $\Leftrightarrow mm_1 = -1$.

The distance between two points with coordinates $(x_1, y_1)$ and $(x_2, y_2)$ is given by $\sqrt{(x_2 - x_1)^2 + (y_2 - y_1)^2}$.

The distance between two points with coordinates $(x_1, y_1, z_1)$ and $(x_2, y_2, z_2)$ is given by $\sqrt{(x_2 - x_1)^2 + (y_2 - y_1)^2 + (z_2 - z_1)^2}$.

The mid-point of $(x_1, y_1)$ and $(x_2, y_2)$, is $(\frac{1}{2}(x_1 + x_2), \frac{1}{2}(y_1 + y_2))$.

The equation of a circle, centre $(a, b)$, radius $r$, is $(x - a)^2 + (y - b)^2 = r^2$.

Area of triangle $= \frac{1}{2}ab \sin C$

## Basic

**1** Find the gradient of each of the following lines.

(a) $y = 3x + 7$     (b) $2y - x = 4$     (c) $x - 3y + 12 = 0$

**2** Find the coordinates of the points of intersection with the axes for each of the following straight lines.

(a) $y = 2x + 6$     *(b) $6y - x = 3$     (c) $x - 4y = 0$

**3** Find the equations of the following lines in the form $y = mx + c$:

*(a) gradient 2, passing through $(3, 7)$,

(b)  gradient $-\frac{1}{2}$, passing through (8, 5),
(c)  gradient $\frac{4}{3}$, passing through $(\frac{1}{2}, 0)$.

**4**  Find the equations of the following lines in the form $ax + by + c = 0$:

(a)  the line passing through $(-2, 3)$ and $(4, -3)$,
(b)  the line passing through $(2, 3)$ and $(-4, 5)$,
(c)  the line passing through $(-\frac{1}{3}, \frac{1}{2})$ and $(-\frac{2}{3}, 1\frac{1}{2})$.

**5**  (a)  Which of the following are parallel to the line $x + 2y = 4$?

(i)  $6y = 1 + 4x$

(ii)  $\dfrac{x}{y - 3} = 2$

(iii)  $\dfrac{x - 3}{2 - y} = 2$

(b)  Which of the following are perpendicular to the line $2x - 3y + 5 = 0$?

(i)  $6y = 1 + 4x$
(ii)  $3x + 2y - 4 = 0$

(iii)  $\dfrac{3 - 2y}{x - 2} = 3$

**6** *(a)  The line joining $(6, a)$ and $(-3, 6)$ has a gradient of $\frac{1}{3}$. What is the value of $a$?

(b)  The line joining the points $(-1, 4)$ and $(x, y)$ has a gradient of $-\frac{1}{3}$. The line joining $(x, y)$ and $(4, 7)$ has a gradient of 2. Find the value of $x$ and the value of $y$.

**7**  Find the lengths of the lines joining the following pairs of points, giving your answers correct to three significant figures.

(a)  $(2, -3)$ and $(4, 7)$
(b)  $(\frac{1}{2}, -\frac{1}{3})$ and $(-\frac{1}{4}, \frac{2}{5})$
(c)  $(2, 3, 7)$ and $(5, 9, 10)$
(d)  $(3, 5, -2)$ and $(-4, 4, -7)$

**8**  $A(2, 3)$, $B(5, 7)$, $C(a, 4)$ are the vertices of an equilateral triangle. Find two possible values for $a$ and calculate the area of triangle $ABC$.

**9**  Find the mid-points of the lines joining the following pairs of coordinates.

(a)  $(2, 7)$ and $(-3, 5)$
(b)  $(-3, -5)$ and $(-7, 11)$
(c)  $(2, -3, 6)$ and $(0, 1, 4)$

**10**  $M(-1, 4)$ is the mid-point of the line $AB$ where $A$ and $B$ have coordinates $(x, y)$ and $(2, 6)$ respectively. Find the coordinates of $A$.

**11** State whether the following are equations of circles. Where they are, give the radius of the circle and the coordinates of the centre.

(a) $x^2 + (y - 2)^2 - 9 = 0$
(b) $x^2 + 2x + 3xy + y^2 = 4$
*(c) $x^2 + 2x + y^2 - 2y - 2 = 0$

**12** The point $P(-2, 5)$ lies on the circumference of a circle, centre $(3, 7)$. Find the equation of the circle and the equation of the tangent to the circle at point $P$.

### Intermediate

**1** The points $A(-1, 1)$, $B(p, 7)$ and $C(5, 10)$ are collinear. Find the value of $p$ and the ratio $AB : BC$.

**2** The perpendicular bisector of $(-3, 3)$ and $(7, 11)$ passes through the point $(6, p)$. Find the value of $p$.

**3** Find the perpendicular distance from $(7, 4)$ to the line $y = -\dfrac{x}{2} + 5$.

**4** Find the area of the triangle formed by the intersection of the lines $2y - 3x + 4 = 0$, $x = 0$ and $y = 0$.

**\*5** Show that the triangle whose vertices are at $A(3, 2)$, $B(1, 5)$, $C(4, 3)$ is isosceles and find the coordinates of point $D$ such that $ABCD$ is a rhombus.

**6** $A$, $B$ and $C$ have coordinates $(5, 7)$, $(3, 3)$ and $(7, 4)$ respectively. A point $D$ lies on $BC$ produced such that $BD = 2BC$. Find the equation of the line $AD$.

**7** Show that $A(3, 4)$, $B(2, 7)$ and $C(8, 9)$ are three vertices of a rectangle. Find the coordinates of the fourth vertex and the area of the rectangle.

**8** The straight lines $y = k^2x + 12$ and $2ky = 4x + 5$ are perpendicular $(k \neq 0)$.

(a) Find the value of $k$.
(b) Find the point of intersection of the two lines.

**9** A triangle is formed by the intersection of the straight lines $y = 2x + 3$, $2y + x = 26$ and $11y = 7x + 18$.

(a) Find the coordinates of the vertices of the triangle.
(b) Show that the triangle is right-angled.
(c) Find the area of the triangle.

**10** A straight line has the equation $\dfrac{2 - x}{3} = \dfrac{y - 4}{5}$.

(a) Write the equation in the form $y = mx + c$.

(b) Find the equation of the straight line which is perpendicular to $\dfrac{2-x}{3} = \dfrac{y-4}{5}$ and which passes through the point $(2, 7)$.

**11** Three points have coordinates $A(-5, 2)$, $B(1, 14)$ and $C(3, 6)$. Find the coordinates of the point of intersection of the line $AB$ and the perpendicular bisector of $AC$.

**12** The cuboid $ABCDEFGH$ is shown. The coordinates of $A$, $B$ and $H$ are $(0, 3, 5)$, $(0, 3, 9)$ and $(4, 9, 5)$ respectively. Write down the coordinates of $G$ and hence find the length of $AG$.

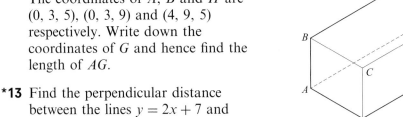

**\*13** Find the perpendicular distance between the lines $y = 2x + 7$ and $y = 2x + 2$.

**14** The circle $x^2 + y^2 - 6x - 8y + 9 = 0$ intersects the $y$-axis at $A$ and $B$ and is a tangent to the $x$-axis at $C$.

(a) Write down the coordinates of point $C$.
(b) Find the length of the chord $AB$.

**15** Find the equation of the circle with diameter $PQ$ where $P$ and $Q$ are the points $(7, 7)$ and $(-1, 3)$ respectively. Show that the point $R(5, 9)$ also lies on the circumference of the circle and find the coordinates of point $S$ such that $RS$ is also a diameter of the circle.

**16** $P(1, 9)$, $Q(4, 8)$ and $R(6, 4)$ lie on the circumference of a circle.

(a) Find the coordinates of the centre of the circle.
(b) Find the radius of the circle.
(c) Write down the equation of the circle.

### Advanced

**1** The straight line passing through the point $P(1, 3)$ and the point $Q(a, 13)$ has gradient $-\dfrac{5}{9}$. Calculate the length of the line segment $PQ$, giving your answer to two decimal places.

**2** A straight line $l$ passes through the point $(6, 10)$ and is perpendicular to the line $m$ which has equation $3y + x = 6$.

(a) Find the equation of $l$.
(b) Find the coordinates of the point of intersection of $l$ and $m$. Deduce the perpendicular distance from the point $(6, 10)$ to $m$.

**3**  The diagram shows a triangle whose vertices are $A(-2, 1)$, $B(1, 7)$ and $C(3, 1)$. The point $L$ is the foot of the perpendicular from $A$ to $BC$, and $M$ is the foot of the perpendicular from $B$ to $AC$.

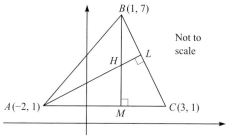

(a)  Find the gradient of the line $BC$.

(b)  Find the equation of the line $AL$.

(c)  Write down the equation of the line $BM$.

The lines $AL$ and $BM$ meet at $H$.

(d)  Find the coordinates of $H$.

(e)  Show that $CH$ is perpendicular to $AB$.

(f)  Find the area of the triangle $BLH$.

[OCR (MEI), 1998]

**4**  The coordinates of points $P$, $Q$ and $R$ are $(0, 2)$, $(4, 6)$ and $(10, 0)$ respectively. $M$ is the mid-point of line $RP$.

(a)  Show that (i) $PQ^2 + QR^2 = RP^2$, (ii) $MP = MQ$.

(b)  Write down the equation of the circle through $P$, $Q$ and $R$.

**5**  The straight line $l$ passes through $A(1, 3\sqrt{3})$ and $B(2 + \sqrt{3}, 3 + 4\sqrt{3})$.

(a)  Calculate the gradient of $l$ giving your answer as a surd in its simplest form.

(b)  Give the equation of $l$ in the form $y = mx + c$, where constants $m$ and $c$ are surds to be given in their simplest form.

(c)  Show that $l$ meets the $x$-axis at the point $C(-2, 0)$.

(d)  Calculate the length of $AC$.

(e)  Find the size of the acute angle between the line $AC$ and the $x$-axis, giving your answer in degrees.

[Edexcel (London), 1996]

**6**  The vertex $A$ of a square $ABCD$ is at the point $(22, 10)$. The diagonal $BD$ has equation $4y - 3x = 24$, and the vertex $B$ is nearer to the origin than $D$.

(a)  Calculate the coordinates of the centre of the square.

(b)  Calculate the coordinates of $B$ and $C$.

(c)  Obtain the equation of the circle which touches the four sides of the square.

[OCR (Cambridge), 1983]

**7** Prove that the line $y = mx + c$ will touch the circle $x^2 + y^2 = 25$ if $c^2 = 25(1 + m^2)$. Hence or otherwise find the equations of the two tangents to this circle from the point $(2, 11)$.
[OCR (Cambridge), 1964]

**8** The points $A$, $B$ have coordinates $(a, 0)$ and $(-a, 0)$ respectively. A point $P$ in the plane of the coordinate axes moves so that $AP : PB = \lambda$, where $\lambda$ is a positive constant. Find the equation of the locus of $P$, and show that, if $\lambda \neq 1$, this locus is a circle. Show that the centre of this circle lies on the axis of $x$, but not between $A$ and $B$.
Find the value of $\lambda$ if the centre of the circle is at the point $C$ on the axis of $x$, where $CB : CA = 3 : 5$.
[OCR (Cambridge), 1973]

**9** The line of gradient $m$ through the point $(p, q)$ cuts the parabola $y^2 = 4ax$ at the points $R$ and $S$.
(a) Show that the coordinates $(X, Y)$ of $M$, the mid-point of $RS$, are given by

$$X = p - \frac{q}{m} + \frac{2a}{m^2} \quad Y = \frac{2a}{m}$$

(Hint: if $\alpha$ and $\beta$ are the roots of $ax^2 + bx + c = 0$, $\alpha + \beta = -\frac{b}{a}$ and $\alpha\beta = \frac{c}{a}$.)

As $m$ varies, the locus of $M$ is a curve.
(b) Find the equation of this curve in the case $p = a$ and $q = 0$. Sketch the curve, showing its relationship to the original parabola.

**10** Prove that the equation $x^2 + y^2 - 7x - qy + 6 = 0$ represents the circle through the points $(1, 0)$, $(6, 0)$ having its centre at the point $A(\frac{7}{2}, \frac{1}{2}q)$; and find the equation of the circle through the points $(0, 2)$, $(0, 3)$ having its centre at the point $B(\frac{1}{2}p, \frac{5}{2})$.
Assuming that the circles intersect, prove that $(p - 7)x = (q - 5)y$ is the equation of the chord common to the two circles. Discuss briefly the case $p = 7$, $q = 5$.
Prove also that, if the circles are so related that the sum of the squares of their radii is equal to $AB^2$, then $7p + 5q = 24$.
[OCR (Cambridge), 1973]

### Revision

**1** Write the equations of the lines $\frac{x - 4}{2} = \frac{2 - y}{3}$ and $3y - 2x + 7 = 0$ in the form $y = mx + c$. State whether the lines are parallel or perpendicular.

**2** The points $A$, $B$ and $C$ have coordinates $(2, 0)$, $(a, 5)$ and $(4, 8)$ respectively. Find two possible values of $a$ such that $AB$ and $BC$ are perpendicular.

**3** Show that the triangle with vertices $(2, 5, 0)$, $(4, 4, -2)$ and $(3, 7, 2)$ is isosceles.

**4** Find the area of the triangle with vertices $A(2, 6)$, $B(10, 6)$, $C(8, 1)$.

**5** Given the points $A(1, -2)$, $B(-1, 5)$, $C(7, 0)$ and $D(3, -3)$, find the point of intersection of the perpendicular bisectors of $AC$ and $BD$.

**6** The parallelogram $ABCD$ has vertices $A(2, 7)$, $B(5, 9)$ and $C(7, 8)$.

   (a) Find the coordinates of vertex $D$.
   (b) Show that the diagonals bisect each other.

**7** (a) Find the equation of the line joining $P(-3, 2)$ and $Q(0, 8)$.
   (b) Show that $R(4, 16)$ lies on $PQ$ produced.
   (c) Find the equation of the line which passes through $R$ and is perpendicular to $PQ$.

**8** Find the equation of the line which passes through the intersection of $y - 3x - 7 = 0$ and $y + 2x + 3 = 0$ and is parallel to the line $2y - 3x - 4 = 0$.

**9** $ABC$ is a triangle in which the coordinates of $A$, $B$ and $C$ are $(-3, 7)$, $(2, 11)$ and $(5, 3)$ respectively. $M$ is the mid-point of $AB$ and $N$ is the mid-point of $BC$.

   (a) Show that $MN$ is parallel to $AC$.
   (b) Find the ratio $MN : AC$.

**10** Find the perpendicular distance between the lines $y = -3x + 1$ and $y = -3x + 6$.

**11** State which of the following are equations of circles. Where they are, find the coordinates of the centre of the circle and the radius.

   (a) $4(x - 3)^2 + (2y - 5)^2 = 16$
   (b) $2(x - 1)^2 + 3(y - 2)^2 = 0$
   (c) $x^2 + y^2 - 6x - 8y = 0$

**12** Find the length of the chord formed by the intersection of the straight line $2y = x - 4$ and the circle $(x - 3)^2 + (y - 2)^2 = 25$.

# 3

# Vector geometry

## 3.1 Addition of vectors; length of vectors; scalar product; angle between two vectors

If $\mathbf{a} = \begin{pmatrix} x_1 \\ y_1 \end{pmatrix}$ and $\mathbf{b} = \begin{pmatrix} x_2 \\ y_2 \end{pmatrix}$ are two vectors, with angle $\theta$ between them, the **scalar product** $\mathbf{a.b} = ab\cos\theta$, where $a = \sqrt{(x_1^2 + y_1^2)}$ and $b = \sqrt{(x_2^2 + y_2^2)}$ are the **magnitudes** of the vectors. The result generalises to three dimensions. Vectors $\mathbf{a}$ and $\mathbf{b}$ are perpendicular $\Leftrightarrow \mathbf{a.b} = 0$.

### Basic

**1** Add the following pairs of vectors.

(a) $\begin{pmatrix} 3 \\ 5 \end{pmatrix} + \begin{pmatrix} 5 \\ 8 \end{pmatrix}$　　　　(b) $\begin{pmatrix} -5 \\ -3 \end{pmatrix} + \begin{pmatrix} 9 \\ -2 \end{pmatrix}$

(c) $(-3\mathbf{i} + 4\mathbf{j}) + (\mathbf{i} - 2\mathbf{j})$

**2** Subtract the following pairs of vectors.

(a) $\begin{pmatrix} 5 \\ 12 \end{pmatrix} - \begin{pmatrix} 3 \\ 8 \end{pmatrix}$　　　　(b) $(4\mathbf{i} + 5\mathbf{j}) - (2\mathbf{i} + 7\mathbf{j})$

(c) $(6\mathbf{i} - 7\mathbf{j}) - (9\mathbf{i} - 9\mathbf{j})$

**3** Find the modulus and argument of each of the following vectors.

(a) $\begin{pmatrix} 4 \\ 6 \end{pmatrix}$　　(b) $\begin{pmatrix} -3 \\ 5 \end{pmatrix}$　　(c) $5\mathbf{i} + 2\mathbf{j}$　　(d) $3\mathbf{i} - \mathbf{j}$

**4** Write each of the following vectors in component form.

(a) 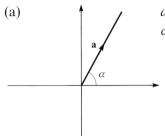 $a = 12$
$\alpha = 60°$

(b) 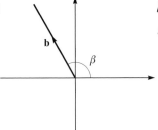 $b = 25$
$\beta = 110°$

(c)

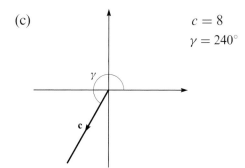

$c = 8$

$\gamma = 240°$

*5  Vectors **p** and **q** are as shown in the diagram.

    (a)  Write **p** and **q** as column vectors.

    (b)  Find **p** + **q**, giving your answer in modulus/argument form.

    (c)  Find 3**p** − 2**q**, giving your answer in modulus/argument form.

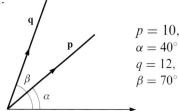

$p = 10$,
$\alpha = 40°$
$q = 12$,
$\beta = 70°$

6  A helicopter has to pick up an emergency medical team from a hospital and fly on to rescue a mountain climber who has been taken ill. The journey from the heliport to the hospital is represented by the vector $\begin{pmatrix} 13 \\ 21 \end{pmatrix}$, and from the hospital to the climbers by $\begin{pmatrix} -15 \\ -8 \end{pmatrix}$. Distances are measured in miles.

    (a)  What vector would represent the direct journey from the heliport to the climber?

    (b)  How much further did the helicopter fly than if it had gone directly to the climber, without collecting the medical team?

7  A ship is sighted at 15 km east and 23 km north of a coastguard station. A yacht is in difficulties 8 km east and 11 km south of the station.

    (a)  Using unit vectors **i** (1 km east) and **j** (1 km north), give the vector of the journey that the ship must make to go to the aid of the yacht.

    (b)  How far will the ship have to travel to reach the yacht?

    (c)  At what bearing should the ship set its course?

8  Find the scalar products of the following pairs of vectors.

    (a)  $\begin{pmatrix} 4 \\ 6 \end{pmatrix}.\begin{pmatrix} 3 \\ 10 \end{pmatrix}$    (b)  $(5\mathbf{i} + 4\mathbf{j}).(3\mathbf{i} - 7\mathbf{j})$

(c)

$$a = 16, \quad \alpha = 25°$$
$$b = 27, \quad \beta = 80°$$

**9**  For each of the following pairs of vectors

(i)   express **a** and **b** in the form $p\mathbf{i} + q\mathbf{j}$,
(ii)  find **a.b** and hence find the angle between **a** and **b**,
(iii) use the diagram to check your answer to part (ii).

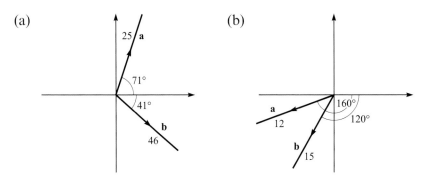

(a)

(b)

**10** For each of the following pairs of vectors,

(i)   find $|\mathbf{a}|$ and $|\mathbf{b}|$,
(ii)  find **a.b**,
(iii) hence find the angle between **a** and **b**.

(a)  $\mathbf{a} = \begin{pmatrix} 5 \\ 7 \end{pmatrix}$  $\mathbf{b} = \begin{pmatrix} 6 \\ -2 \end{pmatrix}$

*(b)  $\mathbf{a} = 3\mathbf{i} - \mathbf{j}$  $\mathbf{b} = 5\mathbf{i} - 2\mathbf{j}$

**11** A photographer is photographing lions using a powerful telescopic lens. He is photographing a male lion at $\begin{pmatrix} 120 \\ 90 \end{pmatrix}$ from his position, when he spots a lioness and her cubs at $\begin{pmatrix} -80 \\ 85 \end{pmatrix}$. Through what angle should he rotate his camera to photograph the lioness?

**12** $p = \begin{pmatrix} 5 \\ 8 \\ 7 \end{pmatrix}$, $\quad q = \begin{pmatrix} 3 \\ 9 \\ 4 \end{pmatrix}$, $\quad r = \begin{pmatrix} 6 \\ -5 \\ -7 \end{pmatrix}$

Find:

(a) $p + q$     (b) $q - r$     (c) $|p|$     (d) $|r|$

(e) $p.q$     (f) $q.r$     (g) the angle between $p$ and $r$

### Intermediate

**1**  $OABC$ is a parallelogram with
$\overrightarrow{OA} = a$,     $\overrightarrow{OC} = c$
$D$ is a point on $CB$ such that
$CD : DB = 1 : 4$
Express in terms of $a$ and $c$:

(a) $\overrightarrow{CD}$     (b) $\overrightarrow{OD}$     (c) $\overrightarrow{AD}$

**\*2**  $OAB$ is a triangle with
$\overrightarrow{OA} = a$,     $\overrightarrow{OB} = b$
$C$ and $D$ are points such that
$OC : CB = 2 : 3$,     $OD : DA = 2 : 3$

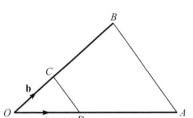

(a) Prove that $\overrightarrow{CD}$ and $\overrightarrow{BA}$ are parallel.

(b) Give the vector $\overrightarrow{OE}$ such that $E$ is
on the line $AB$ and $\overrightarrow{DE}$ is parallel to $\overrightarrow{CB}$.

**3**  For each vector $p$, find the unit vector in the direction of $p$

(a) $p = 3i + 4j$     (b) $p = 10i - 24j$     (c) $p = -4i + 5j$

**4**  If $\overrightarrow{OA} = \begin{pmatrix} 5 \\ 7 \end{pmatrix}$ and $\overrightarrow{OB} = \begin{pmatrix} -7 \\ 10 \end{pmatrix}$, find $\overrightarrow{OC}$ such that $C$ divides $AB$ in the
ratio $3 : 2$.

**\*5**  $OABC$ is a rhombus. Show that
$\overrightarrow{OB}$ is a perpendicular to $\overrightarrow{AC}$.

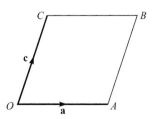

**6**  *OAB* is a triangle. *C, D* and *E* form the mid-points of the sides of the triangle. Show that *OE, BD* and *AC* meet at a point *G* such that *OG* : *GE* = 2 : 1.

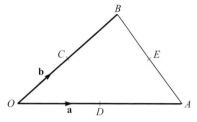

**7**  *ABC* is a triangle such that $\overrightarrow{AB} = 13\mathbf{i} + 12\mathbf{j}$ and $\overrightarrow{BC} = -10\mathbf{i} + 4\mathbf{j}$. Find:

(a)  $\overrightarrow{AC}$,

(b)  the length of each side *AB, BC, AC,*

(c)  each angle in the triangle.

**8**  *OAB* is a triangle. The angle between $\overrightarrow{OA}$ and $\overrightarrow{OB}$ is $\theta$.

$$\mathbf{a} = \begin{pmatrix} 7 \\ 2 \end{pmatrix} \quad \mathbf{b} = \begin{pmatrix} 4 \\ 5 \end{pmatrix}$$

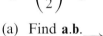

(a)  Find **a.b.**

(b)  Find (i) $|\overrightarrow{AB}|$, (ii) $|\mathbf{a}|$, (iii) $|\mathbf{b}|$, leaving your answers in surd form.

(c)  Show that $\cos\theta = \dfrac{38}{\sqrt{53}\sqrt{41}}$

(d)  Show that $(AB)^2 = a^2 + b^2 - 2ab\cos\theta$

**9**  If $\overrightarrow{OA} = \begin{pmatrix} 3 \\ 2 \\ 8 \end{pmatrix}$ and $\overrightarrow{OB} = \begin{pmatrix} 8 \\ -3 \\ 3 \end{pmatrix}$, find $\overrightarrow{OC}$, such that *C* divides *AB* in the ratio 1 : 4.

**10**  If $\overrightarrow{OP} = 5\mathbf{i} - \mathbf{j} + 4\mathbf{k}$, $\overrightarrow{OQ} = 9\mathbf{i} + 4\mathbf{j} - 2\mathbf{k}$, $\overrightarrow{OR} = 9\mathbf{i} + \mathbf{j} + \mathbf{k}$, $\overrightarrow{OS} = 13\mathbf{i} + 6\mathbf{j} - 5\mathbf{k}$, show that *PQRS* is a parallelogram.

**11**  Show that the angle between the longest diagonal of a cube and an edge is $\cos^{-1}\left(\dfrac{1}{\sqrt{3}}\right)$.

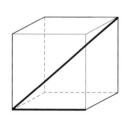

**12**  A hiker sets off up a mountain on a bearing of 22° at an angle of elevation of 8°, at an average speed of 1.4 m s⁻¹. After 20 minutes, he takes the steeper path at an average speed of 1 m s⁻¹, on a bearing of 345°, angle of elevation 13° and walks for 5 km, before stopping to radio his position from his starting point.

(a)  Using components in the directions east, north and vertically upwards, give the column vector of his position when he stopped.
(b)  What was his average speed for the whole journey?

**13** The points $A$, $B$ and $C$ have position vectors $-6\mathbf{i}$, $-3\mathbf{j}$, $3\mathbf{i}+3\mathbf{j}$ respectively.

(a)  Write down $\overrightarrow{AB}$, $\overrightarrow{BC}$.
(b)  Show that (i) $|AB| = |BC|$, (ii) $AB$ is perpendicular to $BC$.
(c)  A square $ABCD$ is formed. Find the position vector of $D$.

**14** Find the angle $PQR$ when $P$, $Q$ and $R$ are the endpoints of the vectors $\mathbf{i}+\mathbf{j}$, $\mathbf{j}-\mathbf{k}$ and $\mathbf{i}-2\mathbf{j}+\mathbf{k}$ respectively.

**15** Vectors $\mathbf{p}$, $\mathbf{q}$, $\mathbf{r}$ are given by

$$\mathbf{p} = 2\mathbf{i} - \mathbf{j} + 2\mathbf{k}$$
$$\mathbf{q} = 5\mathbf{i} + \mathbf{j} - 3\mathbf{k}$$
$$\mathbf{r} = \mathbf{i} + 2\mathbf{j} - 4\mathbf{k}$$

A fourth vector is given by $\mathbf{s} = 3\mathbf{i} + \mathbf{k}$.
Find values of $\alpha$, $\beta$, $\gamma$, such that $\mathbf{s} = \alpha\mathbf{p} + \beta\mathbf{q} + \gamma\mathbf{r}$.

**16** $P$ and $Q$ are two points with coordinates $(1, 2, -2)$ and $(0, 1, -1)$ respectively.

(a)  Show that $\cos POQ = \frac{2}{3}\sqrt{2}$.
(b)  The point $R$ lies on $PQ$ so that $PR : RQ = k : 1 - k$.
  (i)  Find the coordinates of $R$.
  (ii)  If $OR$ is perpendicular to $PQ$, find $k$.
  (iii)  Find the perpendicular distance from $O$ to $PQ$.

**Advanced**

**1** The vector $\begin{pmatrix} 1 \\ \alpha \\ \beta \end{pmatrix}$ is perpendicular to $\begin{pmatrix} 4 \\ 2 \\ 5 \end{pmatrix}$ and to $\begin{pmatrix} -3 \\ 5 \\ 6 \end{pmatrix}$. Find $\alpha$ and $\beta$.

**2** The points $P$, $Q$, $R$ have position vectors $\mathbf{p} = \mathbf{i} - 8\mathbf{j} + 10\mathbf{k}$, $\mathbf{q} = 6\mathbf{i} + 2\mathbf{j}$, $\mathbf{r} = 4\mathbf{i} - 2\mathbf{j} + 4\mathbf{k}$ respectively.

(a)  Show that $P$, $Q$ and $R$ are collinear and find the ratio $PR : RQ$.
(b)  A line $\ell$ passes through $R$ in the direction given by $\mathbf{i} + \frac{5}{2}\mathbf{j} - \frac{1}{2}\mathbf{k}$. Find a vector of the form $a\mathbf{i} + b\mathbf{j} + \mathbf{k}$ that is perpendicular to both $PR$ and $\ell$.

**3** The position vectors of points $A$, $B$ and $C$ are

$$\mathbf{a} = 3\mathbf{i} + 5\mathbf{j} - 2\mathbf{k}, \quad \mathbf{b} = 3\mathbf{i} - 4\mathbf{j} + 7\mathbf{k}, \quad \mathbf{c} = \lambda\mathbf{i} + \mu\mathbf{j} - 3\mathbf{k}$$

(a)  Find a unit vector parallel to $\overrightarrow{AB}$.
(b)  Find values for $\lambda$ and $\mu$ so that $A$, $B$ and $C$ are collinear.
(c)  If $\lambda = 5$ and $\mu = 1$, find the position vector of $D$ so that $ABCD$ is a parallelogram.

**4**  Two points $A$ and $B$ have position vectors **a** and **b** respectively. **a** and **b** are each of unit length and the angle between the vectors is $30°$.

(a)  Write down (i) **a.a**, (ii) **b.b**, (iii) **a.b**.
The point $C$ on the line segment $AB$ is such that $AC = 3CB$.
(b)  Find the position vector **c** of $C$ in terms of **a** and **b**.
(c)  Hence calculate, to two significant figures, (i) the length of **c**, (ii) the angle between **a** and **c**.

**5**  $P$ is a point on the circumference of a circle, centre $O$ and diameter $AB$. The position vectors of $A$ and $P$ are **a** and **p** respectively.
Calculate the scalar product $\overrightarrow{AP}.\overrightarrow{BP}$ and interpret the result geometrically.

**6**  If $A$ and $B$ have position vectors **a** and **b**, find the position vector of the mid-point of $AB$.
Hence prove that the lines joining the mid-points of the opposite sides of a tetrahedron are concurrent.

**7**  $ABCD$ is a tetrahedron and the position vectors of $A$, $B$, $C$ and $D$ with respect to a point $O$ are **a**, **b**, **c**, **d** respectively. Given that the edges $AB$ and $CD$ are perpendicular, show that $\mathbf{a.c} + \mathbf{b.d} = \mathbf{a.d} + \mathbf{b.c}$.
Given also that $BC$ and $AD$ are perpendicular, prove that $AC$ and $BD$ are perpendicular.
[OCR (Cambridge), 1983]

**8**  The points $A$, $B$, $C$, $D$ have position vectors **a**, **b**, **c**, **d** given by

$$\mathbf{a} = \mathbf{i} + 2\mathbf{j} + 3\mathbf{k}, \qquad \mathbf{b} = \mathbf{i} + 2\mathbf{j} + 2\mathbf{k}$$
$$\mathbf{c} = 3\mathbf{i} + 2\mathbf{j} + \mathbf{k}, \qquad \mathbf{d} = 4\mathbf{i} - \mathbf{j} - \mathbf{k}$$

respectively. The point $P$ lies on $AB$ produced and is such that $AP = 2AB$, and the point $Q$ is the mid-point of $AC$.

(i)    Show that $PQ$ is perpendicular to $AQ$.
(ii)   Find the area of the triangle $APQ$.
(iii)  Find a vector perpendicular to the plane $ABC$.
(iv)   Find the cosine of the acute angle between $AD$ and $BD$.

[OCR (Cambridge), 1987]

**9** (i) Show geometrically that, for any two vectors $\mathbf{a}$ and $\mathbf{b}$, $|\mathbf{a}| + |\mathbf{b}| \geq |\mathbf{a} + \mathbf{b}|$. State under what conditions the equality sign holds.

Deduce that, for vectors $\mathbf{a}_1, \mathbf{a}_2, \ldots, \mathbf{a}_n$, $\displaystyle\sum_{r=1}^{n} |\mathbf{a}_r| \geq \left| \sum_{r=1}^{n} \mathbf{a}_r \right|$.

(ii) By choosing the vectors $\mathbf{a}_r$ to be of the form $c_r\mathbf{i} + c_r\mathbf{j} + \mathbf{k}$, for suitable choices of $c_r$, prove that

$$\sum_{r=1}^{n}(2r^2 + 1)^{\frac{1}{2}} \geq [\tfrac{1}{2}n^2(n^2 + 2n + 3)]^{\frac{1}{2}}$$

(iii) Prove that

$$\sum_{r=1}^{n}(5r^2 + 1)^{\frac{1}{2}} \geq [\tfrac{1}{4}n^2(5n^2 + 10n + 9)]^{\frac{1}{2}}$$

[OCR (Cambridge), 1988]

**10** In the triangle $OAB$, $\overrightarrow{OA} = \mathbf{a}$, $\overrightarrow{OB} = \mathbf{b}$ and $OA = OB = 1$. Points $C$ and $D$ trisect $AB$ (i.e. $AC = CD = DB = \tfrac{1}{3}AB$). $X$ and $Y$ lie on the line segments $OA$ and $OB$ respectively, in such a way that $CY$ and $DX$ are pependicular and $OX + OY = 1$. Denoting $OX$ by $x$, obtain a condition relating $x$ and $\mathbf{a}.\mathbf{b}$, and prove that

$$\tfrac{8}{17} \leq \mathbf{a}.\mathbf{b} \leq 1$$

[OCR (STEP), 1989]

## Revision

**1** $\mathbf{p} = 5\mathbf{i} + 10\mathbf{j}, \qquad \mathbf{q} = 3\mathbf{i} - 2\mathbf{j}, \qquad \mathbf{r} = 7\mathbf{i} + 7\mathbf{j}, \qquad \mathbf{s} = -5\mathbf{i} - 9\mathbf{j}$

Find:

(a) $\mathbf{p} + \mathbf{q} + \mathbf{r} + \mathbf{s}$      (b) $\mathbf{p} - \mathbf{q} + \mathbf{r} - \mathbf{s}$
(c) $3\mathbf{p} - 5\mathbf{q}$              (d) $5(\mathbf{q} + \mathbf{s})$

**2** Using the vectors $\mathbf{p}$, $\mathbf{q}$ and $\mathbf{s}$ from question 1, find $\mathbf{x}$ if

$$11\mathbf{x} + 2\mathbf{q} = 5(\mathbf{p} - \mathbf{s})$$

**3** Find: (a) $\mathbf{l} + \mathbf{m} + \mathbf{n}$
          (b) $4\mathbf{m} - 3\mathbf{n}$

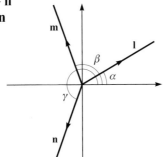

$l = 26, \qquad \alpha = 30°$
$m = 18, \qquad \beta = 110°$
$n = 15, \qquad \gamma = 250°$

**4** Using the vectors **l**, **m** and **n** from question 3, find **y** if

$$3\mathbf{y} - \mathbf{m} = 4(\mathbf{l} + \mathbf{n})$$

Give your answer in component form.

**5** Find the scalar products.

(a) $\begin{pmatrix} 4 \\ -7 \end{pmatrix} \cdot \begin{pmatrix} 10 \\ 5 \end{pmatrix}$     (b) $(3\mathbf{i} + 5\mathbf{j}) \cdot (8\mathbf{i} - 5\mathbf{j})$

(c)

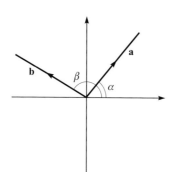

$a = 15, \quad \alpha = 50°$
$b = 10, \quad \beta = 150°$

**6** Find the angle between the following pairs of vectors.

(a) $\begin{pmatrix} -2 \\ 8 \end{pmatrix}$ and $\begin{pmatrix} -5 \\ -9 \end{pmatrix}$     (b) $(3\mathbf{i} - 8\mathbf{j})$ and $(12\mathbf{i} + 15\mathbf{j})$

**7** Find the scalar product of:

(a) $2\mathbf{i}$ and $5\mathbf{j}$     (b) $\begin{pmatrix} 2 \\ 5 \end{pmatrix}$ and $\begin{pmatrix} -15 \\ 6 \end{pmatrix}$

Explain your answers.

**8** $\mathbf{p} = 12\mathbf{i} + 57\mathbf{i}, \quad \mathbf{q} = -0.8\mathbf{i} + 3.8\mathbf{j}, \quad \mathbf{r} = -28\mathbf{i} - 133\mathbf{j}, \quad \mathbf{s} = -95\mathbf{i} + 20\mathbf{j}$
Which pairs of vectors are (a) perpendicular, (b) parallel?

**9** If **a** and **b** are perpendicular, simplify:
(a) $(\mathbf{a} - \mathbf{b}) \cdot (\mathbf{a} - \mathbf{b})$     (b) $(\mathbf{a} - \mathbf{b}) \cdot \mathbf{b} - (\mathbf{b} - \mathbf{a}) \cdot \mathbf{a}$
(c) $(2\mathbf{a} + 3\mathbf{b}) \cdot \mathbf{b}$

**10** $\mathbf{a} = \begin{pmatrix} 4 \\ 3 \\ 8 \end{pmatrix}, \quad \mathbf{b} = \begin{pmatrix} -5 \\ -10 \\ 12 \end{pmatrix}, \quad \mathbf{c} = \begin{pmatrix} 18 \\ -6 \\ 15 \end{pmatrix}$

Find:
(a) $\mathbf{a} + \mathbf{b} + \mathbf{c}$     (b) $\mathbf{a} + \mathbf{c} - 2\mathbf{b}$     (c) $6(\mathbf{a} - \mathbf{b}) + \mathbf{c}$

**11** Using the vectors given in question 10, find the angle between:
(a) **a** and **b**     (b) **b** and **c**     (c) **a** and **c**

**12** A starship is mapping the stars in a newly discovered solar system. Their positions are given as vectors from their sun, with distances measured in billions of kilometres.

$$\text{Planet } \alpha \begin{pmatrix} 0.1 \\ -0.2 \\ 0.05 \end{pmatrix}, \quad \text{planet } \beta \begin{pmatrix} 0.15 \\ -0.08 \\ -0.12 \end{pmatrix}, \quad \text{planet } \gamma \begin{pmatrix} -0.07 \\ 0.15 \\ 0.2 \end{pmatrix}$$

Planet $\alpha$ has a moon. Its vector from the planet is $\begin{pmatrix} 0.01 \\ -0.02 \\ 0.02 \end{pmatrix}$.

(a) Give the position of the moon from the sun.
(b) What is the distance between planet $\beta$ and planet $\gamma$?

(c) The starship's position from the sun is $\begin{pmatrix} 1 \\ 0 \\ 0 \end{pmatrix}$. It sends probes to each

planet. What is the angle between the directions of the probes sent to planet $\alpha$ and planet $\gamma$?

## 3.2   2D vectors; position vectors; ratio theorem; vector equation of a line; intersection of lines

> **Ratio theorem**: if $A$ and $B$ have position vectors $\mathbf{a}$ and $\mathbf{b}$ relative to an origin $O$, and the point $P$ divides $AB$ in the ratio $p:q$, then the position vector of $P$ is given by
>
> $$\mathbf{p} = \frac{1}{p+q}(q\mathbf{a} + p\mathbf{b})$$
>
> The vector equation of the line through the point with position vector $\mathbf{a}$, which is parallel to the vector $\mathbf{b}$, is given by $\mathbf{r} = \mathbf{a} + \lambda\mathbf{b}$. The **median** of a triangle is the line joining a vertex to the mid-point of the opposite side.

### Basic

**1**   $\mathbf{a}$ and $\mathbf{b}$ are the position vectors of $A$ and $B$ respectively. $\mathbf{a} = 2\mathbf{i} + 3\mathbf{j}$ and $\mathbf{b} = \mathbf{i} - 4\mathbf{j}$. Find:

(a) $-\mathbf{a} + 2\mathbf{b}$          (b) $|\mathbf{b} - \mathbf{a}|$
(c) the position vector of the mid-point of $AB$

**\*2**  Given that $\overrightarrow{OA}$ has a magnitude of 65 and has the same direction as the vector $\begin{pmatrix} 5 \\ 12 \end{pmatrix}$, find the coordinates of point $A$.

**\*3**  Show that the point $P$, which divides the line $AB$ internally in the ratio $m:n$, has a position vector $\dfrac{n\mathbf{a} + m\mathbf{b}}{m + n}$, where $\mathbf{a}$ is the position vector of point $A$ and $\mathbf{b}$ is the position vector of point $B$.

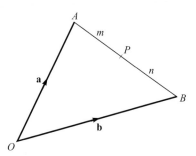

**4**  $A$ and $B$ have position vectors $4\mathbf{i} + 2\mathbf{j}$ and $\mathbf{i} - \mathbf{j}$ respectively. Find the position vector of the point which divides the line $AB$ internally in the ratio $1:2$.

**5**  $P$ and $Q$ have position vectors $2\mathbf{i} + 3\mathbf{j}$ and $10\mathbf{i} + 11\mathbf{j}$ respectively. Find the position vector of the point which divides the line $PQ$ internally in the ratio $3:5$.

**6**  A triangle has vertices $A$, $B$ and $C$ with position vectors $3\mathbf{i} + 3\mathbf{j}$, $5\mathbf{i} + 7\mathbf{j}$ and $9\mathbf{i} - 5\mathbf{j}$ respectively.

   (a)  Find the position vector of $M$, the mid-point of the line $AB$.
   (b)  Show that the position vector of $P$, the point which divides the line $MC$ internally in the ratio $2:3$, is $6\mathbf{i} + \mathbf{j}$.

**7**  A vector equation for the line $\mathbf{r}_1$ is $\begin{pmatrix} x \\ y \end{pmatrix} = \begin{pmatrix} 2 \\ 7 \end{pmatrix} + \lambda \begin{pmatrix} 1 \\ 2 \end{pmatrix}$.

   (a)  By substituting integral values of $\lambda$ from $-3$ to $3$, find the corresponding values of $x$ and $y$ and hence plot the graph of
$$\begin{pmatrix} x \\ y \end{pmatrix} = \begin{pmatrix} 2 \\ 7 \end{pmatrix} + \lambda \begin{pmatrix} 1 \\ 2 \end{pmatrix}.$$

   (b)  Using a similar method, plot the graph of the line $\mathbf{r}_2$ with equation $\begin{pmatrix} x \\ y \end{pmatrix} = \begin{pmatrix} 6 \\ 5 \end{pmatrix} + \mu \begin{pmatrix} -2 \\ 1 \end{pmatrix}$, and hence show that $\mathbf{r}_1$ and $\mathbf{r}_2$ intersect at $(2, 7)$.

   (c)  Write the equations of $\mathbf{r}_1$ and $\mathbf{r}_2$ in the form $y = mx + c$.

**8**  A vector equation for the line $AB$ is

$$\begin{pmatrix} x \\ y \end{pmatrix} = \begin{pmatrix} 3 \\ 6 \end{pmatrix} + \lambda \begin{pmatrix} 3 \\ 2 \end{pmatrix}$$

*(a)  Find $\lambda$ in terms of $x$ and $y$ and hence find a Cartesian equation for the line $AB$.

(b)  Show that $\begin{pmatrix} x \\ y \end{pmatrix} = \begin{pmatrix} 0 \\ 4 \end{pmatrix} + \mu \begin{pmatrix} 6 \\ 4 \end{pmatrix}$ is also a vector equation for the line $AB$.

**9**  $P$ and $Q$ have coordinates (2, 7) and (4, 11) respectively. Find a vector equation for the line which passes through $P$ and $Q$.

**10**  Find a vector equation for the line which passes through the point (1, 4) and is parallel to the vector $3\mathbf{i} + 4\mathbf{j}$.

**11**  Find a vector equation for the line which passes through the point (7, 4) and is perpendicular to the vector $3\mathbf{i} - \mathbf{j}$.

**\*12**  Find the point of intersection of the lines

$$\begin{pmatrix} x \\ y \end{pmatrix} = \begin{pmatrix} 3 \\ 7 \end{pmatrix} + \lambda \begin{pmatrix} 3 \\ -5 \end{pmatrix}$$

and

$$\begin{pmatrix} x \\ y \end{pmatrix} = \begin{pmatrix} 1 \\ 3 \end{pmatrix} + \mu \begin{pmatrix} 7 \\ 3 \end{pmatrix}.$$

### Intermediate

**1**  (a)  Show that $2\mathbf{i} - \mathbf{j}$ is the position vector of a point which lies on the line $2y - x + 4 = 0$.

(b)  Find the value of $k$ such that $5\mathbf{i} + k\mathbf{j}$ is also the position vector of a point on the line $2y - x + 4 = 0$.

**2**  Find the vector equation of the following lines:
(a) · the line through (3, −2) parallel to the vector $\begin{pmatrix} 4 \\ 9 \end{pmatrix}$,

(b)  the line through (4, 7) perpendicular to the vector $\begin{pmatrix} -2 \\ 1 \end{pmatrix}$,

(c)  the line through (3, −2) and (4, 7).

**3**  $ABC$ is a triangle. The position vectors of $A$, $B$ and $C$ are $\mathbf{a}$, $\mathbf{b}$ and $\mathbf{c}$ respectively. $P$, $Q$ and $R$ are the mid-points of $AB$, $BC$ and $CA$ respectively.

(a)  Find the position vectors of $P$, $Q$ and $R$ in terms of $\mathbf{a}$, $\mathbf{b}$ and $\mathbf{c}$.
(b)  Prove that triangles $ABC$ and $QRP$ are similar.

**4**  $A$ and $B$ have position vectors $\mathbf{i} + 5\mathbf{j}$ and $3\mathbf{i} - \mathbf{j}$ respectively. Find the position vector of the point which divides the line $AB$ externally in the ratio $3:1$.

**5**  A triangle has vertices $A$, $B$ and $C$ with position vectors $50\mathbf{i} - 36\mathbf{j}$, $-25\mathbf{i} - 36\mathbf{j}$ and $8\mathbf{i} + 20\mathbf{j}$ respectively.

  (a)  Find the position vector of the point $X$ which divides the line $AC$ internally in the ratio $9:5$.
  (b)  Show that $B\widehat{X}C$ is a right angle, and hence find the area of triangle $ABC$.

**6**  Point $Z$ divides the line $XY$ internally in the ratio $3:2$. If the position vector of $Z$ is $-3\mathbf{i} + \mathbf{j}$, and the position vector of $X$ is $3\mathbf{i} - 2\mathbf{j}$, find the position vector of $Y$.

**7**  Given that $\overrightarrow{OA}$ is $3\mathbf{i} + 6\mathbf{j}$, $|AB| = \sqrt{20}$ and that $AB$ is perpendicular to $OA$, find two possible values for the vector $\overrightarrow{OB}$.

**8**  Given that $\overrightarrow{OA} = 2\mathbf{i} + \mathbf{j}$ and $\overrightarrow{OB} = 8\mathbf{i} - 2\mathbf{j}$, show that the point $P$ with position vector $2p\mathbf{i} + (2 - p)\mathbf{j}$ lies on the line $AB$. Hence find a value of $p$ such that $AP:PB = 2:1$.

**9**  Find a vector equation for the perpendicular bisector of $(-1, 1)$ and $(7, 3)$.

**10**  Lines $\ell_1$, $\ell_2$ and $\ell_3$ have the following vector equations:

$$\ell_1 : \mathbf{r} = \begin{pmatrix} 1 \\ 0 \end{pmatrix} + \lambda \begin{pmatrix} -1 \\ 2 \end{pmatrix}$$

$$\ell_2 : \mathbf{r} = 6\mathbf{i} + \mathbf{j} + \mu(3\mathbf{i} + \mathbf{j})$$

$$\ell_3 : \mathbf{r} = (2 + 2\varphi)\mathbf{i} + (6 + 5\varphi)\mathbf{j}$$

Write the equations of $\ell_1$, $\ell_2$ and $\ell_3$ in the form $y = mx + c$.

**11**  $A$ and $B$ have position vectors $-\mathbf{i} - 8\mathbf{j}$ and $13\mathbf{i} + 13\mathbf{j}$ relative to a fixed point $O$. Point $X$ divides the line $AB$ internally in the ratio $2:p$. Find the value of $p$, given that $O\widehat{X}A$ is $90°$.

**12**  Find whether the following pairs of lines are parallel or intersecting. Where they intersect, find the position vector of the point of intersection.

  *(a)  $\mathbf{r}_1 = -2\mathbf{i} + 4\mathbf{j} + \lambda(14\mathbf{i} + 8\mathbf{j})$
       $\mathbf{r}_2 = -3\mathbf{i} + 9\mathbf{j} + \mu(16\mathbf{i} - 2\mathbf{j})$

  (b)  $\mathbf{r}_1 = (2 + 2\lambda)\mathbf{i} + (11 + 6\lambda)\mathbf{j}$
       $\mathbf{r}_2 = (2 + 3\mu)\mathbf{i} + (5 + 9\mu)\mathbf{j}$

  (c)  $\ell_1 : \begin{pmatrix} x \\ y \end{pmatrix} = \begin{pmatrix} -1 \\ 5 \end{pmatrix} + \lambda \begin{pmatrix} 11 \\ -1 \end{pmatrix}$

  $\ell_2 : \begin{pmatrix} x \\ y \end{pmatrix} = \begin{pmatrix} 0 \\ 1 \end{pmatrix} + \mu \begin{pmatrix} 9 \\ 7 \end{pmatrix}$

**13** In the diagram $\overrightarrow{OA} = i + j$, $\overrightarrow{OB} = 5i + 11j$
and $\overrightarrow{OC} = 15i + 3j$.

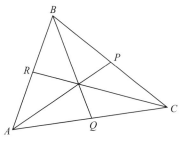

(a) Show that the medians $AP$, $BQ$ and $CR$ are concurrent, and find their point of intersection.

(b) Hence show that this point of intersection divides each median in the ratio $2:1$.

**14** Find the value of $k$ for which the lines $\mathbf{r} = 2i + j + \lambda(ki + 2j)$ and $\mathbf{r} = 3i - j + \mu(2i + j)$ are perpendicular and find the point of intersection of the two lines.

**15** Find the angles between the following pairs of lines.

*(a) $\begin{pmatrix} x \\ y \end{pmatrix} = \begin{pmatrix} 2 \\ 3 \end{pmatrix} + \lambda \begin{pmatrix} 1 \\ 2 \end{pmatrix}$ and $\begin{pmatrix} x \\ y \end{pmatrix} = \begin{pmatrix} 4 \\ -6 \end{pmatrix} + \mu \begin{pmatrix} 3 \\ 1 \end{pmatrix}$

(b) $\mathbf{r} = (5 - 2\lambda)i + 4\lambda j$ and $\mathbf{r} = (5 + \lambda)i + (3 - 7\lambda)j$

**16** Points $A$, $B$, $C$ and $D$ are the four vertices of a rectangle. The position vectors of $A$, $B$ and $C$ are $2i + 2j$, $-i + 7j$ and $8i + 9j$ respectively.

(a) Find the position vector of point $D$.

(b) Find a vector equation for the line which passes through $B$ and $D$.

*(c) Show that the shortest distance from $C$ to the line $BD$ is $\sqrt{17}$.

## Advanced

**1** The position vectors of the vertices $A$, $B$, $C$ of a triangle relative to an origin $O$ are $\mathbf{a}$, $\mathbf{b}$, $\mathbf{c}$. The side $BC$ is produced to $D$ so that $\overrightarrow{CD} = 3\overrightarrow{BC}$. $X$ is the point dividing $AB$ in the ratio $1:2$ and $Y$ is the point dividing $AC$ in the ratio $2:3$.
Prove that $X$, $Y$, $D$ are collinear.

**2** The point $A$ has coordinates $(1, 4)$ and the vector $\overrightarrow{OB} = \begin{pmatrix} 4 \\ -3 \end{pmatrix}$. The line $\ell$ passes through $A$ and is parallel to $\overrightarrow{OB}$.

(a) Find the equation of the line $\ell$.

(b) If $P$ is a point on $\ell$, find the coordinates of $P$ if $|AP| = 6$.

(c) Find the length of the perpendicular from $O$ to $\ell$.

**3** With origin at $O$, $A$ and $B$ have position vectors $\mathbf{a}$, $\mathbf{b}$ respectively.

(i) Write down the position vector of the centroid $G$ of triangle $OAB$ in terms of $\mathbf{a}$ and $\mathbf{b}$.

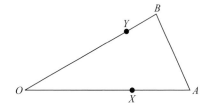

    (ii)  $X$ is the point dividing $OA$ in the ratio $5:4$, and $Y$ is the point dividing $OB$ in the ratio $5:1$. Show that the position vector of the point which divides $XY$ in the ratio $\lambda : 1 - \lambda$ is $\frac{5}{9}(1 - \lambda)\mathbf{a} + \frac{5}{6}\lambda\mathbf{b}$.

    (iii)  Hence show that $XY$ passes through $G$.

[OCR (SMP), 1990]

**4**  $OAB$ is a triangle and the position vectors of $A$ and $B$ relative to $O$ are $\mathbf{a}$ and $\mathbf{b}$ respectively. $C$ is the point on $AB$ produced such that $\overrightarrow{AB} = \frac{1}{n}\overrightarrow{AC}$.

    (a)  Express $\overrightarrow{OC}$ in terms of $\mathbf{a}$ and $\mathbf{b}$.

    (b)  $D$ is a point on $OA$ such that $\overrightarrow{OD} = \frac{1}{m}\overrightarrow{OA}$ and $E$ divides $CD$ in the ratio $\lambda : 1 - \lambda$. Find the position vector of $E$.

    (c)  The line $CD$ meets $OB$ in $F$. Show that the position vector of $F$ is

$$\frac{n}{1 + m(n - 1)}\mathbf{b}.$$

**5**  A curve (an ellipse) is traced out by a point whose position vector is given by $\begin{pmatrix} x \\ y \end{pmatrix} = \begin{pmatrix} 2\cos t \\ \sin t \end{pmatrix}$ as $t$ varies from $0$ to $2\pi$.

    (a)  Write down vectors in the directions of (i) the tangent, (ii) the normal to the curve at this point.

    [*Hint*: you may use the fact that the vectors $\begin{pmatrix} a \\ b \end{pmatrix}$ and $\begin{pmatrix} b \\ -a \end{pmatrix}$ are perpendicular to each other, provided that $a$ and $b$ are not both zero.]

    (b)  Write down an equation in the form $\begin{pmatrix} x \\ y \end{pmatrix} = \begin{pmatrix} * \\ * \end{pmatrix} + \lambda \begin{pmatrix} * \\ * \end{pmatrix}$, where each asterisk is to be replaced by an expression involving $t$, for the normal to the curve at this point.

    (c)  The normal cuts the $x$- and $y$-axes at points $X$ and $Y$ respectively. Find the coordinates of $X$ and $Y$ in terms of $t$.

    (d)  Show that the triangle $OXY$ has area of magnitude $|\frac{9}{8}\sin 2t|$.

    (e)  For what values of $t$ between $0$ and $2\pi$ is the magnitude of area $OXY$ greatest?

[OCR (SMP), 1988]

**6**  $O$ is the origin of position vectors, and points $A$ and $B$ are given by $\overrightarrow{OA} = \mathbf{a}$, $\overrightarrow{OB} = \mathbf{b}$; $R$ is the point dividing $AB$ internally in the ratio $\lambda : \mu$, and $\overrightarrow{OR} = \mathbf{r}$. Write down an expression for $\mathbf{r}$ in terms of $\mathbf{a}$, $\mathbf{b}$, $\lambda$ and $\mu$, and hence show that

$$\frac{\mathbf{r}.\mathbf{a}}{\mathbf{r}.\mathbf{a}} = \frac{\mu a^2 + \lambda \mathbf{a}.\mathbf{b}}{\lambda b^2 + \mu \mathbf{a}.\mathbf{b}}$$

where $a = |\mathbf{a}|$ and $b = |\mathbf{b}|$. Deduce that, when $\lambda : \mu = a : b$, the line $OR$ bisects angle $AOB$.

[OCR (Cambridge), 1976]

7  (a)  A point with position vector $\mathbf{r}_1$ lies on a straight line through the points with position vectors $\mathbf{a}$ and $\mathbf{b}$. Show that the vector equation of the line is $\mathbf{r}_1 = \mathbf{a} + s(\mathbf{b} - \mathbf{a})$ where $s$ is a scalar parameter.
   (b)  A point with position vector $\mathbf{r}_2$ lies on the straight line through the point $\mathbf{a}$ and parallel to the vector $\mathbf{b}$. Show that the equation of the line is $\mathbf{r}_2 = \mathbf{a} + t\mathbf{b}$ where $t$ is a scalar parameter.

   Let $\mathbf{a} = 2\mathbf{i} + 3\mathbf{j}$ and $\mathbf{b} = 3\mathbf{i} + 2\mathbf{j}$. The vector $\mathbf{r}_2$ makes an angle of $30°$ with the $x$-axis. Find the parameter $t$.
   [OCR (Oxford Entrance), 1987]

8  $A$ and $B$ are points with position vectors $\mathbf{a}$ and $\mathbf{b}$ respectively. The line $CD$ is parallel to $AB$ and of the same length as $AB$, and the position vector of $C$ is $\mathbf{c}$. $E$ is the mid-point of $AB$.
   Find the vector equation of the line $CE$. Show that $CE$ trisects $AD$.

9  Let $\mathbf{a}$ and $\mathbf{b}$ be given vectors and $\lambda$ a real positive parameter. The unknown vector $\mathbf{x}$, lying in the plane of $\mathbf{a}$ and $\mathbf{b}$, satisfies the equations

$$|\mathbf{x} - \tfrac{1}{3}(2\mathbf{a} + \mathbf{b})| = \tfrac{1}{3}|\mathbf{a} - \mathbf{b}|,$$
$$\{\mathbf{x} - [(1 - \lambda)\mathbf{a} + \lambda\mathbf{b}]\}.(\mathbf{a} - \mathbf{b}) = 0$$

Find, using a diagram, or otherwise, the values of $\lambda$, where $\lambda > 0$, for which the equations have
   (i)   no solution for $\mathbf{x}$,
   (ii)  one solution for $\mathbf{x}$,
   (iii) more than one solution for $\mathbf{x}$.
   [OCR (Cambridge), 1983]

10 The position vectors of the points $A$, $B$, $C$, referred to an origin $O$ in the plane $ABC$, are given by the *unit* vectors $\mathbf{a}$, $\mathbf{b}$, $\mathbf{c}$. Prove that $\mathbf{a}$, $\mathbf{b}$, $\mathbf{c}$ are connected by a relation of the form $p\mathbf{a} + q\mathbf{b} + r\mathbf{c} = \mathbf{0}$, where $\mathbf{0}$ is the zero vector and $p$, $q$, $r$ are scalar constants.
   Describe the triangle $ABC$ when the relation is

   (i)  $\mathbf{a} + \mathbf{b} + \mathbf{c} = \mathbf{0}$     (ii)  $\mathbf{b} + \mathbf{c} = \mathbf{0}$

   In the general case, the line $AO$ meets the line $BC$ in $U$. Prove that $OU$ is equal to the numerical value of $\dfrac{p}{(q + r)}$.
   [OCR (Cambridge), 1972]

## Revision

1  If the position vector of $A$ is $7\mathbf{i} + 5\mathbf{j}$ and the position vector of the mid-point of $AB$ is $10\mathbf{i} + 4\mathbf{j}$, find:

   (a)  the position vector of $B$,
   (b)  $|AB|$.

**2** $P$ and $Q$ have position vectors $3\mathbf{i} - 2\mathbf{j}$ and $8\mathbf{i} + 3\mathbf{j}$ respectively. Find the position vector of the point which divides the line $PQ$ internally in the ratio $3:7$.

**3** If $OA = \begin{pmatrix} 2 \\ -3 \end{pmatrix}$ and $OB = \begin{pmatrix} 3 \\ 1 \end{pmatrix}$, find the position vector of point $X$, which divides the line $AB$ externally in the ratio $3:2$.

**4** The position vectors of $P$, $Q$ and $R$ relative to a fixed point $O$ are $\begin{pmatrix} 2 \\ 7 \end{pmatrix}$, $\begin{pmatrix} 6 \\ 17 \end{pmatrix}$ and $\begin{pmatrix} -2 \\ 21 \end{pmatrix}$ respectively. Find the point of intersection of the medians of triangle $PQR$.

**5** $ABO$ is an isosceles triangle with $|AB| = |OB|$.
$A$ has position vector $4\mathbf{i} + 8\mathbf{j}$, relative to $O$.
$B$ has position vector $p\mathbf{i} + q\mathbf{j}$, relative to $O$.

(a) Show that $p + 2q = 10$.
(b) Given that $\widehat{ABO} = 90°$ and that $p < q$, find the values of $p$ and $q$.

**6** Points $A$ and $B$ have position vectors $2\mathbf{i} + 3\mathbf{j}$ and $7\mathbf{i} - 2\mathbf{j}$ respectively. Find a vector equation for the line which passes through $A$ and $B$.

**7** Find a vector equation for the line which passes through the point $(2, 4)$ and is parallel to the vector $\mathbf{i} - \mathbf{j}$.

**8** Find a vector equation for the line which passes through the point $(7, 3)$ and is perpendicular to the vector $2\mathbf{i} - 5\mathbf{j}$.

**9** A vector equation for the line $PQ$ is $\begin{pmatrix} x \\ y \end{pmatrix} = \begin{pmatrix} 4 \\ 5 \end{pmatrix} + \lambda \begin{pmatrix} 2 \\ 1 \end{pmatrix}$. State which of the following are also vector equations for the line $PQ$:

$$\ell_1: \begin{pmatrix} x \\ y \end{pmatrix} = \begin{pmatrix} -1 \\ 2 \end{pmatrix} + \mu \begin{pmatrix} 2 \\ 4 \end{pmatrix}$$

$$\ell_2: \begin{pmatrix} x \\ y \end{pmatrix} = \begin{pmatrix} 2 \\ 4 \end{pmatrix} + \varphi \begin{pmatrix} 2 \\ 1 \end{pmatrix}$$

$$\ell_3: \begin{pmatrix} x \\ y \end{pmatrix} = \begin{pmatrix} 0 \\ 2 \end{pmatrix} + \gamma \begin{pmatrix} 6 \\ 3 \end{pmatrix}$$

$$\ell_4: \begin{pmatrix} x \\ y \end{pmatrix} = \begin{pmatrix} 3 \\ 5 \end{pmatrix} + \alpha \begin{pmatrix} 2 \\ 1 \end{pmatrix}$$

$$\ell_5: \begin{pmatrix} x \\ y \end{pmatrix} = \begin{pmatrix} 0 \\ 3 \end{pmatrix} + \beta \begin{pmatrix} 4 \\ 2 \end{pmatrix}$$

**10** Find the angle between the lines

$$\ell_1: \begin{pmatrix} x \\ y \end{pmatrix} = \begin{pmatrix} 3 \\ 2 \end{pmatrix} + \lambda \begin{pmatrix} 2 \\ 1 \end{pmatrix} \quad \text{and} \quad \ell_2: \begin{pmatrix} x \\ y \end{pmatrix} = \begin{pmatrix} 4 \\ 6 \end{pmatrix} + \mu \begin{pmatrix} -3 \\ 2 \end{pmatrix}$$

**11** The square $ABCD$ has vertices with position vectors $3\mathbf{i} + 5\mathbf{j}$, $-3\mathbf{i} + 17\mathbf{j}$, $9\mathbf{i} + 23\mathbf{j}$ and $p\mathbf{i} + q\mathbf{j}$ respectively.

(a) Find the values of $p$ and $q$.
(b) If $X$ divides the line $BC$ internally in the ratio $1:2$ and $Y$ divides the line $AD$ internally in the ratio $5:1$, find a vector equation for the line $XY$.

**12** Lines $\ell_1$, $\ell_2$ and $\ell_3$ have the following vector equations:

$$\ell_1: \mathbf{r} = (1 - 5\alpha)\mathbf{i} + (13 + 3\alpha)\mathbf{j}$$
$$\ell_2: \mathbf{r} = (-2 - 5\beta)\mathbf{i} + (10 + 3\beta)\mathbf{j}$$
$$\ell_3: \mathbf{r} = (-1 + \gamma)\mathbf{i} + (3 + \gamma)\mathbf{j}$$

(a) Show that $\ell_1$ and $\ell_2$ are parallel.
(b) Given that $\ell_3$ intersects $\ell_1$ and $\ell_2$ at $X$ and $Y$ respectively, find the length of $XY$.

## 3.3   3D vectors; equations of lines and planes; intersection of lines and planes

> The vector equation of the plane through the point with position vector $\mathbf{a}$, parallel to the vectors $\mathbf{b}$ and $\mathbf{c}$, is given by $\mathbf{r} = \mathbf{a} + \lambda\mathbf{b} + \mu\mathbf{c}$. The normal vector to the plane $ax + by + cz = d$ is
>
> $$\mathbf{n} = \begin{pmatrix} a \\ b \\ c \end{pmatrix}$$
>
> The vector equation of the plane through the point with position vector $\mathbf{a}$, which is normal to the vector $\mathbf{n}$, is given by $\mathbf{n}.\mathbf{r} = \mathbf{n}.\mathbf{a}$. The perpendicular distance of the point $(x_1, y_1, z_1)$ from the plane $ax + by + cz = d$ is given by
>
> $$\frac{|ax_1 + by_1 + cz_1 - d|}{\sqrt{a^2 + b^2 + c^2}}$$

**Basic**

**1** $A$ and $B$ have position vectors $2\mathbf{i} + \mathbf{j} - \mathbf{k}$ and $-\mathbf{i} - 4\mathbf{j} + 4\mathbf{k}$ respectively. Find the position vector of the point which divides the line $AB$ internally in the ratio $2:3$.

**2**   $P$ and $Q$ have coordinates $(1, 0, 2)$ and $(-2, 3, -1)$. Find the coordinates of point $X$, which divides the line $PQ$ externally in the ratio $5:2$.

**3**   Triangle $ABC$ has vertices with position vectors $2\mathbf{i} + 3\mathbf{j} + \mathbf{k}$, $2\mathbf{i} - 5\mathbf{j} + 5\mathbf{k}$ and $-\mathbf{j} + 8\mathbf{k}$ respectively.

   (a)  Find the position vector of point $X$, which divides the line $AB$ internally in the ratio $3:1$.
   (b)  Show that $\widehat{CXA}$ is a right angle.
   (c)  Hence, or otherwise, find the area of triangle $ABC$.

**\*4**   The vector equation of a line is

$$x\mathbf{i} + y\mathbf{j} + z\mathbf{k} = 2\mathbf{i} + 3\mathbf{j} + 7\mathbf{k} + \lambda(4\mathbf{i} - 2\mathbf{j} + \mathbf{k})$$

Express $\lambda$ in terms of $x$, $y$ and $z$, and hence find the Cartesian equations for the line.

**5**   The Cartesian equations of a line are $\dfrac{x-2}{3} = \dfrac{y-4}{2} = \dfrac{z+1}{4}$. Find a vector equation for the line.

**6**   Find the angle between the lines

$$\mathbf{r}_1 = 2\mathbf{i} + 3\mathbf{j} - \mathbf{k} + \lambda(2\mathbf{i} - \mathbf{j} - 2\mathbf{k}) \quad \text{and} \quad \mathbf{r}_2 = \mathbf{i} - 2\mathbf{j} + \mathbf{k} + \mu(7\mathbf{i} + 4\mathbf{j} - 4\mathbf{k})$$

**7**   Lines $\ell_1$, $\ell_2$ and $\ell_3$ have the following vector equations:

$\ell_1: \mathbf{r} = 2\mathbf{i} + \mathbf{j} + \mathbf{k} + \lambda(\mathbf{i} - 2\mathbf{j} + 2\mathbf{k})$
$\ell_2: \mathbf{r} = 3\mathbf{i} + \mathbf{j} + 2\mathbf{k} + \mu(3\mathbf{i} - 6\mathbf{j} + 6\mathbf{k})$
$\ell_3: \mathbf{r} = 3\mathbf{i} + \mathbf{j} + 3\mathbf{k} + \varphi(\mathbf{i} - 3\mathbf{j} + 2\mathbf{k})$

   (a)  Show that $\ell_1$ and $\ell_2$ are parallel.
   (b)  Show that $\ell_1$ and $\ell_3$ intersect, and find the position vector of their point of intersection.
   (c)  Show that $\ell_2$ and $\ell_3$ are skew (i.e. they do not intersect and are not parallel).

**8**   Find the point of intersection of the line $\mathbf{r} = 5\mathbf{i} + 4\mathbf{j} + 2\mathbf{k} + \lambda(3\mathbf{i} + \mathbf{j} + 3\mathbf{k})$ and the $xy$-plane.

**\*9**   Find Cartesian equations for the following planes.

   (a)  $\mathbf{r}.(2\mathbf{i} + 3\mathbf{j} - \mathbf{k}) = 6$
   (b)  $\mathbf{r} = 2\mathbf{i} + \mathbf{j} - \mathbf{k} + \lambda(2\mathbf{i} + \mathbf{k}) + \mu(-\mathbf{i} - \mathbf{j} + 2\mathbf{k})$

**10**   Find vector equations for the following planes in scalar product form.

   (a)  $4x - 5y + z = 7$
   (b)  $\mathbf{r} = 2\mathbf{i} + \mathbf{j} - \mathbf{k} + \lambda(2\mathbf{i} + 3\mathbf{k}) + \mu(4\mathbf{i} - 2\mathbf{j} + \mathbf{k})$

**11** For each of the following planes find:

  (i)  a unit vector perpendicular to the plane.
  (ii)  the distance of the plane from the origin.

  (a)  $\mathbf{r}.(6\mathbf{i} + 2\mathbf{j} - 3\mathbf{k}) = 14$     (b)  $6x - 9y + 2z = 5$

**12** A plane passes through the points $A(2, 1, 2)$, $B(3, 2, -2)$ and $C(5, 0, -1)$. Find a vector equation for the plane:

  *(a)  in parametric form, (b) in scalar product form.

### Intermediate

**1**  The coordinates of $A$ and $B$ are $2\mathbf{i} - \mathbf{j} + 3\mathbf{k}$ and $6\mathbf{i} + 5\mathbf{j} + \mathbf{k}$ respectively. Show that the line $\mathbf{r} = 4\mathbf{i} + 2\mathbf{j} + 2\mathbf{k} + \lambda(5\mathbf{i} - 3\mathbf{j} + \mathbf{k})$ is a perpendicular bisector of $AB$.

**2**  In parallelogram $OABC$, $\overrightarrow{OA} = 5\mathbf{i} - 24\mathbf{j} + 32\mathbf{k}$ and $\overrightarrow{OB} = 55\mathbf{i} - 30\mathbf{j} + 40\mathbf{k}$.

  (a)  Find $\overrightarrow{OC}$.
  (b)  Find the position vector of point $X$, which divides the line $AC$ in the ratio $1:2$.
  (c)  Show that $O\widehat{X}A$ is a right angle.

**3**  The line which divides $AB$ externally in the ratio $3:1$ also divides $XY$ internally in the ratio $p:q$.
  Given that the position vectors of $A$, $B$, $X$ and $Y$ are $8\mathbf{i} - 3\mathbf{j} + 5\mathbf{k}$, $4\mathbf{i} + \mathbf{j} + \mathbf{k}$, $4\mathbf{i} + 5\mathbf{j} + \mathbf{k}$ and $-\mathbf{i} - 4\mathbf{k}$ respectively, find the values of $p$ and $q$.

**4**  State whether the following pairs of lines are parallel, intersecting or skew.

  (a)  $\mathbf{r} = (2 + 4\lambda)\mathbf{i} + (3 + 2\lambda)\mathbf{j} + (1 - 6\lambda)\mathbf{k}$
      $\mathbf{r} = (2 - 2\mu)\mathbf{i} - \mu\mathbf{j} + (1 + 3\mu)\mathbf{k}$
  (b)  $\mathbf{r} = 3\lambda\mathbf{i} + (1 + \lambda)\mathbf{j} - \lambda\mathbf{k}$
      $\mathbf{r} = (2 - 3\mu)\mathbf{i} + 2\mathbf{j} + (1 + \mu)\mathbf{k}$
  (c)  $\mathbf{r} = (1 + 3\lambda)\mathbf{i} + (2 - \lambda)\mathbf{j} + 2\lambda\mathbf{k}$
      $\mathbf{r} = (5 - 2\mu)\mathbf{i} + (1 + \mu)\mathbf{j} + (5 + \mu)\mathbf{k}$

**5**  Lines $\ell_1$, $\ell_2$ and $\ell_3$ have vector equations

$$\ell_1: \mathbf{r} = \mathbf{i} + 3\mathbf{j} + 4\mathbf{k} + \lambda(\mathbf{i} + c\mathbf{j} + 2\mathbf{k})$$
$$\ell_2: \mathbf{r} = 3\mathbf{i} + 2\mathbf{k} + \mu(-2\mathbf{i} + 2\mathbf{j} - 4\mathbf{k})$$
$$\ell_3: \mathbf{r} = 2\mathbf{i} + \mathbf{j} + \sigma(\mathbf{i} - 4\mathbf{j} + 8\mathbf{k})$$

Find a value for $c$, given that:

  (a)  $\ell_1$ and $\ell_2$ are parallel, (b) $\ell_1$ and $\ell_3$ intersect.

**6** State whether the lines

$$\ell_1: \frac{x-2}{4} = y - 1 = \frac{z}{3} \quad \text{and} \quad \ell_2: \frac{3-x}{2} = \frac{y-1}{2} = z$$

are intersecting or skew and find the angle between them.

**7** For each of the following planes, find:

(i) a unit vector normal to the plane,
(ii) the distance of the plane from the origin.

(a) $\mathbf{r} = \begin{pmatrix} 1 \\ 1 \\ -2 \end{pmatrix} + \lambda \begin{pmatrix} -1 \\ 3 \\ 4 \end{pmatrix} + \mu \begin{pmatrix} 2 \\ 1 \\ 6 \end{pmatrix}$

(b) $\mathbf{r} = \begin{pmatrix} 1 \\ 2 \\ 1 \end{pmatrix} + \lambda \begin{pmatrix} -2 \\ 0 \\ 3 \end{pmatrix} + \mu \begin{pmatrix} 2 \\ 3 \\ -2 \end{pmatrix}$

**8** State whether the following lines are parallel to, intersect or lie within the plane $P: 2x - y + 3z = 5$.

*(a) $\mathbf{r} = -\mathbf{i} + \mathbf{j} + 2\mathbf{k} + \varphi(3\mathbf{i} + 2\mathbf{k})$      (b) $\mathbf{r} = \mathbf{i} + 2\mathbf{k} + \lambda(2\mathbf{i} + \mathbf{j} - \mathbf{k})$

(c) $\mathbf{r} = -2\mathbf{i} + 3\mathbf{k} + \mu(5\mathbf{i} + 4\mathbf{j} - 2\mathbf{k})$      (d) $\mathbf{r} = \mathbf{i} + \mathbf{j} + \chi(3\mathbf{i} + \mathbf{j} - \mathbf{k})$

**\*9** Show that the planes $P_1: \mathbf{r}.(2\mathbf{i} + 3\mathbf{j} - \mathbf{k}) = 7$ and $P_2: \mathbf{r}.(4\mathbf{i} + 6\mathbf{j} - 2\mathbf{k}) = 7$ are parallel and find the distance between them.

**10** Show that the line $\mathbf{r} = 2\mathbf{i} + \mathbf{k} + \lambda(2\mathbf{i} + 2\mathbf{j} - \mathbf{k})$ is parallel to the plane $2x - y + 2z = 5$ and find the distance between the line and the plane.

**11** The Cartesian equations of a line and a plane are:

$$\ell: \frac{x-2}{c} = \frac{y-2}{2} = \frac{3-z}{2}$$

$$P: 4x - y + z = 5$$

Find a value for $c$ given that:

(a) $\ell$ and $P$ are parallel, (b) $\ell$ and $P$ are perpendicular.

**12** Find the acute angle between the normals to the planes

$$P_1: \mathbf{r}.(2\mathbf{i} - 2\mathbf{j} - \mathbf{k}) = 6 \quad \text{and} \quad P_2: \mathbf{r}.(6\mathbf{i} - 2\mathbf{j} + 3\mathbf{k}) = 14$$

**13** (a) Find a vector equation for the line which passes through the point $(-2, 3, -2)$ and is normal to the plane $4x - 2y + z = 5$.
(b) Find the point of intersection of the line and the plane.

**14** (a) Find the Cartesian equation of a plane which passes through the point $(2, 3, -1)$ and whose normal is parallel to the line

$$\mathbf{r} = 5\mathbf{i} - 2\mathbf{j} + 4\mathbf{k} + \lambda(3\mathbf{i} + \mathbf{j} + \mathbf{k})$$

(b) Find the point of intersection of the line and the plane.

**15** Find a Cartesian equation for the plane which contains the lines

$$\mathbf{r} = \mathbf{i} + \mathbf{j} + 2\mathbf{k} + \lambda(4\mathbf{i} + 4\mathbf{k}) \quad \text{and} \quad \mathbf{r} = 3\mathbf{i} + \mathbf{j} + 4\mathbf{k} + \mu(10\mathbf{i} - 4\mathbf{j} + 3\mathbf{k})$$

Hence find the distance of the plane from the origin.

**16** Show that the line of intersection of the planes

$$P_1: \mathbf{r}.\begin{pmatrix} 1 \\ -1 \\ 2 \end{pmatrix} = 7 \quad \text{and} \quad P_2: \mathbf{r}.\begin{pmatrix} 3 \\ -4 \\ 4 \end{pmatrix} = 6$$

is $\mathbf{r} = (-2 + 4\lambda)\mathbf{i} + (3 + 2\lambda)\mathbf{j} + (6 - \lambda)\mathbf{k}$.

### Advanced

**1** The position vectors of three points $A$, $B$, $C$ on a plane ski-slope are
$\mathbf{a} = 4\mathbf{i} + 2\mathbf{j} - \mathbf{k}$, $\mathbf{b} = -2\mathbf{i} + 26\mathbf{j} + 11\mathbf{k}$, $\mathbf{c} = 16\mathbf{i} + 17\mathbf{j} + 2\mathbf{k}$, where the units
are in metres.
  (i)  Show that the vector $2\mathbf{i} - 3\mathbf{j} + 7\mathbf{k}$ is perpendicular to $\overrightarrow{AB}$ and also
       perpendicular to $\overrightarrow{AC}$. Hence find the equation of the plane of the ski-
       slope.
The track for an overhead railway lies along the straight edge $DEF$,
where $D$ and $E$ have position vectors $\mathbf{d} = 130\mathbf{i} - 40\mathbf{j} + 20\mathbf{k}$ and
$\mathbf{e} = 90\mathbf{i} - 20\mathbf{j} + 15\mathbf{k}$, and $F$ is a point on the ski-slope.
  (ii)  Find the equation of the straight line $DE$.
  (iii) Find the position vector of the point $F$.
  (iv)  Show that $\overrightarrow{DF} = 15(-8\mathbf{i} + 4\mathbf{j} - \mathbf{k})$ and hence find the length of the
        track.
[OCR (MEI)]

**2** Within an oil refinery there are two
straight pipelines, $\ell$ joining
$A(-1, 5, -7)$ and $B(3, -1, -7)$ and $\ell'$
joining $C(0, 4, -5)$ and $D(2, -2, -5)$.
(Neglect the diameters of the
pipelines.) It is required to connect $\ell$,
$\ell'$ by a continuous straight link $OEF$
to a station at $O(0, 0, 0)$.
  (i)  Verify that $A$, $B$ lie on the
       plane $\pi$ with equation
       $3x + 2y + z = 0$.
  (ii) Find the parametric vector
       equation of $CD$.
  (iii) If $CD$ meets $\pi$ in $E$, find the
        coordinates of $E$.

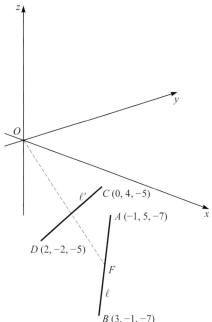

(iv) Explain geometrically why the lines $AB$, $OE$ must intersect, and show that they do so at the point $F(\frac{7}{5}, \frac{7}{5}, -7)$.

(v) Find the angle between the line $OEF$ and the line $AB$.

[OCR (SMP), 1984]

**3** Two points $A$ and $B$ have position vectors $2\mathbf{i} - \mathbf{j} + 2\mathbf{k}$, $4\mathbf{j} + 3\mathbf{k}$ respectively, relative to an origin $O$. The point $C$ divides $AB$ internally in the ratio $\lambda : 1 - \lambda$.

(a) Find the angle $AOB$.

(b) Find the area of triangle $OAB$.

(c) Find the position vector of the point $C$ on $AB$, whose distance from $O$ is $\sqrt{17}$.

(d) Find the perpendicular distance of $O$ from the line $AB$.

**4** Two planes through the origin have equations

(i) $x\cos\alpha + z\sin\alpha = 0$,     (ii) $y\sin\alpha + z\cos\alpha = 0$

where $\alpha$ is an acute angle. Describe them geometrically, in the form 'The plane through the ... -axis, making an angle $\alpha$ with the plane ... $= 0$', each blank being filled by one of the letters $x$, $y$ or $z$.

Write down unit normal vectors to each of the planes. By finding the angle between these vectors, prove that the acute angle $\beta$ between the planes is given by

$$\cos\beta = \tfrac{1}{2}\sin 2\alpha$$

[OCR (SMP), 1984]

**5** The lines $\ell_1$ and $\ell_2$ have equations

$$\mathbf{r} = \begin{pmatrix} 1 \\ 4 \\ 8 \end{pmatrix} + t\begin{pmatrix} 2 \\ 2 \\ 1 \end{pmatrix} \quad \text{and} \quad \mathbf{r} = \begin{pmatrix} 0 \\ 3 \\ 0 \end{pmatrix} + s\begin{pmatrix} 1 \\ 3 \\ -2 \end{pmatrix}$$

respectively. Show that $\ell_1$ and $\ell_2$ are skew. The point $A$ has position vector $\begin{pmatrix} -3 \\ 0 \\ 6 \end{pmatrix}$, and $O$ is the origin. Show that $A$ lies on $\ell_1$, and that $\overrightarrow{OA}$ is perpendicular to $\ell_1$. Show also that the line through $O$ and $A$ intersects $\ell_2$. Denoting the point of intersection by $B$, find the position vector of the reflection of $B$ in $\ell_1$.

[OCR (Cambridge)]

**6** The plane $p$ has equation $3x + 2y - z + 1 = 0$ and the line $\ell$ has Cartesian equations

$$\frac{x - 4}{-1} = \frac{y + 3}{2} = \frac{z - 7}{1}$$

Show that $\ell$ lies in $p$.

The line $m$ has vector equation

$$\mathbf{r} = \begin{pmatrix} 0 \\ 10 \\ 7 \end{pmatrix} + t \begin{pmatrix} 1 \\ 3 \\ 2 \end{pmatrix}$$

and $m$ intersects $p$ at the point $A$. Find the coordinates of $A$.

Write down the Cartesian equation of the plane passing through $A$ and perpendicular to $\ell$. By finding where this plane intersects $\ell$, or otherwise, find a vector equation for the line through $A$ which lies in $p$ and is perpendicular to $\ell$.

[OCR (Cambridge), 1989]

7  $A$ and $B$ are points relative to an origin $O$ such that

$$\overrightarrow{OA} = \begin{pmatrix} 1 \\ 2 \\ 2 \end{pmatrix}, \qquad \overrightarrow{OB} = \begin{pmatrix} 8 \\ 1 \\ 4 \end{pmatrix}$$

Find the vector equation of the line bisecting angle $AOB$.

8  Three lines $\ell_1$, $\ell_2$ and $\ell_3$ have equations

$$\ell_1: \mathbf{r} = \begin{pmatrix} 15 \\ 1 \\ 32 \end{pmatrix} + s \begin{pmatrix} -20 \\ 12 \\ 9 \end{pmatrix}, \quad \ell_2: \mathbf{r} = \begin{pmatrix} 35 \\ 19 \\ -17 \end{pmatrix} + t \begin{pmatrix} 0 \\ 3 \\ -4 \end{pmatrix},$$

$$\ell_3: \mathbf{r} = \begin{pmatrix} 20 \\ 3 \\ -29 \end{pmatrix} + u \begin{pmatrix} 15 \\ 16 \\ 12 \end{pmatrix}$$

where $s$, $t$ and $u$ are scalar parameters.

(i)  Show that each line is perpendicular to each of the other two lines.

(ii)  Show that $\ell_2$ intersects both $\ell_1$ and $\ell_3$, and state the coordinates of $A$ and $B$, the points of intersection.

(iii)  Show that the length of $AB$ is 50 units.

(iv)  A cube has $AB$ as one of its edges, and has two other edges along $\ell_1$ and $\ell_3$. There are four possible positions for the centre $C$ of the cube. Show that the origin is one possible position for $C$, and find another possible position.

[OCR (Cambridge), 1997]

9  $ABC$ is a triangle whose vertices have position vectors $\mathbf{a}$, $\mathbf{b}$, $\mathbf{c}$ respectively, relative to an origin in the plane $ABC$.

Show that an arbitrary point $P$ on the segment $AB$ has position vector $\rho\mathbf{a} + \sigma\mathbf{b}$, where $\rho \geq 0$, $\sigma \geq 0$ and $\rho + \sigma = 1$.

Give a similar expression for an arbitrary point on the segment $PC$, and deduce that any point inside $ABC$ has position vector $\lambda\mathbf{a} + \mu\mathbf{b} + \nu\mathbf{c}$, where $\lambda \geq 0$, $\mu \geq 0$, $\nu \geq 0$ and $\lambda + \mu + \nu = 1$.

Sketch the region of the plane in which the point $\lambda\mathbf{a} + \mu\mathbf{b} + \nu\mathbf{c}$ lies in each of the following cases:

(i) $\lambda + \mu + \nu = -1$, $\lambda \leq 0$, $\mu \leq 0$, $\nu \leq 0$;

(ii) $\lambda + \mu + \nu = 1$, $\nu \leq 0$, $\mu \leq 0$.

[OCR (STEP), 1987]

**10** (i) The points $A$, $B$, $C$ have position vectors $\mathbf{a}$, $\mathbf{b}$, $\mathbf{c}$ (relative to some origin $O$). Given that there exist non-zero scalars $\lambda$, $\mu$, $\nu$ such that $\lambda\mathbf{a} + \mu\mathbf{b} + \nu\mathbf{c} = \mathbf{0}$ and $\lambda + \mu + \nu = 0$, prove that $A$, $B$, $C$ are collinear.

(ii) The three circles shown in the diagram have centres $P_1$, $P_2$, $P_3$ and (unequal) radii $r_1$, $r_2$, $r_3$. The three pairs of exterior tangents meet at $L_1$, $L_2$, $L_3$. Show that, if $P_1$, $P_2$, $P_3$ have position vectors $\mathbf{p}_1$, $\mathbf{p}_2$, $\mathbf{p}_3$, then $L_1$ has position vector

$$\frac{r_2\mathbf{p}_3 - r_3\mathbf{p}_2}{r_2 - r_3}$$

Find similar expressions for the position vectors of $L_2$ and $L_3$, and deduce that $L_1$, $L_2$, $L_3$ are collinear.

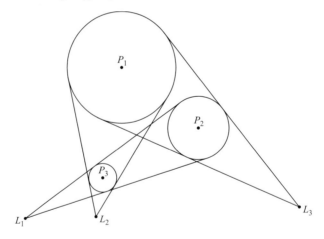

[OCR (SMP), 1979]

## Revision

**1** State whether the following pairs of lines are parallel, intersecting or skew.

(a) $\mathbf{r} = 3\mathbf{i} + 2\mathbf{j} - \mathbf{k} + \lambda(2\mathbf{i} + \mathbf{j} + 4\mathbf{k})$
$\mathbf{r} = 3\mathbf{i} + \mathbf{k} + \mu(-2\mathbf{i} + \mathbf{j} + 5\mathbf{k})$

(b) $\mathbf{r} = 3\mathbf{i} + \mathbf{k} + \lambda(\mathbf{i} + 4\mathbf{k})$
$\mathbf{r} = 2\mathbf{i} + \mathbf{j} + 5\mathbf{k} + \mu(3\mathbf{i} + 12\mathbf{k})$

(c) $\mathbf{r} = \mathbf{j} + \mathbf{k} + \lambda(2\mathbf{i} - 2\mathbf{j} + \mathbf{k})$
$\mathbf{r} = 3\mathbf{i} - \mathbf{k} + \mu(2\mathbf{i} + 2\mathbf{j} - 6\mathbf{k})$

**2**  Find the angle between the lines

$$\mathbf{r} = (2 + 6\lambda)\mathbf{i} + (1 - 3\lambda)\mathbf{j} + 2\lambda\mathbf{k} \quad \text{and} \quad \mathbf{r} = (2 + 4\mu)\mathbf{i} + 7\mathbf{j} + (5 + 3\mu)\mathbf{k}$$

**3**  (a)  Find Cartesian equations for the line $\mathbf{r} = (2 - 3\lambda)\mathbf{i} + (4 + 2\lambda)\mathbf{j} + \lambda\mathbf{k}$.

(b)  Find a vector equation for the line $\dfrac{x - 2}{4} = 1 - y = \dfrac{z}{3}$.

**4**  Lines $\ell_1$ and $\ell_2$ have Cartesian equations

$$\frac{x + 2}{4} = y = \frac{z - 1}{2} \quad \text{and} \quad \frac{x}{2} = \frac{y + 1}{2} = 4 - z \quad \text{respectively}$$

Find the position vector of the point of intersection of $\ell_1$ and $\ell_2$.

**5**  $A$ and $B$ have coordinates $(2, 3, 1)$ and $(6, -1, 5)$ respectively. The perpendicular bisector of the line $AB$ is in the direction of $2\mathbf{i} + 3\mathbf{j} - \mathbf{k}$. Find the point of intersection of the perpendicular bisector and the plane $x = 2$.

**6**  $P$ and $Q$ have position vectors $2\mathbf{i} + \mathbf{j} - 3\mathbf{k}$ and $7\mathbf{i} - 9\mathbf{j} + 7\mathbf{k}$ respectively. The line $\mathbf{r} = 8\mathbf{i} - 2\mathbf{j} + \lambda(4\mathbf{i} + \mathbf{j} - \mathbf{k})$ intersects $PQ$ at point $X$. Show that $X$ divides $PQ$ internally in the ratio $2:3$.

**7**  A plane passes through the points $A(3, 2, -1)$, $B(2, 1, 3)$ and $C(3, -1, 0)$. Find a vector equation for the plane:

(a)  in parametric form, (b) in scalar product form.

**8**  For each of the following planes, find:

(i)   a unit vector normal to the plane,
(ii)  the distance of the plane from the origin.

(a)  $4x - 5y + 7z = 10$
(b)  $\mathbf{r} = 4\mathbf{i} + \mathbf{j} - \mathbf{k} + \lambda(3\mathbf{i} + \mathbf{j} - 2\mathbf{k}) + \mu(5\mathbf{i} - \mathbf{k})$

**9**  State whether the following lines are parallel to, intersect or lie within the plane $\mathbf{r}.(2\mathbf{i} - 2\mathbf{j} - \mathbf{k}) = 6$.

(a)  $\mathbf{r} = 5\mathbf{i} + \mathbf{j} + 2\mathbf{k} + \lambda(2\mathbf{i} + \mathbf{j} + 2\mathbf{k})$  (b)  $\mathbf{r} = 3\mathbf{i} - \mathbf{k} + \mu(2\mathbf{i} + \mathbf{j} + 3\mathbf{k})$
(c)  $\mathbf{r} = 2\mathbf{i} + \mathbf{j} - \mathbf{k} + \varphi(5\mathbf{i} + 2\mathbf{j} + 6\mathbf{k})$  (d)  $\mathbf{r} = 4\mathbf{i} + 2\mathbf{k} + \chi(\mathbf{i} - \mathbf{j} + 4\mathbf{k})$

**10**  Show that the planes

$$P_1\colon 7x - y + 5z = 6 \quad \text{and} \quad P_2\colon 14x - 2y + 10z = 9$$

are parallel, and find the distance between them.

**11**  Find a Cartesian equation for the plane which passes through the point $(2, 1, 0)$ and is parallel to the lines $\mathbf{r} = 2\mathbf{i} + \mathbf{j} - \mathbf{k} + \lambda(3\mathbf{i} + 2\mathbf{j} - \mathbf{k})$ and $\mathbf{r} = 3\mathbf{i} - \mathbf{k} + \mu(2\mathbf{i} + 2\mathbf{j} + \mathbf{k})$. Hence find the distance of the plane from the origin.

**12** The line $\mathbf{r} = 2\mathbf{i} + b\mathbf{j} - 3\mathbf{k} + \lambda(a\mathbf{i} + 2\mathbf{k})$ is contained within the plane $\mathbf{r}.(3\mathbf{i} + \mathbf{j} - 6\mathbf{k}) = 25$. Find the values of $a$ and $b$.

# 4

# Functions

## 4.1 Definitions of functions involving formulae and domains; ranges of functions; graphical representation of functions; composition of functions; inverse functions

The graph of $y = f^{-1}(x)$ is the reflection of the graph of $y = f(x)$ in the line $y = x$.

**Basic**

**1** The function f is defined by

$$f(x) = x^2 - 3, \quad x \in \mathbb{R}$$

Calculate the values of $f(x)$ when:

(a) $x = 4$    (b) $x = 1.5$    (c) $x = -2$    (d) $x = t$

**2** The function g is defined by the rule

$$g(x) = \frac{x}{3x - 2}$$

(a) Evaluate    (i) g(0)    (ii) g(1)    (iii) g(−1).
(b) For what value of $x$ is g($x$) undefined?
(c) Solve the equation g($x$) = $x$.

**3** The functions f and g are defined by

$$f(x) = 3x + 2, \quad x \in \mathbb{R}$$

$$g(x) = 2 - 3x, \quad x \in \mathbb{R}$$

Evaluate:

*(a) fg(2)    (b) gf(2)    (c) ff(−2)    (d) gg(0)

**4** The function f is defined by

$$f(x) = 3x - 4, \quad x \in \mathbb{R}$$

Solve:

*(a) f($x$) = 8    (b) f($x$) = −1    (c) f($x$) = 0    (d) f($x$) = $\frac{1}{2}$

**5** Sketch the graph of each of the following functions.

(a) $f(x) = 2x - 3, x \in \mathbb{R}$  (b) $f(x) = x^2 - 1, x \in \mathbb{R}, x \geq 0$
(c) $g(\theta) = \sin \theta, \theta \in \mathbb{R}, 0 \leq \theta \leq 2\pi$  (d) $h(t) = 2^t, t \in \mathbb{R}$

**6** State the range for each of the following functions.

(a) $f(x) = x^2 - 1, x \in \mathbb{R}$  (b) $f(\theta) = 4 \sin \theta, \theta \in \mathbb{R}$
(c) $g(x) = 2, x \in \mathbb{R}$  (d) $h(t) = \dfrac{1}{t}, t \in \mathbb{R}, t \neq 0$

**7** For each of the following, state the largest domain for which the function is defined.

(a) $f(x) = x^2 - 1$  (b) $f(t) = \dfrac{t + 3}{t + 4}$  (c) $g(x) = \sqrt{x + 3}$
(d) $h(z) = \sqrt[3]{z + 3}$

**8** (a) If $f(x) = 3x + 2$ and $g(x) = 2x - 3$, obtain and simplify the formulae
for:  *(i) $fg(x)$  (ii) $gf(x)$  (iii) $gg(x)$
(b) If $h(x) = 2 - x$
(i) obtain the formula for $hh(x)$,
(ii) explain why the function h is called self-inverse.

**9** $f(x)$ is defined by $f(x) = 5 - x, x \in \mathbb{R}, x > 0$.

(a) State the range of $f(x)$.
(b) Sketch the graph of $|f(x)|$ and hence state the range of $|f(x)|$.
(c) Solve the equation $|f(x)| = 4$.

**10** (a) If $f(x) = x^2 - 3$ and $g(x) = x + 3$, find:
*(i) $fg(x)$  (ii) $gf(x)$

*(b) If $f(x) = \dfrac{x + 1}{x - 2}$ and $g(x) = x + 2$, find the following, simplifying your answers.
(i) $fg(x)$  (ii) $gf(x)$
(c) If $f(x) = \ln x$ and $g(x) = e^{x+1}$, find:
(i) $fg(x)$  (ii) $gf(x)$

**11** For each of the following functions $f(x)$, find the rule for the inverse function $f^{-1}(x)$.

*(a) $f(x) = 3x + 2$  (b) $f(x) = \dfrac{1}{x + 5}$

*(c) $f(x) = \dfrac{x + 3}{2 + x}$  (d) $f(x) = 1 + \ln x$

**12** $f(x) = x^2 + 1, x \in \mathbb{R}, x \geq 0$.

(a) Write down the range for $f(x)$.
(b) Obtain a formula for $f^{-1}(x)$.
(c) Write down the domain and range for $f^{-1}(x)$.

**Intermediate**

**1**   The function f is defined by

$$f(x) = x^2 - 4x - 5, \quad x \in \mathbb{R}$$

Sketch the graph of f(x) and indicate on your graph the solutions of f(x) = 0.

**2**   The function h is defined by

$$h(x) = 1 - 2^{-x}, \quad x \in \mathbb{R}, x \geq 0$$

Sketch the graph of h(x).

**3**   The functions f and g are defined as

$$f(\theta) = \theta \qquad\qquad \theta \in \mathbb{R}, 0 \leq \theta \leq 2\pi$$
$$g(\theta) = 2\cos\theta \qquad \theta \in \mathbb{R}, 0 \leq \theta \leq 2\pi$$

Sketch, on the same axes, the graphs of:
(a)  f(θ)      (b)  g(θ)      (c)  f(θ) + g(θ)

**4**   The functions f and g are defined by

$$f(x) = x^2 - 6, \quad x \in \mathbb{R}; \qquad g(x) = x - 4, \quad x \in \mathbb{R}$$

Solve:
(a)  f(x) = g(x)      (b)  fg(x) = g(x)

**5**   The functions f and g are defined by

$$f(x) = x^2 - 3, \quad x \in \mathbb{R}; \qquad g(x) = x + 3, \quad x \in \mathbb{R}$$

(a)  Obtain the formula for the function gf(x).
(b)  State the range for each of the following functions.
      (i)  f(x)      (ii)  g(x)      (iii)  gf(x)

**6**   The formulae for functions f and g are defined by

$$f(x) = x^2 + 2, \quad g(x) = \sqrt{3 - x}$$

(a)  State the largest possible domain for:
      (i)  f(x)      (ii)  g(x)
(b)  State the largest possible domain and corresponding range for gf(x).

**7**   The formulae for functions f and g are defined by

$$f(x) = \frac{x + 3}{x - 4}, \quad g(x) = \frac{x - 1}{x + 2}$$

(a)  Show that $gf(x) = \dfrac{7}{3x - 5}$.

(b)  State the largest possible domain and corresponding range for:
   (i) f(x)    (ii) g(x)    (iii) gf(x)

**8**  The formulae for functions f and g are defined by

$$f(\theta) = 3\cos\theta, \quad g(\theta) = 2^{\theta}$$

Obtain the formula, define a valid domain and corresponding range for:
(a) gf(θ)    (b) fg(θ)

**9**  The formulae for functions f and g are given as

$$f(x) = x^2 + 5, \quad g(x) = \sqrt{x - 5}$$

Obtain the formula, define a valid domain and corresponding range for:
(a) gf(x)    (b) fg(x)

**10**  The function f is defined by

$$f(x) = (x + 1)^2, \quad x \in \mathbb{R}, x \geq -1$$

Calculate the value of:
(a)  $f^{-1}(16)$    (b)  $f^{-1}(0)$    (c)  $f^{-1}(x)$

**11**  The functions f, g and h are defined by

$$f(x) = 2 - 3x, \quad x \in \mathbb{R}; \quad g(x) = 1 - x, \quad x \in \mathbb{R};$$

$$h(x) = \frac{2 - x}{3}, \quad x \in \mathbb{R}$$

(a)  Show that (i) fg(x) = gf(x), (ii) fh(x) = hf(x).
(b)  Does gh(x) = hg(x)?

**12**  If $f(x) = \dfrac{x + 1}{x - 2}$,

(a)  show that $f(x) = 1 + \dfrac{3}{x - 2}$,

(b)  write down a valid domain and range for f(x),

(c)  show that $f^{-1}(x) = \dfrac{1 + 2x}{x - 1}$,

(d)  write down a valid domain and range for $f^{-1}(x)$.

**13**  Functions g(x) and h(x) are defined by

$$g(x) = 2 - 3x, \quad x \in \mathbb{R}$$

$$h(x) = \frac{1}{x}, \quad x \in \mathbb{R}, x \neq 0$$

The function $f(x)$ is defined by $f(x) = gh(x)$, $x \in \mathbb{R}$, $x \neq 0$.

(a)  Sketch the graph of $f(x)$.
(b)  Write down expressions for:
    (i)  $g^{-1}(x)$    (ii)  $h^{-1}(x)$    (iii)  $h^{-1}(g^{-1}(x))$    (iv)  $f^{-1}(x)$

**14** The functions $f$ and $g$ are defined by
$$f(x) = \sin 2x, \quad x \in \mathbb{R}, 0 \leq x \leq \tfrac{1}{6}\pi$$
$$g(x) = 2 \ln x, \quad x \in \mathbb{R}^+$$

Find, stating the rule and domain:
(a)  $f^{-1}(x)$    (b)  $g^{-1}(x)$    (c)  $gf(x)$

**15** The function $f(x)$ is defined by
$$f(x) = x^2 - 6x + 13, \quad x \in \mathbb{R}, x \geq 3$$

Obtain the inverse function $f^{-1}(x)$, stating its domain and range.

**16** The function $g(x)$ is defined by
$$g(x) = e^{-2x}, \quad x \in \mathbb{R}$$

Obtain the inverse function $g^{-1}(x)$.

## Advanced

**1**  $f(x)$ is an even function, with period 4 and has domain $\mathbb{R}$. For $0 \leq x \leq 2$, $f(x) = 2 - x$.

(a)  Draw the graph of $f(x)$ over the interval $-6 \leq x \leq 6$.
(b)  Write down the equation of $f(x)$ for:
    (i)  $-2 \leq x \leq 0$    (ii)  $2 \leq x \leq 4$    (iii)  $100 \leq x \leq 102$

**2**  (a)  The function $f(x) = [x]$ denotes the greatest integer not exceeding $x$, for example $[2.8] = 2$, $[5] = 5$ and $[-3.4] = 4$.
    (i)  Sketch the graph of $f(x)$, $x \in \mathbb{R}$.
    (ii)  State the range of $f(x)$.
    (iii)  If $g(x) = x - [x]$, sketch the graph of $g(x)$, $x \in \mathbb{R}$.
    (iv)  Solve the equation $f(x) = g(x)$.
    (v)  Solve the equation $fg(x) = gf(x)$.
    (vi)  Evaluate $\int_0^a f(x)\,dx$, where $a \in \mathbb{Z}$.

(b)  The function $m(x) = \max(1, x)$ denotes the maximum of numbers 1 and $x$. Find $\int_0^5 m(x)\,dx$.

**3**  $f(x) = 1 + \sqrt{x}$, $x \in \mathbb{R}$, $x \geq 0$.

(a)  On the same axes, sketch the graphs of $y = f(x)$ and $y = f^{-1}(x)$. State the number of roots of the equation $f(x) = f^{-1}(x)$.
(b)  Solve the equation $f(x) = f^{-1}(x)$.

**4** (a) $h(x) = 2^x$, $x \in \mathbb{R}$. Write down $h^{-1}(x)$.

(b) $f(x) = \ln(1 - \frac{1}{9}x^2)$, $x \in \mathbb{R}$, $0 \leq x < a$. State the largest possible value for $a$ and the corresponding range for $f(x)$.

(c) $g(x) = \sqrt{1 - e^{-x}}$. State the largest possible domain of $g(x)$ and sketch the graph of $y = g(x)$.

**5** $f(x)$ is defined by

$$f(x) = \left| \frac{2x}{x - 3} \right|, \qquad x \in \mathbb{R}, x \neq 3$$

(a) State the range of $f(x)$.

(b) Show algebraically that:

   (i) $x > 3 \Rightarrow f(x) > 2$

   (ii) $x < 0 \Rightarrow f(x) < 2$

(c) Sketch the graph of $f(x)$.

**6** (a) The function f is defined for $x > 1$ by $f(x) = 3x^2 - 6x + 2$.

   (i) By considering the derivative of $f(x)$, show that the inverse function $f^{-1}$ exists.

   (ii) Obtain an expression for $f^{-1}(x)$ and state the domain of $f^{-1}$.

   (iii) Sketch f and $f^{-1}$ on the same axes.

   (iv) State the geometrical relationship between the graphs of f, $f^{-1}$ and the line $y = x$. Use this to find the coordinates of the point of intersection of the graphs of f and $f^{-1}$.

(b) A further function g is defined for $x > 5$ by

$$g(x) = \frac{1}{x - 5}$$

   (i) Find an expression for $gf(x)$.

   (ii) Given that the domain for gf is $x > k$, find the smallest possible value of $k$.

[WJEC, 1994]

**7** $f(x)$ is defined by $f(x) = (x - 2)^2 + 1$, $x \in \mathbb{R}$, $x \geq 2$.

(a) On a single diagram, sketch the graphs of $y = f(x)$, $y = f^{-1}(x)$ and $y = ff^{-1}(x)$.

$g(x)$ is defined by $g(x) = \sqrt{x - 1}$, $x \in \mathbb{R}$.

(b) Find $gf(x)$ for $x \geq 2$.

$h(x)$ is defined by $h(x) = px + q$, $x \in \mathbb{R}$, $p$, $q$ constant.

(c) If $fh(x) = 25x^2 + 20x + 5$, $x \in \mathbb{R}$, $x \geq r$, find the values of $p$, $q$ and $r$.

**8** The functions f, g are defined by

$$f(x) = x^2 + 1 \quad (x \geq 0) \quad \text{and} \quad g(x) = e^{-x} \quad (x \geq 0).$$

(a)  State the ranges of f and g.
(b)  Find expressions for $f^{-1}(x)$ and $g^{-1}(x)$.
(c)  Find an expression for $fg(x)$ and hence solve the equation

$$3fg(x) = 4g(x) + 2$$

(d)

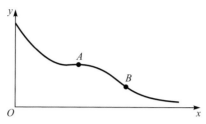

The figure shows a sketch graph of the function h defined by
$h(x) = f(x)g(x)$. Find the $x$ coordinates of the points of inflexion
$A$ and $B$.
[WJEC, 1995]

**9**  The functions $f(x)$ and $g(x)$ are defined by

$$f(x) = \sqrt{3 + x} - x, \quad g(x) = \ln x$$

Find the set of values of $x$ for which $gf(x)$ exists.

**10**  The function $f(x)$ is defined by

$$f(x) = \frac{2x - 3}{x^2 - 3x + 2} \quad (x \text{ is real and } x \neq 1, x \neq 2)$$

Express $f(x)$ in partial fractions.
Sketch the graph given by the equation $y = f(x)$.
Determine an interval in $x$ for which the function f has a unique inverse
g defined for all real values of $x$, and find an expression for that inverse.
[OCR (Cambridge), 1973]

## Revision

**1**  The function $g(x)$ is defined by

$$g(x) = \sqrt{1 - x^2}, \quad x \in \mathbb{R}, -1 \leq x \leq 1$$

Calculate:

(a)  $g(1)$     (b)  $g(0)$     (c)  $g\left(\dfrac{\sqrt{3}}{2}\right)$

**2**  The functions f and g are defined by

$$f(x) = e^x, \quad x \in \mathbb{R}; \quad g(x) = \ln\left(\frac{1}{x}\right), x \in \mathbb{R}^+$$

(a) Calculate the values of:

   (i) gf(0)　　　(ii) gf(5)

(b) Find an expression for gf($x$).

**3**　The function h($\theta$) is defined by

$$h(\theta) = \sin\theta, \quad \theta \in \mathbb{R}, 0 \le \theta \le 2\pi$$

Calculate the values of $\theta$ when:

(a) h($\theta$) = 1　　　(b) h($\theta$) = $\frac{1}{2}$

**4**　The function g($x$) is defined by

$$g(x) = x + \frac{1}{x}, \quad x \in \mathbb{R}^+$$

Sketch the graph of the function g($x$).

**5**　The function f($x$) is defined by f($x$) = $\sqrt{1 - 2x}$. State the largest possible domain for the function f($x$).

**6**　The function h($x$) is illustrated below. Write down a possible formula and domain which define h($x$).

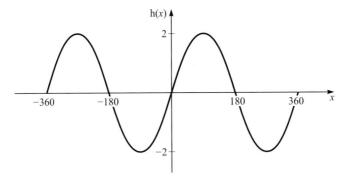

**7**　The function g($x$) is defined by

$$g(x) = \sqrt{1 - e^x}, \quad x \in \mathbb{R}, x \le 0$$

State the range of the function g($x$).

**8**　The functions f and g are defined by

$$f(x) = 3x + 4, \quad x \in \mathbb{R}; \qquad g(x) = 1 - x^2, \quad x \in \mathbb{R}$$

Write down the formula, domain and range of:

(a) fg($x$)　　　(b) gf($x$)

**9** The functions g and h are defined by

$$g(x) = \sqrt{x - 4}, \quad x \in \mathbb{R}, x > 4; \qquad h(x) = \sqrt{1 - x^2}, x \in \mathbb{R}, -1 \le x \le 1$$

State the domain and range for the function hg(x).

**10** The function f(x) is defined by

$$f(x) = \frac{x + 1}{3}, \quad x \in \mathbb{R}$$

Obtain a rule and domain for the inverse function $f^{-1}(x)$.

**11** The function g(x) is defined by

$$g(x) = (x^2 - 4)^{-1}, \quad x \in \mathbb{R}^+, x \ne 2$$

Obtain a rule and domain for the inverse function $g^{-1}(x)$.

**12** The function h(x) is defined by

$$h(x) = \frac{x - 4}{x + 1}, \quad x \in \mathbb{R}, x \ne -1$$

Obtain a formula for:

(a) hh(x)     (b) $h^{-1}(x)$

## 4.2    Algebraic and geometric properties of simple transformations including $f(x) + a, f(x + a), af(x), f(ax)$; composition of transformations up to and including $af(bx + c) + d$

The graph of $y = af(x)$ is the graph of $y = f(x)$, stretched by scale factor $a$ parallel to the $y$-axis.
The graph of $y = f(ax)$ is the graph of $y = f(x)$, stretched

by a scale factor $\dfrac{1}{a}$ parallel to the $x$-axis.

The graph of $y = f(x) + a$ is the graph of $y = f(x)$,

translated by $\begin{pmatrix} 0 \\ a \end{pmatrix}$.

The graph of $y = f(x + a)$ is the graph of $y = f(x)$,

translated by $\begin{pmatrix} -a \\ 0 \end{pmatrix}$.

## Basic

**1** The function $f(x) = x^2$ is illustrated below.

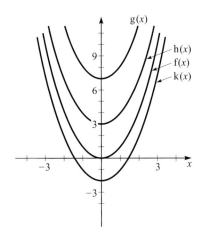

g(x), h(x) and k(x) are translations of f(x).

(a) Write down the formula for:

    (i) g(x)     (ii) h(x)     (iii) k(x)

(b) Complete the identities:
    (i) $g(x) = f(x) + \cdots$
    (ii) $h(x) = f(x) + \cdots$
    (iii) $k(x) = f(x) + \cdots$

**2** For each of the following, describe fully the transformation which maps the graph of f(x) onto the graph of g(x).

(a) $f(x) = 3x$           and   $g(x) = 3x + 2$
(b) $f(x) = (x - 2)^2$     and   $g(x) = (x - 2)^2 + 5$
(c) $f(x) = 5^x$          and   $g(x) = 5^x - 3$
(d) $f(x) = x^2 + 4x + 3$   and   $g(x) = x^2 + 4x + 1$

**3** The function $f(x) = x^3$ is illustrated below.

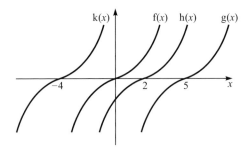

g(x), h(x) and k(x) are translations of f(x).

(a) Write down the formula for:

    (i) $g(x)$      (ii) $h(x)$      (iii) $k(x)$

(b) Write down the equation connecting:

    (i) $g(x)$ and $f(x)$      (ii) $h(x)$ and $f(x)$      (iii) $k(x)$ and $f(x)$

**\*4** (a) If $f(x) = x^2$ show that $f(x - 2) + 1 = x^2 - 4x + 5$.

    (b) Describe fully the transformation which maps $f(x)$ onto $g(x)$ where $g(x) = x^2 - 4x + 5$.

**5** The function $f(x) = 2^x$ is illustrated below.

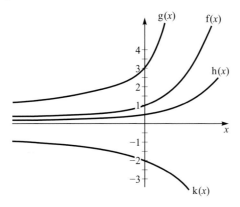

$g(x)$, $h(x)$ and $k(x)$ are one-way stretches of $f(x)$, parallel to the $y$-axis.

(a) Write down the formula for:

    (i) $g(x)$      (ii) $h(x)$      (iii) $k(x)$

(b) Express in terms of $f(x)$:

    (i) $g(x)$      (ii) $h(x)$      (iii) $k(x)$

**6** The function $f(\theta) = \sin \theta$. Sketch the graph of each of the following functions and describe fully the transformation from $f(\theta)$ onto the new function.

(a) $g(\theta) = \sin 3\theta$

(b) $h(\theta) = f(\frac{1}{2}\theta)$

(c) $k(\theta) = f(-2\theta)$

**7** The function $f(x) = |x|$. Sketch the graph of each of the following functions and describe fully the transformation from $f(x)$ onto the new function.

(a) $g(x) = 2f(x) = 2|x|$

(b) $h(x) = f(\frac{1}{2}x) = |\frac{1}{2}x|$

(c) $k(x) = -f(2x) = -|2x|$

**\*8** The functions $f(x) = x^2$ and $g(x)$ are illustrated below.

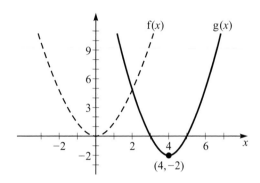

g(x) is obtained from $f(x)$ by a combination of two transformations.

(a) State these transformations.
(b) Express $g(x)$ in terms of $f(x)$.
(c) Hence show algebraically that $g(x) = 2x^2 - 16x + 30$.

**9** The functions $f(x)$, $g(x)$ and $h(x)$ are defined such that

$$g(x) = f(x + b) \quad \text{and} \quad h(x) = g(ax).$$

(a) Explain how:
   (i) the graph of $g(x)$ may be obtained from that of $f(x)$,
   (ii) the graph of $h(x)$ may be obtained from that of $g(x)$.
(b) Show that $h(x) = f(ax + b)$.
(c) Describe the sequence of transformations which maps the graph of $f(x)$ to the graph of $f(ax + b)$.
(d) Sketch the graph of $y = \sin\left(2x + \dfrac{\pi}{3}\right)$

**10** (a) Sketch the graph of:

$$\text{(i)} \quad y = \frac{1}{x} \qquad \text{(ii)} \quad y = \frac{1}{x - a} + b$$

(b) Show that $\dfrac{1}{x - a} + b = \dfrac{bx + 1 - ab}{x - a}$.

**11** $f(x) = \sqrt{4-x}$. Sketch the graph of:

(a) $y = f(x)$    (b) $y = f(-x)$    (c) $y = \frac{1}{2}\{f(x) + f(-x)\}$

**12** The diagram shows the graph of $y = f(x)$.

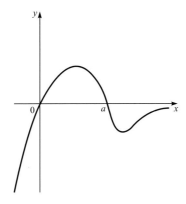

Sketch, on separate diagrams, the graph of:

(a) $y = f(x+b)$    (b) $y = f(-x)$    (c) $y = f(2x)$

## Intermediate

**1** The function $f(x)$ is illustrated below.

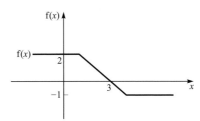

Sketch the graph of:

(a) $f(x+2)$    (b) $f(x)+2$    (c) $f(x-1)-1$

**2** The function $g(x) = x^2$ and $g(x) = f(x+2) - 1$.

(a) Sketch the graph of $f(x)$.
(b) Obtain the formula for $f(x)$.

**3**  The graph of $y = f(x)$ is shown below.

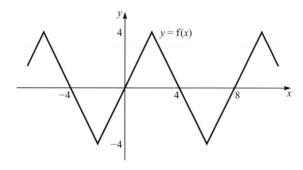

Sketch, on separate diagrams, the graphs of:

(a)  $y = f(x) + 2$      (b)  $y = f(x - 3)$      (c)  $y = f(3x)$

**4**  If $f(x) = \dfrac{2x + 3}{x + 1}$ and $g(x) = \dfrac{1}{x}$ then:

(a)  show algebraically that $f(x - 1) = g(x) + 2$,

(b)  describe fully in words the transformation which maps the graph of $f(x)$ onto the graph of $g(x)$.

**5**  Two sine waves are defined by $f(t) = \sin 2\pi t$ and $g(t) = 0.036 \sin 800\pi t$.

(a)  Sketch the graph of $f(t)$.

(b)  Express $g(t)$ in terms of $f(t)$.

(c)  Describe the transformation that maps $f(t)$ onto $g(t)$ and hence sketch the graph of $g(t)$.

(d)  Write down the equation of a sine wave which has a frequency of 200 cycles per second and an amplitude of 0.05.

**6**  The function $f(x)$ is illustrated below. If $g(x) = f(2x + 1)$, sketch the graph of $g(x)$.

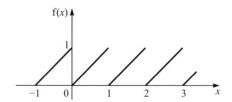

**7**  If $f(x) = 3e^{x-1}$ and $g(x) = 2e^{x+1}$, describe fully in words the transformation which maps the graph of $f(x)$ onto the graph of $g(x)$.

**8**  The function $f(x) = x^2 + 4x - 3$.

(a)  Express $f(x)$ in the form $(x + a)^2 + b$.

(b)  Sketch the graph of $y = f(x)$.

(c)  Sketch the graph of $y = \dfrac{1}{f(x)}$.

9  The function $f(x) = 8x^2 + 5x - 3$ and $g(x) = f(2x - 1)$.
Express $g(x)$ in the form $ax^2 + bx + c$.

10  The function $f(\theta) = \sin(a\theta + b)$ is illustrated below.

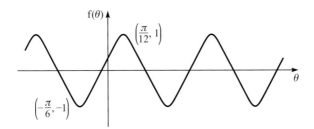

State the values of $a$ and $b$.

11  Sketch the graph of $x = a\left(1 - \cos\dfrac{\pi t}{10}\right)$ for $0 \le t \le 10$.

12  If $f(x) = \dfrac{x + 5}{x - 2} - 1$ and $g(x) = \frac{3}{7}f(3x + 2)$, obtain the formula for $g(x)$ in its simplest form.

13  If $g(x) = \frac{1}{2}f(x + 4) - 5$ and $h(x) = 2g\left(\dfrac{x}{2} - 1\right) + 3$, express $h(x)$ in terms of $f(x)$.

14  The function $f(x) = \dfrac{1}{x}$ can be mapped onto $g(x)$ by a combination of the transformations: an enlargement, parallel to the $x$-axis, scale factor $\frac{1}{2}$; an enlargement, parallel to the $y$-axis, scale factor 3; and a translation $\begin{pmatrix} -\frac{3}{2} \\ 7 \end{pmatrix}$.

(a)  Express $g(x)$ in terms of $f(x)$.

(b)  Hence show that $g(x) = \dfrac{14x + 24}{2x + 3}$.

15  Sketch $f(x) = |x + 2| + |x - 3|$. State the range of $f(x)$.

16  $f(x) = x^2$, $g(x) = x^2 - 6x + 7$ and $h(x) = f\left(\dfrac{x}{2} - 1\right) + 3$

(a)  Show that $x^2 - 6x + 7 = (x - 3)^2 - 2$ and describe fully in words the transformation which maps the graph of $g(x)$ onto the graph of $f(x)$.

(b)  Hence express $f(x)$ in terms of $g(x)$.

(c)  Hence express $h(x)$ in terms of $g(x)$ and describe fully in words the transformations which map the graph of $g(x)$ onto the graph of $h(x)$.

## Advanced

**1**  Describe fully in words the transformation which maps the graph of $f(x)$ onto the graph of $g(x)$, if

(a)  $f(x) = \ln(x+1)$ and $g(x) = \ln x + 2$

(b)  $f(x) = e^{x-1}$ and $g(x) = e^x - 2$

**2**  (a)  Express $3x + 2$ in the form $a(x-3) + b$, clearly stating the value of the constants $a$ and $b$.

(b)  Express $\dfrac{3x+2}{x-3}$ in the form $c + \dfrac{d}{x-3}$.

(c)  Sketch the graph of $y = \dfrac{3x+2}{x-3}$.

(d)  Sketch the graph of $y = \dfrac{4x+5}{x+2}$.

**3**  The function $f(x) = 4x^2 - 24x + 52$.

(a)  Express $f(x)$ in completed square form.

(b)  Show that $0 < \dfrac{1}{4x^2 - 24x + 52} \le a$, where $a$ is to be found.

**4**  The function $f(x) = 5^{2x-1}$ can be mapped onto $g(x)$ by a combination of the transformations: an enlargement, parallel to the $x$-axis, scale factor 2 followed by an enlargement, parallel to the $y$-axis, scale factor $\frac{1}{5}$; and a translation $\begin{pmatrix} -2 \\ -3 \end{pmatrix}$.

(a)  Express $g(x)$ in terms of $f(x)$.

(b)  Hence obtain, in its simplest form, the formula for $g(x)$.

**5**  (a)  The curve $y = 1/x$ is reflected in the line $x = a$. Find its equation.

(b)  The curve $y = f(x)$ is rotated by $180°$ about $(a, 0)$. Show that the equation of the resulting curve is $y = -f(2a - x)$.

**6**  Describe the transformation that maps the graph of $f(x) = ax^2 + c$ onto that of $g(x) = a(x-b)^2 + c$. Sketch the graph of $f(x)$ when:

(a)  $a > 0, c > 0$     (b)  $a > 0, c < 0$     (c)  $a < 0, c > 0$

(d)  $a < 0, c < 0$

Hence describe a simple algebraic test to determine whether $g(x) = 0$ has real, distinct roots.

7  (a)  Sketch the graph of (i) $y = \ln x$, (ii) $y = \ln(x + 3)$.
   (b)  You are given that $\int_1^5 \ln x \, dx = 4.0$ and that $\ln 2 \approx 0.7$. *Without using your calculator*, evaluate:

(i) $\displaystyle \int_{-2}^{2} \ln(2x + 6) \, dx$     (ii) $\displaystyle \int_{3}^{7} \ln(x - 2)^2 \, dx$     (iii) $\displaystyle \int_{0}^{4} \ln(ex + e) \, dx$

8  The function H is defined for all real $x$ by

$$H(x) = 0, \quad x < 0$$
$$H(x) = 1, \quad x \geq 0$$

Evaluate:

(i) $\displaystyle \int_{0}^{2} [H(x) + H(x - 1) + H(x - 2)] \, dx$

(ii) $\displaystyle \int_{0}^{n} \left[ \sum_{r=0}^{n} H(x - r) \right] dx$, where $n$ is a positive integer

[OCR (Cambridge), 1976]

9  Prove that $\int_0^{2a} f(x) \, dx = \int_0^a [f(x) + f(2a - x)] \, dx$.
   Hence, find $\int_0^\pi x \sin x \sin 3x \, dx$.

10  The function f is defined for $0 \leq x \leq \pi$ by $f(x) = 3 \sin x + \sin 3x$.

   (a)  Prove that $f(\frac{1}{2}\pi + x) = f(\frac{1}{2}\pi - x)$ and sketch the graph of f.
   (b)  The function F is defined for $-\pi \leq x \leq \pi$ by

$$F(x) = f(x), \qquad\qquad 0 \leq x \leq \tfrac{1}{2}\pi$$
$$-F(-x), \qquad -\tfrac{1}{2}\pi < x \leq 0$$
$$F(x + \pi), \qquad -\pi \leq x \leq -\tfrac{1}{2}\pi$$
$$F(x - \pi), \qquad \tfrac{1}{2}\pi < x \leq \pi$$

Sketch the graph of $F(x)$.

**Revision**

**1**   The function $f(x) = x^3$ is illustrated below.

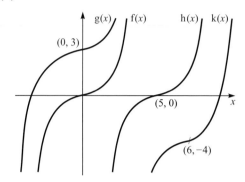

State the values of:

(a)   $a$ and $b$ if $g(x) = f(x + a) + b$
(b)   $c$ and $d$ if $h(x) = f(x + c) + d$
(c)   $s$ and $t$ if $k(x) = f(x + s) + t$

**2**   Describe fully in words the transformation which maps the graph of $f(x)$ onto the graph of $g(x)$, if:

(a)   $f(x) = \cos x$ and $g(x) = \cos\left(x - \dfrac{\pi}{3}\right)$

(b)   $g(x) = f(x) - 2$
(c)   $f(x) = x^3 + 2x - 3$ and $g(x) = (x - 2)^3 + 2x - 1$

**3**   If $f(x) = x + \dfrac{2}{x - 1}$ and $g(x) = f(x - 1) + 2$ then

(a)   describe fully in words the transformation which maps the graph of $f(x)$ onto the graph of $g(x)$,
(b)   obtain the formula for $g(x)$ in its simplest form.

**4**   The function $f(x) = x^2 - 6x + 8$ is illustrated below.

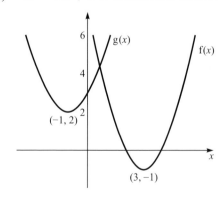

$g(x)$ is a tranlsation of $f(x)$.

(a) Describe fully the transformation which maps the graph of $f(x)$ onto the graph of $g(x)$.

(b) Find the formula for $g(x)$ in the form $x^2 + bx + c$.

5   The function $f(\theta)$ is illustrated below.

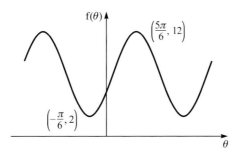

State the values of $a$, $b$ and $c$ if $f(\theta) = a\cos(\theta + b) + c$.

6   (a) Describe fully the transformations which map the graph of $f(x)$ onto the graph of $g(x)$ if:

(i)  $f(x) = \cos x$ and $g(x) = 5\cos\left(x - \dfrac{\pi}{3}\right)$

(ii) $g(x) = f(2x - 1)$

(b) $f(x) = x^3 + 2x - 3$ and $g(x) = 8x^3 + 4x - 1$.

(i)  Show that $g(x) = f(2x) + 2$.

(ii) Describe the transformation that maps $f(x)$ onto $g(x)$.

7   If $f(x) = (x + 1)(x - 2)$ and $g(x) = 2f(x - 1) + 4$ then

(a) describe fully the transformations which map the graph of $f(x)$ onto that of $g(x)$,

(b) show that $g(x) = 2(x - 1)(x - 2)$.

8   The functions $f(x)$ and $g(x)$ are illustrated below.

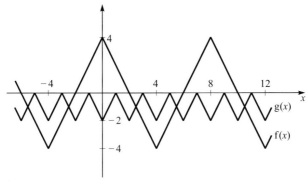

(a) Describe fully the transformation which maps the graph of $f(x)$ onto the graph of $g(x)$.

(b)  Hence express g(x) in terms of f(x).

**9** The diagram shows the graphs of $y = 3^x$ and $y = 3^{x+2}$.

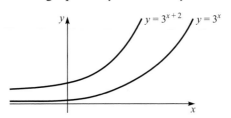

Describe two different transformations which map the graph of $y = 3^x$ onto that of $y = 3^{x+2}$.

**10** The function $f(x) = \dfrac{1}{x}$.

(a)  Sketch, on a single diagram, the graphs of:
     (i)  $y = f(x)$     (b)  $y = f(x+2)$     (iii)  $y = f(x+2)+3$

(b)  Show that $f(x+2)+3 = \dfrac{3x+7}{x+2}$.

**11** If $f(x) = \dfrac{x+3}{x+1} - 1$, find, in its simplest form:

(a)  $f(2x-1)$     (b)  $\frac{3}{2}f(3x-1)$

**12** The function $f(x) = 2^x$ can be mapped onto g(x) by a combination of the transformations: an enlargement, parallel to the x-axis, scale factor $\frac{1}{3}$; an enlargement, parallel to the y-axis, scale factor 2; and a translation $\begin{pmatrix} \frac{1}{3} \\ 0 \end{pmatrix}$.

(a)  Express g(x) in terms of f(x).
(b)  Hence show algebraically that $g(x) = 8^x$.

# 5
## Sequences

## 5.1    Inductive definition and formula for the $n$th term; recognition of periodicity, oscillation, convergence and divergence; formulae for $\sum i^k (k = 1, 2, 3)$

$$\sum_{i=1}^{n} i = \tfrac{1}{2}n(n+1) \qquad \sum_{i=1}^{n} i^2 = \tfrac{1}{6}n(n+1)(2n+1)$$

$$\sum_{i=1}^{n} i^3 = \tfrac{1}{4}n^2(n+1)^2$$

### Basic

**1**   Write down a formula for the $r$th term of each of the following sequences.

(a) $5, 9, 13, 17, \ldots$      (b) $17, 14, 11, 8, \ldots$

(c) $\tfrac{1}{3}, \tfrac{2}{5}, \tfrac{3}{7}, \tfrac{4}{9}, \ldots$      (d) $1, 7, 17, 31, 49, \ldots$

**2**   Find an inductive definition for each sequence.

(a) $1, 5, 9, 13, \ldots$      (b) $3, 4\tfrac{1}{2}, 6\tfrac{3}{4}, \ldots$      (c) $2, 4, 12, 48, 240, \ldots$

**3**   Write down the first five terms of each of the following sequences and state whether they are convergent, divergent, periodic or oscillating.

(a) $u_r = \dfrac{r+1}{r+3}$      (b) $u_1 = 3, u_{r+1} = \dfrac{3u_r}{u_r - 1}$

(c) $u_r = \cos \dfrac{r\pi}{3}$      *(d) $u_1 = 1, u_{r+1} = u_r^2 - u_r + 2$

**4**   A sequence is defined by $u_1 = 2, u_{r+1} = \dfrac{16}{u_r^2}$. Show that the sequence is divergent and oscillating.

**\*5**   Investigate and describe the sequence defined by $u_1 = 2, u_2 = 5$, $u_{r+2} = u_{r+1} + u_r$.

**6**   Evaluate:

(a) $\displaystyle\sum_{r=1}^{6} (r-2)(r+1)$    (b) $\displaystyle\sum_{r=5}^{12} r^2$    (c) $\displaystyle\sum_{r=3}^{6} \dfrac{1}{r(r-2)}$    (d) $\displaystyle\sum_{r=1}^{8} 2^{r+1}$

**7** Write out in full and evaluate:

(a) $\sum_{r=2}^{6} \frac{r+1}{r-1}$    (b) $\sum_{r=1}^{8} (2r-3)$    (c) $\sum_{r=1}^{4} (-1)^r r$

**8** Express in the form $\sum_{r=1}^{n} f(r)$:

(a) $6 + 11 + 16 + 21 + 26$    (b) $\frac{1}{3} + \frac{1}{5} + \frac{1}{7} + \frac{1}{9}$

(c) $1^2 - 2^2 + 3^2 - 4^2 + 5^2$

**9** Write out the terms of $\sum_{i=1}^{4} (-1)^{i+1} \frac{2i}{i+1} x^{2i}$.

**\*10** Find the formula for $\sum_{r=1}^{n} r(r-1)$.

**11** Show that $\sum_{r=1}^{n} (r-2)(r+3) = \frac{1}{3} n(n^2 + 3n - 16)$

**12** Find a formula for $\sum_{r=1}^{n} (8r^3 - 12r^2)$.

## Intermediate

**1** Which of the following sequences converge?

(a) $u_{r+1} = \frac{3}{4} u_r, u_1 = 4$    (b) $u_{r+1} = u_r + 0.1, u_1 = 2$

(c) $u_{r+1} = \frac{3}{u_r - 1}, u_1 = 2$    (d) $u_{r+1} = \frac{u_r}{(u_r + 1)^2}, u_1 = 1$

**2** A sequence is defined by $u_1 = 1, u_{r+1} = \frac{u_r}{u_r + 2}$.

Write down the first five terms and then find an expression for $u_n$.

**3** A sequence is obtained by using the definition $u_{r+1} = \frac{5}{u_r + 2}$. Given that $u_2 = \frac{3}{5} u_3$, find the possible values of $u_1$.

**4** A sequence is defined by $u_{r+1} = \frac{r+1}{r^2} u_r, u_1 = 1$. Find an expression for $u_n$.

**5** A sequence is defined by $u_{r+1} = \frac{u_r}{1 + u_r}, u_1 = a$, where $a$ is a constant.

Find expressions, in terms of $a$ and in their simplest form, for $u_2, u_3$ and $u_4$.

**6**  The sequence $u_1$, $u_2$, $u_3$, ... is defined for all positive $r$ by $u_{r+1} = 5 - ku_r$, where $k$ is a constant.

(a) If $k = 3$ and $u_1 = 2$, find $u_2$, $u_3$ and $u_4$ and describe the behaviour of the sequence.

(b)  (i) Show that $u_3 = 5 - 5k + k^2 u_1$ and that $u_4 = 5 - 5k + k^2 u_2$.
  (ii) If $u_1 = u_3 = 1$, find the value of $k$.
  (iii) Show that, if $k$ is taken to be the smaller of your answers to (ii), the sequence will oscillate, irrespective of the value of $u_1$.

**7**  A sequence giving octagonal numbers is defined by $u_1 = 1$, $u_{r+1} = u_r + 6r + 1$. Write down the first four terms and then find an expression for $u_n$.

**8**  The series $U = 2 \times 3 + 3 \times 5 + 4 \times 7 + \cdots$

(a) Write down an expression for the $r$th term in $U$.
(b) Use the formulae for $\sum r$, $\sum r^2$ to find the sum of the first 12 terms of $U$.

**9**  Find the sum of the series $1 \times 1^2 + 3 \times 2^2 + 5 \times 3^2 + \cdots + 199 \times 100^2$.

**10** Write each of the following series in the form $\sum f(r)$ and, using appropriate results for $\sum r$, $\sum r^2$ and $\sum r^3$, evaluate each sum:

(a) $1 \times 2 + 2 \times 5 + 3 \times 10 + 4 \times 17 + \cdots + 22 \times 485$
(b) $1 \times 3 + 3 \times 6 + 5 \times 9 + 7 \times 12 + \cdots + 21 \times 33$

**11** $\displaystyle\sum_{i=1}^{n} i^2 = \sum_{i=1}^{2n} i$. Find $n$.

**12** Show that:

(a) $2^2 + 4^2 + 6^2 + \cdots + (2n)^2 = \frac{2}{3}n(n+1)(2n+1)$
(b) $1^2 + 3^2 + 5^2 + \cdots + (2n-1)^2 = \frac{1}{3}n(2n+1)(2n-1)$

**13**

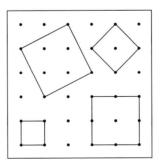

A board has $n^2$ pins hammered into it, forming a square pattern. Squares are made by stretching elastic bands round selected pins as shown. It can be proved that the total number of squares that can be made in this way is

$$\sum_{i=1}^{n}(n-i)i^2$$

Use this formula to work out the total number of squares that can be made on the pinboard shown in the diagram.
[OCR (SMP), 1985]

**14** (a) Show that $\dfrac{1}{i(i+1)} = \dfrac{1}{i} - \dfrac{1}{i+1}$.

*(b) By writing $\dfrac{1}{i(i+1)}$ as partial fractions, show that

$$\sum_{i=1}^{n}\frac{1}{i(i+1)} = 1 - \frac{1}{n+1}$$

(Hint: write out the first few terms.)

**15** Prove that $\displaystyle\sum_{r=1}^{n}\frac{1}{(r+2)(r+3)} = \frac{n}{3(n+3)}$.

**16** Express $\dfrac{3x+2}{x(x+1)(x+2)}$ in partial fractions.

Hence prove that

$$\sum_{r=1}^{n}\frac{3r+2}{r(r+1)(r+2)} = 2 - \frac{1}{n+1} - \frac{2}{n+2}$$

## Advanced

**1** The sequence $u_1, u_2, u_3, \ldots$ is defined by

$$u_1 = 4 \quad \text{and} \quad u_{n+1} = \tfrac{1}{8}u_n \quad \text{for all positive integers } n$$

(i) Find the values of $u_2$, $u_3$ and $u_4$, and state the limit to which the terms in this sequence converge.

(ii) A second sequence $w_1, w_2, w_3, \ldots$ is defined in terms of $u_1, u_2, u_3, \ldots$ by

$$w_n = \sum_{i=1}^{n}u_i \quad \text{for all positive integers } n$$

Find the values of $w_1$, $w_2$ and $w_3$.
Determine the limit to which the terms of the second sequence converge.
[OCR (Cambridge), 1995]

**2** (a) Show that $\dfrac{1}{x} - \dfrac{1}{x+1} = \dfrac{1}{x(x+1)}$.

(b) A sequence $u_1, u_2, u_3, \ldots$ is defined by $u_r = \dfrac{1}{r(r+1)}$.

Write down $u_1$, $u_2$ and $u_3$. You should leave your answers in fractional form.

(c) The terms of the sequence are summed to give a new sequence where

$$w_n = \sum_{r=1}^{n} u_r$$

(i) Write down $w_1$, $w_2$, and $w_3$. Leave your answers in fractional form.

(ii) Use the result $\displaystyle\sum \dfrac{1}{r(r+1)} = \sum \dfrac{1}{r} - \sum \dfrac{1}{r+1}$ to show that

$$w_n = 1 - \dfrac{1}{n+1}$$

(Hint: write out the first few terms.)

(iii) Hence write down the limit of the sum of the infinite series

$$\dfrac{1}{1\times 2} + \dfrac{1}{2\times 3} + \dfrac{1}{3\times 4} + \cdots + \dfrac{1}{r(r+1)} + \cdots$$

**3**

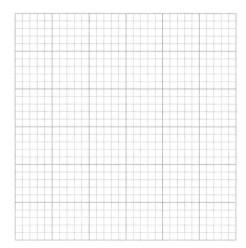

The diagram shows a piece of graph paper 6 cm by 6 cm, divided into 2 mm squares.

(a) Write down the number of squares that are:
   (i) 2 mm by 2 mm     (ii) 8 mm by 8 mm
(b) Calculate the total number of squares.

**4**

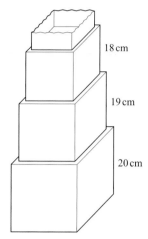

18 cm

19 cm

20 cm

A child's building set consists of 20 cubes, whose sides are 1 cm, 2 cm, 3 cm, ... 20 cm. His mother builds a tower as shown above.

   (a)  If she uses $k$ cubes, find a formula for the total height of the cubes.
   (b)  If she uses 13 cubes, find the total volume of the blocks in m$^3$.

**5**   (i)  If f$(r)$ is a function defined for $r = 0, 1, 2, 3, \ldots$, show that

$$\sum_{r=1}^{n} \{ \mathrm{f}(r) - \mathrm{f}(r-1) \} = \mathrm{f}(n) - \mathrm{f}(0)$$

   (ii)  If $\mathrm{f}(r) = r^2(r+1)^2$, evaluate $\mathrm{f}(r) - \mathrm{f}(r-1)$ and hence determine

$$\sum_{r=1}^{n} r^3.$$

   (iii)  Find the sum of the series $1^3 - 2^3 + 3^3 - 4^3 + \cdots + (2n+1)^3$.

[OCR (STEP), 1995]

**6**  Nina only ever buys a new car on her birthday. Whenever she buys one, she pays £20 000 and keeps it for $n$ years, After $n$ years, she can trade it in for $\dfrac{1}{n+1}$ of the purchase price. In the $i$th year of a car's life the cost of repairs is £500$i$.

   (a)  If Nina keeps the car for $n$ years, calculate:
      (i)  the total cost of buying the car, repairing it and selling it;
      (ii)  the average cost, £$C_n$, of buying, repairing and selling the car.
   (b)  Prove that $C_n < C_{n-1} \Rightarrow n(n+1) < 80$ and hence deduce how long Nina should keep the car before trading it in.

7   Weather records in Aipotu show that, over a long period of time, the probability of the weather changing from being wet one day to dry the next, or vice versa, is $\frac{1}{3}$. The probability that day $n$ is dry is $p_n$.

(a)  Explain why $p_{n+1} = \frac{2}{3}p_n + \frac{1}{3}(1 - p_n)$.
(b)  If the first day is dry,
       (i)   calculate $p_4$,
       (ii)  find a formula for $p_n$ in terms of $n$.

8   A document is repeatedly copied. At any stage the word *woad* has a probability $p(< 1)$ of being copied correctly and a probability $q(< 1)$ of being copied as *wood*, where $p + q = 1$. If it appears in the form *wood* it has a probability $P(< 1)$ of being copied as *wood* and a probability $Q(< 1)$ of being copied as *woad*, where $P + Q = 1$. In the original document the word appears as *woad*. If $U_n$ is the probability that after $n$ copyings it reads *woad*, show that

$$U_{n+1} = Q + (p - Q)U_n$$

If

$$V_n = U_n - \frac{Q}{(q + Q)}$$

prove that $V_{n+1} = (p - Q)V_n$ and obtain the value of $V_n$.
Hence determine the value to which $U_n$ approaches after many copyings.
[OCR (Cambridge), 1968]

9   Let $a_1 = 3$, $a_{n+1} = a_n^3$ for $n \geq 1$. (Thus $a_2 = 3^3$, $a_3 = (3^3)^3$ and so on.)

(i)   What digit appears in the unit place for $a_7$?

(ii)  Show, without using tables, that $a_7 > 10^{100}$.

(iii) What is $\dfrac{a_7 + 1}{2a_7 + 1}$ correct to two places of decimals? Justify your answer.

[OCR (STEP), 1997]

10  You are *given* that

$$\cos(2n + 1)\theta + i\sin(2n + 1)\theta = (\cos\theta + i\sin\theta)^{2n+1}$$

for any real number $\theta$ and any non-negative integer $n$. Use this result to show that

$$\sin(2n+1)\theta = \sin^{2n+1}\theta\left\{(2n+1)\cot^{2n}\theta - \binom{2n+1}{3}\cot^{2n-2}\theta\right.$$

$$\left. + \binom{2n+1}{5}\cot^{2n-4}\theta - \cdots + (-1)^n\right\}$$

Deduce that $x = \cot^2\dfrac{r\pi}{2n+1}$ is a zero of the polynomial

$$(2n+1)x^n - \binom{2n+1}{3}x^{n-1} + \binom{2n+1}{5}x^{n-2} - \cdots + (-1)^n \qquad (1)$$

for $r = 1, 2, \ldots, n$.

Explain why these $n$ values of $x$ are all different. By comparing (1) with its factorised form

$$(2n+1)\left(x - \cot^2\frac{\pi}{2n+1}\right)\left(x - \cot^2\frac{2\pi}{2n+1}\right)\cdots\left(x - \cot^2\frac{n\pi}{2n+1}\right)$$

find an expression for the sum $\displaystyle\sum_{r=1}^{n}\cot^2\frac{r\pi}{2n+1}$.

Use this last result, together with the fact that $\cot\theta < \theta^{-1}$ for $0 < \theta < \frac{1}{2}\pi$, to show that

$$\sum_{r=1}^{n}\frac{1}{r^2} > \frac{\pi^2}{6}\left(1 - \frac{1}{2n+1}\right)\left(1 - \frac{2}{2n+1}\right)$$

You are *given* that (by using a method similar to the above) the following inequality may also be shown to hold:

$$\sum_{r=1}^{n}\frac{1}{r^2} < \frac{\pi^2}{6}\left(1 - \frac{1}{2n+1}\right)\left(1 + \frac{1}{2n+1}\right)$$

Use these results to determine whether or not the infinite series

$$\sum_{r=1}^{\infty}\frac{1}{r^2}$$ converges. If it does, find its sum.

[SMP 'S'/O&C]

## Revision

**1**  State the $r$th term of each of the following sequences.

(a) $1!, 4!, 7!, 10!, \ldots$         (b) $1, \frac{4}{3}, \frac{7}{5}, \frac{10}{7}, \frac{13}{9}, \frac{16}{11}, \ldots$

(c) $3, 7, 15, 31, 63, \ldots$

**2** Write down the first six terms of the sequences whose inductive definitions are given as:

(a) $u_{r+1} = u_r + 3r - 1, u_1 = 2$     (b) $u_{r+1} = \dfrac{r+3}{r} u_r, u_1 = 1$

**3** A sequence is defined by $u_{r+1} = (u_r - 1)^2$. Describe its behaviour for:

(a) $u_1 = 2$     (b) $u_1 = 3$

**4** Two sequences are defined as follows:

(a) $u_i = \dfrac{i^2}{i+2}$     (b) $u_{i+1} = \dfrac{2u_i - 1}{u_i}, u_i = 2$

Write down the first four terms of each sequence and decide in each case whether the sequence is convergent, divergent, oscillating or periodic.

**5** A sequence of numbers $u_1, u_2, u_3, u_4, \ldots$ is formed by taking a starting value of $u$ and using the rule $u_{r+1} = u_r^2 - 1$.

(a) If $u_1 = 1$, calculate $u_2$, $u_3$ and $u_4$. Write down the value for $u_{50}$.
(b) Find the value of $u_1$ for which all values of the sequence are the same.
(c) Describe the behaviour of the sequence when (i) $u_1 = 0$, (ii) $u_1 = 2$.

**6** Find a formula for $\displaystyle\sum_{r=1}^{n} (3r - 2)$.

**7** Express the sum of each of the following series in sigma notation.

(a) $\dfrac{2}{3\times 4} + \dfrac{3}{4\times 5} + \dfrac{4}{5\times 6} + \cdots$     (2n terms)

(b) $2 - 6 + 18 - 54 + \cdots$     (15 terms)

**8** Find the sum of the cubes of the natural numbers from 10 to 20 inclusive.

**9** Find the sum of the series $(n + 2)^2 + (n + 3)^2 + (n + 4)^2 + \cdots + (2n)^2$.

**10** Find the $r$th term and the sum to $n$ terms of the series $5^3 + 9^3 + 13^3 + \cdots$.

**11** Express $\dfrac{1}{(2r - 1)(2r + 1)}$ in partial fractions.

Hence show that $\displaystyle\sum_{r=1}^{n} \dfrac{1}{(2r - 1)(2r + 1)} = \dfrac{n}{2n + 1}$.

**12** $u_1 = 1$, $u_2 = 11$, $u_3 = 29$ and $u_r = ar^2 + br + c$.

Find the values of $a$, $b$, $c$ and $\displaystyle\sum_{r=1}^{n} u_r$.

## 5.2     Arithmetic and geometric series; sum to infinity of a convergent series

For an arithmetic series $a, a + d, a + 2d, \ldots$

$$u_n = a + (n-1)d, \quad S_n = \frac{n}{2}\{2a + (n-1)d\}$$

For a geometric series $a, ar, ar^2, \ldots$

$$u_n = ar^{n-1}, \quad S_n = \frac{a(1 - r^n)}{1 - r} \quad (r \neq 1)$$

the sum to infinity, $S_\infty = \dfrac{a}{1 - r} \quad (|r| < 1)$

**Basic**

**1**  Find (i) the twentieth term, (ii) the $n$th term of the following arithmetic sequences.

   (a)  $4, 7, 10, \ldots$     (b)  $33, 27, 21, \ldots$     (c)  $2, 4.5, 7, \ldots$

**2**  Find (i) the sum of 10 terms, (ii) the sum of $n$ terms of the following arithmetic series.

   (a)  $1, 8, 15, \ldots$     (b)  $10, 6, 2, \ldots$     (c)  $-6, -1\frac{1}{2}, 3, \ldots$

**\*3**  (a)  The $n$th term of a series is $\frac{1}{2}(3n - 1)$. Show that the series is arithmetic and find the sum to 20 terms.

   (b)  An arithmetic series has a sum to $n$ terms of $n(5 - 2n)$. Find the first three terms and the 12th term.

**4**  Find (i) the sixth term, (ii) the $n$th term of the following geometric sequences.

   (a)  $4, 24, 144, \ldots$     (b)  $2, -6, 18, \ldots$     (c)  $6, -3, 1\frac{1}{2}, \ldots$

**5**  Sticky tape is wound into a spiral on a reel. The first complete loop has length 25.00 cm, the second 25.05 cm, the next 25.10 cm and so on, forming a total of 100 loops. What is the total length of tape on the reel?

**6**  Find (i) the sum of 20 terms, (ii) the sum of $n$ terms of the following geometric series, giving your answers in simplified index form where necessary.

   (a)  $4, 12, 36, \ldots$     (b)  $2, -4, 8, \ldots$     (c)  $1, \frac{1}{2}, \frac{1}{4}, \ldots$

**7**  The $n$th term of a geometric series is $3(\frac{3}{2})^{n-2}$. Find the first two terms and the sum to four terms.

**8**   The sum to $n$ terms of a geometric series is $2^{n-1} - \frac{1}{2}$. Find:

(a)  the first term       (b)  the common ratio       (c)  the sixth term

**9**   (a)  5, $a$, 12 are the first three terms of an arithmetic sequence. Find $a$.
(b)  4, $b$, 484 are the first three terms of a geometric sequence. Find $b$.

**10**  Find the sum to infinity of the following series:

(a)  $3, -1, \frac{1}{3}, \ldots$       (b)  $4, 2, 1, \ldots$       (c)  $-6, 2, -\frac{2}{3}$

**11**  (a)  Which of the following geometric series converge?

(i)  $\frac{2}{3} + \frac{4}{9} + \frac{8}{27}$       (ii)  $\frac{3}{2} + \frac{9}{4} + \frac{27}{8}$       (iii)  $\frac{2}{3} - \frac{4}{9} + \frac{8}{27}$

*(b)  For which values of $x$ does the series $1 + 2x + 4x^2 + 8x^3 + \cdots$ converge?

*(c)  Find the range of values of $x$ which makes this geometric series converge and, assuming that $x$ lies within this range, find its sum to infinity.

$$1 - (1 - 2x) + (1 - 2x)^2 - (1 - 2x)^3 + \cdots$$

***12**  The sum to infinity of a geometric series is 6. If the first term of the series is equal to the common ratio, find the value of the tenth term.

## Intermediate

**1**   Carlo has asked his father if he could have his pocket money for April in a special way: 1 lira on the first day, 2 lira on the second day, 4 lira on the third day, 8 lira on the fourth day and so on until the end of the month. If the rate of exchange is 3100 lira to the pound, show that his pocket money on the last day would be equivalent to approximately £173 000 and find the total amount of pocket money he would receive for the whole month.

**2**   Winston invests a sum of money at 6% per annum. How many years does it take him to double his money?

**3**   Find: (a)  $\displaystyle\sum_{i=1}^{12} (3 + 4i)$       (b)  $\displaystyle\sum_{i=1}^{12} 3 \times 4^i$

**4**   Find the sum of all the integers from 1 to 300 excluding those that are multiples of 5 and multiples of 9.

**5**   (a)  How many terms of the arithmetic series $2 + 5 + 8 + \cdots$ are required to make a sum of 13 872?

*(b)  How many terms of the geometric series $5 + 15 + 45 + \cdots$ are required to give a sum greater than 20 000?

**6** Find the value of $n$ which makes the sum of each of the following series greater than 500:

(a) $\sum_{i=1}^{n} (2 + 5i)$    (b) $\sum_{i=1}^{n} 2 \times 5^i$

**7** Find the sum of $n$ terms of the geometric series below and show that, however large $n$ may be, the sum cannot exceed 4.

$$3 + \tfrac{3}{4} + \tfrac{3}{16} + \cdots$$

**8** Colin leaves school and starts a job with a salary of £16 000 in the first year. He receives an annual increase of 4% each year.

(a) Assuming that he works for 40 years, calculate:
　　(i) the amount he will earn in his 40th year,
　　(ii) the total amount that he will earn over the 40 year period.
(b) How many years will he need to work for his total earnings to exceed £1 million?

**9** An arithmetic series has first term $a$, common difference 8. The sum of the first $n$ terms is 12 000.

(a) Find $a$ in terms of $n$.

(b) Show that the $n$th term is $\dfrac{12\,000}{n} + 4(n - 1)$

(c) If the $n$th term is greater than 600, show that $n^2 - 151n + 3000 > 0$ and hence find the range of possible values of $n$.

**\*10** The sum to infinity of a convergent geometric series is equal to the sum to infinity of the squares of its terms. If the first term of the geometric series is $\tfrac{1}{4}$, find its common ratio.

**\*11** Three consecutive terms of an arithmetic series have a sum of 51 and a product of 4641. Find the three terms.

**12** If the sixth term of a geometric series is $-32$ and the eleventh term is 1, find the first term, the common ratio and the sum to infinity.

**13** A sheet of graph paper is marked into 1 mm squares. The line $y = \tfrac{1}{10}x$ is drawn from the origin to the point (400, 40). Find the number of *complete* 1 mm squares within the region bounded by this line, the $x$-axis and the line $x = 400$.

**14** For the geometric series $6 + 2 + \tfrac{2}{3} + \tfrac{2}{9} + \cdots$ find the least number of terms whose sum differs from the sum to infinity by $10^{-5}$.

**15** Meera invests £2000 in a building society account on 1 January 2000 and the same amount on 1 January in each succeeding year. If the building society pays compound interest at 4.5% per annum, calculate how much is in Meera's account on 31 December 2010.

**16** A credit card company charges 1.5% each month on the outstanding balance of a loan. Peter borrows £3000 on 1 January and repays £300 on the first day of each month.

(a) How much does he owe on (i) 31 January, (ii) 1 February, (iii) 1 March?

(b) How much does he owe at the end of the $r$th month?

(c) On which date does he pay off the debt?

## Advanced

**1** The fifth, ninth and twelfth terms of an arithmetic series, with common difference 3, are the first three terms of a geometric series. Show that the geometric series is convergent and find its sum to infinity.

**2** The vicar of St Trinians is raising funds by persuading his parishioners to sell books of raffle tickets. Richard is given a number of books to sell. Each book contains the same number of tickets and the tickets are numbered in sequence. The number on the first ticket of the 4th book is 3558 and the number on the first ticket of the 25th book is 3684.

(a) What is the number on the front of the first book?

(b) How many tickets are in each book?

(c) The last ticket has number 3779. How many books has Richard been given?

**3** Prove that the geometric series below is convergent for all values of $x$ and find the sum of an infinite number of terms of the series.

$$1 + \frac{4x}{5 + x^2} + \left(\frac{4x}{5 + x^2}\right)^2 + \cdots$$

**4** At the beginning of a month, a customer owes a credit card company £1000. In the middle of the month, the customer pays £$A$ to the company, where $A < 1000$, and at the end of the month the company adds interest at a rate of 3% of the amount still owing. This process continues, with the customer paying £$A$ in the middle of each month, and the company adding 3% of the amount outstanding at the end of each month.

(i) Find the value of $A$ for which the customer still owes £1000 at the start of every month.

(ii) Find the value of $A$ for which the whole amount owing is exactly paid off after the second payment.

(iii) Assuming that the debt has not been paid off after 4 payments, show that the amount still owing at the beginning of the 5th month can be expressed as

$$\pounds\{1000R^4 - A(R^4 + R^3 + R^2 + R)\}$$

where $R = 1.03$.

(iv) Show that the value of $A$ for which the whole amount owing is exactly paid off after the $n$th payment is given by

$$A = \frac{1000R^{n-1}(R-1)}{R^n - 1}$$

[OCR (Cambridge), 1996]

**5**   When a ball is dropped from rest at a height $h$ above horizontal ground, it bounces and rises to a height $e^2h$ in a time of $(1+e)\sqrt{\dfrac{2h}{g}}$ seconds, where $e$ is a constant $(0 < e < 1)$ and $g$ is the acceleration due to gravity. If the ball continues to bounce until it comes to rest, find the total distance it travels and show that the total time taken will be

$$\frac{1+e}{1-e}\sqrt{\frac{2h}{g}}$$

**6**   The sum of the first $n$ terms of an arithmetic progression is denoted by the symbol $S_n$. Prove that

$$(q-r)\frac{S_p}{p} + (r-p)\frac{S_q}{q} + (p-q)\frac{S_r}{r} = 0$$

Deduce, or prove otherwise, that if $p + q = 2r$, then

$$\frac{S_p}{p} + \frac{S_q}{q} = 2\frac{S_r}{r}$$

[OCR (Cambridge), 1974]

**7**   (i) By using the formula for the sum of a geometric series, or otherwise, express the number $0.383\,838\,38\ldots$ as a fraction in its lowest terms.

(ii) Let $x$ be a real number which has a recurring decimal expansion

$$x = 0.a_1a_2a_3\ldots$$

so that there exist positive integers $N$ and $k$ such that $a_{n+k} = a_n$ for all $n > N$. Show that

$$x = \frac{b}{10^N} + \frac{c}{10^N(10^k - 1)}$$

where $b$ and $c$ are integers to be found. Deduce that $x$ is rational.
[OCR (STEP), 1996]

**8**   Prove that

$$x + 2x^2 + 3x^3 + 4x^4 + \cdots + nx^n = \frac{nx^{n+2} - (n + 1)x^{n+1} + x}{(x - 1)^2}$$

By writing $x = 1 + y$ and comparing coefficients in the expansions, in ascending powers of $y$, of both sides of this identity, deduce that

$$\sum_{1}^{n} r = \tfrac{1}{2}n(n + 1) \quad \text{and} \quad \sum_{1}^{n} r^2 = \tfrac{1}{6}n(n + 1)(2n + 1)$$

[OCR (Cambridge), 1963]

**9**   The diagram below shows a sequence of points $P_0(1, 1)$, $P_1(\tfrac{1}{2}, \tfrac{1}{3})$, $P_2(\tfrac{1}{4}, \tfrac{1}{9})$, $P_3(\tfrac{1}{8}, \tfrac{1}{27})$.

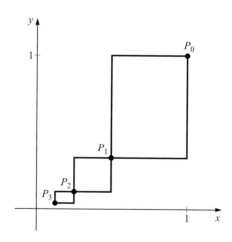

(a)   If this sequence continues, write down the coordinates of $P_k$.
(b)   A series of $n$ rectangles is formed with sides parallel $Ox$, $Oy$ and with $P_k$, $P_{k+1}$ as opposite vertices.
  (i)   Show that the area of the rectangle for which $k = 0$ is $\tfrac{1}{3}$.
  (ii)   Find the limit as $n \to \infty$ of the sum of the areas of these $n$ rectangles.
(c)   A series of circles circumscribes these rectangles.
  (i)   Show that the area of the circle for which $k = 0$ is $\tfrac{25}{144}\pi$.
  (ii)   Find the limit as $n \to \infty$ of the sum of the areas of these $n$ circles.

**10**

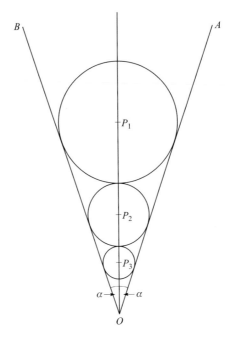

The diagram represents two straight lines $OA$, $OB$ inclined at an angle $2\alpha$. The circle of centre $P_1$ has radius $a$ and touches each of $OA$, $OB$. A sequence of circles is drawn, decreasing in radius, each touching $OA$, $OB$ and its immediate predecessor. Prove that the areas of these circles are in geometric progression. The sum of the first $n$ of these areas is $S_n$ and the sum to infinity of the geometric progression is $S$. Prove that the difference $S - S_n$ is less than $\frac{1}{100}S$ whenever $n$ exceeds

$$1/\log_{10}\left(\frac{1+\sin\alpha}{1-\sin\alpha}\right)$$

Prove also that the area of the first circle is equal to the sum of the areas of all the other circles when $\sin\alpha = 3 - 2\sqrt{2}$.
[OCR (Cambridge), 1974]

## Revision

1   Find the first four terms of the geometric series whose first term is 8 and which converges to a sum of 6.

2   In a physics experiment, a ball is dropped from a height of 490 m and takes 10 seconds to reach a hard surface. After each impact it takes $\frac{3}{5}$ of the previous falling time to rise to its maximum height. How long does it take altogether before it comes to rest?

3   Show that $\log_2 x + \log_4 x + \log_{16} x + \cdots$ is a geometric series and find its sum to infinity.

4 The eighth term of an arithmetic series is 2.5 times the third term and the sum of the first 10 terms is 87.5. Find the first term and the $n$th term.

5 Find the least number of terms of the arithmetic series $5 + 12 + 19 + \cdots$ needed to make a sum exceeding 2000.

6 Three consecutive terms of an increasing arithmetic series are $x + 4, 2x^2, 2x + 6$. Find the possible values of $x$.

7 A small village started with a population of 100 and in 10 years its population increased to 5500. If the population increased annually in a geometric sequence over those years and continued in the same way afterwards, find:

(a) the common ratio to three significant figures,
(b) the population at the end of a further five years, to the nearest thousand.

8 Find three consecutive numbers of a geometric series whose sum is 65 and whose product is 3375.

9 The common ratio of a geometric series is 5. If the sum of the first $2n$ terms is 626 times the sum of the first $n$ terms, find the value of $n$.

10 $p$ and $2q$ are the first two terms of an arithmetic series. If the sum of the first twelve terms is 5 times the sum of the first six terms, find $p$ in terms of $q$. Hence find, in terms of $q$, the 12th term of the series.

11 The sum of the first eight terms of an arithmetic series is 240 and the product of the second and fifth term is 340. Find the common difference.

12 Find the sum to $n$ terms of the series $1 + 3x + 5x^2 + 7x^3 + \cdots$.

## 5.3 $n!$, $\binom{n}{r}$ notation, binomial expansion of $(1 + x)^n$, $n \in \mathbb{Z}^+$

$$n! = n \times (n - 1) \times (n - 2) \times \cdots \times 3 \times 2 \times 1, \qquad 0! = 1$$

$$\binom{n}{r} = \frac{n!}{r!(n - r)!}$$

$$(a + b)^n = a^n + \binom{n}{1}a^{n-1}b + \binom{n}{2}a^{n-2}b + \cdots + \binom{n}{r}a^{n-r}b^r + \cdots$$

$$+ \binom{n}{n-1}ab^{n-1} + b^n \quad (n \in \mathbb{Z}^+)$$

## Basic

**1** Evaluate:

(a) $\dfrac{8!}{3!}$     (b) $\dfrac{10!}{6!\,4!}$

(c) $\dbinom{7}{4}$     (d) $\dbinom{5}{2}$

**2** Expand $(a+b)^3$ and $(a-b)^3$. Hence show that
$$(a+b)^3 - (a-b)^3 = 2b(3a^2 + b^2).$$

**3** Expand $(1+x)^5$. Hence show that
$$(1+x)^5 + (1-x)^5 = 2(1 + 10x^2 + 5x^4).$$

**4** Expand the following as far as the term in $x^3$.

(a) $(1-2x)^8$     (b) $(1+\tfrac{1}{3}x)^6$     (c) $(3+4x)^5$

**5** Simplify $(1+3x)^4 - (1-3x)^4$.

**\*6** Write down the sixth term in the expansion of $(1-2x)^{10}$.

**\*7** Expand $(1+2x)^4$. By substituting a suitable value of $x$, find $1.004^4$, correct to five decimal places.

**8** Expand: (a) $2x(1-x)^4$     (b) $(1+x)(1+2x)^3$

**9** Find the middle term in the expansion of $(1-3x)^8$.

**10** Find the coefficient of $x^6$ in each of the following expansions.

(a) $(1+x^2)^7$     (b) $(3+\tfrac{1}{5}x)^9$

**11** Simplify $(1-\sqrt{2})^4$.

**\*12** Determine the first four terms in the expansion of $(1+2x)^{19}$. Hence find the coefficient of $x^3$ in the expansion of $(3+5x)(1+2x)^{19}$.

## Intermediate

**1** (a) Evaluate $\dfrac{200!}{150!} \times \dfrac{148!}{199!}$.

(b) Simplify $\dfrac{n!}{r!} \times \dfrac{(r+1)!}{(n-2)!}$.

**2** $\dbinom{23}{7} = \dbinom{23}{a}$. State the possible values of $a$.

**3** Expand:

  (a) $(2+x)^4$     (b) $\left(x - \dfrac{1}{x}\right)^4$     (c) $\left(1 - \dfrac{x}{2}\right)^4$

**4** Expand and simplify $\left(x + \dfrac{3}{x}\right)^5 - \left(x - \dfrac{3}{x}\right)^5$.

**5** Expand $(1+x)(1-x)^6$.

**6** When $(1 - \frac{1}{2}x)^n$ is expanded in ascending powers of $x$, the coefficient of $x$ is $-5$.

  (a) Find the value of $n$.
  (b) Find the coefficient of (i) $x^2$, (ii) $x^3$ in the expansion.

**7** The second and fourth terms in the expansion of $(1+x)^n$, where $x$ and $n$ are positive integers, are 36 and 5940 respectively. Find the values of $n$ and $x$.

**8** Find the values of $a$, $b$ and $c$, given that

$$(1 + ax + bx^2)(1 + 3x)^5 = 1 + 16x + 103x^2 + cx^3 + \cdots$$

**9** Expand $(1+y)^5$. By letting $y = 2x + 3x^2$, find the first four terms in ascending powers of $x$ of the expansion of $(1 + 2x + 3x^2)^5$.

**10** Find the first five terms in descending powers of $x$ in the expansion of $(x^2 + 1)^{30}$.

**11** Evaluate $\displaystyle\int_0^1 (1 + 4x^2)^5 dx$.

**12** Simplify $\dfrac{(x+h)^4 - x^4}{h}$.

**13** (a) Expand $(2x + 3y)^6$ as far as the term in $y^2$.
  (b) Use values of $x = 1$ and $y = 0.01$ in your series to obtain an approximate value of $2.03^6$.
  (c) By evaluating the term in $y^3$ in the expansion, state the degree of accuracy of your answer to (b).

**14** Find the term independent of $x$ in the expansion of $\left(2x + \dfrac{3}{x}\right)^8$.

**15** If $x$ is so small that $x^3$ and higher powers of $x$ are negligible, show that

$$(3x - 2)(1 - 5x)^9 \approx -2 + 93x - 1935x^2$$

**16** (a) Simplify: (i) $\dfrac{r+1}{(r+1)!}$     (ii) $(n-1)(n-2)!$

           (iii) $(n-1)! - (r+1)(n-2)!$

   (b) Prove that $\dbinom{n-1}{r+1} - \dbinom{n-2}{r} = \dbinom{n-2}{r+1}$ for all $n \in \mathbb{Z}$, $n > 2$.

### Advanced

**1** Find the term independent of $x$ in the expansion of $\left(ax^2 - \dfrac{b}{x}\right)^9$.

**2** The coefficients of the second, third and fourth terms in the expansion of $(1+x)^n$ are three terms of an arithmetic sequence. Find the value of $n$.

**3** Express $(x+2)^5 - (x-2)^5$ as a polynomial in $x$, and hence find the exact value of $(\sqrt{5}+2)^5 - (\sqrt{5}-2)^5$.
Use the fact that $0 < \sqrt{5} - 2 < \frac{1}{4}$ to deduce that $(\sqrt{5}+2)^5$ differs from an integer by less than $\frac{1}{1024}$.
[OCR (Cambridge), 1990]

**4** The derivative of $f(x)$ is defined to be $f'(x) = \lim\limits_{h \to 0} \dfrac{f(x+h) - f(x)}{h}$.

Use this definition to show that the derivative of $x^n$ is $nx^{n-1}$.

**5** (a)  (i) State the binomial expansion of $(x+y)^4$.
      (ii) If $x+y = 5$ and $xy = 3$, use the expansion in (i) to find the value of $x^4 + y^4$.
  (b)  (i) If $x - y = a$ and $xy = b$, express $x^3 - y^3$ in terms of $a$ and $b$.

      (ii) Without solving for $a$, show that, if $a - \dfrac{1}{a} = 3$, then

        $a^3 - \dfrac{1}{a^3} = 36$.

**6** (a) By expanding $(a+b)^n$ and choosing suitable values of $a$ and $b$, show

     that $2^n - 2 = \displaystyle\sum_{r=1}^{n-1} \binom{n}{r}$.

  (b)  (i) Expand $\left(1 + \dfrac{1}{n}\right)^n$ as a series of powers of $\dfrac{1}{n}$, as far as the term

      in $\left(\dfrac{1}{n}\right)^3$.

      (ii) Show that the term in $\left(\dfrac{1}{n}\right)^2$ simplifies to $\dfrac{1}{2!}\left(1 - \dfrac{1}{n}\right)$ and give a

      similar expression for the term in $\left(\dfrac{1}{n}\right)^3$.

(iii) The base of the natural logarithms, e, may be defined as

$$e = \lim_{n \to \infty} \left(1 + \frac{1}{n}\right)^n.$$

Use this definition to show that $e = 1 + \frac{1}{1!} + \frac{1}{2!} + \frac{1}{3!} + \cdots$

**7** Find the coefficient of $x^6$ in $(1 - 2x + 3x^2 - 4x^3 + 5x^4)^3$.
You should set out your working clearly.
[OCR (STEP), 1996]

**8** By considering the coefficient of $x^n$ in the identity
$(1 - x)^n(1 + x)^n = (1 - x^2)^n$, or otherwise, simplify

$$\binom{n}{0}^2 - \binom{n}{1}^2 + \binom{n}{2}^2 - \binom{n}{3}^2 + \cdots + (-1)^n \binom{n}{n}^2$$

in the cases (i) when $n$ is even, (ii) when $n$ is odd.
[OCR (STEP), 1994]

**9** Write down the binomial expansion of $(1 + x)^n$, where $n$ is a positive integer.

(a) By substituting particular values of $x$ into the above expression, or otherwise, show that, if $n$ is an even positive integer,

$$\binom{n}{0} + \binom{n}{2} + \binom{n}{4} + \cdots + \binom{n}{n}$$

$$= \binom{n}{1} + \binom{n}{3} + \binom{n}{5} + \cdots + \binom{n}{n-1}$$

$$= 2^{n-1}$$

(b) Show that, if $n$ is any positive integer, then

$$\binom{n}{1} + 2\binom{n}{2} + 3\binom{n}{3} + \cdots + \binom{n}{n} = n2^{n-1}$$

Hence evaluate

$$\sum_{r=0}^{n} (r + (-1)^r) \binom{n}{r}$$

[OCR (STEP), 1989]

**10** If $\binom{r}{p} = \frac{r(r-1) \cdots (r-p+1)}{p!}$

where $r$ and $p$ are positive, non-zero integers, prove that:

(a) $\dbinom{r}{p} = 0$, when $r < p$

(b) $\dbinom{r}{p} = \dbinom{r+1}{p+1} - \dbinom{r}{p+1}$

Deduce the value of

$$\sum_{r=1}^{n} \dbinom{r}{p}$$

where $n \geq p$.
[OCR (Cambridge), 1964]

**Revision**

**1** Find the values of:

(a) $\dbinom{10}{6}$    (b) $\dbinom{15}{9}$    (c) $\dfrac{(r+1)!}{(r-1)!}$

**2** Expand $(5x - 2)^4$ in descending powers of $x$.

**3** Simplify $(1 + 2x)^5 - (1 - 2x)^5$.

**4** Expand:

(a) $4x(1 - 2x)^3$    (b) $(1 - x)(1 + x)^4$    (c) $\left(\dfrac{2}{x} + \dfrac{x}{2}\right)^6$

**5** Find the coefficient of $x^3$ in the expansion, in ascending powers of $x$, of $(2 + 3x)^{10}$.

**6** Show that, if $\alpha t$ is small, $(1 + \alpha t)^3 \approx 1 + 3\alpha t$.

**7** In the expansion of $(1 + ax)^n$ the coefficient of $x^2$ equals the coefficient of $x^3$ and the coefficient of $x$ is 4. Find the values of $a$ and $n$.

**8** If $x$ is so small that any terms in $x^3$ or higher powers of $x$ can be neglected, show that

$$(1 - x)^4(1 + 2x)^7 \approx 1 + 10x + 34x^2$$

**9** Find the coefficient of $x^9$ in the expansion of $\left(x^2 + \dfrac{5}{x}\right)^9$.

**10** (a) Expand $(1 + 3x)^6$ as far as the term in $x^2$.
(b) By putting $x = 0.04$, obtain an estimate for $1.12^6$.
(c) By evaluating the term in $x^3$ in the expansion, give an estimate of the error in your answer to part (b).

**11** Find the ratio of the 50th term to the 49th term in the expansion of $(1 + 2x)^{100}$.

**12** Expand $(1 + \frac{1}{2}x - x^2)^p$ in ascending powers of $x$, up to and including the term in $x^3$. Find the value of $p$ which makes the coefficient of $x^3$ equal to zero.

## 5.4    Binomial series

Binomial series:

$$(1 + x)^n = 1 + nx + \frac{n(n-1)}{2!}x^2 + \frac{n(n-1)(n-2)}{3!}x^3 + \cdots$$

### Basic

**1** Expand as far as the term in $x^4$:

(a) $(1 + x)^{1/2}$    (b) $(1 - 2x)^{-2}$

**2** For each of the following, state the range of values of $x$ for which the expansion, in ascending powers of $x$, is valid.

(a) $\left(1 + \frac{3x}{2}\right)^{-3}$    (b) $\dfrac{1}{\sqrt{1 - 4x}}$

**\*3** Write down the first four terms in the expansion of $(1 - x^2)^{-2}$.

**4** Find the first four terms in the expansion of $(4 + x)^{3/2}$.

**\*5** Expand $(1 - x)(1 + 3x)^{1/2}$ in ascending powers of $x$ up to the term in $x^3$. State the values of $x$ for which the expansion is valid.

**6** Show that, when $\dfrac{1}{(1 - x)^2}$ is expressed as a binomial series, the coefficients increase in an arithmetic sequence.

**7** Use the expansion of $(1 + 2x)^{1/2}$ by the binomial series to find the value of $\sqrt{1.04}$ to five significant figures.

**\*8** By first factorising $1 - 3x - 10x^2$, expand $\sqrt{1 - 3x - 10x^2}$ in ascending powers of $x$ up to and including the term in $x^2$.

**9** Expand $\dfrac{1}{\sqrt[3]{27 + x}}$ in ascending powers of $x$ up to the term in $x^2$, stating the range of values of $x$ for which the series is valid.

**10** Find the first three non-zero terms in the expansion, in ascending powers

of $x$, of $\dfrac{x}{1-x}$.

**11** Expand $\dfrac{1}{1+2x}$ in ascending powers of $x$ as far as the term in $x^3$. State

the coefficient of $x^n$.

**12** Show that, for small values of $x$, $\dfrac{1+x}{(1-x)^2} \approx 1 + 3x$.

### Intermediate

**1** If $x$ is so small that $x^4$ and higher powers of $x$ can be neglected, show
that

$$(1-3x)^{-2}(1+2x)^{1/2} = 1 + 7x + \frac{65x^2}{2} + \frac{265x^3}{2}$$

**2** Express $\mathrm{f}(x) = \dfrac{5-x}{(1+x)(1-2x)}$ in the form $\dfrac{A}{(1+x)} + \dfrac{B}{(1-2x)}$ where $A$ and

$B$ are integers to be found. Hence expand $\mathrm{f}(x)$ as a series of ascending
powers of $x$ as far as the term in $x^3$.

**3** Expand $\dfrac{1+x}{(1-4x)^3}$ in ascending powers of $x$ up to and including the term

in $x^3$ and state the values of $x$ for which the expansion is valid.

**4** Expand $\sqrt{\dfrac{1+2x}{1+x}}$ in ascending powers of $x$ up to and including the term

in $x^3$.

**5** Given that $\dfrac{1}{(2+ax)^2} \approx \dfrac{1}{4} - \dfrac{3x}{4} + bx^2$, find the values of $a$ and $b$.

**6** Expand the expression $\dfrac{1}{1+2x-8x^2}$ in ascending powers of $x$ up to and

including the term in $x^3$.

**7** The coefficient of $x^4$ in the expansion of $(1+ax)^n$ is $6\frac{1}{4}$ times the
coefficient of $x^3$ and the coefficient of $x$ is 10. Find the values of $a$ and $n$.

**8** Show that, if $x^3$ and higher powers of $x$ are neglected,

$$\frac{(1+2x)^3 - (1-x)^{1/2}}{1-x^2} = \frac{13x}{2} + \frac{97x^2}{8}$$

**9** Show that, if $x$ is so small that $x^3$ and higher powers of $x$ can be neglected,

$$\sqrt{\frac{1-2x}{1+2x}} = 1 - 2x + 2x^2$$

By putting $x = \frac{1}{30}$, show that $\sqrt{14} \approx \frac{842}{225}$.

**10** If the coefficients of $x$ and $x^2$ in the expansion of $\dfrac{\sqrt{1+ax}}{1+bx}$ are 4 and $11\frac{1}{2}$ respectively, find the two possible values of $a$ and $b$.

**11** Find the first three terms in the expansion of $\left(1 - \dfrac{4}{x}\right)^{1/2}$. By putting $x = 100$, find an approximation to $\sqrt{6}$. Find the percentage error in using this value compared with the value given by your calculator.

**12** The coefficient of $x^4$ in the expansion of $(1-x)\sqrt{1+ax}$ is $\frac{1}{16}$ of the coefficient of $x^2$. Find the value of $a$ which is an integer.

**13** Find the values of the constants $a$ and $b$ if the term of lowest degree in the expansion of $(1+ax)(1-bx^2)^5 - (1-3x)^{1/4}$, in ascending powers of $x$, is the term involving $x^3$.

**14** Express $f(x) = \dfrac{3-2x}{(1-3x)(x+2)}$ in partial fractions and hence express $f(x)$ as a series of ascending powers of $x$, as far as the term in $x^2$. For what values of $x$ is your series valid? Find the coefficient of $x^n$ in the expansion.

**15** Express $f(x) = \dfrac{3x}{(1+x)(2-x)^2}$ in the form $\dfrac{A}{(1+x)} + \dfrac{B}{(2-x)} + \dfrac{C}{(2-x)^2}$.
By finding the values of $A$, $B$ and $C$, expand $f(x)$ in a series of ascending powers of $x$ up to the term in $x^3$. For what values of $x$ is the series valid?

**16** $(1+x)^n$ and $\dfrac{1+ax}{1+bx}$ have identical expansions, as far as the term in $x^2$.
Express $a$ and $b$ in terms of $n$. By taking $n = \frac{2}{3}$ and $x = \frac{1}{8}$, show that $\sqrt[3]{81} \approx \frac{212}{49}$.

## Advanced

**1** Expand $(1+x)^{1/4}$ as far as the term in $x^2$. Hence:

(a) calculate $(1.000\,008)^{1/4}$, giving your answer correct to 13 decimal places;

(b) show that $\sqrt[4]{17} \approx \frac{8317}{4096}$.

**2** If $\dfrac{b}{a}$ is small enough for powers above the third to be neglected, show that

$$\sqrt{a+b} - \sqrt{a-b} = \sqrt{a}\left(\frac{b}{a} + k\frac{b^3}{a^3}\right), \qquad \text{where } k \text{ is to be found}$$

Use this result to find an approximation for $\sqrt{5} - \sqrt{3}$ in the form $\dfrac{p}{q}$. Find an equivalent approximation for $\sqrt{5} + \sqrt{3}$.

**3** The derivative, $f'(x)$, of $f(x)$ is defined by $f'(x) = \lim\limits_{h\to 0} \dfrac{f(x+h) - f(x)}{h}$.

(a) Use this definition to calculate $f'(x)$ when $f(x) = x^{1/2}$.

(b) Explain why using the binomial series in the above definition may not constitute a formal proof.

**4** Find the values of $a$ and $b$ for which the expansion of $\dfrac{1+ax}{1+bx}$ agrees with that of $e^x$ as far as the term in $x^2$. Hence show that $e^{1/20} \approx \frac{41}{39}$.

**5** Express $f(x) = \dfrac{4x+3}{(x+2)(2x-1)}$ in partial fractions. Hence expand $f(x)$ as a series of powers of $\dfrac{1}{x}$, stating the first three terms and the coefficient of $\left(\dfrac{1}{x}\right)^n$. State the range of values of $x$ for which the expansion is valid.

**6** (a) Find the first four terms in the expansion of $\left(1 + \dfrac{3}{x}\right)^{-2}$. State the values of $x$ for which the expansion is valid.

(b) Show that $\left(1 + \dfrac{3}{x}\right)^{-2} = kx^2\left(1 + \dfrac{x}{3}\right)^{-2}$.

(c) Using the value of $k$ that you calculated in (b), find the first four terms in the expansion of $kx^2\left(1 + \dfrac{x}{3}\right)^{-2}$. State the values of $x$ for which the expansion is valid.

(d) Explain why your answers to (a) and (c) are different.

**7** Show that, if $|px| < 1$ and $|qx| < 1$,

$$\frac{p-q}{(1-px)(1-qx)} = \sum_{n=0}^{\infty} c_n x^n$$

expressing $c_n$ in terms of $p$ and $q$.

**8** (a) By considering the expansion of $\dfrac{1}{(1-x^2)^2}$, or otherwise, evaluate the

$n$th derivative of $\dfrac{1}{(1-x^2)^2}$ when $x=0$.

(b) By writing $(1+x)$ as $\frac{1}{2}[1+(1+2x)]$, or otherwise, show that the coefficient of $x^n$ in the expansion of

$$\frac{(1+x)^n}{(1+2x)^2} \quad \text{(where } n \in \mathbb{Z})$$

in ascending powers of $x$ is $(-1)^n(2n+1)$.

[OCR (Cambridge), 1988]

**9** By considering the binomial expansions of $(1+x)^{-2}$ and $(1+x)^{-6}$, or otherwise, find the coefficient of $x^6$ in

$$(1-2x+3x^2-4x^3+5x^4-6x^5+7x^6)^3.$$

[OCR (STEP), 1996]

**10** Given that $b > a > 0$, find, by using the binomial theorem, coefficients $c_m$ ($m = 0, 1, 2, \ldots$) such that

$$\frac{1}{(1-ax)(1-bx)} = c_0 + c_1 x + c_2 x^2 + \cdots + c_m x^m + \cdots, \text{ for } b|x| < 1.$$

Show that $c_m^2 = \dfrac{a^{2m+2} - 2(ab)^{m+1} + b^{2m+2}}{(a-b)^2}$.

Hence, or otherwise, show that

$$c_0^2 + c_1^2 x + c_2^2 x^2 + \cdots + c_m^2 x^m + \cdots = \frac{1+abx}{(1-abx)(1-a^2x)(1-b^2x)}$$

for $x$ in a suitable interval which you should determine.

[OCR (STEP), 1988]

## Revision

**1** For small values of $x$, find cubic polynomials which approximate to the following functions.

(a) $\dfrac{1}{(1+x)^3}$     (b) $\sqrt[3]{1-2x}$

**2** State the first two terms in the expansion of $\sqrt{1+x}$.
By writing $x = \frac{1}{49}$, show that $\sqrt{50} \approx \frac{99}{14}$.

**3** Show that $\sqrt{16 - x^2} \approx 4 - \frac{1}{8}x^2 - \frac{1}{512}x^4$. For what values of $x$ is the expansion valid?

**4** Find a quadratic approximation to $\sqrt{\dfrac{2+x}{1-4x}}$.

**5** The acceleration due to gravity at a height $h$ above sea level is given by

$$g = \frac{g_0 R^2}{(R+h)^2}$$

where $g_0$ is the value of $g$ at sea level and $R$ is the radius of the earth. Show that, if $h$ is small compared with $r$, $g = g_0\left(1 - \dfrac{2h}{R}\right)$.

**6** Express $\dfrac{1+x}{(1-x)(1+5x)}$ in partial fractions and hence expand $f(x)$ in ascending powers of $x$ as far as the fourth term. For what values of $x$ is the series valid?

**7** The coefficient of $x^4$ in the expansion in powers of $x$ of $(1-x)(a+bx)^{-2}$ is zero. Find the value of $\dfrac{a}{b}$.

**8** Using the binomial series, find the value of $\dfrac{1}{\sqrt[4]{15.92}}$ to four decimal places.

**9** Show that, if $x$ is small,

$$\frac{1}{1+2x} - \sqrt{1-4x} \approx 6x^2$$

**10** Show that the first three terms of the expansions of $\sqrt{\dfrac{1-x}{1+x}}$ and $\dfrac{2-x}{2+x}$ are the same.

**11** Express $f(x) = \dfrac{-x-7}{(x+3)(x-1)}$ in partial fractions. If $x$ is large, obtain an expansion of $f(x)$ in ascending powers of $\dfrac{1}{x}$ as far as the term in $\dfrac{1}{x^3}$.

**12** If the coefficient of $x^2$ is $-\dfrac{5}{16}$ of the coefficient of $x$ in the expansion of

$$\sqrt{\frac{1+ax}{4-x}}$$

find the possible values of $a$.

# 6
# Trigonometry

## 6.1 Radian measure; $s = r\theta$, $A = \frac{1}{2}r^2\theta$

> Arc length $s = r\theta$, area of sector $A = \frac{1}{2}r^2\theta$, where $\theta$ is measured in radians.

### Basic

Notation: $3^c$ is shorthand for 3 radians.

**\*1** Convert the following angles from degrees to radians, giving your answers in terms of $\pi$.

    (a) $180°$     (b) $45°$     (c) $270°$     (d) $72°$     (e) $240°$

**2** Calculate, to three significant figures, radian approximations to the following angles.

    (a) $37°$     (b) $230°$     (c) $57.3°$     (d) $2\pi°$     (e) $2\pi^c$

**3** State the degree equivalents for each of the following angles measured in radians.

    (a) $\pi/6$     (b) $\pi/9$     (c) $3\pi/4$     (d) $7\pi/12$     (e) $5\pi/3$

**4** Calculate, to three significant figures, degree approximations to the following angles.

    (a) $2.5$     (b) $1$     (c) $6.283$     (d) $7\pi/13$     (e) $21\pi/11$

**5** For which of the angles $\theta$ below is each of the following true?

    (a) $\sin\theta = \frac{1}{2}$     (b) $\sin\theta = \cos\theta$     (c) $\tan\theta = 1.732$

        (i) $\pi/3$     (ii) $5\pi/4$     (iii) $330°$     (iv) $60°$     (v) $2\pi$
        (vi) $\pi/6$     (vii) $5\pi/6$     (viii) $45°$     (ix) $7\pi/4$

**\*6** (a) Find an exact expression for the magnitude of the base angle $A$ in the isosceles triangle shown.

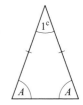

(b)  Find an exact expression for the magnitude of the vertex angle $V$ in the isosceles triangle shown.

(c)  Show that $A - \frac{1}{2}V = \left(\dfrac{90}{\pi}\right)^{\circ}$

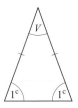

**7**  Calculate the length of the circular arc, whose locus is described by a radius $R$ and angle $\theta$ where:

*(a)  $R = 2\,\text{m}, \theta = 1$          (b)  $R = 5.3\,\text{mm}, \theta = 0.7$
 (c)  $R = 3.67\,\text{km}, \theta = 2\pi$

**8**  A piece of flexible wire of length 15.0 cm is curved into a circular arc. What angle (in radians) will be subtended, if the radius of the arc is:

(a)  15.0 cm          (b)  5.0 cm          (c)  $R$ cm

**9**  The arc of a circle is required to have length $\ell\,$m. State the radius if the angle of the arc is:

(a)  $\dfrac{\pi}{3}$      (b)  $\dfrac{7\pi}{5}$      (c)  $144^{\circ}$      (d)  1.00      (e)  $\alpha$

*\*10**  Which of the following sectors, with radius $r$ and angle $\theta$, differs in area from all the others?

(a)  $r = 5, \theta = 2.88$      (b)  $r = 6, \theta = 2$      (c)  $r = 8, \theta = \frac{9}{8}$
(d)  $r = 1.6, \theta = \frac{225}{8}$      (e)  $r = 3, \theta = 4$

**11**  What angle (in radians) is necessary to define a circular sector, if the area $A$ and radius $r$ are as follows?

(a)  $A = 12.5\,\text{cm}^2, r = 5\,\text{cm}$      (b)  $A = 270\,\text{mm}^2, r = 1.2\,\text{cm}$
(c)  $A = t^2, r = 3t$

**12**  A metallic component to be cut from a sheet of steel has a cross-section in the shape of a circular sector, and on that face must have an area of $153\,\text{cm}^2$ to three significant figures. The tolerance in the equipment permits an angle equal to 2.5 radians to one decimal place.

(a)  Between what two values must the radius of the sector lie? Give your answer to the nearest one tenth of a millimetre.
(b)  What is the maximum permissible percentage error in the radius?

### Intermediate

**1**  The diagram shows a sector of a circle with centre $O$ and radius 4 cm. Angle $AOB = 0.8$ radians. Calculate:

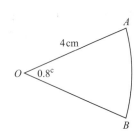

(a)  the length of the arc $AB$
(b)  the area of sector $AOB$

*2 Points $A$ and $B$ lie on the circumference of a circle, radius 17 mm; and the arc $AB$ subtends an angle of 0.3 radians at the centre of the circle. A minor segment of this circle is bounded by arc $AB$ and chord $AB$. Find the area of the minor segment (shaded).

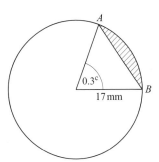

*3

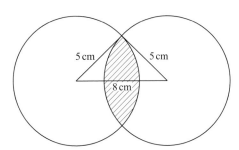

Find the common area enclosed by two circles, both with radius 5 cm, positioned so that their centres are 8 cm apart.

4 Show that the minute hand of a clock turns through $\dfrac{24\pi}{11}$ radians between noon and the next occasion that the minute hand and hour hand are exactly aligned.

5 A sector of land has a perimeter of 250 m, and forms an angle of $\dfrac{\pi}{6}$ radians. Another sector is to be formed with half the perimeter, but the same angle. What proportion of the old area will be occupied by the new sector?

6 The sector, $OAB$, of a circle has radius $r$ cm and perimeter 10 cm. The arc $AB$ subtends an angle $\theta$ at the centre. If the area of the sector is $A$ cm$^2$, show that:

(a) $A = 5r - r^2$
(b) the maximum value of $A$ is $\frac{25}{4}$. At what value of $\theta$ does this occur?

7 A circular pane of glass, of circumference 6.16 m, is to be cut into a number of sectors, before being installed as a 'rose' window. Each sector must be bounded by a strip of lead before the final assembly.

(a) Show that a sector, described by an angle of 0.8 radians, requires just under 2.75 m of strip lead.
(b) If the remainder of the glass is to be cut into five sectors, calculate the *total* amount of strip lead required for the whole window. Explain

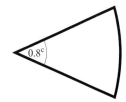

why this is independent of the angles which determine the size of each sector.

**8** A fisherman casts a distance of 80 m, during which the reel spins for 1.8 seconds. Calculate the rate of rotation in radians per second of the reel, which has a 4 cm diameter. What assumptions have been applied in the answer?

**9**

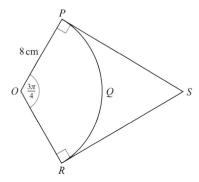

$PQR$ is an arc of a circle, centre $O$, radius 8 cm. $PS$, $RS$ are tangents to the circle at $P$ and $R$ and angle $PQR = \dfrac{3\pi}{4}$. Calculate the area enclosed by $PQRS$. Give your answer to one decimal place.

**10** A pattern-drawing set contains cogs that can either be fixed to the page, or be allowed to rotate around the outer edge of another fixed cog. One such fixed cog has a diameter of 12 cm, and a smaller cog of diameter 5 cm is free to rotate about the perimeter of the larger fixed cog. Through how many radians does the smaller cog turn in one complete revolution of the larger cog?

**11** A sector is to be formed using a rope of length 25 m.

(a) Find an expression for $\theta$, in terms of the perimeter and radius, $r$ m, of the sector. Hence show that the area of the sector is given by $A = \frac{1}{2}r(25 - 2r)$.

(b) By completing the square, or otherwise, find the value of the radius which maximises the area.

(c) Show that the maximum area of the sector is $\frac{625}{16}$ m$^2$.

**12** Two circles of radius 15 cm are constructed so that the centre of one is on the circumference of the other (and vice versa). Show that the common area enclosed by the two circles is given by $75\left(2\pi - \dfrac{3\sqrt{3}}{2}\right)$.

**13** Using calculus, show that the maximum area of any sector of fixed perimeter $p$ always occurs when the angle describing the sector is 2 radians.

**14** (a) Explain why the area of the segment shown in the diagram may be found using the formula: $A = \frac{1}{2}r^2(\theta - \sin\theta)$.

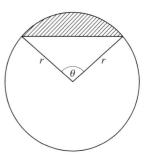

(b) By using the cubic approximation for $\sin\theta$, valid for small $\theta$ (i.e. $\sin\theta \approx \theta - \frac{1}{6}\theta^3$), find an approximate formula for the area of a segment.

(c) Show that when $r = 12$ cm, and $\theta = 0.5$, the error in the approximation is less than 2%.

**15** (a) Write down the equation which must be satisfied if the area of a segment is to be one half the area of the corresponding sector.

(b) Show that this equation simplifies to $2\sin\theta = \theta$.

(c) Demonstrate with a sketch graph that this equation has three solutions.

(d) Using a numerical method, determine the value of the required solution to two decimal places.

**16**

2500 r.p.m.

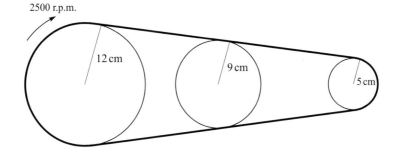

12 cm

9 cm

5 cm

The rate of rotation of three drums is determined by a belt drive which turns each of them simultaneously. If the largest drum turns at 2500 revolutions per minute (r.p.m.) and has a radius of 12 cm, calculate in radians per second the rates of rotation of the other two drums with radii 9 cm and 5 cm respectively.

**Advanced**

**1** (a) Verify that the radius of a sector with perimeter $p$ is given by

$$r = \frac{p}{2 + \theta}$$

(b) Two sectors are bent from wire: one with perimeter 38.4 cm and $\theta = 1.2$, the other with perimeter 39.0 cm and $\theta = 1.0$. Show by considering their areas, or otherwise, that the sector with the shorter perimeter cannot be placed on a plane surface inside the other sector.

2   A semi-circle of area $A$ cm$^2$ is formed by a flexible strip of plastic, which forms the boundary. $k$ strips, identical to this, are joined together to form the boundary of a new semi-circle. Find its area in terms of $k$ and $A$.

3   Two circles, which are positioned so that their centres are 11 cm apart, intersect. If the radii are 9 cm and 4 cm, find the perimeter which bounds the common region of the two circles.

4   $A$ and $B$ are points on a circle, centre $O$. $AC$ is a tangent at $A$ and $AC = $ arc length $AB$. Prove that the shaded area inside the circle is equal to the shaded area outside the circle.

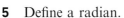

5   Define a radian.
A and $B$ are two points on the circumference of a circle with centre $O$ and radius $r$, where angle $AOB = \theta$ radian ($\theta < \pi$). Prove that the area of the segment bounded by the chord $AB$ and the minor arc $AB$ is $\frac{1}{2}r^2(\theta - \sin\theta)$.
A goat is tethered in a circular enclosure, centre $O$ and radius $r$, by means of a rope of length $\ell$ fixed to a point $P$ on the circumference. $Q$ and $R$ are the points on the circumference furthest from $P$ that the goat can reach, and angle $QPR = \theta$ radian. Show that $\ell^2 = 2r^2(1 + \cos\theta)$, and find an expression in terms of $r$ and $\theta$ for the area of the region that the goat can reach.
[OCR (Cambridge), 1976]

6   The diagram shows a circle, radius $r$ and centre $O$. $A$ and $B$ are points on the circumference, $AT$ is a tangent at $A$ and $\theta < \frac{1}{2}\pi$. If the area enclosed by $AT$, $BT$ and the arc $AB$ is equal to half the area of sector $AOB$, show that $2\tan\theta = 3\theta$.
Find $\theta$, correct to the nearest degree.

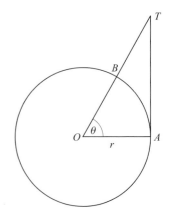

**7** The diagram shows an arc $ABC$ of a circle, with centre $O$ and radius $a$, and the chord $AC$. The length of the arc $ABC$ is $\ell$ and the angle $AOC = \theta$ radians. The area of triangle $AOC$ is equal to one quarter of the area of the sector $OABC$. Show that $x + 4\sin x = 0$, where $x = \ell/a$.

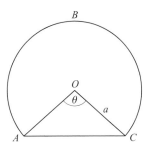

**8**

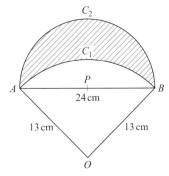

The diagram shows a triangle $OAB$ with $OA = OB = 13$ cm and $AB = 24$ cm. The mid-point of $AB$ is $P$. $C_1$ and $C_2$ are arcs with centres $O$ and $P$ respectively. Find the shaded area between the two arcs, giving your answer correct to one decimal place.

**9** A space-ship is travelling directly towards the centre of a spherical planet of radius $r$. When it is at a distance $h$ from its surface, $p\%$ of the planet's surface is visible. Express $p$ in terms of $r$ and $h$.
(Hint: you may assume that, when two parallel planes, distance $d$ apart, intersect a sphere of radius $r$, the surface area of the sphere between the planes is $2\pi r d$.)

**10**

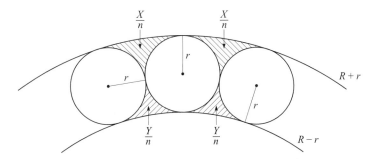

The region $A$ between concentric circles of radii $R + r$, $R - r$ contains $n$ circles of radius $r$. Each circle of radius $r$ touches both the larger circles as well as its two neighbours of radius $r$, as shown in the figure. Find the relationship that must hold between $n$, $R$ and $r$.

Show that $Y$, the total area of $A$ outside the circles of radius $r$ and adjacent to the circle of radius $R - r$, is given by

$$Y = nr\sqrt{R^2 - r^2} - \pi(R - r)^2 - n\pi r^2\left(\frac{1}{2} - \frac{1}{n}\right).$$

Find similar expressions for $X$, the total area of $A$ outside the circles of radius $r$ and adjacent to the circle of radius $R + r$, and for $Z$, the total area inside the circles of radius $r$.

What value does $\dfrac{X + Y}{Z}$ approach when $n$ becomes large?

[OCR (STEP), 1988]

## Revision

1  Convert the following angles from degrees to radians, giving your answers in terms of $\pi$.

(a)  30°      (b)  135°      (c)  210°      (d)  144°      (e)  126°

2  Write down estimates in radians (to one decimal place) for the following angles. Confirm your estimates by calculating correct approximations to three significant figures.

(a)  106°      (b)  200°      (c)  18°      (d)  270°      (e)  95°

3  $ABCD$ is a cyclic quadrilateral, circumscribed by a circle centred at $O$.
Angle $BOC$ is $\dfrac{3\pi}{5}$ and angle $COD$ is $\dfrac{2\pi}{5}$. Find angle $BCD$.

4  A 12.0 cm length of string is to be curved into a circular arc. What angle (measured in radians) will be subtended, if the radius of the arc is:

(a)  36.0 cm      (b)  15.0 cm      (c)  6.0 cm?

5  Write down an expression for the radius $r$ cm of a sector whose area is $A$ cm$^2$ and where the angle describing the sector is $\theta$. Use the expression to calculate the radii when:

(a)  $A = 187.2, \theta = 2.6$      (b)  $A = 126, \theta = 1.75$
(c)  $A = 52.56, \theta = 0.73$

6  (a)  Establish that the angle describing a sector with perimeter $p$ is given by $\theta = (p - 2r)/r$.
   (b)  Hence show that the area of such a sector is identical to that covered by a rectangle with sides $\dfrac{r}{2}$ and $l$, where $l$ is to be stated.

**7**

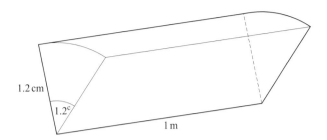

A pressure moulded extrusion is precisely designed to have a cross-sectional area that is a sector of a circle with radius 1.2 cm, and angle 1.2 radians. Each extrusion is exactly 1 m long, but both the radius and the angle may be inaccurate by as much as 7% in the manufacture. What is the possible maximum volume of excess material in any one length?

**8** (a) Prove that the area of a segment may be given by $A = \frac{1}{2}r^2(\theta - \sin\theta)$.

(b) For a fixed value of $r$, sketch the graph of $A$ as $\theta$ varies from 0 to $2\pi$. Comment on the geometrical significance of the variation in gradient.

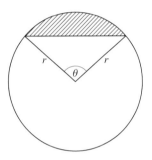

**9** Two mechanical cogs are driven by a motor so that the first with diameter 24 cm turns with an angular speed of 16 rad/s. The second is driven directly by the first, and has a diameter of 18 cm. Through how many complete revolutions does the second cog turn in one minute?

**10** A quadrant of a circle whose diameter is 17 mm is reshaped into a semi-circle.

(a) What is the new radius, if the area is kept constant?

(b) How much area is lost, if the perimeter is kept constant?

**11** A sector has a perimeter of 23 cm, but both the radius $r$ and the angle $\theta$ can vary. Find the values of $r$ and $\theta$ which maximise its area.

**12** Find the area enclosed when two identical circles of radius 10 cm intersect so that their centres are 16 cm apart.

## 6.2    Sine, cosine and tangent functions; their reciprocals, inverses and graphs

|       | 30°                    | 45°                    | 60°                    |
|-------|------------------------|------------------------|------------------------|
| sin   | $\frac{1}{2}$          | $\frac{1}{\sqrt{2}}$   | $\frac{\sqrt{3}}{2}$   |
| cos   | $\frac{\sqrt{3}}{2}$   | $\frac{1}{\sqrt{2}}$   | $\frac{1}{2}$          |
| tan   | $\frac{1}{\sqrt{3}}$   | $1$                    | $\sqrt{3}$             |

$$\tan x \equiv \frac{\sin x}{\cos x} \quad (\cos x \neq 0) \qquad \cot x \equiv \frac{\cos x}{\sin x} \quad (\sin x \neq 0)$$

$$\sec x \equiv \frac{1}{\cos x} \quad (\cos x \neq 0) \qquad \operatorname{cosec} x \equiv \frac{1}{\sin x} \quad (\sin x \neq 0)$$

Principal values: $\quad -\frac{1}{2}\pi \leq \sin^{-1} x \leq \frac{1}{2}\pi$

$$0 \leq \cos^{-1} x \leq \pi$$

$$-\frac{1}{2}\pi < \tan^{-1} x < \frac{1}{2}\pi$$

### Basic

1   In which quadrants do the following trigonometric functions have the stated signs?

(a)  $\sin + ve$               (b)  $\cos - ve$
(c)  $\tan + ve$ and $\sin - ve$     (d)  $\sin - ve$ and $\cos - ve$ and $\tan - ve$
(e)  $\cos - ve$ and $\tan + ve$

2   For values of $x$ in the given range, state whether these expressions will be positive or negative.

(a)  $\sin^2 x \quad \left(\frac{3\pi}{2} < x < 2\pi\right)$      (b)  $\tan^2 x \cos x \quad \left(\frac{\pi}{2} < x < \pi\right)$

(c)  $\cos^3 x \quad \left(\pi < x < \frac{3\pi}{2}\right)$      (d)  $\cos x \sin x \quad \left(\frac{\pi}{2} < x < \pi\right)$

3   Draw an equilateral triangle with sides of length 2 units, adding the altitude of the triangle.

(a)  Using your diagram, prove that $\cos 60° = \frac{1}{2}$.

(b)  Find exact surd values for:
(i)  $\sin 60°$    (ii)  $\tan 60°$    (iii)  $\sin 30°$    (iv)  $\cos 30°$
(v)  $\tan 30°$

4  (a)  What is the exact length of the hypotenuse of an isosceles right-angled triangle with two sides of length $k$ units?
(b)  Derive exact values for the sine, cosine and tangent of $\dfrac{\pi}{4}$.

5  Simplify each of the following expressions to give a single trigonometric function.

*(a)  $\dfrac{1}{\operatorname{cosec} x}$    *(b)  $\cot x \sin x$    (c)  $\sec^2 x \sin x \cos x$

(d)  $\dfrac{\tan x \cot x}{\sin x}$    (e)  $\tan x \operatorname{cosec} x$

6  (a)  Draw a sketch graph of $y = \sin x$ over the range $-180° \le x \le 360°$.
(b)  Use your graph to illustrate that the acute equivalent of $\sin 287°$ is $-\sin 73°$.
(c)  What are the acute equivalents of:
(i)  $\sin 133°$    (ii)  $\sin -76°$    (iii)  $\sin 346°$?

7  Specify the acute equivalents for:

(a)  $\cos 190°$    (b)  $\cos 297°$    (c)  $\cos -150°$
(d)  $\tan 232°$    (e)  $\tan -125°$

8  Consider the graphs of $\sin x$, $\cos x$ and $\tan x$ over the domain $-\pi < x \le \pi$.

(a)  Describe fully the symmetry of each graph.
(b)  State the period of each graph.
(c)  Identify which of the functions is *odd*, which *even*, and which neither.

9  Describe fully the simplest single transformation which maps $y = \cos x$ to each of the following graphs.

(a)  $y = -\cos x$    (b)  $y = 3 \cos x$    (c)  $y = \cos \dfrac{x}{7}$
(d)  $y = \cos\left(x - \dfrac{\pi}{6}\right)$    (e)  $y = \sin x$

10  Find the maximum value taken by each of the following expressions.

*(a)  $7 - 5 \sin x$    (b)  $2 + 3 \cos x$    *(c)  $\frac{1}{2}(1 - \sin^2 x)$

(d)  $\dfrac{1}{2 - \sin x}$    (e)  $\dfrac{5 - 3 \cos x}{3 + 2 \cos x}$

**11** Write down the principal value of:

(a) $\sin^{-1}\frac{1}{2}$    (b) $\cos^{-1}\frac{1}{\sqrt{2}}$    (c) $\tan^{-1}(-1)$

(d) $\sin^{-1}\left(-\frac{\sqrt{3}}{2}\right)$    (e) $\cos^{-1}(-1)$

**12** Find the values of $x$ in the range $0 \le x \le \pi$ that satisfy:

(a) $\sin x = 0.6$    (b) $\sin 2x = 0.6$    (c) $\sin\left(x + \frac{\pi}{6}\right) = 0.6$

### Intermediate

**1** State the exact values of the following trigonometric functions.

(a) $\sin 240°$    (b) $\tan -150°$    (c) $\cos -270°$
(d) $\tan 510°$    (e) $\sin -390°$    (f) $\cos 585°$

**2** State the exact values of:

(a) $\sin\frac{\pi}{3}$    (b) $\cos\frac{5\pi}{4}$    (c) $\tan\frac{5\pi}{3}$    (d) $\cos 7\pi$

**3** Leaving answers as multiples of $\pi$, write down the first three positive values of $\theta$ for which:

(a) $\sin\theta = \frac{\sqrt{3}}{2}$    (b) $\tan\theta = \frac{-1}{\sqrt{3}}$    (c) $\cos\theta = -1$

**4** Evaluate exactly:

*(a) $\sec\frac{\pi}{6} - \cot\frac{\pi}{3}$    (b) $\operatorname{cosec}\left(\frac{-2\pi}{3}\right) + 2\tan\left(\frac{7\pi}{6}\right)$

(c) $\operatorname{cosec}^2\left(\frac{7\pi}{4}\right) - \cot\left(\frac{7\pi}{4}\right)$

**5** (a) Verify graphically that $\sin 237°$ may be written as either
(i) $-\sin 57°$    or    (ii) $-\cos 33°$
(b) In the same way, identify two acute equivalents (in terms of sin and cos or cosec and sec) for:
(i) $\sin 172°$    (ii) $\cos -136°$    (iii) $\operatorname{cosec} 532°$
(iv) $\operatorname{cosec} -74°$    (v) $\sec 398°$

**6** Solve the following equations for $0° \le x \le 90°$.

(a) $\sin x = \frac{\sqrt{3}}{2}$    (b) $\sin 3x = \frac{\sqrt{3}}{2}$    (c) $\sin x = \cos 34°$

(d) $\cos x = \sin 12°$

7  (a)  Write down a vector in the form $\begin{pmatrix} a \\ 0 \end{pmatrix}$, with $a > 0$, which maps the

graph of $y = \sin x°$ onto the graph of $y = \cos x°$.

   (b)  In the same way, state a vector which maps $y = \sin x°$ onto the graph of $y = -\cos x°$.

   (c)  Use your answers to complete the following identities:

   (i)  $\cos x° \equiv \sin (\ldots)$     (ii)  $-\cos x° \equiv \sin (\ldots)$

8  (a)  By considering transformations of the graphs, verify that $\cos(x + \pi)$ may be simplified to give $-\cos x$.

   (b)  Find simplified expressions for: (i) $\sin \left(x + \dfrac{\pi}{2}\right)$ (ii) $\operatorname{cosec} (x - \pi)$

9  The height, $h$ cm, of a bicycle pedal above the ground after $t$ seconds is given by $h = 30 + 16 \sin 2t$

   (a)  What is the height when $t = 0$?

   (b)  What is the maximum height above the ground? What is the first time at which this occurs?

   (c)  How long does it take for the pedal to complete one revolution?

10  (a)  Give a sequence of transformations that will map the graph of the

function $f(x) = \cos x$ onto the graph of $g(x) = 2\cos\dfrac{x}{3} - 5$.

   (b)  Show that this sequence of transformations is not unique.

11  Describe the sequence of transformations that maps the graph of

$y = \cos x$ onto that of $y = 3\cos \left(x - \dfrac{\pi}{5}\right)$.

12  The most general sine wave, in degrees, has the form $A \sin(Bx° + C) + D$.

   *(a)  A sine wave has a maximum at $(34, 5.3)$, and a minimum at $(70, 2.7)$. Given that there are no turning points between these coordinates, draw a sketch to illustrate the curve in this region. Hence, find the values of A and D.

   *(b)  By considering the period of the graph, determine the value of B.

   (c)  Using one or more of the coordinates show that one possible value for C is $-80°$.

13  (a)  State the largest possible domain for: (i) $\sin^{-1} x$ (ii) $\cos^{-1} x$ (iii) $\tan^{-1} x$

   (b)  Sketch a graph of each inverse function, stating the range within which the principal values must lie for the function to be well-defined.

**14** The function $y = f(x)$ is defined by $f(x) = \tan 3x \left(0 < x \le \dfrac{\pi}{12}\right)$.
   (a)  Find an expression for $f^{-1}(x)$.
   (b)  Sketch the graph of $y = f^{-1}(x)$, clearly showing the domain.

**15** Sketch the graph of $y = \operatorname{cosec}^{-1} x$.

**16** Find both the upper and lower bounds of the range for each function, which are defined for all values of $x$.

   *(a)  $f(x) = \sqrt{(1 - \sin^2 x)}$      (b)  $f(x) = (3 + 2\cos x)(3 - 2\cos x)$
   (c)  $f(x) = (\tan x - 3)^2 + 5$      (d)  $f(x) = 4\sec^2 x + 20 \sec x + 14$

   In (d), it may help to rewrite the expression in completed square form.

## Advanced

**1**  For what values of $x$ does $\displaystyle\sum_{k=0}^{\infty} \cos^k x$ converge?

**2**  If $\sin^{-1} x = \dfrac{2\pi}{9}$, find the values of $\cos^{-1} x$.

**3**  Use appropriate graphs to solve the following inequalities for $\theta$ in the given range.

   (a)  $\tan \theta > 1$                $(0 \le \theta < 2\pi)$
   (b)  $\sin 3\theta > 0$               $(0 \le \theta < 2\pi)$
   (c)  $\operatorname{cosec} 3\theta \operatorname{cosec} 5\theta > 0$    $(0 \le \theta < \tfrac{1}{2}\pi)$

**4**  Two functions are defined on the interval $0 \le x \le \pi$:

$$f(x) = \sin \tfrac{1}{2}x, \quad g(x) = \cos 2x$$

   (a)  Explain why one of the functions has an inverse, while the other does not.
   (b)  The domain is now restricted to $0 \le x \le \tfrac{1}{2}\pi$. Evaluate

   (i)  $fg^{-1}(\tfrac{1}{2})$    (ii)  $f^{-1}g\left(\dfrac{\pi}{6}\right)$

**5**  The coordinates $(x, y)$ of a point $P$ satisfy the equation $\sin^2 x + \cos^2 y = 2$. Illustrate these points on a diagram.

**6**  Sketch the following graphs, indicating clearly the turning points.

   (a)  $y = \cos(\cos x)$   $(0 \le x \le 2\pi)$
   (b)  $y = \sin(\sin x)$   $(0 \le x \le 2\pi)$

**7**  Sketch the graph with equation $y = a + b\cos \pi x$, where $a > b > 0$, for $-1 \le x \le 1$. Indicate on your sketch the values of $a$ and $b$.
   The average time taken for my journey to work in the morning varies

according to when I leave home. If I leave at 7.00 the journey time is at its least value of 20 minutes. If I leave at 8.00, when the rush hour is at its worst, the journey time takes its maximum value of 60 minutes. If I leave at 9.00 the roads are quieter and the journey time is back to 20 minutes. I decide to model the average journey time, $y$ minutes, as a function of the time I leave home, measured as $x$ minutes after 8.00. Thus $x$ takes values from $-60$ to $60$. The equation I use is $y = a + b\cos k\pi x$ where $-1 \le kx \le 1$.

(i) Give reasons for the choice of values $a = 40$ and $b = 20$. Find an appropriate value for $k$.

(ii) By considering journeys which begin at 8.30 and 8.31, identify an implausible feature of this model. Do journeys starting at 7.29 and 7.30 indicate similar problems with the model?

(iii) By considering $\dfrac{dy}{dx}$ or otherwise, determine the range of departure times for which the model is implausible.

(iv) Show graphically how a better model, which avoids this implausible feature, might be devised.

[OCR (O&C), 1996]

**8**  Draw a diagram to illusrate, with respect to rectangular Cartesian axes, the square whose sides are $x = 4\pi$, $x = -4\pi$, $y = 4\pi$, $y = -4\pi$. Indicate all the points inside the square for which $\sin y = \sin x$, showing that they consist of two isolated points (at two of the vertices) and a number of straight lines of total length $64\pi\sqrt{2}$.
(The argument giving this number must be clearly stated.)
[OCR (Cambridge), 1972]

**9**  (i) Sketch the locus defined by all the points whose coordinates $(x, y)$ satisfy $0 \le x \le \pi$, $0 \le y \le \pi$ and $\sin x \sin y = \frac{1}{2}$.

(ii) Sketch the regions in the $x$–$y$ plane defined by all the points whose coordinates $(x, y)$ satisfy $-\pi \le x \le \pi$, $-\pi \le y \le \pi$ and $\sin |x| \sin |y| \ge \frac{1}{2}$.

[OCR (Cambridge), 1982]

**10** (a) Use a sketch graph to demonstrate that the equation $x = \tan x$ has an infinite sequence of positive solutions, $\alpha_1, \alpha_2, \ldots$, where $n\pi < \alpha_n < n\pi + \frac{1}{2}\pi$. Consider the equation $\sin x = ax$ ($x > 0$).

(b) Show that the equation
   (i)  has no solutions for $a > 1$,
   (ii) has one solution for $\cos \alpha_2 < a < 1$.

(c) How many solutions does the equation have for $\cos \alpha_{2n} < a < \cos \alpha_{2(n-1)}$, where $n > 1$?

**Revision**

**1**  By sketching appropriate graphs, state the values of $\theta$ for which $f(\theta) > 0$.

    (a)  $f(\theta) = \sin\theta\cos\theta$      (b)  $f(\theta) = 1 + \cos\theta$      (c)  $f(\theta) = \tan\theta - 1$

    (d)  $f(\theta) = \sin 2\theta$      (e)  $f(\theta) = 5\cos\dfrac{\theta}{3}$

**2**  Write down the exact values for each trigonometric function:

    (a)  $\sin\dfrac{\pi}{3}$      (b)  $\cos\dfrac{7\pi}{4}$      (c)  $\tan\dfrac{\pi}{3}$

    (d)  $\csc\dfrac{\pi}{4}$      (e)  $\sec\dfrac{13\pi}{6}$      (f)  $\cot\dfrac{\pi}{4}$

**3**  Determine all the values in the domain $\pi \le \theta \le 3\pi$ for which:

    (a)  $\sin\theta = 1$      (b)  $\cos\theta = -\frac{1}{2}$      (c)  $\tan\theta = \sqrt{3}$

    (d)  $\csc\theta = 0$      (e)  $\sec\theta = \dfrac{2}{\sqrt{3}}$      (f)  $\cot^2\theta = 3$

**4**  (a)  Draw a sketch of $y = \sin x$, and hence verify that $\sin 227°$ may be expressed as $-\sin 47°$.

    (b)  Determine, with a sketch in each case, the acute equivalents for:

        (i)  $\tan 187°$      (ii)  $\sec 129°$      (iii)  $\cos 546°$

**5**  (a)  Identify fully the single transformation that maps:

        (i)  $y = \sin x$      onto      $y = \sin 2x$

        (ii)  $y = \sin 2x$      onto      $y = \sin(2x - 45°)$

        (iii)  $y = \sin(2x - 45°)$      onto      $y = \sin(2x - 45°) + 3$

    (b)  Hence sketch one period of the graph of $y = \sin(2x - 45°) + 3$, identifying the coordinates of the turning points.

**6**  Conrad is playing with a bird whistle on the end of an inelastic string, which is being rotated in a vertical circle, at a constant 120 r.p.m. having started from the downward vertical. If the string is of length 0.82 m, and Conrad's stationary hand is 1.35 m above the ground, find an expression for the height of the whistle after $t$ seconds.

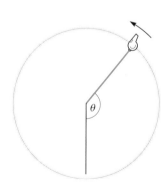

**7** Superimpose the graphs of $\tan\theta$ and $\cot\theta$, with the domain $0 \le \theta \le \pi$. Hence determine the values of $\theta$ for which $\tan\theta - \cot\theta$ is negative.

**8** (a) For the graph with equation $y = 6\sin 5x$, state:
    (i) the period
    (ii) the amplitude
    (iii) the equation of a line of symmetry
  (b) Describe the sequence of transformations that maps the graph of $y = \sin x$ to $y = 6\sin 5x$.

  (c) If $f(x) = 6\sin 5x\left(0 \le x \le \dfrac{\pi}{10}\right)$, sketch the graph of $y = f^{-1}(x)$.

**9** A computer programmer needs to model the motion of the hands of an analogue clock. The centre of the clock will have screen position $(165, 235)$. Using the same unit of measurement the lengths of the hands are 15 and 35 units respectively.

  (a) Show that the tip of the hour hand, starting at noon, may be described by the equations

$$x = 165 + 15\sin\left(\frac{\pi t}{21\,600}\right), \quad y = 235 + 15\cos\left(\frac{\pi t}{21\,600}\right)$$

    where $t$ is measured in seconds.
  (b) Find an equivalent pair of equations for the minute hand.

**10** Determine the range of the following functions over the specified domain.

  (a) $f(x) = 2\sin x - 5 \quad 0° \le x \le 360°$

  (b) $f(x) = \operatorname{cosec}\dfrac{x}{2} \quad 0° \le x \le 180°$

  (c) $f(x) = \sqrt{3}\tan x \quad \pi/6 \le x \le \pi/2$
  (d) $f(x) = 2\sin 3x \quad -\pi \le x \le -\pi/2$

**11** Find the equation of the sine wave, which has a period of $15°$, a turning point located at $(23°, 5.2)$, and a minimum value of 2.8.

**12** When a ray of light passes from air into water, the angle of incidence, $i$, and the angle of refraction, $r$, are related by $\dfrac{\sin i}{\sin r} = 1.3$.

  (a) Find $r$ when $i = 45°$.

  (b) Explain why $\sin r \le \dfrac{1}{1.3}$. Hence state the maximum possible value of $r$.

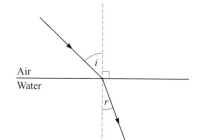

Air
Water

## 6.3    Trigonometric identities including $\sin^2\theta + \cos^2\theta \equiv 1$ etc.; addition formulae; double angle formulae and $R\sin(\theta + \alpha)$

$$\sin^2\theta + \cos^2\theta \equiv 1, \quad 1 + \tan^2\theta \equiv \sec^2\theta,$$
$$\cot^2\theta + 1 \equiv \operatorname{cosec}^2\theta$$
$$\sin(A \pm B) \equiv \sin A \cos B \pm \cos A \sin B$$
$$\cos(A \pm B) \equiv \cos A \cos B \mp \sin A \sin B$$

$$\tan(A \pm B) \equiv \frac{\tan A \pm \tan B}{1 \mp \tan A \tan B}$$

$$\sin 2A \equiv 2\sin A \cos A,$$
$$\cos 2A \equiv \cos^2 A - \sin^2 A \equiv 2\cos^2 A - 1 \equiv 1 - 2\sin^2 A$$

$$\tan 2A \equiv \frac{2\tan A}{1 - \tan^2 A}$$

$$a\sin\theta + b\cos\theta \equiv R\sin(\theta + \alpha) \quad \text{where}$$

$$R = \sqrt{a^2 + b^2} \text{ and } \tan\alpha = \frac{b}{a}$$

### Basic

**1**  Simplify:

(a) $\sqrt{1 - \sin^2\theta}$     (b) $(1 - \sin\theta)(1 + \sin\theta)$

(c) $\dfrac{\sqrt{1 + \tan^2\theta}}{\sqrt{1 - \sin^2\theta}}$     (d) $3\sin^2\theta + 3\cos^2\theta$

**2**  Express $4\cos^2 x - \sin^2 x$ in terms of:

(a) $\sin x$ only   (b) $\cos x$ only

**3**  Show that:

(a) $\dfrac{\sin\theta}{\cos\theta} + \dfrac{\cos\theta}{\sin\theta} \equiv \dfrac{1}{\sin\theta\cos\theta}$

(b) $\sin^4\theta - \cos^4\theta \equiv \sin^2\theta - \cos^2\theta$

(c) $\sqrt{2\sin^2\theta + 6\cos^2\theta - 2} \equiv 2\cos\theta$

**4**  Given that $\sin\beta = \frac{7}{11}$ and that $0 \le \beta \le \frac{1}{2}\pi$, use the given identities to find exact values for:

(a) $\cos\beta$     $(\sin^2\theta + \cos^2\theta \equiv 1)$

(b) $\tan \beta$     $\left(\tan \theta \equiv \dfrac{\sin \theta}{\cos \theta}\right)$

(c) $\cot \beta$     $\left(\cot \theta \equiv \dfrac{1}{\tan \theta}\right)$

(d) $\operatorname{cosec} \beta$     $(\operatorname{cosec}^2 \theta - \cot^2 \theta \equiv 1)$
Verify your answer to (d) directly, from the original value for $\sin \beta$.

*5   Find the values of the constant $k$, which correctly complete each of the following identities

(a) $(\sec^2 \theta - 1)(\operatorname{cosec}^2 \theta - 1) \equiv k$
(b) $(\tan \theta + \cot \theta)\pi \sin \theta \cos \theta \equiv k$
(c) $\sqrt{\sec^2 \theta - \tan^2 \theta} + \sqrt{\operatorname{cosec}^2 \theta - \cot^2 \theta} \equiv k$

6   Simplify:

(a) $\sin \left(\alpha + \dfrac{\pi}{2}\right)$          (b) $\tan(\alpha + \pi)$

(c) $-\cos\left(\dfrac{\pi}{2} - \alpha\right)$          (d) $\operatorname{cosec} 2(\alpha + \pi)$

7   Determine the value of the acute angle $\alpha$ which satisfies:

(a) $\cos 22° = \cos 32° \cos \alpha + \sin 32° \sin \alpha$

(b) $\tan(45° + \alpha) = \dfrac{\tan 37° + \tan 49°}{1 - \tan 37° \tan 49°}$

8   Simplify:

(a) $\sin \theta \cos \theta$     (b) $\dfrac{1 - \cos 2x}{\sin 2x}$     (c) $\sqrt{1 + \cos 4\theta}$

9   Use the identity $\cos 2A \equiv 2\cos^2 A - 1$ to show that $\cos 15° = \frac{1}{2}\sqrt{2 + \sqrt{3}}$ and find a similar expression for $\sin 15°$
Write down an expression for $\cos 75°$.

*10 Determine the value of the acute angle $\alpha$ which satisfies each of these identities.

(a) $12 \sin \theta + 5 \cos \theta \equiv 13 \sin(\theta + \alpha)$
(b) $3 \cos \theta + 4 \sin \theta \equiv 5 \cos(\theta - \alpha)$
(c) $7 \sin \theta - \cos \theta \equiv \sqrt{50} \sin(\theta - \alpha)$

11 Determine the value of the positive constant, $R$, which satisfies each of these identities.

(a) $R \cos(\theta + 30°) \equiv \sqrt{3} \cos \theta - \sin \theta$
(b) $R \sin(\theta - 45°) \equiv \sin \theta - \cos \theta$
(c) $\sqrt{29} \sin(\theta + \alpha) \equiv 5 \sin \theta + R \cos \theta$

**12** Find the coordinates of the maximum point, nearest to the origin, of the following functions.

(a) $y = \cos x + 3 \sin x$
(b) $y = 5 \cos x - 3 \sin x$
(c) $y = 11 \cos 2x + 13 \sin 2x$

### Intermediate

**1** By inspection, find an angle that satisfies the equation:

(a) $\sin^2 \alpha = (1 + \cos 35°)(1 - \cos 35°)$        $0° \leq \alpha \leq 90°$

(b) $1 + \tan^2 2\alpha = \sec^2 \dfrac{\pi}{4}$        $0 \leq \alpha \leq \dfrac{\pi}{4}$

(c) $(\operatorname{cosec} \alpha - \cot \alpha)(\cot 2 + \operatorname{cosec} 2) = 1$    $\pi \leq \alpha \leq 2\pi$

**2** Prove the following identities.
*(a) $\sec^2 \theta + \operatorname{cosec}^2 \theta \equiv \sec^2 \theta \operatorname{cosec}^2 \theta$
*(b) $1 + \tan \theta \sin \theta \sec \theta \equiv \tan \theta \operatorname{cosec} \theta \sec \theta$

(c) $\cos^2 \theta \equiv \dfrac{\operatorname{cosec} \theta - \sin \theta}{\operatorname{cosec} \theta}$

***3** Without using a calculator, evaluate the following expressions, in exact form.

(a) $\sin 59° \cos 14° - \sin 14° \cos 59°$

(b) $\dfrac{\tan 15° + \frac{1}{\sqrt{3}}}{1 - \frac{1}{\sqrt{3}} \tan 15°}$

(c) $\cos^2 30° - \sin^2 30°$

**4** Given that $\sin \alpha = \frac{3}{5}$, $\cos \beta = \frac{5}{13}$, $0 \leq \alpha \leq \frac{1}{2}\pi$ and $0 \leq \beta \leq \frac{1}{2}\pi$, find $\cos \alpha$ and $\sin \beta$ and hence exact values for:

(a) $\cos (\alpha + \beta)$        (b) $\tan (\beta - \alpha)$        (c) $\sin (2\alpha - \beta)$

**5** Using the substitution $t = \tan \theta$, simplify the following expressions.

(a) $\dfrac{2t}{1 + t^2}$        *(b) $\dfrac{1 - t^2}{1 + t^2}$        (c) $\dfrac{2t}{1 - t^2}$

**6** Superimpose the graphs of the following pairs of functions. Use the same axes in each case.

(a) $f(x) = \sin x$,    $g(x) = \sin 2x$        $0 \leq x \leq 2\pi$
(b) $p(x) = \sin 2x$,    $q(x) = \sin x \cos x$    $0 \leq x \leq \pi$
(c) $m(x) = 2 \cos^2 x$, $n(x) = \cos 2x$        $0 \leq x \leq 2\pi$

Comment on the graphs and explain each feature with reference to the given functions.

**7** Prove that $\cos(60° - x) + \sqrt{3}\sin(60° - x) = 2\cos x$. Hence find an exact expression for $\cos 15°$.

**8** One of the following identities is true; the rest are false. Use counter-examples to identify those which are false and prove that the remaining identity is true.

(a) $\sin x + \sin 2x \equiv \sin x(1 + \cos x)$  (b) $\cos 2x + \sin 2x \equiv 1$
(c) $\cot x - \tan x \equiv 2\cot 2x$  (d) $\sin 3x \equiv 3\sin x \cos x$

**9** (a) By rewriting $\sin 3\theta$ in the form $\sin(\theta + 2\theta)$ establish the identity

$$\sin 3\theta \equiv \sin\theta - 2\sin^3\theta + 2\sin\theta\cos^2\theta$$

(b) Hence prove that $\sin 3\theta \equiv 3\sin\theta - 4\sin^3\theta$.

**10** Let two functions be defined by $f(x) = \sin x$, $x \in \mathbb{R}$ and $g(x) = \cos x$, $x \in \mathbb{R}$. Verify that $f(4\alpha) \equiv 2f(\alpha)g(\alpha) - f(2\alpha)\{1 - g(2\alpha)\}$

**11** A ladder mounted on the turntable of a 'Simon Snorkel' fire appliance has fixed length $l$ and is initially inclined at an angle $\alpha$ above the horizontal.

(a) Demonstrate that, when the ladder is raised to an angle of $2\alpha$ above the horizontal, the height of the ladder end above the turntable increases by a factor of $2\cos\alpha$.
(b) Using the identity $4\sin^3\theta \equiv 3\sin\theta - \sin 3\theta$, find an expression for the factor by which the height increases when the ladder is raised from the initial position to an angle of $3\alpha$ above the horizontal. Hence show that trebling the angle in this way can never treble the height.

**12** In an isosceles triangle $ABC$, $AB = AC = 5\,\text{cm}$ and $N$ is the mid-point of $BC$.

(a) Show that $BN = 5\sin\left(\frac{1}{2}A\right)$ and hence derive an expression for the length $BC$.
(b) Using the cosine rule, find an alternative expression for the length $BC$.
(c) Use your results to demonstrate that $\sin^2\left(\frac{1}{2}A\right) \equiv \frac{1}{2}(1 - \cos A)$.

**13** (a) Express $5\cos\theta + 12\sin\theta$ in the form $R\cos(\theta - \alpha)$.
(b) Find the greatest and least values of the expression

$$\frac{1}{5\cos\theta + 12\sin\theta - 7},$$

giving the values of $\theta$ $(0 \le \theta \le 360°)$ for which these occur.

**14** The displacement of a particle along a straight-line track, after $t$ seconds have elapsed, is given by $x_1 = 5\sin(12t + 30)°$. A second particle moving on a neighbouring track has displacement $x_2 = 7\sin(12t + 45)°$.

(a) Rewrite both $x_1$ and $x_2$, separately, in the form $\alpha \sin 12t + \beta \cos 12t$.
(b) Hence find, to two decimal places, the maximum value of $|x_1 - x_2|$, the distance between the particles.

**15** Prove that $1 + \tan \theta \equiv R \sec \theta \cos (\theta - \alpha)$, stating the values of $R$ and $\alpha$. Hence prove that $-a \sec \theta \le 1 + \tan \theta \le a \sec \theta$, $a > 0$, where the minimum value of $a$ is to be found.

**16** (a) Simplify $\cos (2t - \pi/3) + \sin(2t - \pi/6)$.
(b) Find an expression for $\alpha$, in terms of $k$, such that
$$\cos (\theta + k) + \sin (\theta + \alpha) \equiv 0$$

## Advanced

**1** (a) If three angles $A$, $B$ and $C$ are complementary, i.e. $A + B + C = 90°$, prove that $\cos A \cos B \cos C \equiv \sin A \sin B \cos C + \sin A \cos B \sin C + \cos A \sin B \sin C$.
(b) Prove:
  (i) $\sin \theta \equiv \cos \theta(\cot \theta - 2 \cot 2\theta)$
  (ii) $2 \tan 2\theta \equiv (\tan 2\theta - \sin 2\theta) \operatorname{cosec}^2 \theta$

**2** (a) Show that $f(\theta) = 5 \sin 2\theta + 1 - 2 \sin^2 \theta \equiv R \sin(k\theta + \alpha)$, stating the values of $R$, $k$ and $\alpha$. Sketch the graph of $f(\theta)$.
(b) Prove that $\cot \theta + \operatorname{cosec} \theta = \cot \frac{1}{2}\theta$. Hence express $\displaystyle\sum_{r=0}^{n} \operatorname{cosec} 2^r x$ in the form $\cot ax - \cot bx$, where $a$ and $b$ are to be stated.

**3** Two underwater struts ($PA$ and $PB$), both of length $l$, lie in a vertical plane and form part of the supporting structure of an oil-rig. They are inclined to the horizontal as shown in the diagram: $PA$ at $\alpha$ above, and $PB$ at $\beta$ below. The values of acute angles $\alpha$ and $\beta$ are not known and cannot readily be measured. A third reinforcement strut needs to be designed and secured along the line $AB$.

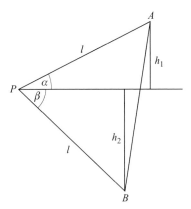

(a) Show that the actual length of $AB$ is given by $\sqrt{2l^2[1 - \cos (\alpha + \beta)]}$.
(b) Using a depthmeter it is possible to ascertain the vertical measurements $h_1$ and $h_2$. Explain, using your answer from (a), why the formula $\sqrt{2l^2 + 2h_1 h_2}$ may be used as an upper bound for the length of the third strut.

4 (a) Use an iterative approach to find a solution, accurate to two decimal places, to the equation $\tan 2\theta = \cos 2\theta + 1$, within the range $0° \le \theta \le 45°$.

(b) Substituting $x = \tan\theta$, show that:

(i) $\tan 2\theta = \dfrac{2x}{1 - x^2}$     (ii) $\cos 2\theta + 1 = \dfrac{2}{1 + x^2}$

(c) Hence obtain an approximation to one root of the equation $x^3 + x^2 + x - 1 = 0$.

5 (a) Sketch graphs of the two functions $f(x) = 5 \sin x$ and $g(x) = 7 \cos x$ on the same axes.

(b) Sketch also the graphs of $r(x) = f(x) + g(x)$ and $s(x) = f(x) - g(x)$. Hence estimate the value of $k$ such that $r(x) \equiv s(x + k)$.

(c) Prove that $k = 2\tan^{-1} 1\frac{2}{5}$.

6 Prove that $\tan^{-1} x + \tan^{-1} y = \tan^{-1} \dfrac{x + y}{1 - xy}$.

7 Show that $4 \sin\theta + 3 \cos\theta$ can be written in the form $R \sin(\theta + \alpha)$, where $R > 0$ and $0 \le \alpha \le \frac{1}{2}\pi$.
Give the values of $R$ and $\alpha$.

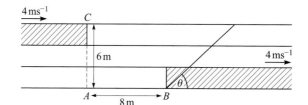

In a shunting yard two long goods trains are travelling in the same direction along parallel tracks at speed $4\,\text{ms}^{-1}$. The gap $AB$ between them is 8 m, and the total distance across both tracks $AC$ is 6 m.
A rail worker wishes to cross in between the passing of the trains. He moves with speed $v$ in a straight line making angle $\theta$ with the track and takes $T$ seconds to cross completely. If he starts from $B$ immediately the first train is clear of him, how far ahead (measured along the track) of the front of the second train is he $t$ seconds later ($t \le T$)?
Find $T$ in terms of $v$ and $\theta$, and hence, or otherwise, show that, if the rail worker is to cross safely, $v$ must not be less than $V$, where

$$V = \frac{12}{4 \sin\theta + 3 \cos\theta}$$

For what value of $\theta$ is $V$ a minimum? Find the minimum value of $V$, and how long the rail worker takes to cross completely at this least possible speed.
[OCR (SMP), 1983]

**8** Prove that $\cot \theta - \cot 2\theta = \operatorname{cosec} 2\theta$.
Replace $\theta$ by $2\theta$ in this identity and deduce that if $0° < \theta < 45°$ then $\cot \theta - \cot 4\theta > 2$.
The acute-angled triangle $ABC$ is such that $B = 4C$. By using the above result, or otherwise, prove that $b^2 - c^2 < 4\Delta$, where $\Delta$ is the area of the triangle.
[OCR (Cambridge), 1967]

**9** (a) Prove that $bc(b - c) + ca(c - a) + ab(a - b) = -(b - c)(c - a)(a - b)$.
(b) Prove that

$$\sin B \sin C \sin (B - C) + \sin C \sin A \sin (C - A) + \sin A \sin B \sin (A - B)$$
$$= -\sin (B - C) \sin (C - A) \sin (A - B) \ .$$

[OCR (Cambridge), 1974]

**10** The points $P_1$ and $P_2$ on the surface of the earth (assumed to be a sphere of radius $r$ and centre $O$) are at the same (northern) latitude $\lambda$, and their respective longitudes are $L_1$ and $L_2$. Show that the length $C$ of the route from $P_1$ to $P_2$ via a circle centre $O$ (called a **great circle**) satisfies the equation

$$\cos \left( \frac{C}{r} \right) = \sin^2 \lambda + \cos^2 \lambda \cos (L_2 - L_1)$$

If the separation in longitude is $90°$ show that either

$$C = 2r \sin^{-1} \left( \frac{\cos \lambda}{\sqrt{2}} \right) \quad \text{or} \quad C = 2\pi r - 2r \sin^{-1} \left( \frac{\cos \lambda}{\sqrt{2}} \right)$$

[OCR (Cambridge), 1967]

## Revision

**1** Prove the identities:

(a) $\sec \theta - \cos \theta \equiv \sin \theta \tan \theta$     (b) $\cot \theta - \sin \theta \cos \theta \equiv \cos^3 \theta \operatorname{cosec} \theta$

**2** Prove the identities:

(a) $(\sec \theta + \cos \theta)(\sec \theta - \cos \theta) \equiv \tan^2 \theta + \sin^2 \theta$
(b) $\sec^4 \theta - \tan^4 \theta \equiv \sec^2 \theta + \tan^2 \theta$

**3** Prove that:

(a) $2 \cos^2 \theta + \cos 2\theta \equiv 3 - 4 \sin^2 \theta$
(b) $\cot \theta (\sin \theta + \sin 2\theta) \equiv 1 + \cos \theta + \cos 2\theta$

**4**  Prove:

(a) $\tan\left(\dfrac{\pi}{4}+\alpha\right) \equiv \cot\left(\dfrac{\pi}{4}-\alpha\right)$

(b) $\sin(A+B) + \sin(A-B) \equiv 2\sin A \cos B$

**5**  Determine which of the following equations are identities.

(a) $\dfrac{1+\cos 2\theta}{\sin 2\theta} = \cot\theta$       (b) $\operatorname{cosec} 2\theta + \cot 2\theta = \cos\theta$

**6**  Prove, using an identity for $\tan(A+B)$, that $\tan 105° = \dfrac{\sqrt{3}+3}{\sqrt{3}-3}$.

**7**  Using the formula for $\cos(A+B)$, or otherwise, obtain an exact value for $\cos 75°$ in the form $a\sqrt{2}(\sqrt{b}-1)$, where $a$ and $b$ are both rational.

**8**  By sketching appropriate graphs, identify the number of solutions to each equation.

(a) $\sin 2\theta = \cos 3\theta$       $0 \le \theta \le \pi$

(b) $\tan\theta = \dfrac{\sin 2\theta}{1-\cos 2\theta},$       $0 < \theta \le 2\pi$

**9**  The following graphs pass through points with coordinates $(0, -1)$ and $(\pi/2, 2)$. Sketch the graphs and in each case find the values of $\alpha$ and $\beta$.

(a) $y = \alpha + \dfrac{\beta \sin x}{1+\cos x}$       (b) $y = \alpha \cos\left(\beta x + \dfrac{\pi}{3}\right)$

**10**  Find the greatest value of $f(\theta)$ for each of the following functions, in the region $0 \le \theta \le \pi$. State the value of $\theta$ at which this occurs.

(a) $f(\theta) = 3\sin\theta + 4\cos\theta$       (b) $f(\theta) = 3\cos\theta - 4\sin\theta$

**11**  (a)  Express $5\cos\theta - 19\sin\theta$ in the form $R\cos(\theta+\alpha)$.
    (b)  Hence obtain an equivalent expression in the form $R\sin(\theta-\alpha)$.

**12**  Find equivalent Cartesian equations for the following parametric curves.

(a) $x = 7 + \cos 2\theta$, $y = 2 - \sin\theta$       (b) $x = \sin^2 2\theta$, $y = \sec\theta$

## 6.4    Solution of trigonometric equations

### Basic

**1**  Solve the following equations for angles in the interval $[0°, 90°]$.

(a)  $\sin\theta = 0.7$       (b)  $\cos\theta = 0.2$       (c)  $\tan\theta = 4.1$
(d)  $3\sin\theta = 2$       (e)  $\cos\theta = 1.2$

**2** Find, to the nearest tenth of a degree, the principal values which are solutions to the following equations.

(a) $\sec \theta = 2.5$                (b) $\tan \theta = -1.3$

(c) $2 \cos \theta + 3 = 1 - 2 \cos \theta$     (d) $\operatorname{cosec} \theta = -5$

**3** Leaving answers as rational multiples of $\pi$, state the principal values which satisfy:

(a) $\tan \theta = -1$             (b) $\cot \theta = \sqrt{3}$      (c) $\sin \theta = -\dfrac{\sqrt{3}}{2}$

(d) $4 - \operatorname{cosec} \theta = 2(3 - \operatorname{cosec} \theta)$      (e) $\tan^2 \theta = 3$

**4** By drawing appropriate sketches, determine how many solutions exist in the specified domain.

(a) $\tan \theta = 0$   $(-\pi < \theta \leq \pi)$      (b) $\sin \theta = -0.5$   $(-\pi \leq \theta < 3\pi/2)$

(c) $\sec \theta = 1$   $(0 \leq \theta \leq 3\pi)$      (d) $\operatorname{cosec} \theta = -2$   $(-2\pi < \theta < -\pi)$

**5** Use the identity $\tan \theta = \dfrac{\sin \theta}{\cos \theta}$ to solve the following equations for angles in the interval $0° \leq \theta \leq 180°$.

(a) $4 \sin \theta = \cos \theta$      (b) $2 \sin \theta + 3 \cos \theta = 0$      *(c) $\tan \theta = \sin \theta$

**6** Solve the following equations for values of $\theta$ in the range $0 \leq \theta \leq 4\pi$. Give your answers to two decimal places.

(a) $5 \cos \theta = 2 \sin \theta$      (b) $\tan \theta = 3 \sin \theta$      (c) $7 \operatorname{cosec} \theta = 11 \sin \theta$

**7** Find all solutions in the range $0 \leq \theta \leq 2\pi$. Give your answers to two decimal places.

(a) $\sin \theta \tan \theta = 0$            *(b) $\sin \theta (\cos \theta - 1) = 0$

(c) $(\tan \theta - 2)(\cot \theta - \frac{1}{2}) = 0$      (d) $(\tan \theta - 3)^2 = 14$

**8** (a) By factorising $6 \sin^2 \theta - 7 \sin \theta + 2$, show that the equation $6 \sin^2 \theta - 7 \sin \theta + 2 = 0$ is satisfied when $\sin \theta = \frac{1}{2}$ and $\sin \theta = \frac{2}{3}$. Hence find all solutions in the range $0° \leq \theta \leq 360°$.

     (b) Solve for $0° \leq \theta \leq 360°$:

         (i) $4 \sin^2 \theta - \sin \theta - 3 = 0$      (ii) $2 \cos^2 \theta - \cos \theta = 0$

**9** (a) Use the identity $\cos^2 \theta = 1 - \sin^2 \theta$ to rewrite the expression $2 \cos^2 \theta + \sin \theta - 2$ in terms of $\sin \theta$ only. Hence find all solutions of $2 \cos^2 \theta + \sin \theta = 2$ in the range $0° \leq \theta \leq 360°$.

     (b) Solve the equation $2 \sin^2 \theta + \cos \theta = -1$ for values of $\theta$ in the range $0° \leq \theta \leq 360°$.

**10** Use a sketch to establish the number of solutions to each equation in the range $0° \leq \theta \leq 360°$, and then find the values to the nearest tenth of a degree.

(a) $\sin 2\theta = 0.5$      (b) $\sin \dfrac{\theta}{2} = 0.7$      (c) $\sin (\theta - 45°) = 0$

**11** Solve the following equations for $0° \le \theta \le 360°$.

*(a)  $3 \sin(2\theta + 30°) = 1$      (b)  $\sqrt{2} \cos(\frac{1}{2}\theta - 45°) = 1$

**12** Find all acute angles for which (a) $\sec 5\theta = 3.8$, (b) $\cot(7\theta + 33°) = 19$.

### Intermediate

**1** Solve the following equations, specifying all solutions in the range $-180° \le x \le 180°$.

(a)  $6 \sin^2 x + \sin x - 2 = 0$      *(b)  $\sin^2 x - 4 \sin x + 1 = 0$
(c)  $2 \tan^2 x + 9 \tan x - 35 = 0$      (d)  $3 \tan^2 x + 5 \tan x + 5 = 0$

**2** Demonstrate that each of the following equations may be simplified to a quadratic involving only $\sin \theta$. (There is no need to solve the equations.)

(a)  $\sin^2 \theta + 5 \cos^2 \theta - 2 \sin \theta = 0$      (b)  $\operatorname{cosec}^2 \theta = 9$

**3** Find all values in the domain $\{x : 0 \le x \le 2\pi\}$ for which:

*(a)  $\tan^2 x + 3 \sec^2 x = 5$      (b)  $(\tan x - 2 \sec x)(\tan x + 2 \sec x) = 11$
(c)  $\sin x \tan x = 3 \cos x$      (d)  $\cot x = 2 \tan x$

**4** Using sketch graphs, determine the number of solutions, $0 \le \theta \le \pi$, which satisfy the equation $a \sin(b\theta + c) + d = 0$, when

(a)  $a = 2, b = 1, c = \frac{1}{2}\pi, d = -1$

(b)  $a = 5, b = 3, c = 0, d = -3$

(c)  $a = -2, b = 1, c = \frac{1}{4}\pi, d = \frac{3}{2}$

(d)  $a = 1, b = \frac{1}{2}, c = \frac{1}{2}\pi, d = -\frac{3}{5}$

**5** Solve the following equations to the nearest tenth of a degree, for $0° \le \theta \le 180°$.

*(a)  $\sin(2\theta - 30°) = -0.52$      (b)  $4 \tan(0.97\theta + 117°) = 11$
(c)  $\sin^2 4\theta = 0.35$      (d)  $\sec(\theta - 27°) = 5$

**6** Use appropriate trigonometrical identities to simplify, and then solve, for values of $\theta$ in the range $-\pi \le \theta \le \pi$:

(a)  $\sin 2\theta = \cos \theta$      (b)  $3 \cos 2\theta + 2 = \sin \theta$      (c)  $\tan 2\theta + 3 \tan \theta = 0$

**7** Solve the inequalities for the given interval:

(a)  $\cos \frac{1}{2}\theta \ge \dfrac{\sqrt{3}}{2}$    $(0 \le \theta \le 2\pi)$      (b)  $\tan \theta < 9 \cot \theta$    $(0 < \theta \le \frac{1}{2}\pi)$

(c) $7\cos^2\theta + 4\cos\theta \le 0$   $(0 \le \theta \le \pi)$

**8** Find all values, $0° \le x < 360°$, which satisfy the equations:

(a) $\operatorname{cosec} x - 2\cot x = 0$    (b) $\tan x + 2\sin x = 0$
(c) $4\cos x\cot x = \sin x$

**9** The functions $f(x)$ and $g(x)$ are defined over the domain $\{x: 0 \le x < 2\pi\}$, by $f(x) \equiv 7\sin x - 5\cos x$,   $g(x) \equiv \sin 2x + \cos 2x$
(a) Solve the equations:
    (i) $f(x) = 0$    (ii) $f'(x) = 0$    (iii) $g(x) = 0$    (iv) $g'(x) = 0$
(b) Hence sketch the graphs of $f(x)$ and $g(x)$.

**10** Solve the equation $\cos 3\theta = \cos\theta$ for $0° \le \theta \le 360°$.

**11** (a) Show that $\sin\theta = \cos(90° - \theta)$.
    (b) Hence solve the following equations for $0° \le \theta \le 360°$.
        (i) $\cos 4\theta = \sin\theta$    (ii) $\sin(\theta - 30°) = \cos(\theta + 45°)$

**\*12** (a) Demonstrate that the expression $3\sin\theta + 4\cos\theta$ may be rewritten as $5\sin(\theta + \alpha)$, where $\alpha$ is an acute angle. State the value of $\alpha$ to two decimal places.
    (b) Hence, or otherwise, solve the equation $3\sin\theta + 4\cos\theta = \frac{7}{2}$, where $\theta$ is acute.

**13** Find all values, $0° \le \theta \le 360°$, where:

(a) $5\sin\theta + 6\cos\theta = 7$    (b) $7\cos\theta = 11\sin\theta - 13$

**14** A smoke alarm emits a loud oscillating signal when activated. The signal comes from two speakers, $A$ and $B$. The volume from the first is given by $V_A = 7\cos 12t$, and from the second by $V_B = 6\sin 12t$. For what percentage of time is the total volume $|V_A + V_B|$ greater than 9 units?

**15** (a)   (i) Write down the first four positive solutions of the equation
$$\tan\theta = \frac{1}{\sqrt 3}.$$
    (ii) Write down the solution of this equation that lies in the interval $[99\pi, 100\pi]$.
    (iii) Write down the general solution of the equation.
  (b) Use the above method to write down the general solution of
$$\sin\theta = \frac{\sqrt 3}{2}.$$

**16** Obtain the exact general solutions (in radians) for:

(a) $\cos\theta = \frac{1}{2}$    (b) $\tan 2\theta = 1$    (c) $\sin\left(\theta - \frac{\pi}{4}\right) = -\frac{1}{2}$
(d) $\tan^2 4\theta = 3$

**Advanced**

1   Show that $\tan\theta + \cot\theta = \dfrac{2}{\sin 2\theta}$.

Hence, or otherwise, solve the equation $\tan\theta + \cot\theta = 4$, giving all the values of $\theta$ between $0°$ and $360°$.
[OCR (Cambridge)]

2   Prove that, for all values of $\theta$, $\sin 3\theta - \cos 3\theta = (\sin\theta + \cos\theta)(2\sin 2\theta - 1)$.
Hence, or otherwise, find the values of $\theta$, such that $0° \le \theta \le 180°$, for which $3(\sin 3\theta - \cos 3\theta) = 2(\sin\theta + \cos\theta)$.
(Where necessary, give your answers correct to $0.1°$.)
[OCR (Cambridge), 1984]

3   Write $\sin\theta + \cos\theta$ in the form $R\sin(\theta + \alpha)$ (where $R$ is a positive constant, and $\alpha$ a constant acute angle in degrees, whose values should be determined).
A bathroom wall is tiled with square tiles measuring $15\,\text{cm} \times 15\,\text{cm}$. The tiles are arranged as shown, with their upper and lower edges tilted to the horizontal but with corresponding vertices in the same vertical line. If each vertical column of tiles lies within two vertical boundaries $18\,\text{cm}$ apart, find the size of the angle $\theta$. Hence calculate (to the nearest mm) the 'overlap' $w$ between one tile and the next.
[OCR (SMP), 1989]

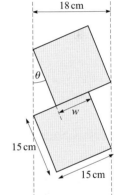

4   Find the general solution of the equation $\tan\theta - \sin\theta = 1 - \cos\theta$.
[OCR (Cambridge), 1983]

5   (a)  The angles $\theta$ and $\varphi$ are acute. If $\theta = \sin^{-1}\dfrac{x}{\sqrt{1+x^2}}$ and
$\varphi = \cos^{-1}\dfrac{1}{\sqrt{1+4x^2}}$ where $\theta + \varphi = \dfrac{3\pi}{4}$, find $x$.
(b)  Solve the equation $\sin\theta + \cos\theta + \sec\theta + \operatorname{cosec}\theta = 0$ for $-\dfrac{\pi}{2} < \theta < \pi$.
[AQA (AEB), 1965]

6   Prove that

$$\operatorname{cosec}\theta - \cot\theta = \tan\tfrac{1}{2}\theta$$

and that

$$\sec\theta - \tan\theta = \tan\left(\tfrac{1}{4}\pi - \tfrac{1}{2}\theta\right)$$

Use one or both of these identities to find:

(i) the angles between 0 and $\pi$ which satisfy the equation
$\operatorname{cosec} 3\theta - \cot 3\theta = \sqrt{3}$

(ii) the two angles between 0 and $\frac{1}{2}\pi$ which satisfy the equation

$$\operatorname{cosec} 2\theta - \cot 2\theta = \sec 5\theta - \tan 5\theta$$

[OCR (Cambridge), 1965]

**7** Given that

$$4 \sin 2y = 3 \sin 2x \quad \text{and} \quad 4 \sin^2 y - 3 \sin^2 x = 2$$

show that $\cos 2x = \frac{1}{9}$ and find the value of $\cos 2y$. Hence, or otherwise, find the angles $x$ and $y$ lying in the interval $[0°, 180°]$, giving your answers to the nearest $0.1°$.
[OCR (Cambridge), 1983]

**8** (a) Find the general solution of the pair of equations

$$\cos x + \sin \alpha = 0, \quad \sin x + \cos \alpha = 0$$

giving $x$ in terms of $\alpha$.
(b) Find the general solution of the simultaneous equations

$$\cos x + \sin y = 1, \quad \sin x + \cos y = \sqrt{3}$$

[OCR (Cambridge), 1986]

**9** Solve the inequality $\tan^{-1}(2x) + \tan^{-1}(\frac{1}{2}x) > 2 \tan^{-1} x$, principal values of the inverse tangent being taken.
[OCR (Cambridge), 1985]

**10** (i) Show that the only solution to the equation $\cos^{10} x - \sin^{10} x = 1$ is of the form $x = n\pi$, where $n$ is an integer.
(ii) The equation $\cos^3 x - \sin^3 x = 1$ has a solution $x_0$, such that $0 < x_0 < 2\pi$. Prove that $\frac{3}{2}\pi \le x_0 < 2\pi$.
Prove also that there is only one such $x_0$ and determine its value.
[OCR (Cambridge), 1981]

## Revision

**1** Find the principal value for $x$ in each of the following trigonometric equations, to the nearest tenth of a degree.

(a) $\sin x = -0.67$     (b) $\cos 2x = 0.31$     (c) $\cot x = 3.2$

(d) $\sec \dfrac{x}{3} = 2.9$

**2** State, as a rational multiple of $\pi$, the smallest positive exact solution when:

(a) $\tan\theta = \sqrt{3}$      (b) $\operatorname{cosec}\theta = -2$      (c) $\sin 5\theta = \dfrac{1}{\sqrt{2}}$

(d) $\cot\theta = -\dfrac{1}{\sqrt{3}}$

**3** (a) Sketch graphs of $f(\theta)$, $g(\theta)$ and $h(\theta)$ over the region $-\pi \le \theta < \pi$, where:

$$f(\theta) = \sin 3\theta + 2, \quad g(\theta) = -\tan\theta, \quad h(\theta) = \cos\left(\theta - \frac{\pi}{3}\right)$$

(b) Hence, or otherwise, determine the number of solutions $-\pi \le \theta \le \pi$, when:

(i) $f(\theta) = 1$      (ii) $g(\theta) = 0$      (iii) $h(\theta) = \frac{1}{2}$

**4** Determine all values of $\theta$ such that $0° \le \theta < 360°$ and:

(a) $(2\sin\theta - 1)(3\cos\theta + 2) = 0$      (b) $(\tan\theta + 5)(2\cos\theta - 5) = 0$
(c) $(\operatorname{cosec}^2\theta - 9)(\sin\theta - \frac{1}{3}) = 0$      (d) $\tan^2\theta - 5\tan\theta - 6 = 0$

**5** Find all angles $\left(\dfrac{\pi}{2} \le \theta < \dfrac{3\pi}{2}\right)$ which satisfy the following equations.

(a) $\sec\theta + 2\tan\theta = 0$      (b) $\operatorname{cosec}\theta(\tan\theta + 3\sin\theta) = 1$
(c) $\tan\theta = \sin\theta$

**6** Determine all acute solutions (if they exist) of the following quadratic equations.

(a) $\sin^2\theta - 3\sin\theta + 1 = 0$      (b) $3\cot^2\theta - 5\cot\theta - 2 = 0$
(c) $11\tan^2\theta + 9\tan\theta + 11 = 0$      (d) $\operatorname{cosec}^2 3\theta + 17\operatorname{cosec} 3\theta - 2 = 0$

**7** Solve:

(a) $\cos 2\theta + \cos\theta = 0$   $(0 < \theta < 2\pi)$      (b) $\sin 2\theta = \cos^2\theta$   $(0 < \theta < \pi)$
(c) $\cos 2\theta = 1 - \sin\theta$   $(0 \le \theta \le \pi)$      (d) $\cos 2\theta < \frac{1}{2}$   $(0 \le \theta \le \pi)$

**8** Describe the method that you would use to solve each of the following equations. (There is no need to find the solution.)

(a) $\sin\theta = 5\cos\theta$      (b) $\sin\theta + \cos\theta = 1$
(c) $2\sin\theta - \cos\theta = 0$      (d) $2\sin^2\theta + \cos\theta = 1$
(e) $\sin 2\theta + \cos\theta = 0$      (f) $\sin\theta + \cos 2\theta = 1$
(g) $\sin 3\theta = \sin\theta$      (h) $\sin 3\theta = \cos\theta$

**9**

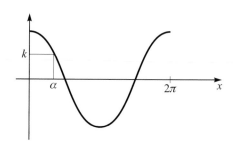

$\alpha$ is an angle $0 < \alpha < \frac{1}{2}\pi$, such that $\cos\alpha = k$. Write down, in terms of $\alpha$, a value of $\theta$ between:

(a)  $\dfrac{3\pi}{2}$ and $2\pi$, such that $\cos\theta = k$

(b)  $3\pi$ and $4\pi$, such that $\cos\theta = -k$

(c)  $\dfrac{\pi}{2}$ and $\pi$, such that $\sin\theta = k$

**10** (a)  Given that $5\sin\theta + 12\cos\theta = R\sin(\theta + \alpha)$, find the values of $R$ and $\alpha$ for which $R > 0$ and $0° < \alpha < 90°$.

(b)  Find all values of $\theta$ between $0°$ and $360°$ satisfying:

    (i)  $5\sin\theta + 12\cos\theta = 4$    (ii)  $5\sin 2\theta + 12\cos 2\theta = 13\sin\theta$

(c)  Find the greatest value of the expression $\dfrac{1}{5\sin\theta + 12\cos\theta + 20}$, stating the smallest positive value of $\theta$ at which this occurs.

**11** (a)  Determine the amplitude of the function $f(t) = 3\sin 2t - 4\cos 2t$.

(b)  (i) Find the values of $f(0)$ and $f'(0)$. (ii) Identify the wavelength.

(c)  Hence sketch the graph of the function for $0 \le t < 5$.

(d)  For what values of $t$, such that $0 \le t < 5$, does $f(t) = \frac{22}{17}$?

**12** Write down the general solutions for the following equations.

(a)  $\cos\theta = -\dfrac{\sqrt{3}}{2}$    (b)  $\sin\frac{1}{2}\theta = \frac{1}{2}$    (c)  $\tan\theta = \cot\theta$

## 6.5    Sum and product formulae

$$\sin(-\theta) \equiv -\sin\theta, \qquad \cos(-\theta) \equiv \cos\theta$$

Sum and difference formulae:

$$2\cos\theta\cos\phi \equiv \cos(\theta+\phi) + \cos(\theta-\phi)$$
$$2\sin\theta\sin\phi \equiv \cos(\theta-\phi) - \cos(\theta+\phi)$$
$$2\sin\theta\cos\phi \equiv \sin(\theta+\phi) + \sin(\theta-\phi)$$

Product formulae:

$$\sin\alpha + \sin\beta \equiv 2\sin\tfrac{1}{2}(\alpha+\beta)\cos\tfrac{1}{2}(\alpha-\beta)$$
$$\sin\alpha - \sin\beta \equiv 2\cos\tfrac{1}{2}(\alpha+\beta)\sin\tfrac{1}{2}(\alpha-\beta)$$
$$\cos\alpha + \cos\beta \equiv 2\cos\tfrac{1}{2}(\alpha+\beta)\cos\tfrac{1}{2}(\alpha-\beta)$$
$$\cos\alpha - \cos\beta \equiv -2\sin\tfrac{1}{2}(\alpha+\beta)\sin\tfrac{1}{2}(\alpha-\beta)$$

### Basic

**1**  Simplify:

  (a) $\sin A + \sin(-A)$      (b) $\cos A + \cos(-A)$

**2**  Express each of the following sums in the form $k\sin A\cos B$.

  (a) $\sin 3\theta + \sin 2\theta$      (b) $\sin 2\theta - \sin 3\theta$      (c) $\sin 5\theta + \sin 5\theta$

  (d) $\sin(2\theta + 30°) + \sin(\theta - 30°)$      (e) $\sin\dfrac{\theta}{3} - \sin\dfrac{\theta}{4}$

**3**  (a)  Evaluate, without using a calculator:
    *(i)  $\sin 75° + \sin 15°$      (ii)  $\sin 75° - \sin 15°$
  (b)  Hence find an exact value for $\sin 75°$.

**4**  Express each of the following sums in the form $k\cos A\cos B$.

  (a) $\cos 2\theta + \cos\theta$                    (b) $\cos 5\theta + \cos 7\theta$

  (c) $\cos 2\theta + \cos\dfrac{\theta}{2}$              (d) $\cos\left(\theta - \dfrac{\pi}{2}\right) + \cos\left(\theta + \dfrac{\pi}{2}\right)$

  (e) $\cos\left(2\theta - \dfrac{\pi}{3}\right) + \cos 2\theta$

**5**  (a)  Sketch, on the same axes, the graphs of (i) $y = \cos 2\theta$ (ii) $y = \cos 4\theta$.
      Hence sketch the graph of $y = \cos 2\theta + \cos 4\theta$.
  (b)  Draw, in addition, a sketch of $y = \cos 3\theta\cos\theta$ and state the identity
      which is illustrated by the answers to parts (a) and (b).

**6**  Express each of the following differences in the form $k\sin A\sin B$.

  (a) $\cos\theta - \cos 2\theta$              (b) $\cos\left(\theta - \dfrac{\pi}{2}\right) - \cos\left(\theta + \dfrac{\pi}{2}\right)$

(c)  $\cos\theta - \cos(-\theta)$           (d)  $\cos 2\theta - \cos\theta$

(e)  $\cos\left(2\theta - \dfrac{\pi}{3}\right) - \cos 2\theta$

**7**   Without using a calculator, evaluate each expression exactly:

*(a)  $\cos 105° - \cos 15°$        (b)  $\sin\dfrac{\pi}{12} + \sin\dfrac{5\pi}{12}$

**\*8**   Prove that $\dfrac{\sin A + \sin B}{\cos A + \cos B} = \tan\left(\dfrac{A + B}{2}\right).$

**9**   Rewrite each of the following products as the sum or difference of two trigonometrical functions.

(a)  $2\sin 3\theta \sin 2\theta$      (b)  $2\sin\theta\sin 6\theta$                        (c)  $-2\cos\theta\cos 3\theta$

(d)  $2\sin 3\theta\cos 3\theta$      (e)  $2\sin\left(\theta + \dfrac{\pi}{2}\right)\sin\left(\theta - \dfrac{\pi}{2}\right)$

**10**  (a)  Express $\cos 3\theta\cos 4\theta$ in the form $k(\cos A + \cos B)$.
(b)  Hence find $\int \cos 3\theta\cos 4\theta\, d\theta$.

**11**  Use the two trigonometrical identities

$$\cos(A + B) \equiv \cos A \cos B - \sin A \sin B$$
$$\cos(A - B) \equiv \cos A \cos B + \sin A \sin B$$

to explain why $\cos(A + B) + \cos(A - B) \equiv 2\cos A \cos B$.
Let $P = A + B$ and $Q = A - B$. Verify that

$$\cos P + \cos Q \equiv 2\cos\tfrac{1}{2}(P + Q)\cos\tfrac{1}{2}(P - Q)$$

**12**  Adapt the method of question 11 to derive the identity

$$\sin P + \sin Q \equiv 2\sin\tfrac{1}{2}(P + Q)\cos\tfrac{1}{2}(P - Q)$$

### Intermediate

**1**   Express each of the following expressions as the product of two trigonometric terms.

(a)  $\sin 2\theta + \sin 3\theta$          (b)  $\sin\theta - \sin\dfrac{\theta}{6}$

(c)  $\cos\theta + \cos 5\theta$          (d)  $\cos\left(2\theta + \dfrac{\pi}{4}\right) - \cos\theta$

(e)  $\sin 2\theta - \sin(-2\theta)$      (f)  $\cos\left(\theta + \dfrac{\pi}{4}\right) + \cos\left(\theta - \dfrac{\pi}{4}\right)$

**2** Rewrite each of the following products as the sum (or difference) of two trigonometric terms.

(a) $\sin\theta\sin 2\theta$

(b) $\cos\dfrac{\theta}{5}\cos 5\theta$

(c) $-\sin 2\theta\cos\theta$

(d) $\sin\theta\cos\theta$

(e) $\sin\left(\theta-\dfrac{\pi}{2}\right)\sin 2\theta$

**3** *(a) Given that $f(x)=\cos 3x$ and $g(x)=\cos 5x$, explain why the solution of $f(x)=g(x)$ can be found by solving $\sin 4x=0$ and $\sin x=0$.

(b) Hence find all such values in the region $0\le x<\pi$.

**4** Express $\sin 2\theta\sin 5\theta$ in the form $a(\cos P-\cos Q)$.
Hence find $\int\sin 2\theta\sin 5\theta\,d\theta$.

**5** (a) Find an expression for $\int f(x)\,dx$, where $f(x)=\sin 3x\cos\left(\tfrac{1}{3}x\right)$.

(b) Hence find, to two decimal places, the area under the graph $y=f(x)$, in the region $0\le x\le\pi/4$.

**6** Find all the values, $0\le\theta\le 2\pi$, for which $\cos 5\theta+\cos 3\theta=0$.

*7 (a) Explain why $|g(\theta)|\le 1$, where $g(\theta)=\sin 3\theta\cos\left(\tfrac{1}{3}\theta\right)$.

(b) Explain why there is no value of $\theta$ for which $|g(\theta)|=1$.

**8** Show that $\sin\theta\cos 2\theta\sin 3\theta$ may be rewritten as $\tfrac{1}{4}(1-\cos 2\theta+\cos 4\theta-\cos 6\theta)$.

**9** Show that the product of any three cosines may be rewritten as the sum of four cosines, that is,
$\cos A\cos B\cos C\equiv k(\cos P+\cos Q+\cos R+\cos S)$, where $k$, $P$, $Q$, $R$ and $S$ are to be expressed in terms of $A$, $B$ and $C$.

*10 Prove that $\sin\theta+\sin 2\theta+\sin 3\theta\equiv 2\sin\theta\cos\theta(2\cos\theta+1)$.

**11** Prove that $\cos\theta+\cos 3\theta+\cos 5\theta\equiv\cos 3\theta(2\cos\theta-1)(2\cos\theta+1)$.

**12** Show that $\cos\theta+\cos\left(\theta+\dfrac{2\pi}{3}\right)+\cos\left(\theta+\dfrac{4\pi}{3}\right)\equiv k$, stating the value of $k$.

**13** Solutions are required to the equation $\cos 5\theta=\sin 3\theta$.

(a) Show that the equation may be rewritten as
$$\sin 3\theta+\sin\left(5\theta-\dfrac{\pi}{2}\right)=0.$$

(b) Use the factor formulae to find all the solutions within the domain $0\le\theta<\pi$.

**14** Simplify $\dfrac{\sin 3\theta + \sin 7\theta}{\sin 3\theta - \sin \theta}$.

**\*15** Find the smallest positive values of $\theta$ for which $\cos\left(2\theta + \dfrac{\pi}{3}\right) = \sin 5\theta$.

**16** (a) Sketch the graph of $y = \cos 8\theta - \cos 6\theta$ for $-\pi \le \theta \le 2\pi$.
 (b) How many *local* maxima lie between one *global* maximum and the next?

## Advanced

**1** Solve, for $0° \le x \le 180°$:

 (a) $\sin(x + 35°) + \sin(x - 85°) = 0.6$
 (b) $\sin(x + 51°)\cos(x + 81°) = 0.2$

**2** (a) Prove $\dfrac{\sin A + \sin 3A + \sin 5A}{\cos A + \cos 3A + \cos 5A} = \tan 3A.$

 (b) Find the general solution of $\sin x + \sin 5x = \sin 3x$.

**3** In the expression $\sin 2P + \sin 2Q + \sin 2R$, $P + Q + R = \pi$. By eliminating $R$ and simplifying the terms, show that
$\sin 2P + \sin 2Q + \sin 2R \equiv 4\sin P \sin Q \sin R$.

**4** Prove that $\sin^2 2\theta - \sin^2 \theta = \sin \theta \sin 3\theta$. Hence or otherwise find all the values of $\theta$ such that $0 \le \theta < 2\pi$ and $\sin^2 2\theta - \sin^2 \theta = 0$.
 [OCR (Cambridge), 1976]

**5** (a) By expressing $\cos 2r\theta \sin \theta$ as the difference of two sines, show that
$$\sum_{r=1}^{n} \cos 2r\theta = \cos(n+1)\theta \sin n\theta \operatorname{cosec} \theta$$
 (b) Find $\displaystyle\sum_{r=1}^{n} \cos r\theta$.

**6** Prove that
$$\frac{\sin(r+2)\theta + \sin(r-2)\theta}{\cos(r+1)\theta - \cos(r-1)\theta} = 2\sin\theta - \operatorname{cosec}\theta$$

Hence explain why the equation
$$\frac{\sin(r+2)\theta + \sin(r-2)\theta}{\cos(r+1)\theta - \cos(r-1)\theta} = 1$$

has a solution which is independent of $r$.
Find the general solution of the equation.

**7** Solve:

(a) $\cos\theta + \cos 2\theta + \cos 4\theta + \cos 5\theta = 0$    $(0 \le \theta \le \pi)$

(b) $2\cos 3\theta - 7\cos 2\theta + 2\cos\theta = 7$        $(0° \le \theta \le 360°)$

**8** Solve $\sin\theta + 2\cos\theta + \sin 2\theta + 2\cos 2\theta = 0$    $(0° \le \theta \le 360°)$.

**9** If $\sin 2A - \sin 2\theta = 2\alpha\cot(A+\theta)$, show that $\alpha + \cos^2 A = \cos^2\theta$.
Find the values of $\theta$ in the range $0 \le \theta < 2\pi$ which satisfy the equation

$$2 - 2\sin 2\theta = \cot\left(\frac{\pi}{4}+\theta\right).$$

**10** Find all the solutions of the equation $\cos 4\theta = \cos 3\theta$.
Hence show that the roots of the equation

$$8x^3 + 4x^2 - 4x - 1 = 0 \text{ are } \cos\frac{2\pi}{7}, \ \cos\frac{4\pi}{7}, \ \cos\frac{6\pi}{7}.$$

Deduce or prove otherwise that $\sec\dfrac{2\pi}{7}\sec\dfrac{4\pi}{7}\sec\dfrac{6\pi}{7} = 8$.

**Revision**

**1** Simplify $\dfrac{\sin A - \sin(-A)}{\cos A + \cos(-A)}$.

**2** Express each of the following expressions as a product.

(a) $\sin\theta + \sin 9\theta$             (b) $\cos 2\theta + \cos 3\theta$

(c) $\sin\dfrac{\theta}{7} - \sin\dfrac{\theta}{6}$          (d) $\sin 3\theta - \sin(\pi - \theta)$

(e) $\cos(2\theta - \pi) - \cos\dfrac{\theta}{2}$    (f) $\cos\left(\theta+\dfrac{\pi}{3}\right) + \cos\left(\theta+\dfrac{\pi}{6}\right)$

**3** Rewrite each of the following products as the sum or difference of two trigonometric terms.

(a) $\sin A \sin 2A$            (b) $\sin A \cos(A+B)$

(c) $\cos(2A - B)\cos(2A + B)$

**4** By applying the appropriate identity, find the exact value of

$$\cos\frac{5\pi}{12} + \cos\frac{\pi}{12}.$$

**5** (a) Express $\sin 45° \cos 15°$ in the form $a(\sin x° + \sin y°)$.
   (b) Hence find the exact value of (i) $\sin 45° \cos 15°$, (ii) $\cos 15°$.

**6** (a) Express $f(x) = \sin 3x + \sin 5x$ in the form $b \sin P \cos Q$.
   (b) Sketch the graph of $y = f(x)$.
   (c) State the period of $y = f(x)$.

**7** Find all the values of $x$, where $\sin(x + 10°) + \sin(x - 10°) = 0$, and $0° \le x < 360°$.

**8** In the region $0 \le \theta \le \pi$, find all the angles $\theta$ for which $\sin\dfrac{7\theta}{2} = \sin\dfrac{9\theta}{2}$.

**9** Prove that $\sin\left(\theta + \dfrac{\pi}{3}\right) \equiv \sin\theta + \sin\left(\theta + \dfrac{2\pi}{3}\right)$.

**10** Determine expressions for $P$, $Q$, $R$ and $S$ (in terms of $A$, $B$ and $C$) such that

$$\sin A + 2\sin B + \sin C \equiv 2(\sin P \cos Q + \sin R \cos S)$$

**11** Find a general expression for the integral $\int (\sin Ax \cos Bx)\,dx$, where $A$ and $B$ are real constants.

Hence evaluate $\displaystyle\int_0^{\frac{\pi}{6}} \sin\dfrac{x}{2} \cos 3x\,dx$ to three decimal places.

**12** (a) Show that $\cos x \cos 2x \cos 3x$ may be written as the sum of three cosines and a constant.
   (b) Hence write down the equation which must be solved to find the $x$-coordinates of the turning points of the graph $y = \cos x \cos 2x \cos 3x$.
   (c) Explain why $x = \dfrac{\pi}{2}$ will be a solution of this equation.

# 7
# Exponential and logarithmic functions

## 7.1 Exponential growth and decay; laws of logarithms; $e^x$ and $\ln x$; solution of $a^x = b$

$$y = a^x \Leftrightarrow x = \log_a y, \quad y = e^x \Leftrightarrow x = \ln y$$
$$\log_a 1 = 0, \quad \log_a a = 1$$
$$\log_a(mn) = \log_a m + \log_a n, \quad \log_a\left(\frac{m}{n}\right) = \log_a m - \log_a n,$$
$$\log_a(m^p) = p \log_a m$$
$$\log_a b = \frac{\log_c b}{\log_c a}$$

### Basic

**1** Sketch, on the same axes, the pairs of graphs:

  (a) (i) $y = 2^x$      (ii) $y = 3^x$
  (b) (i) $y = 2^x$      (ii) $y = 2^{-x}$
  (c) (i) $y = 2^x$      (ii) $y = 3 \times 2^x$

**2** Find $x$ exactly for the following:

  (a) (i) $3^x = 9$      (ii) $4^x = \frac{1}{64}$      *(iii) $10^x = 0.01$
  (b) (i) $2^{x-1} = 8$      (ii) $5^{2x} = 0.2$      (iii) $3^{2x+1} = \frac{1}{27}$
  (c) (i) $5 \times 2^x = 80$      (ii) $3 \times 8^{2x} = 6$      (iii) $4 \times 2^{x+1} = 128$

**3** Sketch, on the same axes, the pairs of graphs:

  (a) (i) $y = e^x$      (ii) $y = e^{-x}$
  (b) (i) $y = e^x$      (ii) $y = 6 \times e^x$
  (c) (i) $y = e^x$      (ii) $y = \ln x$

In each case state the relationship between the curves.

**4** Find the value of each of the following, giving your answer to two significant figures, where appropriate.

  (a) (i) $e^3$      (ii) $3e^{-0.4}$      (iii) $e^0$
  (b) (i) $5\ln 3.1$      (ii) $\ln 0.4$      (iii) $\ln 1$

**5** Find the exact values:

(a) (i) $\log_{10} 100$      (ii) $\log_2 64$      (iii) $\log_{16} 4$

(b) (i) $\log_{10} 0.1$      (ii) $\log_5 0.04$      (iii) $\log_a 1$

(c)*(i) $\log_2 \sqrt{8}$      (ii) $\log_9 27$      (iii) $\log_3 3^4$

**6** Express as a single logarithm:

(a) $\log_a p + \log_a q - \log_a r$      *(b) $2\log_a p - (\log_a q + \log_a r)$

(c) $3\log_a p - 4\log_a r + 0.5\log_a q$

**7** Express in terms of $\log_a p$, $\log_a q$ and $\log_a r$:

(a) $\log_a (pqr^2)$      *(b) $\log_a \left(\dfrac{pq}{r^3}\right)$      (c) $\log_a \sqrt{pq}$

**8** Find the value of $x$ to two significant figures when:

(a) (i) $e^x = 2$      (ii) $\ln x = 2$

(b) (i) $5e^{3x} = 0.3$      (ii) $5\ln 3x = 0.3$

(c)*(i) $3e^{2x-1} = 6$      (ii) $3\ln(2x - 1) = 6$

**9** Find the value of $x$ to three decimal places when:

*(a) $3^x = 10$      (b) $2^{x-3} = 11$      (c) $4^x = 5^{x-1}$

**10** Find $a$ if:

(a) $\log_a 8 = \frac{3}{2}$

(b) $\log_a 25 - \log_a 0.25 = 2$

(c) $\log_a 45 + 4\log_a 2 - 0.5\log_a 81 - \log_a 10 = \frac{3}{2}$

**\*11** The cost of living in a certain country is increasing by 3% each year.

(a) What is the growth factor?

(b) What will be the total percentage increase after (i) 2 years, (ii) 18 months?

(c) Write an expression for the percentage increase after $n$ years.

**12** The mass $x$ kg of a radio-active substance remaining in a sample $t$ hours after starting timing is given by the equation $x = 4e^{-0.2t}$.

(a) What was the mass at the start of timing?

(b) Find the mass left after five years.

(c) Find the time taken for the mass remaining to be half the initial mass.

### Intermediate

**1** Find the value of:

(a) $\log_6 9 + \log_6 4$      (b) $\log_7 \left(\frac{2}{3}\right) + \log_7 \left(\frac{3}{98}\right)$      (c) $\log_{27} 54 - \log_{27} 6$

**2** Simplify:

(a) $e^{\ln x}$     (b) $e^{\ln x + \ln y}$     (c) $e^{2\ln x - \ln y}$     (d) $\ln \sqrt{e^{x+y}}$

**3** Given that $\log_a x = b$, express in terms of $b$:

(a) $\log_a x^3$     (b) $\log_a \dfrac{1}{x^2}$     (c) $\log_a a\sqrt{x}$

**4** Functions $f(x)$ and $g(x)$ are defined to be $f(x) = e^{2x+1} (x \in \mathbb{R})$,
$g(x) = \ln x^{1/2} (x \in \mathbb{R}^+)$.

(a) (i) Find $f^{-1}(x)$     (ii) $g^{-1}(x)$

(b) Show that $g(f(x)) = x + \frac{1}{2}$.

**5** (a) Sketch the curve $y = \log_5 x$.

(b) Solve the simultaneous equations:

$$y = \log_5 x$$
$$y = \frac{1 + \log_5 125x}{5}$$

**6** Solve the equations:

(a) $2^{5t+1} = 12$

(b) $2\log_9 t - \dfrac{3}{\log_9 t} = 1$

(c) $\log_2 t^2 + \log_2 t^3 = 15$     (d) $\log_{10} 20t - \log_{10}(t - 8) = 2$

**\*7** Given that $\log_2 (x - 5y + 4) = 0$ and $\log_2 (x + 1) - 1 = 2\log_2 y$, find $x$ and $y$.

**8** Find the value of $q$ for which:

(a) $\log_q 20 = \log_q 10 + \frac{1}{2}$

(b) $1 + \log_{10} q = \log_{10} 2 - 2\log_{10} 5$

**9** (a) Show that $\log_a b = \dfrac{\log_c b}{\log_c a}$.

(b) Use this result to calculate to three significant figures the value of $\log_4 7$.

(c) If $2\log_y x + 2\log_x y = 5$, show that $\log_y x = 0.5$ or $2$. Hence find all pairs of values of $x$ and $y$ which satisfy the equation above and $xy = 27$.

**\*10** The compound interest on a savings account is 4.2% per annum. After how many years would an initial investment of £2000 exceed £8000?

**11** A colony of bacteria has a growth factor of 4 per hour (i.e. it increases by a factor of 4 each hour). Initially there are 150 bacteria present.

(a) Write an expression for the number of bacteria present after $t$ hours.

(b)  How many bacteria will there be after 30 minutes?

(c)  How long will it take for the number of bacteria to reach 150 000?

**12** A capacitor is a device for storing electrical charge, measured in coulombs. Its charge decays exponentially, so that after 1 second it has lost half its charge (i.e. its half-life is 1 second). It stores 500 coulombs at the start.

(a)  Write an expression for the charge $C$ coulombs stored on the capacitor after $t$ seconds.

(b)  How long will it take the charge stored to drop to one tenth of the initial value?

**13** A fungus has an initial mass of 10 kg and growth factor 1.3 per day.

(a)  Find the mass of fungus after one week.

(b)  Harvesting occurs when the mass of fungus is 250 kg. How long will the farmer have to wait to harvest?

**14** A biologist knows that, after $t$ days, the mass of a certain organism is given by the equation $m = 2e^{0.1t}$ kg.

(a)  What is the mass initially?

(b)  What is the mass after three days?

(c)  How long does it take for the mass to double in size?

**15** A sample of radium decays at a rate which is proportional to its mass. The mass of radium, $m$, is given by the equation $m = m_0e^{-kt}$ where $m_0$ is the initial mass, $k$ is the decay constant and $t$ is the time in years. If the half-life is 1600 years

(a)  find the value of $k$,

(b)  calculate the percentage rate of decrease per century.

**16** A bathful of water is at a temperature of 80 °C in a large room whose temperature is 20 °C. The water cools at a rate which is proportional to its excess temperature $T$ (the difference between its temperature and that of the surroundings). $T$ is given by the equation $T = T_0e^{-kt}$ where $T_0$ is the excess temperature initially, $k$ is the decay constant and $t$ is the time in minutes. The water takes 5 minutes to cool to 70 °C.

(a)  Find the value of the constants $T_0$ and $k$.

(b)  How long does it take the water to reach 60 °C?

## Advanced

**1** Show that, if $\log p + \log q = k \log r$, then $p$, $q^{k-1}$, $q^{k-2}r$ are in geometric progression.

**2** (a) Express $e^{x/3}$ in the form $a^x$, stating the value of $a$ to two decimal places.

(b) Solve the equation $e^{2x} + e^x - 12 = 0$.

**3** (a) If $4^x 5^{3x+1} = 10^{2x+1}$, prove that $x = \dfrac{\log 2}{\log 5}$.

(b) Show that, if $3^x = 4^y$ and $y = 2x - 1$, $x = \dfrac{\ln 4}{\ln \frac{16}{3}}$.

**4** If $M$, $N$, $P$ are the $m$th, $n$th and $p$th terms respectively of a geometric progression, prove that $(n - p)\log M + (p - m)\log N + (m - n)\log P = 0$.
[OCR (Cambridge), 1968]

**5** If $pq = a^2$, prove that $\dfrac{1}{a+p} + \dfrac{1}{a+q} = \dfrac{1}{a}$.

Hence find $\dfrac{3}{7(3 + 7\log_b c)} + \dfrac{1}{7 + 3\log_c b}$.

**6** Solve $\displaystyle\sum_{r=0}^{\infty} e^{1+rx} = 5$.

**7** Solve the equation $\log_2 x + \log_3 x = 1 + \log_4 x$, giving your answer to three significant figures.

**8** Show that the sum of the infinite series

$$\log_2 e - \log_4 e + \log_{16} e - \cdots + (-1)^n \log_{2^{2^n}} e + \cdots$$

is

$$\frac{1}{\ln(2\sqrt{2})}$$

($\log_a b = c$ is equivalent to $a^c = b$.)
[OCR (STEP), 1987]

**9** Sketch the graph of the function f given by $f(x) = \log_x a$, $x \in \mathbb{R}^+$, $x \neq 1$, in the cases

(i) $0 < a < 1$     (ii) $a > 1$

[OCR (Cambridge), 1984]

**10** Let $x$, $p$, $q$, with $pq \neq 1$, be real numbers taking all positive values except 1. By expressing all logarithms to a common base, or otherwise, prove or disprove the following statements:

(i) $\log_p x + \log_{p^2} x^2 + \cdots + \log_{p^n} x^n = \log_p x^n$, where $n$ is a positive integer,

(ii) there exist values of $x$, $p$, $q$ such that
$$\log_p x + \log_q x = \log_{pq} x$$

(iii) there exist values of $p$ and $q$ such that
$$\log_p q + \log_q p < 0$$

[OCR (Cambridge), 1985]

## Revision

**1** Find the exact value of $x$, showing your working:

(a) $\log_2 x = 5$      (b) $\log_3 \frac{1}{81} = x$      (c) $\log_x 125 = 3$

(d) $\log_{64} x = \frac{1}{2}$      (e) $\log_5(x+1) = 2$

**2** (a) Simplify $\ln e^x - e^{\ln 2x}$.

(b) If $e^{3x} = y$ express $x$ in terms of $y$ and find $x$ when $y = 2$.

(c) If $\ln 2x = y$ express $x$ in terms of $y$ and find $x$ when $y = 0.3$.

**3** A car bought for £5000 depreciates by 12% each year.

(a) What is its value after five years?

(b) How long is it before its value is half its original price?

**4** Solve the following equations exactly.

(a) $3^{2x-1} = \frac{1}{27}$      (b) $5^{2x-1} = 25^{-x}$      (c) $8(2^x)^2 = 16^{4x}$

**5** Express as a single logarithm:

(a) $2\log_a p - \frac{1}{2}\log_a q + 3\log_a r$

(b) $2 + \frac{1}{4}\log_a p - \frac{1}{3}\log_a q$

**6** Solve, giving your answers to two significant figures where appropriate:

(a) $2^x = 3$      (b) $3^{x+2} = \frac{1}{3}$      (c) $5^{2x+1} = 7^x$

**7** (a) Show that $\log_x z = \dfrac{1}{\log_z x}$.

(b) Hence find $x$ if (i) $\log_3 x = 4\log_x 3$, (ii) $\log_5 x + 2\log_x 5 = 3$.

**8** The number of worms in a garden doubles each week. Initially the garden has three worms. Find a formula for the population of worms after $t$ weeks. After how many weeks will there be 300 worms?

**9** Given that:

(a) $\log_a x + \log_a 64 = \log_a x^4$, $x > 0$, find $x$

(b) $2\log_2 y - \log_2(2y + 5) = 2$, find $y$

**10** The curve with equation $y = ka^x$ passes through the points $(2, 4)$ and $(4, 2)$. Find the value of the constants $k$ and $a$ exactly.

**11** (a) Solve the simultaneous equations:

$$2\log_2 x = y$$
$$\log_2 2x = y + 4$$

(b) By letting $y = 2^x$, find the exact value of $x$ if $5(2^x) - 4^x = 4$.

**12** The proportion of the British population who do not have a washing machine fell from 81% in 1960 to 24% in 1985. Assuming this can be modelled by an equation $P = ae^{-kt}$, where $t$ is the number of years after 1960,

(a) find the value of the constants $k$ and $a$,

(b) find the year in which the model predicts that at least 50% of all households had a washing machine.

## 7.2    Reduction of laws to linear form

### Basic

**1** The variables $x$ and $y$ are related by a law of the form $y = x^2 + 3$. Plot the graphs of $Y$ against $X$ where (a) $Y = y$, $X = x$, (b) $Y = y$, $X = x^2$ for $-4 \le x \le 4$. Describe the shape of each graph.

**2** Reduce each of the following relationships to their linear form $Y = mX + c$. Give the functions equivalent to $X$ and $Y$ and the constants $m$ and $c$.

(a) $y = ax^2 + c$    (b) $\dfrac{1}{x} + \dfrac{1}{y} = \dfrac{1}{a}$    (c) $xy = a$

**3** The following relationships are in the form $Y = mX + c$.

(i) $\dfrac{y}{x} = ax + b$    *(ii) $\ln y = x \ln b + \ln a$    (iii) $\ln y = n \ln x + \ln a$

(a) Give the functions equivalent to $X$ and $Y$ and the constants $m$ and $c$ in each case.

(b) Rearrange each relationship to make $y$ the subject.

**4**  It is suspected that $x$ and $y$ are related by the laws given below. By expressing the laws in the form $Y = mX + c$, state suitable functions to plot to give a linear graph.

(a) $y = ae^x$    *(b) $\dfrac{a}{x} + \dfrac{b}{y} = 1$    (c) $x^2 + y^2 = 1$

**5**  For each of the following sets of experimental values for the variables $x$ and $y$ and the law which relates them, draw a suitable straight-line graph and use it to find the values of $a$ and $b$ to one significant figure.

(a)

| $x$ | 2 | 4 | 6 | 8 |
|---|---|---|---|---|
| $y$ | 6.1 | 3.6 | −0.1 | −5.5 |

$y = ax^2 + b$

*(b)

| $x$ | 1 | 2 | 3 | 4 |
|---|---|---|---|---|
| $y$ | 15.4 | 24.6 | 47.2 | 88.3 |

$y = ab^x$

(c)

| $x$ | 1 | 3 | 5 | 7 |
|---|---|---|---|---|
| $y$ | −0.5 | 1.5 | 0.83 | 0.7 |

$\dfrac{a}{x} + \dfrac{b}{y} = 1$

**6**  Find the law connecting $x$ and $y$ when the graph of $y$ against $x^2$ is a straight line:

(a)  with gradient 2 passing through the point (0, 3),
(b)  with gradient $\frac{1}{3}$ and $y$-intercept −2,
(c)  passing through the points (0, 4) and ($\frac{1}{4}$, 0).

**7**  Find the law connecting $x$ and $y$ when a graph of $1/y$ against $1/x$ is a straight line:

*(a)  with gradient 5 passing through the point (5, 1),
(b)  with gradient $\frac{1}{4}$ passing through the point (1, 1),
(c)  passing through the points ($\frac{1}{2}$, 2) and (2, $\frac{1}{2}$).

**8**  An object moves from rest so that its distance $y$ metres travelled in time $t$ seconds is satisfied by an equation of the form $y = at^2$ where $a$ is a constant. The results below were recorded.

| $t$ | 0 | 1 | 2 | 3 |
|---|---|---|---|---|
| $y$ | 0 | 3.3 | 13.2 | 29.7 |

Plot $y$ against $t^2$ and draw a line of best fit. From your graph estimate the value of $a$ to one decimal place.

**9** It is known that a variable $y$ depends on $x$ according to a law of the form $y = x^n$. An experiment to find the value of $n$ gave the following results.

| $x$ | 1 | 2 | 3 | 4 | 5 |
|---|---|---|---|---|---|
| $y$ | 1.05 | 15.9 | 84.3 | 260 | 620 |

Plot a graph of $\ln y$ (vertically) against $\ln x$ (horizontally) and draw a line of best fit through the points. Use your graph to estimate the value of $n$ to one significant figure.

**10** The following values of $x$ and $y$ obey a law of the type $y = ax^n$ where $a$ and $n$ are constants. By plotting $\log_{10} y$ against $\log_{10} x$, find the values of $a$ and $n$ to one significant figure.

| $x$ | 1 | 2 | 3 | 4 | 5 |
|---|---|---|---|---|---|
| $y$ | 3 | 12 | 27 | 48 | 75 |

**11** The relationship between $s$ and $t$ is given by $s = at^2 + b$ where $a$ and $b$ are constants. Experimental results for $s$ and $t$ are:

| $t$ | 0.25 | 0.5 | 0.75 | 1.0 | 1.25 |
|---|---|---|---|---|---|
| $s$ | 3.13 | 3.53 | 4.18 | 5.10 | 6.28 |

By plotting $s$ against $t^2$ verify that the relationship is correct and use your graph to estimate the value of $a$ and $b$ to one decimal place.

**12** The variables $R$ and $t$ are thought to be related by the law $R = kt^n$. Using the experimentally obtained values below, show that this law does in fact hold, by drawing a suitable graph. Use your graph to estimate the value of the constants $k$ and $n$.

| $t$ | 1.5 | 2 | 3 | 5 | 7 |
|---|---|---|---|---|---|
| $R$ | 58 | 43.5 | 26.5 | 14.5 | 10 |

**Intermediate**

**1** The following values of $x$ and $y$ satisfy a relation of the form $y = ax^2 + b$.

| $x$ | 0 | 1 | 2 | 2.5 | 3 |
|---|---|---|---|---|---|
| $y$ | −5 | −4 | −1 | 1.25 | 4 |

By drawing a suitable graph, find the values of $a$ and $b$.

**2**  $S$ is proportional to $T^2$. Experimental results are recorded as follows.

| $T$ | 1 | 2 | 3 | 4 | 5 |
|---|---|---|---|---|---|
| $S$ | 3.17 | 12.81 | 28.75 | 51.16 | 80.41 |

Draw a graph of $S$ against $T^2$ and use the gradient of this straight line to find the constant of proportionality correct to one decimal place.

**3**  The relationship between $x$ and $y$ is given by $y = \dfrac{k}{x^2} + c$ where $k$ and $c$ are constants. The following experimental results are recorded.

| $x$ | 0.3 | 0.4 | 0.5 | 0.6 | 0.7 | 0.8 |
|---|---|---|---|---|---|---|
| $y$ | 63.2 | 36.9 | 24.7 | 18.0 | 14.2 | 11.5 |

Draw a graph of $y$ against $\dfrac{1}{x^2}$ and use your graph to find the values of $k$ and $c$ to suitable degrees of accuracy.

**4**  The following values of $x$ and $y$ satsify a relation of the form $y = \dfrac{a}{x} + b$.

By drawing a straight-line graph, find the values of $a$ and $b$ and hence the equation for $y$ in terms of $x$.

| $x$ | 1 | 2 | 3 | 4 | 5 | 6 |
|---|---|---|---|---|---|---|
| $y$ | 16 | 10 | 8 | 7 | 6.4 | 6 |

**5**  An engineer measures the power $P$ (kilowatts) required for a car to travel at various speeds $V$ (km/h). The results are

| $V$ | 40 | 60 | 80 | 100 | 120 | 140 |
|---|---|---|---|---|---|---|
| $P$ | 13.5 | 30.5 | 54 | 84.5 | 122 | 166 |

It is thought that the formula connecting $P$ and $V$ is of the form $\sqrt{P} = kV$ where $k$ is a constant. By drawing a graph of $\sqrt{P}$ against $V$, show that the formula is correct and estimate the constant $k$ to two significant figures.

**6**  A ball is released from the top of a building and its position is recorded every second using an electronic photoflash camera. The following results were obtained, where $d$ is the distance fallen in metres and $t$ is the time taken in seconds.

| $t$ | 0 | 1 | 2 | 3 |
|---|---|---|---|---|
| $d$ | 0 | 4.9 | 19.6 | 44.1 |

It is thought that $t$ and $d$ obey the law $d = \frac{1}{2}gt^2$ where $g$ is a constant. By drawing a suitable straight-line graph and finding its gradient, find the value of $g$.

**7** Two variables $T$ and $V$ are thought to be related by an equation which is either $V = a\sqrt{T} + b$ or $V = \dfrac{a}{T} + b$. Below are four pairs of values of $T$ and $V$.

| $T$ | 1 | 2 | 4 | 10 |
|---|---|---|---|---|
| $V$ | 15.5 | 9.5 | 6.5 | 4.7 |

By drawing suitable graphs, determine the correct equation, giving the values of $a$ and $b$ to two significant figures.

**8** Two quantities $v$ and $p$ are believed to be related by the equation $v = kp^n$. The following experimental data were collected.

| $p$ | 1.1 | 1.3 | 1.4 | 1.7 | 1.9 | 2.2 | 2.5 | 2.8 |
|---|---|---|---|---|---|---|---|---|
| $v$ | 4.61 | 5.93 | 6.63 | 8.87 | 10.48 | 13.05 | 15.81 | 18.74 |

By plotting a suitable straight-line graph, show that the equation holds and find the values of $k$ and $n$.

**9** A zoo keeps an official record of the mass, $x$ kg, and the average daily food intake, $y$ kg, of each adult animal. Four selected pairs of values of $x$ and $y$ are given in the table below.

| Animal | Cheetah | Deer | Rhinoceros | Hippopotamus |
|---|---|---|---|---|
| $x$ | 40 | 170 | 1500 | 3000 |
| $y$ | 1.8 | 5.0 | 33.2 | 50.0 |

Show, by drawing a suitable linear graph on a sheet of 2 mm graph paper, that these values are approximately consistent with a relationship between $x$ and $y$ of the form

$$y = ax^m$$

where $a$ and $m$ are constants.
Use your linear graph to find an estimate of the value of $m$.
The zoo has a bear with mass 500 kg. Assuming that this animal's food intake and mass conform to the relationship mentioned above, indicate a point on your linear graph corresponding to the bear and estimate the bear's average daily food intake.
[AQA (NEAB), 1995]

**10** The following values of $V$ and $I$ were obtained experimentally.

| $V$ | 60 | 80 | 100 | 120 | 140 |
|---|---|---|---|---|---|
| $I$ | 11 | 20.5 | 89 | 186 | 319 |

There was one error made in obtaining the readings. Allowing for this error, show that $V$ and $I$ are related by the law $I = aV^n$ where $a$ and $n$ are constants. Find the probable correct reading and the value of the constant $n$.

11  The following values of $s$ and $t$, obtained experimentally, are thought to follow a law of the type $s = at^n$ where $a$ and $n$ are constants.

| $t$ | 5.1 | 26 | 82 | 200 | 414 |
|---|---|---|---|---|---|
| $s$ | 40 | 60 | 80 | 100 | 120 |

Verify that this is correct by plotting a suitable graph, and find the values of $a$ and $n$.

12  Under certain conditions, a certain strain of bacteria is known to reproduce exponentially according to the law $y = a^x$ where $x$ is the number of days and $y$ is the number of bacteria present. The following results were obtained by experiment.

| $x$ | 0 | 3 | 6 | 9 | 12 |
|---|---|---|---|---|---|
| $y$ | 1 | 5 | 23 | 110 | 530 |

Use these results to estimate the value of the constant $a$ to two significant figures.

13  The population $P$ in millions of a small country was recorded in January of various years and the results are shown in the table below.

| Year | 1968 | 1974 | 1980 | 1985 |
|---|---|---|---|---|
| $P$ | 12.3 | 13.4 | 15.1 | 17.1 |

Given that $P = 10 + ab^t$, where $t$ is the time measured in years from January 1965 and $a$ and $b$ are constants, express $\log_{10}(P - 10)$ as a linear function of $t$.
Draw a suitable line graph for $0 \leq t \leq 20$. Use your graph to estimate the values of $a$ and $b$ to a suitable degree of accuracy.

14  Determine graphically which of the following readings is in error if a law of the form $y^2 = kx^3$ relates the variables $x$ and $y$. Estimate also the value of $k$.

| $x$ | 7 | 8 | 9 | 10 | 11 | 12 |
|---|---|---|---|---|---|---|
| $y$ | 58.6 | 71.6 | 85.4 | 105 | 115 | 131 |

**15** Find the law connecting $x$ and $y$ when:

    (a) the graph of $\ln y$ against $\ln x$ is a straight line with gradient $-2.5$ and intercept 2.5 on the $(\ln x)$-axis,

    (b) the graph of $\log_{10} y$ against $x$ is a straight line with gradient 0.36 and intercept 1.23 on the $(\log_{10} y)$-axis.

**16** During an experiment the following values of $x$ and $y$ were observed.

| $x$ | 0 | 1 | 2 | 3 | 4 |
|---|---|---|---|---|---|
| $y$ | 4 | 5 | 34 | 165 | 516 |

By plotting a suitable straight-line graph show that $x$ and $y$ could be related by a law of the form $y = ax^4 + b$.

Use the graph to estimate (a) the value of $y$ when $x = 2.5$, (b) the value of $x$ when $y = 200$.

## Advanced

**1** Pairs of variables $x$ and $y$ obtained in an experiment are shown below.

| $x$ | 1 | 2 | 3 | 4 | 5 |
|---|---|---|---|---|---|
| $y$ | 4.2 | 10.8 | 19.8 | 31.2 | 45.0 |

It is believed that $x$ and $y$ are related by an equation of the form $y = ax + bx^2$. By plotting a suitable graph, demonstrate that the relationship holds and find values for $a$ and $b$.

**2** A technical manual of ship designs contains the following information about the power needed to propel a 20 metre, round-hulled craft of 127.5 tons displacement at different speeds.

| Speed $V$ in knots | 6 | 7 | 8 | 9 | 10 | 11 | 12 | 15 |
|---|---|---|---|---|---|---|---|---|
| Power $P$ in brake horse power | 36 | 78 | 142 | 240 | 497 | 906 | 1345 | 2126 |

Below is a sketch graph of $P$ against $V$ for $6 \le V \le 12$. This suggests that there may be a relationship between $P$ and $V$ which can be modelled by the equation $P = kV^n$, where $k$ and $n$ are as yet unknown.

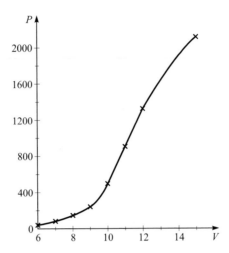

(i) Complete the table of values of ln $V$ and ln $P$. Give the natural logarithms correct to one decimal place. Plot the points on graph paper.

| $V$ | 6 | 7 | 8 | 9 | 10 | 11 | 12 | 15 |
|---|---|---|---|---|---|---|---|---|
| ln $V$ | 1.8 | | 2.1 | | 2.3 | | 2.5 | |
| $P$ | 36 | 78 | 142 | 240 | 497 | 906 | 1345 | 2126 |
| ln $P$ | 3.6 | | 5.0 | | 6.2 | | 7.2 | |

(ii) Comment on the location of the points and, where suitable, join them with a straight line.

(iii) Show how, by taking natural logarithms, the equation $P = kV^n$ can be changed into a linear equation.

(iv) Use the straight line which you have drawn in part (ii) to find an estimate of $n$. Calculate an estimate for $k$, explaining your method.

(v) Comment on the limitations of the equation $P = kV^n$ as a model for the power required to drive this craft at different speeds.

[OCR (MEI)]

3   The population of a country has been recorded at 10-year intervals during the twentieth century. The figures, in millions given to the nearest million, for the years 1910 to 1960 are as follows.

| Year | 1910 | 1920 | 1930 | 1940 | 1950 | 1960 |
|---|---|---|---|---|---|---|
| Population | 37 | 44 | 53 | 64 | 77 | 93 |

One model for population size is given by

$$P = P_0 \times k^n$$

where $P_0$ is the population at some starting date
$\quad\quad$ $P_n$ is the population $n$ years later
and $\quad$ $k$ is a constant.
$\quad$(i) According to this model, what happens to the population in each of the cases:

$\quad\quad$(A) $k > 1$ $\quad\quad$ (B) $k = 1$ $\quad\quad$ (C) $k < 1$?

$\quad$(ii) Complete the table giving $\log_{10} P_n$ for different values of $n$. Notice that $P_0$ is taken to be the population in the year 1900 and so $n$ is the number of years that have elapsed since 1900.

| Year | 1910 | 1920 | 1930 | 1940 | 1950 | 1960 |
|------|------|------|------|------|------|------|
| $n$ | 10 | 20 | | | | 60 |
| $\log_{10} P_n$ | 1.57 | | | | | 1.97 |

$\quad$(iii) Draw the graph of $\log_{10} P_n$ against $n$.
$\quad$(iv) Explain how you can tell from your graph whether the given model gives a good description of the population.
$\quad$(v) Estimate the values of $P_0$ and $k$ from your graph.

The populations in 1970 to 1990 were as follows.

| Year | 1970 | 1980 | 1990 |
|------|------|------|------|
| Population | 110 | 125 | 138 |

$\quad$(vi) Comment on the significance of these figures, bearing in mind the given model.
[OCR (MEI)]

**4** Pairs of values of $t$ and $y$ obtained in an experiment are shown below.

| $t$ | 1 | 2 | 3 | 4 | 5 |
|-----|---|---|---|---|---|
| $y$ | 1.45 | 4.83 | 16.1 | 53.7 | 178 |

Show that the data are consistent with a law of the form $ky = a^{-t}$, stating the values of $a$ and $k$.

**5** The winning times ($t$ seconds) of the Gold medalists in the finals of the $x$-metre events at the 1996 Olympic Games were as follows.

| $x$ | 100 | 200 | 400 | 800 | 1500 | 5000 | 10000 |
|-----|-----|-----|-----|-----|------|------|-------|
| $t$(men) | 9.84 | 19.32 | 43.49 | 102.58 | 215.78 | 787.96 | 1627.34 |
| $t$(women) | 10.94 | 22.12 | 48.25 | 117.73 | 240.83 | 899.88 | 1861.63 |

The speed of the runner, $v\,\mathrm{m\,s^{-1}}$, is given by $v = \dfrac{x}{t}$. By plotting $\dfrac{1}{v}$ against $\log x$, express $t$ as a function of $x$, commenting on any data that do not fit your model.

**6** Reduce each of the following laws to the linear form $Y = mX + c$, clearly stating the values of $X$, $Y$, $m$ and $c$.

(a) $ae^y = x^2 + bx$

(b) $\left(\dfrac{s}{t}\right)^a = be^{-t}$

(c) $y = \dfrac{a}{bx + c}$

(d) $y = \dfrac{1}{(x-a)(x-b)}$

**7** Bode's law for planets, proposed in the eighteenth century, states that the average distance $d$ from the sun is related to its planetary number $n$ (its rank order in distance from the sun) by $d = a + b \times 2^{n-1}$.
The data for the planets are as follows (expressed as multiples of the Earth's average distance from the sun).

| Planet | Number, $n$ | Distance, $d$ |
| --- | --- | --- |
| Venus | 1 | 0.72 |
| Earth | 2 | 1.00 |
| Mars | 3 | 1.52 |
| Asteroids | 4 | 2.90 |
| Jupiter | 5 | 5.20 |
| Saturn | 6 | 9.54 |
| Uranus | 7 | 19.2 |
| Neptune | 8 | 30.1 |
| Pluto | 9 | 39.5 |

(a) Investigate the truth of Bode's law, paying particular attention to Neptune and Pluto, which were discovered after Bode's law was proposed.

(b) The distance of the Earth from the sun is 150 million km. If $D$ is the distance of the planet in millions of kilometres, state the revised form of Bode's law.

**8** The current ($I$ amperes) flowing in an electrical circuit $t$ seconds after a switch is thrown is given below.

| $t$ | 0 | 5 | 10 | 15 | 20 | 25 |
| --- | --- | --- | --- | --- | --- | --- |
| $I$ | 0 | 4.48 | 6.60 | 7.60 | 8.08 | 8.30 |

The current eventually settles to a steady value of 8.50. Theory suggests that the current should obey the law $I = I_0(1 - e^{-kt})$. By reducing the data to linear form, verify that the data obey the law and estimate values for $I_0$ and $k$.

**9** Balmer's formula for the wavelength of the $n$th spectral line of hydrogen is $\lambda_n = A \dfrac{(n+2)^2}{(n+2)^2 - N^2}$, where $A$ and $N$ are constants.

The wavelengths for the first seven lines are

| line $n$ | 1 | 2 | 3 | 4 | 5 | 6 | 7 |
|---|---|---|---|---|---|---|---|
| wavelength $\lambda_n$ | 6563 | 4861 | 4341 | 4102 | 3970 | 3889 | 3835 |

Verify Balmer's formula and find $A$ and $N$.

**10**

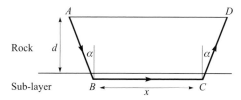

In order to estimate the thickness of a layer of rock, a seismologist generates a small explosion at $A$ (see diagram). Sound travels down to the lower boundary of the rock, where it is refracted, passes through the sub-layer, and follows the path $ABCD$. The sound of the explosion is received at $D$, $T$ seconds later. $A$ and $D$ are on the same horizontal level and the rock is $d$ km thick. $v_1$ and $v_2$ are the speeds of sound (in km s$^{-1}$) in the rock and sub-layer respectively. It is known from the laws of refraction that $\sin\alpha = v_1/v_2$.

(a) Prove that $T = \dfrac{x}{v_2} + \dfrac{2d\cos\alpha}{v_1}$.

(b) The following data are found for various values of $x$.

| $x$ (km) | 0.5 | 1.0 | 1.5 | 2.0 | 2.5 |
|---|---|---|---|---|---|
| $T$ (s) | 0.43 | 0.62 | 0.80 | 0.99 | 1.17 |

It is known that $v_1 = 1.8$ km s$^{-1}$. Estimate $v_2$, $\alpha$ and $d$.

## Revision

**1** Reduce each of the following to the form $Y = mX + c$. In each case give the functions equivalent to $X$ and $Y$ and the constants equivalent to $m$ and $c$.

(a) $x^2 + y^2 = a^2$     (b) $y(ax + b) = 1$     (c) $y = ab^x$

**2** The following table gives sets of values related by the law $\dfrac{a}{x} + \dfrac{b}{y} = 1$.

| $x$ | 3 | 4 | 5 | 6 |
|---|---|---|---|---|
| $y$ | 1.5 | 1 | 0.83 | 0.75 |

Find the values of $a$ and $b$ correct to one significant figure by drawing a suitable graph.

**3**  Find the law connecting $x$ and $y$ when the graph of $\log_{10} y$ against $\log_{10} x$ is a straight line with gradient equal to 0.5 and intercept equal to 0.52 on the $(\log_{10} y)$-axis.

**4**  It is thought that the period $T$ of a planet's year is related to $r$, its mean distance from the sun, by an equation of the form $T = kr^n$ where $k$ and $n$ are constants. If $T$ is measured in Earth-years and $r$ in astronomical units of distance, their values for the six inner planets are:

|       | Mercury | Venus  | Earth | Mars  | Jupiter | Saturn |
|-------|---------|--------|-------|-------|---------|--------|
| $r$   | 0.3871  | 0.7233 | 1.000 | 1.524 | 5.203   | 9.539  |
| $T$   | 0.2408  | 0.6152 | 1.000 | 1.881 | 11.86   | 29.46  |

Use natural logarithms to plot these values as an approximate straight line. From your graph of $\ln T$ against $\ln r$ find the gradient of the graph and hence the values of $n$ and $k$.

**5**  It is believed that the following data satisfy a law of the form $V = pt^q$ where $p$ and $q$ are rational constants.

| $t$ | 0 | 2    | 4    | 6    | 8    |
|-----|---|------|------|------|------|
| $V$ | 0 | 0.47 | 0.67 | 0.82 | 0.94 |

(a)  Express $\ln V$ in terms of $\ln t$ for $t > 0$.
(b)  By drawing a suitable straight-line graph, show that $q \approx \frac{1}{2}$ and $p \approx \frac{1}{3}$.

**6**  The following data are believed to fit a relationship of the form $x^2 y^k = A$ where $k$ and $A$ are constants.

| $x$ | 1    | 2    | 3    |
|-----|------|------|------|
| $y$ | 1.71 | 1.08 | 0.82 |

(a)  Make $y$ the subject of the formula $x^2 y^k = A$.
(b)  Find an expression for $\ln y$ in terms of $\ln x$.
(c)  By drawing a suitable straight-line graph, obtain values for $k$ and $A$ correct to one significant figure.

**7**  The graph of $\ln y$ against $x$ crosses the $x$-axis at $\frac{1}{3}$ and the $(\ln y)$-axis at $\ln y = \frac{2}{3}$.

(a)  Find the equation of the line.
(b)  Express $y$ as a function of $x$ in the form $y = ab^x$ where $a$ and $b$ are constants.

**8**  The times of oscillations, $T$ seconds, of heavy weights on the ends of wires of length $\ell$ metres are given by

| $\ell$ | 2 | 4 | 6 | 8 |
|---|---|---|---|---|
| $T$ | 2.81 | 4.01 | 4.98 | 5.63 |

It is thought that $T$ are $\ell$ are related by the equation $T = k\ell^n$ where $k$ and $n$ are constants.

(a) Use logarithms to plot these readings as an approximate straight line.
(b) Estimate the values of $k$ and $n$ using the graph.
(c) From the graph, find the length of a pendulum whose time of oscillation is 1 second.

9  The mass $m$ kg of a fixed length of wire is given for different diameters $d$ mm of the wire.

| $d$ | 8 | 9.5 | 11 | 13 | 16 | 19 |
|---|---|---|---|---|---|---|
| $m$ | 21.6 | 30.5 | 40.9 | 57.2 | 86.6 | 122 |

By plotting a suitable graph, show that $d$ and $m$ are connected approximately by the relationship $m = kd^2$ where $k$ is a constant.

10  A car costing £5000 depreciates at a rate of 15% each year.

(a) Express its value £$P$ as a function of its age $n$ years.
(b) Use a logarithmic scale to plot its depreciation as a straight-line graph. With the same axes plot the depreciation line when the annual rate is 30%.

11  The frequency $f$ oscillations per second and the interval $x$ semitones of the notes of a C major scale are given below.

| | C | D | E | F | G | A | B | C |
|---|---|---|---|---|---|---|---|---|
| $x$ | 0 | 2 | 4 | 5 | 7 | 9 | 11 | 12 |
| $f$ | 256 | 287 | 323 | 342 | 384 | 431 | 483 | 512 |

Show that $f$ and $x$ are related by a law of the form $f = ka^x$ where $k$ and $a$ are constants. Find the constants $k$ and $a$ to three significant figures.

12  Pairs of numerical values $(x, y)$ are collected from an experiment and it is possible that either of the two following equations may be applicable to the data.

(i)  $ax^2 + by^3 = 1$    $a, b$ constants
(ii)  $y = cx^d$          $c, d$ constants

In each case explain carefully how you would use a graph to examine the validity of the equation. Explain also how you would estimate the value of the constants if you found the equation to be valid from your graph.

# 8

## Differentiation

### 8.1 Differentiation of polynomials, trigonometric, exponential and logarithmic functions; product and quotient rules; composite functions

$$f'(x) = \lim_{h \to 0} \frac{f(x+h) - f(x)}{h}$$

| $f(x)$ | $f'(x)$ | $f(x)$ | $f'(x)$ |
|---|---|---|---|
| $(ax+b)^n$ | $an(ax+b)^{n-1}$ | $\sin^{-1} x$ | $\dfrac{1}{\sqrt{(1-x^2)}}$ |
| $\sin ax$ | $a\cos ax$ | | |
| $\cos ax$ | $-a\sin ax$ | $\tan^{-1} x$ | $\dfrac{1}{1+x^2}$ |
| $\tan ax$ | $a\sec^2 ax$ | | |
| $\sec ax$ | $a\sec ax \tan ax$ | $\ln ax$ | $\dfrac{1}{x}$ |
| $\operatorname{cosec} ax$ | $-a\operatorname{cosec} ax \cot ax$ | $e^{ax}$ | $ae^{ax}$ |
| $\cot ax$ | $-a\operatorname{cosec}^2 ax$ | | |

**Product rule:** if $y = uv$, then $\dfrac{dy}{dx} = v\dfrac{du}{dx} + u\dfrac{dv}{dx}$

**Quotient rule:** if $y = \dfrac{u}{v}$, then $\dfrac{dy}{dx} = \dfrac{v\frac{du}{dx} - u\frac{dv}{dx}}{v^2}$

**Chain rule:** if $y = f(u)$ and $u = g(x)$, then $\dfrac{dy}{dx} = \dfrac{dy}{du} \times \dfrac{du}{dx}$

**Basic**

**1** Find $\dfrac{dy}{dx}$ if $y$ is:

(a) $x^5$  (b) $x^{1/2}$  (c) $\sqrt[3]{x}$  (d) $x^{-1}$

(e) $\dfrac{1}{x^2}$  (f) $\dfrac{1}{\sqrt{x}}$  (g) $\dfrac{1}{x^n}$

**2**   Differentiate the following with respect to $x$.

(a) $3x^7$

(b) $6\sqrt{x}$

(c) $2x^4 - x^3 + 2x$

(d) $5x + 3$

(e) $3$

(f) $3x^4 - \dfrac{x^3}{3} + 4x^2 - \dfrac{x}{2} + 10$

(g) $x + \dfrac{1}{x}$

(h) $x^2 - \dfrac{1}{x^2}$

(i) $x^4 - \dfrac{8}{x^2}$

(j) $3x + \dfrac{4}{x}$

(k) $6x^4 - 4x^6$

(l) $ax^2 + bx + c$

**3**   Using the chain rule, find $f'(x)$ if $f(x)$ is:

(a) $(x+1)^4$

(b) $(2x+3)^5$

(c) $4(x-2)^2$

(d) $3(2-3x)^3$

(e) $(x^2+1)^2$

(f) $(3x^2+1)^4$

(g) $(1-x^2)^6$

(h) $(x^2-x)^5$

(i) $(\sqrt{x}+1)^{10}$

*(j) $\sqrt{1-x}$

(k) $\sqrt{x^2+2}$

(l) $(ax+b)^n$

**4**   Using the chain rule, differentiate the following with respect to $t$.

(a) $(t+3)^{-3}$

(b) $(2t+3)^{-1}$

*(c) $\dfrac{1}{3t+2}$

(d) $\dfrac{1}{\sqrt{(3t+1)}}$

(e) $\dfrac{1}{(3-t^2)^5}$

(f) $\dfrac{1}{(1+\sqrt{t})^2}$

(g) $\dfrac{2}{\sqrt{2+t^2}}$

(h) $\dfrac{1}{(at+b)^n}$

**5**   Using the product rule, find the derivative with respect to $x$ of the following, simplifying your answers.

*(a) $2x(x+1)^3$

(b) $x^2(2x^3+1)^5$

(c) $(x+1)^2(x+2)^3$

(d) $(x^2+2)\sqrt{x}$

(e) $x\sqrt{x^2+2}$

(f) $x^n(x+1)^m$

**6**   Using the quotient rule, find $\dfrac{dy}{dx}$ for the following, simplifying your answers.

(a) $\dfrac{x}{1+x^2}$

(b) $\dfrac{x+1}{x-1}$

(c) $\dfrac{x}{2x^2+1}$

(d) $\dfrac{1-x^2}{1+x^2}$

*(e) $\dfrac{x}{(3x+1)^2}$

(f) $\dfrac{1+\sqrt{x}}{1-\sqrt{x}}$

(g) $\dfrac{x^2+1}{(x+1)^2}$

(h) $\dfrac{x^2}{\sqrt{1+x^2}}$

**7**   For the following functions, find $f'(x)$ if $f(x)$ is:

(a) $2\sin x$

(b) $-4\cos x$

(c) $0.5\tan x$

(d) $\sin 3x$

(e) $\cos 0.5x$

(f) $\tan 6x$

(g) $-3 \sin 2x$    (h) $2 \cos \frac{1}{2} x$    (i) $\frac{1}{6} \tan \frac{1}{6} x$

(j) $3 \sin \pi x - 2 \cos \frac{1}{2} \pi x$    (k) $3 \tan \frac{1}{12} \pi x - 0.5 \sin 2\pi x$    (l) $\sec 7x$

**8**  Differentiate the following with respect to $x$.

*(a) $\sin^2 x$    (b) $\sin x^2$    (c) $\sin 2x$

(d) $\cos^2 x - 3 \sin^2 x$    (e) $4 \tan^2 x$    (f) $6 \sin^3 2x$

(g) $\sqrt{\sin x}$    (h) $4 \cos 3x^2$    (i) $(\sin x + \cos x)^3$

(j) $\sin^2 \pi x$    (k) $\operatorname{cosec} x^2$

**9**  Find $\dfrac{dy}{dx}$ if $y$ is equal to the following.

(a) $2e^x$    (b) $e^{-x}$    (c) $e^{4x}$    (d) $3e^{2x}$    *(e) $e^{x^2}$

(f) $e^{\sin x}$    (g) $e^{1/x}$    (h) $\exp e^x$    (i) $(e^{2x} + 1)^2$    (j) $(e^{2x+1})^2$

**10**  For the following functions $f(x)$, find $f'(x)$, simplifying your answers.

(a) $2 \ln x$    (b) $\ln 2x$    (c) $3 \ln 4x$    *(d) $\ln x^2$

(e) $\ln \sin x$    (f) $\ln(x^2 + 1)$    (g) $(\ln x)^2$

**11**  Using the product or quotient rule, differentiate the following with respect to $x$.

(a) $x \sin x$    (b) $x^2 \cos 4x$    (c) $\dfrac{e^x}{x}$

(d) $x \ln x$    (e) $\dfrac{\ln x}{x^2}$    (f) $x^2 e^{3x}$

(g) $\dfrac{\sin x}{x}$    (h) $\dfrac{\tan x}{x}$    (i) $\dfrac{x^2}{\sin x}$

(j) $e^{2x} \cos \pi x$    (k) $e^{x \sin x}$    (l) $\sin 3x \cos x + \cos 3x \sin x$

(m) $x^2 \sec x$    (n) $\sqrt{x} \cot x$

**12** (a)  (i) By rewriting $y = \sin^{-1} x$ as $x = \sin y$ find $\dfrac{dx}{dy}$.

(ii) Using the fact that $\dfrac{dy}{dx} = \dfrac{1}{dx/dy}$, find $\dfrac{dy}{dx}$ in terms of $x$.

(b) Using a similar method, find $\dfrac{dy}{dx}$ if $y = \tan^{-1} x$.

## Intermediate

**1**  Find the derivative of $y = 2x^3 + 3x^2 - 36x$. Factorise your answer and hence find the values of $x$ for which the derivative is equal to zero.

2  The derivative of the curve $y = ax^3 + 2bx^2 + 3cx$ is $\dfrac{dy}{dx} = 6x^2 + 6x - 6$.

Find the values of the constants $a$, $b$ and $c$, simplifying your answers as much as possible.

3  Given that $f(x) = x \ln(x^3 - 4)$, find the value of $f'(2)$. Leave your answer in terms of natural logarithms.

4  If $y = \dfrac{\ln x}{x}$ show that $\dfrac{dy}{dx} = 0$ when $x = e$.

5  (a)  Find $f'\left(\dfrac{\pi}{3}\right)$ if $f(x) = 2 \sin x - 3 \cos 2x$.

(b)  Find $f'(1)$ if $f(x) = 4x \ln x$.
(c)  Find $f'(0)$ and $f'(1)$ if $f(x) = \exp(x^2 - 2x)$.

6  If $y = 64 \cos x - \dfrac{8 \cos x}{\sin x}$ find the value of $\sin x$ for which $\dfrac{dy}{dx} = 0$.

7  (a)  If $x^4 y = 3$, find $\dfrac{dy}{dx}$ when $x = 1$.

(b)  If $pq = 9$, find the value of $\dfrac{dp}{dq}$ when $q = 3$.

8  If $y = a \cos x - b \sin x$ and $\dfrac{dy}{dx} = 0$ when $x = \dfrac{\pi}{3}$, show that $a = \dfrac{-b}{\sqrt{3}}$.

9  Find the derivatives of the following, simplifying your answers where possible.

(a)  $x^4 + 3x^2$    (b)  $\dfrac{1}{(3 - 2x)^3}$    (c)  $x^2 \cos x$    (d)  $\dfrac{2x + 1}{3x - 1}$

(e)  $\dfrac{x^2 + 1}{x^2 - 1}$    (f)  $\sqrt{x^2 - 1}$    (g)  $\sec^2 x$    (h)  $\cot 5x$

10  Differentiate the following with respect to $x$.

*(a)  $\sin^{-1} 2x$    (b)  $\tan^{-1} x^2$    (c)  $\sin^{-1} \sqrt{x}$

11  Find and simplify the derivative of $\dfrac{x}{1 + x^2} + \tan^{-1} x$.

12  Differentiate the following with respect to $t$.

(a)  $5 \sin^3 3t$    (b)  $\dfrac{\sin t + 1}{\cos t + 1}$    (c)  $2 \sin 2t \cos 3t$    (d)  $\tan^{-1} 3t$

(e)  $\dfrac{\sin t}{e^t}$    (f)  $\ln(1 + \tan^2 t)$

**13 (a)** Use the product rule to differentiate:

(i) $e^{-2x}\cos 2x$    (ii) $3x\ln 2x$    (iii) $e^x \sin x$

**(b)** Use the quotient rule to differentiate:

(i) $\dfrac{x}{1+x}$    (ii) $\dfrac{\tan^{-1} x}{1+x^2}$    (iii) $\dfrac{1-e^{-x}}{1+e^x}$

**14** Differentiate:

(a) $\sqrt{\dfrac{1+4x}{2x-1}}$    (b) $\tan^{-1}\left(\dfrac{1-4x}{4x+1}\right)$    (c) $\dfrac{x^2 \sin x}{\ln x}$

(d) $\dfrac{\exp(-x^2)}{\sqrt{x}}$    (e) $\cos^{-1} x - x\sqrt{1-x^2}$    (f) $\ln(x+\sqrt{1+x^2})$

**15 (a)** Differentiate:

*(i) $\ln\left(\dfrac{x^2}{1+x^2}\right)$    (ii) $\ln\sqrt{1+x}$    (iii) $\ln\left(\dfrac{x^2+1}{2x+1}\right)$

**(b)** Given that $f(x) = \ln\left(\dfrac{1+\sin x}{1-\sin x}\right)$ show that $f'(x) = \dfrac{2}{\cos x}$.

**16 (a)** (i) Differentiate $y = (x^2+1)(x+3)^{-2}$ as a product.

(ii) Now differentiate $y = \dfrac{x^2+1}{(x+3)^2}$ as a quotient.

**(b)** Why should your answers to part (a) be the same? Show that this is the case.

## Advanced

**1** Differentiate with respect to $x$:

(a) $\dfrac{x}{\sqrt{ax^2+b}}$    (b) $\sin(\cos(x^3))$    (c) $e^{\sin^2 x}$

**2** Differentiate $f(x) = x^{-2}$ from first principles.

**3** Differentiate with respect to $x$, simplifying your answers,

(a) $\ln\left(\dfrac{a-x}{a+x}\right)^{1/3}$    (b) $e^{2\ln 3x}$    (c) $\cos^4 x - \sin^4 x$

**4** Given that $f(x) = \dfrac{3x+5a}{x^2-a^2}$, find the values of $a$ for which $f'(12) = 0$.

**5** If $y = e^{-x}(ax+b)$, and $y$ satisfies the differential equation

$\dfrac{d^2 y}{dx^2} + p\dfrac{dy}{dx} + qy = 0$ for all $a$ and $b$, find the values for $p$ and $q$.

**6**  Differentiate the following functions with respect to $x$.

(a) $\cos{(\sin{(ax)})}$     (b) $\dfrac{x^3}{e^x - e^{-x}}$     (c) $\tan^{-1}(e^{-x^3})$

(d) $\displaystyle\int_0^\infty ye^{-xy^2}\,\mathrm{d}y$, where $x$ and $y$ are independent variables and $x > 0$

**7**  Let $f(x) = x - \ln{(1 + x)} - \dfrac{x^2}{2(1 + x)}$, where $x > 0$. Find $f'(x)$ and hence, or otherwise, show that, when $x > 0$, $x > \ln(1 + x) + \dfrac{x^2}{2(1 + x)}$.
[OCR (Cambridge), 1987]

**8**  Differentiate with respect to $x$:

(a) $1 + \operatorname{cosec} 2x - \dfrac{2(\cos^2 x - \sin^2 x)}{\sin 4x}$

(b) $\cos{\{\tan^{-1}(x^2)\}}$
(c) $\sin{(e^x - |x|)}$

**9**  (i) By considering $(1 + x + x^2 + \cdots + x^n)(1 - x)$ show that, if $x \neq 1$,

$$1 + x + x^2 + \cdots + x^n = \frac{(1 - x^{n+1})}{1 - x}$$

(ii) By differentiating both sides and setting $x = -1$ show that

$$1 - 2 + 3 - 4 + \cdots + (-1)^{n-1}n$$

takes the value $-\dfrac{n}{2}$ if $n$ is even and the value $\dfrac{(n + 1)}{2}$ if $n$ is odd.
(iii) Show that

$$1^2 - 2^2 + 3^2 - 4^2 + \cdots + (-1)^{n-1}n^2 = (-1)^{n-1}(An^2 + Bn)$$

where the constants $A$ and $B$ are to be determined.
[OCR (STEP), 1995]

**10** Differentiate from first principles:

(a) $|x^3|$     (b) $x \sin^2 x$

## Revision

**1**  Given that $y = 3x^4 - 4x^3 - 12x^2$ find $\dfrac{\mathrm{d}y}{\mathrm{d}x}$ in factorised form.

**2**  If $f(x) = x^{1/3} + \dfrac{1}{2x - 1}$ find $f'(x)$.

**3** Find $\dfrac{dv}{dt}$ if:

(a)  $v = 4t(t^2 - 1)^3$  (b)  $v = t\sqrt{2 - t}$

**4** A curve is given by $y = \dfrac{x^2 - 5x + 4}{x}$ for $x > 0$. Show that $\dfrac{dy}{dx} = 1 - \dfrac{4}{x^2}$.

**5** Differentiate the following with respect to $t$.

(a)  $e^{2t}\cos t$  (b)  $\sin(t^3 + 4)$  (c)  $\dfrac{\ln t}{t}$  (d)  $\ln(1 - \sin^2 t)$

**6** For $y = x(1 + 2x)^3$ use the product rule to find an expression for $\dfrac{dy}{dx}$, simplifying your answer as far as possible.

**7** Given that $y = \ln\sqrt{1 + x^2}$ show that $\dfrac{dy}{dx} = \dfrac{x}{1 + x^2}$.

**8** Using the quotient rule, differentiate $y = \dfrac{e^x}{1 + e^{-x}}$.

**9** Given that $y = \sin^{-1} 4x$, show that $\dfrac{dy}{dx} = \dfrac{4}{\sqrt{1 - 16x^2}}$.

**10** Show that the result of differentiating $\sqrt{x} + \dfrac{1}{\sqrt{x}}$ with respect to $x$ may be written in the form $\dfrac{x - 1}{2x\sqrt{x}}$.

**11** Find the derivatives of the following functions.

(a)  $\sin 5x$  (b)  $\tan 0.5x$  (c)  $e^{3x}$  (d)  $(1 + x^2)^4$
(e)  $\ln(1 + x^3)$  (f)  $\cos^{-1}(2x)$

**12** Use the quotient rule to differentiate the function $f(x) = \dfrac{x^2}{1 - x^2}$.

## 8.2    Increasing and decreasing functions; rates of change; tangents and normals; maxima, minima and stationary points; points of inflexion; optimisation problems

---

Velocity $v = \dfrac{dx}{dt}$,  acceleration $a = \dfrac{dv}{dt}$

At a stationary point $\dfrac{dy}{dx} = 0$.

For a maximum, $\dfrac{d^2y}{dx^2} < 0$; for a minimum, $\dfrac{d^2y}{dx^2} > 0$.

At a point of inflexion $\dfrac{d^2y}{dx^2} = 0$ and changes sign as $x$ moves across the point.

---

## Basic

**1**  Find the gradient of each of the following curves at the given point.

(a)  $y = 4x^2 - 5x + 1$ at $x = 2$
(b)  $y = x^3 + x^2 - 6$ at $x = 3$
(c)  $y = 2x^3 - 3x^2 + 5x - 1$ at $x = -1$

**2**  Find the equation of the tangent to each of the following curves at the given point.

*(a)  $y = x^2 - 3x + 2$ at $(3, 2)$
(b)  $y = 3x^2 + 4x - 1$ at $(-1, -2)$
(c)  $y = 3x^2 + \dfrac{1}{x^2}$ at $(1, 2)$

**3**  Find the equation of the normal to each of the following curves at the given point.

(a)  $y = 2x^2 - 6x - 6$ at $(2, -10)$
(b)  $y = x^3 - 4x$ at $(3, 15)$
(c)  $y = 3\sqrt{x} + \dfrac{1}{\sqrt{x}}$ at $(1, 4)$

**4**  Find the value(s) of $x$ for which each of the following curves has the gradient given.

(a)  $y = 5x^2 + 2x - 6$,  gradient 2
(b)  $y = x(4x + 1)$,  gradient $-1$
(c)  $y = x(x^2 + 3)$,  gradient 15

**5**  Find the coordinates of the points on the following curves for which the gradient is zero.

(a)  $y = x^2 - 5x + 8$
(b)  $y = x^3 - 15x^2 + 48x + 7$
(c)  $y = x + \dfrac{4}{x}$

**6**  Find the coordinates of the stationary points of:

*(a)  $f(x) = x^2 + 6x - 9$
(b)  $g(x) = (x - 5)(x + 7)$
(c)  $h(x) = x^3 + 5x^2 - 8x + 7$

**7**  Find the turning point(s) for each of the following, distinguishing between maxima and minima. Sketch the curve.

(a)  $y = 3x^2 + 12x - 7$
(b)  $f(x) = x^3 - 6x^2 - 15x + 8$
(c)  $g(x) = x + \dfrac{1}{x}$

**8**  For each of the following, determine the coordinates of the points for which (i) $\dfrac{\mathrm{d}y}{\mathrm{d}x} = 0$ and (ii) $\dfrac{\mathrm{d}^2 y}{\mathrm{d}x^2} = 0$. Sketch the curve.

(a)  $y = 2x^3 - 3x^2 - 36x + 5$
(b)  $y = x^4 - 2x^2$
(c)  $y = (x - 1)(x - 2)(x + 3)$

**9**  A particle moves in a straight line so that, after a time of $t$ seconds, its displacement $s$ metres from a fixed point $O$ is given by $s = 2t^3 - 24t$.

(a)  Find (i) the velocity, (ii) the acceleration of the particle after 4 seconds.
(b)  At what time is the particle stationary?

**10**  A particle moves in a straight line so that its displacement $s$ cm from a fixed point $O$ after time $t$ seconds is given by $s = (2t + 1)(4 - t)$.

(a)  Find its velocity after 10 seconds.
(b)  Show that its acceleration is constant.
(c)  Find the maximum displacement of the particle from $O$.

**\*11**  A groundsman has 80 metres of tape with which to mark out a rectangular enclosure against a brick wall. If the length of each of the two shortest sides is $x$ metres and that of the longest side is $y$ metres, show that the area of the enclosure, $A\,\mathrm{m}^2$ is given by $A = 80x - 2x^2$. Hence find the maximum area that can be enclosed.

**12**  A gardener wishes to build a wooden enclosure with a rectangular cross-section and has available a length of 3 metres of wood. If the lengths of two sides of the rectangle are $x$ metres and $y$ metres respectively, find the area of the enclosure in terms of $x$ and hence find the maximum area that can be enclosed.

## Intermediate

**1**  Find the equation of the tangent to the curve $y = x^2 + \dfrac{1}{x}$ at the point $P$ where $x = 2$. If the tangent intersects the $x$-axis at the point $A$, find the area of triangle $OAP$.

**2**  If $\mathrm{f}(x) = 4 + 2\sin 3x$,

(a)  find the equation of the tangent to the curve at the point where $x = \tfrac{1}{3}\pi$,
(b)  find the coordinates of the points in the interval $[0, \pi]$ for which the gradient of $y = \mathrm{f}(x)$ is equal to 1.

**3**  Find the stationary value of $f(x) = 8x^2 + \dfrac{1}{\sqrt{x}}$. Sketch the curve.

**4**  Calculate the coordinates of the maximum and minimum points on the curve $y = x^2(a - x)^3$, where $a$ is a positive constant.

**5**  A function $h(x)$ is defined by $h(x) = (ax^2 + b)e^{cx}$. It is known that $h(0) = -4$, that $h'(0) = 8$ and that the function has a minimum value at $x = -1$.
Find the values of $a$, $b$, $c$.

**6**  (a)  The table below gives information about the function $f(x)$ which is defined for values of $x$ in the interval $[-1, 10]$. Thus, at the point where $x = 0$, $f(x) = 4$, $f'(x)$ has a positive sign, and $f''(x)$ has a negative sign. Assuming that $f'(x) \neq 0$ at any other point in the interval, use the information to sketch the graph of $f(x)$ for the given domain.

| $x$ | $-1$ | $0$ | $3$ | $8$ | $10$ |
|---|---|---|---|---|---|
| $f(x)$ | 3 | 4 | 8 | 3 | $-2$ |
| $f'(x)$ | $+$ | $+$ | 0 | 0 | $-$ |
| $f''(x)$ | $-$ | $-$ | $-$ | 0 | $-$ |

(b)

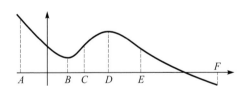

(i)  For the graph shown above, complete the table to show the signs of $f'(x)$ and $f''(x)$ for each of the intervals stated.

| Interval | $AB$ | $BC$ | $CD$ | $DE$ | $EF$ |
|---|---|---|---|---|---|
| $f'(x)$ | | | | | |
| $f''(x)$ | | | | | |

(ii)  State the points at which $f'(x) = 0$.
(iii)  State the points at which $f''(x) = 0$.

**\*7**  If $f(x) = 4x^4 \ln x - x^4$, $x \in \mathbb{R}^+$,

(a)  Find $f'(x)$.
(b)  Find the interval on which $f(x)$ is decreasing.
(c)  Show that the function $y = f(x)$ has one stationary point and hence sketch the curve. (Note: as $x \to 0$, $x^4 \ln x \to 0$.)

**8**  A point $P$ on the curve $y = (x - 2)(x + 3)$ has coordinates $(p, q)$. The tangent to the curve at $P$ meets the $y$-axis at $T$. Show that the length $OT$ is given by $q - p - 2p^2$.

**9**  After time $t$ seconds, the distance of a particle $s$ metres from a fixed point $O$ is given by $s = 3e^{2t} + 12e^{-t}$.

   (a)  Find the time at which the velocity of the particle is zero.
   (b)  Explain why the acceleration of the particle can never be zero.

**\*10**  A closed rectangular box, of width $x$ and depth $y$, is made of cardboard and its length is three times its width. Its volume is $900\,\text{cm}^3$.

   (a)  Show that its surface area $S$ is given by $S = 6x^2 + \dfrac{2400}{x}$.

   (b)  Find the dimensions of the box which has minimum surface area.

**11**  The function $f(x)$ is defined as $f(x) = e^{-x}(x^2 - 3)$.

   (a)  Find $f'(x)$.
   (b)  Find the stationary values of $f(x)$, distinguishing between them.
   (c)  Find the points of inflexion of $f(x)$.
   (d)  Sketch the graph of $y = f(x)$.

**12**  Find the coordinates of all the stationary points of the function

$$y = 2\sin x + \sin 2x \quad \text{in the interval } [0, 2\pi]$$

distinguishing between maxima, minima and points of inflexion. Sketch the graph of $y$ in the given interval.

**13**  The curve $y = 3x^4 + ax^3 + bx^2$ passes through the point $(1, 3)$ and has a stationary point when $x = 2$. Calculate the values of $a$ and $b$ and sketch the curve.

**14**  The line $y = 4x + c$ is a tangent to $y = (x + 3)(x + 1)$ at a point $P$.

   (a)  Find the value of $c$.
   (b)  The tangent intersects the $x$-axis at $A$ and the normal to $P$ intersects the $x$-axis at $B$. Find the area of triangle $PAB$.

**15**  The function $g(x)$ is defined as $g(x) = \dfrac{x - 2}{\sqrt{x^2 + 4}}$

   (a)  Find $g'(x)$.
   (b)  Find the stationary value of $g(x)$ and determine whether it is a maximum or a minimum.
   (c)  Find the points of inflexion of $g(x)$.
   (d)  Sketch the graph of $y = g(x)$.

**16**  (a)  Sketch the curve $y = x^2 + x$.

(b) Show that the equation of the tangent to the curve $y = x^2 + x$ at the point $x = a$ is given by $y = (2a + 1)x - a^2$.

(c) If this tangent passes through the point (2, 5), find the possible values of $a$. Hence write down the equations of the tangents to the curve $y = x^2 + x$ which pass through (2, 5).

### Advanced

**1**  Albert and Victoria each purchase a car for £8000 and wish to know its value in future years. Albert believes that his car will decrease in value by £800 each year, while Victoria estimates that, after $t$ years, her car will be worth £$(8000e^{-0.2t})$. Show that, after 7 years, Albert's estimate of his car's value is greater than that of Victoria while after 8 years, the situation is reversed.

Assuming that the estimates can be modelled as continuous variables, find the value of $t$ for which the ratio of Albert's estimate to Victoria's has its largest value.

**2**

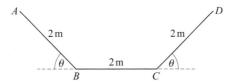

In the diagram $ABCD$ represents the symmetric cross-section of a drainage channel $\left(\text{where } 0 < \theta \leq \frac{1}{2}\pi\right)$. The sides and base are made from sheets of metal of width 2 metres, so that $AB = BC = CD = 2$.

(i) Show that $W$, the area of the cross-section of the channel, is given by

$$W = 4\sin\theta + 2\sin 2\theta$$

(ii) Find the value of $\theta$ for which $W$ is stationary, and show that the stationary value is a maximum.

[OCR (SMP), 1987]

**3**  (a)  The functions f and g are defined by

$$f(x) = x(30 - x)(10 + x) \quad \text{and} \quad g(x) = \frac{100}{f(x)}.$$

where the domain consists of all the real numbers for which the expressions are defined.

(i) Draw a rough sketch of the graph of f, and state the values of $x$ for which $f(x) > 0$.

(ii) Hence, or otherwise, sketch the graph of g.

(b) A hollow cuboid container is to be constructed to hold a given amount of a gas. The gas obeys Boyle's law, such that, when the volume occupied is $v\,\mathrm{cm}^3$ and the pressure is $P\,\mathrm{N\,cm}^{-2}$, then $Pv = 100$. The container is to be manufactured from a strong thin rectangular sheet of material 60 cm × 40 cm. (The net is shown in the diagram, the shaded areas to be discarded.)

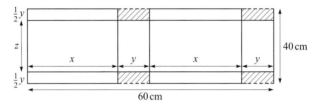

(i) Find an expression for $P$ in terms of $x$.

(ii) Find the minimum value that $P$ can take. (Work to three significant figures.)

[OCR (SMP), 1985]

4 A piece of wire of length 36 cm is to be bent into the shape shown in the diagram, which consists of an equilateral triangle surmounting a rectangle. Show that,

(a) if the length of the base is $x\,\mathrm{cm}$, the area, $A$, is given by

$$A = 18x + \frac{(\sqrt{3} - 6)x^2}{4}$$

(b) when the area is a maximum, the length of the base is

$$\frac{36}{6 - \sqrt{3}}.$$

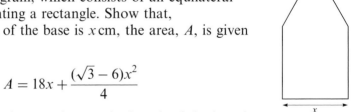

5 A curve has an equation of the form $y = ax^3 + bx^2 - 9x$, where $a$ and $b$ are constants. It is given that the curve has a stationary point when $x = -1$ and also that the tangent to the curve at the point at which $x = 1$ cuts the $y$-axis at the point $(0, 1)$.

Find the values of the constants $a$ and $b$.

Sketch the curve.

Hence sketch the curves

(i) $y^2 = ax^3 + bx^2 - 9x$      (ii) $y = |ax^3 + bx^2 - 9x|$

[OCR (MEI), 1973]

6 A man is standing on level moorland at a point $A$ at distance $a$ from a straight road. He wishes to reach a point $B$ on the road distant

$\sqrt{a^2 + b^2}$ from him. He plans to walk in a straight line to a point $P$ on the road and then to follow the road to $B$. His speed on the road will be constant and equal to $k$ times his speed over the moorland (also constant).

Assuming that $k > 1$, find the position of $P$ in order that the journey will take least time, distinguishing between the cases $kb > \sqrt{a^2 + b^2}$ and $kb \leq \sqrt{a^2 + b^2}$.

[OCR (Cambridge), 1969]

**7**  Prove that, for all positive values of $x$,

$$\frac{e^{x/4}}{x^2 + 16} > \frac{1}{16}$$

**8**  Sketch the curve

$$y = x^n e^{-x} \quad (n \text{ a positive integer, } n > 1)$$

(i)  when $n$ is even,

(ii)  when $n$ is odd.

Prove that the maximum of this curve lies, for all values of $n$, on the curve

$$y = x^x e^{-x}$$

Prove also that, for positive $x$, the gradient of the curve $y = x^n e^{-x}$ decreases for values of $x$ lying in an interval of length $2\sqrt{n}$.

[OCR (Cambridge), 1975]

**9**  Show that $x - x^2 - \ln(1 + x)$ is an increasing function of $x$ if $-\frac{1}{2} < x < 0$ and is a decreasing function of $x$ if $x > 0$.

Show also that $\ln(1 + x) - (x - \frac{1}{3}x^2)$ is an increasing function of $x$ if $-1 < x < 0$ and is a decreasing function of $x$ if $0 < x < \frac{1}{2}$.

Hence, or otherwise, show that $x - x^2 \leq \ln(1 + x) \leq x - \frac{1}{3}x^2$ when $-\frac{1}{2} \leq x \leq \frac{1}{2}$.

[OCR (MEI), 1973]

**10**  (i)  Sketch the curve

$$y = x \cos x$$

for values of $x$ between $-3\pi$ and $3\pi$, making clear its relationship to the lines $y = x$ and $y = -x$.

Prove that the points for which $y$ has a maximum value all lie on the curve.

$$y = +\frac{x^2}{\sqrt{1 + x^2}}$$

(ii)  Given that

$$f(x) = +\frac{x^2}{\sqrt{1+x^2}}$$

and that $x \geq 0$, find the differential coefficients $f'(x)$ and $f''(x)$; and verify that $f''(x) = 0$ when $x = \sqrt{2}$.

Sketch the curve $y = +\dfrac{x^2}{\sqrt{1+x^2}}$

for $x \geq 0$.
[OCR (Cambridge), 1971]

### Revision

**1**  Find the equation of the tangent to the curve $y = 1 + 3\sin 2x$ at the origin. Find the percentage error in using the tangent as an approximation to the curve at the point $x = \pi/3$. Give your answer to one decimal place.

**2**  Show that the equation of the normal to the curve $y = x^2 e^{-3x}$ at the point where $x = 1$ is given by $e^3 y = e^6 x + 1 - e^6$.

**3**  Find the turning values and point of inflexion of the function $y = x^3 + x^2 - 8x - 5$. Sketch the curve.

**4**  Find the turning values and point of inflexion of the function $y = (x+2)^2(4-x)$. Sketch the curve.

**5**  Find the greatest value of $y = \dfrac{2 - 4x^2}{x^2 + 2}$.

**6**  Prove that the function $f(x) = e^{-kx} \sin kx \, (k > 0)$ has a maximum at

$$\left(\frac{\pi}{4k}, \frac{1}{\sqrt{2}} e^{-\pi/4}\right)$$

Find the coordinates of the next stationary value and determine whether it is a maximum or a minimum.

**7**  By investigating the turning values of $f(x) = 5x^3 - x^2 - 8x + 7$, show that the equation $f(x) = 0$ has only one real root, but that $f(x) = 5$ has three real roots. For what values of $k$ does $f(x) = k$ have two real roots?

**8**  A particle moves along the $x$-axis in such a way that, at time $t$ seconds, its distance from the origin $O$ is given by $x = t^2 e^{-2t}$ cm.

(a)  Find the values of $t$ for which the particle is stationary.
(b)  Find the maximum displacement of the particle.

(c)  Find the acceleration of the particle when $t = 1$.

**9** (a)  Show that the function $f(x) = e^{-x}(1 + x^2)$ is a decreasing function for all values of $x$.

  (b)  For the function $g(x) = e^{-x}(3 - x^2)$, determine the intervals for which the function is increasing.

**10**  The function $y = \dfrac{a}{x^2 + bx + c}$ has value 3 when $x = 0$ and has a

stationary point at $x = 1$. When $x = 0$, the graph has gradient $-3$. Find the values of $a$, $b$ and $c$.

**11**

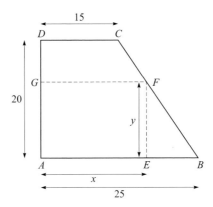

An engineer has a piece of scrap metal with the dimensions (in centimetres) shown in the diagram. He wishes to cut from it a rectangular piece of metal of maximum area. If the length $AE = x$ and $FE = y$, show that $y = 50 - 2x$.
Hence find the maximum area of the rectangle $AEFG$.

**12**  A salt cellar is in the shape of a cylinder with a hemisphere attached to one end. The total volume is to be $120\,\text{cm}^3$. If the radius of the base is $r\,\text{cm}$, show that the surface area is given by $S = \dfrac{5\pi r^2}{3} + \dfrac{240}{r}$ and hence find the radius that will give the minimum surface area.

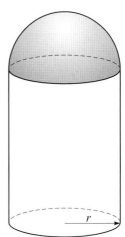

## 8.3    Parametric curves, including the parabola, circle and ellipse; implicit differentiation; logarithmic differentiation

If a curve is expressed parametrically as $x = f(t)$, $y = g(t)$, then

$$\frac{dy}{dx} = \frac{\frac{dy}{dt}}{\frac{dx}{dt}}$$

The parametric equation of a circle, centre $O$, is

$$x = a \sin t, \quad y = a \cos t$$

The parametric equation of an ellipse, centre $O$ with $x$-axis as major axis, is

$$x = a \sin t, \quad y = b \cos t$$

The Cartesian equation of an ellipse, major axis length $a$, minor axis length $b$, is

$$\frac{x^2}{a^2} + \frac{y^2}{b^2} = 1$$

### Basic

**1** (a) Complete the table below and hence plot the curve $x = 3t^2$, $y = 6t$ for $-3 \le t \le 3$.

| $t$ | $-3$ | $-2$ | $-1$ | 0 | 1 | 2 | 3 |
|---|---|---|---|---|---|---|---|
| $x$ | | | | | | | |
| $y$ | | | | | | | |

(b) Plot the following parametric curves for values of $t$ in the interval $-3 \le t \le 3$.

(i) $x = 3t + 1$, $y = 2 - t$     (ii) $x = 4t$, $y = \dfrac{4}{t}$

(iii) $x = t^2 + 2$ $y = t^3$

**2** By eliminating $t$, express $y$ in terms of $x$ for each of the following parametric curves.

(a) $x = 4t^2$, $y = 8t$     (b) $x = 3t$, $y = \dfrac{6}{t}$

(c) $x = t^3$, $y = t^2 + 1$     (d) $x = 2t$, $y = 20t - 5t^2$

**3** For the following curves, defined parametrically, find $\dfrac{dx}{dt}$, $\dfrac{dy}{dt}$ and hence find $\dfrac{dy}{dx}$.

(a) $x = 2t, \quad y = t^2$  (b) $x = 3t^2, \quad y = t^4$
(c) $x = 1 - t^3, \quad y = 1 + t^2$

**4** Find the value of the gradient of the following parametric curves when $u = 2$.

(a) $x = 3u - u^3, \quad y = u^2$  *(b) $x = 2u, \quad y = \dfrac{2}{u}$

(c) $x = \dfrac{u}{1 - u}, \quad y = \dfrac{u^2}{1 - u}$

**5** Find the exact value of $\dfrac{dy}{dx}$ for the following curves when the parameter $\theta = \pi/4$.

(a) $x = \cos\theta, \quad y = \sin\theta$  (b) $x = \sin^2\theta, \quad y = \cos\theta\sin\theta$
(c) $x = \sec\theta, \quad y = \tan\theta$

**6** For the following curves defined parametrically, find $\dfrac{dy}{dx}$ in terms of $t$ and the gradient of the normal to the curves when $t = -1$.

(a) $x = 3t, \quad y = t^2$  (b) $x = t, \quad y = \dfrac{1}{t}$  (c) $x = 2t, \quad y = t^3 - 4t$

**\*7** A curve has parametric equations $x = t(1 + t), \; y = t(1 - t)$.

(a) Find $\dfrac{dy}{dx}$ in terms of $t$.

(b) Deduce the gradient of the curve at the point where $t = 2$ and hence find the equation of the tangent to the curve when $t = 2$.

**8** Use implicit differentiation to differentiate the following with respect to $x$.

(a) $x^2y$  (b) $2xy + y^2$  (c) $\dfrac{x}{y^2}$

**9** Find $\dfrac{dy}{dx}$ in terms of $x$ and $y$ for the following curves by differentiating implicitly.

(a) $x^3 + y^3 = 4$  (b) $x^2 - y^2 = 4$  *(c) $xy = 4$

**10** Find the gradient of the following curves at the given value of $x$.

*(a) $x^2 + y^2 = 25, \quad x = 3$  (b) $4x^2 + 9y^2 = 25, \quad x = 2$
(c) $x^2 + 2y^2 = 8x + 2, \quad x = 4$

**11** Find the equation of the tangent to the following curves at the points specified.

*(a) $x^3 + y^3 = 0$  at $(2, -2)$     (b) $x^2 + (y - 1)^2 = 10$  at $(-1, 4)$
(c) $x^3 y^2 = 25$  at $(1, 5)$

**12** (a) Find an expression for $\dfrac{dy}{dx}$ for the hyperbola $x^2 - y^2 + y = 1$.

(b) Find the value of the gradient of the normal at the point $(-1, 1)$ and hence find the equation of the normal to the curve at this point.

### Intermediate

**1** State the coordinates of the points on the curve $x = 4 \sin \theta$, $y = 5 \cos \theta$ for $\theta = 0$, $\frac{1}{6}\pi$, $\frac{1}{4}\pi$, $\frac{1}{3}\pi$, $\frac{1}{2}\pi$. Hence sketch the section of the curve for which $0 \le \theta \le \frac{1}{2}\pi$.

**2** Find the Cartesian equations for each of the following curves.

(a) $x = 3 - t$,   $y = t^2 - 5$     (b) $x = \dfrac{2t - 1}{t}$,   $y = \dfrac{3t + 4}{t + 1}$

*(c) $x = 2 \sin \theta$,   $y = 3 \cos \theta$

**3** Find $\dfrac{dy}{dx}$ if:

(a) $x = (t + 4)^2$,   $y = t^3 - 1$     (b) $x = at^2$,   $y = 2at$

(c) $x = \cos \theta - \sin \theta$,   $y = 4 \sin \theta$     (d) $x = \dfrac{2u}{u + 2}$,   $y = \dfrac{3u}{u + 3}$

(e) $x = \dfrac{t}{1 - t}$,   $y = \dfrac{t^2}{1 - t}$     (f) $x = e^t - 2t^2$,   $y = e^{2t}$

(g) $x = t$,   $y = \dfrac{12}{t}$

**4** Find the value of $\dfrac{dy}{dx}$ for the following parametric equations at the points stated.

(a) $x = 4 \cos \theta$,   $y = 3 \sin \theta$  at  $\theta = \frac{1}{6}\pi$
(b) $x = 3 \cos \theta + \cos 2\theta$,   $y = 3 \sin \theta - \sin 2\theta$  at  $\theta = \frac{1}{4}\pi$
(c) $x = \sin 2\theta$,   $y = \sin^2 \theta$  at  $\theta = \frac{1}{8}\pi$

**5** For the curve $x = 4t$, $y = t^3 - 12t$,

(a) find $\dfrac{dy}{dx}$ and write down the values of $t$ for which $\dfrac{dy}{dx} = 0$,

(b) write down the $x$- and $y$-coordinates of the turning points on the curve.

**6** For the parametric curves

(a) $x = 2t, \quad y = \sqrt{t} + 3$    (b) $x = \ln t, \quad y = 2t + 3 \ln t$

find: (i) $\dfrac{dy}{dx}$ in terms of $t$,

     (ii) the equation of the tangent to the curve at $t = 1$.

**7** (a) A circle has parametric equations $x = 3 \cos t, \, y = 3 \sin t$. Find

     (i) $\dfrac{dy}{dx}$

     (ii) the equations of the tangent and normal to the curve at the point $(3, 0)$.

   (b) A curve has parametric equations $x = 5 \sec t, \, y = 3 \tan t$ for $-\frac{1}{2}\pi < t < \frac{1}{2}\pi$. Show that at the point with parameter $t$ the gradient of the curve is $\frac{3}{5} \operatorname{cosec} t$.

**8** A curve has parametric equations $x = t^2 + t, \, y = 2t + 1$.

   (a) Find an expression for $\dfrac{dy}{dx}$ in terms of $t$.

   (b) Find the values of $t$ for which $x = 0$ and hence find the coordinates of the points where the curve cuts the $y$-axis. Find the equation of the tangent at each of these points.

**9** A curve has parametric equations $x = \cos \theta, \, y = \sqrt{3} \sin \theta, \, 0 \le \theta \le \pi$.

   (a) The line $y = 3x$ intersects the curve at the point $P$. Find the value of $\theta$ at $P$.

   (b) Show that the tangent to the curve at $P$ has equation $y = 2 - x$.

**10** A curve has parametric equations $x = cp, \, y = \dfrac{c}{p}$, where $c$ is a constant.

   (a) Find the equation of the tangent and normal at the point $R$ with parameter $r$.

   (b) The normal at $R$ meets the curve at the point $S\left(cs, \dfrac{c}{s}\right)$. Show that $s = -\dfrac{1}{r^3}$.

   (c) The tangents at $R$ and $S$ meet at $T$. Assuming $r^2 \ne 1$, find the coordinates of $T$ in terms of $c$ and $r$.

**11** Use implicit differentiation to find $\dfrac{dy}{dx}$ in terms of $x$ and $y$ when:

(a) $x^2 - y^2 = 9$      (b) $\sin x \cos y = 1$      (c) $xy^2 = 16$
(d) $y^2 = 2x + 1$      (e) $x^2 y^3 = 64$      (f) $xy^3 + x^3 y = x - y$
(g) $xy(x - y) = 4$

**12** Find the gradient of the following ellipses at the points on the curve where $x = 1$.

(a) $2x^2 + 3y^2 = 29$      (b) $x^2 - 3x + 2y^2 = 4$
(c) $3(x - 2)^2 + 2y^2 = 7$

**13** Find the equation of the tangent and the normal to $x^3 - xy^2 = 24$ at the point $(-2, 4)$.

**14** If $\tan y = 2x$, show that $\dfrac{dy}{dx} = \dfrac{2}{1 + 4x^2}$.

**15*(a)** If $y = x^x$, express $\ln y$ in terms of $x$. Hence, by differentiating $\ln y$ implicitly, show that $\dfrac{dy}{dx} = x^x(1 + \ln x)$,

(b) Use the method of part (a) to find $\dfrac{d}{dx} 2^x$.

**16** A curve has equation $x^2 - 3xy + 4y^2 = 2$.

(a) Show that $P(2, 1)$ lies on the curve and that, at this point $\dfrac{dy}{dx} = -\tfrac{1}{2}$.

(b) The point $Q(2 + \alpha, 1 + \beta)$ also lies on the curve. If $\alpha$ and $\beta$ are small, express $\beta$ in terms of $\alpha$.

**Advanced**

**1** (a) If $y = \operatorname{cosec}^{-1} x$, find $\dfrac{dy}{dx}$.

(b) By taking logarithms of both sides, differentiate $x^{1/x}$.

**2** (a) If $x^2 + y^2 - 2y = 0$, show that
$$\frac{d^2 y}{dx^2} = \frac{1}{(1 - y)^3}$$

(b) If $x^2 y = a \sin \pi x$, show that
$$x^2 \frac{d^2 y}{dx^2} + 4x \frac{dy}{dx} + (2 + \pi^2 x^2) y = 0$$

**3** (a) A curve has parametric equations $x = at - a\sin t$, $y = a - a\cos t$, where $a$ is a positive constant and $0 < t < 2\pi$.

Prove that $\dfrac{dy}{dx} = \cot\frac{1}{2}t$, and (by writing $\dfrac{d^2y}{dx^2}$ as $\dfrac{d}{dx}\left(\dfrac{dy}{dx}\right)$ and using the chain rule) that $\dfrac{d^2y}{dx^2} = -\dfrac{1}{4a}\operatorname{cosec}^4\frac{1}{2}t$.

Hence show that $y$, regarded as a function of $x$, has a stationary point where $t = \pi$, and determine its nature. Sketch the curve.

(b) A microcomputer is programmed to display two dots $P$, $Q$ on its screen such that, at time $t$ seconds (where $0 < t < \pi$), $P$ is at position

$$\mathbf{r}_1 = a\begin{pmatrix} t - \sin t \\ 1 - \cos t \end{pmatrix} \text{ and } Q \text{ at position } \mathbf{r}_2 = a\begin{pmatrix} t \\ 2 \end{pmatrix}.$$

Show that, at any instant $t$ (where $0 < t < \pi$), the velocity $\mathbf{v}$ of $P$ is in the direction of $PQ$, and that $|\mathbf{v}|^2 = 4a^2 - PQ^2$.

[OCR (O&C)]

**4** Show that the point $P$ with coordinates $x = a\cos\theta$, $y = b\sin\theta$ lies on the ellipse $\dfrac{x^2}{a^2} + \dfrac{y^2}{b^2} = 1$. The tangent to the ellipse at $P$ meets the coordinate axes at the points $Q$ and $R$. Prove that, as $\theta$ varies, the minimum area of triangle $OQR$ is $ab$.

**5** (i) Find the coordinates of the two points of intersection of the line $3y - 2x = 4$ and the parabola $y^2 = 4x$.

(ii) Determine the value of $c$ for which the line $3y - 2x = c$ is a tangent to this parabola. Find the coordinates of the point of contact.

(iii) Show that the equation of the normal at the point $P(p^2, 2p)$ on the parabola is

$$y - 2p = -p(x - p^2).$$

(iv) This normal cuts the parabola again at the point $Q(q^2, 2q)$. Show that, for $p \neq 0$, $q = -\left(p + \dfrac{2}{p}\right)$.

Given that $\widehat{POQ}$ is a right angle, where $O$ denotes the origin, show that $p = \pm\sqrt{2}$.

[WJEC, 1993]

**6** Suppose that $y$ is a function of $x$, with $0 \leqslant y < \left(\frac{1}{2}\pi\right)^{1/2}$ and $0 < x < \left(\frac{1}{2}\pi\right)^{1/2}$, which satisfies $x = y\sin y^2$.

Show that $\dfrac{dy}{dx} = \dfrac{y}{x + 2y^2\sqrt{y^2 - x^2}}$.

[OCR (STEP), 1997]

**7** The coordinates of a moving particle at time $t$ are given by $x = 2a \cos t + a \cos 2t$, $y = 2a \sin t + a \sin 2t$, where $a$ is a positive constant. Find components, parallel to the axes, of (i) the velocity, (ii) the acceleration of the particle.

At certain times during the motion, the velocity of this particle is perpendicular to its acceleration. Find an equation that expresses this condition and show that $t = n\pi$ (where $n$ is an integer) is a solution of the equation.

Find the magnitude of the resultant velocity of the particle at time $t$.
[OCR (Cambridge), 1975]

**8** Given that $a$ is a constant, differentiate the following expressions with respect to $x$.

(i)  $x^a$     (ii)  $a^x$     (iii)  $x^x$     (iv)  $x^{(x^x)}$     (v)  $(x^x)^x$

[OCR (STEP), 1994]

**9** Show that, for $x > 0$, $x^{1/x}$ has its greatest value when $x = $ e. Hence, or otherwise, but without use of a calculator, determine which is the greater of $e^\pi$ and $\pi^e$.
[OCR (Cambridge), 1981]

**10** A curve $C$ is defined parametrically by the equations $x = X(t)$, $y = Y(t)$. The point $Q$ with coordinates $(p, q)$ is a given point not lying on the curve. $P$ is the point on $C$ nearest to $Q$. Show that $t$, the parameter of $P$, satisfies the equation

$$\{p - X(t)\}\frac{dX(t)}{dt} + \{q - Y(t)\}\frac{dY(t)}{dt} = 0$$

Deduce that $Q$ lies on the normal at $P$.
Find the coordinates of the point on the parabola $y^2 = 4ax$, which is nearest to the point $(5a, 52a)$.
[OCR (Cambridge), 1967]

## Revision

**1** Find, in terms of the appropriate parameter, an expression for $\dfrac{dy}{dx}$ for each of the following.

(a)  $x = 1 - 2t, \quad y = t^2 + 5$     (b)  $x = \sqrt{u}, \quad y = \dfrac{1}{u^3}$

(c)  $x = \theta(3\theta - 1)^4, \quad y = \dfrac{\theta}{(3\theta - 1)^4}$

**2** Find $\dfrac{dy}{dx}$ in terms of $t$ if $x = t^3$, $y = t^2 - t$.

Hence find the coordinates of the stationary point on the curve.

3 (a) Find the equations of the tangent and normal to the curve $x = (t+1)^2$, $y = t^2 - 1$ at the point where $t = 1$.

   (b) Find the equation of the normal to the curve $3y^2 - x^2 = 3$ at the point $(3, 2)$.

4 A curve has parametric equations $x = t + e^t$, $y = t + e^{-t}$. Find $\dfrac{dy}{dx}$ in terms of $t$ and the value of $t$ when $\dfrac{dy}{dx} = 0$. Hence find the coordinates of the stationary point.

5 A curve is defined parametrically by the equations $x = 1 + t$, $y = t(t-1)$.

   (a) Find $\dfrac{dy}{dx}$ from these parametric equations.

   (b) Find the Cartesian equation of the curve and differentiate explicitly to find $\dfrac{dy}{dx}$. Show that your two answers are the same.

6 A curve has parametric equations $x = 3t - \ln 3t$, $y = t^3 - \ln t^3$ where $t > 0$. What is the value of $t$ when $\dfrac{dy}{dx} = 3$?

7 Find the equation of the tangent to the cycloid $x = a(2\theta - \sin 2\theta)$, $y = a(1 - \cos 2\theta)$, where $a$ is a constant, at the point where $\theta = \pi/4$ (you may leave $\pi$ in your answer).

8 A circle is described by the parametric equations $x = \cos\theta$, $y = \sin\theta$.

   (a) Find $\dfrac{dx}{d\theta}$, $\dfrac{dy}{d\theta}$ and hence $\dfrac{dy}{dx}$.

   (b) Show that the equation of the tangent at the point with parameter $\theta$ is $y\sin\theta + x\cos\theta = 1$.

   (c) What is the equation of the tangent at the point $(1, 0)$?

9 For the curve with equation $x^2 + xy + y^2 = 3$, find the gradient of the tangent and normal at the point $(-1, -1)$.

10 A curve called the *Witch of Agnesi* has equation $y^2 = \dfrac{3}{x-1}$, $y > 0$. By differentiating implicitly, find its gradient exactly when $x = \frac{1}{2}$.

11 For the curve $3x^2 + y^2 = 4y$,

   (i) show that $\dfrac{dy}{dx} = \dfrac{3x}{(2-y)}$,

(ii)  find the equation of the tangents to the curve at the points where $x = 1$,

(iii)  find when the tangent to the curve is parallel to the $x$-axis.

**12**  A curve is given implicitly by $1 + y\sqrt{x} = y^2 - x$. Show that

$$\frac{dy}{dx} = \frac{y + 2\sqrt{x}}{4y\sqrt{x} - 2x}$$

## 8.4    Curve sketching

In this section, take the domain of the given functions to be $\mathbb{R}$ unless stated otherwise.

**Basic**

**1**  On separate axes, sketch the graph of $y = f(x)$, where $f(x)$ is:

(a) $2^x$  (b) $\sin 3x$  (c) $|x| + 3$  (d) $3 - x^2$

(e) $\tan x$  (f) $x^5$  (g) $\dfrac{1}{\sqrt{x}}$ $(x > 0)$  (h) $e^{-x}$

**2**  Sketch the following straight lines, clearly labelling the intercepts on the $x$- and $y$-axes.

(a) $y = 12x$  (b) $2y = 5x + 12$  (c) $4x + 3y = 24$

(d) $y - 7 = 3(x - 2)$  (e) $\dfrac{y}{3} - \dfrac{x}{5} = 10$

**3**  Illustrate, by sketching, how the following four lines intersect to form a rectangle.

$$7y + 3x = 0, \quad 3y = 7x + 6, \quad 4 - 7y = 3x, \quad \frac{y}{3} - \frac{7x}{9} = 1$$

**4**  Sketch, on separate axes, each of the following quadratic graphs, clearly labelling the intercepts.

(a) $y = (x - 3)(x + 2)$  (b) $y = 2x^2 - 9x - 35$
(c) $y = x^2 - 8x + 16$  (d) $y = x^2 - (\alpha + \beta)x + \alpha\beta$ $(\alpha > 0, \beta > 0)$

**5**  Express each of the following functions in completed square form $k\{(x + p)^2 + q\}$, and hence sketch the graph of $y = f(x)$ against $x$, labelling the turning point and $y$-intercept.

*(a) $f(x) = x^2 + 6x + 2$  *(b) $f(x) = 2x^2 - 20x + 62$
(c) $f(x) = 10 - 6x - 3x^2$  (d) $f(x) = \frac{1}{4}x^2 - 4x + 16$

**6** For each quadratic function, find its intercepts, turning points, orientation and symmetry. Then sketch and label fully each graph.

(a) $y = 7 - x^2$

(b) $y = x^2 - 5x + 6$

(c) $y = (2x - 9)(2 - x)$

(d) $y = 3\{(x + 2)^2 - 1\}$

(e) $y = x(\frac{1}{2}x - 4) + 8$

**7** Using only one set of axes, superimpose sketches of the following six cubic functions.

(a) $p(x) = x^3$

(b) $q(x) = 2x^3$

(c) $r(x) = -2x^3$

(d) $f(x) = (x - 10)^3$

(e) $g(x) = (x - 10)^3 + 10$

(f) $h(x) = (10 - x)^3 + 10$

**8** Labelling clearly both the $y$-intercepts and the roots (i.e. the $x$-intercepts), draw sketches of each of the following factorised cubics.

(a) $f(x) = (x - 3)(x - 2)(x + 5)$

(b) $f(x) = (x + 2)^2(x + 4)$

(c) $f(x) = (3x - 7)(2x + 4)(x - 2)$

(d) $f(x) = x^2(3 - x)$

(e) $f(x) = (x + 5)(x^2 + 4)$

**9** (a) (i) Sketch, on the same axes, the graphs of $f(x) = x^2 + x$ and $g(x) = 14 - x^3$.

   (ii) Use your answer to (i) to state the number of solutions to the equation $x^3 + x^2 + x - 14 = 0$.

   (b) By sketching a suitable pair of graphs, determine the number of solutions to the equation $x^3 + x^2 - 6x = 0$.

**10** On one pair of axes for each part of the question, superimpose the sketches of the three reciprocal functions.

(a) (i) $p(x) = \dfrac{1}{x}$

   (ii) $q(x) = \dfrac{5}{x}$

   (iii) $r(x) = \dfrac{-1}{x}$

(b) (i) $p(x) = \dfrac{1}{x^2}$

   (ii) $q(x) = \dfrac{5}{x^2}$

   (iii) $r(x) = \dfrac{-1}{x^2}$

**\*11** Examine each of the functions below and state the values of $x$ for which the discontinuities will occur.

(a) $f(x) = \dfrac{5}{x - 2}$

(b) $f(x) = \dfrac{1}{(x - 2)(x + 3)}$

(c) $f(x) = \dfrac{1}{x^2 - 7x + 12}$

**12** Sketch the following graphs, stating the coordinates of any turning points and labelling intercepts on the $y$-axis.

(a) $y = x^3 + 3x^2 - 9x + 5$

(b) $y = 2x^3 + 3x^2$

(c) $y = 3x^4 - 8x^3 - 48x^2 + 5$

**Intermediate**

**1** (a) Sketch the graph of each of the following functions.

(i) $\cos\left(x+\dfrac{\pi}{6}\right)$      (ii) $\tan 2x$      (iii) $\sqrt{x-3}\ (x \geq 3)$

(iv) $\dfrac{1}{\sqrt{x}}\ (x > 0)$      (v) $\dfrac{1}{x+5}\ (x \neq -5)$      (vi) $\ln 2x\ (x > 0)$

(vii) $|x^2 - 2|$      (viii) $e^{-x^2}$

(b) Sketch the graph of $y = f(x)$ where $f(x)$ is defined by

$$f(x) = 0 \quad (x < 0)$$
$$x^2 \quad (0 \leq x < 2)$$
$$2x \quad (x \geq 2)$$

**2** (a) Suggest a suitable domain for $g(x) = \sqrt{x-7}$ and hence sketch the graph of $y = g(x)$.

(b) On the same axes, sketch the graph of $y = \dfrac{12}{x}$ and hence determine two successive integers $a$ and $b$ so that the equation $\dfrac{12}{x} = \sqrt{x-7}$ has a solution in the interval $[a, b]$.

**3** Sketch the graphs of the following functions, showing clearly any asymptotes and the intercepts on the $x$- and $y$-axes.

(a) $\dfrac{2}{x+4}$      (b) $\dfrac{5}{(x-2)(x+5)}$      *(c) $\dfrac{x}{x+3}$      (d) $\dfrac{2x+7}{x-3}$

(e) $\dfrac{x}{x^2-16}$      (f) $\dfrac{x^2}{x^2-16}$

**4** A function is defined by $f(x) = x^2 + 2kx + 3$.

(a) Find the coordinates of the turning points of the graph of $f(x)$.
(b) Sketch the graph of $y = f(x)$.
(c) For which values of $k$ does the equation $x^2 + 2kx + 3 = 0$ have no real solutions?

**5** Sketch the graphs of the following functions on the specified domain, where $a > 0$, $b > 0$.

(a) $a\left(1 - \cos\dfrac{\pi t}{5}\right)\ (0 \leq t \leq 5)$      (b) $a + b\sin 2t\ (0 \leq t \leq 2\pi)$

(c) $a\cos^2 t\ (0 \leq t \leq 2\pi)$      (d) $|a\sin t|\ (0 \leq t \leq 2\pi)$

**6** For each of the following functions, sketch the graph of $f(x)$ and, on the same axes, sketch the graph of $\dfrac{1}{f(x)}$.

(a) $f(x) = x^2 + 1$    (b) $f(x) = x^3 - 3$    (c) $f(x) = \cos x$

(d) $f(x) = |x - 2|$

**7** On one pair of axes for each part of the question, use sketches of the first two functions to obtain the graph of the third.

(a) (i) $y = x$    (ii) $y = \dfrac{x+1}{x-3}$    (iii) $y = x + \dfrac{x+1}{x-3}$

(b) (i) $y = x + 5$    (ii) $y = \dfrac{1}{x+7}$    (iii) $y = x + 5 + \dfrac{1}{x+7}$

(c) (i) $y = x^2$    (ii) $y = \dfrac{-1}{x}$    (iii) $y = x^2 - \dfrac{1}{x}$

**8** For each function, (i) sketch the graph, (ii) obtain the inverse function, (iii) sketch the inverse function on the same axes, (iv) superimpose the line $y = x$.

(a) $f(x) = 10 - \dfrac{x}{3}$    (b) $g(x) = \dfrac{9 - 4x}{5}$

(c) $h(x) = x^2 + 1$ $(x \geq 0)$    (d) $k(x) = \dfrac{1}{2x - 5}$ with $x \neq \frac{5}{2}$

**9** For each of the following pairs of functions, use the graphs of $f(x)$ and $g(x)$ to sketch the graph of $f(x)g(x)$.

(a) $f(x) = x$,    $g(x) = \sin x$

(b) $f(x) = x^2$,    $g(x) = e^{-x}$ (assume that $x^2 e^{-x} \to 0$ as $x \to \infty$)

**10** Find the coordinates of the turning points of the graphs, and use this information alone to determine how many distinct roots each cubic has. Illustrate your results with a sketch.

(a) $y = x^3 + x^2 + 5$    (b) $y = x^3 + x^2$

(c) $y = x^3 + x^2 - 1$    (d) $y = x^3 + x^2 - \frac{4}{27}$

**11** Find the $x$-coordinate of the turning points of each cubic giving decimal values to three significant figures. Sketch each graph, labelling the key features.

(a) $y = (x + 3)(x + 5)(x - 1)$    (b) $y = (x - 2)^2(x + 2)$

(c) $y = x(2x + 1)(3x + 2)$

**12 (a)** Sketch the circular graphs given by the following equations.

(i) $x^2 + y^2 = 25$               (ii) $x^2 + (y - 4)^2 = 49$

(iii) $(x - 2)^2 + (y + 3)^2 = \frac{1}{4}$

**(b)** Find the centre and radius of the following circles and hence draw a single sketch with all three circles illustrated.

*(i) $x^2 + y^2 + 6x - 4y + 9 = 0$       (ii) $x^2 + y^2 + 6x - 4y + 4 = 0$

(iii) $x(x + 6) + y(y - 4) = 0$

**13** Sketch the elliptical graphs given by the following equations.

(a) $x^2 + 4y^2 = 100$             (b) $9x^2 + (y - 3)^2 = 36$

(c) $\left(\frac{x}{2} - 1\right)^2 + (2y + 2)^2 = \frac{1}{4}$

**14** By eliminating the parameter $t$, find the Cartesian equation for each graph. Sketch the graph obtaining information from both parametric and Cartesian forms.

(a) $x = t + 2, \quad y = t^2 - 2$       (b) $x = \dfrac{1}{t}, \quad y = \dfrac{1}{t - 1}$

(c) $x = t^2, \quad y = t^3$            (d) $x = t^2 + 6t, \quad y = (t + 3)^2$

**15** For $x > 0$, the function $f(x)$ is given by $f(x) = 2x - x \ln x$. The diagram below shows part of the graph of the function.

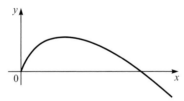

(i) Show that $f(e^3) = -e^3$.

(ii) Find $f'(x)$ and $f''(x)$.

(iii) Show that the curve $y = f(x)$ has just one stationary point and find its coordinates. Verify that $f''(x) < 0$ at this point.

The function $g(x)$ is defined for the domain $x \geq e$. In this domain $g(x) = f(x)$.

(iv) Write down the range of $g(x)$.

(v) Explain why $g(x)$ has an inverse, $g^{-1}(x)$. Sketch, with the same axes, graphs of $y = g(x)$ and $y = g^{-1}(x)$.

Calculate the gradient of the graph of $y = g^{-1}(x)$ at the point where $x = -e^3$.

[OCR (MEI), 1998]

**16** Express $f(x) = \dfrac{3x}{(x-1)(x-4)}$ in partial fractions.

(i) Use your result to write down an expression for $f'(x)$ and show that

$$f''(x) = \frac{-2}{(x-1)^3} + \frac{8}{(x-4)^3}$$

(ii) Find the coordinates of the two stationary points on the graph of f and identify each as a maximum or minimum.

(iii) The graph of f has one point of inflexion. Show that its x-coordinate, $x_0$, satisfies the cubic equation $x^3 - 12x + 20 = 0$. Hence show that $x_0$ lies between $-4$ and $-5$.

(iv) Sketch the graph of f.

[OCR (MEI)]

## Advanced

**1** A curve is given by the parametric equations $x = t^2 - 6$, $y = t(t^2 - 6)$.

(a) Find its Cartesian equation.
(b) Prove that it is symmetrical about the x-axis.
(c) Show that there are no points on the curve for which $x < -6$.

(d) Find the points on the curve for which $\dfrac{dy}{dx} = 0$.

(e) Sketch the curve.

**2** The position of a particle on the screen of an oscilloscope is given in parametric form as:

(a) $x = \sin t$,   $y = \sin 2t$      (b) $x = \sin 2t$,   $y = \sin 3t$

The resulting curves are known as Lissajous' figures.
By using tables of values, and identifying intercepts, sketch the given Lissajous' figures.

**3** For each of the following functions, find the turning points and points of inflexion. Sketch the curve.

(a) $f(x) = x^3 - 6x^2 + 9x + 6$      (b) $f(x) = xe^{-x}$      (c) $f(x) = \dfrac{3}{x} + \ln x$

**4** If $y^2 = x^2(x-2)$, obtain an expression for $\dfrac{dy}{dx}$ in terms of x, and hence show that on the graph of y against x there are no turning points. Show, that, when $x = 2\frac{2}{3}$, $\dfrac{dy}{dx} = \pm\sqrt{6}$ and $\dfrac{d^2y}{dx^2} = 0$.

Sketch the form of the graph of $y$ against $x$, paying special attention to the point $(2, 0)$ and to the points where $\dfrac{d^2y}{dx^2} = 0$.
[OCR (Cambridge)]

5   (a)  Sketch the curves:

$$\text{(i)} \quad y = \frac{(x-3)(x-5)}{(x-1)(x-4)} \qquad \text{(ii)} \quad y^2 = \frac{(x-3)(x-5)}{(x-1)(x-4)}$$

(b) Find the coordinates of the stationary points of $y = \dfrac{(x-a)^2}{x(x-4)}$.

Sketch the curve when (i) $a > 4$, (ii) $2 < a < 4$.

6   (a)  Sketch the graph of $x^2y^2 - x^2 + y^2 = 0$.
    (b)  State the equation of (i) the tangent at the origin, (ii) the asymptotes.

7   Given that $y = \dfrac{x^2 + 2x + 3}{x^2 - 2x - 3}$, form a quadratic equation in $x$ and hence

show that $y$ cannot take values between $-1$ and $\frac{1}{2}$.

8   (a)  The function $f(x)$ is defined by $f(x) = \dfrac{\frac{1}{2}(x^2 - 1) - x}{1 + x^2}$.

Sketch the graph of $y = f(x)$.
    (b)  The function $g(x)$ is defined by $g(x) = \dfrac{a(x^2 - 1) - bx}{1 + x^2}$. Determine the
stationary points of $g(x)$, classifying them as maxima or minima.

9   (i)  Sketch the graph of the curve with equation

$$y = \frac{1}{1 - x^2} \, (x \in \mathbb{R}, x \neq \pm 1).$$

(ii)  Sketch the graph of the curve with equation

$$y = \tan^{-1}\left(\frac{1}{1 - x^2}\right), \quad \text{where } -\tfrac{1}{2}\pi < y < \tfrac{1}{2}\pi$$

for $x \in \mathbb{R}, x \neq \pm 1$, paying particular attention to the shape and gradient of the curve when $x$ is near to $\pm 1$.
[OCR (Cambridge), 1982]

10  Find the stationary points of the function $f$ given by
$f(x) = e^{ax}\cos bx \, (a > 0, b > 0)$. Show that the values of $f$ at the stationary points with $x > 0$ form a geometric progression with common ratio $-e^{a\pi/b}$.

Give a rough sketch of the graph of $f$.
[OCR (STEP), 1987]

## Revision

**1** Determine the area of the quadrilateral bounded by the following four lines:

$$y = x + 1, \quad y = 1 - x, \quad \frac{y}{2} + \frac{x}{3} = 1, \quad 2y = x - 3$$

**2** Sketch the graph of $y = |6 - x|$ and hence solve the equation $|6 - x| = 4$.

**3** Sketch the graphs of the following four quadratic functions.

(a) $f(x) = (x + 3)(x - 5)$      (b) $g(x) = (2x - 3)(3x - 1)$
(c) $h(x) = 2x^2 + 11x - 21$      (d) $k(x) = 3x^2 + 5x + 7$

**4** Locate the turning point for each quadratic, and hence determine the number of roots for each expression.

(a) $y = (2x - 5)^2 - 7$      (b) $y = \left(\frac{x}{3} - 7\right)^2 + 3$

(c) $y = 3x^2 + 15x - 17$      (d) $y = x^2 + 2\alpha x + \alpha^2$

**5** Using one set of axes for each part of the question, draw a graph for the given function and, by superimposing a suitable second graph, find approximate solutions of the equation.

(a) $p(x) = x^2,$      $x^2 = 2x + 5$
(b) $p(x) = 3x - 7,$      $2x^2 - 3x + 7 = 0$
(c) $p(x) = x^2,$      $2x^2 - x - 8 = 0$

**6** Find the coordinates of any stationary points, and hence sketch the curves.

(a) $f(x) = x^3 - 5x^2 - 8x + 4$      (b) $g(x) = x^3 - 9x^2 + 27x + 14$
(c) $h(x) = x^3 + 2x^2 + 5x + 2$      (d) $k(x) = 4x^3 - 3x + 8$

**7** Sketch each cubic, labelling clearly all intercepts.

(a) $y = (x + 1)(x + 2)(x + 3)$      (b) $y = x^2(2x - 1)$
(c) $y = x(x^2 - \alpha^2)$      (d) $y = 2x^3 - x^2 - 6x$

**8** Apply the following transformations in sequence to the graph $y = x^3$, at each stage providing a sketch and giving the equation of the curve.

(a) Translate $y = x^3$ using the vector $\begin{pmatrix} -1 \\ -3 \end{pmatrix}$.

(b) Reflect the result of (a) in the line $y = 0$.
(c) Stretch the result of (b), parallel to the $y$-axis, with factor $\frac{1}{3}$.

**9** State the asymptotes that determine the limiting behaviour of each function.

(a) $p(t) = \dfrac{3}{t+3}$    (b) $p(t) = \dfrac{t}{2t-5}$    (c) $p(t) = \dfrac{(2t+1)(t+2)}{(t+3)(t+4)}$

**10** (a) The graph of the function $f(x)$ is shown below.

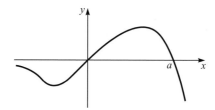

Sketch the graph of

(i) $|f(x)|$  (ii)    $f(-x)$  (iii)    $f(x-a)$

labelling all intercepts.

(b) The graph of $y = f(x)$ is shown below.

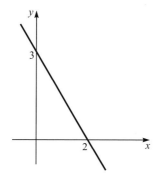

Sketch the graph of

(i) $\dfrac{1}{f(x)}$    (ii) $f^{-1}(x)$    (iii) $f(3x)$

labelling all intercepts and asymptotes.

**11** Use a sketch to illustrate each of the following conics. Explain why they all have the same enclosed area.

(a) $x^2 + (y-3)^2 = 16$    (b) $(2x-5)^2 + \left(\dfrac{y}{2}\right)^2 = 16$

(c) $\left(\dfrac{x}{8}\right)^2 + \left(\dfrac{y}{2}\right)^2 = 1$

**12** By eliminating the parameter $t$, find the Cartesian equation for each graph. Sketch the graph obtaining information from both parametric and Cartesian forms.

(a) $x = 2t + 1$, $y = t^2$    (b) $x = \dfrac{1}{t}$, $y = t + 3$

(c) $x = t^2$, $y = t^2$    (d) $x = 2t$, $y = (t + 3)^2$

## 8.5    Formation of simple differential equations; small angle approximations; Maclaurin's series for simple functions

$$\sin x = x - \frac{x^3}{3!} + \frac{x^5}{5!} - \cdots, \qquad \cos x = 1 - \frac{x^2}{2!} + \frac{x^4}{4!} - \cdots$$

$$e^x = 1 + x + \frac{x^2}{2!} + \frac{x^3}{3!} + \cdots,$$

$$\ln(1 + x) = x - \frac{x^2}{2} + \frac{x^3}{3} - \cdot \quad (-1 < x \le 1)$$

Maclaurin's series: $f(x) = f(0) + xf'(0) + \dfrac{1}{2!}x^2 f''(0) + \cdots$

**Basic**

**1** Match each of the four linear equations, with the corresponding differential equation.

(a) $2y = 7x + 7$    (b) $\dfrac{y}{2} + \dfrac{x}{7} = 5$    (c) $y = -\frac{7}{2}x + c$

(d) $(x - 3) = \frac{7}{2}(y - 4)$

(i) $\dfrac{dy}{dx} = -\frac{7}{2}$    (ii) $\dfrac{dy}{dx} = \frac{2}{7}$    (iii) $\dfrac{dy}{dx} = \frac{7}{2}$    (iv) $\dfrac{dy}{dx} = -\frac{2}{7}$

**2** Which of the following are possible solutions of the differential equation $\dfrac{dy}{dx} = 2$?

(a) $x - \dfrac{y}{2} = 0$    (b) $y = x^2$    (c) $y = 2x + \alpha$    (d) $y - 2x + 7 = 0$

**3** (a) If $y = ax^2 + 2$, find $\dfrac{dy}{dx}$ and hence show that $2y = x\dfrac{dy}{dx} + 4$.

(b) Use the method of part (a) to show that $y = x^2 + 5x + \frac{25}{4}$ is a possible solution of $2y = \dfrac{dy}{dx}(x + \frac{5}{2})$.

**\*4** Show that each of the following differential equations may be satisfied by the quadratic function $f(x) = 3x^2 + 6x + 4$.

(a) $f'(x) = 6x + 6$     (b) $f''(x) = 6$     (c) $f'(x) = (x + 1)f''(x)$

**5** By eliminating the constant $a$, find a first-order differential equation satisfied by:

\*(a) $y = ax^2 - 4$     (b) $y = \dfrac{a}{x} + 1$     (c) $y = ae^{4x}$

**6** Show that the differential equation $\dfrac{d^2 y}{dx^2} = -4y$ may be satisfied by any of:

(a) $y = \sin 2x$     (b) $y = \cos 2x$     (c) $y = \alpha \sin 2x + \beta \cos 2x$

**7** By eliminating the constants $a$ and $b$, find a second-order differential equation satisfied by:

(a) $y = ax^2 + b$     \*(b) $y = ax^2 + bx$     (c) $y = ae^{2x} + be^{-2x}$

**8** Use the approximation $\cos x \approx 1 - \frac{1}{2}x^2$ to find a quadratic approximation to

\*(a) $\cos 3x$     (b) $\cos^2 x$     (c) $\sec x$

**9** (a) Plot the graph of the function $f(x) = x^3 + 2x^2 + 5$ in the region $-1 \le x \le 1$.
(b) Evaluate $f(0)$, $f'(0)$, and $f''(0)$.
(c) Show that the function $g(x) = 2x^2 + 5$ is such that $g(0) = f(0)$, $g'(0) = f'(0)$ and $g''(0) = f''(0)$.
(d) Superimpose the graph of $g(x)$ on the graph of $f(x)$, and verify that, close to zero, $g(x)$ is a good approximation to $f(x)$.

**10**\*(a) Show that the function $f(x) = \sin x$ and the cubic approximation $g(x) = x - \frac{1}{6}x^3$ satisfy the following relations.
(i) $g(0) = f(0)$     (ii) $g'(0) = f'(0)$     (iii) $g''(0) = f''(0)$
(iv) $g'''(0) = f'''(0)$
(b) On the same axes, sketch the graphs of $f(x)$ and $g(x)$ in the interval $-\pi \le x \le \pi$.
(c) Find the percentage error in taking $g(x)$ as $\sin x$ when
$x = $ (i) $\dfrac{\pi}{20}$     (ii) $\dfrac{\pi}{4}$.

**11** (a) Verify that $y = e^x$ and the related second-order Maclaurin series
$$y = 1 + x + \tfrac{1}{2}x^2$$

    (i)  are co-incident when $x = 0$,

    (ii)  have the same first derivative when $x = 0$,

    (iii)  have the same second derivative when $x = 0$,

    (iv)  do not have the same third derivative when $x = 0$.

  (b)  On the same axes, sketch the graph of $e^x$ and $y = 1 + x + \frac{1}{2}x^2$ for $-2 < x < 2$.

  (c)  Find the percentage error in using the Maclaurin series as an approximation for $e^x$ when $x = 0.5$.

**12** Find Maclaurin series for each of the following, as far as the term in $x^2$.

  (a)  $f(x) = e^{-x}$     (b)  $f(x) = \ln(1 + 2x)$     (c)  $f(x) = (1 + 5x)^{1/5}$

## Intermediate

**1**  (a)  If $y = Ax^2$, write down expressions for both $\dfrac{dy}{dx}$ and $\dfrac{d^2y}{dx^2}$.

    (b)  Hence show that this family of quadratics satisfies:

      (i)  $x\dfrac{d^2y}{dx^2} = \dfrac{dy}{dx}$     (ii)  $x^2\dfrac{d^2y}{dx^2} = 2y$

**2**  (a)  Let $f(x) = ax^2 + bx$. Show that $b = f'(x) - 2ax$ and that $a = \frac{1}{2}f''(x)$.

    (b)  Hence show that $f(x) - xf'(x) + \frac{1}{2}x^2f''(x) = 0$.

**\*3**  (a)  Given that $xy - x^2 = 1$, show by implicit differentiation that

$$\frac{dy}{dx} = \frac{2x - y}{x}.$$

    (b)  Hence show that $\dfrac{dy}{dx} = 1 - \dfrac{1}{x^2}$.

**4**  (a)  Show that the parametric equations $x = t^2$, $y = 2t - 1$ satisfy the

differential equation $\dfrac{dy}{dx} = \dfrac{2}{y + 1}$.

    (b)  Find the Cartesian equivalent to $x = t^2$, $y = 2t - 1$ and use it to

verify that $\dfrac{dx}{dy} = \frac{1}{2}(y + 1)$.

**5**  Show that the second-order differential equation $\dfrac{d^2y}{dx^2} - 5\dfrac{dy}{dx} + 6y = 0$, may be satisfied by:

  \*(a)  $y = e^{2x}$     (b)  $y = e^{3x}$     (c)  $y = Ae^{2x} + Be^{3x}$

**6** (a) Use implicit differentiation to show that, if $\sin(x+y) = 0$, then

$$\left(1 + \frac{dy}{dx}\right)\cos(x+y) = 0.$$

*(b) Hence explain why the graph of $\sin(x+y) = 0$ is a collection of straight lines parallel to $y = -x$.

**7** (a) Evaluate expressions for $f'(x)$ and $f''(x)$, in the case where $f(x) = \ln x$. Verify that, in this case, $x^2 f''(x) + x f'(x) = 0$ for all values of $x > 0$.

(b) Show that the same differential equation is also satisfied when $f(x) = \ln(kx)$.

**\*8** If $y = (2x+1)e^{3x}$ satisfies the differential equation $\dfrac{d^2y}{dx^2} + p\dfrac{dy}{dx} + qy = 0$, find the values of $p$ and $q$.

**9** Assuming that the angle $x$ is small enough to neglect terms of $x^3$ and above, use the results $\sin x \approx x$ and $\cos x \approx 1 - \frac{1}{2}x^2$ to find approximations to:

(a) $\dfrac{\sin 2x}{x}$    (b) $\sqrt{1 - \cos 2x}$    (c) $\tan x$    (d) $\dfrac{x\sin 3x}{\cos x}$

**10**

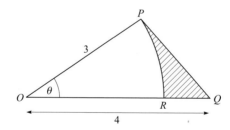

(a) Find an expression for the shaded area, $A$, in terms of $\theta$. Assuming that $\theta$ is small enough for terms in $\theta^3$ and above to be ignored, show that $A \approx \frac{3}{2}\theta$.

(b) Show that the perimeter, $P$, of the shaded area is given by
$P = 1 + 3\theta + (25 - 24\cos\theta)^{1/2}$.
Assuming that $\theta$ is small enough for terms in $\theta^3$ and above to be neglected, express $P$ in the form $a + b\theta + c\theta^2$.

**11** Use the result $f(x) \approx f(0) + xf'(0) + \frac{1}{2}x^2 f''(0)$ to show that $1 - \frac{1}{2}x^2$ is the second-order Maclaurin expansion for $\cos x$.

**12** (a) If $f(x) = \ln(1+x)$, find $f(0)$, $f'(0)$, and $f''(0)$.

(b) Find a second-order Maclaurin series for $\ln(1+x)$.

**13** Find the Maclaurin series, up to and including the term in $x^3$, for:

(a) $\ln(3 + 2x)$    (b) $\sin\left(\dfrac{\pi}{6} + 3x\right)$

**14** Show that, if terms above $x^2$ are ignored, $e^{3x} - \cos x \approx 3x + 5x^2$ and that $\cos 8x \approx 1 - 32x^2$.

Hence find an approximate value for the solution of the equation $e^{3x} - \cos x = \cos 8x$ in the interval $[0, 1]$.

**15** Verify that, for $x > 0$ and all values of the constant $k$, $y = x \ln x + kx$ is a solution of the differential equation $x\dfrac{dy}{dx} = x + y$.

The diagram shows the member of the family of solutions which passes through the point $(1, 1)$. Find the value of $k$ for this curve and the coordinates of the point $A$ where it crosses the $x$-axis.

[OCR (SMP), 1989]

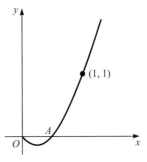

**16** (a) Use the approximations $\ln(1 + x) \approx x - \frac{1}{2}x^2 + \frac{1}{3}x^3$ and $\sin x \approx x - \frac{1}{6}x^3$ to find an approximation for $\ln\sqrt[3]{1 + \sin x}$ in the form $ax + bx^2 + cx^3$.

(b) Find the Maclaurin expansion for $\tan^{-1} x$ as far as the term in $x^3$.

## Advanced

**1** A curve has equation $y = x + \lambda x^2$, where $\lambda$ is a constant. Show that the gradient at the origin does not depend on $\lambda$. Show also that the curve satisfies the differential equation $x\dfrac{dy}{dx} = 2y - x$.

For different values of the constant $\lambda$ the first equation defines a family of curves. Find the equations of the curves of the family which pass through the points:

(i) $(2, 0)$    (ii) $(1, 2)$    (iii) $(2, 2)$

Sketch the graphs of the three equations on the same diagram for positive values of $x$, clearly labelling each graph.

[OCR (SMP), 1984]

**2** Find constants $a$ and $b$ so that, in the expansion of the function $x + a\sin x + bx\cos x$ in ascending powers of $x$, the first non-zero term is the one in $x^5$, and determine the coefficient of that term.

With the same values of $a$ and $b$ find the first non-zero term in the expansion of $1 + (a + b) \cos x - bx \sin x$ in ascending powers of $x$.
[OCR (Cambridge), 1967]

3  (i)  Express $\dfrac{2}{(2 - x)(1 - x)}$ in partial fractions.

Show that, for small values of $x$, $\dfrac{2}{(2 - x)(1 - x)} \approx 1 + kx + \tfrac{7}{4}x^2$,

where $k$ is to be found.

(ii)  By using a suitable small angle approximation for $\cos \theta$, together with the result from part (i), show that, for small values of $\theta$,

$$\frac{2}{(1 + \cos \theta) \cos \theta} \approx 1 + \tfrac{3}{4}\theta^2.$$

(iii)  Given that $\theta$ is small, find an approximate solution of the equation

$$\frac{2}{(1 + \cos \theta) \cos \theta} = 0.99 + \sin^2 \theta$$

[OCR (MEI), 1998]

4  Given that $y = e^x \sin x$,

(a)  show that $\dfrac{dy}{dx} = \sqrt{2}e^x \sin \left( x + \dfrac{\pi}{4} \right)$,

(b)  express $\dfrac{d^2y}{dx^2}$ in the form $ae^x \sin(x + \alpha)$,

(c)  show that $e^x \sin x \approx x + x^2$.

5  The mid-point of the minor arc $AB$ of a circle is $C$, and the arc $AB$ subtends an angle $2\theta$ at the centre of the circle. The chords $AB$ and $AC$ have lengths $x$ and $y$ respectively. Use the expansions of $\sin \tfrac{1}{2}\theta$ and $\sin \theta$, as far as the terms in $\theta^5$, to show that, if $\theta$ is small, then $\tfrac{1}{3}(8y - x)$ is approximately equal to the length of the arc $AB$.
[OCR (Cambridge), 1970]

6  Given that $y = e^{\tan^{-1} x}$, where $\tan^{-1} x$ denotes the principal value, show that

$$(1 + x^2)\frac{dy}{dx} = y$$

By repeated differentiation of this result, show also that

$$(1 + x^2)\frac{d^4y}{dx^4} + 6x\frac{d^3y}{dx^3} + 6\frac{d^2y}{dx^2} = \frac{d^3y}{dx^3}$$

Hence, or otherwise, obtain the expansion of $e^{\tan^{-1} x}$ in ascending powers of $x$ up to and including the term in $x^4$, and show that, when $x$ is small enough for powers above the fourth to be neglected,

$$e^{\tan^{-1} x} = e^x - \tfrac{1}{3}(x^3 + x^4).$$

[OCR (Cambridge), 1986]

**7** The points $A$ and $B$ are fixed in a plane, and $P$ is a variable point which moves in the plane so that $AP = kBP$, where $k$ is a constant such that $0 < k < 1$. The angles $PAB$ and $PBA$, measured in radians, are $x$ and $y$ respectively (see diagram).

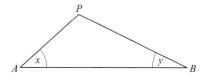

(i) Show that $\sin y = k \sin x$. Deduce that $y \le \sin^{-1}(k)$ for all positions of $P$.

(ii) By differentiation of the equation in part (i), or otherwise, show that

$$\cos y \frac{d^2 y}{dx^2} - \sin y \left(\frac{dy}{dx}\right)^2 = -k \sin x.$$

(iii) By using Maclaurin's series, or otherwise, show that, if $x$ is sufficiently small for powers of $x$ above $x^3$ to be neglected, then

$$y \approx kx + \frac{k(k^2 - 1)}{6} x^3.$$

[OCR (Cambridge), 1991]

**8** The variables $x$ and $y$ are connected by the equation $\dfrac{dy}{dx} = e^{xy}$, and $y = 1$ when $x = 0$. Find $\dfrac{d^2 y}{dx^2}$, and prove that

$$\frac{d^3 y}{dx^3} = e^{xy} \left\{ \left(y + x\frac{dy}{dx}\right)^2 + 2\frac{dy}{dx} + x\frac{d^2 y}{dx^2} \right\}.$$

Find the first four terms in the Maclaurin expansion for $y$.
[OCR (Cambridge), 1972]

**9** If $y = \sin(m \sin^{-1} x)$, where $m$ is a constant, show that:
(i) $y = 0$, when $x = 0$

(ii) $\dfrac{dy}{dx} = m$, when $x = 0$

(iii) $(1 - x^2)\dfrac{d^2 y}{dx^2} - x\dfrac{dy}{dx} + m^2 y = 0$, for all values of $x$

Taking $m = 3$, find constants $p$, $q$, $r$ and $s$ such that $y = p + qx + rx^2 + sx^3$ satisfies conditions (i), (ii) and (iii).

Deduce an expression for $y = \sin(3\sin^{-1} x)$ and verify its correctness by another method.

[OCR (Cambridge), 1967]

**10** Prove that the differential equation

$$\left\{1 + \left(\frac{dy}{dx}\right)^2\right\}\frac{d^3y}{dx^3} - 3\frac{dy}{dx}\left(\frac{d^2y}{dx^2}\right)^2 = 0$$

is satisfied by $x^2 + y^2 + 2gx + 2fy + c = 0$ for arbitrary values of the constants $g$, $f$ and $c$.

[OCR (Cambridge), 1963]

## Revision

**1** Verify that the function $f(x) = 7(x^2 + 2x + 6)$ is a possible solution of the differential equation

$$\left(\frac{x}{2} + 3\right)f''(x) + \tfrac{1}{2}xf'(x) - f(x) = 0$$

**2** Verify that the graph $y = 3x^2 + 8x + \tfrac{16}{3}$ is a possible solution of:

(a) $\dfrac{dy}{dx} = x\dfrac{d^2y}{dx^2} + 8$    (b) $2y = \dfrac{dy}{dx}(x + \tfrac{4}{3})$

**3** Show that the second-order differential equation $\dfrac{d^2y}{dx^2} - 9y = 0$ may be satisfied by:

(a) $y = e^{3x}$    (b) $y = Ae^{3x} + Be^{-3x}$

**4** Show that the second-order differential equation $\dfrac{d^2y}{dx^2} + 9y = 0$, may be satisfied by:

(a) $y = \sin 3x$    (b) $y = A\sin 3x + B\cos 3x$

**5** If $y = e^{-x}\sin 2x$, prove that $\dfrac{d^2y}{dx^2} + 2\dfrac{dy}{dx} + 5y = 0$.

**6** If $y = \tan x$, show that $\dfrac{dy}{dx} = 1 + y^2$. Hence express $\dfrac{d^2y}{dx^2}$ and $\dfrac{d^3y}{dx^3}$ in terms of $y$.

**7**  If $y = ax^2 + \dfrac{b}{x}$,

(a)  show that $x^2 \dfrac{d^2 y}{dx^2} = 2y$,

(b)  find the values for $a$ and $b$, given that $y = 5$ and $\dfrac{dy}{dx} = -8$ when $x = 1$,

(c)  sketch the graph of $y$ against $x$, using the values of $a$ and $b$ from part (b).

**8**  If $xy = a \sin 3x$, prove that $x \dfrac{d^2 y}{dx^2} + 2 \dfrac{dy}{dx} + 9xy = 0$.

**9**  (a)  If $\theta$ is small, find $k$ where $\dfrac{\sin 3\theta}{\sin 5\theta} = k$.

(b)  If $\alpha$ is a small angle, prove that $\sin(x + \alpha) \approx \sin x + \alpha \cos x$ and hence show that the solution to the equation $\sin(x + \alpha) = \cos x$ is given by $x \approx \tan^{-1}(1 - \alpha)$.

**10**  (a)  Find by differentiation the third-order Maclaurin series for $e^{-2x}$ (i.e. a cubic approximation to the graph at $x = 0$).

(b)  Find the percentage error in using the series you have found to evaluate $e^{-0.2}$.

**11**  (a)  Find directly the third-order Maclaurin expansion for $\sin 2x$.

(b)  Verify the result by making an appropriate substitution in the expression $\sin u \approx u - \tfrac{1}{6} u^3$.

**12**  Find the third-order Maclaurin series for:

(a)  $\ln(1 + x)$     (b)  $\ln \dfrac{1 - 2x}{(1 + 2x)^3}$

# 9 Integration

## 9.1 Integration as the reverse of differentiation; integrals of $x^n$, $e^x$, $\dfrac{1}{x}$, $\sin x$ etc.; area under curve; definite integrals

| $f(x)$ | $\int f(x)\,dx$ | $f(x)$ | $\int f(x)\,dx$ |
|---|---|---|---|
| $(ax+b)^n (n \neq -1)$ | $\dfrac{1}{a(n+1)}(ax+b)^{n+1} + c$ | $\dfrac{1}{\sqrt{a^2 - x^2}}$ | $\sin^{-1}\left(\dfrac{x}{a}\right) + c$ |
| $\dfrac{1}{ax+b}$ | $\dfrac{1}{a}\ln|ax+b| + c$ | | |
| $\sin ax$ | $-\dfrac{1}{a}\cos ax + c$ | $\dfrac{1}{a^2 + x^2}$ | $\dfrac{1}{a}\tan^{-1}\left(\dfrac{x}{a}\right) + c$ |
| $\cos ax$ | $\dfrac{1}{a}\sin ax + c$ | | |
| $\sec^2 ax$ | $\dfrac{1}{a}\tan ax + c$ | | |
| $e^{ax}$ | $\dfrac{1}{a}e^{ax} + c$ | | |

The area under the graph of $y = f(x)$ from $x = a$ to $x = b$ is $\int_a^b f(x)\,dx$, provided $f(x) > 0$ for $a \leq x \leq b$.

**Basic**

**1** Integrate the following with respect to $x$.

(a) $3x^4 - x^2$    (b) $\dfrac{2}{x^4}$    (c) $\sqrt{x} + \dfrac{1}{\sqrt{x}}$    (d) $(x+3)(x-4)$

**2** Integrate the following with respect to $x$.

(a) $4x^3 - \sqrt{x}$

(b) $\dfrac{1}{x^2} + \dfrac{1}{x^3}$

*(c) $\dfrac{2+x}{x^5}$

(d) $\dfrac{(x+3)(x-2)}{x^4}$

**\*3** The gradient function of a curve is $4x$ and it passes through the point $(2, 11)$. Find the equation of the curve.

**4** Find the following indefinite integrals.

(a) $\displaystyle\int \dfrac{x^4 - 1}{x^3}\,dx$

(b) $\displaystyle\int (1 + \sqrt{x})^2\,dx$

**5** Find the following indefinite integrals.

(a) $\displaystyle\int \dfrac{4}{x^2} + \sin x\,dx$

*(b) $\displaystyle\int \cos x\,(2 + \tan x)\,dx$

**6** Given that $\dfrac{dP}{dq} = q^3 + 2q - 1$ and that $P = 13$ when $q = 2$, find $P$ as a function of $q$.

**7** Find the value of the following definite integrals.

(a) $\displaystyle\int_3^4 (x^2 + 3x)\,dx$

*(b) $\displaystyle\int_1^2 \left( \dfrac{x^2}{2} - \dfrac{2}{3x^3} \right)dx$

**8** Find the value of the following definite integrals.

(a) $\displaystyle\int_{\frac{\pi}{2}}^{\pi} (\sin x - \cos x)\,dx$

(b) $\displaystyle\int_{\frac{1}{4}}^{\frac{1}{2}} \left( \dfrac{x^2 - 2}{x^3} \right)dx$

(c) $\displaystyle\int_0^1 e^x\,dx$

**9** Find the area under the curve $y = x^2 + 2$ between the ordinates $x = 2$ and $x = 5$.

**\*10** The curve $y = 4x(3 - x)$ cuts the $x$-axis at the points $x = a$ and $x = b$. Find the values of $a$ and $b$. Hence find the area between the curve $y = 4x(3 - x)$ and the $x$-axis from $x = a$ to $x = b$.

**11** Sketch the graph of $y = \dfrac{2}{x}$ for $x > 0$. Find the area between the curve $y = \dfrac{2}{x}$ and the $x$-axis from $x = 2$ to $x = 3$.

**12** Find the area between the curve $y = x^2$ and the $y$-axis from $y = 1$ to $y = 4$.

## Intermediate

**1**  Integrate the following with respect to $x$.

(a) $\dfrac{3x^2}{\sqrt{x}}$     (b) $\left(2x + \dfrac{1}{x}\right)^2$

**2**  Find the following indefinite integrals.

(a) $\displaystyle\int \sqrt{x}\left(2x - \dfrac{1}{x}\right) dx$     (b) $\displaystyle\int \sqrt{\dfrac{1}{x^3}}\, dx$     (c) $\displaystyle\int (\sin^2 x + \cos^2 x)\, dx$

**3**  Given that $\dfrac{dy}{dx} = 2 + 3x^2$ and that $y = 4$ when $x = 0$ find $y$ as a function of $x$.

**4**  A curve has a gradient function of $2x + c$. It crosses the $y$-axis at $(0, -3)$ and the $x$-axis at $(1, 0)$ and $(a, 0)$. Find the equation of the curve and the value of $a$.

**5**  Find the value of the following definite integrals, leaving your answers in surd form.

(a) $\displaystyle\int_{\frac{\pi}{4}}^{\frac{\pi}{2}} 2 \sin x\, dx$     (b) $\displaystyle\int_{\frac{2\pi}{3}}^{\frac{5\pi}{6}} \dfrac{\cos x - 3 \sin x}{2}\, dx$

**6**  (a)  Find the value of:

(i) $\displaystyle\int_2^6 \dfrac{dx}{x}$     (ii) $\displaystyle\int_1^4 \dfrac{2\sqrt{x} - 3}{x^2}\, dx$

(b) Show that $\displaystyle\int_{-1}^1 e^x\, dx = \dfrac{e^2 - 1}{e}$.

**7**  (a)  Show that $\dfrac{2x^2 + 8x - 42}{x^2 - 3x}$ simplifies to an expression of the form $a + \dfrac{b}{x}$, where $a$ and $b$ are constants to be found.

(b) Find $\displaystyle\int_2^4 \dfrac{2x^2 + 8x - 42}{x^2 - 3x}\, dx$

**\*8** Find the values of $p$ and $q$ which satisfy the following simultaneous equations.

$$\int_1^2 (px^2 + q)\, dx = 9$$

$$\int_1^2 (qx + p)\, dx = 6$$

**9** (a) Differentiate $y = \cos^3 x$.
   (b) Hence integrate $\sin x \cos^2 x$ with respect to $x$.

**10** (a) The curve $y = f(x)$ is such that $f'(x) = x^2 + x - 12$. Find $y$ as a function of $x$ given that $y = 20$ when $x = 6$.
   (b) Find the coordinates of the turning points of the curve $y = f(x)$.
   (c) Sketch the curve.

**\*11** A curve has a gradient function of $2x - 2$. The normal to the curve at $P(2, 3)$ also crosses the curve at $Q$. Find the coordinates of $Q$.

**12** Sketch the curve $y = x^2 - 4x$ stating the coordinates of the intercepts with the $x$- and $y$-axes. Find the area enclosed between the curve $y = x^2 - 4x$, the ordinates $x = -2$ and $x = 3$ and the $x$-axis.

**13** The diagram below shows part of the curve $y = \dfrac{1}{x} - 2 \, (x > 0)$ and the line $y = -2x + 1$. Find the coordinates of $P$ and $Q$ and hence find the shaded area.

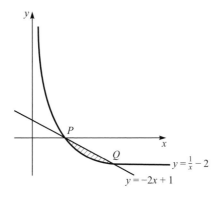

**\*14** Find the area enclosed between $y = \sin x$, $y = \cos x$ and the $x$-axis from $x = 0$ to $x = \frac{1}{2}\pi$.

**\*15** Given that $y = \ln(x - 2)$, find $x$ as a function of $y$. Hence find the area enclosed between $y = \ln(x - 2)$ and the $y$-axis from $y = 2$ to $y = 3$.

**16** The diagram below shows the graphs of $y = x^2 - 2$ and $y = 2x + 1$. Find the shaded area.

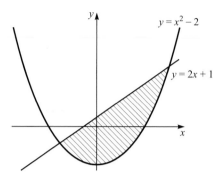

**Advanced**

**1** Find:

(a) $\displaystyle\int_0^n (x - [x])\,dx$ $(n \in \mathbb{Z}^+)$, where $[x]$ means the greatest integer which does not exceed $x$, e.g. $[5.2] = 5$, $[4] = 4$

(b) $\displaystyle\int_0^{n\pi} |\sin x|\,dx$ $(n \in \mathbb{Z}^+)$

(c) $\displaystyle\int_0^{2\pi} |\cos x - 1|\,dx$

**2** $P$ is the point on the curve $y = x^3 - x$ with coordinates $(1, 0)$. The tangent to the curve at $P$ intersects the curve again at $Q$. Find the area of the region bounded by the curve and the line segment $PQ$.

**3** Sketch, on the same diagram, for $x \geq 0$, the graphs of $y = x^{1/2}$ and $y = x^{3/2}$, labelling each graph clearly.
[An accurate plot is not required. You should show the general shape of each curve, particularly near the origin, and give the coordinates of the point(s) of intersection of the curves.]
Show that $x = \frac{1}{2}$ satisfies the equation $x^{1/2} = 2x^{3/2}$ and sketch also on your diagram the curve $y = 2x^{3/2}$.
Show, by integration, that the area of the finite region between the curves $y = x^{1/2}$ and $y = 2x^{3/2}$ is $2^{1/2}/15$.
[OCR (Cambridge), 1988]

**4** By sketching the graph of $y = \dfrac{1}{x^3}$ for $x > 0$, and drawing appropriate rectangles, demonstrate that

$$\frac{1}{2^3} + \frac{1}{3^3} + \frac{1}{4^3} < \int_1^4 \frac{1}{x^3}\,dx$$

Hence show that

$$\sum_{r=1}^{n} \frac{1}{r^3} < \frac{3}{2} - \frac{1}{2n^2}$$

**5**

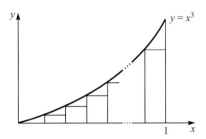

The diagram shows the part of the graph of $y = x^3$ between $x = 0$ and $x = 1$, divided into strips of width $\frac{1}{n}$. Prove that the area of the eight rectangles shown may be written as $A = a \sum_{r=1}^{b} r^3$, where $a$ and $b$ are functions of $n$, to be stated. Given that

$$\sum_{r=1}^{n} r^3 = \frac{n^2(n+1)^2}{4}$$

show that

$$A = \frac{(n-1)^2}{4n^2}$$

and explain how the value of $\int_0^1 x^3 \, dx$ may be deduced from this expression.

**6**  (i)  By considering the area under the curve with equation $y = \frac{1}{x}$ show that

$$\sum_{r=2}^{n} \frac{1}{r} < \int_1^n \frac{1}{x} \, dx < \sum_{r=1}^{n-1} \frac{1}{r}$$

(ii)  Hence show that $\ln n < \sum_{r=1}^{n} \frac{1}{r} < 1 + \ln n$

(iii)  Deduce that $\sum_{r=1}^{n} \frac{1}{r} \to \infty$ as $n \to \infty$.

[OCR (MEI)]

**7**  Sketch the curve whose equation is $xy^2 = (x-a)^2(2a-x)$, where $a > 0$. State the equation of the asymptote to the curve. Find the area of the region enclosed by the loop of the curve. [OCR (Cambridge), 1983]

**8** The tangent to the curve $y = e^x$ at the point $P(p, e^p)$ passes through the origin $O$. Find the value of $p$.

The tangent at the point $A(0, 1)$ to the curve meets the tangent at $P$ in $U$. Prove that the area of the region bounded by the lines $AU$, $UP$ and the arc $AP$ is

$$\frac{e^2 - 3e + 1}{2(e - 1)}$$

[OCR (Cambridge), 1974]

**9** Find constants $a_0$, $a_1$, $a_2$, $a_3$, $a_4$, $a_5$, $a_6$ and $b$ such that

$$x^4(1 - x)^4 = (a_6 x^6 + a_5 x^5 + a_4 x^4 + a_3 x^3 + a_2 x^2 + a_1 x + a_0)(x^2 + 1) + b$$

Hence, or otherwise, prove that

$$\int_0^1 \frac{x^4(1 - x)^4}{1 + x^2} \, dx = \frac{22}{7} - \pi$$

Evaluate $\int_0^1 x^4(1 - x)^4 \, dx$ and deduce that

$$\frac{22}{7} > \pi > \frac{22}{7} - \frac{1}{630}$$

[OCR (STEP), 1997]

**10** Find constants $a_1$, $a_2$, $u_1$ and $u_2$ such that, whenever P is a cubic polynomial,

$$\int_{-1}^1 P(t) \, dt = a_1 P(u_1) + a_2 P(u_2)$$

[OCR (STEP), 1997]

## Revision

**1** Integrate the following with respect to $x$.

(a) $x^2 - x$     (b) $\dfrac{1}{x^2} + \sqrt{x}$

**2** Find the following indefinite integrals.

(a) $\displaystyle\int (\sqrt{x} + 2)(x - 3) \, dx$     (b) $\displaystyle\int \frac{(1 - \sqrt{x})^2}{x} \, dx$

**3** $\dfrac{dx}{dt} = 2t + 4$. Find $x$ in terms of $t$ given that $x = 2$ when $t = 1$.

**4** Find the value of:

(a) $\int_0^3 \left( \dfrac{x^3}{3} - 4x \right) dx$

(b) $\int_1^2 \dfrac{(2x+3)(x-1)}{x} dx$

**5** Find the value of:

(a) $\int_{1.2}^{1.4} (e^x + 2) dx$

(b) $\int_{\frac{\pi}{6}}^{\frac{\pi}{3}} (\cos x - \frac{1}{2}\sin x) dx$, leaving your answer in surd form.

**6** Find the negative value of $k$ which satisfies the equation

$$\int_1^k (x - 3) dx = \int_0^4 \dfrac{3x^2}{4} dx$$

**7** A curve with a gradient function of $3x^2 + 3$ crosses the $x$-axis at $(1, 0)$. Find the equation of the curve and the coordinates of its intersection with the $y$-axis.

**8** By letting $u = 3x$, use the chain rule to differentiate $y = e^{3x}$. Hence find the value of $\int_0^1 e^{3x} dx$.

**9** (a) Find the area between the curve $y = 3\sin x$ and the $x$-axis from $x = 0$ to $x = \pi$.

(b) The diagram below shows the graphs of $y = -x^2 + 2x + 2$ and $y = -\frac{1}{2}x + 3$. Find the area enclosed between them.

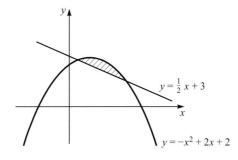

$y = \frac{1}{2}x + 3$

$y = -x^2 + 2x + 2$

**10** For each of the functions $y = f(x)$ shown below, express $\int_a^b f(x)\,dx$ in terms of the areas $A$, $B$ and $C$.

(a)

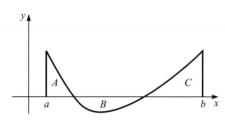

(b)

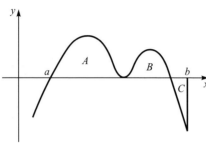

(c)

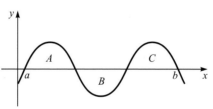

**11** The diagram below shows the graph of $y = 3 - \sqrt{x}\,(x \geq 0)$. Find the area enclosed between the curve and the $y$-axis from $y = 1$ to $y = 2$.

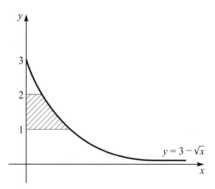

**12** (a) Factorise the expression $y = x^3 + x^2 - 6x$.
  (b) Sketch the graph of $y = x^3 + x^2 - 6x$, stating the coordinates of the intercepts with the axes.
  (c) Find the area between $y = x^3 + x^2 - 6x$ and the $x$-axis from $x = -2$ to $x = 2$.

## 9.2 Integration by inspection, substitution, partial fractions and parts

$$\int \frac{f'(x)}{f(x)}\, dx = \ln |f(x)| + c$$

Integration by parts: $\int u \frac{dv}{dx}\, dx = uv - \int v \frac{du}{dx}\, dx$

### Basic

1 (a) Differentiate (i) $\sin 5x$ (ii) $e^{5x}$ (iii) $\ln(2x + 1)$ (iv) $(3x + 1)^5$
   (b) Use your answers to (a) to find:

   (i) $\displaystyle\int \cos 5x\, dx$     (ii) $\displaystyle\int e^{5x}\, dx$     (iii) $\displaystyle\int \frac{1}{2x + 1}\, dx$

   (iv) $\displaystyle\int (3x + 1)^4\, dx$

2 Integrate the following with respect to $x$.

   (a) $\sin 2x$     (b) $2e^{4x}$     (c) $\dfrac{1}{4x + 1}$     (d) $(7x + 3)^{10}$

3 (a) Use the chain rule to differentiate:

   (i) $(x^3 + 2)^5$     (ii) $\ln (x^2 + 1)$     (iii) $\displaystyle\int \frac{1}{(x^3 - 4)^2}$     (iv) $\sin^4 x$

   (b) Use your answers to (a) to find:

   (i) $\displaystyle\int x^2(x^3 + 2)^5\, dx$     (ii) $\displaystyle\int \frac{x}{x^2 + 1}\, dx$     (iii) $\displaystyle\int \frac{x^2}{(x^3 - 4)^3}\, dx$

   (iv) $\displaystyle\int \sin^3 x \cos x\, dx$

4 Use the method of question 3 to find the following indefinite integrals.

   (a) $\displaystyle\int (4x - 5)^7\, dx$     (b) $\displaystyle\int x(2x^2 - 3)^3\, dx$     *(c) $\displaystyle\int \frac{x}{(3x^2 - 1)^2}\, dx$

   (d) $\displaystyle\int \cos^4 x \sin x\, dx$

5 Use the given substitution to find the following.

   (a) $\displaystyle\int \frac{x^2\, dx}{1 + x^3},\quad u = 1 + x^3$     (b) $\displaystyle\int x^4 \sin (x^5 + 2)\, dx,\quad u = x^5 + 2$

   (c) $\displaystyle\int \frac{\sin x}{\cos x}\, dx,\quad u = \cos x$

**6**   Integrate the following using the given substitutions.

(a) $\displaystyle\int x(1+x)^4\,dx,\quad u=1+x$

*(b) $\displaystyle\int 4x(2x-3)^5\,dx,\quad u=2x-3$

(c) $\displaystyle\int x\sqrt{x+3}\,dx,\quad u=x+3$

(d) $\displaystyle\int 6x(3x-4)^4\,dx,\quad u=3x-4$

**7**   Find each of the following integrals, either by inspection or by using an appropriate substitution.

(a) $\displaystyle\int \dfrac{dx}{5x+2}$   (b) $\displaystyle\int \dfrac{dx}{1-2x}$   (c) $\displaystyle\int \dfrac{dx}{(3x-1)^2}$

**8**   (a) Write $\dfrac{13-x}{x^2+4x-21}$ in partial fractions.

(b) Hence find $\displaystyle\int \dfrac{13-x}{x^2+4x-21}\,dx.$

**9**   Use partial fractions to find the value of $\displaystyle\int_1^5 \dfrac{3x+9}{x^2+8x+7}\,dx$

**10**  Use a method of integration by parts to find the following indefinite integrals.

(a) $\displaystyle\int xe^x\,dx$   *(b) $\displaystyle\int x(x+2)^3\,dx$

**11**  Use a method of integration by parts to find the value of:

(a) $\displaystyle\int_3^4 x(x-3)^4\,dx$   (b) $\displaystyle\int_{\frac{\pi}{2}}^{\pi} x\sin x\,dx$

**12**  The curve with gradient function $e^{2x}$ crosses the $y$-axis at $y=2$. Find the equation of the curve.

## Intermediate

**1**   Write down each of the following integrals.

(a) $\displaystyle\int e^{-x}\,dx$   (b) $\displaystyle\int \sin\dfrac{\theta}{2}\,d\theta$   (c) $\displaystyle\int (2x-4)^7\,dx$

(d) $\displaystyle\int \sec^2 3\theta\,d\theta$

**2** Use inspection to find the following indefinite integrals.

(a) $\int 3(2x - 4)^5 \, dx$ (b) $\int \frac{x^3}{3x^4 - 5} \, dx$

**3** Integrate the following with respect to $x$.

(a) $(e^x + 2)^2$ (b) $(e^x + e^{-x})^2$

**4** Find the value of:

(a) $\int_{\frac{\pi}{4}}^{\frac{\pi}{2}} 3\cos(2\theta - \pi) \, d\theta$

(b) $\int_2^3 2e^{x/2} \, dx$

**5** Use the given substitution to find:

(a) $\int \frac{3x}{x^2 + 9} \, dx, \quad u = x^2 + 9$

(b) $\int x^2 e^{x^3} \, dx, \quad u = x^3$

**6** Use an appropriate substitution to find the value of:

(a) $\int_0^1 -3x^2(x^3 - 2)^5 \, dx$

(b) $\int_0^2 (x^3 - 1)(x^4 - 4x)^3 \, dx$

*(c) $\int_0^{\pi/2} \sin 2\theta \sin \theta \, d\theta$

**7** Integrate the following using appropriate substitutions.

(a) $\int 4x\sqrt{2x - 1} \, dx$ (b) $\int \frac{e^{2x}}{1 - e^x} \, dx$

**8** Using the given substitutions, find the value of:

(a) $\int_2^5 x^2(x - 1)^{\frac{1}{2}} \, dx, \quad x = u^2 + 1$

(b) $\int_4^9 \frac{2}{\sqrt{x} - 1} \, dx, \quad u = \sqrt{x} - 1$

**9** (a) Express $\dfrac{4x - 5}{6x^2 - x - 2}$ in partial fractions.

   (b) Hence, or otherwise, show that

$$\int_{1}^{22} \frac{4x - 5}{6x^2 - x - 2}\, dx = \ln\left(\frac{15}{4}\right)$$

**10** Use partial fractions to find $\displaystyle\int \frac{dx}{x^2 - 9}$.

**11** Use integration by parts to find:

   (a) $\displaystyle\int 2x\cos\left(\frac{x}{3}\right) dx$    (b) $\displaystyle\int xe^{-3x}\, dx$

**12** Use integration by parts to find:

   *(a) $\displaystyle\int \ln x\, dx$    (b) $\displaystyle\int x^2 \sin x\, dx$

**13** (a) Use the quotient rule to differentiate $\dfrac{x^4}{x^2 - 1}$, simplifying your answer.

   (b) Hence find $\displaystyle\int \frac{x^3(x^2 - 2)}{(x^2 - 1)^2}\, dx$.

**14** Find the value of $k$ which satisfies the equation $\displaystyle\int_{-1}^{0} e^{3x}\, dx = \int_{0}^{k} \frac{1}{x + 1}\, dx$, giving your answer to three significant figures.

**15**\*(a) The diagram shows the curve $2y = 3 + \ln x$ $(x > 0)$. Find the shaded area.

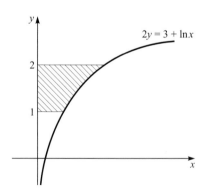

$$2y = 3 + \ln x$$

   (b) A region is described by the inequalities $y \geq x^2$, $y \leq 4$, $8xy \geq 1$. By sketching appropriate graphs show the region on a diagram and hence find its area.

**16** The diagram shows the circle $x^2 + y^2 = 9$ and the line $2y + x = 6$ which intersect at $P$ and $Q$.

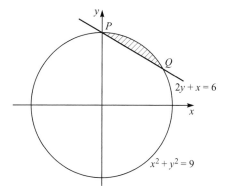

(a) Find the coordinates of $P$ and $Q$.

(b) By using the substitution $x = 3 \sin u$, or otherwise, use integration to find the area of the minor segment formed by the circle and the chord $PQ$.

## Advanced

**1** Let $C = \int_0^\pi e^{-3x} \cos x \, dx$ and $S = \int_0^\pi e^{-3x} \sin x \, dx$.
Show that $C = 3S$ and, using a similar method, express $S$ in terms of $C$. Hence find the values of $C$ and $S$.

**2** An ellipse $E$ has equation $\dfrac{x^2}{a^2} + \dfrac{y^2}{b^2} = 1$, where $a$ and $b$ are positive

constants. Show that the area $A$ of the region enclosed by $E$ is given by

$$A = \frac{4b}{a} \int_0^a \sqrt{a^2 - x^2} \, dx$$

By using the substitution $x = a \sin \theta$, or otherwise, find the value of $A$ in terms of $a$, $b$ and $\pi$.
Show on a sketch the region $R$ of points inside the ellipse $E$ such that $x > 0$ and $y < x$. Given that $a^2 = 3b^2$, find the area of $R$ in terms of $a$ and $\pi$.
[OCR (Cambridge), 1990]

**3** (i) Sketch the graph of $f(x) = \dfrac{1}{4 - x^2}$.

(ii) By using partial fractions, find $\displaystyle\int \frac{dx}{4 - x^2}$,   $|x| < 2$.

(iii) Show that $\displaystyle\int_3^4 \frac{dx}{4 - x^2} = -\frac{1}{4} \ln \frac{5}{3}$, and by reference to the graph of $f$

explain the negative sign in the answer.

(iv) Given $|x| < 2$, use the substitution $x = 2 \sin \theta$ to find $\displaystyle\int \frac{dx}{4 - x^2}$ in terms of $\theta$.
[You may quote $\int \sec \theta \, d\theta = \ln (\sec \theta + \tan \theta) + C$.]

(v) Show that $\sec \theta = \dfrac{2}{\sqrt{4 - x^2}}$, and hence that your solutions to parts (ii)

and (iv) are equivalent to each other.
[OCR (SMP), 1986]

**4**  The two graphs represent $\sin^{-1} x$ and $\cos^{-1} x$. State the coordinates of $A$, $B$, $C$, $D$.

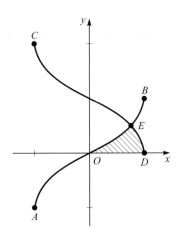

Show that $f(x) = \sin^{-1} x + \cos^{-1} x$ is constant. Find the value of the constant, and deduce the coordinates of $E$.

Use integration by parts to find $\int \sin^{-1} x \, dx$, and *hence* find the area of the shaded region $ODE$.

Alternatively, a neater method of finding the area of region $ODE$ is obtained by dividing up the area into elements parallel to the $x$-axis. Show that this method leads to the same answer as before.

[OCR (SMP), 1986]

**5**  Using integration by parts, show that, if $I_n = \int_0^1 x^n \sqrt{1 - x} \, dx$, then

$$I_n = \frac{2n}{2n + 3} I_{n-1} \quad (n \geq 1)$$

Hence find:

(a)  $I_3$     (b)  $\displaystyle\int_0^{\pi/2} \cos^5 \theta \sin^2 \theta \, d\theta$

**6**  (i)  Suppose that

$$S = \int \frac{\cos x}{\cos x + \sin x} \, dx \quad \text{and} \quad T = \int \frac{\sin x}{\cos x + \sin x} \, dx$$

By considering $S + T$ and $S - T$ determine $S$ and $T$.

(ii)  Evaluate $\displaystyle\int_{\frac{1}{4}}^{\frac{1}{2}} (1 - 4x)\sqrt{\frac{1}{x} - 1} \, dx$ by using the substitution $x = \sin^2 t$.

[OCR (SMP), 1995]

**7** Show that if $f(x) = ax^4 + bx^3 + cx^2 + dx + e$, then

$$\int_{-h}^{h} f(x)\,dx = \frac{h}{3}\{f(-h) + 4f(0) + f(h)\} - \frac{4ah^5}{15}$$

**8** Explain why the use of the substitution $x = \frac{1}{t}$ does not demonstrate that the integrals

$$\int_{-1}^{1} \frac{1}{(1+x^2)^2}\,dx \quad \text{and} \quad \int_{-1}^{1} \frac{-t^2}{(1+t^2)^2}\,dt$$

are equal.

Evaluate both integrals correctly.

[OCR (STEP), 1987]

**9** The functions $f(x)$ and $g(x)$ are given to be non-negative throughout the interval $0 \le x \le \frac{1}{2}\pi$. The greatest and least values of $f(x)$ in that interval are M and m respectively. Using a graphical argument (based on areas) or otherwise, prove that

$$m \int_{0}^{\pi/2} g(x)\,dx \le \int_{0}^{\pi/2} f(x)g(x)\,dx \le M \int_{0}^{\pi/2} g(x)\,dx$$

Deduce that $\displaystyle\int_{0}^{\pi/2} \frac{\sin^2 x\,dx}{1+x^2}$ lies between $\dfrac{\pi}{(4+\pi^2)}$ and $\frac{1}{4}\pi$.

[OCR (Cambridge), 1971]

**10** Find constants $a$, $b$, $c$ and $d$ such that

$$\frac{ax + b}{x^2 + 2x + 2} + \frac{cx + d}{x^2 - 2x + 2} = \frac{1}{x^4 + 4}$$

Show that

$$\int_{0}^{1} \frac{1}{x^4 + 4}\,dx = \frac{1}{16}\ln 5 + \frac{1}{8}\tan^{-1} 2$$

[OCR (STEP), 1997]

## Revision

**1** Integrate with respect to $x$:

(a) $x^3(1 - x^4)^2$     (b) $(x+1)(x^2 + 2x)^5$

**2**  Find the following indefinite integrals.

(a) $\int \dfrac{dx}{e^{2x}}$     (b) $\int \dfrac{dx}{3-x}$

**3**  Use the given substitutions to find:

(a) $\int \dfrac{x}{1-4x}\,dx$,   $u = 1 - 4x$     (b) $\int x(1-2x^2)^4\,dx$,   $u = 1 - 2x^2$

**4**  (a) Write $\dfrac{x+3}{x^2-1}$ in partial fractions.

(b) Hence show that $\displaystyle\int_2^4 \dfrac{x+3}{x^2-1}\,dx = \ln\left(\tfrac{27}{5}\right)$.

**5**  Find the value of $\displaystyle\int_3^4 \dfrac{dx}{(x+3)(x-2)}$.

**6**  Use integration by parts to find:

(a) $\int x\ln x\,dx$     (b) $\int x^2 e^{2x}\,dx$

**7**  Find the value of:

(a) $\displaystyle\int_0^1 2xe^x\,dx$     (b) $\displaystyle\int_0^{\frac{\pi}{2}} \sin\left(\dfrac{\theta}{2}\right)\,d\theta$, leaving your answer in surd form

**8**  Find the values of $p$ which satisfy the equation $\displaystyle\int_0^p \dfrac{2x}{(2x^2-1)^3}\,dx = -\dfrac{3}{4}$.

**9**  Integrate the following with respect to $\theta$.

(a) $2\sin^2 2\theta$     (b) $\cos\theta(1 - \sin^2\theta)$

**10**  The curve with gradient function $\sin\left(2\theta + \dfrac{\pi}{2}\right)$ crosses the x-axis at $\left(\dfrac{7\pi}{12}, 0\right)$. Find the coordinates of the point where the curve crosses the y-axis.

**11**  The diagram below shows the curve $y = \dfrac{x}{x^2+2}$ and the line $y = \dfrac{x}{11}$. Find the shaded area.

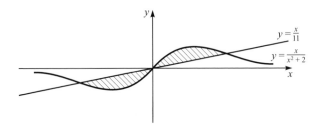

**12** The diagram below shows the curve $y = \dfrac{x^3}{\sqrt{x^2+1}}$. Use the substitution $u^2 = x^2 + 1$ to find the shaded area.

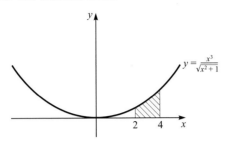

## 9.3      Choice of method of integration

### Basic

Use an appropriate method to find the following indefinite integrals.

**1** $\displaystyle\int (2x^2 - 3x + 4)\,dx$

**2** $\displaystyle\int 2xe^x\,dx$

**3** $\displaystyle\int e^{-4x}\,dx$

**4** $\displaystyle\int x\sqrt{x-2}\,dx$

**5** $\displaystyle\int \frac{2x-3}{(x+1)(x-4)}\,dx$

Evaluate the following definite integrals using an appropriate method.

**\*6** $\displaystyle\int_3^4 x(x-3)^7\,dx$

**7** $\displaystyle\int_2^3 \frac{(x+3)(x-2)}{x^2}\,dx$

**8** $\displaystyle\int_0^{\pi/2} x\cos x\,dx$

**9** $\displaystyle\int_0^1 \frac{3x+13}{(x+3)(x+5)}\,dx$

**10** $\displaystyle\int_1^2 3x(x^2-2)^4\,dx$

**11** Sketch on the same diagram the graphs of $y = 4 - x^2$ and $y = x + 2$. Hence find the area enclosed between the two graphs.

**\*12** The gradient function of a curve is $\dfrac{x}{(x+3)^3}$ and it passes through the points $(0, \frac{1}{2})$ and $(-1, a)$. Find the value of $a$.

### Intermediate

Use an appropriate method to find the following indefinite integrals.

**1** $\displaystyle\int \sin\theta \cos^4\theta \, d\theta$

**2** $\displaystyle\int \frac{(x+1)^2}{2x} \, dx$

**3** $\displaystyle\int \frac{4}{x^2 - 16} \, dx$

**4** $\displaystyle\int x^2 \cos x \, dx$

**5** $\displaystyle\int \frac{x}{2x - 1} \, dx$

**6** $\displaystyle\int \frac{x + 3}{x^2 + 6x + 13} \, dx$

Evaluate the following definite integrals using an appropriate method.

**7** $\displaystyle\int_1^4 (\sqrt{x} - 3)^2 \, dx$

**8** $\displaystyle\int_1^2 xe^{-x} \, dx$

**9** $\displaystyle\int_{\pi/6}^{\pi/3} 4\sin^2 2\theta \, d\theta$

**10** $\displaystyle\int_2^3 \frac{2}{(x-1)(x+5)} \, dx$

**11** $\displaystyle\int_1^2 \ln 2x \, dx$

**12** $\displaystyle\int_0^1 \frac{x^3}{\sqrt{2 - x^2}} \, dx$

**\*13** Given that

$$\frac{dP}{dq} = \frac{3q + 4}{q^2 + 2q}$$

and that $P = \ln 3$ when $q = 1$, find the value of $P$ when $q = 2$.

**14** (a) Sketch the graph of $y = xe^x$.
(b) Find the area enclosed between $y = xe^x$ and the $x$-axis from $x = -2$ to $x = 2$.

**\*15** The points $(-1, 1)$ and $(-2, 21)$ lie on the curve with gradient function $a(2x + 1)^3$. Find the value of $a$.

**16** Find the area enclosed between the curve $y = e^x$ and the $y$-axis from $y = 1$ to $y = 2$.

## Advanced

**1** Find:

(a) $\displaystyle\int \frac{dx}{e^x + 9e^{-x}}$  (b) $\displaystyle\int \cos^3 x \, dx$  (c) $\displaystyle\int \frac{x^2 \, dx}{1 - x^2}$

**2** Find $\dfrac{d}{dx}(x \sin^{-1} x)$ and hence evaluate $\displaystyle\int_0^1 \sin^{-1} x \, dx$.

**3** Evaluate:

(a) $\displaystyle\int_0^5 \sqrt{25 - x^2} \, dx$  (b) $\displaystyle\int_0^{2\pi} |\sin x - \cos x| \, dx$

(c) $\displaystyle\int_0^1 \frac{(\tan^{-1} x)^2 \, dx}{1 + x^2}$

**4** (i) Show that $\displaystyle\int_5^{10} \frac{1}{u} \, du = \ln 2$.

The function $f(x)$ is defined by $f(x) = \dfrac{x}{x^2 + 1}$.

The graph of $y = f(x)$ for positive values of $x$ is shown below.

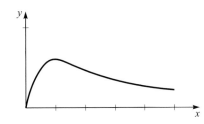

(ii) Calculate $\int_2^3 f(x) \, dx$. [You may wish to use the substitution $u = x^2 + 1$.]

(iii) Show that f(x) is an odd function. Write down the value of $\int_{-3}^{-2} f(x)\,dx$.

(iv) State a transformation which will transform the graph of $y = f(x)$ into the graph of $y = f(x+1)$.

(v) Using parts (iii) and (iv), or otherwise, calculate the value of

$$\int_{-4}^{-3} \frac{x+1}{x^2+2x+2}\,dx.$$

[OCR (MEI), 1998]

5    Given that $y = \sqrt{ax^2 + b}$ and $z = \sqrt{ax^2 + c}$, where $a$, $b$ and $c$ are constants, show that

$$\frac{d}{dx}\ln(y+z) = \frac{ax}{yz}$$

Hence:

(a) show that $\displaystyle\int_0^1 \frac{x\,dx}{\sqrt{x^2+1}\sqrt{x^2+9}} = \ln\left(\frac{\sqrt{2}+\sqrt{10}}{4}\right)$

(b) evaluate $\displaystyle\int_0^1 \frac{dx}{\sqrt{x+1}\sqrt{x+9}}$

6    The integral $I_n$ is given by $I_n = \int_0^{\pi/2} \cos^n\theta\,d\theta$  $(n \geq 2)$. By writing $\cos^n\theta$ as $\cos^{n-1}\theta\cos\theta$, show that

$$I_n = \frac{n-1}{n}I_{n-2}$$

Hence evaluate:

(a) $\displaystyle\int_0^{\pi/2} \cos^6\theta\,d\theta$    (b) $\displaystyle\int_0^{\pi/2} \cos^4\theta\sin^2\theta\,d\theta$

7    Evaluate the integrals:

(i) $\displaystyle\int_0^{\pi/3} \sin^3 x\cos^2 x\,dx$    (ii) $\displaystyle\int_4^9 \frac{1}{(x-1)\sqrt{x}}\,dx$

(iii) $\displaystyle\int_0^{\pi/2} \frac{1}{1+2\cos x}\,dx$

[OCR (Cambridge), 1983]

8    (a) Integrate:

(i) $\displaystyle\int \ln x\,dx$    (ii) $\displaystyle\int (\ln x)^2\,dx$

(b) Prove that $\displaystyle\int_1^3 x[\ln(a^2x^2)]^2\,dx = \frac{1}{2a^2}\int_{a^2}^{9a^2}[\ln y]^2\,dy$

Hence show that $\displaystyle\int_1^3 x[\ln(81x^4)]^2\,dx = 70(\ln 9)^2 - 68\ln 9 + 32.$

9 (a) Find $\displaystyle\int_0^{\pi/2} \frac{1}{(1+\sin x)(1+\cos x)}\,dx.$

(b) Let $[x]$ denote the greatest integer not greater than $x$, so that for example $[\pi] = 3$, $[3] = 3.$ Given that $n$ is a positive integer greater than 1, evaluate

$$\int_1^{e^n} [\ln x]\,dx$$

[OCR (Cambridge), 1983]

10 Prove that $\int_0^{2a} f(x)\,dx = \int_0^a \{f(x) + f(2a - x)\}\,dx.$
Hence, or otherwise, evaluate:

(a) $\displaystyle\int_0^{\pi} x\sin^2 x\,dx$     (b) $\displaystyle\int_0^{\pi} \frac{x\,dx}{1+\frac{1}{2}\sin x}$

[OCR (Cambridge), 1963]

### Revision

The most common methods of integration are:

(a) direct integration, e.g. $\displaystyle\int \frac{1}{\sqrt{1-y^2}}\,dy = \sin^{-1} y + c$

(b) algebraic rearrangement, e.g. $\displaystyle\int \frac{1}{\sqrt{x}}\,dx = \int x^{-\frac{1}{2}}\,dx \cdots$ or

$\displaystyle\int \frac{x^2+1}{x}\,dx = \int x + \frac{1}{x}\,dx \cdots$

(c) trigonometric rearrangement, e.g.

$\displaystyle\int \sin 6x \sin 2x\,dx = \int \frac{1}{2}(\cos 4x - \cos 8x)\,dx \cdots$

(d) inspection, e.g. $\displaystyle\int \frac{2x\,dx}{x^2+1} = \ln(x^2+1) + c$

(e) substitution, e.g. $\displaystyle\int \frac{x}{(3x-2)^2}\,dx$ let $u = 3x - 2 \cdots$

(f)  parts, e.g. $\displaystyle\int xe^{2x}\,dx = \frac{1}{2}xe^{2x} - \int \frac{1}{2}e^{2x}\,dx \cdots$

(g)  partial fractions, e.g. $\displaystyle\int \frac{x+1}{(x+4)(x+3)}\,dx = \int \frac{3}{x+4} - \frac{2}{x+3}\,dx \cdots$

**1**  State which of the above *methods* is the best for finding each of the following integrals. There is no need to find the integral.

(i)  $\displaystyle\int \frac{x^2}{1+x^3}\,dx$

(ii)  $\displaystyle\int \frac{1}{x(4-x)}\,dx$

(iii)  $\displaystyle\int \frac{1}{9+x^2}\,dx$

(iv)  $\displaystyle\int \frac{1}{9-y^2}\,dy$

(v)  $\displaystyle\int \frac{x^3-2}{x^2}\,dx$

(vi)  $\displaystyle\int \sin^5 x \cos x\,dx$

(vii)  $\displaystyle\int \sin^2 x\,dx$

(viii)  $\displaystyle\int \frac{10}{5-2y}\,dy$

(ix)  $\displaystyle\int \frac{10y}{5-2y}\,dy$

(x)  $\displaystyle\int xe^{x^2}\,dx$

(xi)  $\displaystyle\int x^2 e^x\,dx$

(xii)  $\displaystyle\int \frac{x}{(3x+2)^4}\,dx$

(xiii)  $\displaystyle\int (5x+1)^9\,dx$

(xiv)  $\displaystyle\int \frac{x}{\sqrt{1-x^2}}\,dx$

(xv)  $\displaystyle\int \frac{dx}{\sqrt{1-x}}$

(xvi)  $\displaystyle\int \frac{dx}{\sqrt{1-x^2}}$

(xvii)  $\displaystyle\int x^2 \sin x\,dx$

(xviii)  $\displaystyle\int \frac{(x^3-1)^2}{x^4}\,dx$

(xix)  $\displaystyle\int \sin x \cos x\,dx$

(xx)  $\displaystyle\int x \ln x\,dx$

(xxi)  $\displaystyle\int \cos\left(2x+\frac{\pi}{4}\right)\,dx$

(xxii)  $\displaystyle\int \frac{7x+1}{x^2+2x-3}\,dx$

(xxiii)  $\displaystyle\int \frac{x-1}{3x^2-6x+4}$

(xxiv)  $\displaystyle\int \sec^2 3\theta\,d\theta$

(xxv) $\int \dfrac{x+1}{\sqrt{x}}\, dx$

(xxvi) $\int x^2(x^3+1)^4\, dx$

(xxvii) $\int \dfrac{e^x+1}{e^x}\, dx$

(xxviii) $\int \tan^2 x\, dx$

(xxix) $\int \sin 3x \cos 2x\, dx$

(xxx) $\int \dfrac{3}{x^2+2x}$

(xxxi) $\int \dfrac{1}{3x+1}\, dx$

(xxxii) $\int \dfrac{\cos x}{\sin^5 x}\, dx$

(xxxiii) $\int \dfrac{4-6x^2}{(1+2x)^2(1+x)}\, dx$

(xxxiv) $\int \dfrac{dx}{(2x-1)^2}$

(xxxv) $\int \dfrac{dx}{(x+5)^2+2}$

(xxxvi) $\int \dfrac{x}{1+x^4}\, dx$

(xxxvii) $\int \sin^3 x\, dx$

(xxxviii) $\int \dfrac{\cos x - \sin x}{\sin x + \cos x}\, dx$

(xxxix) $\int \sqrt{25-x^2}\, dx$

(xl) $\int x\sqrt{25-x^2}\, dx$

Use an appropriate method to find the following indefinite integrals.

2  $\int \dfrac{x-1}{2x^2-4x+7}\, dx$

3  $\int \dfrac{e^x}{e^x+1}\, dx$

4  $\int 2x \sin x\, dx$

5  $\int \dfrac{4x^3}{\sqrt{x}}\, dx$

Evaluate the following definite integrals using an appropriate method.

6  $\int_3^4 \dfrac{3}{x^2-x-2}\, dx$

7  $\int_6^7 2x(7-x)^6\, dx$

**8** $\displaystyle\int_2^6 \frac{1}{2x-3}\,dx$

**9** $\displaystyle\int_1^4 (\sqrt{x}+x)^2\,dx$

**10** $\displaystyle\int_0^1 xe^{3x}\,dx$

**11** Find the value of $a$ which satisfies the equation $\displaystyle\int_2^3 \frac{ax}{x^2-3}\,dx = \ln 6$.

**12** On the same diagram sketch the graphs of $9x = y^2$ and $9y = x^2$. Find the area enclosed between them.

## 9.4 Problems involving differential equations; solution of simple differential equations of the form $dy/dx = f(x)$; separation of variables

### Basic

**1** Form a differential equation by eliminating the arbitrary constant $A$ from each of the following.

(a) $y = x^3 + A$        (b) $y = A\sin x$       (c) $x = Ae^{3t}$

(d) $\theta = \ln(A + 2t)$

**2** For each of the following, find (i) the general solution and (ii) the particular solution satisfying the given boundary conditions.

*(a) $\dfrac{dy}{dx} = 5x - 2, \quad x = 1, y = 1$

(b) $\dfrac{dy}{dx} = e^{2x} - \sin 2x, \quad x = 0, y = 2$

**3** Give the general solution for each of the equations.

(a) $\dfrac{dy}{dx} = 2x(x^2 + 5)^4$      (b) $\dfrac{dv}{dt} = \dfrac{4t}{t^2 + 5}$

**\*4** A container of liquid is being heated at a rate which is decreasing steadily with time. The temperature $\theta\,^\circ$C after $t$ minutes satisfies the differential equation

$$\frac{d\theta}{dt} = 10 - \frac{8t}{5}$$

Given that the initial temperature is $30\,^\circ$C, find the temperature after 4 minutes. Will the model still be valid after 10 minutes?

**5** When an object is moving in a straight line, its acceleration $t$ seconds after the start of the motion is given by $\dfrac{dv}{dt} = 4 + 3t^2$.

If the initial velocity of the object is $5\,\mathrm{m\,s}^{-1}$, find the velocity $v$ at time $t = 3$ seconds.

**6** Find the general solution of:

(a) $\dfrac{dy}{dx} = 6y$     (b) $\dfrac{dy}{dx} = \dfrac{1}{y+2}$

**7** Eliminate the arbitrary constant $A$ and so form a differential equation.

Give your answer in the form $g(y)\,\dfrac{dy}{dx} = f(x)$.

(a) $y^2 = x^3 + A$     *(b) $\sin y = Ax^2$

**8** A curve passes through the point $(2, \tfrac{1}{2})$ and at the point $(x, y)$ the gradient is given by $\dfrac{dy}{dx} = xy^2$. Find the equation of the curve, giving your answer in the form $y = f(x)$.

**9** Which of the following differential equations can be solved using the method of separating the variables? Solve those to which the method applies.

(a) $\dfrac{dy}{dx} = 2x + xy$     (b) $\dfrac{dy}{dx} = 3x - 2y$

(c) $\dfrac{dy}{dx} = xy + 6$     (d) $3x + 2y\,\dfrac{dy}{dx} = 5$

**\*10** The height $h$ metres of a tree at age $t$ years is given by $dh/dt = 0.4 - 0.03h$. A tree is planted when it is 2 metres high. How high is the tree after 30 years?

**11** A colony of ants grows at a rate proportional to the size of the population, $n$.

(a) Express this as a differential equation relating $n$ and $t$, where $t$ is the time in days since the colony was formed.
(b) The colony has an initial population of 200 and starts to grow at the rate of 75 ants per day. How many ants will there be after 10 days?

**12** The rate, in $\mathrm{cm}^3\,\mathrm{s}^{-1}$, at which a liquid leaks from a container, $t$ seconds after the formation of a hole, is proportional to the volume of the liquid, $V\,\mathrm{cm}^3$, in the container at that instant. At time $t = 0$, $V = 200\,\mathrm{cm}^3$.

(a) Write down a differential equation connecting $V$ and $t$.
(b) Show that $V = Ae^{-kt}$, where $A$ is to be stated.

When $t = 50$, $V = 190$.

(c)  Find $k$.

(d)  Find the time taken for the volume of liquid to fall to $100 \, \text{cm}^3$.

## Intermediate

**\*1**  Find the general solution of:

(a)  $\dfrac{dx}{dt} = 2x^3 t^2$     (b)  $\dfrac{dy}{dx} = y - y \cos x$

**2**  Use the method of separation of variables to find the solution to the differential equations which pass through the given point.

(a)  $\dfrac{dy}{dx} = \sqrt{xy}$,     $(0, 1)$

(b)  $\dfrac{dy}{dx} = \sin x \cos^2 y$,     $(\tfrac{1}{2}\pi, \tfrac{1}{4}\pi)$

(c)  $\dfrac{dy}{dx} - \dfrac{3y}{x} = 0$,     $(2, 4)$

**3**  If $e^{-x^2} \dfrac{dy}{dx} = x(y + 2)^2$, find $y$ in terms of $x$, given that $y = 0$ when $x = 0$.

**4**  Solve the differential equation $(1 - e^{2x}) \tan y \, \dfrac{dy}{dx} = e^{2x}$, $x > 0$, given that $y = \dfrac{\pi}{3}$ when $x = 1$, giving your answer in terms of e.

**5**  Solve the differential equation $x \dfrac{dy}{dx} = y(3 - y)$ where $y = 2$ when $x = 2$, giving $y$ as a function of $x$.

**6**  Solve the equation $2 \tan x \, \dfrac{dy}{dx} + y^2 - 1 = 0$, given that $y = 2$ when $x = \tfrac{1}{2}\pi$.

Give your answer in the form $y = f(x)$.

**\*7**  The depth $h \, \text{cm}$ of water in a pool is initially $140 \, \text{cm}$. It varies with time, $t$ hours, such that

(a)  $\dfrac{dh}{dt} = 0.4 + 0.3 \cos \dfrac{\pi t}{50}$     (b)  $\dfrac{dh}{dt} = 1 - 0.4 e^{t/250}$.

Solve each differential equation and compare the depths after 5 days.

*8  During a spell of freezing weather, the ice on a lake has thickness $h$ mm at time $t$ hours after the start of freezing. At 4.00 p.m., after one hour of freezing weather, the ice is 3 mm thick.

(a) If the rate of increase of $h$ is taken to be proportional to the reciprocal of $h$, write down a differential equation for $h$ involving a constant of proportionality $\lambda$.

(b) Solve the differential equation and hence show that the thickness of the ice is proportional to the square root of the time elapsed from the start of freezing.

(c) Determine the time that the ice will be double the thickness it was at 4.00 p.m.

9  A radio-active substance decays at a rate proportional to its mass. A particular specimen is found to have mass 25.000 g and is decaying at the rate of 0.025 grams per year. There are $m$ grams left after $t$ years.

(a) Write down a differential equation connecting $m$ and $t$.
(b) Find the mass of the specimen after 100 years.
(c) Find how long it will take for the specimen to decay to 5 g.

10  The acceleration, $a\,\mathrm{m\,s^{-2}}$, of a parachute in free fall from an aircraft is given by the equation

$$a = 10 - 0.4v^2$$

where $v$ is its speed in $\mathrm{m\,s^{-1}}$.

(a) Show that $a = v\dfrac{\mathrm{d}v}{\mathrm{d}x}$.

(b) Given that $v = 0$ when $t = 0$, form and solve differential equations for $v$
(i) as a function of time $t$,    (ii) as a function of distance $x$.

11  A boy makes his way to school at a speed which is proportional to the distance he has left to cover. He leaves home, 3 km away from school, running at $12\,\mathrm{km\,h^{-1}}$. Writing his distance from home after time $t$ hours as $x$ km,

(a) write down a differential equation relating $x$ and $t$;
(b) determine how long it takes him to travel $\frac{4}{5}$ of the journey;
(c) determine how long it takes him to reach school.

12  Grain is pouring from a hopper on to a barn floor, where it forms a conical pile whose height, $h$, is increasing at a rate that is inversely proportional to $h^3$. The initial height of the pile is $h_0$ and the height doubles after time $T$. Find, in terms of $T$, the time after which the height has grown to $3h_0$.

**13** In a reservoir which is discharging over a weir, it is know that

$$\frac{dH}{dt} = \frac{64 - H^2}{320}$$

where $H$ metres is the height of the water surface above the sill of the weir after $t$ minutes. If, initially, $H = 1\,\text{m}$, find an expression for $H$ and hence find the greatest value $H$ can reach.

**14** In a chemical reaction, a chemical X has a concentration of $x$ moles per litre. $x$ is known to satisfy the differential equation $\dfrac{dx}{dt} = k(a - x)^2$, where $a$ and $k$ are constants. Given that the initial concentration is zero, find a formula for $x$ at time $t$, expressing your answer in terms of $a$ and $k$.

**15** In a certain process, the rate of production of yeast is $\lambda y$ grams per minute, where $y$ grams is the amount already produced, and yeast is removed at a constant rate of $m$ grams per minute.

(a) Write down a differential equation relating $y$ and the time $t$ measured in minutes.
(b) If initially $q$ grams of yeast were present, find an expression for the amount of yeast at time $t$ minutes.
(c) Deduce that, if $m \le \lambda q$, the supply of yeast is never exhausted.
(d) Find the value of $m$ to three significant figures if $\lambda = 0.004$, $q = 25\,000$ and the supply of yeast is exhausted in 100 minutes.

**\*16** By means of the substitution $y = zx$, where $z$ is a function of $x$, reduce the differential equation of $x\dfrac{dy}{dx} - y = \frac{1}{4}x^2 - y^2$ to a differential equation involving $z$ and $x$ only. Hence solve it, given that $y = 0$ when $x = \ln 2$.

## Advanced

**1**

$x\,\text{cm}$

A cylindrical container has a height of 200 cm. The container was initially full of a chemical but there is a leak from a hole in its base. When the leak is noticed, the container is half-full and the level of the chemical is dropping at a rate of 1 cm per minute.

(i)  On the assumption that the rate of leakage has been constant, calculate for how long the container has been leaking.

(ii)  A more sophisticated model assumes that when the depth of the chemical remaining is $x$ cm, the rate at which the level is dropping is proportional to $\sqrt{x}$. Show that this model leads to the differential equation

$$\frac{dx}{dt} = -\tfrac{1}{10}\sqrt{x}$$

where $t$ is the time in minutes.

Obtain the general solution of this differential equation and hence show that the container has been leaking for about 80 minutes.

[OCR (Cambridge)]

2   The length, $x$, of a certain leaf, at time $t$ (during a period of its growth), is proportional to the amount of water it contains. It may be assumed that during this period the leaf has a constant shape. The leaf absorbs water from the plant at a rate proportional to the length of the leaf, and loses water by evaporation at a rate proportional to the area of the leaf. Show that the growth of the leaf can be represented by the differential equation

$$\frac{dx}{dt} = ax - bx^2$$

where $a$ and $b$ are positive constants.

Solve this equation, given that, when $t = 0$, $x = \dfrac{a}{2b}$.

Hence express $x$ in terms of $t$ and deduce that the length of the leaf never exceeds the value $\dfrac{a}{b}$.

[OCR (Cambridge), 1973]

3   In a simple model of population growth, the rate of increase of the population at any time is taken to be proportional to the population at that time. Treating the size of the population as a continuous variable, this model leads to the differential equation

$$\frac{dP}{dt} = kP$$

where $P$ denotes the size of the population at time $t$ (measured in days), and $k$ is a positive constant.

   (i)  Given that $P = P_0$ when $t = 0$, express $P$ in terms of $k$, $t$ and $P_0$.
   (ii)  In a laboratory experiment, the number of individual cells present in a specimen was 1218 at a certain time, and was 1397 one day later. Find the number of cells after one further day predicted by the model.
   (iii)  Give a reason why this model can never represent a real-world population correctly over the longer term.

Biologists studying a particular population observe that the fertility of individual members in the population appears to be decreasing as time goes on, and that consequently the population is not growing as rapidly as had been expected. They propose that the situation may be modelled mathematically by replacing the constant $k$ in the simple model above by a term of the form $Ke^{-\lambda t}$, where $K$ and $\lambda$ are positive constants. This revised model leads to the differential equation

$$\frac{dP}{dt} = Ke^{-\lambda t}P$$

where $P = P_0$ when $t = 0$.
Show that this model predicts a population that approaches a certain fixed limit, and express this limit in terms of $K$, $\lambda$ and $P_0$.
[OCR (Cambridge), 1995]

**4**   A family of curves is defined by the differential equation

$$\frac{dy}{dx} = \frac{2x - y}{x - y}$$

   (i)  All the members of this family have zero gradient at the points where they cross a certain straight line. What is the equation of this straight line?
   (ii)  All members of this family have infinite gradient at the points where they cross another straight line. What is the equation of this straight line?
   (iii)  On a sketch graph draw the lines referred to in parts (i) and (ii). Label them 'zero gradient' and 'infinite gradient' respectively.

(iv) One of the curves A to D is a member of the family of curves. Which is it?

A    B    C    D

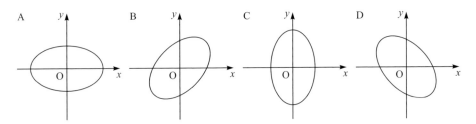

[OCR (SMP), 1990]

**5** Substitute $y = z/x$ in the differential equation

$$\frac{dy}{dx} = \frac{2xy + 1 - 2y}{x(x+2)}$$

to obtain a differential equation relating $z$ and $x$.
Solve this equation and hence find the general solution for $y$ in terms of $x$.
[OCR (Cambridge), 1987]

**6** At time $t$ the volume of water in a lake is $yV_0$, where $V_0$ is the volume at time $t = 0$, and $y$ depends on $t$. As a net result of evaporation and rainfall the volume increases at a rate $ky(2 - y)V_0$, where $k$ is a constant. In addition the volume increases at a rate $3kV_0$ as a result of inflow from a river. Establish a differential equation satisfied by $y$ and deduce the volume of water in the lake at time $t$.
Show that the volume will be $2V_0$ when $t = (1/4k)\log_e 3$.
[OCR (Cambridge), 1970]

**7** By substituting $y(x) = xv(x)$ in the differential equation

$$x^3\frac{dv}{dx} + x^2v = \frac{1 + x^2v^2}{(1 + x^2)v}$$

or otherwise, find the solution $v(x)$ that satisfies $v = 1$ when $x = 1$.
What value does this solution approach when $x$ becomes large?
[OCR (STEP), 1987]

**8** It is given that $y$ satisfies the differential equation

$$(4\cos y + 3\sin y)\frac{dy}{dx} = 4\cos x + 3\sin x$$

and that $y = 0$ when $x = 0$. Prove that the *complete* solution is $y = x$.
[OCR (Cambridge), 1973]

**9** At time $t$ the amounts of two reacting chemicals present in a vessel are $x$ and $y$, being $x_0$ and $y_0$ at time $t = 0$. The reaction proceeds according to the differential equations

$$\frac{dy}{dt} = -kxy, \quad \frac{dx}{dt} = kxy$$

Show that $y - x$ is constant.
[OCR (Cambridge)]

**10** A disease is spreading through a large animal population of fixed size. Initially there are $\lambda$ animals susceptible to the disease (but which have not yet contracted it), $\mu$ animals infected with the disease and no animals immune to it. The rate at which the number of susceptible animals decreases (through their contracting the disease) is proportional to the product of the numbers of susceptible and infected animals, while the rate at which the number of immune animals increases (through infected animals recovering from the disease) is proportional to the number of infected animals. (The disease is never fatal.) Let $\alpha$, $\beta$ denote the constants of proportionality in the two above rates and let $x$, $y$ and $z$ denote the number of susceptible, infected and immune animals (respectively) at any time $t$ (where $t \geq 0$). Write down a system of three differential equations that are satisfied by $x$, $y$, $z$. Show that if $\alpha\lambda > \beta$ then $y$ will increase until $x$ has the value $\beta/\alpha$, and that $y$ will then decrease. Find both $y$ and $z$ as explicit functions of $x$, and deduce that if $\alpha\lambda > \beta$ then $y$ will never exceed the value

$$\lambda + \mu - \frac{\beta}{\alpha}\left(1 + \ln\frac{\alpha\lambda}{\beta}\right)$$

[OCR (SMP), 1977]

## Revision

**1** Find the general solution of:

(a) $\dfrac{dy}{dx} = y^2(x+1)$      (b) $\dfrac{dy}{dx} = \dfrac{\sqrt{x+1}}{y}$

**2** Solve the equation $3x^2\dfrac{dy}{dx} = 1 + x^3$, given that when $x = 2$, $y = \frac{1}{2}$.

**3**  Solve:

(a)  $\dfrac{dy}{dx} = e^{x+3y}$, given that, when $x = 0$, $y = 0$

(b)  $\dfrac{dy}{dx} + \dfrac{\sqrt{1+y^2}}{xy} = 0$, given that, when $x = 1$, $y = \sqrt{3}$

**4**  The gradient of the tangent to a curve at the point $(x, y)$ is given by

$$\frac{dy}{dx} = \frac{1 - y^2}{2xy}$$

Find the equation of the curve which passes through $(2, 3)$.

**5**  The manufacturers of a certain brand of baked beans are concerned that the number of people buying their product at any time $t$ has remained constant for some months. They launch a major advertising programme which results in the number of customers, $p$, increasing at a rate proportional to $\sqrt{p}$. Express, as a differential equation, the progress of sales (a) before advertising, (b) after advertising.

**6**  A circular patch of oil has radius $r$ metres at time $t$ seconds. The rate of increase of $r$ is proportional to $\dfrac{1}{r}$.

(a)  Write down a differential equation connecting $r$ and $t$.
The initial radius of the patch is $2\,\mathrm{m}$ and when $t = 5$, $r = 12$.
(b)  Solve the differential equation.
(c)  When $r = 8$, $t = T$. Find $T$.

**7**  A tank contains water to a depth of $h\,\mathrm{cm}$. Water flows out through a valve. When the valve is opened, the rate at which the depth of water decreases $(\mathrm{cm\,s^{-1}})$ is proportional to the square root of $h$.

(a)  Write down a differential equation relating $h$ and $t$, the time in seconds after the valve has been opened.
The initial depth of water is $625\,\mathrm{cm}$ and when $t = 100$, $h = 400$.
(b)  Calculate a formula for $h$ in terms of $t$.
(c)  Determine how long it takes for the tank to empty.

**8**  In a certain country, the price $p$ of a particular commodity increases with time $t$ at a rate equal to $kp$, where $k$ is a positive constant. Show that, if $p = 1$ when $t = 0$, and $p = \alpha$ when $t = 1$, then, at time $t$, $p = \alpha^t$.

**9**  A liquid is being heated in an oven maintained at a constant temperature of $180\,^{\circ}\mathrm{C}$. It is assumed that the rate of increase in the temperature of the liquid is proportional to $180 - \theta$, where $\theta\,^{\circ}\mathrm{C}$ is the temperature of the liquid at time $t$ minutes. If the temperature of the liquid rises from $0\,^{\circ}\mathrm{C}$

to $120\,^\circ\text{C}$ in 5 minutes, find the temperature of the liquid after a further 5 minutes.

10 The rate at which a body loses speed at any given instant as it travels through a resistive medium is given by $kv^2\,\text{m}\,\text{s}^{-2}$, where $v$ is the speed at that instant and $k$ is a positive constant. If its initial speed is $u$, show that the time taken to halve this speed is $1/ku$ seconds.

11 A ball is thrown vertically upwards with initial speed $u$. Assuming that the air resistance is proportional to the speed of the ball, $v$, the motion may be modelled by the differential equation $\dfrac{dv}{dt} = -g - kv$, where $g$ is the acceleration due to gravity and $k$ is a constant.

(a) Solve the equation to find $v$ in terms of $t$.
(b) Show that the ball reaches its maximum height when

$$t = \frac{1}{k}\ln\left(1 + \frac{ku}{g}\right)$$

12 Solve the equation $\dfrac{dy}{dx} = (y - x)^2$ using the substitution $y = x + v$, where $v$ is a function of $x$, and $y = 2$ when $x = 0$.

## 9.5     Further applications of integration; volumes of revolution; $\int y\,dx = \lim \sum y\,\delta x$

The volume of revolution of the portion of curve $y = f(x)$ between $x = a$ and $x = b$, through $360°$ about the $x$-axis is $\pi \int_a^b y^2\,dx$.

$$\lim_{\delta x \to 0} \sum_{x=a}^{x=b} y\,\delta x = \int_a^b y\,dx$$

**Basic**

1 Find the volume of the solid formed when the area between the curve $y = 2x^2$ for $0 \le x \le 3$ and the $x$-axis is rotated through $360°$ about the $x$-axis.

**2** Find the volume of the solid formed when the area between the curve $y = x + \dfrac{1}{x}$, the $x$-axis and the lines $x = 1$ and $x = 3$ is rotated through $360°$ about the $x$-axis.

**3** Find the volume of the solid formed when the area between the line $y = 2x + 1$, the $x$-axis and the lines $x = 0$ and $x = 4$ is rotated through $360°$ about the $x$-axis.

**4** Sketch the curve $y^2 = 1 - \cos 2x$ for values of $x$ between $0$ and $\pi$. A spindle-shaped solid is in the form obtained by rotating the above portion of the curve through $360°$ about the $x$-axis. Calculate the volume of the solid.

**5** An ellipsoid is formed by rotating the ellipse $\dfrac{x^2}{a^2} + \dfrac{y^2}{b^2} = 1$ through $360°$ about the $x$-axis. Find its volume.

**\*6** A solid is formed by the rotation through $360°$ about the $y$-axis of the part of the curve $y = x^3$ between $y = 1$ and $y = 8$. Show that its volume is $93\pi/5$ cubic units.

**7** A solid $10\,\text{cm}$ high is formed by rotating the area between the curve $y = 5x^2 + 2$ and the $y$-axis through $360°$ about the $y$-axis. Find its volume.

**8** When the region between $y = \ln x$, the axes and the lines $y = 1$ and $y = 5$ is rotated through $360°$ about the $y$-axis, a solid is generated. Find its volume.

**9** The part of the curve $y = 2(x^2 - 4)$ from $x = 2$ to $x = 4$ is rotated through $360°$ about the $y$-axis to form a solid of revolution. Find the volume of the solid which is generated.

**10** The region between the $x$- and $y$-axes and the line $y = 6 - 4x$ is rotated through $360°$ about the $y$-axis. Find, by integration, the volume of the cone that is formed.

**\*11** The rate, $n$ people per hour, at which customers enter a supermarket between 8 a.m. and 1 p.m. is given by $n = 400t \sin(\pi t/5)$, where $t$ is the time in hours after 8 a.m.

(a) How many customers enter in the small time interval $\delta t$?
(b) Find the total number of people who enter the supermarket over the 5 hour period.

**12** The region between the graph $y = e^x$, the axes, and the line $x = -b$ is rotated through $360°$ about the $x$-axis. Find, in terms of $b$, the volume of the solid generated and show that, as $b \to \infty$, the volume remains finite.

**Intermediate**

1  Calculate the volume of the frustrum of a cone formed by rotating the area between the line $y = 2x + 3$, the ordinates $x = 1$ and $x = 4$, and the $x$-axis through $360°$ about the $x$-axis.

2  Find the volume generated when the area under $y = \cos x$ from $x = 0$ to $x = \frac{1}{2}\pi$ is rotated through $360°$ about the $x$-axis.

3  Sketch the graph of $y = 1 + \frac{1}{2}\sin x$ from $x = 0$ to $x = 2\pi$. A vase is formed by rotating the sketched part of the curve through $360°$ about the $x$-axis. Find the volume of the vase.

4  Sketch the parabolas $y^2 = 8x$ and $y^2 = 6x + 4$ and find their points of intersection. A bowl is made by rotating the area enclosed by the curves through $360°$ about the $x$-axis. Find the volume of material used to make the bowl.

5  Find the volume formed when the area between the curve $y^2 = 12x$ and $y = 2x$ is rotated through $360°$ about the $x$-axis.

6  The area in the first quadrant, bounded by the curves $y = \dfrac{9}{x}$, $y = \dfrac{9}{x^2}$ and the line $x = 3$ is rotated once about the $x$-axis. Find the volume of the solid of revolution formed.

7  Find the volume of the solid formed when the region between the graph $y = \dfrac{2}{x}$, the $y$-axis, the lines $y = 1$ and $y = 5$ is rotated through $360°$ about the $y$-axis.

*8  Find the volume of the solid of revolution when the area bounded by the curve $y = e^{2x}$, the $y$-axis and the line $y = e$ is rotated through $360°$ about the $y$-axis.

*9  The internal diameter of a tumbler increases uniformly from $6\,\text{cm}$ to $8\,\text{cm}$ and the tumbler is $12\,\text{cm}$ high. Find a formula for the radius of the tumbler at a height $y\,\text{cm}$, and hence find, by integration, the volume of liquid it would hold when full.

*10  The area of the cross-section of an ellipsoid $y\,\text{cm}$ from one end is given by $A = y(25 - 2y)$. Find the volume of the ellipsoid using integration.

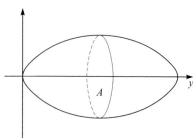

**11** A pyramid, height 6 m, with a rectangular base, length 4 m and width 3 m, is shown in the diagram. A shaded slice is shown $y$ m below the vertex. Write down the lengths of the edges of the slice in terms of $y$ and hence find the area of the slice. If the slice has thickness $\delta y$, write down the volume of the slice and hence, by integration, find the volume of the pyramid.

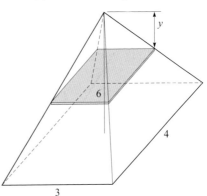

**12** A spinning top, $\pi$ cm high, has cross-section $A$ cm$^2$, $y$ cm from the base, such that $A = e^y \sin y$. By dividing the spinning top into slices, thickness $\delta y$, and summing, find its volume.

**\*13** The thickness of a discus $r$ cm from the centre is given by the formula $t = \dfrac{25 - r^2}{25}$ cm. Find the volume of the discus.

**14** By dividing into annular slices, calculate the mass, in grams, of a circular disc of thickness 0.03 m, radius 0.6 m, if the density $\rho$ kg m$^{-3}$ at radius $r$ is given by $\rho = 4r^2 + 3$.

**15** (a) Find the volume of the portion of the sphere generated by rotating the area inside the circle $x^2 + y^2 = 100$ between the lines $x = -6$ and $x = 6$ through 360° about the $x$-axis.
   (b) What fraction of this volume lies within the cylinder obtained by rotating the line $y = 8$ about the $y$-axis?

**16** Show that the volume of the solid formed by rotating through 360° about the $y$-axis the area bounded by the $y$-axis, the line $y = -1$ and the graph $y = \cos 2x$ for $0 \le x \le \frac{1}{2}\pi$ is $\frac{1}{4}\pi(\pi^2 - 4)$.

### Advanced

**1** The equation $x^2 + y^2 = 1$ represents the circle with centre the origin and radius 1 unit. By considering an approximate region of the circle, or otherwise, show that

$$\int_0^1 \sqrt{1 - x^2}\, dx = \tfrac{1}{4}\pi.$$

The diagram shows the circle with equation $x^2 + (y-1)^2 = 1$, and the region $R$ which is bounded by the circle, the $x$-axis, and the line $x = 1$. Show that the volume of the solid formed when $R$ is rotated through $360°$ about the $x$-axis may be expressed as

$$\pi \int_0^1 [2 - x^2 - \sqrt{1 - x^2}]\,dx$$

Hence find this volume, giving your answer in terms of $\pi$.

[OCR (Cambridge), 1991]

**2**

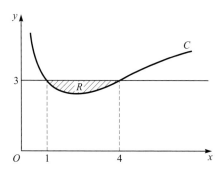

The diagram shows the region $R$ in the first quadrant bounded by the curve $C$ with equation $y = \sqrt{x} + \dfrac{2}{\sqrt{x}}$ and the line $y = 3$. The line and the curve intersect at the points $(1, 3)$ and $(4, 3)$. Calculate the exact area of $R$. Write down the equation of the curve obtained when $C$ is translated by 3 units in the negative $y$-direction.

Hence, or otherwise, show that the volume of the solid formed when $R$ is rotated completely about the line $y = 3$ is given by

$$\pi \int_1^4 \left( x - 6\sqrt{x} + 13 - \frac{12}{\sqrt{x}} + \frac{4}{x} \right) dx$$

and evaluate this integral exactly.

[OCR (Cambridge), 1994]

**3**   The density of population, $p$ people per square kilometre, $x$ km from the centre of a city is given by

$$p = 500(8 - x) \quad (0 \le x \le 8)$$
$$0 \qquad\qquad (x > 8)$$

Calculate the population of the city.

**4**

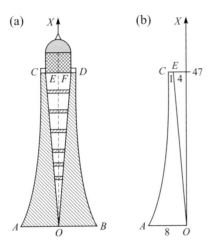

(a)    (b)

Diagram (a) shows the cross-section of a lighthouse of the stone masonry type, built of stone of uniform density $\rho\,\mathrm{kg\,m^{-3}}$. It has base diameter of 16 m at $AB$, narrowing down to a diameter of 10 m at $CD$, 47 metres above $AB$. If the external radius $r$ metres decreases exponentially with the height $x$ metres above $AB$ (i.e. $r = k\mathrm{e}^{-\lambda x}$), state the value of $k$ and show that $\lambda \approx 0.01$.

The interior is of the form of a cone with a vertex $O$ and the base diameter $EF$ of the cone is 8 metres. Show, by rotating the area $AOEC$ (see diagram (b)) through $360°$ about the axis $OX$, that the volume of stone needed to build the main body of the lighthouse is given by

$$\pi \int_0^{47} \left[ 64\mathrm{e}^{-0.02x} - \left(\frac{4x}{47}\right)^2 \right] \mathrm{d}x$$

Evaluate this integral.
[OCR (SMP), 1987]

**5** (a) Find $\displaystyle\int_0^{\frac{1}{2}} \frac{\mathrm{d}x}{(x - \frac{1}{2})^2 + \frac{3}{4}}$.

(b) Express $\dfrac{1}{1 + x^3}$ in the form $\dfrac{A}{1 + x} + \dfrac{Bx + C}{x^2 - x + 1}$.

(c) By expressing your value for $Bx + C$ in the form $p(2x - 1) + q$, evaluate

$$\int_0^{\frac{1}{2}} \frac{\mathrm{d}x}{1 + x^3}$$

(d) A small step is made in the shape obtained by rotating the graph

$$f(x) = \frac{1}{\sqrt{1+x^3}}$$ between $x = 0$ and $x = \frac{1}{2}$ through $360°$ about the

x-axis. Sketch the graph of $f(x)$ and find the volume of the step.

**6**

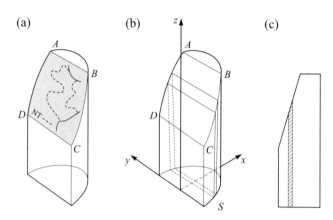

(a)    (b)    (c)

Using suitable substitutions, or otherwise, evaluate

$$I_1 = \int_0^{2.5} \sqrt{25 - x^2}\, dx$$

and

$$I_2 = \int_0^{2.5} x\sqrt{25 - x^2}\, dx$$

A nature-trail map is inscribed on the plane face $ABCD$ of the solid shown in diagrams (a), (b) and (c). In (b), $S$ is that part of the horizontal circle in the $x$, $y$ plane with equation $x^2 + y^2 = 25$ for which $x > 0$. The solid consists of the part of the right circular half-cylinder with base $S$ and axis vertical that lies below the plane $z = 10 + 4x$ for $0 \leq x \leq 2.5$ and below the plane $z = 20$ for $2.5 \leq x \leq 5$.

(i) Show that the volume of the part of the solid cut off by the vertical plane through $AB$ for which $x > 2.5$ is given by $250\pi - 40I_1$.

(ii) By considering the element sketched in (b), with side view shaded in (c), show that the volume of the other part of the solid is given by $20I_1 + 8I_2$. Hence show that the volume of the complete solid is approximately 663 cubic units.

[OCR (SMP), 1991]

**7** A viscous liquid flows through a tube of circular cross-section, radius 4 cm. The speed $v$ of the liquid $r$ cm from the centre is given by $v = 0.2(16 - r^2)\,\text{cm s}^{-1}$. By considering the flow through an annulus of radius $r$ cm and thickness $\delta r$, find the volume of liquid that flows through the tube in one hour.

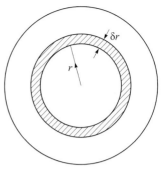

**8** A uniform solid right circular cylinder of radius $a$ and height $2a$ stands on a horizontal plane. Rectangular coordinate axes $Ox$, $Oy$ are taken in the plane of the base, with $O$ at the centre of the base. The cylinder is cut into two equal parts by the plane which passes through the line $x = -a$ and makes an angle of $45°$ with the horizontal. Justify the formula

$$\int_{-a}^{a} 2(x + a)\sqrt{a^2 - x^2}\,\mathrm{d}x$$

for the volume of the lower half, and verify by calculation of the integral that the volume is $\pi a^3$.
[OCR (Cambridge)]

**9** If $\dfrac{\mathrm{d}}{\mathrm{d}x}[(A \sin \beta x - B \cos \beta x)\mathrm{e}^{-\alpha x}] = \mathrm{e}^{-\alpha x} \cos \beta x$, ]express $A$ and $B$ in terms of the constants $\alpha$ and $\beta$.

For purposes of streamlining, a capsule is constructed so that it is bounded by the surface of revolution obtained by rotating the curve $y = \mathrm{e}^{-x} \sin x\, (0 \leq x \leq \pi)$, about the axis of $x$. Show that a good approximation to the volume of the capsule is $\frac{1}{8}\pi$.
[OCR (Cambridge), 1968]

**10** A spherical planet of radius $a$ has a variable density f$(r)$ which depends only on the distance $r$ from the planet's centre. Show that the average density of the planet is

$$3 \int_0^1 t^2 \mathrm{f}(at)\,\mathrm{d}t$$

Find the average density correct to two significant figures in each of the three cases:

(i) $\mathrm{f}(r) = \exp\left[\left(-\dfrac{r}{a}\right)^3\right]$, where $\exp(x)$ denotes $\mathrm{e}^x$

(ii) $\mathrm{f}(r) = \exp\left(-\dfrac{r}{a}\right)$

(iii) $f(r) = \dfrac{a^2 r}{(a+r)^3}$

[OCR (Cambridge), 1970]

## Revision

**1**  Find the volume of the solid formed when the area between the curve
$y = \dfrac{1}{x-1}$ for $2 \leq x \leq 5$ and the $x$-axis is rotated through $360°$ about the
$x$-axis.

**2**  The part of the curve $x^2 y = x^4 + 4$ between the ordinates $x = 1$ and
$x = 2$ is rotated through $360°$ about the $x$-axis. Calculate the volume
generated.

**3**  A cone is formed by rotating the area between the line $y = \dfrac{r}{h}x$, the $x$-axis
and the line $x = h$ through $360°$ about the $x$-axis. Find the volume of the
cone.

**4**  The inner surface of a vessel is formed by rotating the curve $x^2 = y - 3$
through $360°$ about the $y$-axis. Show that, if the vessel contains liquid to
a depth $h$ cm, the volume of liquid is $\frac{1}{2}\pi h^2$ cm$^3$.

**5**  Find the volume of the solid formed by rotating the area between
$y = 2\sqrt{x}$, the $y$-axis, $2 \leq 4 \leq 4$, through $360°$ about the $y$-axis.

**6**  Find the capacity of a container which is formed by rotating the curve
$y = x^3 + \frac{1}{2}$, between $y = 1\frac{1}{2}$ and $y = 8\frac{1}{2}$, through $360°$ about the $y$-axis.

**7**  Find the volume generated when the region between the curve
$y = \ln(1 + x)$ for $0 \leq y \leq 3$ and the $x$- and $y$-axes is rotated through
$360°$ about the $y$-axis.

**8**  Sketch the curves $y = \frac{1}{4}x^2$ and $y = \frac{1}{5}(x^2 + 4)$. The area between the two
curves is rotated through $360°$ about the
$y$-axis. Find the volume of the material
used to make the bowl.

**9**  A yoghurt container has a circular cross-
sectional area. Its height is $7$ cm and the
radii of its base and top are $3$ cm and $5$ cm
respectively. At height $h$ cm above the
base, the radius is $r$ cm.

(a)  Express $r$ in terms of $h$.
(b)  Use integration to calculate the
volume of the container.

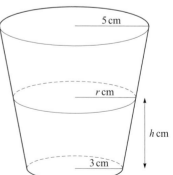

**10** The region enclosed by the curve $y = (b/a)\sqrt{a^2 - x^2}$ and the lines $y = 0$, $x = 0$, $x = \frac{1}{2}a$ is rotated through $360°$ about the $x$-axis. Show that the volume of the solid of revolution is $\frac{11}{24}\pi ab^2$.

**11** The diagram shows a container whose height is $\pi$ metres and whose internal cross-sectional area is given by $A = 12 - 3\cos y$, where $y$ is measured in metres from half-way up the container. By considering a thin slice of thickness $\delta y$, at a height $y$ from the centre, find the capacity of the container.

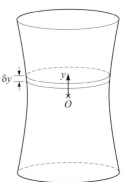

**12** Oil flows through a horizontal pipeline of radius 20 cm. Because of its viscosity, it flows faster down the middle of the pipe than it does near the wall. At a distance $r$ cm from the axis of the pipe the speed of flow is $(200 - \frac{1}{2}r^2)$ cm s$^{-1}$. The figure shows a cross-section of the pipe, looking along the axis of flow; taking the area of the shaded region to be approximately $2\pi r \delta r$ cm$^2$, write in the form of an integral the total volume rate of flow of oil down the pipe, and evalute this numerically in cm$^3$ s$^{-1}$ correct to two significant figures.
[SMP/O&C]

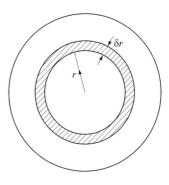

# 10
# Numerical methods

## 10.1    Absolute and relative errors; $\delta y \approx (dy/dx)\delta x$

> **Relative error** in $x$, $r_x = \dfrac{e_x}{x}$, where $e_x$ is the absolute error in $x$.
>
> **Percentage error** in $x = 100 \times$ relative error
>
> If $y = f(x)$, the error in $y$, $\delta y$, corresponding to a small error $\delta x$ in $x$ is given by $\delta y \approx \dfrac{dy}{dx}\delta x$.

### Basic

**1**   Express the following to two decimal places.

(a)  30.5689       (b)  1.2835       (c)  2.801
(d)  0.333 33      (e)  28.5         (f)  2.2349

**2**   Express the following to three significant figures.

(a)  1.367         (b)  201.51             (c)  0.068 425
(d)  1.217 217     (e)  $4.605 \times 10^{-8}$   (f)  0.999 99

**3**   The following measurements are given to the nearest centimetre. For each measurement give the minimum and maximum possible value.

(a)  57 cm     (b)  40 cm     (c)  128 cm

**4**   State the minimum and maximum values for the following, given that they are recorded to the nearest millimetre.

(a)  248 mm    (b)  72.6 cm    (c)  1.5 cm
(d)  3.762 m   (e)  4.500 m    (f)  100 cm

**5**   State the absolute error in each of the following, assuming they are recorded to the given degree of accuracy.

(a)  921 (to the nearest whole number)
(b)  3500 (to the nearest hundred)
(c)  3500 (to three significant figures)
(d)  6.176 (to three decimal places)

**6** The following numbers are recorded to the given accuracy and their absolute error is given. Give the range of values possible for each number, expressing your answers in the form $l \leq A < u$.

(a) $A = 3\,\mathrm{m}$    (abs. error 10 cm)
(b) $A = 50\,\mathrm{kg}$    (abs. error 2 kg)
(c) $A = 8.5\,\mathrm{cm}^2$    (abs. error $0.05\,\mathrm{cm}^2$)

**7** $A = 5.6\,\mathrm{cm}$ and $b = 3.8\,\mathrm{cm}$ are both given to the nearest millimetre. Give the range of values possible for each of the following.

(a) $A$           (b) $B$           (c) $A + B$
(d) $A - B$       (e) $2A$          (f) $2A + B$

**8** Find the relative error in each of the following.

*(a) 5.8 seconds measured to the nearest tenth of a second
(b) 0.082 km measured to the nearest metre
(c) 32000 kg measured to the nearest tonne

**9** Find the percentage error in each of the following.

(a) 0.014 recorded to three decimal places
(b) 1 h 30 min recorded to the nearest minute
(c) 170 recorded to the nearest 10

**10** $P = 92\,\mathrm{mm}$ and $Q = 160\,\mathrm{mm}$ are given to the nearest millimetre. Find the minimum and maximum values for each of the following, giving your answer to four significant figures.

(a) $P \times Q$       (b) $\dfrac{P}{Q}$       (c) $P^2 + Q^2$

**\*11**

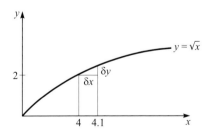

Given that $y = \sqrt{x}$,

(a) state the value of $\dfrac{\mathrm{d}y}{\mathrm{d}x}$ at $x = 4$,

(b) use the approximation $\delta y \approx \dfrac{\mathrm{d}y}{\mathrm{d}x}\delta x$ to find the value of $\delta y$ when $x = 4$ and $\delta x = 0.1$,

(c)  use the result of (b) to find an approximate value for $\sqrt{4.1}$, without using a calculator,

(d)  find the percentage error in your answer to (c).

**12** Using the approximation $\delta y \approx \dfrac{dy}{dx}\,\delta x$ find a value for $\delta y$ for the following functions at the given points.

(a)  $y = x^2 + 3x$ at $x = 1$, given $\delta x = 0.2$
(b)  $y = \sin x$ at $x = 0.3$, given $\delta x = 0.01$
(c)  $y = e^{2x}$ at $x = -0.5$, given $\delta x = 0.03$

## Intermediate

**1**  The following numbers are given correct to the number of significant figures shown. Evaluate the expressions giving the minimum and maximum values possible. Hence express the answers to the calculations to as many significant figures as possible.

(a)  $3.64 + 5.28$

(b)  $101.8 - 100.1$

(c)  $2 \times 10^{-3} \times 5.6 \times 10^4$

(d)  $\dfrac{31 \times 22}{0.4}$

**2**  The dimensions of a rectangle, measured to the nearest centimetre, are 5 cm and 7 cm. Find the greatest and least possible values for the area and for the perimeter.

**3**  The wording on a matchbox claims that it holds 150 matches but evidence suggests that this is only correct to the nearest 5 matches. If a single match measures 4.8 cm $\pm$ 1 mm, find:

(a)  the minimum length of a single matchbox, given that the matches are not allowed to lie diagonally in the box;
(b)  the maximum length covered if the matches from five matchboxes are laid end to end.

**4**  The ancient Egyptians used an approximate value of 3.16 for $\pi$. Archimedes calculated $\pi$ as $3\frac{10}{71}$. What is:

(a)  the absolute error in using the Egyptian value for $\pi$?
(b)  the percentage error in using Archimedes' value for $\pi$?

**5**  Copy and complete the following table giving absolute, relative and percentage errors. Give your answers to an appropriate degree of accuracy.

|  | Value | Abs. error | Rel. error | % error |
|---|---|---|---|---|
| $A$ | 3.1 | 0.05 | 0.016 | 1.6% |
| $B$ | 1.8 | 0.05 | | |
| $A + B$ | | | | |
| $2A$ | | | | |
| $B^2$ | | | | |
| $\dfrac{A}{B}$ | | | | |
| $\dfrac{1}{A - B}$ | | | | |

**\*6** (a) Show that $\dfrac{1}{\sqrt{2} - 1} = \sqrt{2} + 1$.

(b) Two students use the value of 1.41 as a three significant figure approximation to $\sqrt{2}$. The first calculates $\sqrt{2} + 1$ and the second calculates $\dfrac{1}{\sqrt{2} - 1}$.

   (i) What is the absolute error (to two significant figures) in using 1.41 as an approximation to $\sqrt{2}$.

   (ii) What is the absolute error in the first student's calculation? Give your answer to two significant figures.

   (iii) What is the relative error in the result of the second student's calculation? Give your answer to two significant figures.

   (iv) Which of the two calculations is more accurate?

**7** A circular pond has an island in the centre (see diagram). The outer radius of the pond is measured as 6.4 m and the radius of the island as 2.3 m. Both values are measured to an accuracy of one decimal place. Areas are calculated using the calculator value for $\pi$.

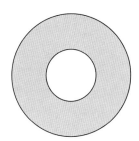

(a) What is the greatest possible area of the island?

(b) What is the least possible area of the pond (i.e. the shaded area in the diagram)?

**8** Various rational approximations for $\pi$ have been used over the centuries including the following:

The Rhind papyrus uses $\pi \approx \left(\frac{4}{3}\right)^4$.

A Chinese mathematician Tsu Ch'ung-chih used $\pi \approx \frac{355}{113}$.

A Hindu mathematician gave as his value $\pi \approx \frac{3927}{1250}$.
Many GCSE questions use the approximation $\pi \approx \frac{22}{7}$.
For each of these approximations, find to a suitable degree of accuracy:

(a)  the absolute error     (b)  the percentage error

**9**  A student attempts to calculate the height of a tree by measuring the angle of elevation of the top of the tree from a point $A$ on the ground approximately 30 m from the foot of the tree (see diagram). If the student measures the angle of elevation as 55°, correct to the nearest degree, and the distance of 30 m with an accuracy of ±1 m, find:

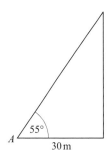

(a)  the maximum absolute error
(b)  the percentage error
in calculating the height of the tree. Give your answers correct to two significant figures.

**10**  The speed of a satellite in orbit changes from $v_1 = 6200\,\text{m s}^{-1}$ to $v_2 = 6400\,\text{m s}^{-1}$, where both speeds are correct to two significant figures.

(a)  What is the maximum absolute error in $v_2 - v_1$?

(b)  What is the maximum relative error in $\dfrac{v_2 - v_1}{v_1}$?

**11**  The formula for the variance $\sigma^2$ of a frequency distribution is

$$\sigma^2 = \frac{\sum fx^2}{n} - \left(\frac{\sum fx}{n}\right)^2$$

In a certain calculation $n = 50$, $\sum fx = 3782.49$ and $\sum fx^2 = 286\,160.838$.

(a)  Calculate $\sigma^2$ to an accuracy of four significant figures.
(b)  The values of $\sum fx$ and $\sum fx^2$ are now rounded to the nearest integer before calculation. Find the percentage error in $\sigma^2$.
(c)  Comment on your answers.

**12**  (a)  Solve the equation $2.50 \cos 2x = 2.10$ ($0° < x < 90°$).
(b)  Given that 2.50 and 2.10 are measurements which are accurate to two decimal places, find the range of possible values for $x$.
(c)  Use your answer to (b) to state the value of $x$ to an appropriate degree of accuracy.

**13**  Two numbers $x_1$ and $x_2$ have absolute errors $e_1$ and $e_2$ respectively. Find expressions for:

(a)  the maximum possible values for $x_1$ and $x_2$,
(b)  the maximum value for the product $x_1 x_2$,

  (c)  the absolute error in the product $x_1 x_2$,

  (d)  the relative error of the product $x_1 x_2$.

**14** (a)  Find the slope of the tangent to $y = x^2$ at $x = 1$.

    (b)  By assuming that the graph of $y = x^2$ is linear to the neighbourhood of $x = 1$, find $\delta y$, the change in $y$, for the given changes in $x$:

      (i)  $\delta x = 0.05$      (ii)  $\delta x = 0.01$      (iii)  $\delta x = 0.0001$

    (c)  Use your answers to (b) to find approximate values for $y$ at:

      (i)  $x = 1.05$      (ii)  $x = 1.01$      (iii)  $x = 1.0001$

    (d)  By calculating the true value of $x$ at these points, find the percentage error in your values to part (c) giving your answers to three significant figures.

**15** The volume, $V$, of a sphere of radius $r$ is given by the formula $V = \frac{4}{3}\pi r^3$.

    (a)  Explain why, if the radius is increased by a small amount $\delta r$, the volume increases by an amount $\delta V \approx 4\pi r^2 \delta r$.

    (b)  Show that $\dfrac{\mathrm{d}V}{V} = 3\dfrac{\delta r}{r}$.

    (c)  If the radius increases by 5%, what is the approximate percentage increase in volume?

**\*16** A liquid is dropped into a piece of absorbent paper and forms a circular disc. When the radius is 2 cm, the next drop increases the radius by 3 mm. Estimate the corresponding increase in area.

## Advanced

**1**

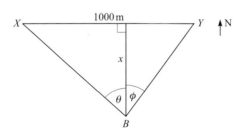

A navigator on a boat at $B$ sights two reference points $X$ and $Y$ which are known to be exactly 1000 m apart, with $Y$ due east of $X$. The angles $\theta$ and $\phi$, shown in the diagram, are measured, and the distance $x$ m from $B$ due north to the line $XY$ is calculated from the formula

$$x = \frac{1000}{\tan\theta + \tan\phi}$$

Given that the measured values of the angles are $\theta = 52°$ and $\phi = 15°$, each correct to the nearest degree,

(i)  find, correct to one decimal place, the greatest and least possible values of $x$,

(ii) estimate the greatest possible relative error in taking $x$ to be

$$\frac{1000}{\tan 52° + \tan 15°}$$

[OCR (Cambridge)]

2  A rectangular enclosure is to be made for a hamster. One side is wooden and the other three sides are formed from wire netting (see diagram). The width of the enclosure, $x$, is measured as 85 cm to the nearest centimetre. The amount of netting available is $3 \, \text{m} \pm 10 \, \text{cm}$. Calculate the maximum area.

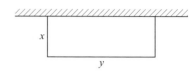

3  Solve the equation $2.7 + \cos 3.0x = 3.3$ in the range $0° < x < 90°$, assuming (a) the coefficients are exact, (b) each coefficient is accurate to two significant figures. Give your answer in an appropriate form.

4  [In this question you will need the following formulae: volume of cylinder $= \pi r^2 h$; curved surface area of cylinder $= 2\pi rh$; volume of sphere $= \frac{4}{3}\pi r^3$; surface area of sphere $= 4\pi r^2$.]

The figure shows a cross-section of a water container in the shape of a circular cylinder of height $h$ and radius $r$ with a hemisphere of radius $r$ at each end. Write down expressions for the volume $V$ and external surface area $S$ of the container in terms of $h$ and $r$.

Given that $V = 36\pi$, show that $S = \dfrac{72\pi}{r} + \dfrac{4\pi r^2}{3}$.

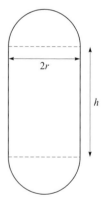

(a)  Find the minimum value of $S$.

(b)  It is decided to take $r = 4$. Show that any subsequent small increase $\delta r$ in $r$ results in an increase $\delta S$ in $S$ given by $\delta S = \dfrac{37\pi}{6}$.

(c)  A different radius results in the value of $S$ being 125. Show that one possible value of $r$ lies between 4.07 and 4.08.

Another possible value of $r$ lies between 2 and 3. Find its value correct to one decimal place.

[WJEC, 1994]

5  The side $a$ of a triangle $ABC$ is calculated from the formula

$$a^2 = b^2 + c^2 - 2bc \cos A$$

If small errors $\beta$ and $\gamma$ occur in $b$ and $c$ respectively, show that, if terms in $\beta^2$, $\gamma^2$ and $\beta\gamma$ are neglected, then the resulting small error $\alpha$ in $a$ is given approximately by

$$a\alpha = (b - c\cos A)\beta + (c - b\cos A)\gamma.$$

Find also an expression for the approximate error $\delta$ in the area of the triangle calculated from the formula $\Delta = \frac{1}{2}bc\sin A$.
If the sides $b$ and $c$ are given 42 mm and 24 mm respectively, each to the nearest mm, and $A$ is $60°$ exactly, calculate values for $a$ and $\Delta$, and estimate in each case the maximum error in the value obtained.
[OCR (Cambridge), 1972]

6  In order to calculate the volume $V$ and the total surface area $A$ of a solid cone of given semi-vertical angle $\theta$, the slant height $s$ of the cone is measured. If there is a small error $\sigma$ in the measurement of $s$, show that, if powers of $\sigma$ greater than the first are neglected, then the resulting error $v$ in $V$ is given approximately by

$$v = \pi s^2 \sigma \sin^2 \theta \cos \theta$$

Find also an expression for the approximate error $a$ in $A$.
Taking $s = 21$ mm and $\theta = 45°$, calculate the values of $V$ and $A$.
If the value of $s$ is only correct to the nearest mm, whereas $\theta$ is exact, estimate the maximum errors in your calculated values of $V$ and $A$.
[OCR (Cambridge), 1973]

7  (i)  Two quantities $P$ and $Q$ whose nominal values are $a$ and $b$ (both positive) are subject to small errors of maximum amount $\alpha$ and $\beta$ respectively (both positive) so that the value of $P$ lies between $a - \alpha$ and $a + \alpha$, and that of $Q$ lies between $b - \beta$ and $b + \beta$. Show that, to the first order in $\alpha$ and $\beta$, the maximum magnitudes of the errors in the values of the product $PQ$ and the quotient $P/Q$ are $b\alpha + a\beta$ and $\alpha/b + a\beta/b^2$ respectively.
   (ii)  If the size of angle $X$ is $\theta$ radian, subject to a small error $\phi$ radian, show that to the first order in $\phi$ the error in $\sin X$ is $\phi\cos\theta$.
   (iii)  $B$ and $C$ are the base angles of a triangle $ABC$. Use (i) and (ii) to estimate the maximum errors to which $\sin B\sin C$ and $\sin B/\sin C$ are liable when $B = 65° \pm 1'$ and $C = 55° \pm 1'$.
[OCR (Cambridge), 1975]

8  Given that $\alpha = 2.732$ to four significant figures, and no further information, prove that $\alpha^2$ is certainly greater than 7.461 and less than 7.467. It is given that the positive root $\beta$ of the equation $x^2 - 2x - 2 = 0$ is 2.732 to four significant figures. What limits can be placed on the value of $\beta^2$?
[OCR (Cambridge), 1974]

**9** If $n$ and $k$ are positive integers such that $n \geq 1$ and $1 \leq k \leq 9$ prove that $2k10^{n-1} - 1 > k10^{n-1}$ except for one exceptional pair of values of $n$ and $k$. Find these exceptional values.

The positive number $N$, when rounded to $p$ significant figures, gives a number $N_R$ which is correct to $q$ decimal places and has $k$ as its first significant digit. Show that

$$N_R - \tfrac{1}{2} \times 10^{-q} \leq N \leq N_R + \tfrac{1}{2} \times 10^{-q}$$

and deduce that, if $p > q$,

$$N \geq k10^{p-q-1} - \tfrac{1}{2} \times 10^{-q}$$

Hence show that

$$\frac{|N - N_R|}{N} < \frac{1}{k10^{p-1}}$$

for all values of $N$ except one.
[OCR (Cambridge), 1976]

**10** In a triangle $ABC$ the increments in the angles $A$, $B$ and $C$ resulting from a small increment $\delta a$ in the length of the side $a$ are respectively $\delta A$, $\delta B$ and $\delta C$. Show that, approximately, $\delta A : \delta B : \delta C = (-a) : b \cos C : c \cos B$.
[OCR (Cambridge), 1968]

## Revision

**1** Each of the following numbers is given to three significant figures.

(a) $1.25 \times 10^6$    (b) $50\,300$    (c) $0.006\,71$    (d) $960$    (e) $0.405$

In each case calculate:
   (i) the maximum possible value,
   (ii) the absolute error,
   (iii) the relative error.

**2** Three quantities $a$, $b$ and $c$ are measured. The results, rounded to three significant figures, were $a = 2.45$, $b = 5.72$, $c = 3.56$.
Find the upper and lower bounds of:

(a) $b - a$    (b) $\dfrac{c^2}{b - a}$

**3** A triangle $ABC$ has a right angle at $B$. The sides $AB$ and $BC$ are measured to the nearest millimetre and found to be $AB = 6.2\,\text{cm}$ and $BC = 12.9\,\text{cm}$. Calculate

(a) the minimum length of side $AC$,
(b) the maximum possible area of triangle $ABC$.

**4**  A trapezium has dimensions as shown. All measurements are correct to the nearest millimetre. Find:

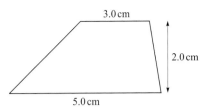

3.0 cm

2.0 cm

5.0 cm

   (a)  the maximum possible area of the trapezium,

   (b)  the relative error in the area,

   (c)  the percentage error in each of the dimensions given in the diagram.

**5**  $\sqrt{2}$ and $\sqrt{3}$ are recorded to one decimal place as 1.4 and 1.7.

   (a)  Using the correct values according to your calculator, express the absolute and relative errors for each of these approximations.

   (b)  Use these values of $\sqrt{2}$ and $\sqrt{3}$ to find approximations for $\sqrt{6}$ and $\sqrt{600}$.
      Calculate the relative errors for these new approximations.

**6**  Exbridge is measured as 20.3 miles south of Otting as the crow flies, and Whyford is 38.3 miles from Otting on a bearing of 050°. Both measurements are given to the nearest tenth of a mile and the bearing is correct to the nearest degree.
Calculate the greatest distance, as the crow flies, from Exbridge to Whyford.

**7**  A parachutist is in free fall. Her speed increases from $25\,\mathrm{m\,s}^{-1}$ to $40\,\mathrm{m\,s}^{-1}$, during which time she falls 70 m. All values are given to two significant figures. Use the formula $v^2 = u^2 + 2as$, where $u$ is the initial speed, $v$ the final speed and $s$ the distance fallen, to find the greatest and least possible values for her acceleration $a$ in $\mathrm{m\,s}^{-2}$, assuming that it stays constant for this period.

**8**  A right-angled triangle can be drawn with integer lengths 3 cm, 4 cm and 5 cm. A student attempts to draw this triangle, using a ruler for the two shorter sides and joining the end points to form the hypotenuse. His measurements are accurate to the nearest 2 mm.

   (a)  Assuming the right angle is accurately drawn, what is the largest possible value for the hypotenuse?

   (b)  Assuming the right angle can only be drawn accurately to the nearest degree, calculate the relative error in the length of the hypotenuse.

**9**  Children's wooden cuboid blocks are manufactured with dimensions 16 cm × 8 cm × 4 cm. The dimensions are accurate to the nearest tenth of a millimetre.

   (a)  Calculate the minimum volume of a block.

(b)  Six blocks are placed on top of each other. Calculate their
(i) minimum height, (ii) maximum height.

**10** When $x$ is small then $\dfrac{1}{1-x}$ can be approximated by $1+x+x^2$.

Find the percentage error involved in this approximation when:

(a)  $x = 0.1$      (b)  $x = 0.2$      (c)  $x = 0.5$

**11** (a)  If $y = \sin x$ explain why the error, $\delta y$, resulting from a small error, $\delta x$
in $x$, is given by $\delta y \approx \cos x \, \delta x$
(b)  The absolute error in measuring the angle $x$ is 0.05 radians.
Calculate the absolute error in $y = \sin x$ at the points:

(i)  $x = 0.5$      (ii)  $x = 0.6$      (iii)  $x = 1$      (iv)  $x = 1.2$

**12** The distance, $x$ metres, at which an amplifier of power $P$ watts is audible,
is given by the formula $x = 50\sqrt{P}$. If the power is increased by a small
amount $\delta P$, the audible distance is increased by $\delta x$.

(a)  Express $\delta x$ in terms of $P$ and $\delta P$.

(b)  Hence show that $\dfrac{\delta x}{x} \approx \dfrac{\delta P}{2P}$.

(c)  If the power is increased by 3%, by what percentage is the audible
distance increased.

## 10.2     Locating roots of equations by sign changes; simple iterative methods including Newton–Raphson, bisection method, $x_n = g(x_{n-1})$; failure of iterative methods; cobweb and staircase diagrams

Newton–Raphson formula for solving $f(x) = 0$,

$$x_{n+1} = x_n - \frac{f(x_n)}{f'(x_n)}$$

### Basic

In this exercise, give answers to three decimal places unless stated otherwise.

**1**  Evaluate $f(x) = x^4 - 7x^2 + 3x + 4$ for integer values of $x$ from $-3$ to 3.
Use your table to give integer bounds for the zeros of the function.

**2**  Show that f($x$) changes sign between $n$ and $n+1$ for the following functions.

(a)  $f(x) = 2x^3 - 5x + 1$,   $n = 1$
(b)  $f(x) = x^3 + x + 8$,   $n = -2$
(c)  $f(x) = 3 - 12x - 4x^2$,   $n = 0$

**3**  Sketch pairs of graphs you could use to solve the following equations. Use your graphs to state the interval(s) containing the roots.

(a)  $9 - x^2 = 2^x$     (b)  $x^3 = x^2 - 4$     (c)  $\dfrac{1}{x^2} = x - 5$     (d)  $x3^x = 1$

**4**  A root of $x^3 - 3x + 7 = 0$ lies in the interval $[-3, -2]$.
(a)  Evaluate $x^3 - 3x + 7$ at $x = -3, -2.5, -2$ and hence give an interval of width 0.5 which contains the root.
(b)  Use the bisection method once more to find a smaller interval which contains the root.

**5**  For each of the following,
(i)  find all the intervals containing the solutions,
(ii)  use a decimal search to find the solutions to two decimal places.

*(a)  $x^3 + 3x^2 - 7 = 0$     (b)  $x^2 + 2^x - 9 = 0$     (c)  $2x + \dfrac{1}{x^2} - 9 = 0$

**6**  Draw a sketch of the graph of $y = \ln(1 + x^2) - 2$. From your graph give integer bounds for the roots of the equation $\ln(1 + x^2) - 2 = 0$. Use a decimal search to find the roots of the equation to one decimal place.

**7**  Use simple iteration with the given starting values to find three more approximations to the solution of the given equations.

(a)  $x_{n+1} = \sqrt{\dfrac{3x_n}{5}}$,   $x_1 = 1$

(b)  $x_{n+1} = \sqrt{\dfrac{200}{x_n}}$,   $x_1 = 3$

(c)  $x_{n+1} = \sqrt[3]{x_n + 5}$,   $x_1 = 2$

**8**  The cube root button on a calculator is not working and an iterative method is to be used to find the cube root of 60.

*(a)  The iteration $x_{n+1} = \sqrt{\sqrt{60x_n}}$ can be used to solve this problem. Show how it can be obtained.
(b)  Give a value for the closest integer to the solution, $x_1$.

(c)  Use this iteration, with starting value $x_1$ and showing all intermediate values, to find the cube root of 60.

9  (a)  Show that $x^3 - 3x^2 - 2 = 0$ can be rearranged to give the following iterative formulae.

*(i)  $x_{n+1} = \sqrt[3]{3x_n^2 + 2}$ 　　　　(ii)  $x_{n+1} = \dfrac{2}{x_n^2 - 3x_n}$

(iii)  $x_{n+1} = \sqrt{\dfrac{x_n^3 - 2}{3}}$ 　　　　(iv)  $x_{n+1} = 3 + \dfrac{2}{x_n^2}$

(b)  For each iteration, use $x_1 = 4$ as a starting value and calculate at least five new values. Comment on your answers.

10  The Newton—Raphson method uses the iteration $x_{n+1} = x_n - \dfrac{f(x_n)}{f'(x_n)}$

to find solutions to $f(x) = 0$. Find expressions for $x_{n+1}$ for the following functions.

*(a)  $f(x) = 2x^3 - 5x + 1$
(b)  $f(x) = x^3 + x + 8$
(c)  $f(x) = 2\sin x - x$

11  Use the Newton–Raphson iteration formulae from question 10 to find three further approximations to $f(x) = 0$ using the given starting value $x_1$.

(a)  $f(x) = 2x^3 - 5x + 1,$ 　　$x_1 = 1$
(b)  $f(x) = x^3 + x + 8,$ 　　　$x_1 = -2$
(c)  $f(x) = 2\sin x - x,$ 　　　$x_1 = 2$

12  Use Newton–Raphson iteration to find the roots of $x^2 - 3.6x + 1.7 = 0$.

## Intermediate

1  Sketch graphs of $y = 5\sin \tfrac{1}{2}x$ and $y = x^2$ on the same axes. Find integer bounds for the non-zero solution to $5\sin \tfrac{1}{2}x = x^2$.

2  Evaluate $f(x) = \cos 2x - x^2$ for $-2 \le x \le 2$ where $x$ is a natural number. Show from sign changes that $f(x) = 0$ has solutions in the intervals $[-1, 0]$ and $[0, 1]$. (Remember to use radian mode.)

3  Use a graphical method to find a first approximation $x_1$ to the root of the following equations, where $x_1$ is the closest integer which is less than the root.

(a)  $e^x = 6 - 2x$
(b)  $x^2 - 2x = \ln(1 + x)$
(c)  $\sin(\tfrac{1}{4}\pi - x) = x + 1$

**4** (a) Find consecutive integer bounds for the solution of $\ln x + x = 0$.
   (b) Use the bisection method to find an interval of width 0.125 which contains this root.

**5** The function f is defined by $f(x) = \dfrac{4}{x+2} - e^x$ for $x \in \mathbb{R}$, $x \neq -2$

   (a) Find $f(0)$ and $f(1)$ and explain why this shows that there is a solution to $f(x) = 0$ between 0 and 1.
   (b) Use a decimal search, showing all the stages in your working, to find an interval of width 0.1 which contains the solution to $f(x) = 0$.

**6** A rectangle which is believed to have artistically pleasing dimensions is known as the **golden rectangle**. The lengths of its sides are in the ratio $\phi : 1$, where $\phi$ is known as the **golden ratio**.
A golden rectangle can be split up into two pieces: a square and another golden rectangle.

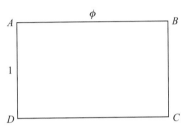

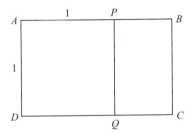

   *(a) Using the similarity of rectangles $ABCD$ and $PBCQ$, show that
   $$\phi^2 - \phi = 1.$$
   (b) Show how the iteration
   $\phi_{n+1} = \sqrt{1 + \phi_n}$ may be obtained from (a).
   (c) Taking $\phi_1 = 1.5$ as a first approximation, find a value for the golden ratio correct to three decimal places.

**\*7** On the same axes, sketch the graphs of $y = 0.5 \cos x$ and $y = x$ for $-\pi/6 \le x \le \pi/2$.
Indicate on your graph where the solution to $x = 0.5 \cos x$ lies.
Using $x_1 = 1$ as a first approximation, find $x_2$ and $x_3$ to two decimal places using the simple iteration $x_{n+1} = 0.5 \cos x_n$.
Mark $x_1$, $x_2$ and $x_3$ on your graph and draw a cobweb diagram to illustrate the iteration.

**8** Sketch $y = x$ and $y = 2.5 \cos x$ on the same axes. Use simple iteration with $x_1 = 1$ to find the three further approximations to $x = 2.5 \cos x$.
Draw a cobweb diagram to explain why this iteration fails to converge.

**\*9** Using Newton–Raphson iteration, find, correct to three significant figures, the root of the equation $0.5 \sin 2x + x = \frac{1}{4}\pi$.

**10** The cubic equation $x^3 - 3x - 1 = 0$ has three zeros. Use Newton–Raphson iteration with different starting values to find all three roots correct to two decimal places. Show that the sum of the roots is equal to zero.

**11** A function is defined by $f(x) = x \sin 2x$, $x > 0$. A graph of this function shows that there is a local maximum close to $x = 1$.

  (a) Differentiate this function and obtain an equation which can be used to find this local maximum.
  (b) Use a suitable numerical method to find the value of $x$ at which this maximum occurs, to three significant figures.

**12** Newton–Raphson iteration is to be used to solve the equation $x^3 + ax + b = 0$.

  (a) Find $a$ and $b$ if the iterative formula is given by

$$x_{n+1} = \frac{2x_n^3 + 5}{3x_n^2 + 2}$$

  (b) Using your values for $a$ and $b$, sketch the graph of the cubic and use your graph to find a first approximation to the root.
  (c) Apply the Newton–Raphson method to obtain a solution to the cubic correct to three decimal places.

**13** (a) Show that the iterative formula $x_{n+1} = x_n(2 - ax_n)$ is a rearrangement of the equation $x = \frac{1}{a}$ where $a$ is a constant.
  (b) By taking $a = 3$ and $x_1 = 0.5$, find $x_2$, $x_3$ and $x_4$.

**14** (a) Show that the equation $x^6 + 3x^2 - 7 = 0$ has a root in the interval $[1, 2]$.
  (b) Find an iteration of the form $x_{n+1} = (ax_n^2 + b)^{1/c}$ which can be used to solve the equation.
  (c) Find a solution to the equation which is accurate to two significant figures.

**15** A chord $PQ$ of a circle, radius $r$, subtends an angle $\theta$ at the centre.

  (a) Show that the area of the minor segment cut off by $PQ$ is $\frac{1}{2}r^2(\theta - \sin\theta)$.
  (b) If the shaded area is $\frac{1}{3}$ of the area of the circle, use Newton–Raphson's method to find the value of $\theta$. Give your answer in radians.

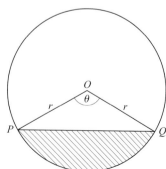

**16** Show that $f(x) = \dfrac{2x - 1}{5 - x^2}$ changes sign in the intervals $[-3, -2]$, $[0, 1]$ and $[2, 3]$.

Show, with the aid of a sketch, that $f(x) = 0$ actually has only one solution.

## Advanced

**1** Mavis wants to buy a computer originally advertised at £400, so she starts to do a paper round. She puts a fixed amount of her earnings each week into a savings account, which with interest produces *total* savings after $t$ weeks of approximately £$2500(e^{0.002t} - 1)$.

Meanwhile the price of the computer drops by an average of £2 a week. Find whether she will have saved enough to buy the computer after 50 weeks.

Now take the formula for her savings to be exact, and assume that the price falls by exactly £2 a week. Find an equation for the number of weeks she will need to work before she has enough money to buy the computer. Show that this equation can be put into the form

$$t = a \ln (b - ct)$$

where $a$, $b$ and $c$ are numbers. By carrying out 5 steps of the iteration

$$t_{n+1} = a \ln (b - ct_n)$$

starting with the first approximation $t_0 = 50$, find the solution of this equation, rounding up your answer to the next highest integer.
[OCR (O&C)]

**2** The figure illustrates a cross-section of a circular tunnel of radius 5 metres. $AB$ is a chord of length $2x$ metres. Because of drainage, the area of the minor segment defined by $AB$ must be $\frac{1}{10}$ of the area of the circle.

Show that $2.5\pi = 25 \arcsin(x/5) - x\sqrt{25 - x^2}$.

Show that this equation may be written in the form
$$x = 5 \sin \left[ \frac{\pi}{10} + \frac{x}{25} \sqrt{25 - x^2} \right]$$

By using an iterative method based on this formula, or otherwise, find $x$ correct to three significant figures.
[OCR (O&C), 1995]

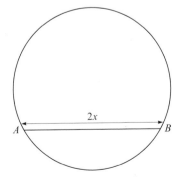

**3** On the same diagram sketch the curves with equations

(i) $y^2 = 9x$    (ii) $y = x^2(1 + x)$

clearly labelling each curve.

Deduce that the equation $x^3(1 + x)^2 - 9 = 0$ has exactly one real root.

Denoting this root by $\alpha$, find an integer $n$ such that $n < \alpha < n + 1$, and, taking $n$ as a first approximation, use the Newton–Raphson method to find a second approximation to $\alpha$, giving two places of decimals in your answer.

[OCR (Cambridge), 1986]

**4**   A curve $C$ has equation $y = \dfrac{\sin x}{x}$, where $x > 0$. Show that the $x$-coordinates of all turning points of $C$ satisfy the equation $x = \tan x$. By considering the graphs of $y = x$ and $y = \tan x$, or otherwise, show that the smallest positive root of the equation $x = \tan x$ lies between $\pi$ and $\frac{3}{2}\pi$. This smallest positive root is denoted by $\alpha$. An attempt to calculate the value of $\alpha$ is made by using the Newton–Raphson method applied to the equation $\tan x - x = 0$ with the initial approximation given by $x_0 = 4$. Calculate $x_1$ and $x_2$, and explain with the aid of a sketch why, in this case, $x_1$ is a worse approximation to $\alpha$ than $x_0$ is.

Use the Newton–Raphson method with a suitable initial approximation, or any other method, to find the value of $\alpha$, correct to three significant figures.

[OCR (Cambridge), 1988]

**5**   Find the coordinates of the stationary points on the graph of $y = x^3 + x^2$. Sketch the graph and hence write down the set of values for the constant $k$ for which the equation $x^3 + x^2 = k$ has three distinct real roots.

The positive root of the equation $x^3 + x^2 = 0.1$ is denoted by $\alpha$.

(i)   Find a first approximation to $\alpha$ by linear interpolation on the interval $0 \le x \le 1$.

(ii)  With the aid of a suitable figure, indicate why, in this case, linear interpolation does not give a good approximation to $\alpha$.

(iii) Find an alternative first approximation to $\alpha$ by using the fact that if $x$ is small then $x^3$ is negligible compared with $x^2$.

[OCR (Cambridge), 1991]

**6**   (a) By means of an appropriate sketch, find the range of values of $k$ for which $\sin x - kx = 0$ has exactly one solution between $x = 0$ and $x = \pi$.

(b) Show that, if $k = \alpha$, where $\alpha$ is positive and close to zero, then the equation has a solution close to $x = \pi$.

(c) By using the Newton–Raphson formula, show that a better approximation is $x = \pi(1 - \alpha + \alpha^2)$.

**7**   The positive integers $m$ and $n$ are such that $m > n$. Find, for the equation $f(x) = 0$, where $f(x) = x \cos x - 2n\pi$, the number of roots lying in the interval $0 \le x \le 2m\pi$.

Given that $N$ is an integer very much greater than $n$, show that a first approximation to the root of the equation $f(x) = 0$ in the interval $2N\pi \leq x \leq (2N+1)\pi$ is $(2N+\frac{1}{2})\pi$. By applying the Newton–Raphson method to the equation $f(x) = 0$, show that a second approximation is

$$(2N+\tfrac{1}{2})\pi - \frac{2n}{(2N+\frac{1}{2})}$$

[OCR (Cambridge), 1981]

**8**  A root of the equation $f(x) = 0$ is to be found by means of the iterative scheme

$$x_{n+1} = F(x_n)$$

together with the initial approximation $x_0$. Draw four separate diagrams to illustrate the convergence of the scheme if $\left|\dfrac{dF}{dx}\right| < 1$ and the divergence of the scheme if $\left|\dfrac{dF}{dx}\right| > 1$, the derivatives being evaluated for a value of $x$ near to $x_0$. Your diagrams should show, on the $x$-axis, the positions of $x_0$, $x_1$ and $x_2$. The equation $2x^3 + 2x^2 - 2x - 1 = 0$ has a real root, $X$, satisfying $-1 < X < 0$. Show that the iterative scheme defined by $x_{n+1} = x_n^3 + x_n^2 - \frac{1}{2}$, together with the initial approximation $x_0$, will converge to $X$ if $-1 < x_0 < \frac{1}{3}$.
[OCR (Cambridge), 1982]

**9**  By drawing appropriate graphs, or otherwise, show that the iteration defined by

$$x_{n+1} = \tfrac{1}{3}\left(2x_n + \frac{a}{x_n^2}\right), \quad a > 0, \ x_0 > 0$$

converges. Determine the limit, $L$, of $x_n$.
The error in the $n$th iterate is $\varepsilon_n$, so that $x_n = L + \varepsilon_n$. Show that $\varepsilon_{n+1} \approx a^{-1/3}\varepsilon_n^2$.
[OCR (Cambridge), 1985]

**10**  The relation $x_{n+1} = x_n - \dfrac{x_n^2 - 100}{2x_n}$ gives successive approximations to the root, 10, of the equation $x^2 - 100 = 0$.
The approximations are taken to start at the value $x_1 = 11$. Prove that $x_2, x_3, x_4, \ldots$ decrease steadily while always remaining greater than 10. Find a value of $n$ for which $x_n - 10$ is less than $20^{-15}$. (If you guess a solution, your statement must be fully verified.)
[OCR (Cambridge), 1972]

**Revision**

1   Find consecutive integer bounds for all the positive roots of the following equations.

(a)  $y = \sqrt{1-x} = 5 - x^2$
(b)  $y = 6 + 9x - 2x^2$
(c)  $y = x^2 - 5x + 3$
(d)  $y = xe^x + 3x^2 - 4$

2   Use Newton–Raphson iteration to find the solution to $\sin 2x = 5x + 1$. Give your answer to two significant figures.

3   The graph of $y = \dfrac{1}{x-2}$ and $y = 4x - x^2$ are illustrated below.

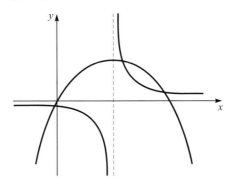

(a)  Give integer bounds for the solutions of the equation

$$\frac{1}{x-2} = 4x - x^2.$$

(b)  Show that the equation can be written as $x = \dfrac{1}{(x-2)(4-x)}$.

(c)  The iterative formula $x_{n+1} = \dfrac{1}{(x_n - 2)(4 - x_n)}$ leads to the negative solution.

Use the iteration to find this solution to three significant figures.

4   Show that the equation $2\sin\theta - \theta = 0$ has a root between $\theta = 1.6$ and $\theta = 2.8$. This interval is to be bisected in order to find a closer approximation to the root. Let the centre of the given interval, $\theta_1 = 2.2$, be the first approximation. Carry out further interval bisection to find $\theta_2$ and $\theta_3$.

5   The solution to $5\cos x = 10x$ is positive and close to $x = 0$. Use a decimal search to find the solution to two decimal places.

6   The following equations have solutions in the given intervals. Use a decimal search to find the solution to two decimal places.

(a)  $xe^x - 3x^2 + 3 = 0$,  $[-1, 0]$
(b)  $\sin^2 x - 0.3 = 0$,  $[5, 6]$

**7** Use the given iteration formulae and the starting values to find three further approximations.

(a) $x_{n+1} = \dfrac{2}{x_n - 3}$,     $x_1 = 0$

(b) $x_{n+1} = 0.5 \cos x_n$,     $x_1 = 1$
(c) $x_{n+1} = 0.1 \exp(x_n) - 3$,     $x_1 = -2$

**8** The solution to $3x e^x = 1$ is to be found using simple iteration. The equation is rearranged to give $x_{n+1} = \frac{1}{3} e^{-x_n}$.

(a) Carefully sketch the graphs of $y = x$ and $y = \frac{1}{3} e^{-x}$ on the same axes.
(b) Use the iteration with $x_1 = 1$ to find $x_2$, $x_3$ and $x_4$.
(c) Use these four values and a cobweb diagram on your graph to illustrate how this method works.

**9** Show that each equation has a root between $x = 3$ and $x = 4$ and find this root correct to two decimal places.

(a) $x^3 - 3x^2 - 2 = 0$
(b) $2x^2 - x^3 + 6x = 0$
(c) $2x^2 - 6.2x - 1.7 = 0$

**10** (a) Find two consecutive integers $a$ and $b$ which are lower and upper bounds for the root of the equation $2x^2 + 5 - x^3 = 0$.
(b) Sketch the graph of $y = 2x^2 + 5 - x^3$ and mark on your graph the two points $P$ and $Q$ corresponding to $x = a$ and $x = b$.
(c) The line through $P$ and $Q$ crosses the $x$-axis at $R$. Find the coordinates of $R$ and hence give an approximation to the root of the equation in (a).

**11** The Newton–Raphson method is to be used to find the roots of the quadratic equation $x^2 + 5x - 3 = 0$.

(a) Show that the Newton–Raphson formula leads to the iteration

$$x_{n+1} = \frac{x_n^2 + 3}{2x_n + 5}$$

(b) Use this iteration to find the roots correct to three decimal places. Show all intermediate calculations.

**12** (a) Copy and complete the table for the following function:
$y = x^3 - 8x + 5$

| $x$ | $-4$ | $-3$ | $-2$ | $-1$ | $0$ | $1$ | $2$ | $3$ | $4$ |
|---|---|---|---|---|---|---|---|---|---|
| $y$ | $-27$ | | | | $5$ | | | $8$ | |

(b) Three possible rearrangements of $y = 0$ are shown below.

(i)  $x = \frac{1}{8}(x^3 + 5)$

(ii)  $x = \frac{1}{8}(16x - x^3 - 5)$

(iii)  $x = \dfrac{2x^3 - 5}{3x^2 - 8}$

Only one of these rearrangements can be used to find all solutions to $y = 0$. Identify which one it is and use it to find all three solutions correct to three decimal places.

## 10.3    Numerical integration; solution of differential equations using numerical methods

> **Trapezium rule:**
>
> $$\int_{x_0}^{x_n} f(x)\,dx \approx \frac{1}{2}h\{y_0 + y_n + 2(y_1 + y_2 + \cdots + y_{n-1})\}$$
>
> **Simpson's rule:**
>
> $$\int_{x_0}^{x_n} f(x)\,dx \approx \frac{1}{3}h\{(y_0 + y_n) + 4(y_1 + y_3 + \cdots + y_{n-1})$$
> $$+ 2(y_2 + y_4 + \cdots + y_{n-2})\}$$
>
> where $n$ must be even.

### Basic

**1**  A curve passes through the following points.

| $x$ | 0.2 | 0.4 | 0.6 | 0.8 | 1.0 | 1.2 |
|---|---|---|---|---|---|---|
| $y$ | 3.20 | 3.39 | 3.56 | 3.72 | 3.84 | 3.93 |

Use the trapezium rule to estimate the area under the curve from $x = 0.2$ to $x = 1.2$.

**2**  Use the trapezium rule with five strips to estimate the area under the curve $y = \dfrac{2}{\sqrt{1 - 7x}}$ between $x = -1$ and $x = 0$.

Is your answer an underestimate or an overestimate?

3   Use the mid-ordinate rule to find an approximate value for the area under the curve between $x = 0$ and $x = 10$ which passes through the following points.

| $x$ | 1 | 3 | 5 | 7 | 9 |
|-----|-----|-----|-----|-----|-----|
| $y$ | 35.83 | 18.39 | 9.44 | 4.85 | 2.49 |

Plot these points and show on your graph how the mid-ordinate method works.

4   Use the mid-ordinate rule with four strips to estimate the area under the curve $y = 1/x^2$ from $x = 3$ to $x = 4$. Give your answer to three decimal places.

5   Use Simpson's rule with six strips to estimate $\displaystyle\int_0^3 \frac{1}{1 + x^2}\, dx$, giving your final answer correct to three significant figures.

*6   Use Simpson's rule with three ordinates to estimate the value of

$$\int_0^1 x \sin x\, dx$$

7   The area under a velocity–time graph represents the distance travelled. The speed of a car in the rush hour, given in $m\,s^{-1}$, is given at 10 second intervals as follows:

| $t$ s | 0 | 10 | 20 | 30 | 40 | 50 | 60 | 70 | 80 | 90 |
|-------|-----|-----|-----|-----|-----|-----|-----|-----|-----|-----|
| $v\,m\,s^{-1}$ | 12 | 10 | 0 | 5 | 2 | 8 | 10 | 6 | 8 | 3 |

Use the trapezium rule to estimate the distance travelled by the car during the 90 second period. Explain why your estimate may not be a very good one.

8   (a)   Use Simpson's rule to find an estimate for $\int_2^3 (x^4 + 3x - 1)\, dx$ using
        (i) two strips, (ii) four strips.
        Give your answers to three decimal places.
   (b)   Find the percentage error in each case.

9   The graph of $y = \cos 2x$ crosses the $x$-axis at $(\pi/4, 0)$. Use the trapezium rule with four strips to find an estimate for $\int_0^{\pi/4} \cos 2x\, dx$.
   Sketch the graph of $y = \cos 2x$ and shade in the area represented by your answer.

**10** The equation of the normal distribution in statistics is $y = \dfrac{1}{\sqrt{2\pi}}e^{-x^2/2}$.

Statistical tables give the area under this curve between $x = -1$ and $x = 1$ as approximately 0.68. Use a numerical method to confirm this value.

**11** A differential equation is given as $\dfrac{dy}{dx} = 0.2y$. A particular solution to this

equation passes through the point $(0, 1)$.
Using steps of 0.5 for $x$, estimate a value for $y$ at $x = 1$ by copying and completing the following table.

| $x$ | $y$ | $\delta x$ | $\dfrac{dy}{dx}$ | $\delta y$ |
|-----|-----|-----|-----|-----|
| 0 | 1 | 0.5 | 0.2 | 0.1 |
| 0.5 | 1.1 | 0.5 | | |
| 1 | | | | |

**\*12** A solution to the differential equation $\dfrac{dy}{dx} = x + y$ passes through the

point with coordinates $(2, 3)$. Use a numerical method with step sizes of 0.2 for $\delta x$ to find an approximation for $y$ at $x = 3$.

### Intermediate

**1** (a) Use the trapezium rule with four strips to estimate the area under $y = \sin x$ from $x = 0$ to $x = \frac{1}{2}\pi$, giving your answer to four significant figures.
  (b) Use algebraic integration to find the exact value of this area.
  (c) Find the relative error involved in using the trapezium method.

**2** The area between the curve $y = 4x - x^3$, the $x$-axis, $x = 0$ and $x = 2$ is to be calculated numerically using the trapezium rule with five strips.

  (a) Sketch the curve $y = 4x - x^3$, showing clearly where the zeros occur. Shade in the required area on your graph.
  (b) Copy and complete the table below.

| $x$ | 0 | 0.4 | 0.8 | 1.2 | 1.6 | 2 |
|-----|-----|-----|-----|-----|-----|-----|
| $y$ | | | | | | |

  (c) Apply the trapezium rule to find an approximation to the given area.
  (d) Use algebraic integration to find an exact value for $\int_0^2 (4x - x^3)\,dx$.
  (e) Show that the percentage error in the numerical value is 4%.

**3** (a) Sketch the graph of $f(x) = \sqrt{\sin x}$ for $0 \le x \le \pi$.
   (b) Complete the table below.

| $x$ | $\pi/12$ | $\pi/4$ | $5\pi/12$ |
|---|---|---|---|
| $\sqrt{\sin x}$ | | | |

   (c) Use the mid-ordinate rule to estimate:

   (i) $\displaystyle\int_0^{\pi/2} \sqrt{\sin x}\, dx$     (ii) $\displaystyle\int_0^{\pi} \sqrt{\sin x}\, dx$

**4** A water carafe with a circular cross-section is shown in the diagram and an estimate of its volume is required.
The total height of the carafe is 22 cm and its circumference, $C$, is measured at various heights and recorded as follows:

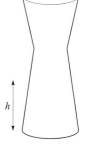

| $h$ cm | 1 | 3 | 5 | 7 | 9 | 11 | 13 | 15 | 17 | 19 | 21 |
|---|---|---|---|---|---|---|---|---|---|---|---|
| $C$ cm | 30 | 27.5 | 25 | 23 | 21.5 | 20 | 19 | 21 | 23 | 26 | 30 |

   (a) Calculate the cross-sectional area at each height.
   (b) State a suitable rule which may be used to determine an approximation to the volume of the carafe.
   (c) Assuming that the glass has negligible thickness, use your calculations to determine whether the carafe is big enough to hold a litre of water.

**5** Use Simpson's rule to find an estimate for $\int_0^2 \sqrt{4 - x^2}\, dx$ using
   (a) four strips     (b) eight strips

   The true value for this integral is $\pi$. Find the relative error in each of your two estimates.

**6** (a) Sketch the graph of $y = 3 + 2x - x^2$, clearly showing the points of intersection with the axes.
   (b) Find the area enclosed by the $x$-axis and the curve $y = 3 + 2x - x^2$ using Simpson's rule with:
   (i) two strips     (ii) four strips     (iii) eight strips

   Comment on your answers.

**\*7** An estimate for $\displaystyle\int_0^{\pi/2} \cos x\, dx$ is required. Use Simpson's rule with two strips to show that this estimate is $\frac{1}{12}\pi(1 + 2\sqrt{2})$.
Find the exact value using algebraic integration and find the percentage error in the estimate obtained using Simpson's rule.

**8** (a) Sketch the cubic $y = x^3 - 7x^2 + 12x$ showing where it crosses the $x$-axis.

(b) Use the mid-ordinate rule with strips of width 0.5 to find an estimate for the total area enclosed by the curve and the $x$-axis.

(c) Use your answer to find an estimate for $\int_0^4 (x^3 - 7x^2 + 12x)\,dx$.

**9** The solution to the differential equation $\dfrac{dy}{dx} = e^{-y}$ passes through the point with coordinates $(0, 0)$.

(a) Use a numerical method to find an estimate for $y$ when $x = 1$ using $\delta x = 0.5$.

(b) Verify that $y = \ln(1 + x)$ is the solution to the differential equation.

(c) Find the absolute error in your estimate for $y$ in (b).

**10** A piece of moulding is shown in the diagram. The moulding is 6 m long, the width $OC$ is 1.5 cm and the curved section from $A$ to $B$ has equation $y = e^{0.5x^2}$. Use the trapezium rule with six strips to estimate the area of the cross-section, $OABC$. Hence obtain an estimate for the volume of the moulding, giving your answer to two significant figures.

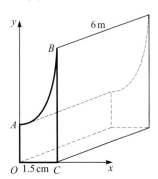

**11** During a 12 second interval along a motorway the speed of a car is recorded six times as follows.

The speed is measured in kilometres per hour and the time in seconds.

| $t$ s | 1 | 3 | 5 | 7 | 9 | 11 |
|---|---|---|---|---|---|---|
| $v$ km h$^{-1}$ | 100 | 105 | 108 | 113 | 112 | 104 |

Estimate, in metres, the distance covered during this 12 seconds of motion.

**12** A student wishes to compare the accuracy of the trapezium rule and Simpson's rule when estimating the area under a graph. The curve chosen is $y = 16 - x^4$ from $x = 0$ to $x = 2$ using four strips.

(a) Calculate this area using both methods, giving your answers to four significant figures.

(b) Find the exact value for the area using algebraic integration and comment on the accuracy of the two methods.

**13** A cup of coffee is served at a temperature of 90 °C in a room temperature of 20 °C.

(a) The coffee is left undrunk for the first 10 minutes. Sketch a graph which represents the temperature of the coffee during those 10 minutes.

(b) The rate of cooling of the coffee is given by the differential equation
$\dfrac{\mathrm{d}T}{\mathrm{d}t} = 4 - 0.2T$ where $t$ is the time in minutes and $T$ the temperature in °C.

Use a numerical method with step sizes of 2 minutes to estimate the temperature of the coffee after 10 minutes.

**14** A winner's rostrum is 20 cm high as shown in the diagram. It has a square cross-section and its width, $w$ cm, is measured at different heights and recorded:

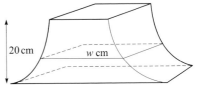

| $h$ cm | 1 | 3 | 5 | 7 | 9 | 11 | 13 | 15 | 17 | 19 |
|--------|----|----|----|----|----|----|----|----|----|----|
| $w$ cm | 80 | 70 | 61 | 53 | 46 | 40 | 36 | 33 | 31 | 30 |

Use these data to estimate the volume of the rostrum.

**15** An ornamental roof tile is shown in the diagram. It is symmetric about the vertical line through $B$ and the width $OD$ is 8 cm. The curved section $AB$ has equation $y = 0.1\sqrt{1 + x^6} + 4$. Use the mid-ordinate rule with four strips to find an estimate for the area of the whole tile.

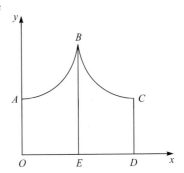

**16** A differential equation is given by

$$\frac{\mathrm{d}y}{\mathrm{d}x} = -\frac{9x}{16y}.$$

A curve satisfying this equation passes through (0, 3).

(a) Copy and complete the following table and hence find an estimate for $y$ when $x = 0.8$.

| $x$ | $y$ | $\delta x$ | $\dfrac{\mathrm{d}y}{\mathrm{d}x}$ | $\delta y$ |
|-----|-----|------------|------------------------------------|------------|
| 0 | 3 | 0.2 | 0 | 0 |
| 0.2 | 3 | 0.2 | | |
| 0.4 | | | | |
| 0.6 | | | | |
| 0.8 | | | | |

(b)  Show that the parametric equations $x = 4 \sin t$, $y = 3 \cos t$ represent a curve which passes through $(0, 3)$ and satisfies the differential equation $\dfrac{dy}{dx} = -\dfrac{9x}{16y}$.

(c)  Use the parametric equations in (b) to find the first positive value of $t$ corresponding to $x = 0.8$. Use this value to find $y$ corresponding to $x = 0.8$ and find the percentage errror in your answer to (a).

## Advanced

**1**   A solid metal object of uniform density $3.4 \times 10^3 \, \mathrm{kg\,m^{-3}}$ is in the form of a solid of revolution of length $2\,\mathrm{m}$. At a distance $x\,\mathrm{m}$ from one end, the radius is $y\,\mathrm{m}$. Values of $x$ and $y$ are given in the table.

| $x$ | 0 | 0.5 | 1.0 | 1.5 | 2.0 |
|-----|-----|-----|-----|-----|-----|
| $y$ | 0.4 | 0.7 | 0.9 | 1.0 | 0.6 |

Estimate the mass of the object.

**2**   $g(x)$ is an even function.
(a)  Use Simpson's rule to prove that $\int_{-0.5}^{0.5} g(x)\,dx \approx \frac{1}{3}\{g(0.5) + 2g(0)\}$ and deduce an approximation for $\int_0^{0.5} g(x)\,dx$.
(b)  Write down the corresponding expression for $\int_{-0.5}^{0.5} g(x)\,dx$ using the trapezium rule.

**3**   (a)  Find an exact expression for $\int_0^k e^{2x/k}\,dx$.

(b)  Use Simpson's rule to show that an approximate value of this integral is $\dfrac{k}{6}(1 + 4e + e^2)$.

(c)  By equating your answers to (a) and (b), find an approximate numerical value for e.
(d)  Show that the corresponding approximation found using the trapezium rule is e $= 3$.

**4**   If left undisturbed, the population $P$ of rats on an isolated island would increase at a rate of 3% of its current value every day. However, predators kill the rats at a rate of $1.2\sqrt{P}$ per day.
(a)  Express $\dfrac{dP}{dt}$ in terms of $P$, where $t$ is the time in days.
(b)  If when $t = 0$ the population is 2000 rats, use a step-by-step method, with step length 10, to estimate how it will change over the next 20 days.

(c) For what initial value of $P$ is the population stable? State what happens to $P$ if the population exceeds this.

5   $x$, $y$ and $t$ satisfy the simultaneous differential equations

$$\frac{\mathrm{d}x}{\mathrm{d}t} = x - y, \qquad \frac{\mathrm{d}y}{\mathrm{d}t} = 2x$$

If $x = 20$ and $y = 5$ when $t = 0$, use a step-by-step method, with step length 0.2, to estimate values for $x$ and $y$ when $t = 1$.

6   Verify that $\int \ln x \, \mathrm{d}x = x \ln x - x + c$, where $c$ is an arbitrary constant. Use the trapezium rule with trapezia of unit width to find an estimate for $\int_2^3 \ln x \, \mathrm{d}x$. Explain with the aid of a sketch why the trapezium rule underestimates the value of the integral in this case, and calculate, correct to one significant figure, the percentage error involved.

By again using trapezia of unit width, show that, when $n$ is a positive integer greater than 1, the trapezium rule approximation to $\int_2^{n+1} \ln x \, \mathrm{d}x$ is

$$\ln (n!) + \tfrac{1}{2} \ln \left( \frac{n+1}{2} \right)$$

[OCR (Cambridge), 1986]

7

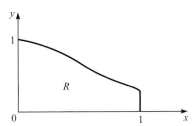

The diagram (not to scale) shows the region $R$ bounded by the axes, the curve $y = (x^2 + 1)^{-3/2}$ and the line $x = 1$. The integral

$$\int_0^1 (x^2 + 1)^{-3/2} \, \mathrm{d}x$$

is denoted by $I$.

(i) Use the trapezium rule, with ordinates at $x = 0$, $x = \tfrac{1}{2}$ and $x = 1$, to estimate the value of $I$, giving your answer correct to two significant figures.

(ii) Use the substitution $x = \tan \theta$ to show that $I = \tfrac{1}{2} \sqrt{2}$.

(iii) By using the trapezium rule, with the same ordinates as in part (i), or otherwise, estimate the volume of the solid formed when $R$ is rotated completely about the $x$-axis, giving your answer correct to two significant figures.

[OCR (Cambridge), 1989]

**8**  Establish the inequalities, when $0 \leq x \leq 1$,

$$2 \geq \sqrt{4 - x^2 + x^4} \geq \sqrt{4 - x^2} > 0$$

Deduce that

$$0.5 < \int_0^1 \frac{dx}{\sqrt{4 - x^2 + x^4}} < 0.524$$

Use Simpson's rule with four strips to evaluate the integral and verify that your answer satisfies the above inequalities.
[OCR (MEI), 1972]

**9**  Prove that $I \equiv \int_0^1 (1 - x^2)^{1/2} \, dx = \frac{1}{4}\pi$.
Obtain an estimate of the value of $I$ by using Simpson's rule with four intervals. Show geometrically that

$$I + \tfrac{1}{2} = 2 \int_0^{1/\sqrt{2}} (1 - x^2)^{1/2} \, dx$$

and, by applying Simpson's rule with four intervals to the integral

$$\int_0^{1/\sqrt{2}} (1 - x^2)^{1/2} \, dx$$

obtain a second estimate of the value of $I$.
Explain why the second method gives a better approximation than the first method to the value of $I$.
[OCR (MEI), 1973]

**10**  Determine constants $a$, $b$ and $c$ such that the numerical integration formula

$$\int_0^{2h} x^{1/2} F(x) \, dx \approx (2h)^{1/2} [aF(0) + bF(h) + cF(2h)]$$

is exact for all quadratic expressions $F(x)$.
Use your formula to evaluate $\int_0^4 x^{1/2}(3x^2 + 2x + 1) \, dx$ and check that your result is exact.
[OCR (Cambridge), 1982]

## Revision

**1**  Plot the following points on a graph and use the trapezium rule to estimate the area under the graph from $x = 0$ to $x = 10$.

| x | 0 | 1 | 2 | 3 | 4 | 5 | 6 | 7 | 8 | 9 | 10 |
|---|---|---|---|---|---|---|---|---|---|---|----|
| y | 14 | 12 | 10 | 8.3 | 6.6 | 5.3 | 4.2 | 3.4 | 3.1 | 3.3 | 4 |

Does your answer overestimate or underestimate the true area?

**2** Use the mid-ordinate rule with five strips to estimate the area enclosed by the curve $y = x^2 \sin(x + \frac{1}{2}\pi)$ and the $x$-axis from $x = 0$ to $x = 1$.

**3** (a) Find an estimate of $\int_{-2}^{2} e^{-x/5} \, dx$ using Simpson's rule with four strips.

    (b) Evaluate this integral precisely.

    (c) Find the percentage error involved in using Simpson's rule.

**4** (a) Sketch the curve $y = 24x + 6x^2 - 3x^3$ in the region $-4 \le x \le 6$.

    (b) Use the trapezium rule with strips of width 1 to find the total area enclosed by the $x$-axis and the curve $y = 24x + 6x^2 - 3x^3$.

**5** The table below represents the cross-sectional area of a tree trunk at various heights above the ground.

| $h$ m | 0.5 | 1.5 | 2.5 | 3.5 | 4.5 | 6.5 |
|-------|-----|-----|-----|-----|-----|-----|
| $A$ m$^2$ | 0.5 | 0.48 | 0.47 | 0.47 | 0.46 | 0.44 |

Use the mid-ordinate rule to estimate the volume of wood in the first 7 m of the tree trunk.

**6** (a) Taking step size 1, draw up a table of values for $y = ax(4 - x)$, where $a$ is a constant, from $x = 0$ to $x = 4$.

    Hence use Simpson's rule with four strips to show that the area enclosed by this curve is approximately $\dfrac{32a}{3}$.

    (b) Evaluate the integral $\int_0^4 ax(4 - x) \, dx$. Comment on your result.

**7** The rate of growth of a population is proportional to the size of the population and is described by the differential equation $\dfrac{dP}{dt} = 0.02P$, where $t$ is measured in years. Assuming the size of the population was 25 000 in 2000, use a step-by-step method to estimate the size of the population in the year 2030. Is your answer an underestimate or an overestimate?

**8** Use the trapezium rule with six ordinates to estimate $\int_0^1 \sqrt{x} \tan^{-1} x \, dx$.

**9** Sketch the graph of $y = \ln(2x + 1)$ and show on your diagram the area obtained by using the mid-ordinate rule, with three strips, to estimate the area under the graph from $x = 0$ to $x = 2$.

Calculate this area using the mid-ordinate rule and give your answers to three decimal places.

**10** The diagram shows a section of the

graph $y = \dfrac{x+1}{\sqrt{1+x+x^3}}$ from $x = 0$ to

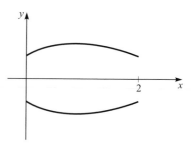

$x = 2$, together with its reflection in the
x-axis. Use Simpson's rule with intervals
of width 0.5 to find the volume generated
by rotating the graph about the x-axis.

**11** $x$ and $y$ are related according to the equation $\dfrac{dy}{dx} = e^{x+y}$ and when $x = 0$,

$y = 0$. Using a step size of 0.2, estimate the value of $y$ when $x = 1$.

**12 (a)** Use the trapezium rule, with step width 0.25, to estimate

$$\int_0^1 \frac{3}{1+x^2}\, dx,$$ giving your answer correct to four decimal places.

**(b)** Use direct integration to show that $\displaystyle\int_0^1 \frac{3}{1+x^2}\, dx = \frac{3}{4}\pi.$

**(c)** Find the percentage error in using the trapezium rule to estimate

$$\int_0^1 \frac{3}{1+x^2}\, dx$$

**(d)** What would be the percentage error in using the trapezium rule to

estimate $\displaystyle\int_0^1 \frac{30}{1+x^2}\, dx?$

# 11

# Proof

## 11.1 Use of mathematical symbols and language – $\Rightarrow$, $\Leftarrow$, $\Leftrightarrow$, if and only if, converses, necessary and sufficient conditions; construction of mathematical arguments; proof by contradiction and disproof by counter-example

### Basic

1  Prove that $\sin 120° = \sqrt{3}/2$.

*2  Use the identities for $\sin(A + B)$ and $\sin(A - B)$ to verify that
$$\sin(A + B) + \sin(A - B) \equiv 2 \sin A \cos B$$

*3  Show that the cube of an odd number is always odd. (Hint: write the number in the form $2r + 1$.)

4  Insert the correct conditional symbol ($\Rightarrow$, $\Leftarrow$, or $\Leftrightarrow$) to complete each of the following statements.

(a)  $2x - 1 = 0$ _____ $x = \frac{1}{2}$     (b)  $x^2 - 4 = 0$ _____ $x = 2$
(c)  $x = 3$ _____ $x^2 = 3x$     (d)  $x^3 = 1$ _____ $x = 1$

5  Find a counter-example to disprove the following statements.

(a)  The product of two consecutive integers is always bigger than their sum.
(b)  For any real number $x$, $x^2 > x$.

6  For each of the following statements:
(i)  state whether it is true or false,
(ii)  give the converse statement,
(iii)  state whether the converse is true or false.

(a)  $\tan x = \sqrt{3} \Rightarrow x = 60°$     (b)  $x^2 = 49 \Rightarrow x = 7$
(c)  $y = \ln x \Rightarrow \dfrac{dy}{dx} = \dfrac{1}{x}$     (d)  If $\cos x = 1$, then $\sin x = 0$.
(e)  In triangle $PQR$, $PQ = PR \Rightarrow \angle PQR = \angle PRQ$.

**7** Complete the following statements by inserting **if, only if** or **if and only if.**

(a) $x - 3 = 0$ _____ $x = 3$

(b) $x(x + 1) = 20$ _____ $x = 4$

(c) $x = 7$ _____ $x^2 - 49 = 0$

**8** Insert the correct conditional symbol ($\Rightarrow$, $\Leftarrow$, or $\Leftrightarrow$) to complete the following statements:

(a) $ABC$ is a right-angled triangle _____ the square of the hypotenuse is equal to the sum of the squares of the other two sides.

(b) $PQRS$ is a rhombus _____ the diagonals are perpendicular

(c) The volume of a given solid is $\frac{1}{3} \times$ base area $\times$ height _____ the solid is a cone.

**9** Insert the words **necessary, sufficient** or **necessary and sufficient** to complete the following statements.

(a) A _____ condition that $2(x - 3) > 6$ is that $x > 6$.

(b) A _____ condition that $4 - x < 0$ is that $x > 4$.

(c) A _____ condition that $x \geq 3$ is that $x^2 \geq 9$.

**10** Prove that $x^2 + ax + 4$ has no real roots when $|a| < 4$.

**11** What is wrong with the following argument that $2 = 1$?

Assume that $a = b$.

| | |
|---|---|
| Multiplying both sides by $a$ | $a^2 = ab$ |
| Subtract $b^2$ from both sides | $a^2 - b^2 = ab - b^2$ |
| Factorise | $(a + b)(a - b) = (a - b)b$ |
| Divide both sides by $a - b$ | $a + b = b$ |
| Let $a = b = 1$ | $2 = 1$ |

**\*12** (a) Use a method of proof by contradiction to show that $\sqrt{6}$ is irrational.

(b) If the method (a) is applied in an attempt to show that $\sqrt{4}$ is irrational, at what point does the proof break down?

## Intermediate

**1** Prove that $\sin 75° + \cos 75° = \sqrt{\frac{3}{2}}$.

**2** Prove that:

**\*(a)** a square number cannot have a last digit of 2, 3, 7 or 8,

(b) a cube number can have any last digit.

**3** What is wrong with each of the following arguments?

*(a) To prove that $1 - 2\cos^2\theta = 2\sin^2\theta - 1$:

| | |
|---|---|
| Assume that | $1 - 2\cos^2\theta = 2\sin^2\theta - 1$ |
| Add 1 to both sides | $2 - 2\cos^2\theta = 2\sin^2\theta$ |
| Add $2\cos^2\theta$ to both sides | $2 = 2\sin^2\theta + 2\cos^2\theta$ |
| Factorise | $2 = 2(\sin^2\theta + \cos^2\theta)$ |
| Since $\sin^2\theta + \cos^2\theta = 1$ | $2 = 2$, so the result is proved. |

(b) To prove that $\frac{1}{8} > \frac{1}{4}$:

| | |
|---|---|
| We know that | $3 > 2$ |
| Multiply both sides by $\log(\frac{1}{2})$ | $3\log(\frac{1}{2}) > 2\log(\frac{1}{2})$ |
| Using $p\log m = \log(m^p)$ | $\log(\frac{1}{2})^3 > \log(\frac{1}{2})^2$ |
| Removing logs | $(\frac{1}{2})^3 > (\frac{1}{2})^2$ |
| Hence | $\frac{1}{8} > \frac{1}{4}$ |

**4** Prove that:

(a) $\dfrac{\cos(A + B)}{\cos(A - B)} \equiv \dfrac{1 - \tan A \tan B}{1 + \tan A \tan B}$    (b) $\cot A - \cot B \equiv -\dfrac{\sin(A - B)}{\sin A \sin B}$

**5** Prove that the solution of the equation $ax^2 + bx + c = 0$ is

$$x = \frac{-b \pm \sqrt{b^2 - 4ac}}{2a}.$$

**6** Prove that the sum of the first $n$ terms of an arithmetic series is

$$\frac{n}{2}\{2a + (n - 1)d\}.$$

**7** 'A 3-digit number minus its reverse is always a multiple of 99.'
Example: $572 - 275 = 297 = 3 \times 99$

(a) Show that this statement is correct for the 3-digit numbers 271 and 488.

*(b) Prove that this statement is correct for all 3-digit numbers.

(c) What is the connection between the multiple of 99 and the original 3-digit number?

**8** Insert the correct conditional symbol ($\Rightarrow$, $\Leftarrow$, or $\Leftrightarrow$) to complete the following statements.

(a) $f(x) = x^2 + 4$ _____ $f'(x) = 2x$

(b) $g(x) = \dfrac{1}{x} + 2$ _____ $g(x) = \dfrac{2x+1}{x}$

(c) $h(x)$ has a maximum at $(1, -1)$ _____ $h(x) = x^2 - 2x$

**9** Complete the following statements by inserting **if, only if** or **if and only if**.

(a) $\dfrac{x}{x+7} = \dfrac{4}{x+1}$ _____ $x = 7$

(b) $\dfrac{x}{x+1} = \dfrac{x+2}{x+4}$ _____ $x = 2$

(c) $x^2 + 3 = 3x + \dfrac{1}{x}$ _____ $x = 1$

**10** Insert the words **necessary, sufficient** or **necessary and sufficient** to complete the following statements.

(a) A _____ condition that $|x - 2| = 4$ is that $x = -2$ or $x = 6$.
(b) A _____ condition that $|x^3 + 1| = 7$ is that $x = -2$.
(c) A _____ condition that $|x^2 - 12| = 4$ is that $x = 4$ or $x = -4$.
(d) A _____ condition for the equation of a line to be $y = 2x + 3$ is that the gradient of the line is 2.
(e) A _____ condition for the line to cross the axis at $(0, 4)$ is that the equation of the line is $y = x + 4$.
(f) A _____ condition for the equation of a line to be $y = 4x + 5$ is that the gradient of the line is 4 and its $y$-intercept is 5.

**11** Prove that, if $p$ and $q$ are positive integers with $p > q$, $p - q$ is even $\Leftrightarrow$ $p + q$ is even.

**12** Decide whether each of the following statements is true or false. If the statement is true, prove that it is true. If the statement is false, find a counter-example to show that it is false.

(a) $n(2n + 3)(n - 1)$ is even for all integer values of $n$.
(b) $a - b > 0 \Rightarrow a^4 - b^4 > 0$.
(c) The product of two irrational numbers is always irrational.
(d) The function $f(n) = n^2 + n + 41$ ($n \in \mathbb{Z}^+$) will generate only prime numbers.

**13** For each of the following statements:
  (i) state whether it is true or false,
  (ii) give the converse statement,
  (iii) state whether the converse is true or false.
(a) If $x = y$, then $x^2 = y^2$.
(b) If $f(a) = 0$ then $x - a$ is a factor of $f(x)$.

(c)   f(x) has a maximum at $x = a \Rightarrow f'(a) = 0$.

(d)   For all integers $m$, $n$, if $m + n$ is even, then $m$ and $n$ are both even.

(e)   For any real $x$, if $x^2 - x$ is positive then $x$ is negative.

**14** Use a proof by contradiction to show that the following statements are correct.

(a)   If $x^3$ is odd, then $x$ is odd.

(b)   There is no real value of $x$ which satisfies $\dfrac{1}{2-x} + \dfrac{x}{4}$.

**15** If f(x) and g(x) are both real functions of $x$, prove that
$(fg(x))^{-1} = g^{-1}(f^{-1}(x))$.

**16** Prove that $\sqrt{3}$ is irrational.

## Advanced

**1**   Use a proof by contradiction to prove that there are no positive integers $p$ and $q$ such that $p^2 - q^2 = 2$.

**2**   Prove that, if $a$, $b$ and $c$ are distinct real numbers, it is impossible to find values of $a$, $b$ and $c$ such that they are simultaneously: successive numbers in an arithmetic sequence; and, taken in the same order, successive numbers in a geometric sequence.

**3**   For any two real numbers $x$ and $y$, let max$\{x, y\}$ denote the greater of $x$ and $y$ and min $\{x, y\}$ denote the smaller of $x$ and $y$. Show that, if $a$, $b$ and $c$ are positive real numbers, max $\{$min$\{a, b\}$, min$\{b, c\}$, min$\{a, c\}\} =$ min$\{$max$\{a, b\}$, max$\{b, c\}$, max$\{a, c\}\}$.
Does your result hold for *any* real numbers?

**4**   Explain the errors in the following.

(a)   $\displaystyle\int_{-\frac{1}{2}}^{\frac{1}{2}} \dfrac{1}{\sqrt{1-x^2}}\, dx = [\sin^{-1} x]_{-\frac{1}{2}}^{\frac{1}{2}} = \dfrac{\pi}{6} - \dfrac{7\pi}{6} = -\pi$

(b)   $\displaystyle\int_{-\frac{1}{2}}^{\frac{1}{2}} \sqrt{1-x^2}\, dx = \int_{\frac{3}{4}}^{\frac{3}{4}} \sqrt{u}(-\tfrac{1}{2})\dfrac{1}{\sqrt{1-u}}\, du$   (putting $u = 1 - x^2$)

(c)   $\displaystyle\int_{\frac{2\pi}{3}}^{\frac{5\pi}{6}} \dfrac{\sec^2 x}{1 + \tan x}\, dx = [\ln(1 + \tan x)]_{2\pi/3}^{5\pi/6}$

**5**   Let $n$ be a positive integer.

(i)   Factorise $n^5 - n^3$, and show that it is divisible by 24.

(ii)   Prove that $2^{2n} - 1$ is divisible by 3.

(iii)   If $n - 1$ is divisible by 3, show that $n^3 - 1$ is divisible by 9.

[OCR (STEP), 1996]

**6**  A real function f is **even** if, for all $x$ in its domain, $f(-x) = f(x)$ and **odd** if, for all $x$ in its domain, $f(-x) = -f(x)$.

  (i)  Prove that any real function can be expressed as the sum of an even function and an odd function.

  (ii)  Determine whether the following statements are true or false, justifying your answers:

  (a)  a *necessary* condition that $\int_{-a}^{a} f(x)\,dx = 0$ is that f be odd in $[-a, a]$.
  (b)  a *sufficient* condition that $\int_{-a}^{a} f(x)\,dx = 0$ is that f be odd in $[-a, a]$

  (iii)  Prove that, if f and g are odd, then $f \circ g$ is odd. State the corresponding results when

  (a)  f is odd and g is even,    (b)  f is even and g is odd.

  [OCR (Cambridge), 1983]

**7**  The function $L(x)$ has the property that

$$L(x_1) + L(x_2) = L(x_1 x_2) \quad (x_1 > 0, x_2 > 0)$$

Without making any further assumptions about $L(x)$, prove that:

  (a)  $L(1) = 0$     (b)  $L\left(\dfrac{1}{x}\right) = -L(x)$

  (c)  $L(x_1) - L(x_2) = L\dfrac{x_1}{x_2}$

  (d)  $L(x^n) = nL(x) \quad (n \in \mathbb{Z}^+)$

  (e)  $L(x^{1/n}) = \dfrac{1}{n}L(x) \quad (n \in \mathbb{Z}^+)$

  (f)  $L(x^s) = sL(x)$  (where $s$ is any rational number)

**8**  From the facts
$$
\begin{aligned}
1 &= 0 + 1 \\
2 + 3 + 4 &= 1 + 8 \\
5 + 6 + 7 + 8 + 9 &= 8 + 27 \\
10 + 11 + 12 + 13 + 14 + 15 + 16 &= 27 + 64
\end{aligned}
$$
guess a general law. Prove it.
Hence, or otherwise, prove that

$$1^3 + 2^3 + 3^3 + \cdots + N^3 = \tfrac{1}{4}N^2(N + 1)^2 \quad \text{for every positive integer } N.$$

[You may assume that $1 + 2 + 3 + \cdots + n = \tfrac{1}{2}n(n + 1)$.]
[OCR (STEP), 1994]

**9**  The function f satisfies $f(0) = 1$ and
$$f(x - y) = f(x)f(y) - f(a - x)f(a + y)$$
for some fixed number $a$ and all $x$ and $y$. Without making any further assumptions about the nature of the function show that $f(a) = 0$. Show that, for all $t$,

(i)  $f(t) = f(-t)$          (ii)  $f(2a) = -1$
(iii)  $f(2a - t) = -f(t)$      (iv)  $f(4a + t) = f(t)$

Give an example of a non-constant function satisfying the conditions of the first paragraph with $a = \pi/2$. Give an example of a non-constant function satisfying the conditions of the first paragraph with $a = -2$.
[OCR (STEP), 1994]

**10**  The Tour de Clochemerle is not yet as big as the rival Tour de France. This year there were five riders, Arouet, Barthes, Camus, Diderot and Eluard, who took part in five stages. The winner of each stage got 5 points, the runner up 4 points and so on down to the last rider who got 1 point. The total number of points acquired over the five stages was the rider's score. Each rider obtained a different score overall and the riders finished the whole tour in alphabetical order with Arouet gaining a magnificent 24 points. Camus showed consistency by gaining the same position in four of the five stages and Eluard's rather dismal performance was relieved by a third place in the fourth stage and first place in the final stage. Explain why Eluard must have received 11 points in all and find the scores obtained by Barthes, Camus and Diderot. Where did Barthes come in the final stage?
[OCR (STEP), 1995]

## Revision

**1**  Prove that, if $A$, $B$ and $C$ are the angles in a triangle, then
$\sin C = \sin(A + B)$

**2**  Show that the curve $y = x^2 - 4$ and the straight line $y = mx - 8$ will intersect if and only if $m \geq 4$ or $m \leq -4$.

**3**  Prove that:

(a)  the product of three consecutive numbers will be divisible by 6,
(b)  the product of $n$ consecutive numbers will be divisble by $n!$.

**4**  Prove that the sum of the first $n$ terms of a geometric progression is

$$a\left(\frac{1 - r^n}{1 - r}\right)$$

**5** 'Think of a 3-digit number, reverse it and then subtract, e.g.
$472 - 274 = 198$. Now reverse the new number and add the new number
to its reverse: $198 + 891 = 1089$. The answer will always be 1089!'

(a) Show that this 'trick' works for the 3-digit numbers 581 and 721.
(b) Find a counter-example to show that this statement is not true for
all 3-digit numbers.

**6** Insert the correct conditional symbol ($\Rightarrow$, $\Leftarrow$, or $\Leftrightarrow$) to complete the
following statements:

(a) $\cos x = \dfrac{\sqrt{3}}{2}$ _____ $x = 30°$

(b) $\tan x = \dfrac{a}{b}$ _____ $\tan(90° - x) = \dfrac{b}{a}$

(c) $x = 30°$ or $150°$ _____ $\sin x = \frac{1}{2}$

**7** Insert the words **necessary**, **sufficient** or **necessary and sufficient** to
complete the following statements.

(a) A _____ condition that $\dfrac{1}{x} < \dfrac{2}{3}$ is that $x > \dfrac{3}{2}$.

(b) A _____ condition that $x(x - 2) > 8$ is that $x > 4$.
(c) A _____ condition that $x > 2$ is that $x^3 > 8$.

**8** Prove that $\sin 15° = \dfrac{\sqrt{2 - \sqrt{3}}}{2}$.

In questions 9 and 10, decide whether the statement is true or false.
If the statement is true, prove that it is true.
If the statement is false, find a counter-example to show that it is false.

**9** $n$, $2n + 10$ and $3n - 10$ are the three sides of a right-angled triangle if and
only if $n = 25$.

**10** For all values of $x$, $\sin^4 x - \cos^4 x = \sin^2 x - \cos^2 x$.

In questions 11 and 12, use the method of proof by contradiction to show that
the statements are correct.

**11** If $x^3$ is even, then $x$ is even.

**12** For all positive values of $x$, $\dfrac{x}{8} + \dfrac{2}{x} \geq 1$.

# Answers and solutions

## Chapter 0 Background knowledge

### 0.1

**1** (a) $2 \times 3 \times 5$    (b) $7^2$
(c) $53$    (d) $2^2 \times 3 \times 7$
(e) $2^2 \times 3^3$    (f) $3^2 \times 7 \times 11$
(g) $2^3 \times 11 \times 13$    (h) $3^3 \times 7^2 \times 11$

**2** (a) $2$    (b) $7$    (c) $6$
(d) $8$    (e) $14$    (f) $13$
(g) $63$    (h) $17$

**3** (a) $30$    (b) $14$    (c) $210$
(d) $12$    (e) $25$    (f) $385$
(g) $924$    (h) $126$

**4** (a) $\frac{1}{5}$    (b) $\frac{3}{25}$    (c) $\frac{2}{3}$

(d) $\frac{1}{5}$    (e) $\frac{3}{4}$    (f) $\frac{1}{4}$

(g) $\dfrac{3a}{4}$    (h) $\dfrac{2ab}{11}$

**5** (a) $18$    (b) $16$    (c) $12$
(d) $56$    (e) $35$    (f) $6a$
(g) $ax$    (h) $2a$

**6** (a) $\frac{17}{12}$    (b) $\frac{3}{35}$    (c) $\frac{54}{91}$
(d) $\frac{1}{24}$    (e) $4\frac{5}{8}$    (f) $2\frac{5}{9}$
(g) $2\frac{25}{28}$    (h) $6\frac{1}{15}$

**7** (a) $\dfrac{17a}{12}$    (b) $\dfrac{3a}{35}$

(c) $\dfrac{5}{a}$    (d) $\dfrac{3b + 2a}{ab}$

(e) $\dfrac{u + v}{uv}$    (f) $\dfrac{5a - 2}{a^2}$

(g) $\dfrac{pq - 2}{q}$    (h) $\dfrac{3c - 5b}{abc}$

**8** (a) $4$    (b) $\frac{3}{8}$    (c) $\frac{12}{35}$
(d) $\frac{4}{15}$    (e) $\frac{6}{35}$    (f) $\dfrac{6a}{11b}$
(g) $1$    (h) $3x + 2$

**9** (a) $9$    (b) $\frac{2}{3}$    (c) $\frac{5}{2}$
(d) $\frac{27}{20}$    (e) $\frac{15}{14}$    (f) $\dfrac{6b}{11a}$
(g) $x^2$    (h) $\dfrac{1}{x}$

**10** $\frac{78}{79}$

**11** (a) $13$   (b) (i) $\frac{1}{4}$    (ii) $\dfrac{1}{n}$

**12** $29$

### 0.2

**1** (a) $a^7$    (b) $a^{13}$    (c) $a^4$
(d) $6a^5$    (e) $5a^9$    (f) $4a^7$

**2** (a) $x^7$    (b) $p$    (c) $x^{11}$
(d) $3a^5$    (e) $\frac{3}{2}a^2$    (f) $\dfrac{a}{3b}$

**3** (a) $a^{15}$    (b) $16a^4$    (c) $25a^6$
(d) $5a^6$    (e) $16a^8$    (f) $27a^6 b^9$

**4** (a) $x$    (b) $x^3$    (c) $ab$
(d) $2a$    (e) $-x^2$    (f) $3a^5 b^2$

**5** (a) $1 + 2x^2 + x^4$    (b) $9 - 6a^3 + a^6$
(c) $x^4 - 2 + \dfrac{1}{x^4}$

**6** (a) $x + x^4$    (b) $3x^4 + 2$
(c) $25x^2$    (d) $5x + 3y - 4xy$

## 0.3

**1**  (a)  $x = 6, y = 8$
  (b)  $x = 10.5$
  (c)  $x = \frac{11}{3}, y = \frac{7}{3}$
  (d)  $x = 5, y = 21$
  (e)  $x = 9, y = \frac{8}{3}$
  (f)  $x = 6, y = \frac{15}{4}$
  (g)  $x = 7.5, y = 5$

**2**  $y = \dfrac{rx}{h}$

**3**  $(\frac{20}{13}, 0)$

**4**  (a)  $4:9$   (b)  $8:27$

**5**  $\frac{128}{9} \approx 14.2$ kg

**6**  (a)  $135.7$ cm
  (b)  $100 \times \sqrt[3]{\dfrac{x}{400}} = 10 \times \sqrt[3]{2.5x}$

  (c)

## 0.4

**1**  (a)  $12 + 3a$      (b)  $12 - 18a$
  (c)  $a^2 + 3a$      (d)  $2a^2 + 3ab$
  (e)  $15a^2 - 6ab$      (f)  $2x + 3$

**2**  (a)  $x^2 + 7x + 10$
  (b)  $x^2 + x - 12$
  (c)  $6x^2 + 13x + 5$
  (d)  $25x^2 - 4$
  (e)  $9a^2 + 12a + 4$
  (f)  $2p^2 + pq - 15q^2$
  (g)  $x^2 + 4 + \dfrac{4}{x^2}$
  (h)  $2x^3 + 6x^2 + x + 3$

**3**  (a)  $4(x + 2y)$      (b)  $x(x - 3)$
  (c)  $x(5x + 2y)$      (d)  $2\pi r(r + h)$
  (e)  $t(u + \frac{1}{2}at)$      (f)  $x^3(2 + 3x)$

**4**  (a)  $(x + 1)(x + 3)$
  (b)  $(x + 3)(x - 1)$
  (c)  $(a - 3)^2$
  (d)  $(x + 5)(x + 2)$
  (e)  $(p + 6)(p - 5)$
  (f)  $(2a + 1)(a + 3)$
  (g)  $(2y + 1)(3y - 5)$
  (h)  $(p + 2q)(p - 2q)$
  (i)  $(p - 2q)(p + 6q)$
  (j)  $(3p - 8q)(5p + 2q)$
  (k)  $(3x + 5y)^2$
  (l)  $(5a - 2)(2a + 7)$

**5**  (a)  $x + 2$      (b)  $x + 2$
  (c)  $x + 2$      (d)  $4 - x$

**6**  (a)  $x = -1, y = 5$
  (b)  $x = 2, y = 3$
  (c)  $x = 4, y = -2$
  (d)  $x = 5, y = 7$
  (e)  $x = 3, y = -4$
  (f)  $x = 1, y = -6$
  (g)  $x = \frac{1}{2}, y = \frac{2}{3}$
  (h)  $x = 1, y = -2$

**7**  (a)  $x^3 - 1$
  (b)  $a^3 + 3a^2b + 3ab^2 + b^3$
  (c)  $a^4 + 6a^3b + 10a^2b^2 + 6ab^3 + b^4$
  (d)  $x^2 - 2$

**8**  (a)  $4ab$      (b)  $x + 1$
  (c)  $x + 2$

**9**  (a)  No solution; parallel lines
  (b)  Infinite number of solutions; lines coincide

## 0.5

**1**  (a)  $3$      (b)  $-2$
  (c)  $-\frac{7}{2}$      (d)  $\frac{5}{8}$
  (e)  $1$      (f)  $-\frac{31}{7}$
  (g)  $\pm 9$      (h)  $\pm 5$
  (i)  $\pm 4$      (j)  $-3$
  (k)  $0$ or $7$      (l)  $\pm 2$
  (m)  $0$ or $4$      (n)  $-3$ or $7$
  (o)  $-4, -\frac{2}{3}, \frac{3}{2}$

**2**  (a) $C = Q/V$

(b) $r = \dfrac{C}{2\pi}$

(c) $C = \frac{5}{9}(F - 32)$

(d) $m = \dfrac{y - c}{x}$

(e) $\ell = \frac{1}{2}P - w$

(f) $a = \dfrac{2S}{n} - \ell$

(g) $a = \dfrac{v^2 - u^2}{2s}$

(h) $a = \dfrac{2(s - ut)}{t^2}$

(i) $d = \dfrac{u - a}{n - 1}$

(j) $d = \dfrac{2}{n - 1}\left(\dfrac{s}{n} - a\right)$

**3**  (a) $c = \sqrt{\dfrac{E}{m}}$    (b) $r = \sqrt[3]{\dfrac{3V}{4\pi}}$

(c) $r = \sqrt{\dfrac{3V}{\pi h}}$    (d) $x = \sqrt{\dfrac{4}{y}}$

(e) $v = \sqrt{u^2 + \dfrac{2I}{m}}$    (f) $x = \frac{1}{4}(y - 3)^2$

(g) $\ell = \dfrac{gT^2}{4\pi^2}$    (h) $r = \sqrt{\dfrac{A}{\pi} + r_1^2}$

(i) $x = \dfrac{1}{y} + a$    (j) $a = \sqrt{c^2 - b^2}$

**5**  $V = \dfrac{r}{2}(S - 2\pi r^2)$

## 0.6

**1**  Gradient 4, y-intercept 2

**2**  (a) 5, −2    (b) −3, 1
(c) $\frac{1}{2}$, 0    (d) −3, −4
(e) $y = 2x + 5$    (f) $y = 6x - 2$
(g) $y = 7x + \frac{1}{2}$    (h) $y = x$
(i) 2, $\frac{1}{2}$    (j) $\frac{2}{5}$, 0

**4**  (a) $y = 5x + 10$    (b) $y = 2x - 2$
(c) $y = -\frac{3}{5}x + 3$    (d) $y = 7$
(e) $x = 3$

**5**  $y = -\frac{1}{2}x + 3$

**6**  (a) (6, 0)    (b) (0, 4)

## 0.7

**1**  (a) 5
(b) $\sqrt{(x_2 - x_1)^2 + (y_2 - y_1)^2}$

**2**  (a) 13    (b) $\sqrt{10}$
(c) $3\sqrt{2}$    (d) $\sqrt{34}$

**4**  (6, 4)

**5**  (i) $OP = \sqrt{x^2 + y^2}$

(ii) $PR = \sqrt{(x - 4)^2 + (y - 3)^2}$;

$8x + 6y = 25$

## 0.8

**1**  (a) 38.7°    (b) 33.7°    (c) 66.4°
(d) 36.9°

**2**  (a) 3.7    (b) 7.1    (c) 10.3
(d) 2.8    (e) 10.0    (f) 9.3
(g) 1    (h) 1

**3**  (a) (i) 1    (ii) $\sqrt{2}$

(b) (i) $\dfrac{1}{\sqrt{2}}$    (ii) $\dfrac{1}{\sqrt{2}}$    (iii) 1

**4**  (a) 6.6    (b) 6.7    (c) 11.0
(d) 35.7°    (e) 30.3°    (f) 122.4°

**5**  (a) 6.7    (b) 12.8    (c) 10.6
(d) 17.6°    (e) 82.8°    (f) 133.4°

**6**  (a) $B = 37°$, $AC = 4.1$, $BC = 6.8$
(b) $X = 106.6°$, $Y = 48.2°$, $Z = 25.2°$

## 0.9

**1**  (a) $15\pi$ cm$^3$    (b) $36\pi$ cm$^3$

(c) $12\pi$ cm$^3$    (d) $\dfrac{256\pi}{3}$ cm$^3$

(e) $144\pi$ cm$^3$

**2**  (a) $240\pi \, \text{cm}^3$    (b) $132\pi \, \text{cm}^2$

**3**  (a) $5.10 \times 10^8 \, \text{km}^2$
     (b) $1.08 \times 10^{12} \, \text{km}^3$

**4**  $4.32 \, \text{cm}$

**6**  $2970 \, \text{m}^3$, assuming the balloon is a complete sphere

**7**  $381 \, \text{cm}^3$

**8**  $29\,060 \, \text{cm}^3$

## 0.10

**1**  (a) 60    (b) $6\sqrt{2}$    (c) 30

**2**  (a) (i) $8 \, \text{cm}$    (ii) $53.1°$
     (b) $97.2°$
     (c) $43.3 \, \text{cm}^2$; $61.4 \, \text{cm}^2$

**3**  (a) (i) $12 \, \text{cm}$    (ii) $67.4°$
     (b) $11.25 \, \text{cm}$
     (c) $90 + \theta$

**4**  $3.71 \, \text{cm}$

**5**  $0.53°$; the Earth has negligible radius; the sun is spherical; distance is measured to the centre of the sun

# Chapter 1 Algebra

## 1.1

### Basic

**1** (a) 1    (b) 3    (c) $\frac{1}{27}$

**2** (a) $6x^3y^2$    (b) $3xy$    (c) $x^{3/2}$

**3** (a) 3    (b) $-3$    (c) $-2$

**4** (a) 18       (b) $9^{x-1}$

   (c) $\dfrac{12^x}{6^x} = \dfrac{(2 \times 6)^x}{6^x}$

          $= \dfrac{2^x \times 6^x}{6^x}$

          $= 2^x$

**5** (a) $x$    (b) $1 + \dfrac{1}{x}$    (c) $x^2 + 2x$

**6** $x^{-2/5}$

**7** (a) $3\sqrt{5}$    (b) $4\sqrt{3}$    (c) 0

**8** (a) $\sqrt{12}$    (b) $\sqrt{80}$    (c) $\sqrt{a^4b}$

**9** (a) $\dfrac{\sqrt{2}}{2}$    (b) $\dfrac{\sqrt{3}}{2}$    (c) $\dfrac{5 - \sqrt{5}}{5}$

**10** (a) $-2 + 2\sqrt{5}$    (b) $4 + 3\sqrt{3}$

   (c) $\dfrac{\sqrt{2}+1}{\sqrt{2}-3} = \dfrac{(\sqrt{2}+1)(\sqrt{2}+3)}{(\sqrt{2}-3)(\sqrt{2}+3)}$

         $= \dfrac{2 + 4\sqrt{2} + 3}{2 - 9}$

         $= \dfrac{5 + 4\sqrt{2}}{-7}$

         $= \dfrac{-5}{7} - \dfrac{4\sqrt{2}}{7}$

   (d) $\dfrac{8 - \sqrt{5}}{59}$

**11** $\sin\alpha = \dfrac{\sqrt{2}}{10}$; $\cos\alpha = \dfrac{7\sqrt{2}}{10}$

**12** (a) $-1 \pm 2\sqrt{2}$    (b) $\frac{3}{2} \pm \dfrac{\sqrt{11}}{2}$

### Intermediate

**1** (a) $\frac{2}{3}$    (b) $\frac{2}{3}$    (c) 512

**2** (a) 12    (b) 18    (c) 0

**3** (a) $x^2$    (b) $x^{5/6}$    (c) $x^{-2}$

**4** $a = 12, b = 6$

**5** $a - b$

**6** (a) $(x+3)^2 + 2(x+3)(x+3)^2$

    $= (x+3)^2\{1 + 2(x+3)\}$

    $= (x+3)^2(2x+7)$

   (b) $32^{\frac{1}{2}} - 18^{\frac{1}{2}} = (16 \times 2)^{\frac{1}{2}} - (9 \times 2)^{\frac{1}{2}}$

     $= 16^{\frac{1}{2}}2^{\frac{1}{2}} - 9^{\frac{1}{2}}2^{\frac{1}{2}}$

     $= 4 \times 2^{\frac{1}{2}} - 3 \times 2^{\frac{1}{2}}$

     $= 2^{\frac{1}{2}}$

   (c) $2x\sqrt{\dfrac{1}{x^2} - \dfrac{1}{4}} = \sqrt{4x^2}\sqrt{\dfrac{1}{x^2} - \dfrac{1}{4}}$

     $= \sqrt{4x^2\left(\dfrac{1}{x^2} - \dfrac{1}{4}\right)}$

     $= \sqrt{4 - x^2}$

**7** $3\sqrt{2},\ 2\sqrt{5},\ 2\sqrt{6},\ 5,\ 2\sqrt{7}$

**8** (a) 4    (b) $-1$    (c) $4\sqrt{2} - 2\sqrt{5}$

**9** (a) 2

   (b) (i) 3, 0    (ii) 1, 0    (iii) 1, 3

**10** $x = 0, y = 1$

**11** $\cos \beta = \dfrac{4\sqrt{3}}{7}$, $\tan \beta = \dfrac{\sqrt{3}}{12}$

**12** (a) (i) $1 + \sqrt{3}$    (ii) $7 + 4\sqrt{3}$

(iii) $\dfrac{43}{44} + \dfrac{3\sqrt{5}}{44}$

(b) (i) $\sqrt{2} - 1$    (ii) $\dfrac{1}{7} + \dfrac{3\sqrt{2}}{14}$

(iii) $-5 - 3\sqrt{3}$

**13** (a) $9 + 4\sqrt{5} = (a + b\sqrt{5})(a + b\sqrt{5})$
$= a^2 + 2ab\sqrt{5} + 5b^2$
$= (a^2 + 5b^2) + 2ab\sqrt{5}$
$\Rightarrow 9 = a^2 + 5b^2$    (1)
$4 = 2ab$    (2)

From equation (2) $a = \dfrac{2}{b}$

Substituting in (1) gives
$9 = \dfrac{4}{b^2} + 5b^2$

$\Rightarrow 5b^4 - 9b^2 + 4 = 0$
$(5b^2 - 4)(b^2 - 1) = 0$
$b^2 = \tfrac{4}{5}$ or $1$

$b = \pm\dfrac{2}{\sqrt{5}}$ or $\pm 1$

Substituting in (2) gives
$a = \pm\sqrt{5}$ or $\pm 2$
Using $a = \pm\sqrt{5}$, $b = \pm\dfrac{2}{\sqrt{5}}$ gives the
answer $\pm(\sqrt{5} + 2)$.
Using $a = \pm 2$, $b = \pm 1$, gives the
same answer $\pm(2 + \sqrt{5})$.

(b) $\pm(1 - 3\sqrt{2})$

(c) $\pm(1 - 2\sqrt{3})$

**14** (a) $\dfrac{7}{6} \pm \dfrac{\sqrt{61}}{6}$    (b) $2 \pm \sqrt{5}$    (c) $2$

**15** $a = 2, b = 5$

**16** (a) $\dfrac{2}{3} + \dfrac{5\sqrt{2}}{6}$    (b) $5 - 3\sqrt{3}$

(c) $-3 - 2\sqrt{3}$    (d) $\dfrac{26}{7} + \dfrac{17\sqrt{2}}{7}$

## Advanced

**1** $\dfrac{49}{9}$, $11$

**2** $-1, 32$

**3** $p + q^2 s + 2q\sqrt{ps}$

**4** $2\sqrt{3}, 4\sqrt{3}$;    (i) $2\sqrt{3} < x < 4\sqrt{3}$

(ii) $\pm 1.86, \pm 2.63$

**5** (a) $\dfrac{a + b + 2\sqrt{ab}}{a - b}$

(c) $4y + 1, 4y + 2$

**6** (a) $x + 1$    (b) $\tfrac{1}{2}$

**7** (a) $\dfrac{1}{2}, \dfrac{\sqrt{3}}{2}, \dfrac{1}{\sqrt{2}}, \dfrac{1}{\sqrt{2}}, \dfrac{\sqrt{3}}{2}, \dfrac{1}{2}$

(b) (i) $\dfrac{\sqrt{3} - 1}{2\sqrt{2}}$    (ii) $\dfrac{\sqrt{3} - 1}{2\sqrt{2}}$

(iii) $\dfrac{\sqrt{3} + 1}{2\sqrt{2}}$

**9** (a) $a - b\sqrt{2}$
(b) $ac + 2bd + (ad + bc)\sqrt{2}$

## Revision

**1** (a) $\tfrac{1}{2}$    (b) $\tfrac{3}{2}$    (c) $16$

**2** (a) $x^{5/2}$    (b) $x^{5/2}$    (c) $x^2$

**3** (a) $-6$    (b) $-\tfrac{1}{2}$    (c) $-1$ or $2$

**4** (a) $2^x$    (b) $\dfrac{x}{\sqrt{x} - 1}$    (c) $x - 4$

**5** (a) $4\sqrt{2}$    (b) $8\sqrt{3}$    (c) $12\sqrt{7}$

**6** (a) $4\sqrt{5}$    (b) $30\sqrt{3}$    (c) $19$

**7** (a) $\dfrac{2\sqrt{5}}{5}$    (b) $1 + \dfrac{2\sqrt{3}}{3}$

(c) $\dfrac{3}{2} + \dfrac{\sqrt{7}}{2}$

**8** (a) $174 - 70\sqrt{5}$    (b) $0 - \sqrt{3}$

**9** $a = \pm 2, b = \pm 3$

**10** (a) $2 + \sqrt{3}$    (b) $\pm 2 \pm 3\sqrt{5}$

**11** (a) $\dfrac{3}{2} \pm \dfrac{\sqrt{17}}{2}$    (b) $\dfrac{5}{6} \pm \dfrac{\sqrt{61}}{6}$

(c) $0, \ 1$

**12** (a) $\dfrac{-3}{2} - \dfrac{5\sqrt{3}}{6}$    (b) $\dfrac{3}{4} - \dfrac{\sqrt{5}}{4}$

## 1.2

## Basic

**1** (a) $x(x - 5)$    (b) $(2x - 7)(2x + 7)$
(c) $(x - 16)(x + 3)$

**2** (a) (i) 4    (ii) $-2$
(b) (i) 5    (ii) 0
(c) $(1 - x)(1 + 2x^2)$
$\quad = -2x^3 + 2x^2 - x + 1;$
(i) degree $= 3$
(ii) coefficient of $x^2 = 2$

**3** (a) 3    (b) 2    (c) 6

**4** (a) $5x^2 - 2x + 1$
(b) $(x + 5)(x^2 + x - 1) - (x + 3)^2$
$\quad = x^3 + 6x^2 + 4x - 5$
$\quad \quad -(x^2 + 6x + 9)$
$\quad = x^3 + 6x^2 + 4x - 5 - x^2$
$\quad \quad -6x - 9$
$\quad = x^3 + 5x^2 - 2x - 14$
(c) $-x^2 - x + 26$

**5** (a) $x^4 - 5x^3 + 7x^2 - 2x - 3$
(b) $x^4 + x^3 - 2x^2 + 3x - 1$
(c) $x^4 - 8x^3 + 6x^2 + 40x + 25$

**6** When $x = 2,$
$y = 2^4 + 2^3 - 7 \times 2^2 + 5 \times 2 - 6 = 0$

**7** (a) $f(x) = 3x^4 - 2x^3 + x^2 - 3x + 1$
$f(2) = 3 \times 2^4 - 2 \times 2^3 + 2^2 - 3 \times 2 + 1$
$\quad = 31$
So, by the remainder theorem, the
remainder when $f(x)$ is divided by
$(x - 2)$ is 31.
(b) $-14$    (c) 1

**8** (a) 4    (b) 0
(c) $f(x) = (x - 2)(x^2 + 4x + 3)$
$\quad = (x - 2)(x + 3)(x + 1)$

**9** (a) $(x - 3)(x + 2)(x + 1)$
(b) $(x + 2)(x - 2)(x + 5)$
(c) $(x + 3)^2(x + 7)$

**10** (a) (i)    (b) (vi)    (c) (iv)
(d) (iii)    (e) (v)    (f) (ii)

**11** (a) (v)    (b) (i)    (c) (vi)
(d) (iii)    (e) (iv)    (f) (ii)

**12** (a) (vi)    (b) (i)    (c) (iii)
(d) (v)    (e) (ii)    (f) (iv)

## Intermediate

**1** (a)

(b)

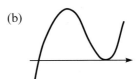

(c)

(d)

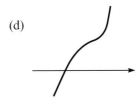

(e)

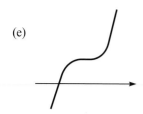

**2**  $f(x) = (1 - x)(2x + 1)(x + 3)$

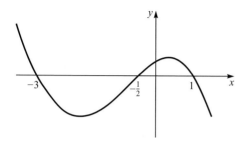

$x < -3, -\frac{1}{2} < x < 1$

**3**  $f(x) = (x - a)(x + a)(x^2 + a^2)$; two real roots

**4**  (a) $8x^5 + 18x^4 - 5x^3 - 14x^2 + 8x - 5$
(b) $4x^2 + 11x + 2$
(c) $16x^3 + 12x^2 - 2x + 1$

**5**  $p = -2, q = 3, r = 12$

**6**  (a) Assume $y = kx^n$.
When $x = 1, y = \frac{1}{4}$,
$\frac{1}{4} = k \times 1^n \Rightarrow k = \frac{1}{4}$
When $x = 2$,
$4 = \frac{1}{4} \times 2^n \Rightarrow 2^n = 16 \Rightarrow n = 4$
So $y = \frac{1}{4}x^4$

(b) $y = -\sqrt{2x}$

(c) $y = \dfrac{3}{x}$

(d) $y = 2x^3$

(e) $y = -\dfrac{x^5}{8}$

(f) $y = \frac{1}{2}(x - 2)^2(x + 2)^2$

**7**  (a) $-4, -2, -1, 1.5$

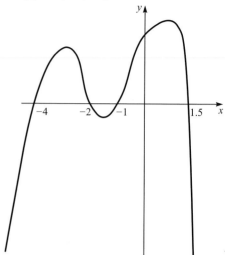

(b) $-4 < x < -2$ or $-1 < x < 1.5$

**8**  $(x - 4)(x^2 + x + 3)$ has one real root.

**9**  $a = 3, b = 1$

**10**  $f(x) = (x^2 - 1)(x^2 - 9)$
$= (x - 1)(x + 1)(x - 3)(x + 3)$

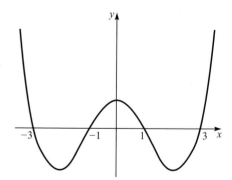

**11**  (a) $y = \sqrt{x + 4}$
(b) The graph cuts the $x$-axis at $-3$, $-1, +1$ and touches at 3. Hence
$y = k(x + 3)(x + 1)(x - 1)(x - 3)^2$
When $x = 0, y = -3$,
$-3 = -27k \Rightarrow k = \frac{1}{9}$
$y = \frac{1}{9}(x + 3)(x + 1)(x - 1)(x - 3)^2$
(c) $y = -(x + 1)^2(x - 3)^2$

**12** $f(x) = x(x-6)^2$

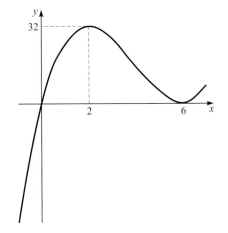

Maximum value $= 32; 0 < k < 32$

**13** $a = 9, b = 1$;
$f(x) = (x-1)(2x+3)(x+4)$;
$x \le -4$ or $-1.5 \le x \le 1$

**14** (a) $f(x) = (x+1)(2x-3)(x-3)$
(b)

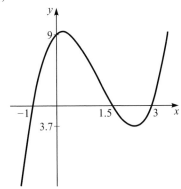

(c) (i) 3    (ii) 1    (iii) 3
    (iv) 3    (v) 3

**15** (a) $x = 4$

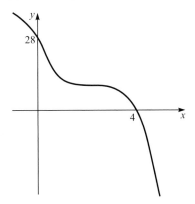

(b) $y = -x + 16$
(c) $(1, 15), (3, 13)$

**16** (a) Roots $5, -1$; maximum $(-1, 0)$,
minimum $(3, -32)$
(b) (i) $k = -5$ or $k = -9$
(ii) $-9 < k < -5$
(iii) $k < -9$ or $k > -5$

## Advanced

**1** $a = -13, b = -1$

**2** (b) $p < -5$ or $p > 3$

**3** (a) $\frac{1}{2}$, 3    (b) $\pi/3, \pi, 5\pi/3$
(c) $-0.693, 1.099$

**4** $\frac{1}{2}a$

**5** $p = q = 1, r = s = 2; 20\,002$

**6** $k = 14, x + 1$

**7** $7, -7, -7, 7$

**8** (a) $x^3 + 3x^2 + 5x + 5$

**9** $r(r-1)(r+1); r(r-1)(r+1)(r^2+1)$;
$r(r-1)(r+1)(r^2-r+1)(r^2+r-1)$;
No.

**10** $s_3 = 57, s_4 = 186; 6, 4.24, 3.85$; tends
to $\alpha$

## Revision

**1**  (a)  (i) $x^2(x-3)(x+3)$
   (ii) $(x+1)(x-3)(x-5)$
   (b) $-2$

**2**  (b) $(2x-1)(x-2)(x+3)$
   (c) $x = \frac{1}{2}, 2, -3$

**3**  $f(x) = (x+1)(x-3)(x^2+x+1)$;
   two real roots

**4**  $a = 0, b = -13; (x+3)(x-4)(x+1)$

**5**  $-\frac{1}{4} < x < 1$ or $x > 4$

**6**  $x = -2$ and $x = 1$; minima $(-2, 0)$
   and $(1, 0)$, maximum $(-\frac{1}{2}, 5\frac{1}{16})$

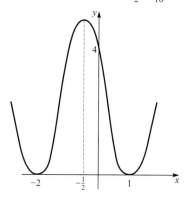

**7**  $a = -8, b = -4$

**8**  $y = 2x + 3; (-1, 1)$

**9**  (a)

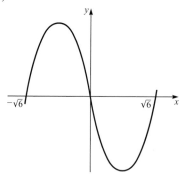

   (b) (i) $y = -3x + 2$   (ii) $(2, -4)$
   (c) $-1 < x < 4$ or $x > 5$

**10**  $k = 28, x = -7$ or $k = -80, x = 5$

**11**  $-4$

**12**  (a) $p = 5, q = 23$;
   $f(x) = (5x - 2)(x + 3)(x + 2)$
   (b) $-3 < x < -2$ or $x > \frac{2}{5}$

## 1.3

## Basic

**1**  (a)

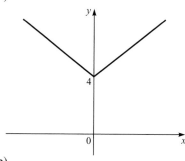

   (b)

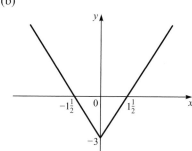

   (c)

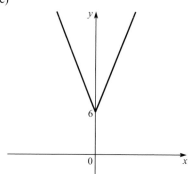

**2**  (a) $x = \pm 3$     (b) $x = \pm 2$
   (c) $x = \pm 1$

**3** (a)

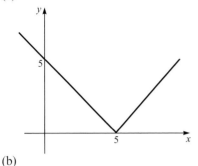

(b)

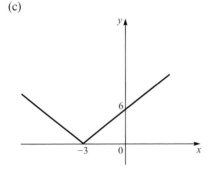

(c)

**4** (a) 4,1    (b) 1, −7
(c) 2, −4$\frac{2}{3}$

**5** (a) $x = -1$    (b) $x = 4$

**6** (a) $x \le 4$    (b) $x < \frac{1}{4}$
(c) $3(4x - 1) - 2(1 + 2x) > 4(x + 3) + 5$
Removing brackets and simplifying
gives
$$8x - 5 > 4x + 17$$
$$4x - 5 > 17$$
$$4x > 22$$
$$x > 5.5$$

**7** (a) $-2 \le x \le 2$
(b) $x > 3, x < -4.2$
(c) $|2x - 5| < |x - 7|$
Since both sides of the inequality are
positive (or zero) for all real values of
$x$, we can square both sides.
So $(2x - 5)^2 < (x - 7)^2$
$4x^2 - 20x + 25 < x^2 - 14x + 49$
giving $3x^2 - 6x - 24 < 0$
or $x^2 - 2x - 8 < 0$
Factorise $(x - 4)(x + 2) < 0$

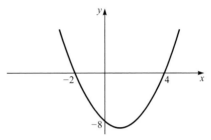

A sketch of the graph $x^2 - 2x - 8$ is
shown above which demonstrates that
the values of $x$ which satisfy the
inequality are where the graph lies
below the $x$-axis, i.e. $-2 < x < 4$.

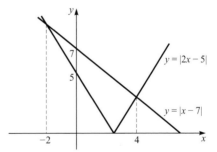

This question can also be done by
drawing the graphs of $y = |2x - 5|$
and $y = |x - 7|$ on the same axes, as
shown, and then finding the values of
$x$ where the line $y = |2x - 5|$ is 'lower'
than the line $y = |x - 7|$.

**8** (a) $-5, \frac{2}{3}$    (b) $-\frac{3}{5}, 3$
(c) $\pm 4$    (d) $-0.36, 8.36$
(e) $0.76, -0.26$    (f) $0.64, -3.14$

**9** (a) $-3 \le x \le 4$    (b) $-\frac{2}{3} \le x \le \frac{1}{4}$
(c) $-5 < x < -\frac{3}{4}$

**10** (a) $(x+1)^2 + 2$

**11**

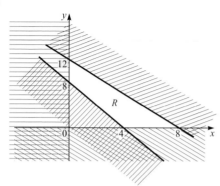

**12** (a) $(-1, -3), (4, 12)$

(b) $x - y = 4$                    (1)

$3x^2 + 4xy + y^2 = 0$        (2)

From equation              (1)

$x = y + 4$                      (3)

Substituting for $x$ in equation (2)

$3(y + 4)^2 + 4y(y + 4) + y^2 = 0$

Removing brackets

$3y^2 + 24y + 48 + 4y^2 + 16y + y^2$
$= 0$

Simplifying:  $8y^2 + 40y + 48 = 0$

$y^2 + 5y + 6 = 0$

Factorising:    $(y + 3)(y + 2) = 0$

$y = -3$ or $y = -2$

Substituting in (3): $x = 1$ or $x = 2$

Solutions of the equations are:

$(1, -3)$ and $(2, -2)$.

**13** (a) $3, 2$          (b) $2\frac{1}{2}, -2$

(c) $-\frac{3}{5}, -1\frac{2}{5}$      (d) $-\frac{1}{3}, 2\frac{2}{3}$

**14** (a) $x^2 - 3x - 4 = 0$

(b) $18x^2 - 3x - 1 = 0$

(c) $5x^2 + 12x + 4 = 0$

# Intermediate

**1** (a)

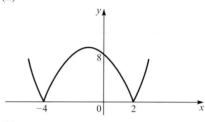

(b)

**2** (a) $-4.61, -3.24, 1.24, 2.61$

(b) $-6.47, 2.47$

**3** (a) $x < -4, x > 3$

(b) $x > 3, -1 < x < 2$

(c) $x < -7, -1 < x < 2$

**4** (a) $-8 \leq x < -3$

(b) $x \leq -\frac{1}{2}, 1 \leq x \leq 3$

**5** (a) (i) $3x(x + 5) = 9x - 2$

Rearranging in the form

$ax^2 + bx + c = 0$,

$3x^2 + 15x = 9x - 2$

$3x^2 + 6x + 2 = 0$

Dividing by 3:  $x^2 + 2x + \frac{2}{3} = 0$

$x^2 + 2x = -\frac{2}{3}$

Halving the coefficient of $x$,

squaring the result and adding to

both sides,

$x^2 + 2x + 1 = -\frac{2}{3} + 1$

$(x + 1)^2 = \frac{1}{3}$

$x + 1 = \pm 0.577$

$x = -0.42$ or $-1.58$

(ii) $1.82, -0.82$

(b) (i) $x < -4, x > 5$

(ii) $x \geq 0.21, x < -1.21$

**6**   $-1 \le x \le 1.5, x \ge 4$

**7**   (a) $(1, -2)$
   (b) $(1, 1), (\frac{1}{4}, -\frac{5}{4})$
   (c) $(2, 6), (6, 2), (-2, -6), (-6, -2)$

**8**   $\frac{5}{12}$

**9**   Line $y = 3x + 7$, circle
   $(x - 2)^2 + (y - 4)^2 = 25$; points of
   intersection $(-2, 1), (\frac{3}{5}, 8\frac{4}{5})$

**10**  (a) $\sqrt{5}, 2\sqrt{5}$
   (b) $\sqrt{5} < x < 2\sqrt{5}$
   (c) $x = \pm 1.50, \pm 2.11$

**11**  (a) $4\frac{2}{7} < x < 6$      (b) $1\frac{2}{5} \le x \le 11$

**12**  $(2, -3), (3, -2)$

**13**  (a) $\frac{1}{9}$      (b) $2\frac{1}{27}$      (c) $\frac{1}{12}$

**14**  (a) $3x^2 + 12x - 8 = 0$
   (b) $\alpha, \beta$ are the roots of the equation
   $3x^2 + 6x - 2 = 0$.
   Then $\alpha + \beta = -2$ and $\alpha\beta = -\frac{2}{3}$.
   The equation to be found has
   roots $\alpha^2, \beta^2$.
   Sum of these roots $= \alpha^2 + \beta^2$
   $= (\alpha + \beta)^2 - 2\alpha\beta$
   $= 4 + \frac{4}{3} = \frac{16}{3}$
   Product of these roots
   $= \alpha^2\beta^2 = (\alpha\beta)^2 = \frac{4}{9}$
   The required equation is therefore
   $x^2 - \frac{16}{3}x + \frac{4}{9} = 0$
   i.e. $9x^2 - 48x + 4 = 0$
   (c) $3x^2 + 36x + 28 = 0$

**16**  $\frac{1}{3}, -2\frac{2}{3}$

## Advanced

**1**   $(\frac{1}{2}, \frac{1}{3}); (\frac{1}{6}, \frac{7}{9})$

**3**   (a) $k$ takes all real values.
   (b) $f(x) \le -\frac{1}{2}, f(x) \ge -\frac{1}{3}$

**4**   $-1 \le p \le 3; p = 2, x = -\frac{1}{2}$

**6**   (a) $x = -a + b + c, y = a - b + c,$
   $z = a + b - c;$

   $x = \dfrac{abc}{-bc + ac + ab},$
   $y = \dfrac{abc}{bc - ac + ab},$
   $z = \dfrac{abc}{bc + ac - ab}$

   (b) $(9, 2); (3, -2)$

**7**

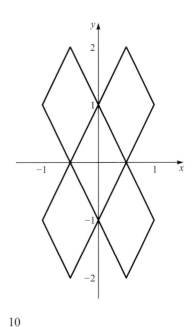

**8**   $10$

**9**   $c \ge 4$
   $\theta = 2n\pi \pm \cos^{-1}\frac{4}{5},$
   $\phi = 2m\pi + \sin^{-1}\frac{1}{5}$
   $\theta = 2n\pi \pm \cos^{-1}\frac{4}{5},$
   $\phi = (2m + 1)\pi - \sin^{-1}\frac{1}{5}$
   $\theta = 2n\pi \pm \cos^{-1}\frac{1}{5},$
   $\phi = 2m\pi + \sin^{-1}\frac{4}{5}$
   $\theta = 2n\pi \pm \cos^{-1}\frac{1}{5},$
   $\phi = (2m + 1)\pi - \sin^{-1}\frac{4}{5}$
   where   $n, m \in \mathbb{Z}$

**10**  $k > 2, x = y = z; k = 2, x = y = z = 0$

## Revision

**1**

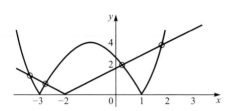

Four solutions

**2** (a) $-2 \le x \le 1$    (b) $x \ge 2, x \le -5\frac{1}{3}$

**3** (a) $-12 < x < 5$
  (b) $x < \frac{1}{4}, x > 2\frac{1}{2}$
  (c) $1 < x \le 4, x \le -1$

**4** $-1 < p < 2$

**5** (a) $\pm 2, \pm 3$    (b) $-3, 5$

**6** $(-1, 3); (3\frac{2}{3}, \frac{2}{3})$

**7** $p = -\frac{1}{3}$

**8** $c < -1\frac{1}{3}$   $c > 1\frac{1}{3}$

**9** $-\frac{8}{9} < q < 0$

**10** (b)

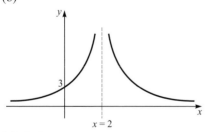

  (c) 0, 4
  (d) $x < 0, x > 4$

**11** $x \le -5$ or $x \ge 1$

**12** (a) $rx^2 + qx + p = 0$
  (b) $p^2 x^2 - (q^2 - 2pr)x + r^2 = 0$
  (c) $px^2 + 3qx + 9r = 0$

## 1.4

### Basic

**1** (a) $\frac{31}{20}$    (b) $\dfrac{9a - 7b}{63}$

  (c) $\dfrac{2y + 3x}{xy}$

**2** (a) $-2$   (b) $\frac{8}{5}$   (c) $\frac{-5}{2}$

**3** (a) $40 = 12a + 15b$
  (b) $221 = a - 3b$
  (c) Multiply throughout by all of the
    denominators, i.e. by $4x(x + 1)$.
    $28(x + 1) = 12x + x(x + 1)$
    $28x + 28 = 12x + x^2 + x$
    $0 = x^2 - 15x - 28$

**4** (a) $a = 2, b = 1$
  (b) $a = 1, b = 3$
  (c) $a = 2, b = 3, c = 2$
  (These solutions are *not* unique.)

**5** (a) $\dfrac{5x + 7}{(x + 1)(x + 2)}$

  (b) $\dfrac{2x + 26}{(x - 3)(x + 5)}$

  (c) $\dfrac{1}{(2x + 1)(3x + 2)}$

**7** (b) These values 'eliminate' each of $A$
    and $B$ in turn.
  (c) $A = 4, B = 2$

**8** (a) Multiply throughout by all of the
    denominators, i.e. by
    $(2x + 1)(x + 2)$.
    $A(x + 2) + B(2x + 1) \equiv x + 8$
    When $x = -2 : -3B = 6$, giving
    $B = -2$

    When $x = -\frac{1}{2} : \dfrac{3A}{2} = \frac{15}{2}$, giving
    $A = 5$

  (b) $A = \frac{1}{7}, B = -\frac{4}{7}$

**9** (a) $\dfrac{3}{2x+3}+\dfrac{-1}{x-2}$

(b) $\dfrac{1}{2(x-1)}+\dfrac{-1}{2(x+1)}$

(c) $\dfrac{1}{2(x-1)}+\dfrac{1}{2(x+1)}$

(d) $\dfrac{5}{3(2x+1)}-\dfrac{8}{3(5x+4)}$

**11** (a) False    (b) False
(c) True

**12** (a) $\dfrac{-2}{x-5}+\dfrac{3}{x+3}$

(b) $\dfrac{3}{2x+3}+\dfrac{3}{x-3}$

(c) $\dfrac{1}{4(2x+1)}+\dfrac{1}{4(2x-1)}$

## Intermediate

**1** (a) $\dfrac{3}{x+2}-\dfrac{2}{2x+1}$    since

$$\dfrac{4x-1}{(2x+1)(x+2)}\equiv\dfrac{A}{2x+1}+\dfrac{B}{x+2}$$

Multiply throughout by both of the denominators, i.e. by $(2x+1)(x+2)$.
$A(x+2)+B(2x+1)\equiv 4x-1$
When $x=-2: -3B=-9$, giving
$B=3$
When $x=-\frac{1}{2}: \frac{3A}{2}=-3$, giving
$A=-2$

(b) $\dfrac{2}{3(3x+4)}+\dfrac{1}{6(3x-1)}$

(c) $\dfrac{1}{x+3}-\dfrac{1}{2(5x-1)}$

**2** $\dfrac{-1}{x+1}-\dfrac{2}{x+2}+\dfrac{3}{x-3}$

**4** (a) $A=1, B=1$

(b)

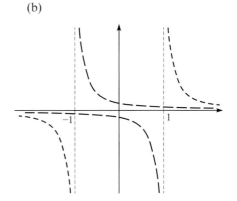

(c)

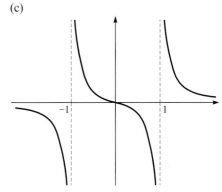

**5** $\dfrac{1}{x-2}-\dfrac{1}{2x+1}$

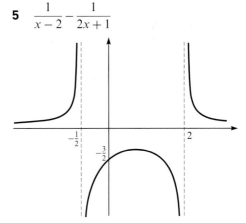

**6** (b) $(2x+3)(x^2+x+1)$
(c) $x^2+x+1$ *cannot* be factorised, as $b^2<4ac$ in the quadratic formula.

**7** (a) $(Ax + B)(x - 2) + C(x^2 + 1)$
$\equiv 7x + 1$
$x = 2 \Rightarrow 5C = 15$, hence $C = 3$
Multiplying out,
$Ax^2 + Bx - 2Ax - 2B + Cx^2$
$+ C \equiv 7x + 1$
$(A + C)x^2 + (B - 2A)x + C - 2B$
$\equiv 7x + 1$
Equating coefficients of $x^2$ gives
$A + C = 0$, hence $A = -3$
Set $x = 0$
$C - 2B = 1$, hence $B = 1$

(b) $\dfrac{5x + 4}{(2x + 3)(x^2 + x + 1)}$
$\equiv \dfrac{Ax + B}{x^2 + x + 1} + \dfrac{C}{2x + 3}$

Multiply throughout by both of
the denominators, i.e. by
$(2x + 3)(x^2 + x + 1)$.
$(Ax + B)(2x + 3) + C(x^2 + x + 1)$
$\equiv 5x + 4$
Note: when $x = -\frac{3}{2}$ the expression
will simplify.
$(2A + C)x^2 + (3A + 2B + C)x$
$+ (3B + C) \equiv 5x + 4$
Using $x = -\dfrac{3}{2}, \dfrac{7C}{4} = -\dfrac{7}{2}$;
and hence $C = -2$.
When $x = 0$, $3B + C = 4$; and
hence $B = 2$.
Equating the coefficients of $x^2$, we
have $2A + C = 0$. Hence $A = 1$

**8** (b) (i) $\dfrac{1}{x + 3} + \dfrac{4}{(x + 3)^2}$

(ii) $\dfrac{5}{x - 4} + \dfrac{17}{(x - 4)^2}$

**9** $(x - 1)$ must be a factor that repeats
twice; thus
$x^3 + 3x^2 - 9x + 5$
$\equiv (x - 1)^2(Ax + B)$
$x^3 + 3x^2 - 9x + 5$
$\equiv (x^2 - 2x + 1)(Ax + B)$
$x^3 + 3x^2 - 9x + 5$
$\equiv Ax^3 + (B - 2A)x^2$
$+ (A - 2B)x + B$

Comparing coefficients, or
substituting values: $B = 5$, and hence
$A = 1$.
$x^3 + 3x^2 - 9x + 5 \equiv (x - 1)^2(x + 5)$
Partial fractions follow as usual,
giving

$$\dfrac{2}{x - 1} + \dfrac{2}{(x - 1)^2} - \dfrac{2}{x + 5}$$

**10** (a) $A = 1, B = -14, C = 74$

(b) $\dfrac{1}{(2x + 3)^2} - \dfrac{3}{(2x + 3)^3}$

**11** (b) $1 + \dfrac{5}{x + 2} - \dfrac{4}{x + 3}$

(c) $a = 4, b = 3, c = 5$

**12** (b) $A = 1, B = 3$

(c) $2x^2 + x + 1$ may not be factorised.

**13** (a) 3 and $3x^2 - 10x + 25$

(b) $3 + \dfrac{1}{x} + \dfrac{2}{x - 5} + \dfrac{10}{(x - 5)^2}$

## Advanced

**1** (a) $\dfrac{b}{x + a} + \dfrac{b}{x - a}$

(b) $\frac{1}{2}\left(\dfrac{b - a}{x - a} + \dfrac{b + a}{x + a}\right)$

**2** (a) $\dfrac{1}{2(n - 1)} - \dfrac{1}{2(n + 1)}$

(b) $\frac{1}{2} + \frac{1}{4} - \frac{1}{10} - \frac{1}{12}$

**3** $x^4 + 1$; $\dfrac{x/2\sqrt{2} + \frac{1}{2}}{x^2 + \sqrt{2}x + 1} + \dfrac{\frac{1}{2} - x/2\sqrt{2}}{x^2 - 2\sqrt{x} + 1}$

**4** $3(-1)^n n!\left(\dfrac{1}{(x + 1)^{n+1}} + \dfrac{2 \times 3^n}{(3x - 2)^{n+1}}\right)$

**5** (a) $\dfrac{3}{n^2} - \dfrac{2}{(n + 2)^2}$

**6**

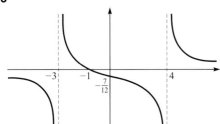

**7**  (b) $\frac{1}{4}$

(c)  21

**8**  $\frac{2}{x-1} + \frac{1}{x-2} + \frac{1}{x-3}; \frac{17 \pm \sqrt{17}}{8}$

**9**  $\frac{1}{2}\left(\frac{1}{1-x} - \frac{1}{1+x}\right); A = \frac{1}{2}\sec\alpha,$

$B = -\frac{1}{2}\sec\alpha$

**10**  $(n+1)!$

## Revision

**2**  (a)  $A = -9, B = 5$
(b)  $A = 10, B = -5$

**3**  (a)  $\frac{3}{2x+1} - \frac{1}{x-1}$

(b)  $\frac{2}{3(3x+1)} + \frac{5}{3(3x-1)}$

**4**  (a)  The partial fractions yield

$\frac{1}{x-2} - \frac{1}{x}.$

**5**  $A = 2, B = -5, C = 2$

**6**  (a)  $(x+5)(x^2 - x + 2)$

(b)  $\frac{7}{x+5} + \frac{2x-1}{x^2 - x + 2}$

**7**  (a)  $\frac{5}{x-2} + \frac{10}{(x-2)^2}$

(b)  $\frac{1}{2x-3} + \frac{1}{(2x-3)^2}$

**8**  $\frac{2}{x+1} - \frac{4}{(x+1)^2} + \frac{2}{(x+1)^3}$

**9**  $A = \frac{4}{3}, B = 2, C = -3$

**10**  (b)  $A = -\frac{2}{3}, B = \frac{17}{3}$

(c)  $\frac{2}{3}x + \frac{17}{9}\ln(3x+1) + c$

**11**  The partial fractions yield

$\frac{4}{1-3x} - \frac{9}{1+2x} \approx 30x - 5.$

**12**  (a)  $-\frac{1}{2x} - \frac{1}{x^2} + \frac{3}{2(x-2)}$

(b)  $\frac{1}{x} - \frac{x}{x^2+1}$

(c)  $\frac{1}{x+1} + \frac{1}{(x+1)^2}$

(d)  $2 + \frac{3}{2x+1}$

## 1.5

### Basic

**1**  (a)  $\pm 1$        (b)  $\pm 2$

(c)  $\pm i$        (d)  $\pm 3i$

(e)  $\pm\frac{i}{2}$        (f)  $\pm 1.2i$

**2**  (a)  $-1$
(b)  $-i$
(c)  i
(d)  Since we know about $i^2$, rewrite
$(-i)^{100} = \{(-i)^2\}^{50} = (-1)^{50} = 1$

**3**  (a)  $2i$        (b)  $-12 - 8i$
(c)  $2a$        (d)  $2bi$

**4**  (a)  $-1 + 2i$
(b)  $-6 - 3i$
(c)  $-5 + 10i$
(d)  $\frac{37}{3}i$
(e)  $(a^2 - b^2) + 2abi$
(f)  $a^2 + b^2$

**5**  (b)  Expand the 'awkward' expression
separately:
$z^2 = (1 + 2i)^2 = (1 + 2i)(1 + 2i)$
$= 1 + 2i + 2i - 4 = -3 + 4i$
Hence $z^2 + 3 = 4i.$

**6**

| $z^*$ | $z+z^*$ | $z-z^*$ | $zz^*$ | $\frac{1}{zz^*}$ |
|---|---|---|---|---|
| $1-i$ | 2 | $2i$ | 2 | $\frac{1}{2}$ |
| 1 | 2 | 0 | 1 | 1 |
| $-i$ | 0 | $2i$ | 1 | 1 |
| $2+3i$ | 4 | $-6i$ | 13 | $\frac{1}{13}$ |
| $a-bi$ | $2a$ | $2bi$ | $a^2+b^2$ | $1/(a^2+b^2)$ |

Since $a$ and $b$ are real, and $zz^* = a^2+b^2$, this must also be real, and positive.

**7** (a) $\frac{5}{2}-\frac{1}{2}i$
   (b) $\frac{6}{5}$
   (c) $\frac{1}{18}+\frac{1}{12}i$

**8** (a) $\frac{2}{5}+\frac{1}{5}i$
   (b) $\dfrac{2i}{5+7i} \times \dfrac{5-7i}{5-7i} = \dfrac{10i+14}{25+49} = \dfrac{7+5i}{37}$
   (c) $2+3i$
   (d) $(a-bi)/(a^2+b^2)$

**9** Radius $= 5$

**10** (a) $3, \pi/2$
   (b) $\sqrt{5}, 1.1$
   (c) $\sqrt{10}, 0.32$
   (d) $2, -\pi/2$
   (e) $2\sqrt{2}, -3\pi/2$

**11** $\frac{7}{\sqrt{2}}+\frac{7}{\sqrt{2}}i, -\frac{6}{\sqrt{2}}+\frac{6}{\sqrt{2}}i, -0.35-3.98i$

**12** (b) Rectangle
   (c) Area $= 4ab$ units$^2$

## Intermediate

**1** (a) $-2-8i$
   (b) $-10+5i$
   (c) $-i$

**2** 1

**3** (a) $z^2+2z+5=0$

Since $(z+1)^2 \equiv z^2+2z+1$, we can rewrite the original equation as:
$(z+1)^2+4=0$, i.e. $(z+1)^2=-4$
Hence $(z+1) = \pm 2i$, giving, finally,
$z = -1 \pm 2i$.
   (b) $\frac{3}{2} \pm \frac{\sqrt{3}}{2}i$          (c) $\frac{3}{2}+\frac{1}{2}i$

**4** (a) $\frac{1}{2} \pm i$          (b) $\frac{1}{3} \pm \frac{2}{3}i$
   (c) $\frac{1}{7}(1 \pm i\sqrt{55})$

**5** (a) $z=-2$ is a root, and therefore $(z+2)$ is a factor.
   By division or inspection:
   $z^3+2z^2+z+2 = (z+2)(z^2+0z+1)$;
   and so, since $(z^2+1) = (z+i)(z-i)$
   $z^3+2z^2+z+2 = (z+2)(z+i)(z-i)$
   as required
   (b) $(z+2)(z-2-i)(z-2+i)$

**6** (a) $z = \dfrac{-5 \pm 3}{8i} = \dfrac{(5 \pm 3)i}{8} = i$ or $\dfrac{i}{4}$

**7** (a) $a=4, b=15$
   (b) When two complex numbers are equal, both the real and imaginary components must have the same value: i.e. $a+2b=1$ and $-\frac{b}{3}=\frac{1}{2}$
   Hence, $b=-\frac{3}{2}$, and $a=4$.
   (c) $a=7, b=-3$

**9** (b) $z^2+z+1, z = -\frac{1}{2} \pm \frac{\sqrt{3}}{2}i$
   (c) $[1,0], [1, 2\pi/3], [1, -2\pi/3]$

**10** (a) Rotation centre $(0,0)$ through $\pi/2$
   (b) Enlargement centre $(0,0)$, scale factor 2
   (c) Reflection in $x$-axis

**11** (a) $[6, \pi/2]$
   (b) $[-1, \pi/7]$
   (c) $[5, \pi/2]$
   (d) $[1, \theta_1 + \theta_2]$
   (e) $[r, \theta]$
   (f) $[15, -\pi/2]$

**12** (c) $[2, 4\pi/5], [2, -2\pi/5], [2, -4\pi/5], [2, 0]$

**13** (c) $[2, \pi/3], [\sqrt{2}, -\pi/4]$
   (d) $[\sqrt{2}, 7\pi/17]$

**14** (b) $A = 2, B = -1$ or $A = -2, B = 1$

**15** (b) $[\sqrt{r}, \theta/2 - \pi]$
(c) $[3, \pi/8][3, -7\pi/8]$

## Advanced

**1** (a) (i) $-3 \pm 5i$
(ii) $\sqrt{34} \pm 2.1$
(iii) 10
(b) (i) $w^2 = -2i, w^3 = -2 - 2i, w^4 = -4$
(ii) $p = -4, q = 2$
(iii) $1 - i, 1 + i$

**2** $a^2 - b^2 - 2iab; \pm(2 + i); \pm(2 - i);$
$\pm(2 \pm i); z^2 - 4z + 5)(z^2 + 4z + 5)$

**3** (b) $\arg \alpha = \pi/4; \arg \beta = 5\pi/6$
(c) $8, -11\pi/12$

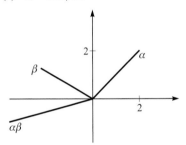

(d) Perpendicular bisector of points representing $\alpha, \beta$
(e) $13\pi/24$

**4** $c = (1 - a) - i, d = 1 + (1 - a)i$

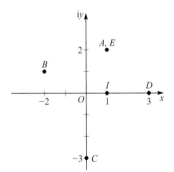

$90°$ anti-clockwise about $O$, $90°$ anti-clockwise about $I$, $90°$ anti-clockwise about $O$, $90°$ anti-clockwise about $I$

**5** $\pm\sqrt{3}, \pm 2\pi/3$
(a) $z^2 + 2z + 4 = 0$
(b) $\pm(1/\sqrt{2} + i\sqrt{3/2})$

**6** (a)

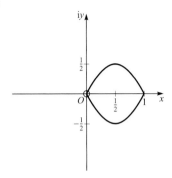

(b) $625; -4 \pm 3i, 3 + 4i$

**7** (a) $\dfrac{(-1 \pm \sqrt{1 - 4\omega^2 LC})i}{2\omega C}$

**9** $s = \pm i$

**10** $2 - i, 1 + i$ or $3 - i, -i$ or $3 - 2i, -2$

## Revision

**1** (a) $4 + 3i$    (b) $4 + 3i$
(c) $5 + 6i$    (d) $5 + 6i$

**3** $1 + i$ in each case

**4** (b) $\frac{1}{2}, 5 - 11i, 5 + 11i$

**5** (a) $-8 + 7i$    (b) $\sqrt{113}, 2.42$

**6** (a) $\frac{1}{2}(-5 \pm i\sqrt{43})$    (b) $\frac{1}{6}(1 \pm i\sqrt{107})$
(c) $2i, -3i$

**7** $z^3 - 6iz^2 - 11z + 6i = 0$ or a multiple of this equation

**8** $\pm(3 + 5i)$

**9** (a) $1 + 2\sqrt{2}$    (b) $2 + 4\sqrt{2}$

**10** (a)

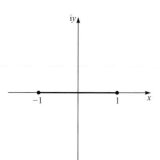

(b)

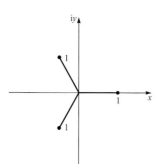

(c)

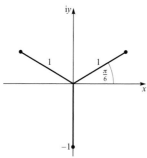

$$[1, \pi/6]^3 = [1^3, 3 \times \pi/6] = [1, \pi/2] = i$$

**11** (a)

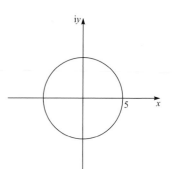

(b)

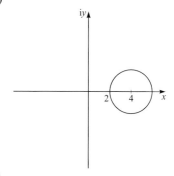

(c)

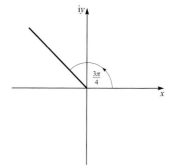

**12** (a)  $-\theta^2, -i\theta^3, \theta^4, i\theta^5$

# Chapter 2 Coordinate geometry

## 2.1

### Basic

**1** (a) 3   (b) $\frac{1}{2}$   (c) $\frac{1}{3}$

**2** (a) $(0, 6)$ and $(-3, 0)$
   (b) When $x = 0, 6y = 3$
   $\qquad\qquad y = \frac{1}{2}$   $(0, \frac{1}{2})$
   $\qquad$ When $y = 0, 0 - x = 3$
   $\qquad\qquad x = -3$   $(-3, 0)$
   (c) $(0, 0)$

**3** (a) Gradient $= 2 \Rightarrow y = 2x + c$
   When $x = 3, y = 7 \Rightarrow 7 = 2 \times 3 + c$
   So $c = 1$
   Hence $y = 2x + 1$
   (b) $y = -\frac{1}{2}x + 9$
   (c) $y = \frac{4}{3}x - \frac{2}{3}$

**4** (a) $y + x - 1 = 0$
   (b) $3y + x - 11 = 0$
   (c) $2y + 6x + 1 = 0$

**5** (a) (iii)
   (b) (ii), (iii)

**6** (a) $\dfrac{6 - a}{-3 - 6} = \dfrac{1}{3}$
   $\qquad 18 - 3a = -9$
   $\qquad\qquad 27 = 3a$
   $\qquad\qquad 9 = a$
   (b) $x = 2, y = 3$

**7** (a) 10.2   (b) 1.05
   (c) 7.35   (d) 8.66

**8** $a = 1$ or 9; $25\sqrt{3}/4$

**9** (a) $(-\frac{1}{2}, 6)$   (b) $(-5, 3)$
   (c) $(1, -1, 5)$

**10** $(-4, 2)$

**11** (a) Yes, 3, $(0, 2)$
   (b) No
   (c) $x^2 + 2x + y^2 - 2y = 2$
   $\qquad (x + 1)^2 - 1 + (y - 1)^2 - 1 = 2$
   $\qquad (x + 1)^2 + (y - 1)^2 = 4$
   $\qquad$ so, it is a circle, radius 2, centre
   $\qquad (-1, 1)$

**12** $(x - 3)^2 + (y - 7)^2 = 29$; $2y + 5x = 0$

### Intermediate

**1** 3;   2 : 1

**2** 2

**3** $\sqrt{5}$ units

**4** $\frac{4}{3}$ units$^2$

**5**

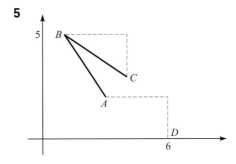

$$\overrightarrow{BC} = \begin{pmatrix} 3 \\ -2 \end{pmatrix} \therefore \overrightarrow{AD} = \begin{pmatrix} 3 \\ -2 \end{pmatrix} \therefore D(6, 0)$$

**6** $x + 3y = 26$

**7**  $(9, 6)$, 20 units$^2$

**8**  (a)  $-\frac{1}{2}$    (b)  $(-4, 11)$

**9**  (a)  $(4, 11), (10, 8), (-1, 1)$
   (c)  37.5 units$^2$

**10**  (a)  $y = -\frac{5}{3}x + \frac{22}{3}$
   (b)  $5y = 3x + 29$

**11**  $(-2.5, 7)$

**12**  $(4, 9, 9)$, $\sqrt{68}$ units

**13**

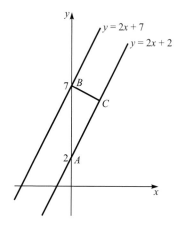

Gradient of $BC = -\frac{1}{2}$ and it intersects
the $y$-axis at $(0, 7)$.
Equation of $BC$ is $y = -\dfrac{x}{2} + 7$.

$C$ is the intersection of $y = -\dfrac{x}{2} + 7$
and $y = 2x + 2$   (1)
$$-\frac{x}{2} + 7 = 2x + 2$$
$$5 = \frac{5x}{2}$$
$$x = 2$$
Substituting in (1) gives $y = 6$, hence
$C$ is the point $(2, 6)$.

Length  $BC = \sqrt{(7 - 6)^2 + (0 - 2)^2}$
$\qquad\qquad = \sqrt{5}$ units

**14**  (a)  $(3, 0)$
   (b)  $\sqrt{28}$ units

**15**  $(x - 3)^2 + (y - 5)^2 = 20$; $(1, 1)$

**16**  (a)  $(1, 4)$
   (b)  5
   (c)  $(x - 1)^2 + (y - 4)^2 = 25$

## Advanced

**1**  20.59

**2**  (a)  $y = 3x - 8$
   (b)  $(3, 1)$; $3\sqrt{10}$

**3**  (a)  $-3$          (b)  $y = \frac{1}{3}x + \frac{5}{3}$
   (c)  $x = 1$          (d)  $(1, 2)$
   (f)  $\frac{15}{4}$ units$^2$

**4**  (b)  $(x - 5)^2 + (y - 1)^2 = 26$

**5**  (a)  $\sqrt{3}$        (b)  $y = \sqrt{3}x + 2\sqrt{3}$
   (d)  6          (e)  $60°$

**6**  (a)  $(16, 18)$
   (b)  $(8, 12)$ and $(10, 26)$
   (c)  $x^2 + y^2 - 32x - 36y + 530 = 0$

**7**  $3y - 4x = 25$, $7x + 24y = 125$

**8**  $x^2 + y^2 + 2a(\lambda^2 + 1)x + (\lambda^2 + 1)a^2$
   $= 0$; $(\lambda^2, 1)$; $\lambda = \sqrt{5/3}$

**9**  (b)  $Y^2 = 2a(X - a)$

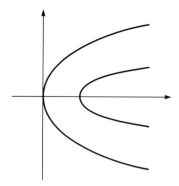

**10**  $x^2 + y^2 - px - 5y + 6 = 0$

# Revision

**1**  $y = -\frac{3}{2}x + 8$; $y = \frac{2}{3}x - \frac{7}{3}$;
perpendicular

**2**  $7$ or $-1$

**4**  $20$ units$^2$

**5**  $(3, 2)$

**6**  (a) $(4, 6)$

**7**  (a) $y = 2x + 8$     (c) $2y + x = 36$

**8**  $2y - 3x - 8 = 0$

**9**  (b) $1 : 2$

**10**  $\sqrt{2.5}$ units

**11**  (a) $(3, \frac{5}{2}), 2$     (c) $(3, 4), 5$

**12**  $\sqrt{80}$ units

# Chapter 3 Vector geometry

## 3.1

### Basic

**1** (a) $\begin{pmatrix} 8 \\ 13 \end{pmatrix}$    (b) $\begin{pmatrix} 4 \\ -5 \end{pmatrix}$

(c) $-2\mathbf{i} + 2\mathbf{j}$

**2** (a) $\begin{pmatrix} 2 \\ 4 \end{pmatrix}$    (b) $2\mathbf{i} - 2\mathbf{j}$

(c) $-3\mathbf{i} + 2\mathbf{j}$

**3** (a) $2\sqrt{13}, 56.3°,$    (b) $\sqrt{34}, 121.0°$

(c) $\sqrt{29}, 21.8°$    (d) $\sqrt{10}, -18.4°$

**4** (a) $6\mathbf{i} + 6\sqrt{3}\mathbf{i}$

(b) $-8.55\mathbf{i} + 23.49\mathbf{j}$

(c) $-4\mathbf{i} - 4\sqrt{3}\mathbf{j}$

**5** (a) $p = 10, \alpha = 40°, \mathbf{p} = \begin{pmatrix} 10\cos 40° \\ 10\sin 40° \end{pmatrix}$

$= \begin{pmatrix} 7.66 \\ 6.43 \end{pmatrix}$

$p = 12, \beta = 70°, \mathbf{q} = \begin{pmatrix} 12\cos 70° \\ 12\sin 70° \end{pmatrix}$

$= \begin{pmatrix} 4.10 \\ 11.28 \end{pmatrix}$

(b) $\mathbf{p} + \mathbf{q} = \begin{pmatrix} 7.66 + 4.10 \\ 6.43 + 11.28 \end{pmatrix}$

$= \begin{pmatrix} 11.8 \\ 17.7 \end{pmatrix}$

$|\mathbf{p} + \mathbf{q}| = \sqrt{11.8^2 + 17.7^2} = 21.3$

$\arg(\mathbf{p} + \mathbf{q}) = \tan^{-1}\left(\frac{17.7}{11.8}\right) = 56.4°$

or $236.4°$

From diagram,

$0° < \arg(p + q) < 90°$ giving

$|\mathbf{p} + \mathbf{q}| = 21.3; \arg(\mathbf{p} + \mathbf{q}) = 56°$

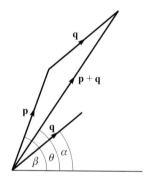

(c) $3\mathbf{p} - 2\mathbf{q} = \begin{pmatrix} 22.98 \\ 19.29 \end{pmatrix} - \begin{pmatrix} 8.20 \\ 22.56 \end{pmatrix}$

$= \begin{pmatrix} 14.8 \\ -3.3 \end{pmatrix}$

$|3\mathbf{p} - 2\mathbf{q}| = \sqrt{14.8^2 + (-3.3)^2} = 15.1$

$\arg(3\mathbf{p} - 2\mathbf{q}) = \tan^{-1}\left(\frac{-3.3}{14.8}\right) = -12.5°$

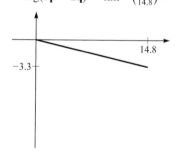

**6** (a) $\begin{pmatrix} -2 \\ 13 \end{pmatrix}$ miles

(b) 28.55 miles

**7** (a) $-7\mathbf{i} - 34\mathbf{j}$    (b) 34.7 km

(c) $191.6°$

**8** (a) 72    (b) $-13$    (c) 247.8

**9** (a) (i) $\mathbf{a} = \begin{pmatrix} 8.14 \\ 23.64 \end{pmatrix}, \mathbf{b} = \begin{pmatrix} 34.72 \\ -30.17 \end{pmatrix}$

(ii) $-430.6$

(iii) $112°$

(b) (i) $\mathbf{a} = \begin{pmatrix} -11.28 \\ -4.10 \end{pmatrix}$,

$\mathbf{b} = \begin{pmatrix} -7.50 \\ -13.00 \end{pmatrix}$

(ii) $137.9$

(iii) $40°$

**10** (a) (i) $|\mathbf{a}| = \sqrt{74}, |\mathbf{b}| = 2\sqrt{10}$

(ii) $16$     (iii) $72.9°$

(b) (i) $|\mathbf{a}| = \sqrt{3^2 + (-1)^2} = \sqrt{10}$

$|\mathbf{b}| = \sqrt{5^2 + (-2)^2} = \sqrt{29}$

(ii) $\mathbf{a.b} = 3 \times 5 + (-1) \times (-2)$
$= 15 + 2 = 17$

(iii) $\mathbf{a.b} = ab\cos\theta$

$\Rightarrow 17 = \sqrt{10} \times \sqrt{29}\cos\theta$

$\Rightarrow \cos\theta = \dfrac{17}{\sqrt{290}} = 0.998$

so $\theta = 3.6°$

**11** $96.4°$

**12** (a) $\begin{pmatrix} 8 \\ 17 \\ 11 \end{pmatrix}$     (b) $\begin{pmatrix} -3 \\ 14 \\ 11 \end{pmatrix}$

(c) $11.75$     (d) $10.49$
(e) $115$       (f) $-55$
(g) $118.6°$

## Intermediate

**1** (a) $\frac{1}{5}\mathbf{a}$          (b) $\mathbf{c} + \frac{1}{5}\mathbf{a}$

(c) $\mathbf{c} - \frac{4}{5}\mathbf{a}$

**2** (a) $\vec{BA} = \mathbf{a} - \mathbf{b}$

$\vec{CD} = \mathbf{d} - \mathbf{c} = \frac{2}{5}\mathbf{a} - \frac{2}{5}\mathbf{b} = \frac{2}{5}\vec{BA}$

Thus $\vec{CD}$ is a multiple of $\vec{BA}$ and so is parallel.

(b) $\vec{OE} = \vec{OD} + \vec{DE}$
$= \vec{OD} + \vec{CB}$
$= \frac{2}{5}\mathbf{a} + \frac{3}{5}\mathbf{b}$

**3** (a) $\frac{3}{5}\mathbf{i} + \frac{4}{5}\mathbf{j}$

(b) $\frac{1}{13}(5\mathbf{i} - 12\mathbf{j})$

(c) $\frac{1}{\sqrt{41}}(-4\mathbf{i} + 5\mathbf{j})$

**4** $\frac{11}{5}\begin{pmatrix} -1 \\ 4 \end{pmatrix}$

**5** $\vec{OB} = \vec{OA} + \vec{AB}$
$= \vec{OA} + \vec{OC}$
$= \mathbf{a} + \mathbf{c}$
$\vec{AC} = \mathbf{c} - \mathbf{a}$
$\vec{OB}.\vec{AC} = (\mathbf{a} + \mathbf{c}).(\mathbf{c} - \mathbf{a})$
$= \mathbf{a.c} - \mathbf{a.a} + \mathbf{c.c} - \mathbf{c.a}$
$= 0$, since $\mathbf{a.c} = \mathbf{c.a}$ and
$|\mathbf{c}| = |\mathbf{a}|$, so $\mathbf{a.a} = \mathbf{c.c}$
Hence $\vec{OB}$ is perpendicular to $\vec{OA}$.

**7** (a) $3\mathbf{i} + 16\mathbf{j}$

(b) $|AB| = \sqrt{313}$,
$|BC| = \sqrt{116}, |AC| = \sqrt{265}$

(c) $A = 36.7°, B = 64.5°, C = 78.8°$

**8** (a) $38$

(b) (i) $3\sqrt{2}$  (ii) $\sqrt{53}$  (iii) $\sqrt{41}$

**9** $\begin{pmatrix} 4 \\ 1 \\ 7 \end{pmatrix}$

**12** (a) $\begin{pmatrix} -0.64 \\ 6.25 \\ 1.36 \end{pmatrix}$

(b) $1.08\,\mathrm{m\,s^{-1}}$

**13** (a) $6\mathbf{i} - 3\mathbf{j}, 3\mathbf{i} + 6\mathbf{j}$

(c) $-3\mathbf{i} + 6\mathbf{j}$

**14** $55.5°$

**15** $\alpha = 3, \beta = -1, \gamma = 2$

**16** (b) (i) $(1 - k, 2 - k, k - 2)$     (ii) $\frac{5}{3}$

(iii) $\sqrt{6}/3$

## Advanced

**1**  $\alpha = 3, \beta = -2$

**2**  (a)  $3:2$
(b)  $a = 8, b = -3$

**3**  (a)  $(1/\sqrt{2})(-\mathbf{j} + \mathbf{k})$
(b)  $\lambda = 3, \mu = 6$
(c)  $5\mathbf{i} + 10\mathbf{j} - 12\mathbf{k}$

**4**  (a)  (i) 1      (ii)  1      (iii)  $\sqrt{3}/2$
(b)  $\frac{1}{4}\mathbf{a} + \frac{3}{4}\mathbf{b}$
(c)  (i) 0.97      (ii)  $23°$

**5**  0; angle in a semi-circle is a right angle

**8**  (ii) 1      (iii)  $\mathbf{j}$      (iv)  $10/\sqrt{102}$

**10  a.b** $= \dfrac{2}{9x^2 - 9x - 2}$

## Revision

**1**  (a)  $10\mathbf{i} + 6\mathbf{j}$
(b)  $14\mathbf{i} + 28\mathbf{j}$
(c)  $40\mathbf{j}$
(d)  $-10\mathbf{i} - 55\mathbf{j}$

**2**  $\mathbf{x} = 4\mathbf{i} + 9\mathbf{j}$

**3**  (a)  $\begin{pmatrix} 11.23 \\ 15.82 \end{pmatrix}$      (b)  $\begin{pmatrix} -9.23 \\ 109.94 \end{pmatrix}$

**4**  $\mathbf{y} = \begin{pmatrix} 21.13 \\ 4.18 \end{pmatrix}$

**5**  (a)  5      (b)  $-1$      (c)  $-26.05$

**6**  (a)  $136.9°$      (b)  $120.8°$

**7**  (a)  0      (b)  0

Each pair of vectors is perpendicular.

**8**  (a)  **p** and **s**; **r** and **s**
(b)  **p** and **r**

**9**  (a)  $a^2 + b^2$      (b)  $a^2 - b^2$
(c)  $3b^2$

**10**  (a)  $\begin{pmatrix} 17 \\ -13 \\ 35 \end{pmatrix}$      (b)  $\begin{pmatrix} 32 \\ 17 \\ -1 \end{pmatrix}$

(c)  $\begin{pmatrix} 72 \\ 72 \\ -9 \end{pmatrix}$

**11**  (a)  $72.7°$      (b)  $67.8°$
(c)  $40.3°$

**12**  (a)  $\begin{pmatrix} 0.11 \\ -0.22 \\ 0.07 \end{pmatrix}$

(b)  0.451 billion km
(c)  $13.2°$

## 3.2

## Basic

**1**  (a)  $-11\mathbf{j}$      (b)  $5\sqrt{2}$
(c)  $\frac{1}{2}(3\mathbf{i} - \mathbf{j})$

**2**  $\overrightarrow{OA} = \begin{pmatrix} 5\lambda \\ 12\lambda \end{pmatrix}$

$\sqrt{(5\lambda)^2 + (12\lambda)^2} = 65$

$\sqrt{25\lambda^2 + 144\lambda^2} = 65$

$\sqrt{169\lambda^2} = 65$
$13\lambda = 65$
$\lambda = 5$
Therefore $A = (25, 60)$

**3** $\vec{OP} = \mathbf{a} + \dfrac{m}{m+n}\vec{AB}$

$= \mathbf{a} + \dfrac{m}{m+n}(\mathbf{b} - \mathbf{a})$

$= \dfrac{\mathbf{a}(m+n) + m(\mathbf{b} - \mathbf{a})}{m+n}$

$= \dfrac{\mathbf{a}m + \mathbf{a}n + \mathbf{b}m - \mathbf{a}m}{m+n}$

$= \dfrac{\mathbf{a}n + \mathbf{b}m}{m+n}$

**4** $3\mathbf{i} + \mathbf{j}$

**5** $5\mathbf{i} + 6\mathbf{j}$

**6** (a) $4\mathbf{i} + 5\mathbf{j}$

**7** (a)

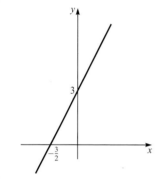

(b)

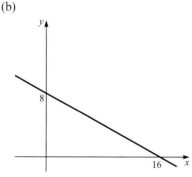

(c) $\mathbf{r}_1 : y = 2x + 3$, $\mathbf{r}_2 : y = -\tfrac{1}{2}x + 8$

**8** (a) $x = 3 + 3\lambda \Rightarrow \lambda = \dfrac{x - 3}{-3}$

$y = 6 + 2\lambda \Rightarrow \lambda = \dfrac{y - 6}{-2}$

Hence $\dfrac{x - 3}{-3} = \dfrac{y - 6}{-2} \Rightarrow y = \tfrac{2}{3}x + 4$

**9** $\mathbf{r} = (2 + \lambda)\mathbf{i} + (7 + 2\lambda)\mathbf{j}$ for example

**10** $\mathbf{r} = (1 + 3\lambda)\mathbf{i} + (4 + 4\lambda)\mathbf{j}$

**11** $\mathbf{r} = (7 + \lambda)\mathbf{i} + (4 + 3\lambda)\mathbf{j}$

**12** Equating $x$- and $y$- coordinates,

$$3 + 3\lambda = 1 + 7\mu \qquad (1)$$

$$7 - 5\lambda = 3 + 3\mu \qquad (2)$$

$(1) \times 5$ gives $15 + 15\lambda = 5 + 35\mu \qquad (3)$

$(2) \times 3$ gives $21 - 15\lambda = 9 + 9\mu \qquad (4)$

$(3) + (4)$ gives $36 = 14 + 44\mu$

$$\tfrac{1}{2} = \mu$$

Hence $\begin{pmatrix} x \\ y \end{pmatrix} = \begin{pmatrix} 1 \\ 3 \end{pmatrix} + \tfrac{1}{2}\begin{pmatrix} 7 \\ 3 \end{pmatrix} = \begin{pmatrix} 4\tfrac{1}{2} \\ 4\tfrac{1}{2} \end{pmatrix}$

The point of intersection is $(4\tfrac{1}{2}, 4\tfrac{1}{2})$.

## Intermediate

**1** (b) $\tfrac{1}{2}$

**2** (a) $\mathbf{r} = \begin{pmatrix} 3 \\ -2 \end{pmatrix} + \lambda\begin{pmatrix} 4 \\ 9 \end{pmatrix}$

(b) $\mathbf{r} = \begin{pmatrix} 4 \\ 7 \end{pmatrix} + \lambda\begin{pmatrix} 1 \\ 2 \end{pmatrix}$

(c) $\mathbf{r} = \begin{pmatrix} 3 \\ -2 \end{pmatrix} + \lambda\begin{pmatrix} 1 \\ 9 \end{pmatrix}$

**3** (a) $\mathbf{p} = \tfrac{1}{2}(\mathbf{a} + \mathbf{b})$, $\mathbf{q} = \tfrac{1}{2}(\mathbf{b} + \mathbf{c})$,
$\mathbf{r} = \tfrac{1}{2}(\mathbf{a} + \mathbf{c})$

**4** $4\mathbf{i} - 4\mathbf{j}$

**5** (a) $23\mathbf{i}$    (b) $2100$ units$^2$

**6** $-7\mathbf{i} + 3\mathbf{j}$

**7** $\begin{pmatrix} -1 \\ 8 \end{pmatrix}$ or $\begin{pmatrix} 7 \\ 4 \end{pmatrix}$

**8** 3

**9** $r = (3 + \lambda)i + (2 - 4\lambda)j$

**10** $\ell_1 : y = -2x + 2$,  $\ell_2 : y = \frac{1}{3}x - 1$
$\ell_3 : y = \frac{5}{2}x + 1$

**11** 5

**12** (a) Direction of $r_1$ is $14i + 8j$.
Direction of $r_2$ is $16i - 2j$.
Angle between lines is angle
between direction vectors. These
are clearly not parallel, so they
intersect.
When they intersect $r_1 = r_2$ i.e.
$(-2 + 14\lambda)i + (4 + 8\lambda)j$
$= (-3 + 16\mu)i + (9 - 2\mu)j$
i.e. $-2 + 14\lambda = -3 + 16\mu$
and $4 + 8\lambda = 9 - 2\mu$
Solving gives $\lambda = \frac{1}{2}, \mu = \frac{1}{2}$ and the
point of intersection is
$-2i + 4j + \frac{1}{2}(14i + 8j) = 5i + 8j$

(b) Parallel
(c) Intersecting; $\frac{9}{2}(i + j)$

**13** (a) $(7, 5)$

**14** $-1; (3, -1)$

**15** (a) Angle between lines is angle
between direction vectors, i.e.

angle between $\begin{pmatrix} 1 \\ 2 \end{pmatrix}$ and $\begin{pmatrix} 3 \\ 1 \end{pmatrix}$.

$\begin{pmatrix} 1 \\ 2 \end{pmatrix} \cdot \begin{pmatrix} 3 \\ 1 \end{pmatrix}$
$= \sqrt{1^2 + 2^2}\sqrt{3^2 + 1^2}\cos\theta$
$\Rightarrow 5 = \sqrt{5}\sqrt{10}\cos\theta$
$\Rightarrow \theta = 45°$

(b) 161.6°

**16** (a) $11i + 4j$
(b) $(-1 + 4\lambda)i + (7 - \lambda)j$
(c) Let $P$ be the point with
parameter $\mu$ on $BD$ such that
$CP \perp BD$ i.e.
$\vec{OP} = (-1 + 4\mu)i + (7 - \mu)j$
Direction of $\vec{BD}$ is $4i - j$
Direction of $\vec{CP}$ is $(-1 + 4\mu)i$
$+ (7 - \mu)j - (8i + 9j)$
$= (-9 + 4\mu)i + (-2 - \mu)j$

$\vec{CP}.\vec{BD} = 0$
$\Rightarrow 4(-9 + 4\mu) - (-2 - \mu) = 0$
$\Rightarrow \mu = 2$
Hence $\vec{CP} = -i - 4j$ so
perpendicular distance $= |CP|$
$= \sqrt{17}$

## Advanced

**2** (a) $r = \begin{pmatrix} 1 \\ 4 \end{pmatrix} + \lambda\begin{pmatrix} 4 \\ -3 \end{pmatrix}$

(b) $\begin{pmatrix} 5.8 \\ 0.4 \end{pmatrix}$ or $\begin{pmatrix} -3.8 \\ 7.6 \end{pmatrix}$

(c) 3.8

**3** (i) $\frac{1}{3}a + \frac{1}{3}b$

**4** (a) $nb - (n-1)a$

(b) $\left\{\frac{\lambda}{m} - (1 - \lambda)(n - 1)\right\}a + n(1 - \lambda)b$

**5** (a) $\begin{pmatrix} -2\sin t \\ \cos t \end{pmatrix}, \begin{pmatrix} \cos t \\ 2\sin t \end{pmatrix}$

(b) $\begin{pmatrix} x \\ y \end{pmatrix} = \begin{pmatrix} 2\cos t \\ \sin t \end{pmatrix} + \lambda\begin{pmatrix} \cos t \\ 2\sin t \end{pmatrix}$

(c) $X(\frac{3}{2}\cos t, 0), Y(0, -3\sin t)$
(e) $t = \pi/4, 3\pi/4, 5\pi/4, 7\pi/4$

**6** $r = \dfrac{\mu a + \lambda b}{\lambda + \mu}$

**7** $\frac{5\sqrt{3}}{23} - \frac{12}{23}$

**8** $r = c + \mu[\frac{1}{2}(a + b) - c]$

**9** (i) $\lambda < 0, \lambda > \frac{2}{3}$     (ii) $\lambda = 0, \lambda = \frac{2}{3}$
(iii) $0 < \lambda < \frac{2}{3}$

**10** (i) Equilateral
(ii) Right-angled at $A$

## Revision

**1** (a) $13i + 3j$     (b) $\sqrt{40}$

**2** $\frac{1}{2}(9i - j)$

**3**   $5\mathbf{i} + 9\mathbf{j}$

**4**   $(2, 15)$

**5**   (b) $p = -2, q = 6$

**6**   $\mathbf{r} = (2 + \lambda)\mathbf{i} + (3 - \lambda)\mathbf{j}$

**7**   $\mathbf{r} = (2 + \lambda)\mathbf{i} + (4 - \lambda)\mathbf{j}$

**8**   $\mathbf{r} = (7 + 5\lambda)\mathbf{i} + (3 + 2\lambda)\mathbf{j}$

**9**   $\ell_2$ and $\ell_5$

**10**   $119.7°$

**11**   (a)  15 and 11
       (b)  $(1 + 4\lambda)\mathbf{i} + (19 - 3\lambda)\mathbf{j}$

**12**   (b) $3\sqrt{2}$

## 3.3

## Basic

**1**   $\frac{4}{5}\mathbf{i} - \mathbf{j} + \mathbf{k}$

**2**   $(-4, 5, -3)$

**3**   (a)  $2\mathbf{i} - 3\mathbf{j} + 4\mathbf{k}$   (c)  $4\sqrt{30}$ units$^2$

**4**   Comparing coefficients of $\mathbf{i}, \mathbf{j}$ and $\mathbf{k}$
       $x = 2 + 4\lambda, \quad y = 3 - 2\lambda,$
       $z = 7 + \lambda$
       Therefore $(\lambda =)\dfrac{x - 2}{4} = \dfrac{3 - y}{2} = z - 7$

**5**   $\mathbf{r} = 2\mathbf{i} + 4\mathbf{j} - \mathbf{k} + \lambda(3\mathbf{i} + 2\mathbf{j} + 4\mathbf{k})$

**6**   $48.2°$

**7**   (b)  $5\mathbf{i} - 5\mathbf{j} + 7\mathbf{k}$
       (c)  $\ell_2$ and $\ell_3$ have direction vectors
            $3\mathbf{i} - 6\mathbf{j} + 6\mathbf{k}$ and $\mathbf{i} - 3\mathbf{j} + 2\mathbf{k}$
            respectively.
            They are clearly not parallel.
            If $\ell_2$ and $\ell_3$ intersect,

$(3 + 3\mu)\mathbf{i} + (1 - 6\mu)\mathbf{j} + (2 + 6\mu)\mathbf{k}$
$= (3 + \varphi)\mathbf{i} + (1 - 3\varphi)\mathbf{j} + (3 + 2\varphi)\mathbf{k}$

$$\Rightarrow 3 + 3\mu = 3 + \varphi \qquad (1)$$
$$1 - 6\mu = 1 + 3\varphi \qquad (2)$$
$$2 + 6\mu = 3 + 2\varphi \qquad (3)$$
$$(1) \Rightarrow 3\mu = \varphi$$
$$(2) \Rightarrow -6\mu = 3\varphi$$

$\Rightarrow \mu = \varphi = 0$, which is inconsistent
with (3)
Hence $\ell_2$ and $\ell_3$ have no common
point and are skew.

**8**   $(3, \frac{10}{3}, 0)$

**9**   (a)  $(x\mathbf{i} + y\mathbf{i} + z\mathbf{k}).(2\mathbf{i} + 3\mathbf{j} - \mathbf{k}) = 6$
            therefore $2x + 3y - z = 6$
       (b)  $x = 2 + 2\lambda - \mu \qquad (1)$
            $y = 1 - \mu \qquad\qquad (2)$
            $z = -1 + \lambda + 2\mu \quad (3)$
            $(1) - (2) \quad x - y = 1 + 2\lambda \quad (4)$
            $(3) + 2 \times (2) \quad z + 2y = 1 + \lambda \quad (5)$
            From (5), $z + 2y - 1 = \lambda$
            Substituting in (4)
            $x - y = 1 + 2(z + 2y - 1)$
            $x - y = 1 + 2z + 4y - 2$
            $x - 5y - 2z = -1$

**10**   (a)  $\mathbf{r}.(4\mathbf{i} - 5\mathbf{j} + \mathbf{k}) = 7$
        (b)  $\mathbf{r}.(3\mathbf{i} + 5\mathbf{j} - 2\mathbf{k}) = 13$

**11**   (a)  (i)  $\begin{pmatrix} \frac{6}{7} \\ \frac{2}{7} \\ -\frac{3}{7} \end{pmatrix}$   (ii)  2

        (b)  (i)  $\begin{pmatrix} \frac{6}{11} \\ -\frac{9}{11} \\ \frac{2}{11} \end{pmatrix}$   (ii)  $\frac{5}{11}$

**12**   (a)  Any point in the plane has
            position vector
            $$\mathbf{r} = \vec{OA} + \lambda\vec{AB} + \mu\vec{AC}$$
            Hence $\mathbf{r} = 2\mathbf{i} + \mathbf{j} + 2\mathbf{k} + \lambda(\mathbf{i} + \mathbf{j} - 4\mathbf{k})$
            $\qquad\qquad + \mu(3\mathbf{i} - \mathbf{j} - 3\mathbf{k})$
        (b)  $\mathbf{r}.(7\mathbf{i} + 9\mathbf{j} + 4\mathbf{k}) = 31$

## Intermediate

**2** (a) $50\mathbf{i} - 6\mathbf{j} + 8\mathbf{k}$
(b) $20\mathbf{i} - 18\mathbf{j} + 24\mathbf{j}$

**3** $p = 2, q = 3$

**4** (a) Parallel
(b) Skew
(c) Intersecting

**5** (a) $-1$     (b) $-3$

**6** Skew; $101.3°$

**7** (a) (i) $\begin{pmatrix} \frac{2}{3} \\ \frac{2}{3} \\ -\frac{1}{3} \end{pmatrix}$     (ii) $2$

(b) (i) $\begin{pmatrix} \frac{9}{11} \\ -\frac{2}{11} \\ \frac{6}{11} \end{pmatrix}$     (ii) $1$

**8** (a) Taking $\mathbf{r}_1$ as $x\mathbf{i} + y\mathbf{j} + z\mathbf{k}$,
$$x = -1 + 3\varphi, \quad y = 1, \quad z = 2 + 2\varphi$$
$\mathbf{r}_1$ intersects $P$ when
$2x - y + 3z = 5$
$$\Rightarrow 2(-1 + 3\varphi) - 1 + 3(2 + 2\varphi) = 5$$
$$\Rightarrow \varphi = \frac{1}{6}$$
Here $\mathbf{r}_1$ intersects $P$ at $(-\frac{1}{2}, 1, \frac{7}{3})$.
(b) Parallel
(c) Lies within
(d) Intersects

**9** Normal to $P_1$ is $\mathbf{n}_1 = 2\mathbf{i} + 3\mathbf{j} - \mathbf{k}$;
normal to $P_2$ is $\mathbf{n}_2 = 4\mathbf{i} + 6\mathbf{j} - 2\mathbf{k}$
Since $\mathbf{n}_2 = 2\mathbf{n}_1$ the planes are parallel.
Distance of $O$ from $P_1$
$$= \frac{7}{\sqrt{2^2 + 3^2 + 1^2}} = \frac{7}{\sqrt{14}}$$

Distance of $O$ from $P_2$
$$= \frac{7}{\sqrt{4^2 + 6^2 + 2^2}} = \frac{7}{2\sqrt{14}}$$

Hence distance of $P_1$ from $P_2$
$$= \frac{7}{\sqrt{14}} - \frac{7}{2\sqrt{14}} = \frac{\sqrt{14}}{4}$$

**10** $\frac{1}{3}$

**11** (a) $1$     (b) $-8$

**12** $51.8°$

**13** (a) $-2\mathbf{i} + 3\mathbf{j} - 2\mathbf{k} + \lambda(4\mathbf{i} - 2\mathbf{j} + \mathbf{k})$
(b) $(2, 1, -1)$

**14** (a) $3x + y + z = 8$
(b) $(\frac{28}{11}, -\frac{31}{11}, \frac{35}{11})$

**15** $4x + 7y - 4z = 3; \frac{1}{3}$

## Advanced

**1** (i) $2x - 3y + 7z = -5$
(ii) $\mathbf{r} = 130\mathbf{i} - 40\mathbf{j} + 20\mathbf{k}$
$+ \lambda(-40\mathbf{i} + 20\mathbf{j} - 5\mathbf{k})$
(iii) $10\mathbf{i} + 20\mathbf{j} + 5\mathbf{k}$     (iv) $135$ m

**2** (ii) $\mathbf{r} = \begin{pmatrix} 0 \\ 4 \\ -5 \end{pmatrix} + \lambda \begin{pmatrix} 2 \\ -6 \\ 0 \end{pmatrix}$

(iii) $(1, 1, -5)$

(iv) $O, A, B, E$ lie in the same plane.
(v) $86.9°$

**3** (a) $82.3°$     (b) $7.43$

(c) $\begin{pmatrix} \frac{2}{5} \\ 3 \\ \frac{14}{5} \end{pmatrix}$     (d) $2.71$

**4** (i) $y, z$; normal $\begin{pmatrix} \cos \alpha \\ 0 \\ \sin \alpha \end{pmatrix}$

(ii) $x, y$; normal $\begin{pmatrix} 0 \\ \sin \alpha \\ \cos \alpha \end{pmatrix}$

**5** $-5\mathbf{i} + 10\mathbf{k}$

**6** $(-2, 4, 3);$   $-x + 2y + z = 13;$
$\mathbf{r} = (-2\mathbf{i} + 4\mathbf{j} + 3\mathbf{k})$
$+ \lambda(13\mathbf{i} - 11\mathbf{j} + 19\mathbf{k})$

**7** $\mathbf{r} = \lambda \begin{pmatrix} 11 \\ 7 \\ 10 \end{pmatrix}$

**8** (ii) $A(35, -11, 23), B(35, 19, -17)$
(iv) $(30, 32, 24)$ or $(70, 8, 6)$ or
$(40, 24, -18)$

**9** (i)

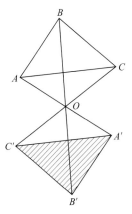

(ii)

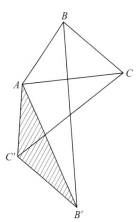

## Revision

**1** (a) Skew
(b) Parallel
(c) Intersecting

**2** $31.0°$

**3** (a) $\dfrac{2 - x}{3} = \dfrac{y - 4}{2} = z$

(b) $\mathbf{r} = -2\mathbf{i} + \mathbf{j} + \lambda(4\mathbf{i} - \mathbf{j} + 3\mathbf{k})$

**4** $2\mathbf{i} + \mathbf{j} + 3\mathbf{k}$

**5** $(2, -2, 4)$

**7** (a) $\mathbf{r} = 3\mathbf{i} + 2\mathbf{j} - \mathbf{k} + \lambda(-\mathbf{i} - \mathbf{j} + 4\mathbf{k})$
$+ \mu(-3\mathbf{j} + \mathbf{k})$
(b) $\mathbf{r}.(11\mathbf{i} + \mathbf{j} + 3\mathbf{k}) = 32$

**8** (a) (i) $\dfrac{1}{3\sqrt{10}} \begin{pmatrix} 4 \\ -5 \\ 7 \end{pmatrix}$   (ii) $\dfrac{\sqrt{10}}{3}$

(b) (i) $\dfrac{1}{5\sqrt{3}} \begin{pmatrix} 1 \\ 7 \\ 5 \end{pmatrix}$   (ii) $\dfrac{2\sqrt{3}}{5}$

**9** (a) Lies within
(b) Intersects
(c) Parallel
(d) Lies within

**10** $\dfrac{\sqrt{3}}{10}$

**11** $4x - 5y + 2z = 3; \dfrac{\sqrt{5}}{5}$

**12** $a = 4, b = 1$

# Chapter 4 Functions

## 4.1

## Basic

**1** (a) 13   (b) −0.75
   (c) 1   (d) $t^2 - 3$

**2** (a) (i) −0.5   (ii) 1   (iii) 0.2
   (b) $\frac{2}{3}$   (c) 0, 1

**3** (a) $fg(2) = f(-4)$
   $= -10$
   (b) −22   (c) −10   (d) −4

**4** (a) $f(x) = 8 \Rightarrow 3x - 4 = 8$
   $3x = 12$
   $x = 4$
   (b) 1   (c) $\frac{4}{3}$   (d) 1.5

**5** (a)

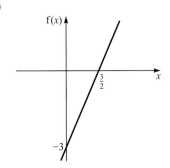

(b)

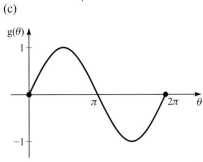

(c)

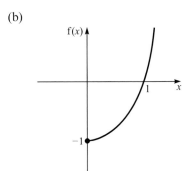

(d)

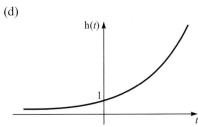

**6** (a) $f(x) \in \mathbb{R}, f(x) \geq -1$
   (b) $f(\theta) \in \mathbb{R}, -4 \leq f(\theta) \leq 4$
   (c) 2
   (d) $h(t) \in \mathbb{R}, h(t) \neq 0$

**7** (a) $\mathbb{R}$
   (b) $t \in \mathbb{R}, t \neq -4$
   (c) $x \in \mathbb{R}, x \geq -3$
   (d) $z \in \mathbb{R}$

**8** (a) (i) $fg(x) = f(2x - 3)$
$= 3(2x - 3) + 2$
$= 6x - 9 + 2$
$= 6x - 7$
(ii) $6x + 1$    (iii)  $4x - 9$
(b) (i) $x$
(ii) $hh(x)$ is the identity function, so $h(x)$ is the inverse of $h(x)$, i.e. the function is its own inverse (self-inverse).

**9** (a) $x \in \mathbb{R}, x < 5$
(b)

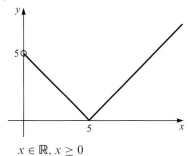

$x \in \mathbb{R}, x \geq 0$
(c)  $1, 9$

**10** (a) (i) $fg(x) = f(x + 3)$
$= (x + 3)^2 - 3$
$(= x^2 + 6x + 6)$
(ii) $x^2$

(b) (i) $f(x + 2) = \dfrac{x + 2 + 1}{x + 2 - 2}$

$= \dfrac{x + 3}{x}$

$\left(= 1 + \dfrac{3}{x}\right)$

(ii) $g\left(\dfrac{x + 1}{x - 2}\right) = \dfrac{x + 1}{x - 2} + 2$

$= \dfrac{(x + 1) + 2(x - 2)}{x - 2}$

$= \dfrac{x + 1 + 2x - 4}{x - 2}$

$= \dfrac{3x - 3}{x - 2}$

$= \dfrac{3(x - 1)}{x - 2}$

(c) (i) $x + 1$    (ii)  $xe^x$

**11** (a)  Let $y = 3x + 2$ and rearrange.
$y - 2 = 3x$

$x = \dfrac{y - 2}{3} \Rightarrow f^{-1}(x) = \dfrac{x - 2}{3}$

(b) $f^{-1}(x) = \dfrac{1}{x} - 5$

(c)  $y = \dfrac{x + 3}{2 + x}$

$y(2 + x) = x + 3$
$2y + xy = x + 3$
$xy - x = 3 - 2y^*$
$x(y - 1) = 3 - 2y$

$x = \dfrac{3 - 2y}{y - 1}$

$\Rightarrow f^{-1}(x) = \dfrac{3 - 2x}{x - 1}$

*alternatively $2y - 3 = x - xy$
$2y - 3 = x(1 - y)$

$x = \dfrac{2y - 3}{1 - y}$

$\Rightarrow f^{-1}(x) = \dfrac{2x - 3}{1 - x}$

(d) $f^{-1}(x) = e^{x-1}$

**12** (a) $f(x) \in \mathbb{R}, f(x) \geq 1$
(b) $f^{-1}(x) = \sqrt{x - 1}$
(c)  Domain $x \in \mathbb{R}, x \geq 1$;
range $f^{-1}(x) \in \mathbb{R}, f^{-1}(x) \geq 0$

## Intermediate

**1**

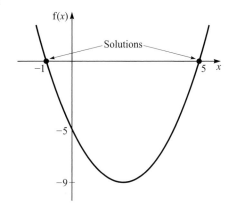

**2**

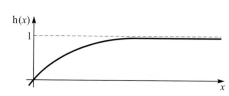

**3**   $\theta$ is measured in radians.

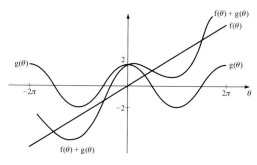

**4**   (a) $-1, 2$   (b)   $2, 7$

**5**   (a) $gf(x) = x^2$
   (b) (i) $f(x) \in \mathbb{R}, f(x) \geq -3$
   (ii) $\mathbb{R}$
   (iii) $gf(x) \in \mathbb{R}, gf(x) \geq 0$

**6**   (a) (i) $\mathbb{R}$   (ii) $x \in \mathbb{R}, \ x \leq 3$
   (b) Domain $x \in \mathbb{R}, -1 \leq x \leq 1$; range
   $gf(x) \in \mathbb{R}, 0 \leq gf(x) \leq 1$

**7**   (b) (i) Domain $x \in \mathbb{R}, x \neq 4$; range
   $f(x) \in \mathbb{R}, f(x) \neq 1$
   (ii) Domain $x \in \mathbb{R}, x \neq -2$; range
   $g(x) \in \mathbb{R}, g(x) \neq 1$
   (iii) Domain $x \in \mathbb{R}, x \neq 4$ or $\frac{5}{3}$;
   range $gf(x) \in \mathbb{R}, gf(x) \neq 1$ or $0$

**8**   (a) $gf(\theta) = 2^{3\cos\theta}$; domain $\mathbb{R}$;
   range $gf(\theta) \in \mathbb{R}, -\frac{1}{8} \leq gf(\theta) \leq 8$
   (b) $fg(\theta) = 3\cos(2^\theta)$; domain $\mathbb{R}$;
   range $fg(\theta) \in \mathbb{R}, -3 \leq fg(\theta) \leq 3$

**9**   (a) $gf(x) = +x$; domain $\mathbb{R}$;
   range $gf(x) \in \mathbb{R}, gf(x) \geq 0$
   (b) $fg(x) = x$; domain $x \in \mathbb{R}, x \geq 5$;
   range $= fg(x) \in \mathbb{R}, fg(x) \geq 5$

**10**   (a) $3$   (b) $-1$   (c) $\sqrt{x} - 1$

**11**   (a) (i) $fg(x) = gf(x) = 3x - 1$
   (ii) $fh(x) = hf(x) = x$
   (b) Yes

**12**   (b) Domain $x \in \mathbb{R}, x \neq 2$; range
   $f(x) \in \mathbb{R}, f(x) \neq 1$
   (d) Domain $x \in \mathbb{R}, x \neq 1$; range
   $f^{-1}(x) \in \mathbb{R}, f^{-1}(x) \neq 2$

**13** (a)

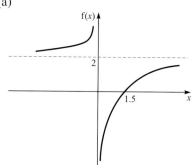

   (b) (i) $\dfrac{2-x}{3}$   (ii) $\dfrac{1}{x}$

   (iii) $\dfrac{3}{2-x}$   (iv) $\dfrac{3}{2-x}$

**14** (a) $\frac{1}{2}\sin^{-1} x, 0 \leq x \leq \sqrt{3}/2$
   (b) $e^{x/2}, x \in \mathbb{R}$
   (c) $2\ln\sin 2x, 0 < x \leq \pi/6$

**15** $f^{-1}(x) = 3 + \sqrt{x-4}$; domain
   $x \in \mathbb{R}, x \geq 4$; range
   $f^{-1}(x) \in \mathbb{R}, f^{-1}(x) \geq 3$

**16** $g^{-1}(x) = \ln(1/\sqrt{x}), x \in \mathbb{R}^+$

## Advanced

**1** (a)

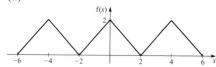

   (b) (i) $y = 2 + x$
   (ii) $y = -2 + x$
   (iii) $y = 102 - x$

**2**   (a)  (i)

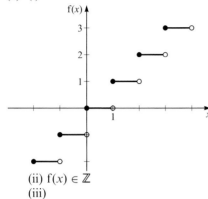

(ii) $f(x) \in \mathbb{Z}$
(iii)

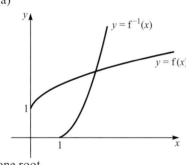

(iv) 0   (v) $x \in \mathbb{R}$   (vi) $\frac{1}{2}a(a-1)$
(b)  13

**3**   (a)

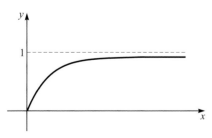

one root
(b)  $\frac{1}{2}(3 + \sqrt{5})$

**4**   (a)  $\ln x / \ln 2 (x > 0)$
(b)  $a = 3, f(x) \leq 0$
(c)  $x \geq 0$

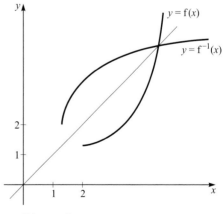

**5**   (a)  $f(x) \geq 0$
(c)

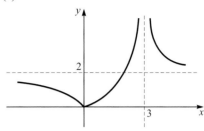

**6**   (a)  (ii) $1 + \sqrt{(x+1)/3}, x > -1$
(iii)

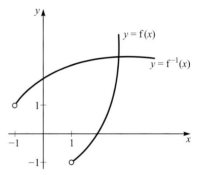

(iv)  $f^{-1}$ is reflection of f in
$y = x$; $(2, 2)$

(b)  (i) $\dfrac{1}{3x^2 - 6x - 3}$     (ii) $1 + \sqrt{2}$

**7**   (a)

(b)  $x - 2$
(c)  $p = 5, q = 4, r = -2/5$

**8** (a) $f(x) \geq 1; 0 < g(x) \leq 1$

(b) $f^{-1}(x) = \sqrt{(x-1)}$;
$g^{-1}(x) = \ln(1/x)$

(c) $e^{-2x} + 1$; 0 or $\ln 3$

(d) $x = 1, 3$

**9** $-3 \leq x < \frac{1}{2}(1 + \sqrt{13})$

**10** $\dfrac{1}{x-1} + \dfrac{1}{x-2}$

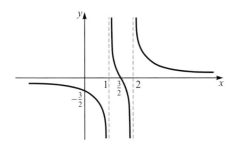

$1 < x < 2$;

$f^{-1}(x) = \dfrac{3x + 2 + \sqrt{x^2 + 4}}{2x}$    $(x \neq 0)$

$3/2$   $(x = 0)$

## Revision

**1** (a) 0     (b) 1     (c) $\frac{1}{2}$

**2** (a) (i) 0     (ii) $-5$
(b) $-x$

**3** (a) $\pi/2$     (b) $\pi/6, 5\pi/6$

**4**

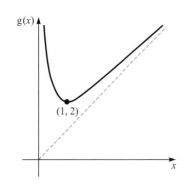

$g(x)$

$(1, 2)$

**5** $x \in \mathbb{R}, x \leq \frac{1}{2}$

**6** $h(x) = 2 \sin x, x \in \mathbb{R}$,
$-360° \leq x \leq 360°$

**7** $g(x) \in \mathbb{R}, 0 \leq g(x) < 1$

**8** (a) $fg(x) = 7 - 3x^2$; domain $\mathbb{R}$; range
$fg(x) \in \mathbb{R}, fg(x) \leq 7$
(b) $gf(x) = -9x^2 - 24x - 15$; domain
$\mathbb{R}$; range $gf(x) \in \mathbb{R}, gf(x) \leq 1$

**9** Domain $x \in \mathbb{R}, 4 < x \leq 5$; range
$hg(x) \in \mathbb{R}, 0 \leq hg(x) < 1$

**10** $f^{-1}(x) = 3x - 1, x \in \mathbb{R}$

**11** $g^{-1}(x) = \sqrt{4 + 1/x}, x \in \mathbb{R}^+$

**12** (a) $hh(x) = \dfrac{3x + 8}{3 - 2x}$

(b) $h^{-1}(x) = \dfrac{x + 4}{1 - x}$

## 4.2

## Basic

**1** (a) (i) $g(x) = x^2 + 7$
(ii) $h(x) = x^2 + 3$
(iii) $k(x) = x^2 - 2$
(b) (i) $g(x) = f(x) + 7$
(ii) $h(x) = f(x) + 3$
(iii) $k(x) = f(x) - 2$

**2** (a) Translation $\begin{pmatrix} 0 \\ 2 \end{pmatrix}$

(b) Translation $\begin{pmatrix} 0 \\ 5 \end{pmatrix}$

(c) Translation $\begin{pmatrix} 0 \\ -3 \end{pmatrix}$

(d) Translation $\begin{pmatrix} 0 \\ -2 \end{pmatrix}$

**3** (a) (i) $g(x) = (x - 5)^3$
(ii) $h(x) = (x - 2)^3$
(iii) $k(x) = (x + 4)^3$
(b) (i) $g(x) = f(x - 5)$
(ii) $h(x) = f(x - 2)$
(iii) $k(x) = f(x + 4)$

**4** (a) $f(x - 2) + 1 = (x - 2)^2 + 1$
$= (x - 2)(x - 2) + 1$
$= x^2 - 4x + 4 + 1$
$= x^2 - 4x + 5$

(b) Translation, $\begin{pmatrix} 2 \\ 1 \end{pmatrix}$

**5** (a) (i) $g(x) = 3 \times 2^x$
(ii) $h(x) = \frac{1}{2} \times 2^x$
(iii) $k(x) = -2 \times 2^x$
(b) (i) $g(x) = 3f(x)$
(ii) $h(x) = \frac{1}{2}f(x)$
(iii) $k(x) = -2f(x)$

**6** (a) One-way stretch, scale factor $\frac{1}{3}$, parallel to $\theta$-axis

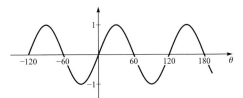

(b) One-way stretch, scale factor 2, parallel to $\theta$-axis

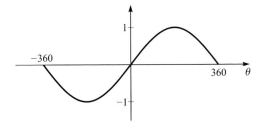

(c) One-way stretch, scale factor $-\frac{1}{2}$, parallel to $\theta$-axis *or* a reflection in the $y$-axis followed by a one-way stretch, scale factor $\frac{1}{2}$, parallel to $\theta$-axis

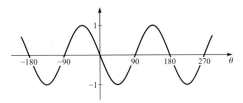

**7** (Other answers are possible.)
(a) One-way stretch, scale factor 2, parallel to $y$-axis

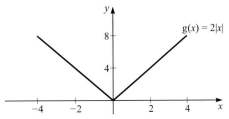

$g(x) = 2|x|$

(b) One-way stretch, scale factor 2, parallel to $x$-axis

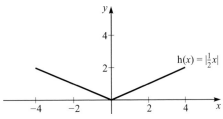

$h(x) = |\frac{1}{2}x|$

(c) A reflection in the $x$-axis, followed by a one-way stretch, scale factor $\frac{1}{2}$, parallel to the $x$-axis

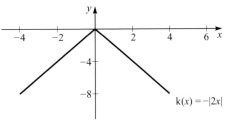

$k(x) = -|2x|$

**8** (a) A one-way stretch, scale factor 2, parallel to the $y$-axis, followed by a translation through

$$\begin{pmatrix} 4 \\ -2 \end{pmatrix}$$

(b) $g(x) = 2f(x - 4) - 2$

(c) $g(x) = 2(x - 4)^2 - 2$
$= 2(x - 4)(x - 4) - 2$
$= 2(x^2 - 8x + 16) - 2$
$= 2x^2 - 16x + 32 - 2$
$= 2x^2 - 16x + 30$

**9** (a) (i)  Translation $\begin{pmatrix} -b \\ 0 \end{pmatrix}$

(ii) One-way stretch, parallel to $x$-axis, scale factor $1/a$

(c) Translation $\begin{pmatrix} -b \\ 0 \end{pmatrix}$ followed by

one-way stretch, parallel to $x$-axis, scale factor $1/a$, *or* one-way stretch, parallel to $x$-axis, scale factor $1/a$, followed by translation $\begin{pmatrix} -b/a \\ 0 \end{pmatrix}$

(d)

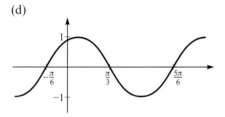

**10** (a) (i)

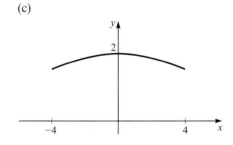

(ii)

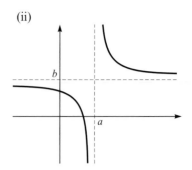

**11** (a)

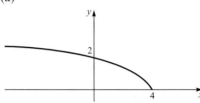

(b)

(c)

**12** (a)

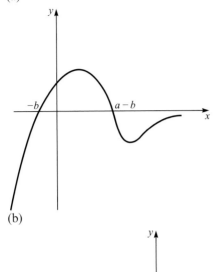

(b)

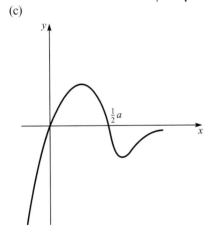

(c)

# Intermediate

**1** (a)

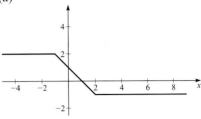

(b)

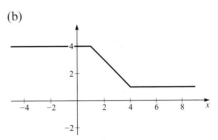

(c)

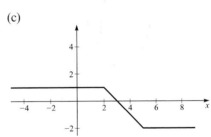

**2** (a)

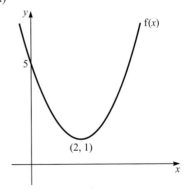

(b)  $f(x) = (x-2)^2 + 1$

**3** (a)

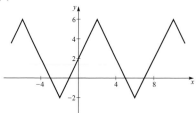

(b)

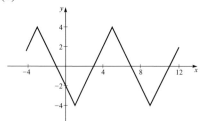

(c)

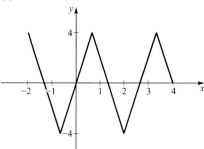

**4** (b) Translation $\begin{pmatrix} 1 \\ -2 \end{pmatrix}$

**5** (a)

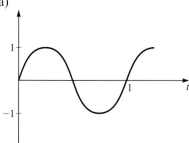

(b) $g(t) = 0.036f(400t)$
(c) One-way stretch, scale factor 0.036, parallel to $y$-axis, followed by one-way stretch, scale factor $\frac{1}{400}$, parallel to $x$-axis

(d) $0.05 \sin 400\pi t$

**6**

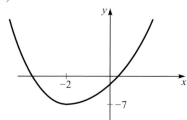

**7** Translation $\begin{pmatrix} -2 \\ 0 \end{pmatrix}$

One-way stretch, scale factor $\frac{2}{3}$, parallel to $y$-axis

**8** (a) $(x + 2)^2 - 7$
(b)

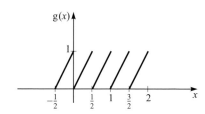

(c)

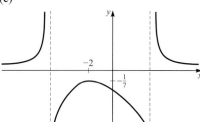

**9** $32x^2 - 22x$

**10** $a = 4$ and $b = \pi/6$

**11**

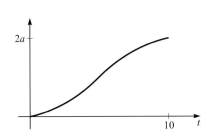

**12** $g(x) = \dfrac{1}{x}$

**13** $h(x) = f\left(\dfrac{x}{2} + 3\right) - 7$

**14** (a) $g(x) = 3f(2x + 3) + 7$

**15**

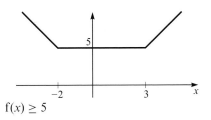

$f(x) \geq 5$

**16** (a) Translation $\begin{pmatrix} -3 \\ 2 \end{pmatrix}$

(b) $f(x) = g(x + 3) + 2$

(c) $h(x) = g\left(\dfrac{x}{2} + 2\right) + 5$

One-way stretch, scale factor 2, parallel to $x$-axis,

followed by a translation $\begin{pmatrix} -4 \\ 5 \end{pmatrix}$

*or* translation $\begin{pmatrix} -2 \\ 5 \end{pmatrix}$

followed by one-way stretch, scale factor 2, parallel to $x$-axis

## Advanced

**1** (a) Translation $\begin{pmatrix} 1 \\ 2 \end{pmatrix}$

(b) Translation $\begin{pmatrix} -1 \\ -2 \end{pmatrix}$

**2** (a) $3x + 2 = 3(x - 3) + 11$

(b) $3 + \dfrac{11}{x - 3}$

(c)

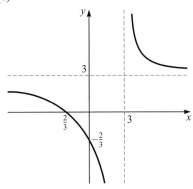

(d)

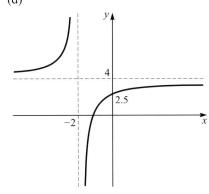

**3** (a) $4\{(x - 3)^2 + 4\}$   (b) $a = \frac{1}{16}$

**4** (a) $g(x) = \frac{1}{5}f\left(\dfrac{x}{2} + 1\right) - 3$

(b) $g(x) = 5^x - 3$

**5** (a) $y = \dfrac{1}{2a - x}$

**6**  Translation $\begin{pmatrix} b \\ 0 \end{pmatrix}$

(a)

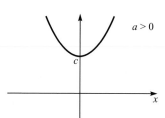

$a > 0$

(b)

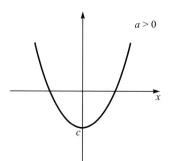

$a > 0$

(c)

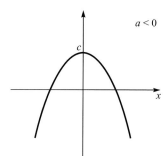

$a < 0$

(d)

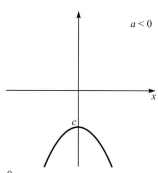

$a < 0$

$ac < 0$

**7**  (a)  (i)

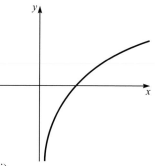

(ii)

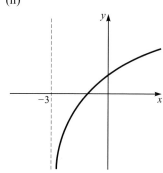

(b)  (i) 6.8      (ii) 8.0      (iii) 8.0

**8**  (i) 3      (ii) $\dfrac{n(n+1)}{2}$

**9**  0

**10**  (a)

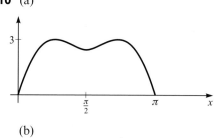

(b)

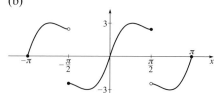

# Revision

**1** (a) $a = 0, b = 3$
(b) $c = -5, d = 0$
(c) $s = -6, t = -4$

**2** (a) Translation $\begin{pmatrix} \pi/3 \\ 0 \end{pmatrix}$

(b) Translation $\begin{pmatrix} 0 \\ -2 \end{pmatrix}$

(c) Translation $\begin{pmatrix} 2 \\ 4 \end{pmatrix}$

**3** (a) Translation $\begin{pmatrix} 1 \\ -2 \end{pmatrix}$

(b) $g(x) = \dfrac{x(x-1)}{x-2}$

**4** (a) Translation $\begin{pmatrix} -4 \\ 3 \end{pmatrix}$

(b) $g(x) = x^2 + 2x + 3$

**5** $a = 5, b = -5\pi/6, c = 7$

**6** (a) (i) Translation $\begin{pmatrix} \pi/3 \\ 0 \end{pmatrix}$; one-way stretch, scale factor 5, parallel to $y$-axis
(ii) One-way stretch, scale factor $\frac{1}{2}$, parallel to $x$-axis, followed by a translation, $\begin{pmatrix} \frac{1}{2} \\ 0 \end{pmatrix}$

(b) (ii) Translation $\begin{pmatrix} 0 \\ 2 \end{pmatrix}$

one-way stretch, scale factor $\frac{1}{2}$, parallel to $x$-axis

**7** (a) Translation $\begin{pmatrix} 1 \\ 0 \end{pmatrix}$ followed by one-way stretch, scale factor 2, parallel to $y$-axis followed by translation $\begin{pmatrix} 0 \\ 4 \end{pmatrix}$

**8** (a) One-way stretch, scale factor $\frac{1}{4}$, parallel to $x$-axis;
one-way stretch, scale factor $\frac{1}{2}$ parallel to $y$-axis;
translation $\begin{pmatrix} 0 \\ 2 \end{pmatrix}$; reflection in $x$-axis
(b) $g(x) = -\frac{1}{2} f(4x) - 2$

**9** Translation $\begin{pmatrix} -2 \\ 0 \end{pmatrix}$

*or* one-way stretch, scale factor 9, parallel to $y$-axis

**10** (a)

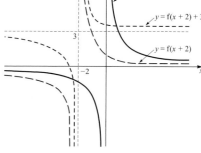

**11** (a) $1/x$     (b) $1/x$

**12** (a) $g(x) = 2f(3x - 1)$

# Chapter 5 Sequences

## 5.1

### Basic

**1** (a) $4r + 1$  (b) $20 - 3r$

(c) $\dfrac{r}{2r + 1}$  (d) $2r^2 - 1$

**2** (a) $u_1 = 1, u_{r+1} = u_r + 4$
(b) $u_1 = 3, u_{r+1} = \frac{3}{2}u_r$
(c) $u_1 = 2, u_{r+1} = (r + 1)u_r$

**3** (a) $\frac{2}{4}, \frac{3}{5}, \frac{4}{6}, \frac{5}{7}, \frac{6}{8}$, convergent to 1
(b) $3, \frac{9}{2}, \frac{27}{7}, \frac{81}{20}, \frac{243}{61}$, convergent to 4
and oscillating
(c) $0.5, -0.5, -1, -0.5, 0, 5$, periodic
and divergent
(d) $u_1 = 1$; putting $r = 1, 2, 3, 4$ into
the given definition we have

$$u_2 = u_1^2 - u_1 + 2 = 2$$
$$u_3 = u_2^2 - u_2 + 2 = 4$$
$$u_4 = u_3^2 - u_3 + 2 = 14$$
$$u_5 = u_4^2 - u_4 + 2 = 184$$

The sequence is divergent.

**5** $u_1 = 2, u_2 = 5$.
Substituting $r = 1, 2, 3, 4$, etc. into the
definition $u_{r+2} = u_{r+1} + u_r$ gives

$$u_3 = u_2 + u_1 = 5 + 2 = 7$$
$$u_4 = u_3 + u_2 = 12$$
$$u_5 = 19, u_6 = 31, \text{ etc.}$$

This is a divergent sequence similar in
structure to the Fibonacci sequence.

**6** (a) 58  (b) 620
(c) $\frac{17}{30}$  (d) 1020

**7** (a) $\frac{3}{1} + \frac{4}{2} + \frac{5}{3} + \frac{6}{4} + \frac{7}{5} = 9\frac{17}{30}$

(b) $-1 + 1 + 3 + 5 + 7 + 9 + 11 + 13$
$= 48$
(c) $-1 + 2 - 3 + 4 = 2$

**8** (a) $\displaystyle\sum_{r=1}^{5}(5r + 1)$

(b) $\displaystyle\sum_{r=1}^{4}\frac{1}{2r + 1}$

(c) $\displaystyle\sum_{r=1}^{5}(-1)^{r+1}r^2$

**9** $x^2 - \frac{4}{3}x^4 + \frac{3}{2}x^6 - \frac{8}{5}x^8$

**10** $\displaystyle\sum_{r=1}^{n} r(r - 1) = \sum_{r=1}^{n}(r^2 - r)$

$$= \sum_{r=1}^{n} r^2 - \sum_{r=1}^{n} r$$

$$= \frac{n(n + 1)(2n + 1)}{6} - \frac{n(n + 1)}{2}$$

$$= \frac{n(n + 1)}{6}(2n + 1 - 3)$$

$$= \frac{n(n + 1)(n - 1)}{3} = \frac{1}{3}n(n^2 - 1)$$

**12** $2n(n + 1)(n^2 - n - 1)$

### Intermediate

**1** (a), (c) and (d)

**2** $1, \frac{1}{3}, \frac{1}{7}, \frac{1}{15}, \frac{1}{31}$;  $u_n = \dfrac{1}{2^n - 1}$

**3**  $3$ or $-\frac{11}{3}$

**4**  $\dfrac{n}{(n-1)!}$

**5**  $\dfrac{a}{1+a}, \dfrac{a}{1+2a}, \dfrac{a}{1+3a}$

**6**  (a)  $-1, 8, -19$; oscillating
(b)  (ii) $k = 1, 4$

**7**  $1, 8, 21, 40$;    $u_n = 3n^2 - 2n$

**8**  (a)  $(r+1)(2r+1)$
(b)  $1546$

**9**  $50\,666\,650$

**10**  (a)  $\displaystyle\sum_{r=1}^{22} r(r^2 + 1)$;  $64\,262$

(b)  $\displaystyle\sum_{r=1}^{11} 3r(2r - 1)$;  $2838$

**11**  $5$

**13**  $105$

**14**  (b)  $\displaystyle\sum_{i=1}^{n} \frac{1}{i(i+1)} = \sum_{i=1}^{n}\left(\frac{1}{i} - \frac{1}{i+1}\right)$

$= \left(\frac{1}{1} - \frac{1}{2}\right) + \left(\frac{1}{2} - \frac{1}{3}\right)$

$+ \left(\frac{1}{3} - \frac{1}{4}\right) + \cdots$

$+ \left(\frac{1}{n} - \frac{1}{n+1}\right)$

$= 1 - \dfrac{1}{n+1}$

**16**  $\dfrac{1}{x} + \dfrac{1}{x+1} - \dfrac{2}{x+2}$

## Advanced

**1**  (i)  $\frac{1}{2}, \frac{1}{16}, \frac{1}{128}$; limit $0$
(ii)  $w_1 = 4$, $w_2 = 4\frac{1}{2}$, $w_3 = 4\frac{9}{16}$;
limit $\frac{32}{7}$

**2**  (b)  $\frac{1}{2}, \frac{1}{6}, \frac{1}{12}$
(c)  (i) $\frac{1}{2}, \frac{2}{3}, \frac{3}{4}$    (iii) $1$

**3**  (a)  (i) $900$    (ii) $729$
(b)  $9455$

**4**  (a)  $\frac{1}{2}k(41 - k)$    (b)  $0.043\,316\,\text{m}^3$

**5**  (ii)  $\frac{1}{4}n^2(n+1)^2$   (iii)  $(4n+1)(n+1)^2$

**6**  (a)  (i) $250n\left(n + 1 + \dfrac{80}{n+1}\right)$

(ii) $250\left(n + 1 + \dfrac{80}{n+1}\right)$

(b)  8 years

**7**  (b)  (i) $\frac{14}{27}$    (ii) $\frac{1}{2}(1 + (\frac{1}{3})^{n-1})$

**8**  $\dfrac{Q}{q + Q}$

**9**  (i)  $3$    (iii)  $0.50$

**10**  $\frac{1}{3}n(2n - 1)$; converges to $\frac{1}{6}\pi^2$

## Revision

**1**  (a)  $u_r = (3r - 2)!$

(b)  $u_r = \dfrac{3r - 2}{2r - 1}$

(c)  $u_r = 2^{r+1} - 1$

**2**  (a)  $2, 4, 9, 17, 28, 42$
(b)  $1, 4, 10, 20, 35, 36$

**3**  (a)  Periodic, oscillating
(b)  Divergent

**4**  (a)  $\frac{1}{3}, 1, \frac{9}{5}, \frac{16}{6}$, diverges
(b)  $2, \frac{3}{2}, \frac{4}{3}, \frac{5}{4}$, converges to $1$

**5**  (a)  $0, -1, 0$; $u_{50} = 0$
(b)  $\frac{1}{2}(1 \pm \sqrt{5})$
(c)  (i) Oscillates between $0$ and $-1$
(ii) Diverges

**6**  $\frac{1}{2}n(3n - 1)$

**7**  (a)  $\displaystyle\sum_{r=1}^{2n} \frac{r+1}{(r+2)(r+3)}$

(b)  $\displaystyle\sum_{r=1}^{15} 2(-1)^{r-1}3^{r-1}$

**8**   42 075

**9**   $\frac{1}{6}(14n^3 + 3n^2 - 11n - 6)$

**10**   $(4r + 1)^3$; $n(16n^3 + 48n^2 + 46n + 15)$

**11**   $\dfrac{\frac{1}{2}}{2r - 1} - \dfrac{\frac{1}{2}}{2r + 1}$

**12**   $a = 4, b = -2, c = -1$;

$\dfrac{n}{3}(3n^2 + 4n + 2)$

## 5.2

## Basic

**1**   (a) (i) 61      (ii) $3n + 1$
        (b) (i) $-81$   (ii) $39 - 6n$
        (c) (i) 49.5    (ii) $\frac{1}{2}(5n - 1)$

**2**   (a) (i) 325      (ii) $\frac{1}{2}n(7n - 5)$
        (b) (i) $-80$   (ii) $n(12 - 2n)$
        (c) (i) $142\frac{1}{2}$   (ii) $\frac{1}{4}n(9n - 33)$

**3**   (a) $1, 2\frac{1}{2}, 4, 5\frac{1}{2}\ldots$; sum $= 305$

        (b) $n = 1$, $S_1 = 1 \times (5 - 2) = 3$,
            1st term $= 3$
            $n = 2$, $S_2 = 2 \times (5 - 4) = 2$,
            2nd term $= S_2 - S_1 = -1$
            $n = 3$, $S_3 = 3 \times (5 - 6) = -3$,
            3rd term $= S_3 - S_2 = -5$
            Common difference $= -4$
            12th term $= 3 + 11(-4) = -41$

**4**   (a) (i) 31 104      (ii) $4 \times 6^{n-1}$
        (b) (i) $-486$     (ii) $2(-3)^{n-1}$
        (c) (i) $-\frac{3}{16}$   (ii) $6(-\frac{1}{2})^{n-1}$

**5**   27.475 m

**6**   (a) (i) $2(3^{20} - 1)$      (ii) $2(3^n - 1)$
        (b) (i) $-\frac{2}{3}(2^{20} - 1)$
            (ii) $\frac{2}{3}\{1 - (-\frac{2}{3})^n\}$
        (c) (i) $2\{1 - (\frac{1}{2})^{20}\}$
            (ii) $2\{1 - (\frac{1}{2})^n\}$

**7**   $2, 3; \frac{65}{4}$

**8**   (a) $\frac{1}{2}$      (b) 2      (c) 16

**9**   (a) $\frac{17}{2}$      (b) 44

**10**   (a) $2\frac{1}{4}$      (b) 8      (c) $-4\frac{1}{2}$

**11**   (a) (i) and (iii)
         (b) Common ratio is $r = 2x$.
             Series converges if $-1 < r < 1$
             i.e. $-1 < 2x < 1$
             i.e. $-\frac{1}{2} < x < \frac{1}{2}$
         (c) Common ratio is $r = -(1 - 2x)$.
             Series converges if $-1 < r < 1$,
             i.e. $-1 < -(1 - 2x) < 1$
             Solving gives $0 < x < 1$

         Sum to infinity $= \dfrac{1}{1 - r} = \dfrac{1}{2 - 2x}$

**12**   Let $a$ be the first term and $r$ the
         common ratio.

         Given    $\dfrac{a}{1 - r} = 6$ and $a = r$,

                  $\dfrac{r}{1 - r} = 6 \Rightarrow r = 6 - 6r$

                  $\Rightarrow r = \frac{6}{7}$

                  $\Rightarrow a = \frac{6}{7}$

         tenth term $= ar^9$
                    $= (\frac{6}{7})^{10}$

## Intermediate

**1**   £346 368 to nearest £

**2**   12  years

**3**   (a) 348      (b) 67 108 860

**4**   31 896

**5**   (a) 96
        (b) Sum to $n$ terms of the series

            $= \dfrac{5(3^n - 1)}{3 - 1} > 20\,000$

            $\Rightarrow 3^n - 1 > 8000$
            $\Rightarrow 3^n > 8001$
            Taking logs   $n \log 3 > \log 8001$
                          $\Rightarrow n > 8.18$
            i.e. $n = 9$

**6**   (a) 14      (b) 4

**7**  $4\{1 - (\frac{1}{4})^n\}$

**8**  (a) (i) £73 862     (ii) £1 520 408
(b) 32 years

**9**  (a)  $a = \dfrac{12\,000}{n} - 4n + 4$

(c)  $1 \le n \le 23$ or $n \ge 128$

**10**  Let the series be $\frac{1}{4}, \frac{1}{4}r, \frac{1}{4}r^2, \dots$

Sum to infinity is $\dfrac{\frac{1}{4}}{1 - r}$

Series of squares of terms is

$\frac{1}{16}, \frac{1}{16}r^2, \frac{1}{16}r^4, \dots$

Sum to infinity is $\dfrac{\frac{1}{16}}{1 - r^2}$

Equating these   $\dfrac{\frac{1}{4}}{1 - r} = \dfrac{\frac{1}{16}}{1 - r^2}$

$\Rightarrow \frac{1}{4}(1 - r^2) = \frac{1}{16}(1 - r)$
$\Rightarrow 4(1 - r)(1 + r) = 1 - r$
Since $r \ne 1$,   $4(1 + r) = 1$
$\Rightarrow r = -\frac{3}{4}$

**11**  Let the terms be $a - d, a, a + d$ (the algebra is easier than for $a, a + d, a + 2d$).

Sum is $a - d + a + a + d = 3a = 51$
Hence $a = 17$

Product is $(a - d)a(a + d)$
$= a(a^2 - d^2) = 4641$
$\Rightarrow 17(17^2 - d^2) = 4641$
$\Rightarrow d = \pm 4$
The terms are 13, 17, 21.

**12**  $1024, -\frac{1}{2}, 682\frac{2}{3}$

**13**  4350

**14**  13

**15**  £28 928.06

**16**  (a) (i) 3045     (ii) 2745
(iii) 2786.18
(b) $3000 \times 1.015^r - 20\,300$
$(1.015^{r-1} - 1)$
(c) 1 December

## Advanced

**1**  Common ratio $= \frac{3}{4}$; $S_\infty = -192$

**2**  (a) 3540     (b) 6     (c) 40

**3**  $\dfrac{5 + x^2}{5 - 4x + x^2}$

**4**  (i) 29.13     (ii) 507.39

**5**  $h\dfrac{1 + e^2}{1 - e^2}$

**7**  (i) $\frac{38}{99}$
(ii) $b = a_1 a_2 a_3 \dots a_N$,
$c = a_{N+1} a_{N+2} \dots a_{N+k}$

**9**  (a) $\left(\frac{1}{2^k}, \frac{1}{3^k}\right)$  (b) (ii) $\frac{2}{5}$  (c) (iii) $5\pi/24$

## Revision

**1**  $8, -\frac{8}{3}, \frac{8}{9}, -\frac{8}{27}$

**2**  40 seconds

**3**  $2 \log_2 x$

**4**  $2, \dfrac{3n + 1}{2}$

**5**  24

**6**  $-\frac{5}{4}, 2$

**7**  (a) 1.56     (b) 51 000

**8**  45, 15, 5

**9**  4

**10**  $p = -2q$; $42q$

**11**  $d = 8$ or $-56$

**12**  $\dfrac{1 - (2n - 1)x^n}{1 - x} + \dfrac{2x(1 - x^{n-1})}{(1 - x)^2}$

## 5.3

## Basic

**1**  (a) 6720    (b) 210    (c) 35
(d) 10

**2**  $a^3 + 3a^2b + 3ab^2 + b^3$;
$a^3 - 3a^2b + 3ab^2 - b^3$

**3**  $1 + 5x + 10x^2 + 10x^3 + 5x^4 + x^5$

**4**  (a) $1 - 16x + 112x^2 - 448x^3$
(b) $1 + 2x + \frac{5}{3}x^2 + \frac{20}{27}x^3$
(c) $243 + 1620x + 4320x^2 + 5760x^3$

**5**  $24x + 216x^3$

**6**  $(1 - 2x)^{10} = 1 + \binom{10}{1}(-2x)$

$$+ \binom{10}{2}(-2x)^2 + \ldots$$

Sixth term is $\binom{10}{5}(-2x)^5$

$$= \frac{10!}{5!5!}(-2)^5 x^5$$

$$= \frac{10 \times 9 \times 8 \times 7 \times 6}{5 \times 4 \times 3 \times 2 \times 1} \times (-32)x^5$$

$$= -8064x^5$$

**7**  $(1 + 2x)^4 = 1 + 8x + 24x^2$
$+ 32x^3 + 16x^4$
Substituting $x = 0.002$ gives

$$1.004^4 = 1 + 8 \times 0.002 + 24$$

$$\times 0.000\,004 + \ldots$$

$$\approx 1.016 + 0.000\,096$$

$$\approx 1.016\,096$$

$$\approx 1.016\,10 \text{ to 5 decimal places}$$

**8**  (a) $2x - 8x^2 + 12x^3 - 8x^4 + 2x^5$
(b) $1 + 7x + 18x^2 + 20x^3 + 8x^4$

**9**  $5670x^4$

**10**  (a) 35    (b) $\dfrac{2268}{15\,625}$

**11**  $17 - 12\sqrt{2}$

**12**  $(1 + 2x)^{19} = 1 + 38x + \dfrac{19 \times 18}{2 \times 1} \times 4x^2$

$$+ \frac{19 \times 18 \times 17}{3 \times 2 \times 1} \times 8x^3 + \ldots$$

$$= 1 + 38x + 684x^2$$
$$+ 7752x^3 + \ldots$$

In the expansion of $(3 + 5x)(1 + 2x)^{19}$
the coefficient of $x^3$ will be given by
$3 \times 7752 + 5 \times 684 = 26\,676$

## Intermediate

**1**  (a) $\frac{4}{447}$
(b) $n(n - 1)(r + 1)$

**2**  7 or 16

**3**  (a) $16 + 32x + 24x^2 + 8x^3 + x^4$
(b) $x^4 - 4x^2 + 6 - 4/x^2 + 1/x^4$
(c) $1 - 2x + \frac{3}{2}x^2 - \frac{1}{2}x^3 + \frac{1}{16}x^4$

**4**  $30x^3 + \dfrac{540}{x} + \dfrac{486}{x^5}$

**5**  $1 - 5x + 9x^2 - 5x^3 - 5x^4$
$+ 9x^5 - 5x^6 + x^7$

**6**  (a) 10    (b) (i) $\frac{45}{4}$    (ii) $-15$

**7**  $n = 12, x = 3$

**8**  $a = 1, b = -2, c = 330$

**9**  $1 + 5y + 10y^2 + 10y^3 + 5y^4 + y^5$;
$1 + 10x + 55x^2 + 200x^3$

**10**  $x^{60} + 30x^{58} + 435x^{56} + 4060x^{54}$
$+ 27\,405x^{52}$

**11**  366.41

**12**  $4x^3 + 6x^2h + 4xh^2 + h^3$

**13**  (a) $64x^6 + 576x^5y + 2160x^4y^2$
(b) 69.976
(c) 0.004

**14**  90 720

**16** (a) (i) $\dfrac{1}{r!}$    (ii) $(n-1)!$

(iii) $(n-r-2)(n-2)!$

## Advanced

**1**  $84a^3b^6$

**2**  7

**3**  $20x^4 + 160x^2 + 64; 1364$

**5**  (a) (i) $x^4 + 4x^3y + 6x^2y^2 + 4xy^3 + y^4$
(ii) 343
(b) (i) $a^3 + 3ab$

**6**  (b) (i) $1 + 1 + \dfrac{1}{2!}\dfrac{(n-1)}{n}$

$+ \dfrac{1}{3!}\dfrac{(n-1)(n-2)}{n^2}$

(ii) $\dfrac{1}{3!}\left(1-\dfrac{1}{n}\right)\left(1-\dfrac{2}{n}\right)$

**7**  369

**8**  (i) 0    (ii) $(-1)^{n/2}\dbinom{n}{\frac{1}{2}n}$

**9**  $n2^{n-1}$

**10**  $\dfrac{(n+1)\cdots(n-p+1)}{(p+1)!}$

## Revision

**1**  (a) 210    (b) 5005    (c) $r(r+1)$

**2**  $625x^4 - 1000x^3 + 600x^2 - 160x + 16$

**3**  $20x + 160x^3 + 64x^5$

**4**  (a) $4x - 24x^2 + 48x^3 - 32x^4$
(b) $1 + 3x + 2x^2 - 2x^3 - 3x^4 - x^5$
(c) $64/x^6 + 96/x^4 + 60/x^2 + 20 + \frac{15}{4}x^2$
$+ \frac{3}{8}x^4 + \frac{1}{64}x^6$

**5**  414 720

**7**  $a = \frac{1}{2}, n = 8$

**9**  10 500

**10**  (a) $1 + 18x + 135x^2$
(b) 1.936
(c) 0.03

**11**  $104x/49$

**12**  $1 + \frac{1}{2}px + \frac{1}{8}p(p-9)x^2$
$+ \frac{1}{48}p(p-1)(p-26)x^3$;    $p = 26$

## 5.4

### Basic

**1**  (a) $1 + \frac{1}{2}x - \frac{1}{8}x^2 + \frac{1}{16}x^3 - \frac{5}{128}x^4$
(b) $1 + 4x + 12x^2 + 32x^3 + 80x^4$

**2**  (a) $-\frac{2}{3} < x < \frac{2}{3}$    (b) $-\frac{1}{4} < x < \frac{1}{4}$

**3**  Using the binomial series

$$(1+x)^n = 1 + nx + \frac{n(n-1)}{2!}x^2$$
$$+ \frac{n(n-1)(n-2)}{3!}x^3 + \cdots$$

and substituting $-x^2$ for $x$ and $-2$ for $n$ we have

$$(1-x^2)^{-2} = 1 + (-2)(-x^2)$$
$$+ \frac{-2 \times -3}{2!}(-x^2)^2$$
$$+ \frac{-2 \times -3 \times -4}{3!}(-x^2)^3$$
$$= 1 + 2x^2 + 3x^4 + 4x^6$$

**4**  $8 + 3x + \frac{3}{16}x^2 - \frac{1}{128}x^3$

**5**  $(1-x)(1+3x)^{1/2}$

$$= (1-x)\left(1 + \frac{3}{2}x + \frac{\frac{1}{2} \times -\frac{1}{2}}{2!}9x^2\right.$$

$$\left. + \frac{\frac{1}{2} \times -\frac{1}{2} \times -\frac{3}{2}}{3!}27x^3 + \cdots\right)$$

$$= (1-x)(1 + \frac{3}{2}x - \frac{9}{8}x^2 + \frac{27}{16}x^3 + \cdots)$$

$$= 1 + \tfrac{3}{2}x - \tfrac{9}{8}x^2 + \tfrac{27}{16}x^3 - x - \tfrac{3}{2}x^2$$
$$+ \tfrac{9}{8}x^3 + \cdots$$
$$= 1 + \tfrac{1}{2}x - \tfrac{21}{8}x^2 + \tfrac{45}{16}x^3$$

The expansion is valid for
$-1 < 3x < 1$,   i.e. $-\tfrac{1}{3} < x < \tfrac{1}{3}$.

**7**    1.0198

**8**    $1 - 3x - 10x^2 = (1 - 5x)(1 + 2x)$

$$\sqrt{(1 - 5x)(1 + 2x)} = (1 - 5x)^{1/2}(1 + 2x)^{1/2}$$
$$= (1 - \tfrac{5}{2}x - \tfrac{25}{8}x^2 + \cdots)$$
$$\times (1 + x - \tfrac{1}{2}x^2 + \cdots)$$
$$= 1 + x - \tfrac{1}{2}x^2 - \tfrac{5}{2}x$$
$$\quad - \tfrac{5}{2}x^2 - \tfrac{25}{8}x^2$$
$$= 1 - \tfrac{3}{2}x - \tfrac{49}{8}x^2$$

**9**    $\tfrac{1}{3} - \tfrac{1}{243}x + \tfrac{2}{19683}x^2$; $-27 < x < 27$

**10**   $x + x^2 + x^3$

**11**   $1 - 2x + 4x^2 - 8x^3 + \cdots$; $(-1)^n 2^n$

## Intermediate

**2**    $A = 2, B = 3$; $5 + 4x + 14x^2 + 22x^3$

**3**    $1 + 13x + 108x^2 + 736x^3$; $-\tfrac{1}{4} < x < \tfrac{1}{4}$

**4**    $1 + \tfrac{1}{2}x - \tfrac{5}{8}x^2 + \tfrac{13}{16}x^3$

**5**    $a = 3, b = \tfrac{27}{16}$

**6**    $1 - 2x + 12x^2 - 40x^3$

**7**    $a = -5, n = -2$

**10**   $a = 2, b = -3$; $a = -18, b = -13$

**11**   $1 - \dfrac{2}{x} - \dfrac{2}{x^2}$; 2.4495; $4 \times 10^{-4}\%$

**12**   $a = -1$

**13**   $a = -\tfrac{3}{4}, b = \tfrac{27}{160}$

**14**   $\dfrac{1}{1 - 3x} + \dfrac{1}{x + 2}$; $\tfrac{3}{2} + \tfrac{11}{4}x + \tfrac{73}{8}x^2$;

$$-\tfrac{1}{3} < x < \tfrac{1}{3}; \quad 3^n + \dfrac{(-1)^n}{2^{n+1}}$$

**15**   $A = -\tfrac{1}{3}, B = -\tfrac{1}{3}, C = 2$; $\tfrac{3}{4}x + \tfrac{9}{16}x^3$;
     $-1 < x < 1$

**16**   $a = \dfrac{1 + n}{2}$; $b = \dfrac{1 - n}{2}$

## Advanced

**1**    $1 + \tfrac{1}{4}x - \tfrac{3}{32}x^2$

     (a) 1.000 001 999 994 0

**2**    $k = \tfrac{1}{8}$; $\tfrac{129}{256}$; $\tfrac{512}{129}$ or $\tfrac{127}{32}$

**3**    (a) $\tfrac{1}{2}x^{-1/2}$

     (b) The argument is circular. The binomial series is usually derived from the Maclaurin expansion of $(1 + x)^n$, which assumes the derivative of $x^n$. More formal proofs can be carried out, but these are beyond the scope of A level.

**4**    $a = \tfrac{1}{2}, b = -\tfrac{1}{2}$

**5**    $\dfrac{1}{x + 2} + \dfrac{2}{2x - 1}$;

$$\left(\dfrac{2}{x}\right) - \dfrac{3}{2}\left(\dfrac{1}{x}\right)^2 + \dfrac{17}{4}\left(\dfrac{1}{x}\right)^3 + \cdots$$

$$+ \left(\dfrac{1}{2^{n-1}} + (-2)^{n-1}\right)\left(\dfrac{1}{x}\right)^n = \cdots, |x| > 2$$

**6**    (a) $1 - \dfrac{6}{x} + \dfrac{27}{x^2} - \dfrac{108}{x^3}$; $x < -3, x > 3$

     (b) $k = \tfrac{1}{9}$

     (c) $\dfrac{x^2}{9} - \dfrac{2x^3}{27} + \dfrac{x^4}{27} - \dfrac{4x^5}{243}$; $-3 < x < 3$

(d)  Each is valid for a different range of $x$. Thus there is no value of $x$ which is common to the two series.

**7**  $p^{n+1} - q^{n+1}$

**8**  (a)  0, $n$ odd; $(1 + \frac{1}{2}n)n!$, $n$ even

**9**  462

**10**  $\dfrac{a^{m+1} - b^{m+1}}{a - b}$ ; $-\dfrac{1}{b^2} < x < \dfrac{1}{b^2}$

## Revision

**1**  (a)  $1 - 3x + 6x^2 - 10x^3$

(b)  $1 - \frac{2}{3}x - \frac{4}{9}x^2 - \frac{40}{81}x^3$

**2**  $1 + \frac{1}{2}x$

**3**  $-4 < x < 4$

**4**  $\sqrt{2}(1 + \frac{9}{4}x + \frac{207}{32}x^2)$

**6**  $\dfrac{\frac{1}{3}}{1 - x} + \dfrac{\frac{2}{3}}{1 + 5x}$;  $1 - 3x + 17x^2 - 83x^3$;

$-\frac{1}{5} < x < \frac{1}{5}$

**7**  $-\frac{5}{4}$

**8**  0.5006

**11**  $\dfrac{1}{x + 3} - \dfrac{2}{x - 1}$, $-\dfrac{1}{x} - \dfrac{5}{x^2} + \dfrac{7}{x^3}$

**12**  $a = 2$  or  $-\frac{1}{4}$

# Chapter 6 Trigonometry

## 6.1

### Basic

**1** Converting from degrees to radians requires: degrees $\to \div 180 \to \times \pi \to$ radians, since there are $\pi$ radians in $180°$.

(a) $\pi$  (b) $\dfrac{\pi}{4}$  (c) $\dfrac{3\pi}{2}$  (d) $\dfrac{\pi}{5}$

(e) $\dfrac{4\pi}{3}$

**2** (a) 0.646  (b) 4.01  (c) 1.00
 (d) 0.110  (e) 6.28

**3** (a) $30°$  (b) $20°$  (c) $135°$
 (d) $105°$  (e) $300°$

**4** (a) $143°$  (b) $57.3°$  (c) $360°$
 (d) $96.9°$  (e) $344°$

**5** (a) $\dfrac{\pi}{6}, \dfrac{5\pi}{6}$  (b) $45°, \dfrac{5\pi}{4}$

(c) none, although $\tan\theta \approx 1.732$ for $\dfrac{\pi}{3}, 60°$

**6** (a) There are $\pi$ radians in a triangle; hence the base angle $= \frac{1}{2}(\pi - 1)$.
 (b) In a similar way, the vertex angle $= \pi - 2$.
 (c) $A - \frac{1}{2}V = \frac{1}{2}(\pi - 1) - \frac{1}{2}(\pi - 2)$
 $= \frac{1}{2}^{c} = (90/\pi)^{c}$.

**7** (a) Length of arc $= R\theta = 2\,\text{m}$
 (b) 3.71 mm  (c) 23.06 km

**8** (a) 1  (b) 3  (c) $\dfrac{15}{R}$

**9** (a) $\dfrac{3\ell}{\pi}$ m  (b) $\dfrac{5\ell}{7\pi}$ m

(c) $\dfrac{5\ell}{4\pi}$ m  (d) $\ell$ m  (e) $\dfrac{\ell}{\alpha}$ m

**10** Using area of sector $= \frac{1}{2}r^2\theta$,
 (a) $\frac{1}{2}r^2\theta = \frac{1}{2} \times 5^2 \times 2.88 = 36$ units$^2$
 and similarly all others equal 36 units$^2$, apart from (e), which equals 18 units$^2$.

**11** (a) 1  (b) $\frac{15}{4}$  (c) $\frac{2}{9}$

**12** (a) $10.94 \le r \le 11.19\,\text{cm}$
 (b) 1.2%

### Intermediate

**1** (a) 3.2 cm  (b) 6.4 cm$^2$

**2** The area of a sector is given by $\frac{1}{2}r^2\theta$, and for a triangle $\frac{1}{2}ab\sin C$. In this case the triangle has area
 $\frac{1}{2}(17\,\text{mm})^2 \sin 0.3 \approx 42.70\,\text{mm}^2$. Hence the area of the minor segment
 $\approx \frac{1}{2}(17\,\text{mm})^2\, 0.3 - 42.70\,\text{mm}^2$
 $\approx 0.65\,\text{mm}^2$

**3** The common area consists of two equal minor segments. The radius forming the segments is 5 cm.
 Angle of sector $= 2\cos^{-1}\left(\frac{4}{5}\right) \approx 1.287$
 using the obvious right-angled triangle
 Area of each sector $= \frac{1}{2}r^2\theta = \frac{1}{2} \times 5^2$
 $\times 1.287 \approx 16.09$
 Area of each right-angled triangle
 $= \frac{1}{2} \times 3 \times 4 = 6\,\text{cm}^2$
 Hence the required area is
 $A \approx 2 \times 16.09 - 4 \times 6 = 8.18\,\text{cm}^2$

**5** $\frac{1}{4}$

**6** (b) 2

**7** (b) 12.04 m

**8** $(20\,000/9)$ rad/s *if* (i) the reel does not reduce in diameter as the line is cast, (ii) the reel rotates at a uniform rate, throughout the time.

**9** 79.1 cm$^2$

**10** $24\pi/5$

**11** (a) $\theta = (25 - 2r)/r$    (b) $r = 6.25$ m

**14** (b) $\frac{1}{12}r^2\theta^3$
    (c) The percentage error is 1.26%

**15** (a) $\frac{1}{2}r^2(\theta - \sin\theta) = \frac{1}{4}r^2\theta$
    (d) 1.90

**16** $1000\pi/9, 200\pi$

## Advanced

**2** $k^2A$ cm$^2$

**3** 13.35 cm

**5** $r^2(\pi + \theta\cos\theta - \sin\theta)$

**6** 55°

**8** 87.4 cm$^2$

**9** $p = \dfrac{50h}{r+h}$

**10** $\sin\dfrac{\pi}{n} = \dfrac{r}{R}$;

$X = \pi(R+r)^2 - n\pi r^2\left(\dfrac{1}{2}+\dfrac{1}{n}\right)$

$\quad - nr\sqrt{R^2 - r^2}$;

$Z = n\pi r^2$; $\dfrac{4}{\pi} - 1$

## Revision

**1** (a) $\dfrac{\pi}{6}$    (b) $\dfrac{3\pi}{4}$    (c) $\dfrac{7\pi}{6}$

  (d) $\dfrac{4\pi}{5}$    (e) $\dfrac{7\pi}{10}$

**2** (a) 1.85    (b) 3.49
  (c) 0.314    (d) 4.71
  (e) 1.66

**3** $\dfrac{\pi}{2}$

**4** (a) $\frac{1}{3}$    (b) $\frac{4}{5}$    (c) 2

**5** $r = \sqrt{\dfrac{2A}{\theta}}$

  (a) 12 cm
  (b) 12 cm
  (c) 12 cm

**6** (b) $l = p - 2r$

**7** 19.44cm$^3$

**8** (b)

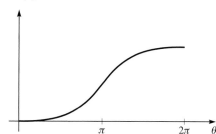

As $\theta$ approaches $\pi$, i.e. the segment approaches a semi-circle, the rate $dA/d\theta$ reaches a maximum. Subsequently, as $\theta > 2\pi$ and it forms a major segment, the gradient decreases to zero when $\theta = 2\pi$.

**9** 203

**10** (a) 6.01 mm    (b) 2.01 mm$^2$

**11** $r = 5.75$ cm, $\theta = 2$

**12** 32.7 cm$^2$

## 6.2

### Basic

**1** (a) 1, 2      (b) 2, 3      (c) 3
   (d) None      (e) 3

**2** (a) +ve      (b) −ve      (c) −ve
   (d) −ve

**3** (b) (i) $\dfrac{\sqrt{3}}{2}$   (ii) $\sqrt{3}$   (iii) $\dfrac{1}{2}$

   (iv) $\dfrac{\sqrt{3}}{2}$   (v) $\dfrac{1}{\sqrt{3}}$

**4** (a) $k\sqrt{2}$

   (b) $\sin\dfrac{\pi}{4} = \cos\dfrac{\pi}{4} = \dfrac{1}{\sqrt{2}}$, $\tan\dfrac{\pi}{4} = 1$

**5** (a) $\dfrac{1}{\operatorname{cosec} x} = \{(\sin x)^{-1}\}^{-1} = \sin x$

   (b) $\cot x \sin x = \dfrac{1}{\tan x}\sin x$

   $= \dfrac{1}{\sin x/\cos x}\sin x$

   $= \dfrac{\cos x}{\sin x}\sin x = \cos x$

   (c) $\tan x$   (d) $\operatorname{cosec} x$   (e) $\sec x$

**6** (c) (i) $\sin 47°$
   (ii) $-\sin 76°$
   (iii) $-\sin 14°$

**7** (a) $-\cos 10°$      (b) $\cos 63°$
   (c) $-\cos 30°$      (d) $\tan 52°$
   (e) $\tan 55°$

**8** $y = \sin x$:
   (a) Rotational symmetry:
       order 2, about (0, 0)
   (b) $2\pi$
   (c) odd
   $y = \cos x$:
   (a) Reflection symmetry in the line
       $x = 0$
   (b) $2\pi$
   (c) even
   $y = \tan x$:
   (a) Rotational symmetry: order 2,
       about (0, 0)
   (b) $\pi$
   (c) odd

**9** (a) Reflection in the line $y = 0$
   (b) Stretch: factor 3, $y$-direction
   (c) Stretch: factor 7, $x$-direction
   (d) Translation $\begin{pmatrix} \pi/6 \\ 0 \end{pmatrix}$
   (e) Translation $\begin{pmatrix} \pi/2 \\ 0 \end{pmatrix}$

**10** (a) $-1 \le \sin x \le 1 \Rightarrow -5 \le 5\sin x \le 5$
    Hence $12 \ge 7 - 5\sin x \ge 2$ and
    max value is 12.
    (b) 5
    (c) $-1 \le \sin x \le 1 \Rightarrow 0 \le \sin^2 x \le 1$
    Hence $0 \le \frac{1}{2}(1 - \sin^2 x) \le \frac{1}{2}$ and
    maximum value is $\frac{1}{2}$.
    (d) 1
    (e) 8

**11** (a) $\pi/6$      (b) $\pi/4$
    (c) $-\pi/4$      (d) $-\pi/3$
    (e) $\pi$

**12** (a) 0.64, 2.50      (b) 0.32, 1.25
    (c) 0.12, 1.97

### Intermediate

**1** (a) $-\sqrt{3}/2$      (b) $1/\sqrt{3}$
   (c) 0      (d) $-1/\sqrt{3}$
   (e) $-1/2$      (f) $-1/\sqrt{2}$

**2** (a) $\sqrt{3}/2$      (b) $-1/\sqrt{2}$
   (c) $-\sqrt{3}$      (d) $-1$

**3** (a) $\pi/3, 2\pi/3, 7\pi/3$
   (b) $5\pi/6, 11\pi/6, 17\pi/6$
   (c) $\pi, 3\pi, 5\pi$

**4** (a) $\sec\dfrac{\pi}{6} - \cot\dfrac{\pi}{3}$

   $= \left(\cos\dfrac{\pi}{6}\right)^{-1} - \left(\tan\dfrac{\pi}{3}\right)^{-1}$

   $= \left(\dfrac{\sqrt{3}}{2}\right)^{-1} - (\sqrt{3})^{-1}$

   $= \dfrac{2}{\sqrt{3}} - \dfrac{1}{\sqrt{3}} = \dfrac{1}{\sqrt{3}}$

   (b) $\dfrac{-2}{\sqrt{3}} + \dfrac{2}{\sqrt{3}} = 0$

   (c) $2 + 1 = 3$

**5** (b) (i) $\sin 8°$,  $\cos 82°$
(ii) $-\cos 44°$,  $-\sin 46°$
(iii) $\operatorname{cosec} 8°$,  $\sec 82°$
(iv) $-\operatorname{cosec} 74°$,  $-\sec 16°$
(v) $\operatorname{cosec} 52°$,  $\sec 38°$

**6** (a) $60°$     (b) $20°$ or $40°$
(c) $56°$     (d) $78°$

**7** (a) $\begin{pmatrix} 270° \\ 0 \end{pmatrix}$     (b) $\begin{pmatrix} 90° \\ 0 \end{pmatrix}$

(c) (i) $x° - 270°$     (ii) $x° - 90°$

**8** (a)

$\cos(x + \pi)$

(b) (i) $\cos x$     (ii) $-\operatorname{cosec} x$

**9** (a) $30\,\text{cm}$
(b) $46$ cm; $t = \pi/4 \approx 0.78$
(c) $\pi \approx 3.1\,\text{s}$

**10** (a) Stretch, factor 2 parallel to the
$y$-axis, $x$-axis invariant; stretch,
factor 3 parallel to the $x$-axis,
$y$-axis invariant;

translation $\begin{pmatrix} 0 \\ -5 \end{pmatrix}$

(b) For example: reverse the order of
the stretches, *or* begin with

translation $\begin{pmatrix} 0 \\ -\frac{5}{2} \end{pmatrix}$

**11** Stretch, factor 3 parallel to the $y$-axis,

followed by translation $\begin{pmatrix} \pi/5 \\ 0 \end{pmatrix}$ or vice
versa

**12**

(a) The range of the function is
$2.7 \le y \le 5.3$.
$A$ is the amplitude, i.e.
$(5.3 - 2.7)/2 = 1.3$.
$D$ is the average of
$2.7$ and $5.3 = 4.0$.
(b) The period of the graph
$= 2(70 - 34) = 72$.
Hence the graph has been
stretched by factor $\frac{1}{5}$ in the
$x$-direction: i.e. $x \to 5x$ i.e. $B = 5$.

**13** (a) (i) $-1 \le x \le 1$
(ii) $-1 \le x \le 1$
(iii) $\mathbb{R}$
(b) $\sin^{-1} x$

$$-\frac{\pi}{2} \le x \le \frac{\pi}{2}$$

$\cos^{-1} x$

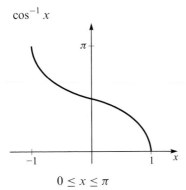

$0 \le x \le \pi$

$\tan^{-1} x$

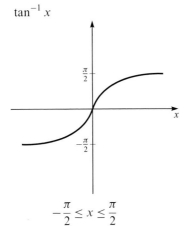

$-\dfrac{\pi}{2} \le x \le \dfrac{\pi}{2}$

**14** (a) $f^{-1}(x) = \frac{1}{3} \tan^{-1} x$

(b)

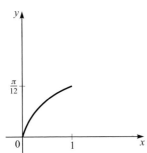

**15**

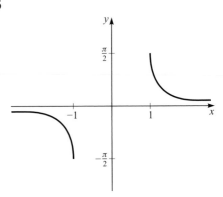

**16** (a) $-1 \le \sin x \le 1 \Rightarrow 0 \le \sin^2 x \le 1$
Hence $0 \le f(x) \le 1$.
(b) 9, 5
(c) $\infty$, 5
(d) $\infty$, $-11$

## Advanced

**1** $x \ne n\pi, n \in \mathbb{Z}$

**2** $2n\pi \pm 5\pi/18, n \in \mathbb{Z}$

**3** (a) $\pi/4 < \theta < \pi/2,\ 5\pi/4 < \theta < 3\pi/2$
(b) $0 < \theta < \pi/3,\ 2\pi/3 < \theta < \pi$,
$4\pi/3 < \theta < 5\pi/3$
(c) $0 < \theta < \pi/5,\ \pi/3 < \theta < 2\pi/5$

**4** (a) $\cos 2x$ is a two–one mapping
within the given domain, e.g.
$\cos 2(\pi/4) = \cos 2(3\pi/4) = 0$
(b) (i) $\sin(\pi/12) \approx 0.26$     (ii) $\pi/3$

**5**

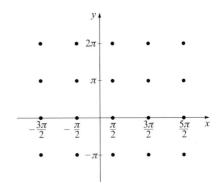

**6** (a)

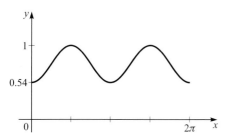

(b)

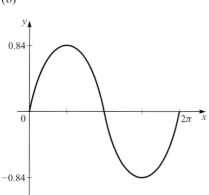

**7**

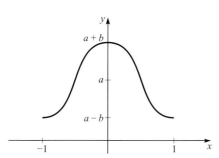

(i)   $k = \frac{1}{60}$

(ii)  An 8.31 start would arrive before an 8.30 start; no

(iii) 8.24 to 8.36

(iv) Adjust the shape of the curve by stretching the steeper portions to reduce the gradient.

**8**

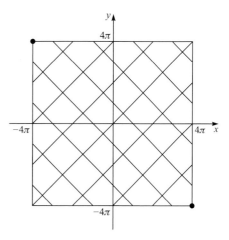

**9** (i)

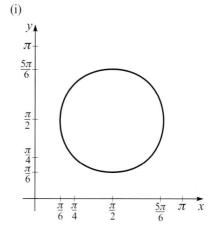

(ii)

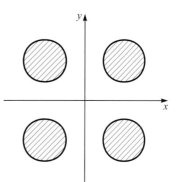

**10** (c)  $2n - 1$

## Revision

**1** (a) $-180° < \theta < -90°, 0° < \theta < 90°$
   $180° < \theta < 270°$
   (b) $\theta \neq \pm 180°$
   (c) $-135° < \theta \leq -90°, 45° < \theta \leq 90°$,
   $225° < \theta \leq 270°$
   (d) as (a)
   (e) $-180° \leq \theta < 270°$

**2** (a) $\sqrt{3}/2$    (b) $1/\sqrt{2}$    (c) $\sqrt{3}$
   (d) $\sqrt{2}$       (e) $2/\sqrt{3}$
   (f) 1

**3** (a) $\theta = 5\pi/2$
   (b) $\theta = 4\pi/3, 8\pi/3$
   (c) $\theta = 4\pi/3, 7\pi/3$
   (d) none
   (e) $\theta = 11\pi/6, 13\pi/6$
   (f) $\theta = 7\pi/6, 11\pi/6, 13\pi/6, 17\pi/6$

**4** (b) (i) $\tan 7°$
   (ii) $-\sec 51°$
   (iii) $-\cos 6°$

**5** (a) (i) Stretch, factor $\frac{1}{2}$, parallel to
   $x$-axis

   (ii) Translation $\begin{pmatrix} \frac{45}{2} \\ 0 \end{pmatrix}$

   (iii) Translation $\begin{pmatrix} 0 \\ 3 \end{pmatrix}$

   (b)

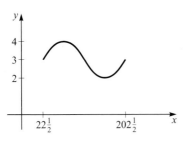

   $(67.5°, 4)$ and $(157.5°, 2)$

**6** $h = 1.35 - 0.82 \cos 4\pi t$

**7** $0 \leq \theta < \pi/4, \pi/2 \leq \theta < 3\pi/4$

**8** (a) (i) $2\pi/5$    (ii) 6
   (iii) $x = \pi/10$ or $3\pi/10$ etc.
   (b) Stretch factor $\frac{1}{5}$ in $x$-direction,
   factor 6 in $y$-direction
   (c)

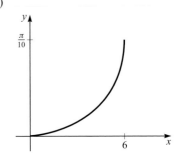

**9** (b) $x = 165 + 35 \sin(\pi t/1800)$;
   $y = 235 + 35 \cos(\pi t/1800)$

**10** (a) $-7 \leq f(x) \leq -3$
   (b) $f(x) \geq 1$
   (c) $f(x) \geq 1$
   (d) $-2 \leq f(x) \leq 2$

**11** $y = 1.2 \sin(24x - 102°) + 4$
   This is not unique: $-102°$ may be
   replaced with $-102° \pm 360°n$.

**12** (a) $33.0°$    (b) $50.3°$

## 6.3

### Basic

**1** (a) $\cos \theta$       (b) $\cos^2 \theta$
   (c) $\sec^2 \theta$     (d) 3

**2** (a) $4 - 5 \sin^2 x$
   (b) $5 \cos^2 x - 1$

**4** (a) $6\sqrt{2}/11$    (b) $7/6\sqrt{2}$
   (c) $6\sqrt{2}/7$     (d) $11/7$

**5** (a) $(\sec^2 \theta - 1)(\operatorname{cosec}^2 \theta - 1)$
   $\equiv \tan^2 \theta \cot^2 \theta \equiv 1$
   (b) $\tan \theta + \cot \theta \equiv \dfrac{\sin \theta}{\cos \theta} + \dfrac{\cos \theta}{\sin \theta}$
   $\equiv \dfrac{\sin^2 \theta + \cos^2 \theta}{\sin \theta \cos \theta}$

Hence

$$(\tan\theta + \cot\theta)\pi\,\sin\theta\,\cos\theta$$

$$\equiv (\sin^2\theta + \cos^2\theta)\pi \equiv \pi$$

(c) $\sqrt{\sec^2\theta - \tan^2\theta}$

$\qquad + \sqrt{\operatorname{cosec}^2\theta - \cot^2\theta} \equiv 1 + 1 \equiv 2$

**6** (a) $\cos\alpha$　　　(b) $\tan\alpha$
　　(c) $-\sin\alpha$　　(d) $\operatorname{cosec}2\alpha$

**7** (a) $10°$　　(b) $41°$

**8** (a) $\frac{1}{2}\sin 2\theta$　　　(b) $\tan x$
　　(c) $\sqrt{2}\cos 2\theta$

**9** $\frac{1}{2}\sqrt{2 - \sqrt{3}}$

**10** (a) $12\sin\theta + 5\cos\theta = 13\sin(\theta + \alpha)$
　　　i.e. $12\sin\theta + 5\cos\theta \equiv$
　　　$13\sin\theta\cos\alpha + 13\cos\theta\sin\alpha$
　　　Hence $13\cos\alpha = 12$, and
　　　　　　$13\sin\alpha = 5$.
　　　(Note: $\sin\alpha$ and $\cos\alpha$ are positive, so
　　　$\alpha$ is acute.)
　　　Dividing, $\tan\alpha = \frac{5}{12}$; and thus
　　　$\alpha \approx 22.6°$.
　　(b) $3\cos\theta + 4\sin\theta \equiv 5\cos(\theta - \alpha)$
　　　i.e. $3\cos\theta + 4\sin\theta \equiv$
　　　$5\cos\theta\cos\alpha + 5\sin\theta\sin\alpha$.
　　　Hence $5\cos\alpha = 3$,
　　　and　$5\sin\alpha = 4$.
　　　(Note: $\sin\alpha$ and $\cos\alpha$ are positive, so
　　　$\alpha$ is acute.)
　　　Dividing, $\tan\alpha = \frac{4}{3}$ and thus $\alpha \approx 53.1°$.
　　(c) $7\sin\theta - \cos\theta \equiv \sqrt{50}\sin(\theta - \alpha)$
　　　i.e. $7\sin\theta - \cos\theta \equiv$
　　　$\sqrt{50}\sin\theta\cos\alpha - \sqrt{50}\cos\theta\sin\alpha$.
　　　Hence $\sqrt{50}\cos\alpha = 7$,
　　　and　$\sqrt{50}\sin\alpha = 1$.
　　　Dividing, $\tan\alpha = \frac{1}{7}$ and thus $\alpha \approx 8.1°$.

**11** (a) $2$　　(b) $\sqrt{2}$　　(c) $2$

**12** (a) $(\tan^{-1}3, \sqrt{10})$
　　(b) $(\tan^{-1} -\frac{3}{5}, \sqrt{34})$
　　(c) $(\frac{1}{2}\tan^{-1}\frac{13}{11}, \sqrt{290})$

## Intermediate

**1** (a) $35$　　(b) $\pi/8$　　(c) $2$

**2** (a) It is required to prove

$$\sec^2\theta + \operatorname{cosec}^2\theta \equiv \sec^2\theta\operatorname{cosec}^2\theta.$$

$\text{RHS} \equiv \sec^2\theta\operatorname{cosec}^2\theta$

$$\equiv \frac{1}{\cos^2\theta\sin^2\theta}$$

$\text{LHS} \equiv \sec^2\theta + \operatorname{cosec}^2\theta$

$$\equiv \frac{1}{\cos^2\theta} + \frac{1}{\sin^2\theta}$$

$$\equiv \frac{\sin^2\theta + \cos^2\theta}{\cos^2\theta\sin^2\theta}$$

$$\equiv \frac{1}{\cos^2\theta\sin^2\theta}$$

Hence $\text{LHS} \equiv \text{RHS}$ as required.
(b) To prove

$1 + \tan\theta\sin\theta\sec\theta \equiv \tan\theta\operatorname{cosec}\theta\sec\theta$:

$\text{LHS} \equiv 1 + \tan\theta\sin\theta\sec\theta$

$$\equiv 1 + \frac{\sin\theta}{\cos\theta}\sin\theta\frac{1}{\cos\theta}$$

$$\equiv 1 + \frac{\sin^2\theta}{\cos^2\theta}$$

$$\equiv 1 + \tan^2\theta$$

$$\equiv \sec^2\theta$$

$\text{RHS} \equiv \tan\theta\operatorname{cosec}\theta\sec\theta$

$$\equiv \frac{\sin\theta}{\cos\theta}\frac{1}{\sin\theta}\frac{1}{\cos\theta}$$

$$\equiv \frac{1}{\cos^2\theta}$$

$$\equiv \sec^2\theta$$

Hence $\text{LHS} \equiv \text{RHS}$ as required.

**3** (a) $\sin 59°\cos 14° - \sin 14°\cos 59°$
　　　$= \sin(59° - 14°) = \sin 45° = 1/\sqrt{2}$

　　(b) $\dfrac{\tan 15° + \frac{1}{\sqrt{3}}}{1 - \frac{1}{\sqrt{3}}\tan 15°}$

　　　$= \dfrac{\tan 15° + \tan 30°}{1 - \tan 30°\tan 15°}$

　　　$= \tan(15° + 30°) = \tan 45° = 1$

(c) $\cos^2 30° - \sin^2 30°$
$= \cos(2 \times 30°) = \cos 60° = 1/2$

**4** (a) $-\frac{16}{65}$    (b) $\frac{33}{56}$    (c) $\frac{36}{325}$

**5** (a) $\sin 2\theta$

(b) $\dfrac{1 - t^2}{1 + t^2} \equiv \dfrac{1 - \tan^2 \theta}{1 + \tan^2 \theta}$

$\equiv \dfrac{1 - \tan^2 \theta}{\sec^2 \theta}$

$\equiv (1 - \tan^2 \theta) \cos^2 \theta$

$\equiv (\cos^2 \theta - \sin^2 \theta) \equiv \cos 2\theta.$

(c) $\tan 2\theta$

**6** (a)

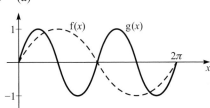

g(x) has half the period of f(x)

(b)

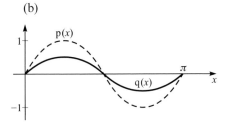

q(x) has half the amplitude of p(x)

(c)

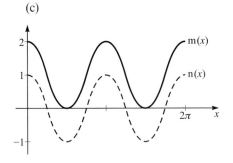

$m(x) \equiv n(x) + 1$

**7** $\dfrac{1}{2\sqrt{2}}(1 + \sqrt{3})$

**8** (c) is true.

**11** (b) $3 - 4\sin^2 \alpha$

**12** (a) $10 \sin(A/2)$
(b) $5\sqrt{2(1 - \cos A)}$

**13** (a) $13 \cos(\theta - 67.4°)$
(b) min $\frac{1}{20}$ when $x = 67.4°$,
max $\frac{1}{6}$ when $x = 247.4°$

**14** (a) $x_1 = \dfrac{5\sqrt{3}}{2}\sin 12t + \dfrac{5}{2}\cos 12t.$

$x_2 = \dfrac{7}{\sqrt{2}}\sin 12t + \dfrac{7}{\sqrt{2}}\cos 12t$

(b) $|x_1 - x_2| \approx 2.53$ units

**15** $R = \sqrt{2}, \alpha = 45°; a = \sqrt{2}$

**16** (a) 0
(b) $\alpha = k - \pi/2$

## Advanced

**2** (a) $R = \sqrt{26}, k = 2, \alpha \approx 0.197$

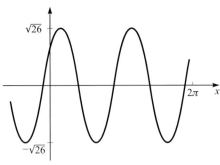

(b) $a = \frac{1}{2}, b = 2^n$

**4** (a) $28.53°$
(c) $0.544$

**5**   (b) $k \approx 1.75°$

**7**   $R = 5, \alpha \approx 0.64; vt \cos\theta + 8 - 4t;$
$T = 6/v \sin\theta; \theta \approx 0.93, V = 2.4, 4.2\,\mathrm{s}$

## Revision

**5**   (a) is an identity.

**7**   $a = \frac{1}{4}, b = 3$

**8**   (a) 3      (b) 4

**9**   (a)

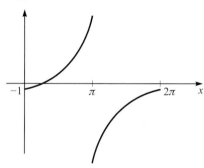

$\alpha = -1, \beta = 3$
(b)

$\alpha = -2,$
$\beta = \frac{4}{3} + 4k\ (k \in \mathbb{Z})$

**10**  (a) 5, 0.64      (b) 3, 0

**11**  (a) $\sqrt{386}\cos(\theta + \tan^{-1}\frac{19}{5})$
(b) $-\sqrt{386}\sin(\theta - \tan^{-1}\frac{5}{19})$

**12**  (a) $x = 2y(4 - y)$
(b) $x = 4(y^2 - 1)/y^4$

## 6.4

### Basic

**1**   (a) 44.4°              (b) 78.5°
(c) 76.3°              (d) 41.8°
(e) No solution

**2**   (a) 66.4°      (b) −52.4°
(c) 120°       (d) −11.5°

**3**   (a) $-\pi/4$      (b) $\pi/6$      (c) $-\pi/3$
(d) $\pi/6$       (e) $\pm\pi/3$

**4**   (a) 2      (b) 3      (c) 2      (d) None

**5**   (a) 14.0°
(b) 123.7°
(c) $\tan\theta = \sin\theta \Leftrightarrow \dfrac{\sin\theta}{\cos\theta} = \sin\theta$

$\Leftrightarrow \sin\theta = \sin\theta\cos\theta$
$\Leftrightarrow \sin\theta(1 - \cos\theta) = 0$

Hence either $\sin\theta = 0$   or   $\cos\theta = 1$

Thus $\theta = 0°, 180°$   or   $\theta = \cos^{-1} 1,$
i.e. $0°$
Thus $\theta = 0°$ or $180°$

**6**   (a) 1.19, 4.33, 7.47, 10.62
(b) 0, 1.23, 3.14, 5.05, 6.28, 7.51,
9.42, 11.34, 12.57
(c) 0.92, 2.22, 4.07, 5.36, 7.21, 8.50,
10.35, 11.64

**7**   (a) 0.00, 3.14, 6.28
(b) $\sin\theta(\cos\theta - 1) = 0$
Hence either

$\sin\theta = 0$   or   $\cos\theta - 1 = 0$

Thus

$\theta = 0, \pi, 2\pi$   or   $\theta = 0, 2\pi$

Thus

$\theta = 0.00, 3.14, 6.28.$

(c) 1.11, 4.25
(d) 1.42, 2.50, 4.57, 5.65

**8** (a) 30°, 41.8°, 138.2°, 150°
   (b) (i) 90°, 228.6°, 311.4°
       (ii) 60°, 90°, 270°, 300°

**9** (a) $\sin\theta - 2\sin^2\theta$; 0°, 30°, 150°,
       180°, 360°
   (b) 180°

**10** (a) 4: 15.0°, 75.0°, 195.0°, 255.0°
    (b) 2: 88.9°, 271.1°
    (c) 2: 45.0°, 225.0°

**11** (a) $\sin(2\theta + 30°) = \frac{1}{3}$
       $\Rightarrow 2\theta + 30° = (19.47°), 160.53°,$
       $379.47°, 520.53°, 739.47°$
       $\Rightarrow 2\theta = (-10.5°), 130.53°,$
       $349.47°, 490.53°, 709.47°$
       We can discard $-10.5°$ since it is
       outside the required range, so
       $\theta = 65.3°, 174.7°, 245.3°, 354.7°$
    (b) 0°, 180°

**12** (a) 14.9°, 57.1°, 86.9°
    (b) 21.4°, 47.1°, 72.9°

## Intermediate

**1** (a) $-138.2°, -41.8°, 30.0°, 150.0°$
   (b) $\sin^2 x - 4\sin x + 1 = 0$
       Using the quadratic formula, or
       completing the square,

       $$\sin x = \{4 \pm \sqrt{(16 - 4)}\}/2$$

       $$= 2 \pm \sqrt{3} \approx 3.732 \text{ or } 0.268$$

       Since $\sin x < 1$, the only possible
       value is $\sin x \approx 0.268$.
       Thus $x = 15.5°$ or $164.5°$
   (c) $-111.8°, -81.9°, 68.2°, 98.1°$
   (d) No solutions

**2** (a) $4\sin^2\theta + 2\sin\theta - 5 = 0$
   (b) $\sin^2\theta = \frac{1}{9}$

**3** (a) $\tan^2 x + 3\sec^2 x = 5$
       $\Leftrightarrow \tan^2 x + 3(1 + \tan^2 x) = 5$
       $\Leftrightarrow 4\tan^2 x = 2$
       $\Leftrightarrow \tan x = \pm\sqrt{\frac{1}{2}}$
       Thus $x = 0.62, 2.53, 3.76, 5.67.$

   (b) None
   (c) $\pi/3, 2\pi/3, 4\pi/3, 5\pi/3$
   (d) 0.62, 2.53, 3.76, 5.67

**4** (a) 1      (b) 4
   (c) 2      (d) 1

**5** (a) $\sin(2\theta - 30°) = -0.52$
       Now $90° < \theta < 180°$, therefore
       $150° < 2\theta - 30° < 330°$
       $\sin^{-1}(-0.52) = -148.7°, -31.3°,$
       $211.3°, 328.7°,$
       $2\theta - 30° = 211.3°$ or $328.7°$
       Thus $\theta = 120.7°$ or $179.3°$.
   (b) 137.1°
   (c) 9.1°, 35.9°, 54.1°, 80.9°, 99.1°,
       125.9°, 144.1°, 170.9°
   (d) 105.5°

**6** (a) $\pm\pi/2, \pi/6, 5\pi/6$
   (b) $-\pi/2, 0.99, 2.16,$
   (c) $0, \pm\pi, \pm0.91, \pm2.23$

**7** (a) $0 \le \theta \le \pi/3$
   (b) $0 < \theta < 1.25$
   (c) $\frac{1}{2}\pi \le \theta \le 2.2$

**8** (a) 60°, 300°
   (b) 0°, 120°, 180°, 240°
   (c) 63.4°, 116.6°, 243.4°, 296.6°

**9** (a) (i) 0.62, 3.76
       (ii) 2.19, 5.33
       (iii) $3\pi/8, 7\pi/8, 11\pi/8, 15\pi/8$
       (iv) $\pi/8, 5\pi/8, 9\pi/8, 13\pi/8$
   (b)

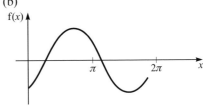

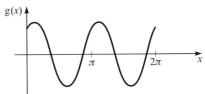

**10**  $0°, 90°, 180°, 270°, 360°$

**11**  (b)  (i)  $18°, 90°, 162°, 210°, 234°, 306°$
$330°$
(ii)  $37.5°, 217.5°$

**12**  (a)  $3\sin\theta + 4\cos\theta \equiv R\sin(\theta + \alpha)$
$\equiv R\cos\alpha\sin\theta + R\sin\alpha\cos\theta$
Equating coefficients of $\sin\theta$ and $\cos\theta$ gives $R\cos\alpha = 3$ and
$$R\sin\alpha = 4$$
Squaring and adding these simultaneous equations gives
$R^2(\cos^2\alpha + \sin^2\alpha) = 3^2 + 4^2$
i.e. $R^2 = 25$,   giving $R = 5$
Hence $5\cos\alpha = 3 \Rightarrow$
$\alpha = \cos^{-1}\frac{3}{5} \approx 0.93$
(b)  $3\sin\theta + 4\cos\theta = \frac{7}{2}$
$\Leftrightarrow 5\sin(\theta + \alpha) = \frac{7}{2}$
$\Leftrightarrow \theta + \alpha = \sin^{-1}\frac{7}{10} \approx 0.77$ or $2.37$
Hence, looking for acute values,
$\theta \approx 1.44$.

**13**  (a)  $13.4°, 66.1°$    (b)  $118.1°, 126.9°$

**14**  $13.9\%$

**15**  (a)  (i)  $\frac{\pi}{6}, \pi + \frac{\pi}{6}, 2\pi + \frac{\pi}{6}, 3\pi + \frac{\pi}{6}$

(ii)  $99\pi + \frac{\pi}{6}$    (iii)  $n\pi + \frac{\pi}{6}$

(b)  $n\pi + (-1)^n\left(\frac{\pi}{3}\right)$

**16**  (a)  $\pm\frac{\pi}{3} + 2n\pi$

(b)  $\frac{\pi}{8} + \frac{n\pi}{2}$

(c)  $\frac{\pi}{12} + 2n\pi, \ -\frac{7\pi}{12} + 2n\pi$

(d)  $\pm\frac{\pi}{12} + \frac{n\pi}{4}$

## Advanced

**1**  $15°, 75°, 195°, 255°$

**2**  $28.2°, 61.8°, 135°$

**3**  $\sqrt{2}\sin(\theta + 45°)$;
$\theta = 13.1°$;   $w = 11.5\,\text{cm}$

**4**  $2n\pi, n\pi + \frac{\pi}{4}$

**5**  (a)  $x = \sqrt{\dfrac{13 + \sqrt{153}}{8}} \approx 1.78$

(b)  $-\pi/4, 3\pi/4$

**6**  (i)  $2\pi/9, 8\pi/9$ (ii) $\pi/14, 5\pi/14$

**7**  $-\frac{2}{3}; x = 41.8°, y = 65.9°$
or   $x = 138.2°, \ y = 114.1°$

**8**  (a)  $2n\pi - \frac{\pi}{2} - \alpha$    (b)  $2n\pi + \frac{\pi}{3}$

**9**  $x < -1, 0 < x < 1$

**10**  (ii)  $\frac{3}{2}\pi$

## Revision

**1**  (a)  $-42.1°$    (b)  $36.0°$
(c)  $17.4°$    (d)  $209.5°$

**2**  (a)  $\frac{1}{3}\pi$    (b)  $\frac{7}{6}\pi$
(c)  $\frac{1}{20}\pi$    (d)  $\frac{2}{3}\pi$

**3**  (a)

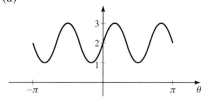

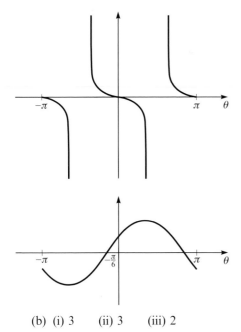

(b) (i) 3     (ii) 3     (iii) 2

**4**   (a)  30.0°, 131.8°, 150.0°, 228.2°
       (b)  101.3°, 281.3°
       (c)  19.5°, 160.5°, 199.5°, 340.5°
       (d)  80.5°, 135.0°, 260.5°, 315.0°

**5**   (a)  $7\pi/6$     (b)  $2\pi/3, 4\pi/3$     (c)  $\pi$

**6**   (a)  0.39     (b)  0.46
       (c)  None     (d)  1.07

**7**   (a)  $\pi/3, \pi, 5\pi/3$
       (b)  0.46, $\pi/2$
       (c)  0, $\pi/6, 5\pi/6, \pi$
       (d)  $\pi/6 < \theta < 5\pi6$

**8**   (a)  $\sin\theta/\cos\theta = \tan\theta$
       (b)  $R\sin(\theta + \alpha)$
       (c)  $\sin\theta/\cos\theta = \tan\theta$
       (d)  $\sin^2\theta = 1 - \cos^2\theta$
       (e)  $\sin 2\theta = 2\sin\theta\cos\theta$
       (f)  $\cos 2\theta = 1 - 2\sin^2\theta$
       (g)  $3\theta = \theta, \pi - \theta$, etc
       (h)  $\sin\theta = \cos(\frac{1}{2}\pi - \theta)$ etc

**9**   (a)  $2\pi - \alpha$     (b)  $3\pi + \alpha$
       (c)  $\frac{1}{2}\pi + \alpha$

**10**  (a)  $13\sin(\theta + 67.4°)$
       (b)  (i)  94.7° or 310.5°
            (ii)  37.5°, 157.5°, 277.5°, 292.6°
       (c)  $\frac{1}{7}$ when $\theta = 202.6°$

**11**  (a)  5
       (b)  (i)  $f(0) = -4, f'(0) = 6$
            (ii)  Wavelength $= \pi$
       (c)

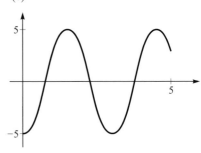

       (d)  0.59, 1.90, 3.74

**12**  (a)  $\pm(5\pi/6) + 2n\pi$
       (b)  $2n\pi + (-1)^n(\pi/3)$
       (c)  $\pm(\pi/4) + n\pi$

## 6.5

### Basic

**1**   (a)  0     (b)  $2\cos A$

**2**   (a)  $2\sin(5\theta/2)\cos(-\theta/2)$
       (b)  $2\sin(-\theta/2)\cos(5\theta/2)$
       (c)  $2\sin 5\theta\cos 0$
       (d)  $2\sin(3\theta/2)\cos(\frac{1}{2}\theta + 30°)$
       (e)  $2\sin(\theta/24)\cos(7\theta/24)$

**3**   (a)
       (i)  $\sin 75° + \sin 15° = 2\sin 45°\cos 30°$
       $$= 2 \times \frac{1}{\sqrt{2}} \times \frac{\sqrt{3}}{2}$$
       $$= \frac{\sqrt{3}}{\sqrt{2}}$$
       (ii)  $\dfrac{1}{\sqrt{2}}$

       (b)  $\dfrac{\sqrt{3}+1}{2\sqrt{2}}$

**4** (a) $2\cos(3\theta/2)\cos(-\theta/2)$
(b) $2\cos 6\theta\cos(-\theta)$
(c) $2\cos(5\theta/4)\cos(3\theta/4)$
(d) $0\ (k=0)$
(e) $\cos(2\theta-\pi/6)\cos(\pi/6)$
(Note: in this question the results for $A$ and $B$ are interchangeable.)

**5** (a)

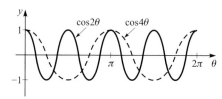

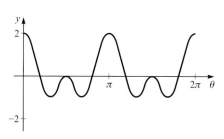

(b) $\cos 2\theta+\cos 4\theta\equiv 2\cos 3\theta\cos\theta$

**6** (a) $-2\sin(3\theta/2)\sin(-\theta/2)$
(b) $2\sin\theta\sin(\pi/2)$
(c) $0\ (k=0)$
(d) $-2\sin(3\theta/2)\sin(\theta/2)$
(e) $\sin(2\theta-\pi/6)\sin(\pi/6)$

**7** (a) $\cos 105°-\cos 15°$
$$=-2\sin 60°\cos 45°$$
$$=-2\times\frac{\sqrt{3}}{2}\times\frac{1}{\sqrt{2}}$$
$$=\frac{-\sqrt{3}}{\sqrt{2}}$$
(b) $\dfrac{\sqrt{3}}{\sqrt{2}}$

**8** $\dfrac{\sin A+\sin B}{\cos A+\cos B}=\dfrac{2\sin(\frac{A+B}{2})\cos(\frac{A-B}{2})}{2\cos(\frac{A+B}{2})\cos(\frac{A-B}{2})}$
$$=\dfrac{\sin(\frac{A+B}{2})}{\cos(\frac{A+B}{2})}$$
$$=\tan(\tfrac{A+B}{2})$$

**9** (a) $\sin 5\theta-\sin\theta$
(b) $\cos 5\theta-\cos 7\theta$
(c) $-\cos 2\theta-\cos 4\theta$
(d) $\sin 6\theta$
(e) $-1-\cos 2\theta$

**10** (a) $\frac{1}{2}(\cos 7\theta+\cos\theta)$
(b) $\frac{1}{14}\sin 7\theta+\frac{1}{2}\sin\theta$

## Intermediate

**1** (a) $2\sin\dfrac{5\theta}{2}\cos\dfrac{\theta}{2}$

(b) $2\cos\dfrac{7\theta}{12}\sin\dfrac{5\theta}{12}$

(c) $2\cos 3\theta\cos 2\theta$

(d) $-2\sin\left(\dfrac{3\theta}{2}+\dfrac{\pi}{8}\right)\sin\left(\dfrac{\theta}{2}+\dfrac{\pi}{8}\right)$

(e) $2\sin 2\theta$     (f) $\sqrt{2}\cos\theta$

**2** (a) $\frac{1}{2}(\cos\theta-\cos 3\theta)$

(b) $\dfrac{1}{2}\left(\cos\dfrac{26\theta}{5}+\cos\dfrac{24\theta}{5}\right)$

(c) $-\frac{1}{2}(\sin\theta+\sin 3\theta)$

(d) $\frac{1}{2}\sin 2\theta$

(e) $\frac{1}{2}\left\{\cos\left(\theta+\dfrac{\pi}{2}\right)-\cos\left(3\theta-\dfrac{\pi}{2}\right)\right\}=$
$\frac{1}{2}(\sin 3\theta-\sin\theta)$

**3** (a) $\cos 3x=\cos 5x$
Hence $\cos 3x-\cos 5x=0$
giving $2\sin 4x\sin x=0$
Therefore either $\sin 4x=0$
or $\sin x=0$
However, note that, whenever $\sin x=0$, it is also true that $\sin 4x=0$.

(b) $0,\dfrac{\pi}{4},\dfrac{\pi}{2},\dfrac{3\pi}{4}$

**4** $\frac{1}{2}(\cos 3\theta-\cos 7\theta)$
$\frac{1}{6}\sin 3\theta-\frac{1}{14}\sin 7\theta+\text{constant}$

**5**  (a) $\dfrac{-3}{20}\cos\dfrac{10x}{3} - \dfrac{3}{16}\cos\dfrac{8x}{3} + \text{constant}$

(b)  $0.56$ units$^2$

**6**  $\dfrac{\pi}{8}, \dfrac{3\pi}{8}, \dfrac{\pi}{2}, \dfrac{5\pi}{8}, \dfrac{7\pi}{8}, \dfrac{9\pi}{8}, \dfrac{11\pi}{8}, \dfrac{3\pi}{2},$
$\dfrac{13\pi}{8}, \dfrac{15\pi}{8}$

**7**  (a)  Since $|\sin 3\theta| \le 1$ and
$|\cos(\frac{1}{3}\theta)| \le 1$, then $|g(\theta)| \le 1$.

(b)  If $|g(\theta)| = 1$, then $|\sin 3\theta| = 1$
and $|\cos(\frac{1}{3}\theta)| = 1$.
Consider the sets of values for
which these statements are true.

$|\sin 3\theta| = 1$ when $\theta = \dfrac{\pi}{6} + n\dfrac{\pi}{3}$

$|\cos(\frac{1}{3}\theta)| = 1$ when $\theta = 3n\pi$
There are no values in common.

**9**  $\frac{1}{4}\{\cos(A+B+C) + \cos(B+C-A) + \cos(A+B-C) + \cos(A+C-B)\}$

**10**  LHS $\equiv \sin\theta + \sin 2\theta + \sin 3\theta$
$\equiv (\sin\theta + \sin 3\theta) + \sin 2\theta$
$\equiv 2\sin 2\theta \cos\theta + \sin 2\theta$
$\equiv \sin 2\theta(2\cos\theta + 1)$
$\equiv 2\sin\theta\cos\theta(2\cos\theta + 1) \equiv$ RHS

**12**  $k = 0$

**13**  (b)  $\dfrac{\pi}{16}, \dfrac{5\pi}{16}, \dfrac{9\pi}{16}, \dfrac{12\pi}{16}, \dfrac{13\pi}{16}$

**14**  $\dfrac{\sin 5\theta}{\sin\theta}$

**15**  $\sin 5\theta - \cos\left(2\theta + \dfrac{\pi}{3}\right) = 0$

i.e.  $\cos\left(5\theta - \dfrac{\pi}{2}\right) - \cos\left(2\theta + \dfrac{\pi}{3}\right) = 0$

Thus  $\sin\left(\dfrac{7\theta}{2} - \dfrac{\pi}{12}\right)\sin\left(\dfrac{3\theta}{2} - \dfrac{5\pi}{12}\right) = 0$

Hence either $\sin\left(\dfrac{7\theta}{2} - \dfrac{\pi}{12}\right) = 0$

or $\sin\left(\dfrac{3\theta}{2} - \dfrac{5\pi}{12}\right) = 0$

The smallest value is when $\dfrac{7\theta}{2} - \dfrac{\pi}{12} = 0$,

giving $\theta = \dfrac{\pi}{42}$.

**16**  (a)

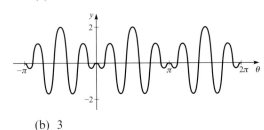

(b)  3

## Advanced

**1**  (a)  $61.9°$ or $168.1°$
(b)  $146.1°$ or $171.9°$

**2**  (b)  $\dfrac{n\pi}{3}, \, n\pi \pm \dfrac{\pi}{6}$

**4**  $0, \dfrac{\pi}{3}, \dfrac{2\pi}{3}, \pi, \dfrac{4\pi}{3}, \dfrac{5\pi}{3}$

**5**  (b)  $\cos\frac{1}{2}(n+1)\theta \sin\frac{1}{2}n\theta \, \text{cosec} \, \frac{1}{2}\theta$

**6**  $n\pi + (-1)^{n+1}\left(\dfrac{\pi}{6}\right), \, 2n\pi + \dfrac{\pi}{2}$

**7**  (a)  $\dfrac{\pi}{6}, \dfrac{\pi}{3}, \dfrac{\pi}{2}, \dfrac{5\pi}{6}, \pi$

(b)  $90°, 104.5°, 255.5°, 270°$

**8**  $77.7°, 180°, 197.7°, 317.7°$

**9**  $\dfrac{\pi}{6}, \dfrac{5\pi}{6}, \dfrac{7\pi}{6}, \dfrac{11\pi}{6}$

**10**  $\dfrac{2n\pi}{7}$

## Revision

**1**  $\tan A$

**2**  (a)  $2\sin 5\theta \cos 4\theta$
(b)  $2\cos\dfrac{5\theta}{2}\cos\dfrac{\theta}{2}$

(c) $-2\cos\dfrac{13\theta}{84}\sin\dfrac{\theta}{84}$

(d) $2\sin\theta\cos 2\theta$

(e) $-2\cos\dfrac{5\theta}{4}\cos\dfrac{3\theta}{4}$

(f) $2\cos\left(\theta+\dfrac{\pi}{4}\right)\cos\dfrac{\pi}{12}$

**3** (a) $\frac{1}{2}(\cos A-\cos 3A)$

(b) $\frac{1}{2}\{\sin(2A+B)-\sin B\}$

(c) $\frac{1}{2}(\cos 4A+\cos 2B)$

**4** $\sqrt{3}/\sqrt{2}$

**5** (a) $\frac{1}{2}(\sin 60^{\circ}+\sin 30^{\circ})$

(b) (i) $\frac{1}{4}(1+\sqrt{3})$   (ii) $\frac{1}{4}(\sqrt{2}+\sqrt{6})$

**6** (a) $2\sin 4x\cos x$

(b)

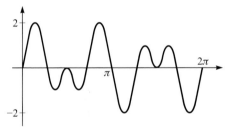

(c) $2\pi$

**7** $0^{\circ}$ or $180^{\circ}$

**8** $0,\dfrac{\pi}{8},\dfrac{3\pi}{8},\dfrac{5\pi}{8},\dfrac{7\pi}{8}$

**10** $P=\frac{1}{2}(A+B),Q=\frac{1}{2}(A-B),$
$R=\frac{1}{2}(B+C),S=\frac{1}{2}(B-C)$

**11** $-\frac{1}{2}\left\{\dfrac{1}{A+B}\cos(A+B)x+\right.$
$\left.\dfrac{1}{A-B}\cos(A-B)x\right\}+\text{constant}$

0.032

**12** (a) $\frac{1}{4}(\cos 6x+\cos 4x+\cos 2x+1)$

(b) $6\sin 6x+4\sin 4x+2\sin 2x=0$

# Chapter 7 Exponential and logarithmic functions

## 7.1

Basic

**1** (a)

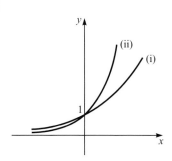

(b)

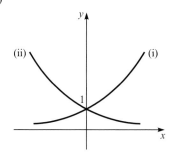

(c)

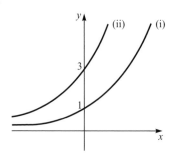

**2** (a) (i) 2   (ii) $-3$
    (iii) $10^x = 0.01 = 1/100$
          $= 1/10^2 = 10^{-2}$
          $\Rightarrow x = -2$

  (b) (i) 4   (ii) $-\frac{1}{2}$   (iii) $-2$
  (c) (i) 4   (ii) $\frac{1}{6}$   (iii) 4

**3** (a)

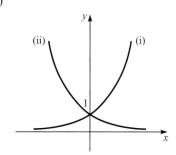

(ii) is the reflection of (i) in the y-axis.

(b)

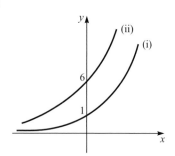

(ii) is (i) stretched by a factor of 6 parallel to the y-axis.

(c)

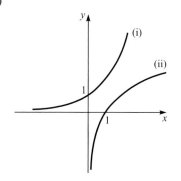

(ii) is the reflection of (i) in $y = x$.

4   (a) (i) 20        (ii) 2.0        (iii) 1
    (b) (i) 5.7       (ii) −0.92      (iii) 0

5   (a) (i) 2         (ii) 6          (iii) $\frac{1}{2}$
    (b) (i) −1        (ii) −2         (iii) 0
    (c) (i) $\log_2 \sqrt{8} = \frac{1}{2}\log_2 8$
        $= \frac{1}{2}\log_2 2^3 = \frac{3}{2}\log_2 2 = \frac{3}{2}$
    (ii) $\frac{3}{2}$   (iii) 4

6   (a) $\log_a(pq/r)$
    (b) $\log_a p^2 - \log_a(qr)$
        $= \log_a p^2 - \log_a(qr)$
        $= \log_a(p^2/qr)$
    (c) $\log_a\{(p^3\sqrt{q})/r^4\}$

7   (a) $\log_a p + \log_a q + 2\log_a r$
    (b) $\log_a p + \log_a q - \log_a r^3$
        $= \log_a p + \log_a q - 3\log_a r$
    (c) $\frac{1}{2}(\log_a p + \log_a q)$

8   (a) (i) 0.69      (ii) 7.4
    (b) (i) −0.94     (ii) 0.35
    (c) (i) $e^{2x-1} = 2 \Rightarrow 2x - 1 = \ln 2$
                $\Rightarrow x = (\ln 2 + 1)/2$
                $= 0.85$
    (ii) 4.2

9   (a) $x\ln 3 = \ln 10$
        $\Rightarrow x = \ln 10/\ln 3 = 2.096$
    (b) 6.459
    (c) 7.213

10  (a) 4       (b) 10       (c) 4

11  (a) 1.03
    (b) (i) $t = 2$ years,
            $p = (1.03)^2 = 1.0609\%$,
            6.09% increase
        (ii) $t = 1.5$ years,
             $p = (1.03)^{1.5} = 1.0453$,
             4.53% increase
    (c) $p = 100\{(1.03)^n - 1\}$

12  (a) 4 kg
    (b) 1.47 kg
    (c) 3.47 years

## Intermediate

1   (a) 2       (b) −2       (c) $\frac{2}{3}$

2   (a) $x$                 (b) $xy$
    (c) $x^2/y$             (d) $\frac{1}{2}(x + y)$

3   (a) $3b$                (b) $-2b$
    (c) $1 + \frac{1}{2}b$

4   (a) (i) $\frac{1}{2}(\ln x - 1)$      (ii) $e^{2x}$

5   (a)

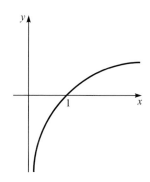

    (b) $x = 5, y = 1$

6   (a) 0.52               (b) 27 or $\frac{1}{9}$
    (c) 8                  (d) 10

**7**  $\log_2(x - 5y + 4) = 0$
$\Rightarrow x - 5y + 4 = 1$    (1)
Writing (1) as $\log_2 2$ enables the laws of logs to be applied.

$$\log_2(x + 1) - 1 = 2\log_2 y$$
$$\Rightarrow \log_2(x + 1) - \log_2 2 = 2\log_2 y$$
$$\Rightarrow \log_2(x + 1)/2 = \log_2 y^2$$
$$\Rightarrow \tfrac{1}{2}(x + 1) = y^2 \quad (2)$$

Solving (1) and (2) simultaneously gives $x = -\tfrac{1}{2}, y = \tfrac{1}{2}$ or $x = 7, y = 2$.

**8**  (a) 4    (b) $\tfrac{1}{125}$

**9**  (b) 1.40
    (c)  $x = 3, y = 9$ or $x = 9, y = 3$

**10**  After one year an investment of £2000 is worth £2000 × 1.042.
After two years it is worth
£2000 × 1.042² and
after $n$ years it is worth
£2000 × 1.042$^n$.
Hence we require
£2000 × 1.042$^n$ > £8000
$\Rightarrow 1.042^n > 4$
Taking logs gives

$$\log 1.042^n > \log 4 \Rightarrow n\log 1.042 > \log 4$$

$$\Rightarrow n > \frac{\log 4}{\log 1.042}$$

$$= 33.7$$

Thus $n = 34$ years

**11**  (a)  $x = 150 \times 4^t$    (b)  300
    (c)  5 hours

**12**  (a)  $C = 5000 \times (\tfrac{1}{2})^t$ or $500\mathrm{e}^{-0.69t}$
    (b)  3.32 seconds

**13**  (a)  62.7 kg    (b)  13 days

**14**  (a)  2 kg    (b)  2.7 kg
    (c)  7 days

**15**  (a)  0.000 43    (b)  4.2%

**16**  (a)  $T_0 = 60, k = 0.036$
    (b)  11.1 minutes

## Advanced

**2**  (a)  1.40    (b)  ln 3

**5**  $\tfrac{1}{7}$

**6**  −0.78

**7**  1.85

**9**  (i)

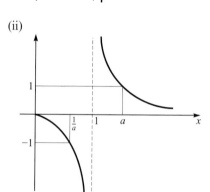

(ii)

**10**  (i) True    (ii) False    (iii) True

## Revision

**1**  (a)  32    (b)  −4
    (c)  5    (d)  8
    (e)  24

**2**  (a)  $-x$
    (b)  $x = \tfrac{1}{3}\ln y$, 0.23
    (c)  $x = \tfrac{1}{2}\mathrm{e}^y$, 0.67

**3** (a) £2639
  (b) 5.4 years

**4** (a) $-1$
  (b) $\frac{1}{4}$
  (c) $\frac{3}{14}$

**5** (a) $\log_a(p^2 r^3/\sqrt{q})$
  (b) $\log_a(a^2 p^{1/4} q^{1/3})$

**6** (a) 1.6
  (b) $-3$
  (c) $-1.3$

**7** (b) (i) 9 or $\frac{1}{9}$    (ii) 5 or 25

**8** $P = 3 \times 2^t$, 7 weeks

**9** (a) 4
  (b) 10

**10** $k = 8, a = 1/\sqrt{2}$

**11** (a) $x = \frac{1}{8},\ y = -6$
  (b) 0, 2

**12** (a) $k = 0.049, a = 81$
  (b) 1970

# 7.2

## Basic

**1** (a)

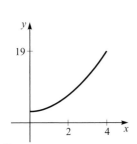

Parabolic

(b)

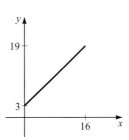

Linear

**2** (a) $X = x^2,\ Y = y, m = a, c = c$
  (b) $X = 1/x,\ Y = 1/y, m = 1,$
     $c = 1/a$
  (c) $X = 1/x,\ Y = y, m = a, c = 0$

**3** (a) (i) $X = x,\ Y = y/x, m = a, c = b$
     (ii) Linear form is $Y = mX + c$,
        Comparing
        $$\ln y = \ln b \times x + \ln a,$$
        $$X = x,\ Y = \ln y,$$
        $$m = \ln b,$$
        $$c = \ln a$$
     (iii) $X = \ln x,\ Y = \ln y, m = n,$
        $c = \ln a$
  (b) (i) $y = ax^2 + bx$
     (ii) $\ln y = x \ln b + \ln a = \ln(ab^x),$
        therefore $y = ab^x$
     (iii) $y = ax^n$

**4** (a) $\ln y = x + \ln a$; plot $\ln y$ against $x$.
  (b) Rearranging $\dfrac{a}{x} + \dfrac{b}{y} = 1$ gives
     $$\frac{b}{y} = -\frac{a}{x} + 1$$
     Dividing by $b$ gives
     $$\frac{1}{y} = \left(-\frac{a}{b}\right)\left(\frac{1}{x}\right) + \frac{1}{b}$$
     Comparing the linear form
     $$Y = mX + c,\ Y = \frac{1}{y},\ X = \frac{1}{x}$$
     so plot $\dfrac{1}{y}$ against $\dfrac{1}{x}$
  (c) $y^2 = -x^2 + 1$; plot $y^2$ against $x^2$

**5** (a) $y$ against $x^2$, $a \approx -0.2$, $b \approx 7$

(b) $y = ab^x$ therefore

$$\ln y = \ln ab^x$$
$$= \ln a + \ln b^x$$
$$= \ln a + x \ln b,$$

so plot $\ln y$ against $x$,

| $x$ | 1 | 2 | 3 | 4 |
|---|---|---|---|---|
| $\ln y$ | 2.73 | 3.20 | 3.85 | 4.48 |

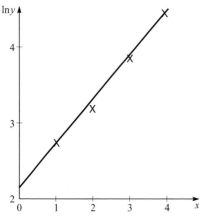

Gradient of this graph $= 0.58$
Therefore $\ln b \approx 0.58$,
$b \approx e^{0.458} \approx 1.79 \approx 2$
$y$-intercept $\approx 2.1$ therefore
$\ln a \approx 2.1$, $a \approx e^{2.1} \approx 8$

(c) $1/y$ against $1/x$, $a \approx 2$, $b \approx 0.5$

**6** (a) $y = 2x^2 + 3$
(b) $y = \frac{1}{3}x^2 - 2$
(c) $y = -16x^2 + 4$

**7** (a) $1/y = m/x + c$,
therefore $1/y = 5/x + c$.
Substituting $x = 5$, $y = 1$ gives
$1/1 = 5/5 + c \Rightarrow c = 0$, giving
$1/y = 5/x$ or $y = \frac{1}{5}x$
(b) $1/y = 1/(4x) + 3/4$
(c) $1/y = -1/x + 5/2$

**8** $a \approx 3.3$

**9** $n \approx 4$

**10** $a \approx 3$, $n \approx 2$

**11** $a \approx 2.1$, $b \approx 3.0$

**12** $k \approx 100$, $n \approx -1.2$

## Intermediate

**1** $a = 1$, $b = -5$

**2** 3.2

**3** $k \approx 5.4$, $c \approx 3$

**4** $a = 12$, $b = 4$, $y = 12/x + 4$

**5** $k \approx 0.092$

**6** $g = 9.8$

**7** $V = 12/T + 3.5$

**8** $n \approx 1.5$, $k \approx 4$

**9** $m = 0.77$–$0.79$; $12$–$14$ kg

**10** $I = 36.6$ not $I = 20.5$, $n \approx 4$

**11** $a \approx 30$, $n \approx 0.25$

**12** $a \approx 1.7$

**13** $\log_{10}(P - 10) = \log_{10} a + t \log_{10} b$;
$a \approx 1.9$, $b \approx 1.07$

**14** $y = 105$ should be $y = 100$; $k \approx 10$

**15** (a) $y \approx 12.2 \times x^{-2.5}$
(b) $y \approx 17 \times 2.3^x$

**16** (a) 81
(b) 3.15

# Advanced

**1**   $a = 3, b = 1.2$

**2**   (i)

| ln $V$ | 1.9 | 2.2 | 2.4 | 2.7 |
|---|---|---|---|---|
| ln $P$ | 4.4 | 5.5 | 6.8 | 7.7 |

(iv) $n \approx 5.2$; $k \approx 0.003$
(v) $P = kV^n$ is a good model within the range $6 \le V \le 12$.

**3**   (i) (A) exponential growth;
(B) Constant $P$; (C) Exponential decay
(ii)

| $n$ | 10 | 20 | 30 | 40 | 50 | 60 |
|---|---|---|---|---|---|---|
| $\log_{10} P_n$ | 1.57 | 1.64 | 1.72 | 1.81 | 1.89 | 1.97 |

(iv) The graph is linear, so it is a good model.
(v) $k \approx 1.015$; $P_0 \approx 32$
(vi) The model is a reasonable fit for 1970, but is an overestimate for 1980 and 1990.

**4**   $a \approx 3.3$; $k \approx 2.3$

**5**   Men's $t \approx 0.02x(\ln x + 0.1)$;
Women's $t \approx 0.02x(\ln x + 0.7)$
100 m includes a significant proportion of the total time accelerating from rest.

**6**   (a) $X = x$,   $Y = \dfrac{e^y}{x}$,   $m = \dfrac{1}{a}$,
$c = \dfrac{b}{a}$

(b) $X = t$,   $Y = \ln \dfrac{s}{t}$,   $m = -\dfrac{1}{a}$,
$c = \dfrac{1}{a} \ln b$

(c) $X = x$,   $Y = \dfrac{1}{y}$,   $m = \dfrac{b}{a}$,
$c = \dfrac{c}{a}$

(d) $X = x$,   $Y = x^2 - \dfrac{1}{y}$,   $m = a + b$,
$c = -ab$

**7**   (a) With $a = 0.4, d = 0.29$, the law is a good fit up to $n = 7$, but a poor fit for $n = 8, 9$.
(b) $D \approx 60 + 43.5 \times 2^{n-1}$

**8**   $I_0 = 8.5, k \approx 0.15$

**9**   $N \approx 2.0, A \approx 3650$

**10**   (b) $v_2 \approx 2.52$ km s$^{-1}$; $\alpha = 41.4°$;
$d \approx 300$ m

# Revision

**1**   (a) $y^2 = -x^2 + a^2$, $X = x^2$, $Y = y^2$,
$m = -1, c = a^2$
(b) $1/y = ax + b$, $X = x$, $Y = 1/y$,
$m = a, c = b$
(c) $\ln y = x \ln b + \ln a$, $X = x$,
$Y = \ln y, m = \ln b, c = \ln a$

**2**   $a \approx 2, b \approx 0.5$

**3**   $y \approx 3.3\sqrt{x}$

**4**   $n \approx 1.5, k \approx 1$

**5**   $\ln V = q \ln t + \ln p$

**6**   (a) $y = (A/x^2)^{1/k}$
(b) $\ln y = (1/k) \ln A - (2/k) \ln x$
(c) $k \approx 3, A \approx 5$

**7**   (a) $\ln y = -2x + \frac{2}{3}$
(b) $y \approx 1.95(0.14)^x$

**8**   (b) $k \approx 2, n \approx 0.5$
(c) 0.25 m

**10**   (a) $P \approx 5000 \times 0.85^n$

(b)

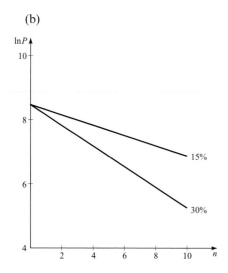

**11**  $k \approx 256, a \approx 1.06$

**12**  (i)  $y^3 = (-a/b)x^2 + 1/b$;
      plot $y^3$ against $x^2$;
      $X = x^2, Y = y^3$,
      $m = -a/b, c = 1/b$
   (ii)  $\ln y = d \ln x + \ln c$;
      plot $\ln y$ against $\ln x$;
      $X = \ln x, Y = \ln y$,
      $m = d, c = \ln c$

# Chapter 8 Differentiation

## 8.1

### Basic

**1** (a) $5x^4$    (b) $1/(2\sqrt{x})$
    (c) $1/(3x^{2/3})$    (d) $-1/x^2$
    (e) $-2/x^3$    (f) $-1/(2x^{3/2})$
    (g) $-nx^{-n-1}$

**2** (a) $21x^6$
    (b) $3/\sqrt{x}$
    (c) $8x^3 - 3x^2 + 2$
    (d) $5$
    (e) $0$
    (f) $12x^3 - x^2 + 8x - \frac{1}{2}$
    (g) $1 - 1/x^2$
    (h) $2x + 2/x^3$
    (i) $4x^3 + 16/x^3$
    (j) $3 - 4/x^2$
    (k) $24x^3(1 - x^2)$
    (l) $2ax + b$

**3** (a) $4(x + 1)^3$
    (b) $10(2x + 3)^4$
    (c) $8(x - 2)$
    (d) $-27(2 - 3x)^2$
    (e) $4x(x^2 + 1)$
    (f) $24x(3x^2 + 1)^3$
    (g) $-12x(1 - x^2)^5$
    (h) $5(2x - 1)(x^2 - x)^4$
    (i) $5(\sqrt{x} + 1)^9/\sqrt{x}$
    (j) Let $u = 1 - x, f(x) = \sqrt{u}$
    Differentiating

$$\frac{du}{dx} = -1, \qquad f'(u) = \frac{1}{2\sqrt{u}}$$

Using the chain rule

$$f'(x) = f'(u) \times \frac{du}{dx}$$

$$= \frac{1}{2\sqrt{u}} \times -1$$

$$= -\frac{1}{(2\sqrt{1 - x})}$$

    (k) $x/\sqrt{x^2 + 2}$
    (l) $na(ax + b)^{n-1}$

**4** (a) $-3(t + 3)^{-4}$
    (b) $-2(2t + 3)^{-2}$
    (c) Let $u = 3t + 1$, $y = 1/u$.
    Differentiating

$$\frac{du}{dt} = 3, \qquad \frac{dy}{du} = -\frac{1}{u^2}$$

Using the chain rule

$$\frac{dy}{dt} = \frac{dy}{du} \times \frac{du}{dt}$$

$$= -\frac{1}{u^2} \times 3$$

$$= \frac{-3}{(3t + 2)^2}$$

    (d) $-1.5/(3t + 1)^{1.5}$
    (e) $10t/(3 - t^2)^6$
    (f) $-1/\{(1 + \sqrt{t})^3 \sqrt{t}\}$
    (g) $-t(2 + t^2)^{-1.5}$
    (h) $-na(at + b)^{-n-1}$

**5** (a) Let $y = uv$ where $u = 2x$,
    $v = (x + 1)^3$.

$$\frac{du}{dx} = 2, \qquad \frac{dv}{dx} = 3(x + 1)^2$$

Using the product rule

$$\frac{dy}{dx} = u\frac{dv}{dx} + v\frac{du}{dx}$$

$$= 6x(x+1)^2 + 2(x+1)^3$$

$$= 2(x+1)^2\{3x + (x+1)\}$$

$$= 2(x+1)^2(4x+1)$$

(b)  $2x(2x^3+1)^4(17x^3+1)$
(c)  $(x+1)(x+2)^2(5x+7)$
(d)  $(x^2+2)/(2\sqrt{x}) + 2x\sqrt{x}$
(e)  $\sqrt{x^2+2} + x^2/\sqrt{x^2+2}$
(f)  $x^{n-1}(1+x)^{m-1}(nx+mx+n)$

6  (a)  $(1-x^2)/(1+x^2)^2$
   (b)  $-2/(x-1)^2$
   (c)  $(-2x^2+1)/(2x^2+1)^2$
   (d)  $-4x/(1+x^2)^2$
   (e)  Let $y = u/v$ where $u = x$,
        $v = (3x-1)^2$.
        Differentiating

$$\frac{du}{dx} = 1, \quad \frac{dv}{dx} = 6(3x-1)$$

Using the quotient rule

$$\frac{dy}{dx} = \frac{\left(v\frac{du}{dx} - u\frac{dv}{dx}\right)}{v^2}$$

$$= \frac{(3x+1)^2 - 6x(3x+1)}{(3x+1)^4}$$

$$= \frac{(3x+1)(3x+1-6x)}{(3x+1)^4}$$

$$= \frac{1-3x}{(3x+1)^3}$$

(f)  $1/\{(1-\sqrt{x})^2\sqrt{x}\}$
(g)  $2(x-1)/(x+1)^3$
(h)  $2x/\sqrt{1+x^2} - x^3/(1+x^2)^{1.5}$

7  (a)  $2\cos x$
   (b)  $4\sin x$
   (c)  $0.5\sec^2 x$
   (d)  $3\cos 3x$
   (e)  $-0.5\sin 0.5x$
   (f)  $6\sec^2 6x$
   (g)  $-6\cos 2x$
   (h)  $-\sin 0.5x$
   (i)  $\frac{1}{36}\sec^2\frac{1}{6}x$

(j)  $\pi(3\cos\pi x + \sin\frac{1}{2}\pi x)$
(k)  $\pi(0.25\sec^2\frac{1}{12}\pi x - \cos 2\pi x)$
(l)  $7\sec 7x\tan 7x$

8  (a)  Let $y = u^2$ where $u = \sin x$.
        Differentiating

$$\frac{dy}{du} = 2u, \quad \frac{du}{dx} = \cos x$$

Using the chain rule

$$\frac{dy}{dx} = \frac{dy}{du} \times \frac{du}{dx}$$

$$= 2u\cos x$$

$$= 2\sin x\cos x$$

(b)  $2x\cos x^2$
(c)  $2\cos 2x$
(d)  $-8\sin x\cos x$
(e)  $8\tan x\sec^2 x$
(f)  $36\sin^2 2x\cos 2x$
(g)  $\cos x/(2\sqrt{\sin x})$
(h)  $-24x\sin 3x^2$
(i)  $3(\sin x + \cos x)^2(\cos x - \sin x)$
(j)  $2\pi\sin\pi x\cos\pi x$
(k)  $-2x\csc x^2\cot x^2$

9  (a)  $2e^x$
   (b)  $-e^{-x}$
   (c)  $4e^{4x}$
   (d)  $6e^{2x}$
   (e)  Let $y = e^u$ where $u = x^2$.
        Differentiating

$$\frac{dy}{du} = e^u, \quad \frac{du}{dx} = 2x$$

Using the chain rule

$$\frac{dy}{dx} = \frac{dy}{du} \times \frac{du}{dx}$$

$$= 2xe^u$$

$$= 2x\exp x^2$$

(f)  $\cos x\,e^{\sin x}$
(g)  $-e^{1/x}/x^2$
(h)  $\exp(x + e^x)$
(i)  $4e^{2x}(e^{2x}+1)$
(j)  $4e^{4x+2}$

**10** (a) $2/x$
    (b) $1/x$
    (c) $3/x$
    (d) Let $y = \ln u$ where $u = x^2$.
       Differentiating

$$\frac{dy}{du} = \frac{1}{u}, \quad \frac{du}{dx} = 2x$$

       Using the chain rule

$$\frac{dy}{dx} = \frac{dy}{du} \times \frac{du}{dx}$$

$$= \frac{2x}{u} = \frac{2x}{x^2} = \frac{2}{x}$$

    (e) $\cot x$
    (f) $2x/(x^2 + 1)$
    (g) $2\ln x/x$

**11** (a) $x\cos x + \sin x$
    (b) $2x(\cos 4x - 2x\sin 4x)$
    (c) $\{(x-1)e^x\}/x^2$
    (d) $1 + \ln x$
    (e) $(1 - 2\ln x)/x^3$
    (f) $xe^{3x}(2 + 3x)$
    (g) $(x\cos x - \sin x)/x^2$
    (h) $(x\sec^2 x - \tan x)/x^2$
    (i) $x(2\sin x - x\cos x)/\sin^2 x$
    (j) $e^{2x}(-\pi\sin\pi x + 2\cos\pi x)$
    (k) $(x\cos x + \sin x)e^{x\sin x}$
    (l) $4(\cos x \cos 3x - \sin x \sin 3x)$
    (m) $x\sec x(2 + x\tan x)$
    (n) $\cot x/(2\sqrt{x}) - \sqrt{x}\csc^2 x$

**12** (a) (i) $dx/dy = \cos y$
      (ii) $dy/dx = 1/\sqrt{1 - x^2}$
    (b) $1/(1 + x^2)$

## Intermediate

**1**   $2, \ -3$

**2**   $a = 2, b = 1.5, c = -2$

**3**   $6 + \ln 4$

**5**   (a) $1 + 3\sqrt{3}$     (b) $4$
    (c) $-2, 0$

**6**   $0.5$

**7**   (a) $-12$     (b) $-1$

**9**   (a) $2x(x^2 + 3)$
    (b) $6/(3 - 2x)^4$
    (c) $x(2\cos x - x\sin x)$
    (d) $-5/(3x - 1)^2$
    (e) $-4x/(x^2 - 1)^2$
    (f) $x/\sqrt{x^2 - 1}$
    (g) $2\sec^2 x \tan x$
    (h) $-5\csc^2 5x$

**10** (a) Let $y = \sin^{-1} u$ where $u = 2x$.
      Differentiating

$$\frac{dy}{du} = \frac{1}{\sqrt{1 - u^2}}, \ \frac{du}{dx} = 2$$

      Using the chain rule

$$\frac{dy}{dx} = \frac{dy}{du} \times \frac{du}{dx}$$

$$= \frac{2}{\sqrt{1 - u^2}}$$

$$= \frac{2}{\sqrt{1 - 4x^2}}$$

    (b) $\dfrac{2x}{(1 + x^4)}$

    (c) $\dfrac{1}{2\sqrt{x - x^2}}$

**11**   $\dfrac{2}{(1 + x^2)^2}$

**12** (a) $45\sin^2 3t \cos 3t$
    (b) $(1 + \sin t + \cos t)/(\cos t + 1)^2$
    (c) $-6\sin 2t\sin 3t + 4\cos 2t\cos 3t$
    (d) $3/(1 + 9t^2)$
    (e) $(\cos t - \sin t)/e^t$
    (f) $2\tan t$

**13** (a) (i) $-2e^{-2x}(\sin 2x + \cos 2x)$
      (ii) $3(1 + \ln 2x)$
      (iii) $e^x(\sin x + \cos x)$

    (b) (i) $\dfrac{1}{(1 + x)^2}$

      (ii) $\dfrac{1 - 2x\tan^{-1} x}{(1 + x^2)^2}$

      (iii) $\dfrac{2 + e^{-x} - e^x}{(1 + e^x)^2}$

**14** (a) $\dfrac{-3}{(2x-1)^{1.5}\sqrt{1+4x}}$

(b) $\dfrac{-4}{16x^2+1}$

(c) $x\left(\dfrac{2\sin x}{\ln x}+\dfrac{x\cos x}{\ln x}+\dfrac{\sin x}{(\ln x)^2}\right)$

(d) $\dfrac{-(1+4x^2)}{2x\sqrt{x}\,e^{x^2}}$

(e) $-2\sqrt{1-x^2}$

(f) $\dfrac{1}{\sqrt{1+x^2}}$

**15** (a) (i) Let $y=\left(\ln\dfrac{x^2}{1+x^2}\right)$

$= 2\ln x - \ln(1+x^2),$
using the laws of logs

$\dfrac{dy}{dx}=\dfrac{2}{x}-\dfrac{2x}{1+x^2}$

which simplifies to

$\dfrac{2}{x(1+x^2)}$

(ii) $\dfrac{1}{2(1+x)}$

(iii) $\dfrac{2(x^2+x-1)}{(2x+1)(x^2+1)}$

**16** (a) $\dfrac{2x}{(x+3)^2}-\dfrac{2(x^2+1)}{(x+3)^3}$

## Advanced

**1** (a) $\dfrac{(a-1)x^2+b}{(ax^2+b)^{3/2}}$

(b) $-3x^2\sin(x^3)\cos(\cos(x^3))$

(c) $\sin 2x\,e^{\sin^2 x}$

**3** (a) $\dfrac{-2a}{3(a^2-x^2)}$     (b) $18x$

(c) $-2\sin 2x$

**4**   $-4,-36$

**5**   $p=2, q=1$

**6**   (a) $-a\cos(ax)\sin(\sin(ax))$

(b) $\dfrac{3x^2(e^x-e^{-x})-x^3(e^x+e^{-x})}{(e^x-e^{-x})^2}$

(c) $\dfrac{-3x^2e^{-x^3}}{1+e^{-2x^3}}$

(d) $-\dfrac{1}{2x^2}$

**7**   $\dfrac{x^2}{2(1+x)^2}$

**8**   (a) 0

(b) $\dfrac{-2x^3}{(1+x^4)^{3/2}}$

(c) $\left(e^x-\dfrac{|x|}{x}\right)\cos(e^x-|x|)$

**9**   (iii) $A=B=\frac{1}{2}$

**10** (a) $3x|x|$
(b) $x\sin 2x+\sin^2 x$

## Revision

**1**   $12x(x-2)(x+1)$

**2**   $1/(3x^{2/3})-2/(2x-1)^2$

**3**   (a) $4(t^2-1)^2(7t^2-1)$
(b) $-t/(2\sqrt{2-t})+\sqrt{2-t}$

**5**   (a) $e^{2t}(2\cos t-\sin t)$
(b) $3t^2\cos(t^3+4)$
(c) $(1-\ln t)/t^2$
(d) $-2\tan t$

**6**   $(1+2x)^2(8x+1)$

**8**   $3/(1+e^{-x})^2$

**11** (a) $5\cos 5x$          (b) $0.5\sec^2 0.5x$
(c) $3e^{3x}$               (d) $8x(1+x^2)^3$
(e) $3x^2/(1+x^3)$          (f) $-2\sqrt{1-4x^2}$

**12** $2x/(1-x^2)^2$

## 8.2

### Basic

**1** (a) 11     (b) 33     (c) 17

**2** (a) Gradient of tangent is given by
$\mathrm{d}y/\mathrm{d}x$.

$$\frac{\mathrm{d}y}{\mathrm{d}x} = 2x - 3$$

At $x = 3$, $\dfrac{\mathrm{d}y}{\mathrm{d}x} = 3$

Tangent is a straight line,
$y = mc + c$, with gradient 3.

$$y = 3x + c \quad (1)$$

Tangent passes through (3, 2).
Substituting in (1)

$$2 = 3 \times 3 + c$$

$$\Rightarrow c = -7$$

Hence   $y = 3x - 7$
(b) $y = -2x - 4$
(c) $y = 4x - 2$

**3** (a) $y = -\frac{1}{2}x - 9$
(b) $23y + x = 348$
(c) $y = -x + 5$

**4** (a) 0     (b) $-\frac{1}{4}$     (c) $\pm 2$

**5** (a) (2.5, 1.75)
(b) (2, 21), (8, −57)
(c) (2, 4), (−2, −4)

**6** (a) $f'(x) = 2x + 6$
At a stationary point, $f'(x) = 0$,
i.e. $2x + 6 = 0 \Rightarrow x = -3$ and,
since $f(-3) = -18$, the
stationary point is $(-3, -18)$
(b) $(-1, -36)$
(c) $(2/3, 4\frac{5}{27})$, $(-4, 55)$

**7** (a)

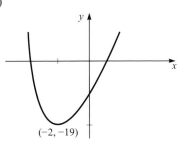

$(-2, -19)$ min.

(b)

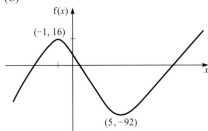

$(-1, 16)$ max; $(5, -92)$ min.

(c)

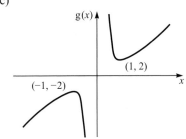

$(-1, -2)$ max.; $(1, 2)$ min.

**8** (a)

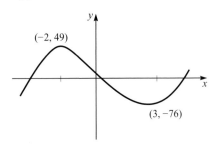

(i) $(3, -76)$; $(-2, 49)$
(ii) $(\frac{1}{2}, -13\frac{1}{2})$

(b)

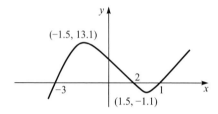

(i) $(-1, -1)$; $(0, 0)$; $(1, -1)$
(ii) $(-1/\sqrt{3}, -5/9)$;
   $(1/\sqrt{3}, -5/9)$

(c)

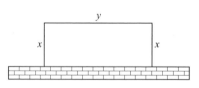

(i) $(-1.53, 13.13)$;
   $(1.53, -1.13)$
(ii) $(0, 6)$

**9**   (a) (i) 72 m s$^{-1}$    (ii) 48 m s$^{-2}$
   (b) 2 s

**10** (a) $-33$ cm s$^{-1}$
   (c) $10\frac{1}{8}$ cm

**11**

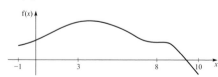

Since total length of tape is 80 m,

$$2x + y = 80 \quad (1)$$

$$A = xy \quad (2)$$

From (1)

$$y = 80 - 2x$$

Substituting in (2)

$$A = x(80 - 2x)$$

$$= 80x - 2x^2$$

$$\frac{\mathrm{d}A}{\mathrm{d}x} = 80 - 4x$$

To find maximum area, need to find
where $\mathrm{d}A/\mathrm{d}x = 0$,

$$\frac{\mathrm{d}A}{\mathrm{d}x} = 0 \Rightarrow 80 - 4x = 0$$

$$\Rightarrow x = 20\,\mathrm{m}$$

Hence max. area $= 800\,\mathrm{m}^2$ since
$y = 40\,\mathrm{m}$

**12**  $A = 1.5x - x^2$; $\frac{9}{16}\,\mathrm{m}^2$

## Intermediate

**1**   $4y = 15x - 12$; 1.8

**2**   (a) $y = -6x + 2\pi + 4$
   (b) $(0.47, 5.97)$, $(1.63, 2.03)$,
      $(2.56, 5.97)$

**3**

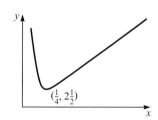

   $2\frac{1}{2}$ at $x = \frac{1}{4}$

**4**   $(0, 0)$, $(a, 0)$, $(2a/5, 108a^5/3125)$

**5**   $a = 2, b = -4, c = -2$

**6**   (a)

(b) (i)

| Interval EF | AB | | BC | CD | DE |
|---|---|---|---|---|---|
| f'(x)– | + | | + | – | + |
| f''(x)+ | + | | – | – | + |

(ii) $B, D$          (iii) $C, E$

**7**   (a)  Using the product rule,

$$f'(x) = 4x^4 \times \frac{1}{x} + 16x^3 \ln x - 4x^3$$

$$= 16x^3 \ln x$$

(b)  $f(x)$ is decreasing when $f'(x) < 0$.
Hence

$$16x^3 \ln x < 0$$

$$x \in \mathbb{R}^+, \quad \text{so} \quad 16x^3 > 0. \text{ Hence}$$

$$\ln x < 0$$

$$\Rightarrow 0 < x < 1$$

(c)  $f(x)$ has a stationary point when
$f'(x) = 0$. Since $16x^3 > 0$, it
follows that $\ln x = 0$. Hence
$x = 1$, giving stationary point
$(1, -1)$.

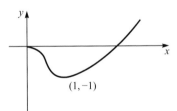

**9**   (a)  0.23
(b)  Because acceleration
$= 12(e^{2t} + e^t)$,
which is always positive

**10**   (a)  Dimensions of box are $x, y, 3x$.
Since volume is $900\,\text{cm}^3$,

$$x \times y \times 3x = 900$$

$$\text{i.e. } y = \frac{300}{x^2} \quad (1)$$

Surface area

$$= 2x \times y + 2x \times 3x + 2y \times 3x$$

$$= 6x^2 + 8xy$$

Substituting for $y$ from (1), gives

$$S = 6x^2 + 8x \times \frac{300}{x^2}$$

$$= 6x^2 + \frac{2400}{x}$$

(b)  For minimum surface area,
require $dS/dx = 0$.

$$12x - \frac{2400}{x} = 0$$

$$\Rightarrow 12x = \frac{2400}{x}$$

$$\Rightarrow x^2 = 200$$

Thus $x = 5.85$, $3x = 17.54$ and
$y = 300/x^2 = 8.77$,
giving dimensions
$5.85\,\text{cm} \times 17.54\,\text{cm} \times 8.77\,\text{cm}$.

**11**   (a)  $e^{-x}(2x - x^2 + 3)$
(b)  max. $12e^{-3}$ at $x = 3$;
min $-2e$ at $x = -1$
(c)  $(-0.24, -3.72)$; $(4.24, 0.22)$
(d)

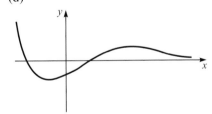

**12**   $(\pi/3, 3\sqrt{3}/2)$ maximum;
$(5\pi/3, -3\sqrt{3}/2)$ minimum;
$(\pi, 0)$ point of inflexion

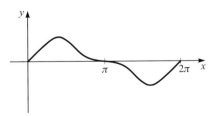

**13** $a = -12, b = 12$

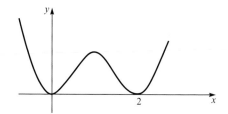

**14** (a) 3    (b) 19.125

**15** (a) $2x/(x^2 + 4)^{3/2}$
(b) $(-2, -\sqrt{2})$, minimum
(c) 0.56, $-3.56$
(d)

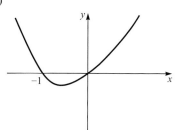

**16** (a)

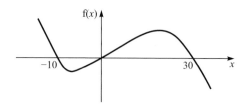

(c) $y = 3x - 1; y = 7x - 9$

## Advanced

**1** 5

**2** (ii) $\pi/3$

**3** (a) (i)

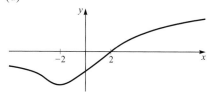

(ii)

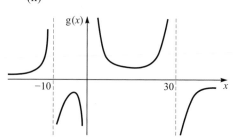

(b) (i) $P = \dfrac{100}{x(30 - x)(10 + x)}$

(ii) 0.0165

**5** $a = 1, b = -3$

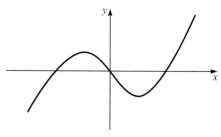

(i)

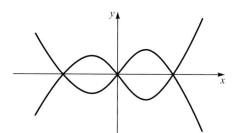

(ii)

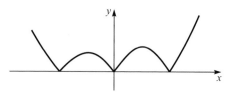

**6** Let $C$ be the nearest point to $A$ on the road. Then, if $bk > \sqrt{a^2 + b^2}$
$PC = a/\sqrt{k^2 - 1}$.
If $bk \le \sqrt{a^2 + b^2}$, then walk directly to $B$.

**8**  (i)

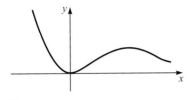

(ii)

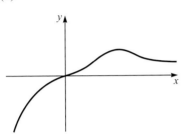

**10** (i)

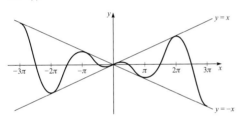

(ii)

$$f'(x) = \frac{2x + x^3}{(1 + x^2)^{3/2}};$$

$$f''(x) = \frac{2 - x^2}{(1 + x^2)^{5/2}}$$

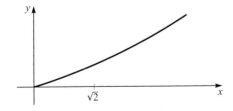

## Revision

**1**  $y = 6x + 1; 15.1\%$

**3**  $(-2, 7)$ maximum;
$(\frac{4}{3}, -11.5)$ minimum;
$(-\frac{1}{3}, -2.26)$ inflexion

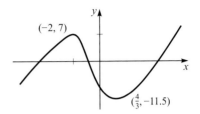

**4**  $(-2, 0)$ minimum;
$(2, \ 32)$ maximum;
$(0, \ 16)$ inflexion

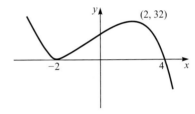

**5**  1

**6**  $(5\pi/4k, -(1/\sqrt{2})e^{-5\pi/4})$, minimum

**7**  $2\frac{13}{25}$ and $10\frac{11}{27}$

**8**  (a) 0, 1
(b) $e^{-2}$ cm
(c) $-2e^{-2}$ cm s$^{-2}$

**9**  (b) $x < -1$ and $x > 3$

**10**  $a = -6, b = -2, c = -2$

**11**  312.5 cm$^2$

**12**  $r = \sqrt[3]{(72/\pi)} \approx 2.84$ cm

## 8.3

### Basic

**1** (a)

| x | 27 | 12 | 3 | 0 | 3 | 12 | 27 |
|---|---|---|---|---|---|---|---|
| y | $-18$ | $-12$ | $-6$ | 0 | 6 | 12 | 18 |

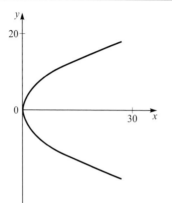

(b) (i)

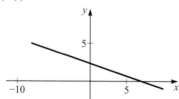

(ii)

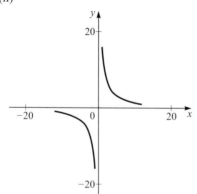

(iii)

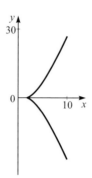

**2** (a) $y = \pm 4\sqrt{x}$

(b) $y = \dfrac{18}{x}$

(c) $y = x^{2/3} + 1$

(d) $y = 10x - \tfrac{5}{4}x^2$

**3** (a) $2, 2t, t$

(b) $6t, 4t^3, \tfrac{2}{3}t^3$

(c) $-3t^2, 2t, -\dfrac{2}{3t}$

**4** (a) $-\tfrac{4}{9}$

(b) Differentiating with respect to $u$,

$$\frac{\mathrm{d}x}{\mathrm{d}u} = 2, \quad \frac{\mathrm{d}y}{\mathrm{d}u} = \frac{-2}{u^2}$$

$$\frac{\mathrm{d}y}{\mathrm{d}x} = \frac{\mathrm{d}y/\mathrm{d}u}{\mathrm{d}x/\mathrm{d}u} = \frac{-2/u^2}{2} = \frac{-1}{u^2}$$

When $u = 2$, $\mathrm{d}y/\mathrm{d}x = -\tfrac{1}{4}$

(c) 0

**5** (a) $-1$    (b) 0    (c) $\sqrt{2}$

**6** (a) $\tfrac{2}{3}t, \tfrac{3}{2}$    (b) $-\dfrac{1}{t^2}, 1$

(c) $\tfrac{1}{2}(3t^2 - 4)$

**7** (a) $x = t + t^2, \mathrm{d}x/\mathrm{d}t = 1 + 2t,$
$y = t - t^2, \mathrm{d}y/\mathrm{d}t = 1 - 2t$
Thus $\mathrm{d}y/\mathrm{d}x = (1 - 2t)/(1 + 2t)$

(b) When $t = 2$, $x = 2 + 4 = 6$,
    $y = 2 - 4 = -2$, and
    $dy/dx = (1 - 4)/(1 + 4) = -\frac{3}{5}$
    Equation of tangent is

$$y = -\tfrac{3}{5}x + c.$$

This passes through $(6, -2)$, so

$$-2 = -\tfrac{3}{5} \times 6 + c \Rightarrow c = \tfrac{8}{5}.$$

Therefore $y = -\tfrac{3}{5}x + \tfrac{8}{5}$

    or   $5y + 3x - 8 = 0$

**8**  (a) $2xy + x^2 \dfrac{dy}{dx}$

    (b) $2x \dfrac{dy}{dx} + 2y + 2y \dfrac{dy}{dx}$

    (c) $\dfrac{1}{y^2} - \left(\dfrac{2x}{y^3}\right) \dfrac{dy}{dx}$

**9**  (a) $-x^2/y^2$
    (b) $x/y$
    (c) Using the product rule and
        differentiating with respect to $x$,

$$x \dfrac{dy}{dx} + y = 0$$

    Rearranging gives

$$\dfrac{dy}{dx} = \dfrac{-y}{x}$$

**10** (a) Differentiating with respect to $x$,

$$2x + 2y \dfrac{dy}{dx} = 0$$

$$\Rightarrow \dfrac{dy}{dx} = -\dfrac{x}{y}$$

    When $x = 3$,

$$9 + y^2 = 25 \Rightarrow y = \pm 4$$

    Thus

$$\dfrac{dy}{dx} = \pm \dfrac{3}{4}.$$

    (b) $\pm \tfrac{8}{9}$
    (c) $0$

**11** (a) $y = -x$
    (b) $3y = x + 13$
    (c) $2y = -15x + 25$

**12** (a) $2x/(2y - 1)$
    (b) $2y = x + 3$

## Intermediate

**1**  $(0, 5)$, $(2, 4.33)$, $(2.83, 3.54)$, $(3.46, 2.5)$,
    $(4, 0)$

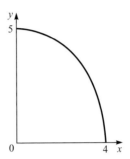

**2**  (a) $y = x^2 - 6x + 4$

    (b) $y = \dfrac{11 - 4x}{3 - x}$

    (c) $\sin \theta = x/2$,   $\cos \theta = y/3$
        Since $\sin^2 \theta + \cos^2 \theta = 1$,
        $(x/2)^2 + (y/3)^2 = 1$
        $\Rightarrow x^2/4 + y^2/9 = 1$

**3**  (a) $\dfrac{3t^2}{2(t + 4)}$

    (b) $1/t$

    (c) $\dfrac{-4 \cos \theta}{\sin \theta + \cos \theta}$

    (d) $\dfrac{9(u + 2)^2}{4(u + 3)^2}$

    (e) $2t - t^2$
    (f) $2e^{2t}(e^t - 4t)$
    (g) $-12/t^2$

**4**  (a) $-3\sqrt{3}/4$      (b) $6\sqrt{2} - 9$
    (c) $\tfrac{1}{2}$

**5**  (a) $\tfrac{1}{4}(3t^2 - 12)$; $2, -2$
    (b) $(8, -16)$, $(-8, 16)$

**6**  (a) (i) $1/(4\sqrt{t})$   (ii) $4y - x - 14 = 0$
       (b) (i) $2t + 3$   (ii) $y = 5x + 2$

**7**  (a) (i) $-\cot t$   (ii) $x = 3, y = 0$

**8**  (a) $2/(2t + 1)$
       (b) $0, -1; (0, 1), (0, -1); y = 2x + 1,$
       $y = -2x - 1$

**9**  (a) $\pi/3$

**10** (a) $r^2y + x = 2cr; ry = r^3x - cr^4 + c$
       (c) $\left(\dfrac{-2cr}{r^4 - 1}, \dfrac{2cr^3}{r^4 - 1}\right)$

**11** (a) $x/y$
       (b) $\cot x \cot y$
       (c) $-y/2x$
       (d) $1/y$
       (e) $-2y/3x$
       (f) $\dfrac{1 - 3x^2y - y^3}{3xy^2 + x^3 + 1}$
       (g) $\dfrac{y^2 - 2xy}{x^2 - 2xy}$

**12** (a) $\pm 2/9$
       (b) $\pm\sqrt{3}/12$
       (c) $\pm 3\sqrt{2}/4$

**13** $4y - x - 18 = 0, y + 4x + 4 = 0$

**15** (a) $\ln y = \ln x^x = x \ln x$, using laws of
           logs. Differentiating implicitly,

$$\frac{1}{y}\frac{dy}{dx} = x \times \frac{1}{x} + 1 \times \ln x$$

$$= 1 + \ln x$$

$$\Rightarrow \frac{dy}{dx} = y(1 + \ln x) = x^x(1 + \ln x)$$

       (b) $2^x \ln 2$

**16** (b) $\beta = -\tfrac{1}{2}\alpha$

## Advanced

**1**  (a) $\dfrac{-1}{x\sqrt{x^2 - 1}}$   (b) $x^{\frac{1}{x}-2}(1 - \ln x)$

**3**  (a) Maximum

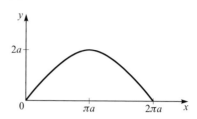

**5**  (i)  $(1, 2), (4, 4)$
       (ii) $\tfrac{9}{2}; (\tfrac{9}{4}, 3)$

**7**  (i)  $-2a \sin t - 2a \sin 2t,$
            $2a \cos t + 2a \cos 2t$
       (ii) $-2a \cos t - 4a \cos 2t,$
            $-2a \sin t - 4a \sin 2t;$
            $\sin t = 0, 4a|\cos\tfrac{1}{2}t|$

**8**  (i) $ax^{a-1}$   (ii) $a^x \ln a$   (iii) $x^x(1 + \ln x)$
       (iv) $x^{x^x+x-1}[1 + x \ln x(1 + \ln x)]$
       (v) $x^{x^2+1}(1 + 2\ln x)$

**9**  $e^\pi > \pi^e$

**10** $(16a, 8a)$

## Revision

**1**  (a) $-t$   (b) $\dfrac{-6}{u^{7/2}}$
       (c) $-\dfrac{1 + 9\theta}{(15\theta - 1)(3\theta - 1)^8}$

**2**  $\dfrac{2t - 1}{3t^2}, (\tfrac{1}{8}, -\tfrac{1}{4})$

**3**  (a) $y = 0.5x - 2, y = -2x + 8$
       (b) $y = -2x + 8$

**4**  $\dfrac{1 - e^{-t}}{1 + e^t}, 0, (1, 1)$

**5**  (a) $2t - 1$   (b) $2x - 3$

**6**  $\sqrt{3}$

**7**  $2y = 2x + 4a - \pi a$

**8**  (a)  $-\sin\theta, \cos\theta, -\cot\theta$
   (c)  $x = 1$

**9**  $-1, 1$

**10**  $-6\sqrt{5}/5$

**11**  (ii)  $y = 3x - 2, y = -3x + 6$
   (iii)  $(0, 0), (0, 4)$

## 8.4

## Basic

**1**  (a)

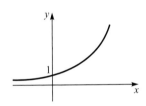

(b)

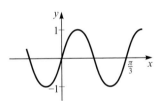

(c)

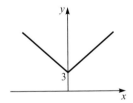

(d)

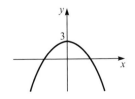

(e)

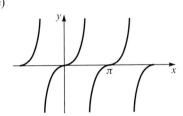

(f)

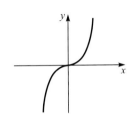

(g)

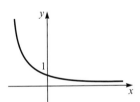

(h)

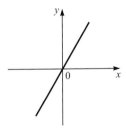

**2**  (a)

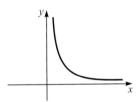

(b)

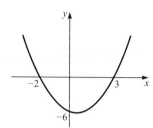

(c)

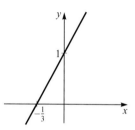

(d)

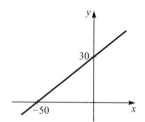

(e)

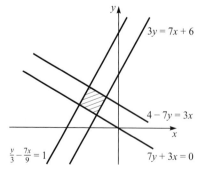

**3**

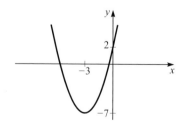

**4**  (a)

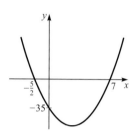

(b)

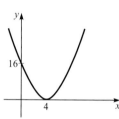

(c)

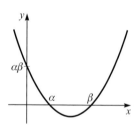

(d)

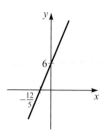

**5**  (a)  $x^2 + 6x + 2 = (x+3)^2 - 9 + 2$
$$= (x+3)^2 - 7$$
So minimum is at $(-3, -7)$

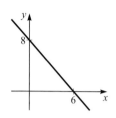

(b) $2x^2 - 20x + 62$
$$= 2\{x^2 - 10x + 31\}$$
$$= 2\{(x - 5)^2 - 25 + 31\}$$
$$= 2\{(x - 5)^2 + 6\}$$
So minimum is at (5, 12)

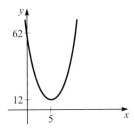

(c) $13 - 3(x + 1)^2$

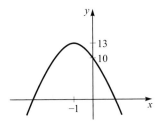

(d) $\frac{1}{4}(x - 8)^2$

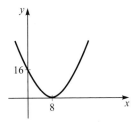

**6**

(a)

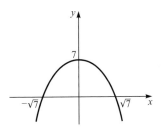

(b)

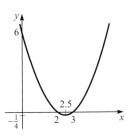

(c)

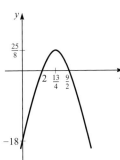

(d)

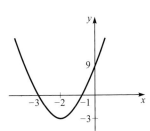

(e)

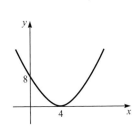

**7**

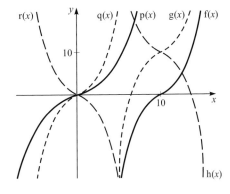

**8**

(a)

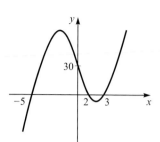

(b)

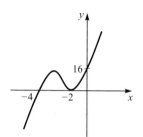

(c)

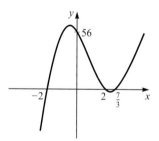

(d)

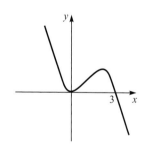

(e)

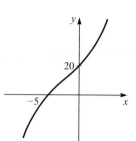

**9**　(a)　(i)

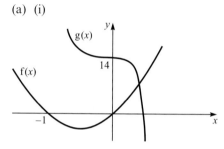

(ii)　One

(b)　Three

**10**　(a)

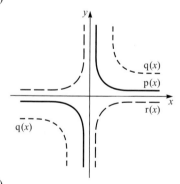

(b)

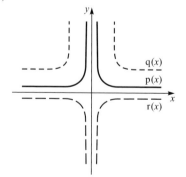

**11** Discontinuities occur when the function is not defined. In these cases, this is where the denominator is zero.
(a) $x - 2 = 0$ when $x = 2$
(b) $x = 2$ or $x = 3$
(c) $x^2 - 7x + 12 = 0$
$\Rightarrow (x - 3)(x - 4) = 0$
$\Rightarrow x = 3$ or $x = 4$

**12** (a) $(-3, 32), (1, 0)$

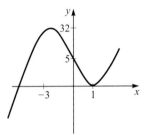

(b) $(-1, 1), (0, 0)$

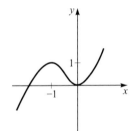

(c) $(-2, -75), (0, 5), (4, -507)$

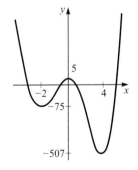

## Intermediate

**1** (a) (i)

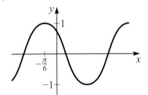

(ii)

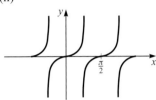

(iii)

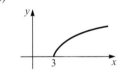

(iv)

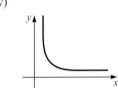

(v)

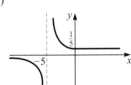

(vi)

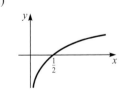

(vii)

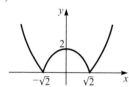

(viii)

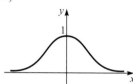

(b)

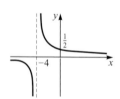

**2** (a) $x \geq 7$

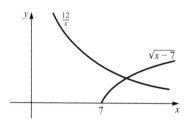

(b) 8 and 9

**3** (a)

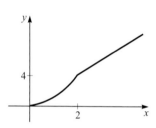

(b)

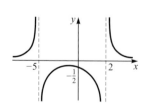

(c) When $x + 3 = 0$, i.e. $x = -3$, the denominator is zero.
Hence a vertical asymptote is $x = -3$.
As $x \rightarrow \pm\infty$, $\dfrac{x}{x+3} \rightarrow 1$

$\Bigg($since, dividing top and bottom

by $x$ gives $\dfrac{1}{1 + 3/x}$ and $\dfrac{3}{x} \rightarrow 0\Bigg)$

Hence $y = 1$ is a horizontal asymptote and, since $x < x + 3$, the graph approaches from below as $x$ increases.

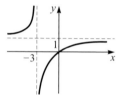

(d)

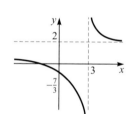

(e)

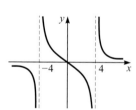

(f)

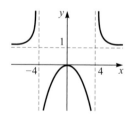

**4** (a) $(-k, 3 - k^2)$

(b)

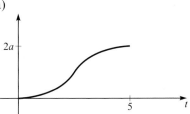

(c) $-\sqrt{3} < k < \sqrt{3}$

**5** (a)

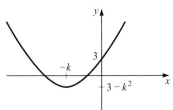

(b)

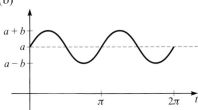

(c)

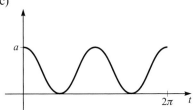

(d)

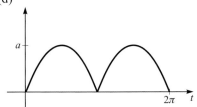

**6** (a)

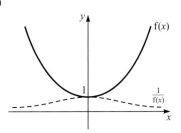

(b)

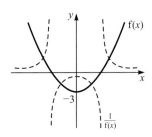

(c)

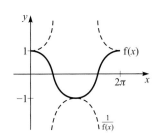

(d)

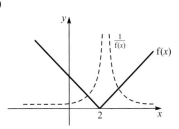

**7** (a)

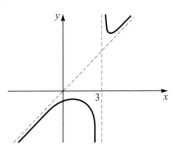

(b)

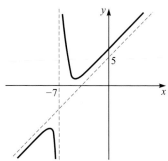

(c)

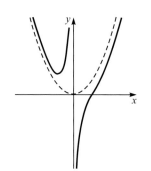

**8**    (a)  $f^{-1}(x) = 3(10 - x)$

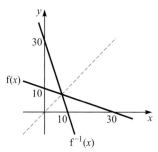

(b)  $g^{-1}(x) = \frac{1}{4}(9 - 5x)$

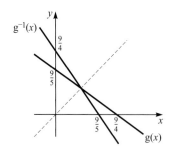

(c)  $h^{-1}(x) = \sqrt{x} - 1$

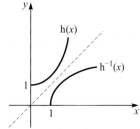

(d)  $k^{-1}(x) = \frac{1}{2x} + \frac{5}{2}$

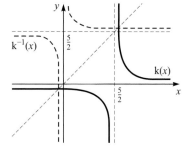

**9**    (a)

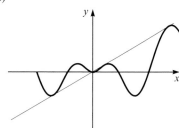

(b)

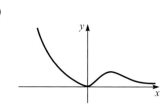

**10**    (a)  $(0, 5), (-\frac{2}{3}, \frac{139}{27})$; one

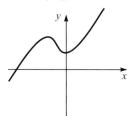

(b)  $(0, 0), (-\frac{2}{3}, \frac{4}{27})$; two

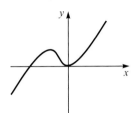

(c)  $-0.189, -0.589$

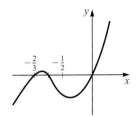

(c)  $(0, -1), (-\frac{2}{3}, -\frac{23}{27})$; one

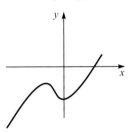

**12** (a) (i)

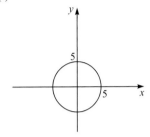

(d)  $(0, -\frac{4}{27}), (-\frac{2}{3}, 0)$; two

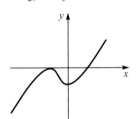

(ii)

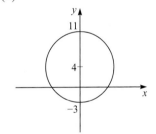

**11** (a)  $-0.569, -4.10$

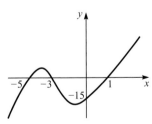

(ii)

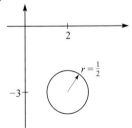

(b)  $-\frac{2}{3}, 2$

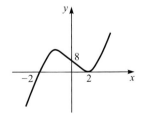

(b) (i) $x^2 + 6x + y^2 - 4y + 9 = 0$
$\Rightarrow (x+3)^2 - 9 + (y-2)^2$
$-4 + 9 = 0$
$\Rightarrow (x+3)^2 + (y-2)^2 = 4,$
a circle, centre $(-3, 2)$,
radius 2
(i)–(iii)

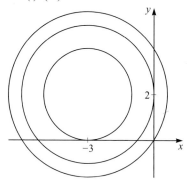

**13** (a)

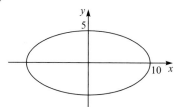

(b)

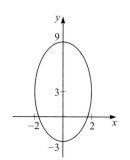

(c)

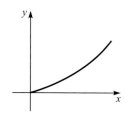

**14** (a) $y = x^2 - 4x + 2$

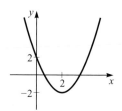

(b) $y = \dfrac{x}{1-x}$

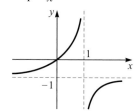

(c) $y^2 = x^3 (x \geq 0)$

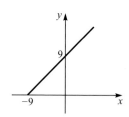

(d) $y = x + 9 \ (x \geq -9)$

**15** (ii) $1 - \ln x; -\dfrac{1}{x}$   (iii) (e, e)
(iv) $x \le e$   (v) $\dfrac{x}{2} \cdot \dfrac{1}{2}$

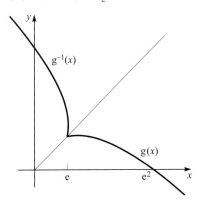

**16** $-\dfrac{1}{x-1} + \dfrac{4}{x-4}, \dfrac{1}{(x-1)^2} - \dfrac{4}{(x-4)^2}$

(ii) $(2, -3)$ maximum;
$(-2, -\tfrac{1}{3})$ minimum

(iv)

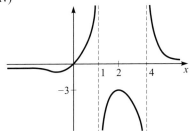

## Advanced

**1** (a) $y^2 = x^2(x+6)$
(d) $(-4, \pm 4\sqrt{2})$
(e)

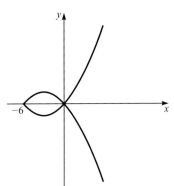

**2** (a)

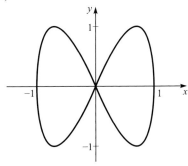

(b)

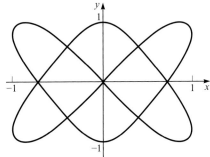

**3** (a) $(1, 10)$ maximum,
$(3, 6)$ minimum,
$(2, 8)$ point of inflexion

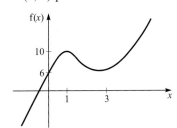

(b) $(1, e^{-1})$ maximum,
$(2, 2e^{-2})$ point of inflexion

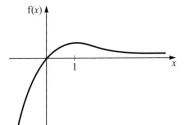

(c)  (3, 2.1) minimum,
    (6, 2.3) point of inflexion

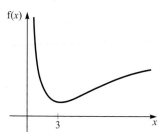

**4**  $\dfrac{3x - 4}{2\sqrt{x - 2}}$

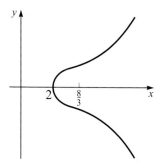

**5**  (a)  (i)

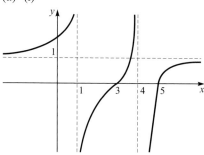

(ii)

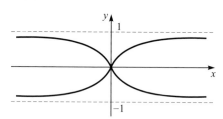

(b)  $(a, 0)$, $\left(\dfrac{2a}{a - 2}, \dfrac{a(4 - a)}{4}\right)$

(i)

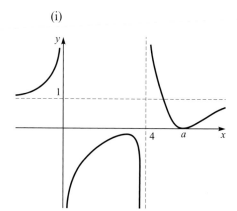

(ii)

**6**  (a)

(b)  (i)  $y = \pm x$
    (ii)  $y = \pm 1$

**8** (a)

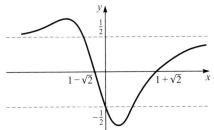

maximum at $-\sqrt{2} - 1$
minimum at $\sqrt{2} - 1$;

(b) maximum at $\dfrac{-2a - \sqrt{b^2 + 4a^2}}{b}$,

minimum at $\dfrac{-2a + \sqrt{b^2 + 4a^2}}{b}$

**9** (i)

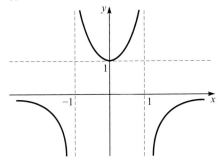

(ii) gradient $= \pm 2$

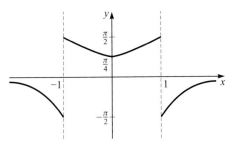

**10**

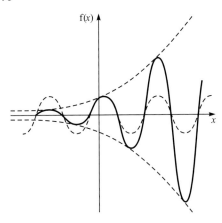

## Revision

**1** Area $= \dfrac{43}{15}$

**2**

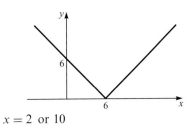

$x = 2$ or $10$

**3** (a)

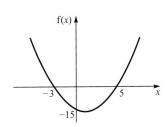

(b)

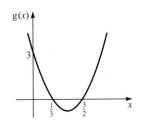

(c)

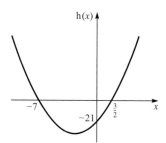

(c)  None

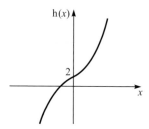

(d)

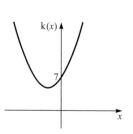

(d)  $(-\frac{1}{2}, 9), (\frac{1}{2}, 7)$

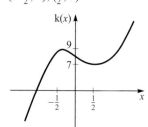

**4**  (a)  $(\frac{5}{2}, -7)$, two
    (b)  $(21, 3)$, none
    (c)  $(-\frac{5}{2}, -\frac{143}{4})$, two
    (d)  $(-\alpha, 0)$, one

**5**  (a)  $-1.4, 3.4$
    (b)  No solutions
    (c)  $-1.8, 2.3$

**6**  (a)  $(-\frac{2}{3}, 6.8), (4, -44)$

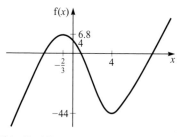

    (b)  $(3, 41)$

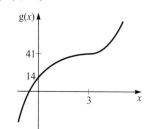

**7**  (a)

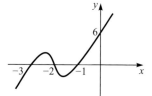

    (b)

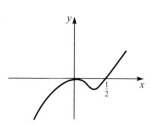

    (c)

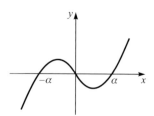

(d)

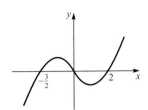

(iii)

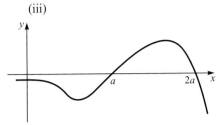

**8**

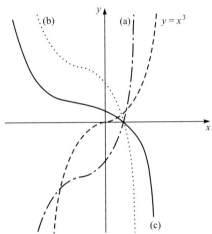

(a) $y = (x+1)^3 - 3$
(b) $y = 3 - (x+1)^3$
(c) $y = 1 - \frac{1}{3}(x+1)^3$

**9**  (a)  $t = -3, p(t) = 0$
(b)  $t = \frac{5}{2}, p(t) = \frac{1}{2}$
(c)  $t = -3, t = -4, p(t) = 2$

**10** (a) (i)

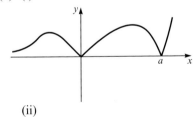

(ii)

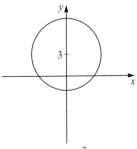

(b) (i)

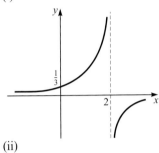

(ii)

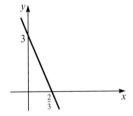

(iii)

**11** (a)

Area $= \pi \times 4^2 = 16\pi$

(b)

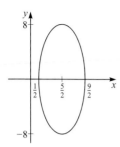

Area $= \pi \times 2 \times 8 = 16\pi$

(c)

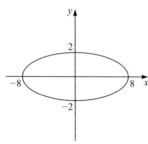

Area $= \pi \times 8 \times 2 = 16\pi$

12  (a)  $y = \frac{1}{4}(x-1)^2$

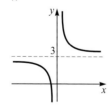

(b)  $y = \dfrac{1}{x} + 3$

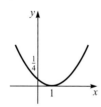

(c)  $y = x \; (x \geq 0)$

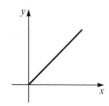

(d)  $y = \frac{1}{4}x^2 + 3x + 9$

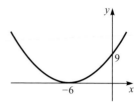

## 8.5

### Basic

1  (a)  $dy/dx = \frac{7}{2}$        (b)  $dy/dx = -\frac{2}{7}$
   (c)  $dy/dx = -\frac{7}{2}$       (d)  $dy/dx = \frac{2}{7}$

2  (a), (c) and (d)

3  (a)  $2ax$

4  (a)  Since $f(x) = 3x^2 + 6x + 4$, then, differentiating, $f'(x) = 6x + 6$ as required.
   (b)  $f''(x) = 6$ similarly
   (c)  Consider the more complicated expression on the right-hand side:
   $(x+1)f''(x) = (x+1) \times 6$
   $= 6x + 6 = f'(x)$ as required

5  (a)  If        $y = ax^2 - 4$        (1)

$$\frac{dy}{dx} = 2ax \qquad (2)$$

It is easier to eliminate $ax$, so multiply (2) by $x$, giving

$$x\frac{dy}{dx} = 2ax^2$$

From (1), $ax^2 = y + 4$, so substituting gives

$$x\frac{dy}{dx} = 2(y+4)$$

   (b)  $x\dfrac{dy}{dx} = 1 - y$

   (c)  $\dfrac{dy}{dx} = 4y$

**7** (a) $x\dfrac{d^2y}{dx^2} = \dfrac{dy}{dx}$

(b) $y = ax^2 + bx$    (1)

$\dfrac{dy}{dx} = 2ax + b$    (2)

$\dfrac{d^2y}{dx^2} = 2a$    (3)

Multiplying (2) by $x$ gives

$x\dfrac{dy}{dx} = 2ax^2 + bx$

$= ax^2 + ax^2 + bx$

$= ax^2 + y$

From (3) $a = \frac{1}{2}d^2y/dx$ so
$x\,dy/dx = \frac{1}{2}x^2 d^2y/dx^2 + y$

(c) $d^2y/dx^2 = 4y$

**8** (a) $1 - (3x)^2/2 = 1 - 9x^2/2$

(b) $1 - x^2$

(c) $1 + \frac{1}{2}x^2$

**9** (a), (d)

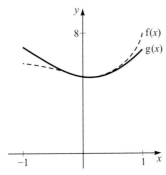

(b) 5, 0, 4

**10** (a) $f(x) = \sin x$     $f(0) = 0$
$g(x) = x - \frac{1}{6}x^3$    $g(0) = 0$

$f'(x) = \cos x$     $f'(0) = 1$
$g'(x) = 1 - \frac{1}{2}x^2$    $g'(0) = 1$

$f''(x) = -\sin x$     $f''(0) = 0$
$g''(x) = -x$    $g''(0) = 0$

$f'''(x) = -\cos x$    $f'''(0) = -1$
$g'''(x) = -1$    $g'''(0) = -1$

(b)

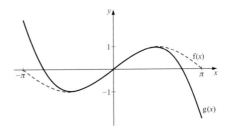

(c) (i) 0.0005%
   (ii) 0.3%

**11** (b)

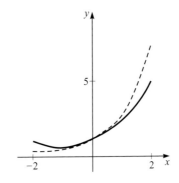

(c) 1.4%

**12** (a) $1 - x + \frac{1}{2}x^2$

(b) $2x - 2x^2$

(c) $1 + x - 2x^2$

## Intermediate

**1** (a) $dy/dx = 2Ax$, $d^2y/dx^2 = 2A$

**3** (a) Differentiate $xy - x^2 = 1$ with respect to $x$, giving

$y + x\dfrac{dy}{dx} - 2x = 0$

Hence $x(dy/dx) = 2x - y$; and thus

$\dfrac{dy}{dx} = \dfrac{2x^2 - y}{x}.$

(b) Multiply $\dfrac{2x - y}{x}$ by $\dfrac{x}{x} = 1$ to give

$$\frac{dy}{dx} = \frac{2x^2 - yx}{x^2}$$

and, since $xy - x^2 = 1$,

$$\frac{dy}{dx} = \frac{x^2 - 1}{x^2}$$

Hence $dy/dx = 1 - 1/x^2$.

**4**   (b) $x = \frac{1}{4}(y + 1)^2$

**5**   (a) $y = e^{2x}$ and so $dy/dx = 2e^{2x}$ and $d^2y/dx^2 = 4e^{2x}$. Now,
$4e^{2x} - 5(2e^{2x}) + 6(e^{2x}) = 0$ as required.

**6**   (b) From (a) *either* $1 + dy/dx$ *or* $\cos(x + y) = 0$, but $\cos(x + y)$ cannot be zero because $\sin(x + y) = 0$. Hence $1 + dy/dx = 0$, giving a gradient of $-1$.

**7**   (a) $f'(x) = 1/x$, $f''(x) = -1/x^2$

**8**   $y = e^{3x}(2x + 1)$

$$\frac{dy}{dx} = 3e^{3x}(2x + 1) + 2e^{3x}$$

$$= 6xe^{3x} + 5e^{3x}$$

$$\frac{d^2y}{dx^2} = 18xe^{3x} + 6e^{3x} + 15e^{3x}$$

$$= 18xe^{3x} + 21e^{3x}$$

Thus

$$\frac{d^2y}{dx^2} + p\frac{dy}{dx} + qy$$

$$= 18xe^{3x} + 21e^{3x}$$

$$+ p(6xe^{3x} + 5e^{3x}) + qe^{3x}(2x + 1)$$

$$= xe^{3x}(18 + 6p + 2q)$$

$$+ e^{3x}(21 + 5p + q)$$

$$= 0$$

Hence   $18 + 6p + 2q = 0$
and      $21 + 5p + q = 0$
Solving  simultaneously gives $p = -6$, $q = 9$.

**9**   (a) 2        (b) $\sqrt{2}x$
        (c) $x$     (d) $3x^2$

**10**  (b) $2 + 3\theta + 6\theta^2$

**12**  (a) $f(0) = 0$, $f'(0) = 1$, $f''(0) = -1$
        (b) $\ln(1 + x) \approx x - \frac{1}{2}x^2$

**13**  (a) $\ln 3 + \frac{2}{3}x - \frac{2}{9}x^2 + \frac{8}{81}x^3$
        (b) $\frac{1}{2} + \frac{3\sqrt{3}}{2}x - \frac{9}{4}x^2 - \frac{9\sqrt{3}}{4}x^3$

**14**  0.13

**15**  $k = 1$; $(e^{-1}, 0)$

**16**  (a) $\frac{1}{3}x - \frac{1}{6}x^2 + \frac{1}{18}x^3$
        (b) $x - \frac{1}{3}x^3$

## Advanced

**1**   (i) $y = x - \frac{1}{2}x^2$      (ii) $y = x^2 + x$
        (iii) $y = x$

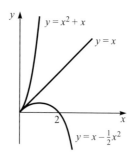

**2**   $a = -\frac{3}{2}, b = \frac{1}{2}; \frac{1}{120}; \frac{1}{24}x^4$

**3**   (a) $\dfrac{2}{1 - x} - \dfrac{2}{2 - x}, k = \frac{3}{2}$
        (c) $\theta = \pm 0.2$

**4**   (b) $2e^x \sin(x + \frac{\pi}{2})$

**6**  $1 + x + \frac{1}{2}x^2 - \frac{1}{6}x^3 - \frac{7}{24}x^4$

**8**  $e^{xy}(x\dfrac{dy}{dx} + y); \ 1 + x + \dfrac{1}{2}x^2 + \dfrac{1}{2}x^3$

**9**  $3x - 4x^3$

## Revision

**6**  $d^2y/dx^2 = 2y + 2y^3,$
$d^3y/dx^3 = 2 + 8y^2 + 6y^4$

**7**  (b)  $a = -1, b = 6$
(c)

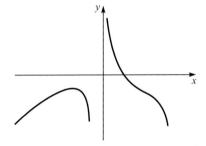

**9**  (a)  $\frac{3}{5}$

**10**  (a)  $1 - 2x + 2x^2 - \frac{4}{3}x^3$
(b)  $0.008\%$

**11**  (a)  $\sin 2x \approx 2x - \frac{4}{3}x^3$

**12**  (a)  $x - \frac{1}{2}x^2 + \frac{1}{3}x^3$
(b)  $-8x + 4x^2 - \frac{32}{3}x^3$

# Chapter 9 Integration

## 9.1

### Basic

**1** (a) $\dfrac{3x^5}{5} - \dfrac{x^3}{3} + c$

(b) $\dfrac{-2}{3x^3} + c$

(c) $\dfrac{2x^{3/2}}{3} + 2x^{1/2} + c$

(d) $\dfrac{x^3}{3} - \dfrac{x^2}{2} - 12x + c$

**2** (a) $x^4 - \dfrac{2x^{3/2}}{3} + c$

(b) $-\dfrac{1}{x} - \dfrac{1}{2x^2} + c$

(c) $\displaystyle\int \dfrac{2+x}{x^5}\,dx$

$= \displaystyle\int \left(\dfrac{2}{x^5} + \dfrac{1}{x^4}\right) dx$

$= -\dfrac{1}{2x^4} - \dfrac{1}{3x^3} + c$

(d) $-\dfrac{1}{x} - \dfrac{1}{2x^2} + \dfrac{2}{x^3} + c$

**3** $\dfrac{dy}{dx} = 4x$

$\Rightarrow y = 2x^2 + c$

$y = 11$ when $x = 2$ $\Rightarrow 11 = 8 + c$

$\Rightarrow c = 3$

$\Rightarrow y = 2x^2 + 3$

**4** (a) $\dfrac{x^2}{2} + \dfrac{1}{2x^2} + c$

(b) $x + \dfrac{x^2}{2} + \dfrac{4x^{3/2}}{3} + c$

**5** (a) $-\dfrac{2}{x} - \cos x + c$

(b) $\displaystyle\int \cos x(2 + \tan x)\,dx$

$= \displaystyle\int \cos x \left(2 + \dfrac{\sin x}{\cos x}\right) dx$

$= \displaystyle\int (2\cos x + \sin x)\,dx$

$= 2\sin x - \cos x + c$

**6** $P = \tfrac{1}{4}q^4 + q^2 - q + 7$

**7** (a) $22\tfrac{5}{6}$

(b) $\displaystyle\int_1^2 \left(\dfrac{x^2}{2} - \dfrac{2}{3x^3}\right) dx = \left[\dfrac{x^3}{6} + \dfrac{1}{3x^2}\right]_1^2$

$= (\tfrac{8}{6} + \tfrac{1}{12}) - (\tfrac{1}{6} + \tfrac{1}{3})$

$= \tfrac{11}{12}$

(c) $e - 1$

**8** (a) $2$ (b) $\ln 2 - 12$

**9** $45$

**10** When $y = 0$, $4x(3 - x) = 0$

$\Rightarrow x = 0$ or $3$

$\displaystyle\int_0^3 4x(3 - x)\,dx = \int_0^3 (12x - 4x^2)\,dx$

$= \left[6x^2 - \dfrac{4x^3}{3}\right]_0^3$

$= (54 - 36) - (0 - 0)$

$= 18 \text{ units}^2$

**11**  $0.811 \text{ units}^2$

**12**  $4\frac{2}{3} \text{ units}^2$

## Intermediate

**1**  (a)  $\dfrac{6x^{5/2}}{5} + c$

   (b)  $\dfrac{4x^3}{3} + 4x - \dfrac{1}{x} + c$

**2**  (a)  $\dfrac{4x^{5/2}}{5} - 2x^{1/2} + c$

   (b)  $\dfrac{-2}{\sqrt{x}} + c$

   (c)  $x + c$

**3**  $y = 2x + x^3 + 4$

**4**  $y = x^2 + 2x - 3; \ -3$

**5**  (a)  $\sqrt{2}$   (b)  $1 - \sqrt{3}$

**6**  (a)  (i) $\ln 3$   (ii) $-0.25$

**7**  (a)  $a = 2, b = 14$
   (b)  $4 + 14 \ln 2$

**8**  Evaluating the first integral,

$$\left[ \frac{px^3}{3} + qx \right]_1^2 = 9$$

which simplifies to
$$7p + 3q = 27 \quad (1)$$

Evaluating the second integral,

$$\left[ \frac{qx^2}{2} + px \right]_1^2 = 6$$

which simplifies to
$$3q + 2p = 12 \quad (2)$$

Solving equations (1) and (2) gives
$p = 3$ and $q = 2$.

**9**  (a)  $\dfrac{dy}{dx} = -3 \sin x \cos^2 x$

   (b)  $-\frac{1}{3}\cos^3 x + c$

**10**  (a)  $y = \dfrac{x^3}{3} + \dfrac{x^2}{2} - 12x + 2$

   (b)  $(-4, 36\frac{2}{3}), (3, -20\frac{1}{2})$

   (c)

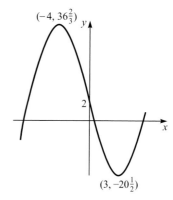

$(-4, 36\frac{2}{3})$

$(3, -20\frac{1}{2})$

**11**  Gradient of tangent at $P$ is 2.
Hence gradient of normal at $P$ is $-\frac{1}{2}$
Equation of normal at $P$ is

$$\frac{y - 3}{x - 2} = -\frac{1}{2}$$
$$\Rightarrow y = -\tfrac{1}{2}x + 4 \quad (1)$$

Since $\dfrac{dy}{dx} = 2x - 2$, the equation of the
curve is

$$y = x^2 - 2x + c$$

Substituting $(2, 3)$ gives

$$3 = 4 - 4 + c$$
$$\Rightarrow c = 3$$
$$\text{so } y = x^2 - 2x + 3 \quad (2)$$

Equating (1) and (2)

$$-\tfrac{1}{2}x + 4 = x^2 - 2x + 3$$
$$-x + 8 = 2x^2 - 4x + 6$$
$$2x^2 - 3x - 2 = 0$$
$$(2x + 1)(x - 2) = 0$$

Hence, when $x = -\frac{1}{2}$, substituting in
(1) gives $y = 4\frac{1}{4}$
The coordinates of $Q$ are $(-\frac{1}{2}, 4\frac{1}{4})$.

**12**

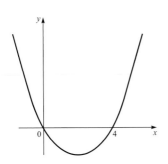

$19\frac{2}{3}$ units$^2$

**13** $(\frac{1}{2}, 0)$; $(1, -1)$; $0.0569$ units$^2$

**14**

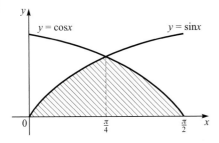

By symmetry,

$$\text{area} = 2 \int_0^{\pi/4} \sin x \, dx$$

$$= 2 \left[ -\cos x \right]_0^{\pi/4}$$

$$= 2 \left[ \left( \frac{-1}{\sqrt{2}} \right) - (-1) \right]$$

$$= 2 \left[ 1 - \frac{1}{\sqrt{2}} \right]$$

$$= 2 - \sqrt{2} \text{ units}^2$$

**15** $y = \ln(x - 2)$
$e^y = x - 2$
$x = e^y + 2$

$$\int_2^3 (e^y + 2) \, dy = \left[ e^y + 2y \right]_2^3$$

$$= 14.7 \text{ units}^2$$

**16** $10\frac{2}{3}$ units$^2$

## Advanced

**1**   (a) $\frac{1}{2}n$     (b) $2n$     (c) $2\pi$

**2**   $6\frac{3}{4}$ units$^2$

**3**

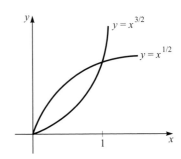

**5**   $a = 1/n^4$, $b = n - 1$

**7**

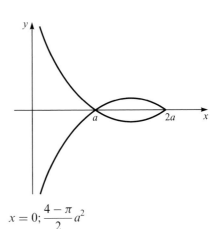

$x = 0$; $\dfrac{4 - \pi}{2} a^2$

**8**   $p = 1$

**9**   $a_6 = 1$, $a_5 = -4$, $a_4 = 5$, $a_3 = 0$,
$a_2 = -4$; $a_1 = 0$, $a_0 = 4$, $b = -4$; $\frac{1}{630}$

**10**   $u_1 = \dfrac{1}{\sqrt{3}}$, $u_2 = -\dfrac{1}{\sqrt{3}}$, $a_1 = a_2 = 1$

# Revision

**1** (a) $\dfrac{x^3}{3} - \dfrac{x^2}{2} + c$

(b) $-\dfrac{1}{x} + \dfrac{2x^{3/2}}{3} + c$

**2** (a) $\dfrac{2x^{5/2}}{5} - 2x^{3/2} + x^2 - 6x + c$

(b) $\ln x - 4x^{1/2} + x + c$

**3** $x = t^2 + 4t - 3$

**4** (a) $-11\frac{1}{4}$    (b) $4 - 3\ln 2$

**5** (a) $1.14$    (b) $\dfrac{\sqrt{3} - 1}{4}$

**6** $-3$

**7** $y = x^3 + 3x - 4;\ (0, 4)$

**8** $3\mathrm{e}^{3x};$    $6.36$

**9** (a) $6$ units$^2$    (b) $\frac{9}{16}$ units$^2$

**10** (a) $A - B + C$    (b) $A + B - C$
(c) $A - B + C$

**11** $2\frac{1}{3}$ units$^2$

**12** (a) $x(x + 3)(x - 2)$
(b)

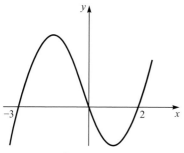

(c) $16$ units$^2$

# 9.2

## Basic

**1** (a) (i) $5\cos 5x$    (ii) $5\mathrm{e}^{5x}$

(iii) $\dfrac{2}{2x + 1}$    (iv) $15(3x + 1)^4$

(b) (i) $\frac{1}{5}\sin 5x + c$    (ii) $\frac{1}{5}\mathrm{e}^{5x} + c$

(iii) $\frac{1}{2}\ln(2x + 1) + c$
(iv) $\frac{1}{15}(3x + 1)^5 + c$

**2** (a) $-\frac{1}{2}\cos 2x + c$

(b) $\frac{1}{2}\mathrm{e}^4 x = c$

(c) $\frac{1}{4}\ln(4x + 1) + c$

(d) $\frac{1}{77}(7x + 3)^{11} + c$

**3** (a) (i) $15x^2(x^3 + 2)^4$    (ii) $\dfrac{2x}{x^2 + 1}$

(iii) $\dfrac{-6x^2}{(x^3 - 4)^3}$    (iv) $4\sin^3 x \cos x$

(b) (i) $\frac{1}{15}(x^3 + 2)^5 + c$
(ii) $\frac{1}{2}\ln(x^2 + 1) + c$

(iii) $\dfrac{-1}{6(x^3 - 4)^2} + c$    (iv) $\frac{1}{4}\sin^4 x + c$

**4** (a) $\frac{1}{32}(4x - 5)^8 + c$
(b) $\frac{1}{16}(2x^2 - 3)^4 + c$

(c) $\displaystyle\int \dfrac{x}{(3x^2 - 1)^2}\,dx$

$= \displaystyle\int x(3x^2 - 1)^{-2}\,dx$

Now $\dfrac{d}{dx}(3x^2 - 1)^{-1} = -6x(3x^2 - 1)^{-2}$

so $\displaystyle\int x(3x^2 - 1)^{-2}\,dx = -\frac{1}{6}(3x^2 - 1)^{-1}$

$= \dfrac{-1}{6(3x^2 - 1)} + c$

(d) $-\frac{1}{5}\cos^5 x + c$

**5** (a) $\frac{1}{3}\ln(1+x^3)+c$

(b) $-\frac{1}{5}\cos(x^5+2)+c$

(c) $-\ln\cos x+c$

**6** (a) $\dfrac{(1+x)^5(5x-1)}{30}+c$

(b) $u=2x-3\Rightarrow 4x=2u+6$

$\dfrac{du}{dx}=2\Rightarrow dx=\dfrac{du}{2}$

$\displaystyle\int\dfrac{(2u+6)}{2}u^5\,du$

$\displaystyle=\int(u^6+3u^5)\,du$

$=\dfrac{u^7}{7}+\dfrac{u^6}{2}+c$

$=u^6\left(\dfrac{u}{7}+\dfrac{1}{2}\right)+c$

$=u^6\dfrac{(u+7)}{14}+c$

$=\dfrac{(2x-3)^6(4x+1)}{14}+c$

(c) $\frac{2}{5}(x+3)^{3/2}(x-7)+c$

(d) $\dfrac{(3x-4)^5(15x+4)}{45}+c$

**7** (a) $\frac{1}{5}\ln(5x+2)+c$

(b) $-\frac{1}{2}\ln(1-2x)+c$

(c) $\dfrac{-1}{3(3x-1)}+c$

**8** (a) $\dfrac{1}{x-3}-\dfrac{2}{x+7}$

(b) $\ln|x-3|-2\ln|x+7|+c$

**9** $\ln 6\frac{3}{4}$

**10** (a) $xe^x-e^x+c$

(b) $u=x,\ v=\frac{1}{4}(x+2)^4$

$\dfrac{du}{dx}=1,\dfrac{dv}{dx}=(x+2)^3$

$\displaystyle\int x(x+2)^3\,dx=\dfrac{x(x+2)^4}{4}-\int\frac{1}{4}(x+2)^4\,dx$

$=\dfrac{x(x+2)^4}{4}-\dfrac{(x+2)^5}{20}+c$

$=\dfrac{(x+2)^4}{4}\left(x-\dfrac{x+2}{5}\right)+c$

$=\dfrac{(x+2)^4}{4}\left(\dfrac{4x-2}{5}\right)+c$

$=\dfrac{(x+2)^4(2x-1)}{10}+c$

**11** (a) $\frac{23}{30}$    (b) $\pi-1$

**12** $y=\frac{1}{2}(e^{2x}+3)$

## Intermediate

**1** (a) $-e^{-x}+c$

(b) $-2\cos\frac{1}{2}\theta+c$

(c) $\frac{1}{16}(2x-4)^8+c$

(d) $\frac{1}{3}\tan 3\theta+c$

**2** (a) $\frac{1}{4}(2x-4)^6+c$

(b) $\frac{1}{12}\ln(3x^4-5)+c$

**3** (a) $\frac{1}{2}e^{2x}+4e^x+4x+c$

(b) $\frac{1}{2}e^{2x}+2x-\frac{1}{2}e^{-2x}+c$

**4** (a) $\frac{3}{2}$    (b) 7.05

**5** (a) $\frac{3}{2}\ln(x^2+9)+c$    (b) $\frac{1}{3}e^{x^3}+c$

**6** (a) $10\frac{1}{2}$    (b) 256

(c) $\displaystyle\int_0^{\pi/2}\sin 2\theta\sin\theta\,d\theta$

$\displaystyle=\int_0^{\pi/2}2\sin\theta\cos\theta\sin\theta\,d\theta$

$\displaystyle=\int_0^{\pi/2}2\sin^2\theta\cos\theta\,d\theta$

$=[\frac{2}{3}\sin^3\theta]_0^{\pi/2}=\frac{2}{3}$

**7** (a) $\frac{4}{15}(2x-1)^{3/2}(3x+1)+c$

(b) $c-e^x-\ln|1-e^x|$

**8** (a) 65.8    (b) $4(1+\ln 2)+c$

**9** (a) $\dfrac{2}{2x+1} - \dfrac{1}{3x-2}$

**10** $\frac{1}{6}\ln\left|\dfrac{x-3}{x+3}\right| + c$

**11** (a) $6x\sin\left(\dfrac{x}{3}\right) + 18\cos\left(\dfrac{x}{3}\right) + c$

  (b) $\dfrac{-xe^{-3x}}{3} - \dfrac{e^{-3x}}{9} + c$

**12** (a) $u = \ln x,\ v = x$

  $\dfrac{du}{dx} = \dfrac{1}{x},\qquad \dfrac{dv}{dx} = 1$

  $\displaystyle\int \ln x\,dx = x\ln x - \int 1\,dx$

  $= x\ln x - x + c$

  (b) $-x^2\cos x + 2x\sin x + 2\cos x + c$

**13** (a) $\dfrac{2x^3(x^2-2)}{(x^2-1)^2}$

  (b) $\dfrac{x^4}{2(x^2-1)} + c$

**14** $k = 0.373$

**15** (a) $2y = 3 + \ln x$

  $2y - 3 = \ln x$

  $e^{(2y-3)} = x$

  $\displaystyle\int_1^2 e^{2y-3}\,dy = \left[\tfrac{1}{2}e^{2y-3}\right]_1^2$

  $= \tfrac{1}{2}e - \tfrac{1}{2}e^{-1}$

  $= 1.18$

  (b)

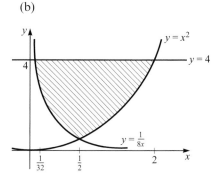

4.90 units$^2$

**16** (a) $P(0, 3),\ Q(2.4, 1.8)$

  (b) $0.573$ units$^2$

## Advanced

**1** $S = -3C + 1 + e^{-3\pi}$;

  $C = \frac{3}{10}(1 + e^{-3\pi})$,

  $S = \frac{1}{10}(1 + e^{-3\pi})$

**2** $A = \pi ab$;   $R = 5\pi a^2/12\sqrt{3}$

**3** (i)

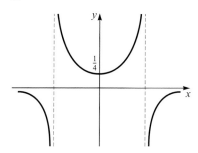

  (ii) $\frac{1}{4}\ln\left(\dfrac{2+x}{2-x}\right) + c$

  (iii) Graph is below axis.

  (iv) $\frac{1}{2}\ln(\sec\theta + \tan\theta) + c$

**4** $A(-1, -\frac{1}{2}\pi),\ B(1, \frac{1}{2}\pi),\ C(-1, \pi),$

  $D(1, 0)$;

  $\sin^{-1} x + \cos^{-1} x = \frac{1}{2}\pi$;

  $(1/\sqrt{2}, \frac{1}{4}\pi);\ x\sin^{-1} x + \sqrt{1-x^2}$;

  $\sqrt{2} - 1$

**5** (a) $\frac{32}{315}$    (b) $\frac{8}{105}$

**6** (i) $S = \frac{1}{2}\{x + \ln(\sin x + x)\}$,

    $T = \frac{1}{2}\{x - \ln(\sin x + \cos x)\}$

  (ii) $\dfrac{1}{2} - \dfrac{3\sqrt{3}}{8}$

**8** $x = 1/t$ is not defined for the whole interval $[-1, 1]$; $\frac{1}{4}\pi + \frac{1}{2};\frac{1}{2} - \frac{\pi}{4}$

**10** $a = \frac{1}{8},\ b = \frac{1}{4},\ c = -\frac{1}{8},\ d = \frac{1}{4}$

## Revision

**1** (a) $-\frac{1}{12}(1-x^4)^3 + c$

(b) $\frac{1}{12}(x^2 + 2x)^6 + c$

**2** (a) $-\frac{1}{2}e^{-2x} + c$

(b) $-\ln|3 - x| + c$

**3** (a) $-\frac{1}{16}(4x + \ln|1 - 4x|) + c$

(b) $-\frac{1}{20}(1 - 2x^2)^5 + c$

**4** (a) $\dfrac{2}{x-1} - \dfrac{1}{x+1}$

**5** $\frac{1}{5}\ln(\frac{12}{7})$

**6** (a) $\frac{1}{2}x^2(\ln x - \frac{1}{2}) + c$

(b) $\frac{1}{2}x^2 e^{2x} - \frac{1}{2}xe^{2x} + \frac{1}{4}e^{2x} + c$

**7** (a) 2    (b) $2 - \sqrt{2}$

**8** $\pm\dfrac{1}{2}, \pm\dfrac{\sqrt{3}}{2}$

**9** (a) $\theta - \frac{1}{4}\sin 4\theta + c$

(b) $\sin\theta - \frac{1}{3}\sin^3\theta + c$

**10** $(0, \frac{1}{4})$

**11** 0.887 units$^2$

**12** 20.7 units$^2$

## 9.3

## Basic

**1** $\dfrac{2x^3}{3} - \dfrac{3x^2}{2} + 4x + c$

**2** $2xe^x - 2e^x + c$

**3** $-\frac{1}{4}e^{-4x} + c$

**4** $\frac{2}{15}(x-2)^{3/2}(3x+4) + c$

**5** $\ln|x - 4| + \ln|x + 1| + c$

**6** Let $u = x - 3$. Then $du = dx$.
When $x = 3, u = 0$
When $x = 4, u = 1$

$$\int_0^1 (u + 3)u^7)\,du$$

$$= \int_0^1 (u^8 + 3u^7)\,du$$

$$= \left[\frac{u^9}{9} + \frac{3u^8}{8}\right]_0^1$$

$$= \frac{35}{72}$$

**7** $\ln(\frac{3}{2})$

**8** $\dfrac{\pi}{2} - 1$

**9** $\ln(\frac{32}{15})$

**10** 9.9

**11**

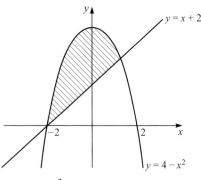

4.5 units$^2$

**12** $y = \int \dfrac{x}{(x+3)^3}\, dx$

Let $u = x + 3$. Then $du = dx$.

$$y = \int \frac{u-3}{u^3}\, du$$

$$= \int (u^{-2} - 3u^{-3})\, du$$

$$= -u^{-1} + \frac{3u^{-2}}{2} + c$$

$$= \frac{-1}{x+3} + \frac{3}{2(x+3)^2} + c$$

$$= \frac{-2(x+3)+3}{2(x+3)^2} + c$$

$$= \frac{-2x-3}{2(x+3)^2} + c \quad (1)$$

Substituting $(0, \tfrac{1}{2})$ gives $\tfrac{1}{2} = -\tfrac{3}{18} + c$
$\Rightarrow \tfrac{2}{3} = c$

Substituting $(-1, a)$ in (1) gives

$a = -\tfrac{1}{8} + \tfrac{2}{3}$

$\Rightarrow a = \tfrac{13}{24}$

## Intermediate

**1** $\dfrac{-\cos^5 \theta}{5} + c$

**2** $\tfrac{1}{4}x^2 + x + \tfrac{1}{2}\ln|x| + c$

**3** $\dfrac{1}{2}\ln\left|\dfrac{x-4}{x+4}\right| + c$

**4** $x^2 \sin x + 2x \cos x - 2\sin x + c$

**5** $\tfrac{1}{4}(2x + \ln|2x-1|) + c$

**6** $\tfrac{1}{2}\ln(x^2 + 6x + 13) + c$

**7** $6\tfrac{1}{2}$

**8** $0.330$

**9** $\dfrac{\pi}{3} + \dfrac{\sqrt{3}}{2}$

**10** $0.187$

**11** $\ln 8 - 1$

**12** $0.219$

**13** $P = \displaystyle\int \frac{3q+4}{q^2 + 2q}\, dq$

$$\frac{3q+4}{q^2+2q} \equiv \frac{A}{q} + \frac{B}{q+2}$$

$3q + 4 \equiv A(q+2) + Bq$
Let $q = 0$; $4 = 2A \Rightarrow A = 2$
Let $q = -2$; $-2 = -2B \Rightarrow B = 1$

So $P = \displaystyle\int \left(\frac{2}{q} + \frac{1}{q+2}\right) dq$

$$P = 2\ln|q| + \ln|q+2| + c$$

Substituting $P = \ln 3$, $q = 1$, gives

$$\ln 3 = 2\ln 1 + \ln 3 + c$$

$$\Rightarrow c = 0$$

When $q = 2$,

$$P = 2\ln 2 + \ln 4$$

$$\Rightarrow P = \ln 16$$

**14** (a)

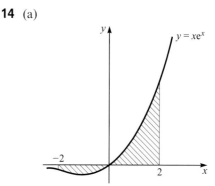

(b) $8.98$ units$^2$

**15** $y = \displaystyle\int a(2x+1)^3\, dx$

$y = \dfrac{a}{8}(2x+1)^4 + k \qquad (1)$

Substituting $(-1, 1)$ in (1),

$$1 = \frac{a}{8}(-1)^4 + c \Rightarrow 8 = a + 8c \qquad (2)$$

Substituting $(-2, 21)$ in (1),

$$21 = \frac{a}{8}(-3)^4 + c \Rightarrow 168 = 81a + 8c \qquad (3)$$

$(3) - (2) \Rightarrow 160 = 80a$

so    $a = 2$

**16**  $(\ln 4 - 1)$ units$^2$

## Advanced

**1**  (a) $\tan^{-1}\left(\frac{e^x}{3}\right) + c$

(b) $\sin x - \frac{1}{3}\sin^3 x + c$

(c) $\frac{1}{2}\ln\left(\frac{1 + x}{1 - x}\right) - x + c$

**2**  $\sin^{-1} x + \frac{x}{\sqrt{1 - x^2}}; \frac{1}{2}\pi - 1$

**3**  (a) $25\pi/4$     (b) $4\sqrt{2}$
(c) $\pi^3/192$

**4**  (ii) $\frac{1}{2}\ln 2$   (iii) $-\frac{1}{2}\ln 2$

(iv) Translation through $\binom{-1}{0}$
(v) $-\frac{1}{2}\ln 2$

**5**  (b) $2\ln\left(\frac{\sqrt{2} + \sqrt{10}}{4}\right)$

**6**  (a) $5\pi/32$     (b) $\pi/32$

**7**  (i) $\frac{47}{480}$  (ii) $\ln\frac{3}{2}$  (iii) $\frac{1}{\sqrt{3}}\ln\left(\frac{\sqrt{3} + 1}{\sqrt{3} - 1}\right)$

**8**  (a) (i) $x\ln x - x + c$
(ii) $x(\ln x)^2 - 2x\ln x + 2x + c$

**9**  (a) $2(1 - \ln 2)$     (b) $\frac{1}{2}(n - 1)n$

**10**  (a) $\pi^2/4$
(b) $2\pi^2/3\sqrt{3}$

## Revision

**1**  (i)   inspection
(ii)   partial fractions
(iii)   direct integration
(iv)   partial fractions
(v)   algebraic rearrangement
(vi)   inspection
(vii)   trigonometric  rearrangement
(viii)   inspection
(ix)   substitution
(x)   inspection
(xi)   parts
(xii)   substitution
(xiii)   inspection
(xiv)   substitution
(xv)   substitution
(xvi)   direct integration
(xvii)   parts
(xviii)   algebraic rearrangement
(xix)   inspection
(xx)   parts
(xxi)   inspection
(xxii)   partial fractions
(xxiii)   inspection
(xxiv)   direct integration
(xxv)   algebraic rearrangement
(xxvi)   inspection
(xxvii)   algebraic rearrangement
(xxviii)   trigonometric rearrangement
(xxix)   trigonometric rearrangement
(xxx)   partial fractions
(xxxi)   inspection
(xxxii)   substitution
(xxxiii)   partial fractions
(xxxiv)   substitution
(xxxv)   substitution
(xxvi)   substitution
(xxxvii)   trigonometric rearrrangement
(xxxviii)   inspection
(xxxix)   substitution
(xl)   substitution.

**2**  $\frac{1}{4}\ln(2x^2 - 4x + 7) + c$

**3**  $\ln(e^x + 1) + c$

**4**  $-2x\cos x + 2\sin x + c$

**5**  $\frac{8}{7}x^{7/2} + c$

**6**  $\ln \frac{8}{5}$

**7**  $1\frac{3}{4}$

**8**  $\ln 3$

**9**  53.3

**10**  4.57

**11**  $a = 2$

**12**

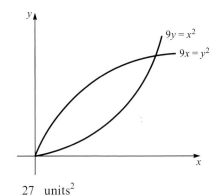

$9y = x^2$

$9x = y^2$

27  units$^2$

## 9.4

## Basic

**1**  (a)  $dy/dx = 3x^2$
   (b)  $\tan x \, dy/dx = y$
   (c)  $dx/dt = 3x$
   (d)  $d\theta/dt = 2e^{-\theta}$

**2**  (a)  (i) $dy/dx = 5x - 2$

$$\Rightarrow y = \int (5x - 2) \, dx$$

$$= \tfrac{5}{2}x^2 - 2x + c, \text{ which is}$$
the general solution

   (ii) But, when $x = 1, y = 1$, so
   $1 = \frac{5}{2}1^2 - 2 \times 1 + c$.
   Thus $c = \frac{1}{2}$ and the particular
   solution which gives $y = 1$
   when $x = 1$ is $y = \frac{5}{2}x^2 - 2x + \frac{1}{2}$
   (b)  (i)  $y = \frac{1}{2}e^{2x} + \frac{1}{2}\cos 2x + c$
   (ii) $y = \frac{1}{2}e^{2x} + \frac{1}{2}\cos 2x + 1$

**3**  (a)  $y = \frac{1}{5}(x^2 + 5)^5 + c$
   (b)  $v = 2\ln |t^2 + 5| + c$

**4**  $\dfrac{d\theta}{dt} = 10 - \dfrac{8t}{5}$

$$\theta = \int \left(10 - \frac{8t}{5}\right) dt$$

$$= 10t - \frac{4t^2}{5} + c$$

When $t = 0$, $\theta = 30$, so $30 = c$.
Hence $\theta = 10t - 4t^2/5 + 30$ and so,
when $t = 4$, $\theta = 40 - 12.8 + 30 = 57.2$.
When $t = 10$, $d\theta/dt = 10 - (80/5) = -6$,
which indicates that the container is
being cooled.

**5**  44 m s$^{-1}$

**6**  (a)  $y = Ae^{6x}$
   (b)  $y^2 + 4y = 2x + A$

**7**  (a)  $2y \, dy/dx = 3x^2$
   (b)  $\sin y = Ax^2 \Rightarrow \cos y \, dy/dx = 2Ax$,
   differentiating implicitly but

$$A = \frac{\sin y}{x^2}$$

   so   $\cos y \dfrac{dy}{dx} = \dfrac{2x \sin y}{x^2}$

$$\Rightarrow \frac{\cos y}{\sin y} \frac{dy}{dx} = \frac{2}{x}$$

$$\Rightarrow \cot y \frac{dy}{dx} = \frac{2}{x}$$

**8**  $y = \dfrac{2}{8 - x^2}$

**9**  (a)  $y = Ae^{(1/2)x^2} - 2$
   (b)  Cannot be solved
   (c)  Cannot be solved
   (d)  $y^2 = 5x - 3x^2/2 + c$

**10**  $dh/dt = 0.4 - 0.3h$ can be solved by separating variables.

$$\frac{1}{0.4 - 0.03h}\frac{dh}{dt} = 1$$

$$\int\frac{1}{0.4 - 0.03h}\,dh = \int 1\,dt$$

$$-\frac{100}{3}\ln|0.4 - 0.03h| = t + c$$

$$\ln(0.4 - 0.03h) = -0.03t + A$$

$$0.4 - 0.03h = e^{-0.03t + A}$$

$$= e^{-0.03t}e^{A} = Be^{-0.03t}$$

When $t = 0, h = 2 \Rightarrow 0.34 = B$

Hence $0.4 - 0.03h = 0.34\,e^{-0.03t}$
When $t = 30, 0.4 - 0.03h = 0.34\,e^{-0.9}$,
giving $h \approx 8.7$ m

**11**  (a)  $dn/dt = 0.375n$
(b)  Over 8500 ants

**12**  (a)  $dV/dt = -kV$
(b)  $A = 200$
(c)  0.00103
(d)  676 s

## Intermediate

**1**  (a)  $dx/dt = 2x^3t^2$ is solved by separating variables.
$$\frac{1}{x^3}\frac{dx}{dt} = 2t^2$$
i.e.  $\displaystyle\int\frac{1}{x^3}\,dx = \int 2t^2\,dt$

which gives  $-\dfrac{1}{2x^2} = \dfrac{2t^3}{3} + c$

(b)  $dy/dx = y - y\cos x$
$$= y(1 - \cos x)$$
Separating variables leads to
$$\int\frac{1}{y}\,dy = \int(1 - \cos x)\,dx$$
$$\Rightarrow \ln y = x - \sin x + c$$
$$\Rightarrow y = e^{x - \sin x + c} = e^{x - \sin x}e^{c}$$
so, writing $e^{c} = A, y = Ae^{x - \sin x}$

**2**  (a)  $y = (\frac{1}{3}x^{3/2} + \frac{1}{2})^2$
(b)  $\tan y = 1 - \cos x$
(c)  $y = \frac{1}{2}x^3$

**3**  $y = \dfrac{2e^{x^2} - 2}{2 - e^{x^2}}$

**4**  $\cos^2 y = \dfrac{1 - e^{2x}}{4(1 - e^2)}$

**5**  $y = \dfrac{3x^3}{4 + x^3}$

**6**  $y = \dfrac{1 + 3\sin x}{3\sin x - 1}$

**7**  (a)  $\dfrac{dh}{dt} = 0.4 + 0.3\cos\dfrac{\pi t}{50}$

Thus $h = \displaystyle\int\left(0.4 + 0.3\cos\frac{\pi t}{50}\right)dt$

$$= 0.4t + \frac{15}{\pi}\sin\frac{\pi t}{50} + c$$

When $t = 0, h = 140 \Rightarrow c = 140$
When $t = 5, h = 2 + \dfrac{15}{\pi}\sin\dfrac{\pi}{10} + 140$

$$= 143.5 \text{ cm}$$

(b)  $\dfrac{dh}{dt} = 1 - 0.4e^{t/250}$

Thus  $h = \displaystyle\int(1 - 0.4e^{t/250})\,dt$

$$= t - 100e^{t/250} + c$$
$t = 0, h = 140 \Rightarrow c = 240$
$t = 5, h = 5 - 100e^{0.02} + 240$
$$= 143.0 \text{ cm}$$

**8**  (a)  The rate of increase of $h$ is given by $dh/dt$ and $dh/dt \propto 1/h$. Hence the differential equation is
$dh/dt = \lambda/h$.
(b)  Separating the variables gives
$h\,dh/dt = \lambda$.
Hence $\displaystyle\int h\,dh = \int \lambda\,dt$
$$\Rightarrow \tfrac{1}{2}h^2 = \lambda t + c$$
When $t = 0, h = 0 \Rightarrow c = 0$
To find $\lambda$, use the information that when $t = 1, h = 3$. Thus $\frac{9}{2} = \lambda \times 1$

So the thickness of the ice at time
$t$ is given by $\frac{1}{2}h^2 = \frac{9}{2}t$
i.e. $h^2 = 9t$ or $h = 3\sqrt{t}$, as
required
(c) When $h = 6$, $\sqrt{t} = 2$, so $t = 4$
Hence the time that the thickness
of ice is 6 mm is 7.00 p.m.

**9** (a) $dm/dt = -0.001m$
(b) 22.6 g
(c) 1610 years

**10** (b) (i) $dv/dt = 10 - 0.4v^2$;
$$v = \frac{5(1 - e^{-4t})}{1 + e^{-4t}}$$
(ii) $v\,dv/dx = 10 - 0.4v^2$;
$$v = 5\sqrt{1 - e^{-0.8x}}$$

**11** (a) $dx/dt = 4(3 - x)$
(b) 24 minutes
(c) He never reaches school.

**12** $16T/3$

**13** $H = \dfrac{72 - 56e^{-t/20}}{9 + 7e^{-t/20}}$, $H \to 8\,\mathrm{m}$

**14** $x = \dfrac{a^2kt}{1 + akt}$

**15** (a) $dy/dt = \lambda y - m$
(b) $y = m/\lambda + (q - m/\lambda)e^{\lambda t}$
(d) 303 grams

**16** $x\,dy/dx - y = \frac{1}{4}x^2 - y^2$
Let $y = zx$. By the product rule,
$$\frac{dy}{dx} = z + x\frac{dz}{dx}$$
$$xz + x^2\frac{dz}{dx} - xz = \frac{1}{4}x^2 - z^2x^2$$
$$\Rightarrow 4x^2\frac{dz}{dx} = x^2 - 4z^2x^2$$
$$\Rightarrow 4\frac{dz}{dx} = 1 - 4z^2,$$
dividing through by $x^2$
This can now be solved by separating
variables and using partial fractions

to give $z = \dfrac{\frac{1}{2}e^x - 1}{2 + e^x}$

Now, $y = xz = \dfrac{x(\frac{1}{2}e^x - 1)}{2 + e^x}$

## Advanced

**1** (i) 100 minutes   (ii) $x = (-\frac{1}{20}t + c)^2$

**2** $x = \dfrac{a}{b(1 + e^{-at})}$.

**3** (i) $P = P_0 e^{kt}$   (ii) 1602
(iii) Real world would place a finite
limit on growth.
$P = P_0 e^{K/\lambda}$

**4** (i) $y = 2x$   (ii) $y = x$   (iv) B

**5** $\dfrac{dz}{dx} = \dfrac{3z + 1}{x + 2}$;   $y = \dfrac{A(x + 2)^3 - 1}{3x}$

**6** $\dfrac{dy}{dt} = k(3 + 2y - y^2)$;   $\dfrac{V_0(3 - e^{-4kt})}{1 + e^{-4kt}}$

**7** $v^2 = \dfrac{3x^2 - 1}{x^2(1 + x^2)}$;   $v \to 0$

**10** $dx/dt = -\alpha xy$; $dy/dt = \alpha xy - \beta y$;
$dz/dt = \beta y$
$$y = \frac{\beta}{\alpha}\ln\frac{x}{\lambda} - x + \lambda + \mu$$
$$z = -\frac{\beta}{\alpha}\ln\frac{x}{\lambda}$$

## Revision

**1** (a) $y = -\dfrac{1}{\frac{1}{2}x^2 + x + c}$
(b) $y^2 = \frac{4}{3}(x + 1)^{3/2} + c$

**2** $y = \dfrac{x^2}{6} - \dfrac{1}{3x}$

**3** (a) $y = -\frac{1}{3}\ln(4 - 3e^x)$
(b) $y^2 = (2 - \ln x)^2 - 1$

**4** $y^2 = 16/x + 1$

**5**  (a) $dp/dt = 0$
   (b) $dp/dt = k\sqrt{p}$

**6**  (a) $dr/dt = k/r$
   (b) $\frac{1}{2}r^2 = kt + c$
   (c) $\frac{15}{7}$

**7**  (a) $dh/dt = -k\sqrt{h}$
   (b) $h = (25 - \frac{1}{20}t)^2$
   (c) $500\,\text{s}$

**9**  $160\,^{\circ}\text{C}$

**11**  (a) $v = \left(\dfrac{g}{k} + u\right)e^{-kt} - \dfrac{g}{k}$

**12**  $y = x + \dfrac{3 + e^{2x}}{3 - e^{2x}}$

## 9.5

## Basic

**1**  $972\pi/5\ \text{units}^3$

**2**  $40\pi/3\ \text{units}^3$

**3**  $364\pi/3\ \text{units}^3$

**4**

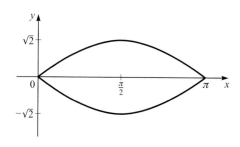

$\pi^2\ \text{units}^3$

**5**  $\dfrac{4\pi ab^2}{3}\ \text{units}^3$

**6**

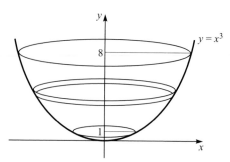

Divide into thin discs, radius $x$,
thickness $\delta y$.
Volume of disc $\delta V = \pi x^2 \delta y$
Hence total volume

$$V = \lim_{\delta y \to 0} \sum \delta V = \int_1^8 \pi x^2\, dy$$

Since   $y = x^3$, $x = y^{1/3}$ and $x^2 = y^{2/3}$

Hence   $V = \displaystyle\int_1^8 \pi y^{2/3}\, dy$

$$= \dfrac{93\pi}{5}$$

**7**  $10\pi\ \text{units}^3$

**8**  $34\,590\ \text{units}^3$

**9**  $240\pi\ \text{units}^3$

**10**  $9\pi/2\ \text{units}^3$

**11**  (a) $\delta n = $ number per hour $\times$ time
   interval $= 400t\ \sin(\pi t/5)\delta t$
   (b) $n = \displaystyle\lim_{\delta t \to 0} \sum \delta n$

$$= \int_0^5 400t\ \sin(\pi t/5)\, dt,\ \text{which,}$$

   after integrating by parts, gives
   3180

**12**  $\dfrac{\pi}{2}(1 - e^{-2b})$

## Intermediate

**1**  $201\pi\ \text{units}^3$

**2**  $\frac{1}{4}\pi^2\ \text{units}^3$

**3**

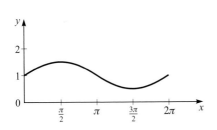

$9\pi^2/4$ units$^3$

**4**

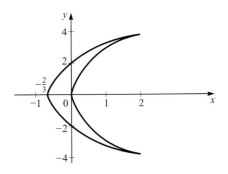

(2, 4) and (2, −4);
volume $= 16\pi/3$ units$^3$

**5**   $18\pi$ units$^3$

**6**   $9\ln 3 - 6$ units$^3$

**7**   $16\pi/5$ units$^3$

**8**   $V = \pi \int_1^e x^2\, dy$ where $y = e^{2x}$

Rearranging, $x = \frac{1}{2}\ln y$, giving

$$V = \pi \int_1^e \left(\tfrac{1}{2}\ln y\right)^2 dy$$

$$= \tfrac{1}{4}\pi \int (\ln y)^2\, dy,$$

which, integrating by parts, gives

$$\tfrac{1}{4}\pi\left[y(\ln y)^2\right]_1^e - \int_1^e 2y\,\frac{1}{y}(\ln y)^2\, dy$$

$$= \tfrac{1}{4}\pi\left[y(\ln y)^2\right]_1^e - \int_1^e 2(\ln y)\, dy$$

$$= \tfrac{1}{4}\pi\left[y(\ln y)^2\right]_1^e - \left\{\left[2y\ln y\right]_1^e\right.$$

$$\left. - \int_1^e 2y\frac{1}{y}dy\right\}$$

$$= \tfrac{1}{4}\pi(e - 2) \text{ units}^3$$

**9**

Consider a thin slice, radius $r$,
thickness $\delta y$.
Volume of slice $\delta V = \pi r^2 \delta y$  (1)
From the diagram, we can use similar
triangles to find $r$ in terms of $y$.

$$\frac{4}{12+h} = \frac{r}{y+h} = \frac{3}{h}$$

Thus $h = 36$ and $r = \tfrac{1}{12}y + 3$
Using (1), total volume

$$V = \lim_{\delta y \to 0}\sum \delta V = \int_0^{12} \pi(\tfrac{1}{12}y + 3)^2 dy$$

$$= 148\pi \text{ cm}^3$$

**10**

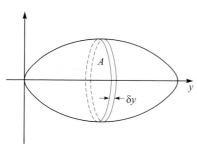

Divide the ellipsoid into thin slices, perpendicular to the $y$-axis.
Let the thickness of the slice be $\delta y$.
Volume of slice
$$\delta V = A\delta y = y(25 - 2y)\delta y$$
Total volume
$$= \lim_{\delta y \to 0} \sum \delta V = \int_0^{12.5} y(25 - 2y)dy$$
$$= 651 \text{ cm}^3$$

**11** Length $= \frac{2}{3}y$, width $= \frac{1}{2}y$, area $= \frac{1}{3}y^2$;
volume $= \frac{1}{3}y^2\delta y$; $24\,\text{m}^3$

**12** $\frac{1}{2}(e^\pi + 1)\,\text{cm}^3$

**13**

Divide the discus into concentric cylinders, radii $r$, $r + \delta r$, thickness $t$.
Cross-sectional area $\delta A = 2\pi r\delta r$
Volume of cylinder,
$$\delta V = \delta A \times t = 2\pi r\delta r \times t$$
$$= 2\pi r \times \frac{25 - r^2}{25}\delta r$$

Total volume
$$= \lim_{\delta r \to 0} \sum \delta V = \int_0^5 \frac{2}{25}(25r - r^3)dr$$
$$= 25\pi/2 \text{ cm}^3$$

**14** 86 grams

**15** (a) $1056\pi \text{ units}^3$
(b) $\frac{8}{11}$

## Advanced

**1** $\left(\frac{5}{3} - \frac{\pi}{4}\right)\pi \text{ units}^3$

**2** $\frac{1}{3} \text{ units}^2$; $y = \sqrt{x} + \frac{2}{\sqrt{x}} - 3$;
$(4\ln 4 - \frac{11}{2})\pi \text{ units}^3$

**3** 268 000

**4** $k = 8$; 5339

**5** (a) $\dfrac{\pi}{3\sqrt{3}}$

(b) $\dfrac{1}{3}\left[\dfrac{1}{x+1} + \dfrac{-x+2}{x^2 - x + 1}\right]$

(c) $\frac{1}{6}\left(\ln 3 + \dfrac{\pi}{\sqrt{3}}\right)$

(d)

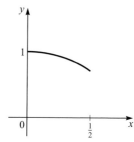

$\dfrac{\pi}{6}\left(\ln 3 + \dfrac{\pi}{\sqrt{3}}\right) \text{ units}^3$

**6** $I_1 = \frac{25}{4}\left(\dfrac{\pi}{3} + \dfrac{\sqrt{3}}{2}\right) \approx 11.96$; $I_2 \approx 14.60$

**7** $0.29\text{m}^3$

**9** $A = \dfrac{\beta}{\alpha^2 + \beta^2}$, $B = \dfrac{\alpha}{\alpha^2 + \beta^2}$

**10** (i) $1 - e^{-1}$  (ii) $6 - 15e^{-1}$
(iii) $\frac{51}{8} - 9\ln 2$

## Revision

**1**  $\frac{3}{4}\pi$ units$^3$

**2**  $\dfrac{283\pi}{15}$ units$^3$

**3**  $\frac{1}{3}\pi r^2 h$ units$^3$

**5**  $\dfrac{(64-8\sqrt{2})\pi}{5}$ units$^3$

**6**  $\dfrac{93\pi}{5}$ units$^3$

**7**  521.6 units$^3$

**8**

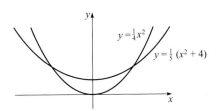

$8\pi$ units$^3$

**9**  (a)  $r = \frac{2}{7}h + 3$

   (b)  $\dfrac{343\pi}{3}$ cm$^3$

**11**  $(12\pi - 6)\,\text{m}^3$

**12**  $130\,000\,\text{cm}^3\,\text{s}^{-1}$

# Chapter 10 Numerical methods

## 10.1

### Basic

**1**  (a) 30.57  (b) 1.28
  (c) 2.80  (d) 0.33
  (e) 28.50  (f) 2.23

**2**  (a) 1.37  (b) 202
  (c) 0.0684  (d) 1.22
  (e) $4.61 \times 10^{-8}$  (f) 1.00

**3**  (a) 56.5, 57.5  (b) 39.5, 40.5
  (c) 127.5, 128.5

**4**  (a) 247.5, 248.5 mm
  (b) 72.55, 72.65 cm
  (c) 1.45, 1.55 cm
  (d) 3.7615, 3.7625 m
  (e) 4.4995, 4.5005 m
  (f) 99.95, 100.05 cm

**5**  (a) 0.5  (b) 50
  (c) 5  (d) 0.0005

**6**  (a) $2.90 \leq A < 3.10$
  (b) $48 \leq A < 52$
  (c) $8.45 \leq A < 8.55$

**7**  (a) $5.55 \leq A < 5.65$
  (b) $3.75 \leq B < 3.85$
  (c) $9.30 \leq A + B < 9.50$
  (d) $1.70 \leq A - B < 1.90$
  (e) $11.1 \leq 2A < 11.3$
  (f) $14.85 \leq 2A + B < 15.15$

**8**  (a) If 5.8 is measured to nearest $\frac{1}{10}$ s,
  maximum absolute error $= 0.05$.

$$\text{Relative error} = \frac{\text{absolute error}}{\text{exact value}}$$
$$= \frac{0.05}{5.8}$$
$$= 0.009$$
  (b) 0.006
  (c) 0.02

**9**  (a) 3.6%  (b) 0.6%
  (c) 2.9%

**10**  (a) $14590 \leq P \times Q < 14850$
  (b) $0.5701 \leq \dfrac{P}{Q} < 0.5799$
  (c) $33810 \leq P^2 + Q^2 < 34320$

**11**  (a) If $y = \sqrt{x}$, $dy/dx = \frac{1}{2}x^{-1/2}$.
  At $x = 4$, $dy/dx = 0.25$.
  (b) $\delta y \approx 0.25 \times \delta x = 0.25 \times 0.1$
  $= 0.025$
  (c) We know that $\sqrt{4} = 2$.
  So taking $x = 4$ and $\delta x = 0.1$
  gives $y = \sqrt{4} = 2$ and $\delta y = 0.025$.
  Hence $\sqrt{4.1} \approx 2 + 0.025 = 2.025$
  (d) From a calculator,
  $\sqrt{4.1} = 2.024\,845\,7$
  Absolute error $= 0.000\,15$
  $$\text{Relative error} = \frac{0.000\,15}{2.0248}$$
  $= 0.000\,076$
  Percentage error $= 0.000\,076 \times 100$
  $\approx 0.008\%$

**12**  (a) 1  (b) 0.009 55 (NB radians)
  (c) 0.022

## Intermediate

**1**  (a) [8.91, 8.93)      8.9 to 2 s.f
    (b) [1.6, 1.8)      2 to 1 s.f.
    (c) [83.25, 141.25)   100 to 1 s.f.
    (d) [1457, 2025)    No answer,
        although in practice, 2000
        could be quoted with some
        confidence

**2**  Area [29.25, 41.25); perimeter [22, 26)

**3**  (a) 4.9 cm    (b) 37.975 m

**4**  (a) 0.018    (b) 0.02%

**5**

|     |        | Abs. error | Rel. error | % error |
|-----|--------|-----------|-----------|---------|
| $A$ | 3.1    | 0.05      | 0.016     | 1.6%    |
| $B$ | 1.8    | 0.05      | 0.028     | 2.8%    |
| $A+B$ | 4.9  | 0.1       | 0.020     | 2.0%    |
| $2A$ | 6.2   | 0.1       | 0.016     | 1.6%    |
| $B^2$ | 3.24 | 0.183     | 0.056     | 5.6%    |
| $\dfrac{A}{B}$ | 1.7222 | 0.0778 | 0.045 | 4.5% |
| $\dfrac{1}{A-B}$ | 0.769 | 0.0641 | 0.083 | 8.3% |

**6**  (a) $\dfrac{1}{\sqrt{2}-1} \times \dfrac{\sqrt{2}+1}{\sqrt{2}+1} = \dfrac{\sqrt{2}+1}{2-1}$

        $= \sqrt{2}+1$

    (b) (i) $\sqrt{2} \approx 1.414\,21\ldots$
        Hence absolute error
            $\approx 1.4142 - 1.41$
            $\approx 0.0042$
        (ii) True value $\approx 1.4142\ldots + 1$
            $\approx 2.4142\ldots$
        Calculated value $= 2.41$
        Hence error $\approx 0.0042$
        (iii) Calculated value

            $= \dfrac{1}{1.41-1} = \dfrac{1}{0.41}$

            $\approx 2.4390\ldots$

Absolute error
    $= 2.4390 - 2.4142\ldots$
    $= 0.0248$
Relative error
    $= \dfrac{0.0248}{2.4142\ldots} \approx 0.010(2)$
(iv) The first student has a lower
    absolute error.

**7**  (a) 17.3 m$^2$    (b) 109.3 m$^2$

**8**

|   | $\pi$ | $(4/3)^4$ | 355/113 |
|---|-------|-----------|---------|
| (a) Abs. error | 0.019 | | $2.7 \times 10^{-7}$ |
| (b) % error | 0.6% | | $8.5 \times 10^{-6}$% |

|   | $\pi$ | 3927/1250 | 22/7 |
|---|-------|-----------|------|
| (a) Abs. error | $7.3 \times 10^{-6}$ | | 0.0013 |
| (b) % error | $2.3 \times 10^{-4}$% | | 0.04% |

**9**  (a) 2.3    (b) 5.3%

**10**  (a) 100    (b) 0.51

**11**  (a) 0.3245
    (b) 558%
    (c) Very large errors introduced,
        because difference is small in
        comparison to size of each term

**12**  (a) 16.43°
    (b) 16.23° − 16.62°
    (c) 16.4° ± 0.2°

**13**  (a) $x_1 + e_1, x_2 + e_2$
    (b) $x_1 x_2 + x_1 e_2 + x_2 e_1 + e_1 e_2$
    (c) $x_1 e_2 + x_2 e_1 + e_1 e_2$
    (d) $\dfrac{x_1 e_2 + x_2 e_1 + e_1 e_2}{x_1 x_2}$

**14**  (a) 2
    (b) (i) 0.1
        (ii) 0.02
        (iii) 0.0002
    (c) (i) 1.1
        (ii) 1.02
        (iii) 1.0002
    (d) (i) 0.2%
        (ii) 0.01%
        (iii) $1 \times 10^{-6}$%

**15** (c)  15%

**16**  $A = \pi r^2 \Rightarrow \mathrm{d}A/\mathrm{d}r = 2\pi r$
$\Rightarrow \delta A = 2\pi r \delta r$
$r = 2,\ \delta r = 0.3$
$\Rightarrow \delta A = 2 \times \pi \times 2 \times 0.3$
$= 1.2\pi\ \mathrm{cm}^2$

## Advanced

**1** (i)  632.7, 659.7   (ii) 0.02

**2**  $11\,914.5\ \mathrm{cm}^2$

**3** (a)  17.7°     (b)  17.7° ± 2.8°

**4**  $V = \pi r^2 h + \frac{4}{3}\pi r^3;\ S = 2\pi rh + 4\pi r^2$
(a)  $36\pi$
(c)  2.1

**5**  $\delta = \frac{1}{2}(b\gamma + c\beta)\sin A;$
$a = 36.5 \pm 0.45\ \mathrm{mm};$
$\Delta = 436.5 \pm 14.3\ \mathrm{mm}^2$

**6**  $2\pi s\sigma \sin\theta(1 + \sin\theta);\ 3430\ \mathrm{mm}^3;$
$1673\ \mathrm{mm}^2;\ 245\ \mathrm{mm}^3;\ 79.6\ \mathrm{mm}^2$

**7** (iii) $2.5 \times 10^{-4};\ 3.8 \times 10^{-4}$

**8**  7.463 − 7.465

**9**  $n = k = 1$

## Revision

**1**

|       | (a)                | (b)        | (c)       |
|-------|--------------------|------------|-----------|
| (i)   | $1.255 \times 10^6$ | 50 350     | 0.006 715 |
| (ii)  | 5000               | 50         | 0.000 005 |
| (iii) | 0.004              | 0.000 99   | 0.000 74  |

|       | (d)       | (e)     |
|-------|-----------|---------|
| (i)   | 960.5     | 0.4055  |
| (ii)  | 0.5       | 0.0005  |
| (iii) | 0.000 52  | 0.001   |

**2** (a)  3.26, 3.28     (b)  3.853, 3.899

**3** (a)  14.25 cm     (b)  40.47 cm$^2$

**4** (a)  8.3025 cm$^2$
(b)  0.038
(c)  1.67%, 1%, 2.5%

**5** (a)  0.014, 0.01; 0.032, 0.019
(b)  2.38, 0.028; 23.8, 0.028

**6**  53.84 miles

**7**  6.45 m s$^{-2}$, 7.48 m s$^{-2}$

**8** (a)  5.14 cm     (b)  0.032

**9** (a)  510.88 cm$^3$
(b)  (i) 23.97 cm   (ii) 96.03 cm

**10** (a)  0.1%     (b)  0.8%
(c)  12.5%

**11** (b)  (i) 0.044   (ii) 0.041   (iii) 0.027
(iv) 0.018

**12** (a)  $\dfrac{25}{\sqrt{P}}\delta P$
(c)  1.5%

## 10.2

## Basic

**1**

| $x$    | −3 | −2  | −1 | 0 | 1 | 2  | 3  |
|--------|----|-----|----|---|---|----|----|
| $f(x)$ | 13 | −14 | −5 | 4 | 1 | −2 | 31 |

Zeros in $[-3, -2], [-1, 0], [1, 2], [2, 3]$

**2**

|        | (a) |   | (b) |    | (c) |     |
|--------|-----|---|-----|----|-----|-----|
| $x$    | 1   | 2 | −2  | −1 | 0   | 1   |
| $f(x)$ | −2  | 7 | −2  | 6  | 3   | −13 |

**3** (a)

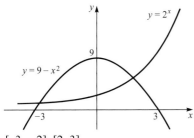

$[-3, -2], [2, 3]$

(b)

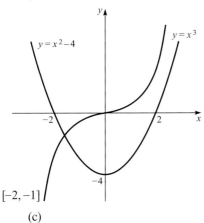

$[-2, -1]$

(c)

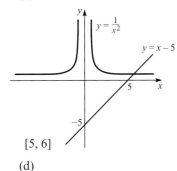

$[5, 6]$

(d)

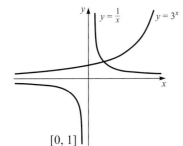

$[0, 1]$

**4** (a)

| $x$ | $-3$ | $-2.5$ | $-2$ |
|---|---|---|---|
| $y$ | $-11$ | $-1.125$ | $5$ |

Root in $-2.5 < x < -2$

(b) $-2.5 < x < -2.25$

**5** (a) (i) From a sketch, there is clearly
only one solution
If $f(x) = x^3 + 3x^2 - 7$,
$f(1) = -3, f(2) = 13$.
Hence there is a solution in the
interval $[1, 2]$.
(ii) The solution appears to be
closer to $x = 1$ than $x = 2$,
so try $x = 1.3$.
$f(1.3) = 0.3$, so solution lies
between 1.0 and 1.3.
$f(1.2) = -0.95$, so solution lies
between $x = 1.2$ and $x = 1.3$.
The solution appears to be
nearer to 1.3 than 1.2, so try
$x = 1.27, 1.28$ and $1.29$.
$f(1.27) = -0.11, f(1.28) = 0.01$
and $f(1.29) = 0.14$
Hence the solution lies between
1.27 and 1.28.
Now $f(1.275) = -0.05$, so the
solution lies between 1.275
and 1.28.
Hence, the solution is 1.28 to
two decimal places.
(b) (i) $[-3, -2], [2, 3]$
(ii) $-2.98, 2.14$
(c) (i) $[-1, 0], [0, 1], [4, 5]$
(ii) $-0.32, 0.35, 4.48$

**6**

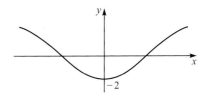

Roots in $[-3, -2]$ and $[2, 3]$;
$x = -2.5, 2.5$

**7**

| | $x_1$ | $x_2$ | $x_3$ | $x_4$ |
|---|---|---|---|---|
| (a) | 1 | 0.775 | 0.682 | 0.640 |
| (b) | 3 | 2.857 | 2.892 | 2.884 |
| (c) | 2 | 1.913 | 1.905 | 1.904 |

**8** (a) $x^3 = 60$
Hence $x^4 = 60x$
and so $x^2 = \sqrt{60x}$
which gives $x = \sqrt{\sqrt{60x}}$
(b) $x_1 = 4$
(c) 3.915

**9** (a) (i) $x^3 = 3x^2 + 2$
Take the cube root of each side, $x = \sqrt[3]{3x^2 + 2}$
(b) (i) 3.68, 3.50, 3.38, 3.31, 3.27
slowly converges (to 3.20)
(ii) 0.5, $-1.6$, 0.27, $-2.7$, 0.13, $-5.4$      oscillates, diverges
(iii) 4.5, 5.5, 7.5, 11.8, 23.3
diverges
(iv) 3.125, 3.205, 3.195, 3.196, 3.196      converges rapidly

**10** (a) If $f(x) = 2x^3 - 5x + 1$,
$f'(x) = 6x^2 - 5$
Hence, substituting in the formula,

$$x_n - \frac{2x_n^3 - 5x_n + 1}{6x_n^2 - 5}$$

(b) $x_n - \dfrac{x_n^3 + x_n + 8}{3x_n^2 + 1}$

(c) $x_n - \dfrac{2 \sin x_n - x_n}{2 \cos x_n - 1}$

**11** (a) 3, 2.184, 1.722
(b) $-1.846$, $-1.834$, $-1.834$
(c) 1.901, 1.896, 1.895

**12** 0.559, 3.041

## Intermediate

**1**

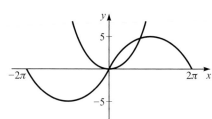

$x \in [2, 3]$

**2**

| $x$ | $-2$ | $-1$ | 0 | 1 | 2 |
|---|---|---|---|---|---|
| $f(x)$ | $-4.65$ | $-1.42$ | 1 | $-1.42$ | $-4.65$ |

**3** (a) $x_1 = 1$       (b) $x_1 = 2$
(c) $x_1 = -1$

**4** (a) $x \in [0, 1]$
(b) $0.5 < x < 0.625$

**5** (a) $f(0) = 1$, $f(1) = -1.38$, change of sign
(b) [0.4, 0.5]

**6** (a) $\dfrac{AB}{BC} = \dfrac{BC}{PB}$

Hence $\dfrac{\phi}{1} = \dfrac{1}{\phi - 1}$

giving $\phi(\phi - 1) = 1$
i.e. $\phi^2 - \phi = 1$
(c) 1.618

**7**

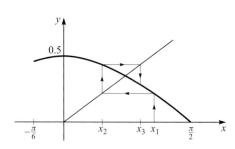

$x_1 = 1$, $x_2 = 0.27$, $x_3 = 0.48$

**8**   $x_2 = 1.35, x_3 = 0.54, x_4 = 2.14$

(b)

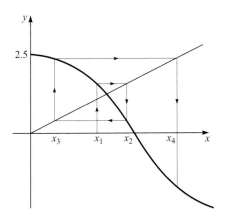

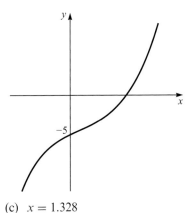

(c)  $x = 1.328$

**9**   (a)  $f(x) = 0.5 \sin 2x + x - \frac{1}{4}\pi$

From graph sketch, $f(x) = 0$ has a solution in [0, 1]
Newton–Raphson formula:

$$x_{n+1} = x_n - \frac{0.5 \sin 2x_n + x_n - \frac{1}{4}\pi}{\cos 2x_n + 1}$$

$$x_1 = 1 \Rightarrow x_2 = 1 - \frac{0.5 \sin 2(1) + 1 - \frac{1}{4}\pi}{\cos 2(1) + 1}$$

$$= -0.146$$

Substituting $x_2 = -0.146$ into the formula gives $x_3 = 0.403$.
Continuing the process,
$x = 0.416$ to 3 s.f.

**10**  $-1.53, -0.35, 1.88$

**11**  (a)  $f'(x) = \sin 2x + 2x \cos 2x = 0$
(b)  $x = 1.01$

**12**  (a)  $a = 2, b = -5$

**13**  (b)  $x_2 = 0.25, x_3 = 0.3125,$
$x_4 = 0.3320$

**14**  (b)  $x_{n+1} = (7 - 3x^2)^{1/6}$
(c)  1.2

**15**  (b)  2.605

**16**

| $x$ | $-3$ | $-2$ | 0 | 1 | 2 | 3 |
|---|---|---|---|---|---|---|
| $f(x)$ | 1.75 | $-5$ | $-0.2$ | 0.25 | 3 | $-1.25$ |

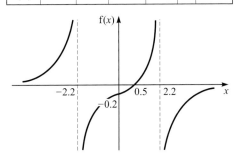

## Advanced

**1**   No; $2500(e^{0.002t} - 1) = 400 - 2t$;
$t = 500 \ln(1.16 - 0.0008t)$; 55

**2**   3.63

**3**

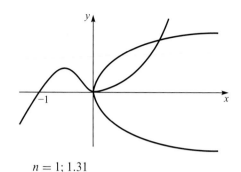

$n = 1; 1.31$

**4**   $x_1 = 61, x_2 = 238; 4.49$

**5**   $(0, 0), (-\frac{2}{3}, \frac{4}{27})$
$0 < k < \frac{4}{27}$
(i)   0.05   (iii) 0.3

**6**   (a)  $0 < k < 1$

**7**   $2(m - n)$

**9**   $L = \sqrt[3]{a}$

**10**  $n = 5$

## Revision

**1**   (a)  $[-2, -1]$          (b)  [5, 6]
(c)  [0, 1] and [4, 5]   (d)  [0, 1]

**2**   −0.32

**3**   (a)  $[-1, 0], [2, 3], [3, 4]$
(c)  −0.115

**4**   $\theta_2 = 1.9$   $\theta_3 = 1.75$

**5**   0.45

**6**   (a)  −0.94      (b)  5.70

**7**   (a)  −0.667, −0.545, −0.564
(b)  0.270, 0.482, 0.443
(c)  −2.986, −2.995, −2.995

**8**   (b)  $x_2 = 0.12, x_3 = 0.29, x_4 = 0.25$
(c)

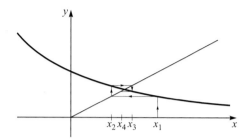

**9**   (a)  3.20      (b)  3.65      (c)  3.35

**10**  (a)  $a = 2, b = 3$
(b)

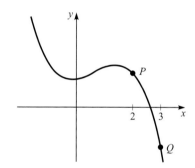

$P(2, 5), Q(3, -4)$
(c)  (2.56, 0); $x = 2.56$

**11**  (b)  −5.541 and 0.541

**12**  (a)

| $a$ | −4 | −3 | −2 | −1 | 0 | 1 | 2 | 3 | 4 |
|---|---|---|---|---|---|---|---|---|---|
| $y$ | −27 | 2 | 13 | 12 | 5 | −2 | −3 | 8 | 37 |

(b)  (iii) −3.100, 0.661, 2.439

# 10.3

## Basic

**1**   3.615 units$^2$

**2**   1.065 units$^2$; overestimate

**3**   142 units$^2$

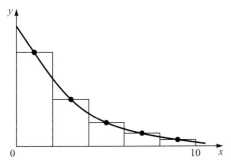

**4**   0.083 units$^2$

**5**   1.25

**6**   Tabulating values of $f(x) = x \sin x$
with interval width $h = 0.5$:

| $x$ | 0 | 0.5 | 1 |
|---|---|---|---|
| $x \sin x$ | 0 | 0.2397 | 0.8415 |

NB radians!

Simpson's rule gives area under
graph as

$$\frac{h}{3}\{f(0) + 4f(0.5) + f(1)\}$$

$$= \frac{0.5}{3}\{0 + 4 \times 0.2397 + 0.8415\}$$

$$= 0.30 \text{ to 2 d.p.}$$

**7**   565 m; not a 'smooth' curve – lots of
sudden changes in speed

**8**   (a)   (i) 48.709   (ii) 48.701
     (b)   (i) 0.2%   (ii) 0.002%

**9**   0.494

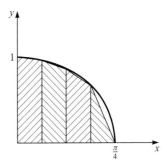

**11**

| $x$ | $y$ | $\delta x$ | $\dfrac{dy}{dx}$ | $\delta y$ |
|---|---|---|---|---|
| 0 | 1 | 0.5 | 0.2 | 0.1 |
| 0.5 | 1.1 | 0.5 | 0.22 | 0.11 |
| 1 | 1.21 | | | |

**12**   Initially $x = 2, y = 3$, so

$$\frac{dy}{dx} = 2 + 3 = 5.$$

Now

$$\delta y \approx \frac{dy}{dx} \delta x = 5 \times 0.2 = 1$$

Thus, new coordinates are
$x = 2 + \delta x = 2 + 0.2 = 2.2$ and
$y = 3 + \delta y = 3 + 1 = 4$.

| $x$ | $y$ | $\delta x$ | $\dfrac{dy}{dx}$ | $\delta y$ |
|---|---|---|---|---|
| 2 | 3 | 0.2 | 5 | 1 |
| 2.2 | 4 | 0.2 | 6.2 | 1.24 |
| 2.4 | 5.24 | 0.2 | 7.64 | 1.528 |
| 2.6 | 6.768 | 0.2 | 9.368 | 1.8736 |
| 2.8 | 8.6416 | 0.2 | 11.4416 | 2.28832 |
| 3 | 10.93 | | | |

## Intermediate

**1** (a) 0.9871 units²    (b) 1 unit²
(c) 0.013

**2** (a)

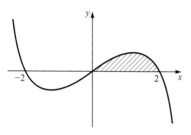

(b)

| x | 0 | 0.4 | 0.8 | 1.2 | 1.6 | 2 |
|---|---|-----|-----|-----|-----|---|
| y | 0 | 1.536 | 2.688 | 3.072 | 2.304 | 0 |

(c) 3.84 units²
(d) 4
(e) $\dfrac{4 - 3.84}{4} \times 100 = 4\%$

**3** (a)

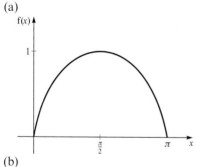

(b)

| x | $\pi/12$ | $\pi/4$ | $5\pi/12$ |
|---|----------|---------|-----------|
| $\sqrt{\sin x}$ | 0.509 | 0.841 | 0.983 |

(c) (i) 1.22   (ii) 2.44

**4** (a)

| h cm | 1 | 3 | 5 | 7 | 9 | 11 | 13 | 15 | 17 | 19 | 21 |
|------|---|---|---|---|---|----|----|----|----|----|----|
| C cm | 30 | 27.5 | 25 | 23 | 21.5 | 20 | 19 | 21 | 23 | 26 | 30 |
| A cm² | 71.62 | 60.18 | 49.74 | 42.10 | 36.78 | 31.83 | 28.73 | 35.09 | 42.10 | 53.79 | 71.62 |

(b) Mid-ordinate rule
(c) Yes, 1047.2 cm³, just over a litre

**5** (a) 3.084, rel. error 0.018
(b) 3.121, rel. error 0.0066

**6** (a)

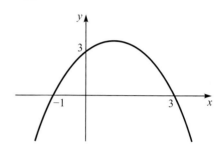

(b) (i) $10\frac{2}{3}$   (ii) $10\frac{2}{3}$   (iii) $10\frac{2}{3}$
Simpson's rule fits points to a quadratic so gives exact answer to any quadratic integral.

**7** $h = \frac{1}{4}h\pi$
Hence

$$\int_0^{\pi/2} \cos x \, dx \approx \frac{1}{3} \times \frac{1}{4}\pi\{\cos 0$$
$$+ 4\cos\tfrac{1}{4}\pi + \cos\tfrac{1}{2}\pi\}$$
$$= \frac{\pi}{12}\left\{1 + 4 \times \frac{1}{\sqrt{2}} + 0\right\}$$
$$= \frac{\pi}{12}\{1 + 2\sqrt{2}\} \quad (\approx 1.002\,28)$$

By integration, exact value = 1
Percentage error
$$= \frac{(1.002\,28 - 1)}{1} \times 100 = 0.23\%$$

**8** (a)

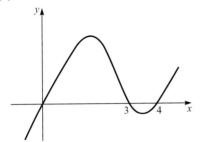

(b) $11.406 + 0.656 = 12.062$ units$^2$
(c) $11.406 - 0.656 = 10.75$

**9** (a)

| $x$ | $y$ | $\delta x$ | $\dfrac{\mathrm{d}y}{\mathrm{d}x}$ | $\delta y$ |
|-----|-----|------------|-------------------------------------|------------|
| 0   | 0   | 0.5        | 1                                   | 0.5        |
| 0.5 | 0.5 | 0.5        | 0.607                               | 0.303      |
| 1   | 0.803 |          |                                     |            |

(c) 0.11

**10** 2.34 cm$^2$; volume 1400 cm$^3$

**11** 357 m

**12** (a) Trapezium 24.94, Simpson's 25.58
(b) 25.6; Simpson's more accurate

**13** (a)

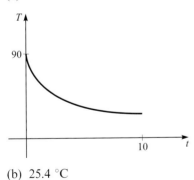

(b) 25.4 °C

**14** 51 600 cm$^3$

**15** 44.6 cm$^2$

**16** (a)

| $x$ | $y$ | $\delta x$ | $\dfrac{\mathrm{d}y}{\mathrm{d}x}$ | $\delta y$ |
|-----|-----|------------|-------------------------------------|------------|
| 0   | 3   | 0.2        | 0                                   | 0          |
| 0.2 | 3   | 0.2        | $-0.0375$                           | $-0.0075$  |
| 0.4 | 2.9925 | 0.2     | $-0.0752$                           | $-0.015$   |
| 0.6 | 2.9775 | 0.2     | $-0.1134$                           | $-0.0227$  |
| 0.8 | 2.955 |           |                                     |            |

(c) $t = \sin^{-1}(0.2) = 0.201$, $y = 2.939$,
% error 0.5%

## Advanced

**1** $1.4 \times 10^4$ kg

**2** (a) $\frac{1}{6}\{g(0.5) + 2g(0)\}$
(b) $g(0) + g(0.5)$

**3** (a) $\frac{1}{2}k(e^2 - 1)$     (c) 2.73

**4** (a) $\mathrm{d}P/\mathrm{d}t = 0.03P - 1.2\sqrt{P}$;
(b) $P = 2137$ when $t = 20$
(c) 1600

**5** $x = 20.6$, $y = 52.1$

**6** 3.636, 0.7%

**7** (i) 0.70  (iii) 1.7 units$^3$

**8** 0.509

**9** 0.771; 0.785

**10** $a = \dfrac{8h}{105}$, $b = \dfrac{32h}{35}$, $c = \dfrac{12h}{35}$

## Revision

**1** 65.2 units$^2$, overestimate

**2** 0.239 units$^2$

**3**  (a)  4.107 559 6
(b)  4.107 523 3 to 7 d.p.
(c)  0.000 9%

**4**  (a)

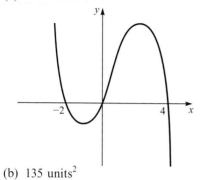

(b)  135 units$^2$

**5**   2.82 m$^3$

**6**  (a)

| $x$ | 0 | 1 | 2 | 3 | 4 |
|---|---|---|---|---|---|
| $y$ | 0 | $3a$ | $4a$ | $3a$ | 0 |

(b)  $32a/3$; Simpson's rule is exact for quadratic functions.

**7**   43200; underestimate

**8**   0.349

**9**

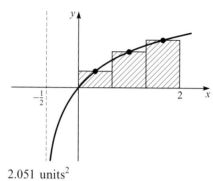

2.051  units$^2$

**10**  7.48 units$^2$

**11**  5.161

**12**  (a)  2.3484     (c)  0.3%
(d)  0.3%

# Chapter 11 Proof

## 11.1

### Basic

**2**  LHS $\equiv \sin(A + B) + \sin(A - B)$
$\equiv \sin A \cos B + \cos A \sin B$
$+ \sin A \cos B - \cos A \sin B$
$\equiv \sin A \cos B + \sin A \cos B$
$\equiv 2 \sin A \cos B$
$\equiv$ RHS

**3**  Any odd number is of the form $2r+1$.
Let $n = 2r + 1$, so
$$n^3 = (2r + 1)^3$$
$$= (2r)^3 + 3(2r)^2 + 3(2r) + 1$$
$$= 2(4r^3 + 6r^2 + 3r) + 1,$$
which is also odd

**4**  (a) $\Leftrightarrow$      (b) $\Leftarrow$      (c) $\Rightarrow$
(d) $\Leftrightarrow$

**5**  (a) $1 \times 2 \neq 1 + 2$      (b) $(\frac{1}{2})^2 \neq \frac{1}{2}$

**6**  (a) (i) False
(ii) $x = 60° \Rightarrow \tan x = \sqrt{3}$
(iii) True
(b) (i) False   (ii) $x = 7 \Rightarrow x^2 = 49$
(iii) True
(c) (i) True   (ii) $\dfrac{dy}{dx} = \dfrac{1}{x} \Rightarrow y = \ln x$
(iii) False
(d) (i) True
(ii) If $\sin x = 0$ then $\cos x = 1$
(iii) False
(e) (i) True
(ii) In $\triangle PQR$, $\angle PQR = \angle PRQ \Rightarrow$
$PQ = PR$   (iii) True

**7**  (a) If and only if
(b) If
(c) Only if

**8**  (a) $\Leftrightarrow$      (b) $\Rightarrow$      (c) $\Leftarrow$

**9**  (a) Necessary and sufficient
(b) Necessary and sufficient
(c) Necessary

**11**  If $a = b, a - b = 0$ and it is invalid to divide by zero

**12**  (a) Let $\sqrt{6} = a/b$, where $a$ and $b$ are integers with no common factors.

Thus $b\sqrt{6} = a$
$\Rightarrow \quad 6b^2 = a^2$
$\Rightarrow \quad a^2 = 2(3b^2)$, so $a^2$ is even

If $a^2$ is even, then $a$ must also be even.
Let $a = 2p$, where $p$ is an integer.
Then $6b^2 = 4p^2$
$\Rightarrow \quad 3b^2 = 2p^2$
$\Rightarrow \quad 3b^2$ is even,

therefore $b^2$ is even
If $b^2$ is even, then $b$ must be even.
But, if $a$ is even and $b$ is even, they have a common factor of 2.
This is a contradiction of the original statement.
Hence the statement $\sqrt{6} = a/b$ is false.
Thus $\sqrt{6}$ cannot be expressed as a fraction in its lowest terms and is therefore irrational.

(b) The line in (a) $6b^2 = 4p^2$ becomes $4b^2 = 4p^2$.
Hence $b^2 = p^2$ and we can no longer conclude that $b$ must be even.

## Intermediate

**2** (a) When a number is squared, its last digit is found from the square of the last digit of the original number.
If we consider all the possible last digits (using proof by exhaustion), we have $0^2 = 0$, $1^2 = 1, 2^2 = 4, 3^2 = 9, 4^2 = 16$, $5^2 = 25, 6^2 = 36, 7^2 = 49, 8^2 = 64$, $9^2 = 81$.
Thus the only possible final digits are 0, 1, 4, 5, 6, 9.

**3** (a) The fact that a true conclusion has been reached in an argument does not prove that the initial statement is true. It is possible to start with a false statement (e.g. $1 = 2$), apply a series of valid steps (e.g. multiplying both sides by 0 to give $1 \times 0 = 2 \times 0$) and arrive at a true conclusion (e.g. $0 = 0$).
(b) $\log \frac{1}{2} < 0$. Hence the direction of the inequality changes.

**7** (b) Consider the number $abc$.
$abc = 100a + 10b + c$
Reversing gives
$cba = 100c + 10b + a$.
$abc - cba = (100a + 10b + c)$
$\qquad\qquad -(100c + 10b + a)$
$\qquad\quad = 99a - 99c$
$\qquad\quad = 99(a - c)$,
which is a multiple of 99
(c) To find the multiple of 99, subtract the last digit from the first.

**8** (a) $\Rightarrow$    (b) $\Leftrightarrow$    (c) $\Leftarrow$

**9** (a) If

(b) If and only if
(c) If and only if

**10** (a) Necessary and sufficient
(b) Sufficient
(c) Sufficient
(d) Necessary
(e) Sufficient
(f) Necessary and sufficient

**12** (a) True    (b) False
(c) False    (d) False

**13** (a) (i) True
(ii) If $x^2 = y^2$ then $x = y$
(iii) False
(b) (i) True
(ii) If $x - a$ is a factor of $f(x)$ then $f(a) = 0$
(iii) True
(c) (i) True
(ii) $f'(a) = 0 \Rightarrow f(x)$ has a maximum at $x = a$
(iii) False
(d) (i) False
(ii) For all integers $m$, $n$, if $m$ and $n$ are both even then $m + n$ is even
(iii) True
(e) (i) False
(ii) For any real $x$, if $x$ is negative then $x^2 - x$ is positive
(iii) True

## Advanced

**3** Yes

**4** (a) Principal values of $\sin^{-1} x$ have not been used.
(b) $u = 1 - x^2$ is not 1–1 on $[-\frac{1}{2}, \frac{1}{2}]$.
(c) $1 + \tan 2\pi/3 < 0$, so the ln is not defined.

**6** (i) $g(x) = \frac{1}{2}\{g(x) + g(-x)\}$
$\qquad\qquad + \frac{1}{2}\{g(x) - g(-x)\}$
(ii) (a) False  (b) True
(iii) (a) Even  (b) Even

**8** $\displaystyle\sum_{(n-1)^2+1}^{n^2} r = (n - 1)^3 + n^3$

**9**   $f(x) = \cos x$

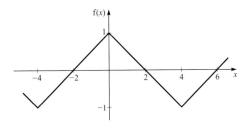

**10**  Barthes 15, Camus 13, Diderot 12; Barthes came last in the final stage.

# Revision

**5**   (b)  For example, 111

**6**   (a)  $\Leftarrow$        (b)  $\Leftrightarrow$        (c)  $\Rightarrow$

**7**   (a)  Necessary and sufficient
      (b)  Sufficient
      (c)  Necessary and sufficient

**9**   False $(n = 50/3$ also$)$

**10**  True